Insurance coverage	511	Publicity	266
Insurance terms	684	Punctuation	340
Insured mail	633	Question mark	356
Interest tables	785	Quotation marks	357
International mail	641	Records management	409
International time	455	Records retention	426
International trade	576	Reference sources	212
Interviewing	26	Registered mail	631
Introductions	45	Report writing	238
Invitations	185	Reports, mechanics	250
Itinerary	469	Roman numerals	378
Law terms	688	Securities transactions	521
Legal citations	225	Semicolon	360
Letter make-up	86	Signs and symbols	771
Letter models	174	Simplifying office procedures	38
Letter writing	144	Social Security	556
Listening	33	Special characters, typing	400
Mail, domestic	623	Special delivery	631
Marketing terms	694	Spelling guide	285
Meetings	51	Statistical material, typing	394
Memorandums	261	Stock market terms	705
Merit rating	34	Subject filing	410
Methods and procedures	38	Tables, typing technique	394
Microform records	428	Tabular presentation	228
Military correspondence	116	Talking to groups	20
Military time	783	Taxes	543
Military titles	135	Telegrams	447
Minutes of meetings	68	Telephone services	442
Numbers, use	372	Telephone technique	11
Numerical filing	415	Teletype messages	463
Office supervision	25	Tickler files	417
Organizing data	241	Time zones	448
Outlining	243	Training	28
Overseas calls	19	Transcribing dictation	162
Parcel post	628	Travel arrangements	466
Parentheses	353	Typing pointers	384
Parliamentary procedure	60	Underlining	379
Period (punctuation)	355	U.S. foreign service posts	621
Personal effectiveness	1	Volume formulas	787
Personnel terms	699	Weights and measures	753
Possessives	315	Wills	536
Postal regulations	623	Wire services	447
Postal services, nonmail	653	Word division	380
Press releases	266	Word usage	323
Printer's copy	275	Words often confused	293
Proofreading	278	Xerox copies	438
Protection of documents	571	ZIP Code addressing	109

New Standard Reference for Secretaries and Administrative Assistants

J. Harold Janis

Professor of Business Communication
New York University

Margaret H. Thompson

Consultant, Office Practices and Communications
Formerly Faculty, Graduate School of Business Administration
University of California, Los Angeles

New Standard Reference for Secretaries and Administrative Assistants

MACMILLAN PUBLISHING CO., INC.
New York

COLLIER MACMILLAN PUBLISHERS
London

MACMILLAN PUBLISHING CO., INC.
866 THIRD AVENUE, NEW YORK, NEW YORK 10022

COLLIER-MACMILLAN CANADA, LTD.

Library of Congress catalog card number: 78–150074

Printing   5 6 7 8 9   Year   7 8 9

Preface

This book is intended primarily as an authoritative reference and guide for secretaries and administrative assistants. It will also answer many questions that arise daily in the work of supervisors, department heads, individuals in business for themselves, and others with staff or management responsibilities. What these positions have in common—and what this book shares with them—is an overriding concern with effective communication: talking, writing, meeting with people, winning cooperation, finding and processing information, and managing the details of these operations smoothly and competently.

Though these broad aims are shared by all, the routes to accomplishment will vary in individual circumstances. Does the situation call for an impressively typed letter? Telephone tact? Speaking skill? Correct form in addressing a bishop? More efficient filing procedures? A good source of trade information overseas? The correct word? Parliamentary rules? Proofreading like a professional? Setting up a statistical table? The list could be carried to indefinite length. What this book has tried to do is organize much of the diverse information the business communicator may need, make it easy to find, and show how it can serve its intended purpose.

For the secretary the chapters having universal application are those on personal effectiveness, meetings, letter form, correct usage, punctuation, mechanical style, and typing pointers. Other chapters, like those on letter writing, information handling, report preparation, and publicity and editorial work, are designed to help out in advanced areas of competence.

For department heads and supervisors, the parts of greatest utility are probably those on group communication, supervision, conference arrangements, dictation techniques, improvement of correspondence procedures, data processing, report writing, and office services. For executives and proprietors of businesses, the value of this material is supplemented by the chapters on financial and tax considerations, and international trade.

For those concerned with the training of personnel, the numerous sections on secretarial practice and language usage may serve both as the text for in-service courses and as a guide to standards for all secretaries, stenographers, typists, and other personnel.

For the professional man and woman, for the writer of letters and reports, for the speaker, for the conference chairman or attendee, for the office editor, for the research assistant—and for all others who need to know where to find business information, how to use and interpret technical business terms, how to phrase business ideas, and how to work with others—this book can be mined for a variety of useful data.

To help the reader in his search for information, there is first of all a table of contents that identifies the subject matter of each chapter and of each section within each chapter. In the text, the chapters and many of the sections also have their own table of contents. In some instances, an alphabetical arrangement is used within a section or chapter to permit easy reference. A shortened index on the inside covers and a complete index at the end of the book ensure that any topic treated will readily be found.

The contents of this book rely heavily on the business and academic experience of both authors. Both have spent many years as writers, speakers, teachers, and consultants to business in areas related to communications, secretaryship, and employee training and education. In all instances, material has been carefully selected to represent the usages and practices of current business. A list of organizations to which the authors are especially indebted follows this preface. Much of the material has also been proved out in the courses and training programs the authors have conducted and in other books and manuals they have written.

Teachers will find ample coverage of the material needed in an advanced course in secretaryship. The additional business data may be viewed as a bonus useful for reference and special projects.

J. H. J.
M. H. T.

This book is helpful in preparing for the nationwide examination for secretaries sponsored by the National Secretaries Association through its Institute for Certifying Secretaries. Members and nonmembers alike may take a six-part examination for the title of Certified Professional Secretary. Information about the examination and the qualifications of candidates may be obtained from the Association, 1103 Grand Avenue, Suite 410, Kansas City, Missouri 64106.

Acknowledgments

The authors appreciate the assistance given by the following organizations, including the many individuals in them who, without regard for their own convenience, provided information and materials for this book.

Aerospace Corporation
American Airlines
American Telephone and Telegraph Company
Burroughs Corporation
Federal Reserve Bank of New York
General Electric Company
Hobbs, Dorman & Company, Inc.
International Business Machines Corporation
International Telephone and Telegraph Company
The Macmillan Company
Manufacturers Hanover Trust Company
National Cash Register Company
New York Telephone Company
Olivetti Underwood Corporation
Pan American World Airways
Random House
The Singer Company
United States Department of Commerce
Western Union
The Wilson Jones Company

Authorities Consulted

This is only a partial list. Names of other works are scattered through the text.

Arnold, Robert R., Harold C. Hill, and Aylmer V. Nichols. *Introduction to Data Processing*. New York: John Wiley, 1966.

Auger, B. Y. *How to Run More Effective Meetings*. New York: Grosset & Dunlap, 1964.

Bingham, W. Van Dyke, and Bruce V. Moore. *How to Interview,* 4th rev. ed. New York: Harper & Row, 1959.

Carter, Byron L. *Data Processing for the Small Business*. New York: McFadden Books, 1966.

Doris, Lillian, and Besse May Miller. *Complete Secretary's Handbook,* 3d ed. Englewood Cliffs, N.J.: Prentice-Hall, 1970.

Douglass, Paul. *Communication Through Reports*. Englewood Cliffs, N.J.: Prentice-Hall, 1957.

Federal Reserve Bank of New York. *Secretarial Handbook*. New York, 1964.

Fluharty, George W., and Harold R. Ross. *Public Speaking*. New York: Barnes & Noble, 1966.

Flynn, Patricia. *The Complete Secretary*. New York: Pitman, 1965.

Grange, William J., and others. *Manual for Corporation Officers*. New York: Ronald Press, 1967.

Greenwood, W. John. *The Standard Business Guide and Correspondents' Handbook*. New York: Halcyon House, 1940.

Herrmann, Irvin A. *Office Methods, Systems, and Procedures*. New York: Ronald Press, 1950.

Heyel, Carl. *Computers, Office Machines, and the New Information Technology*. New York: Macmillan, 1969.

Hicks, Charles B., and Irene Place. *Office Management,* 2nd ed. Boston: Allyn and Bacon, 1962.

Holm, James N. *Productive Speaking for Business and the Professions*. Boston: Allyn and Bacon, 1967.

Hutchinson, Lois Irene. *Standard Handbook for Secretaries*. 8th ed. New York: McGraw-Hill, 1969.

Janis, J. Harold. *The Business Research Paper: A Manual of Style*. New York: Hobbs, Dorman & Co., 1967.

————. *A Guide to Writing Reports at the Federal Reserve Bank of New York*. Federal Reserve Bank of New York [1969].

————. *Writing and Communicating in Business*. New York: Macmillan, 1964.

————. *Writing Better Letters*. New York: Manufacturers Hanover Trust Company, 1968.

Kahn, Gilbert, Theodore Yerian, and Jeffrey R. Stewart, Jr. *Progressive Filing and Records Management.* New York: Gregg Publishing Division, McGraw-Hill, 1962.

Keithley, Erwin M., and Margaret H. Thompson. *English for Modern Business.* Homewood, Ill.: Richard D. Irwin, 1966.

Lutz, R. R. *Graphic Presentation Simplified.* New York: Funk & Wagnalls, 1949.

Measures, Howard. *Styles of Address,* 2nd ed. New York: Thomas Y. Crowell, 1969.

Melcher, Daniel, and Nancy Larrick. *Printing and Production Handbook,* 3d ed. New York: McGraw-Hill, 1966.

Nicholson, Margaret. *A Practical Style Guide for Authors and Editors.* New York: Holt, Rinehart and Winston, 1967.

Reisman, S. J. *A Style Manual for Technical Writers and Editors.* New York: Macmillan, 1962.

Rogers, Anna C. *Graphic Charts Handbook.* Washington, D.C.: Public Affairs Press, 1961.

Stafford, Alison R., and Billie Jean Culpepper. *The Science-Engineering Secretary.* Englewood Cliffs, N.J.: Prentice-Hall, 1963.

Taintor, Sara Augusta, and Kate M. Monro. *The Secretary's Handbook,* 9th ed. New York: Macmillan, 1969.

Terry, George R. *Principles of Management,* 5th ed. Homewood, Ill.: Richard D. Irwin, 1968.

U.S. Department of the Air Force. *Guide to Air Force Writing.* Washington, D.C.: Government Printing Office, 1960.

U.S. Government Organization Manual 1969–70. Office of the Federal Register, National Archives and Record Service, General Services Administration.

U.S. Government Printing Office. *Style Manual,* rev. ed. Washington, D.C., 1967.

Wanous, S. J., and L. W. Erickson. *The Secretary's Book,* rev. ed. New York: Ronald Press, 1952.

Weeks, Bertha M. *How to File and Index,* rev. ed. New York: Ronald Press, 1956.

Wylie, Harry L. (ed.). *Office Management Handbook,* 2nd ed. New York: Ronald Press, 1958.

Contents

1.	**PERSONAL EFFECTIVENESS**	1
1.1	Opportunities in the Changing Office Environment	1
1.2	Appointments and Visitors	4
1.3	Using the Telephone	11
1.4	Talking to Groups	20
1.5	Office Supervision	25
1.6	Business Etiquette	41
2.	**MEETINGS**	51
2.1	Conference Arrangements	52
2.2	Parliamentary Procedure	60
2.3	Minutes	68
2.4	Conventions and Large-Scale Meetings	78
3.	**LETTER MAKE-UP**	86
3.1	Letter Form and Style	86
3.2	Letters to Government and the Military: Format and Security Precautions	115
3.3	Forms of Address	134
4.	**LETTER WRITING**	144
4.1	Effective Letters	144
4.2	Dictation Techniques	155
4.3	Taking and Transcribing Dictation	159
4.4	Improving Correspondence Procedures	164
4.5	A Treasury of Model Letters	174
5.	**HANDLING BUSINESS INFORMATION**	194
5.1	Data Processing	194
5.2	Information Sources	210
5.3	Footnotes and Bibliographies	219
5.4	Tabular Presentation	228
5.5	Graphic Presentation	231
6.	**REPORT PREPARATION**	238
6.1	Planning the Report	238
6.2	Writing the Report	246

6.3   The Report in Finished Form   250
6.4   Memorandums   261

7.   **PUBLICITY AND EDITORIAL WORK**   266
7.1   The Press Release   266
7.2   Editing   271
7.3   Preparing Copy for the Printer   275
7.4   Proofreading   278

8.   **CORRECT ENGLISH USAGE**   284
8.1   Spelling Guide   285
8.2   Words Often Confused   293
8.3   Glossary of Common Grammatical Terms   303
8.4   Grammar Review   308
8.5   Dictionary of English Usage   323

9.   **PUNCTUATION**   340
9.1   Apostrophe   340
9.2   Brackets   341
9.3   Colon   341
9.4   Comma   343
9.5   Dash   347
9.6   Ellipsis   348
9.7   Exclamation Point   348
9.8   Hyphen   349
9.9   Parentheses   353
9.10 Period   355
9.11 Question Mark   356
9.12 Quotation Marks   357
9.13 Semicolon   360

10.   **MECHANICAL STYLE**   362
10.1 Abbreviations   362
10.2 Capitals   365
10.3 Numbers   372
10.4 Underlining   379
10.5 Word Division   380

11.   **TYPING POINTERS**   384
11.1 Improving Typing Efficiency   384
11.2 Typing Statistical Material   394
11.3 Typing Special Characters, Formulas, and Equations   400

12.	**OFFICE SERVICES**	409
12.1	Records Management	409
12.2	Duplicating and Copying	431
12.3	Telephone and Wire Services	442
12.4	Travel Arrangements	466
13.	**FINANCIAL AND TAX CONSIDERATIONS**	484
13.1	Banking	484
13.2	Credit	496
13.3	Insurance	511
13.4	Securities Transactions	521
13.5	Estate Planning—The Will	536
13.6	Taxes	543
13.7	Social Security	556
13.8	Protection and Replacement of Important Documents	571
14.	**INTERNATIONAL TRADE**	576
14.1	Doing Business Abroad	576
14.2	Foreign Countries, Their Capitals, and Descriptive National Terms	604
14.3	Foreign Money and Its Value	607
14.4	Customs Regulations	612
14.5	U.S. Foreign Service Posts	621
15.	**POSTAL REGULATIONS**	623
15.1	Domestic Mail	623
15.2	International Mail	641
15.3	Nonmail Postal Services	653
16.	**DICTIONARY OF BUSINESS TERMS**	657
16.1	Accounting	657
16.2	Banking	662
16.3	Data Processing	668
16.4	Economics	678
16.5	Government	682
16.6	Insurance	684
16.7	Law	688
16.8	Marketing	694
16.9	Personnel	699
16.10	Stock Market	705
17.	**LIST OF STANDARD ABBREVIATIONS**	709
18.	**WEIGHTS AND MEASURES**	753

APPENDICES

A. *Signs and Symbols*   771
B. *Greek Alphabet*   775
C. *Six-Year Holiday Timetable*   776
D. *State Holidays*   778
E. *Twenty-four-Hour Military Time*   783
F. *Number of Days Between Dates*   784
G. *Simple Interest Tables*   785
H. *Decimal Equivalents of Fractions*   786
I. *Common Volume Formulas*   787
J. *Common Area Formulas*   788

INDEX   789

1

Personal Effectiveness

Whatever else a responsible job entails, it puts a high premium on the ability of the individual to deal with others face to face and over the telephone.

That is what this chapter is all about. Following a brief overview of the prospects offered by the modern office, it recommends effective procedures for making appointments, meeting visitors, maintaining poise, exerting personal influence, and improving administrative and human relations skills.

CONTENTS

1.1 Opportunities in the Changing Office Environment   p. 1
1.2 Appointments and Visitors   p. 4
1.3 Using the Telephone   p. 11
1.4 Talking to Groups   p. 20
1.5 Office Supervision   p. 25
1.6 Business Etiquette   p. 41

1.1 OPPORTUNITIES IN THE CHANGING OFFICE ENVIRONMENT

The office is changing. No other fact about business life is so important to you if you are making your career in a secretarial or administrative position.

Characteristically, change shuts off opportunity for some and opens new avenues of advancement for others. This section is intended to help you measure your future course.

In summary, you can look for these developments.

1. The spread of mechanical and electronic processes puts additional value on human communication—in person, on the telephone, and by letter.

2. The rising uses of business information open the doors to talent in such areas as research, writing, and editing.

3. The increasing interdependence of all parts of the organization offers greater scope for the exercise of human relations and administrative talents.

1

4. Rapid changes in jobs and personnel place additional responsibilities on key people to train others to succeed them and to substitute for them in their absence.

5. The constantly growing ties between business and government and between domestic companies and the international business community have created a need for new types of data useful to both the secretary and the executive.

The Impact of Automation.   The most revolutionary office development has been the introduction of labor-saving equipment, notably in the area of data processing. The consequences are enormous. Work has been redistributed. Jobs have been eliminated or redefined. Even the executive's functions have been updated and remade to take advantage of the speed and wealth of data provided by the computer.

With the replacement by the machine of many functions formerly performed by people, human contact has in some respects become a scarce commodity in business. That circumstance has only enhanced the value of the secretary. For it is reassuring to have in the organization a compatible being who can provide a wide range of "unprogrammed" services, from greeting a visitor and answering a telephone to booking a luncheon or arranging the details of a meeting.

Automation has not only reinforced the need for many of the secretary's traditional services, but it has also opened new vistas for her. Machines now absorb much of the drudgery and time that used to be spent in copying, calculating, and other clerical chores. Favored by the trust and responsibility she already enjoys, the secretary thus finds it easy to move up to work of a creative or an administrative nature. It is now not unusual for the upgraded secretary to have a staff of her own, with the responsibilities of hiring, training, and supervising. This trend has been accelerated by a number of factors, not the least of which are the proliferation of administrative positions and the increasing professionalization of the secretary.

The Information Explosion.   Another important development in business is the dramatic rise in the production, accessibility, and uses of information. The computer has multiplied the amount of information available and has aided in its processing, but a great deal still needs to be done by conventional gathering, reporting, and interpreting methods. Among the most interesting tasks performed by the modern secretary or administrative assistant are those relating to the information function, including report preparation and publicity and editorial work. These require not only a high level of verbal skills, but an acquaintance with the sources of business information, research procedures, graphic techniques, and printing requirements.

The overload of words produced by modern office machines and the businessman's thirst for information present further challenges to the secretary who wishes to protect her employer from the worst consequences of the avalanche. Thus she may be called on to monitor incoming messages, sort out the "junk mail," divert some mail to other persons in the organization, and make sure that no information of consequence escapes her employer's attention. She may also be encouraged to answer letters and initiate correspondence either for her own or for her employer's signature.

Another manifestation of the information explosion is the enormous growth in the number of meetings and conferences of all sorts and on all levels. The secretary's responsibilities have grown commensurately, for she is expected to set up meetings for her employer, take minutes, and follow up to see that the decisions made at meetings are communicated to others and implemented. The secretary–administrator will also attend meetings and participate actively in them as chairman, speaker, or member of a discussion group.

Interdependence and the Need for Cooperation. A change especially evident to the executive is the growing interdependence of all parts of the business organization. Before computerization and the so-called systems approach to management, departments and offices worked more or less independently in their particular areas of responsibility. Today there is a strong realization of the influence of one function or event upon another, and as a consequence there is a far greater coordination of effort and a far greater need for communication and cooperation among the various elements that constitute the organization. This condition of mutual dependency requires that an executive know a great deal about techniques and events elsewhere in the organization; it also requires frequent contact with other members of the organization through meetings, memorandums, and the telephone.

The change in the executive's responsibilities is reflected in those of his secretary or administrative assistant. She no longer exists only in the small world created by her employer; rather, her duties now require her to reach out to all parts of the organization. In the process, she makes new contacts, increases her usefulness to her employer, and broadens her knowledge and opportunities. She is helped along by her adaptability and the respect she gains from her personal qualities and her ability to communicate effectively.

Providing for Continuity of Service. In any list of the changes taking place in business today, the growth of training would rank high. Many factors account for this trend: the more rapid movement of workers from company to company and job to job, business growth and change, and the need for workers trained in the specific methods and operations of the organization. The training given by the company may take place on the job, in company classrooms, or off the premises in independent schools and colleges. The training is usually supplemented by the issuance of written instructions in the form of memorandums, bulletins, manuals, and the like.

In the realm of training, the key assistants share the responsibility for counseling new employees and overseeing their work. Because her work is visible, the secretary especially is expected to set high standards of performance and to demonstrate in her own production how those standards can be met. To provide for the contingencies of illness and absence for business reasons, she is also well advised to train a back-up secretary to take over for her when necessary. Such foresightedness actually works to her own advantage because knowing that she has a competent replacement gives her peace of mind when her absence is unavoidable, and the presence of a replacement allays the panic her employer might otherwise feel. She also has less reason to worry about work piling up for her return.

Business, Government—and the World.   Two more facets of modern business need to be mentioned. The first is the increased involvement of business with government. The second is the growing international flavor of American business through its relations with foreign markets and foreign business organizations. Both developments contribute enormously to the complexity of business operations and put tremendous demands on the executive and the secretary for information not usually found in ordinary business sources. Such information ranges from methods of addressing letters to the military to knowing whether you call a native of Cameroon a Cameroon or a Cameroonian (it's Cameroonian). Another side effect of government and world business is the additional travel demands on the executive, with all that those demands mean to the secretary in terms of itinerary, tickets, hotel accommodations, and communications.

Our purpose in this section has been to point up new opportunities and new problems that must be faced in today's office environment. Succeeding sections and chapters will attempt to provide information and guidance through which those opportunities can be opened and the problems solved.

1.2   APPOINTMENTS AND VISITORS

The executive's appointments must be handled efficiently to avoid conflicts of time and to make sure visitors are received courteously and promptly. The secretary who arranges the appointments and meets the visitors must herself set an example of competence, poise, and charm.

Making Appointments.   Proficiency in making appointments for an employer requires a close knowledge of his working day, his work habits, and his business acquaintances and friends. With some experience the secretary is usually able to classify and screen visitors according to the degree of accessibility the employer wishes to grant them. Such a classification might follow a pattern like this:

1. Close business associates and friends and members of the family, who may walk in unannounced if the executive is alone.

2. Employees and customers who ask to see the executive and who may come in at almost any time without an appointment.

3. Salesmen and others who may have special hours or days set aside for them, with or without an appointment.

4. Those in any category for whom an appointment must be made in advance.

5. Those whom the executive prefers not to see.

Records.   Systematic records are the best insurance that appointments will be meticulously kept (Figure 1-1).

1. Record every appointment on your employer's calendar and on your own. Information should include the name, the purpose of the call, the time, and—if not in your employer's own office—the place.

2. On the same calendars, record standing appointments and regularly scheduled meetings as far ahead as the dates are known.

3. For additional convenience, type a daily, weekly, or monthly appointment schedule that your employer can keep on his desk or take with him (Figure 1-2).

4. Keep in your own address file the names of all visitors, with their business connections and phone numbers, so that you will be able to communicate with them if necessary.

5. Consider keeping a day book, listing all visitors, with the time and purpose of their visit. This is often valuable in reconstructing events at a later date.

Coordination. The success of any visit requires careful planning and much communication.

1. At the beginning of the day, review appointments and meetings, and gather necessary materials well in advance.

2. Check at least once a day with your employer to make sure neither he nor you have made an appointment without the other's knowledge.

3. When your employer's plans are changed, notify conferees immediately and arrange new appointments.

4. If your company receptionist screens all visitors, give her a list of your employer's appointments, so that she may recognize visitors by name and announce them promptly.

5. In the instance of a luncheon meeting hosted by your employer, see that reservations are made well in advance and that the maître d'hôtel is informed of time of arrival, number in party, and any special requirements in seating, service, menu, and so on.

6. Never make an appointment for your employer unless you are sure he desires it. If you have any doubts, check with him first. Where only the time is in doubt, make a tentative appointment subject to later confirmation.

7. When an appointment requiring your employer to leave the office is

A MONTHLY CALENDAR for desk or wall shows at a glance the distribution of tasks for the period—makes it easy to balance the work load.

A WEEKLY CALENDAR gives a clear view of activities within the Monday to Friday span—and on weekends, too.

A DAILY CALENDAR pinpoints specific tasks, appointments, meetings, etc. for specific times of the day. It also has space for notes.

A POCKET CALENDAR allows the executive to check appointments when he is away from the office. It should include important names, addresses, and telephone numbers.

Figure 1-1   Types of calendars.

WEEKLY APPOINTMENT SCHEDULE

April 12	MONDAY	9:30 a.m.	Weekly staff meeting. Board Room.
		10:00 a.m.	Mr. Denton Peters, AVCO Mfg. Co.
		12:30 p.m.	Luncheon speaker, City Bankers Association, Union Club, Park Avenue and 69th Street.
		3:00 p.m.	Telephone Mr. Paul Smith, San Francisco Office.
		8:00 p.m.	Opera.
April 13	TUESDAY	10:00 a.m.	Pension Committee meeting. Your office.
		12:00 noon	Lunch with Mr. David Knauth, Lawyers Club, 115 Broadway.
		2:30 p.m.	Telephone conference, Regional Sales Managers.
		3:30 p.m.	Miss Doris Walley, candidate for position of Research Assistant.
		7:00 p.m.	New York Coliseum. Inspection of company's Trade Show Exhibit (Booth 29, Main Floor, rear).

Figure 1-2   Part of a weekly appointment schedule.

made more than a few days in advance, telephone the day before the meeting —or at least before your employer leaves the office—to confirm the appointment.

Greeting the Visitor.   Whatever your employer's attitude is toward individual callers, it is your job to be cordial to everyone, yet ward off unwanted intrusions.

General Procedure.   The greeting accorded a visitor will range from normal courtesy to flattering attention, depending on his importance and his relations with the employer. The following procedure is minimal.

1. Look up from your work as soon as the visitor arrives at your desk and greet him by name, if you know him, or by asking pleasantly, "May I help you?"

2. Practiced callers usually give their names, but if a caller does not, obtain it tactfully by asking, "Who shall I say is calling?"

3. If a visitor has an appointment, you will say, depending on the circumstances:

> Mr. Todd is expecting you. Go right in.
> I'll tell Mr. Todd you're here.
> Mr. Todd is on the phone right now. Will you have a seat? I'll tell him you're here as soon as he's through.

4. If a wardrobe is available, it is considerate to take the waiting visitor's hat and coat.

5. If an important visitor must be kept waiting, he will be less fretful if you engage him in light conversation for a few minutes. If the wait is to be extended, offer a newspaper or magazine.

Visitors Without Appointments.   A visitor who comes in without an appointment must be handled with special care. You do not want to be in the position of turning away a person whose business or goodwill may mean a lot to your company and one whom your employer would therefore most certainly want to see. For that reason it is always a good idea to ascertain who the individual is and what business brings him to your office. When the visitor's identity and purpose have been weighed, you may decide to announce him immediately. Such an instance would occur infrequently, however. More often, the visitor without an appointment would be asked (1) to wait until the person he wants to see is available, (2) to see another person, (3) to come back at another time, (4) to let you try to help, or (5) to write a letter stating his business. The following paragraphs may suggest what to say in a number of different situations.

> Mr. Brown is engaged now. Will you let me know what you wish to see him about? Perhaps I can help.
> Mr. Brown is working on a special project and can't be disturbed. But I'm sure that Mr. Wiley can help.
> If you'll let me know what you want, I'll see that Mr. Brown hears about it. You can call me later in the day for his answer.

Mr. Brown has a personal list of charities. But if you'd like him to consider your organization, the best thing to do would be to write him a letter enclosing some of your literature.

Job interviews are customarily given in our Personnel Department. If you'd like to see someone there, I'll give Mr. Blaine a ring and tell him you're coming.

I'm sure Mr. Brown would be interested in your company's machine. But you'd stand a much better chance of getting him to consider it if you went through channels. The best man to see is Mr. McLean in the Purchasing Department.

When a visitor is offensively persistent after you have told him your employer cannot see him, you might say in an even-tempered voice:

I'm only carrying out Mr. Brown's instructions and he'll be angry with me and with you if I disobey them. I've already suggested the best way of reaching him. I'm sure you'll accomplish a lot more in that way than by any other.

Business Associates. Visits from persons in the same organization follow special rules. Many executives have open-door policies that permit at least close associates to walk in unannounced. Others who do not have this privilege may be told, "I'll see if he's in," "I'll call you when he's free," or "He'll be free at eleven. Why not drop back then? I'll tell him you're coming."

Refreshments. If a visit coincides with a morning or afternoon coffee break, bring two cups of coffee, but if the visitor refuses, serve your employer anyway. If the visit is to be short, or if it is undesirable to extend the visit, wait until the visitor leaves before serving coffee.

If you are receiving the visitor, you should also offer coffee if the situation warrants; but if coffee is refused, it may be desirable to postpone your own refreshments until the visitor leaves. Certainly, it would be impolite to have anything more than coffee while the visitor abstains.

Interruptions. If your employer must be interrupted while a visitor is in his office, it may be better to call him on the telephone or to take in a note than to speak to him openly; he may not care to advertise the subject of the interruption to his visitor. If you do interrupt the discussion, excuse yourself first. In any case, make sure the interruption is brief.

If a telephone call comes for a visitor who is already closeted with your employer, offer to take the message for him; but if the caller insists on talking to him, interrupt the meeting by saying, "Mr. Jones, I have a telephone call for you." You may suggest that he take the call in your office or in a more private place if he prefers.

Ending the Visit. It is the secretary's responsibility to see that the executive is free for his next appointment. The procedure to be followed may need to be discussed with the executive when the secretary first assumes the job. They may agree that she should interrupt in person with such a statement as, "Mr. Brown, your next visitor has arrived for his appointment." When, in any case, the executive expects a garrulous visitor, he may leave instructions to employ a ruse to end the meeting. Thus he may ask you to telephone him, or hand him a note, or go in and say, "It's time for your meeting, Mr. Brown."

The experienced host will usually anticipate the need to cut a visit short by saying to the visitor when he arrives, "I have a meeting at three, but I'm sure that will give us plenty of time to talk." During the visit the host may also signal the end of the meeting by saying, for example, "Let's continue this discussion some other time."

Hosting the Visitor.   Anyone interviewing a visitor has special responsibilities. If the meeting has been arranged in advance, you should consider what the objective is and work out a strategy for achieving it most effectively. If necessary, brief yourself on the situation by consulting whatever records are available and bring to the interview any papers or other materials that may be needed.

Consider also what questions you will ask and how you will answer the questions you anticipate from the visitor. If you do not wish to be disturbed, arrange to have your telephone attended by someone else. If the interview is unanticipated, make a quick appraisal of the situation to determine what objective the interview will serve, then plan your remarks to bring it to a prompt and successful conclusion. The following points will apply in almost all situations.

1. Greet the visitor cordially. After the initial "hello," show the visitor to a chair and put him at his ease. A matter of common interest makes a good starting point. It may be the weather, a reference to a mutual acquaintance, a compliment, or the reason for the interview.

> The Excelsior Company? I love their TV commercials. Do you have anything to do with them?
> We thought we might find some applications here for your Supergraph duplicator.
>   I wonder if you can give me some idea of the cost?
> Mr. Brown asked me to give you whatever help I can.

2. Channel your remarks. Direct your own and your visitor's remarks into channels that will help you complete your business as quickly as possible. Asking a question or briefly summarizing the visitor's main point may help to bring the interview to a conclusion.

3. Adapt to the visitor. Consider the visitor's feelings and don't let your impatience prevent you from suggesting what is best for him. For example, instead of telling a salesman that his product is decidedly inferior to the one you are now using, perhaps you could say, "We are satisfied with the Ace transcribing machine that we are using. Let us know when your company develops new products, however, and we will be interested in seeing them."

4. Avoid controversial issues. And try not to argue with the visitor if he raises them. You might gloss over statements with which you disagree by such remarks as:

You're certainly entitled to your opinion.
I'm sure you have your reasons for thinking so.

5. Use caution in speaking. Be careful about offering personal opinions about people, especially about members of your own organization, and don't give any information about your company that is not already publicly available unless you have previously cleared it with your superior.

6. Don't pass the buck. Refer the visitor to someone else in the organization only if necessary; don't do it just to pass off an unwanted caller on some hapless co-worker.

7. Close the interview conclusively and pleasantly. For example:

That's as much information as I can give you. I hope it will be useful to you.
Then I'll expect you to send me the specifications and price. Can you do that by Wednesday? Good. It was very kind of you to give me so much of your time.
Now, if you'll put in a letter the information you just gave me, I'll be able to take up your request with Mr. Brown. You'll do that, won't you? It was so nice talking to you.

1.3 USING THE TELEPHONE

The telephone is the most accessible and useful of all business machines, and the easiest to operate. Used correctly, it can save enormous amounts of time, reduce correspondence and travel, and make friends for the user and his company. No other machine makes possible such close human contact with customers, prospective customers, employees, suppliers, and others.

A big advantage of the telephone over writing is that it provides for immediate response or feedback, and thus permits both parties to work out differences on the spot. It is probably not used nearly as much as it should be.

This section tells how to be personally effective when using the telephone. For a detailed description of available telephone services for business, see Section 12.3, "Telephone and Wire Services."

Telephone Technique. Clear speech and a pleasing telephone personality are essential to all who wish to use the instrument effectively. Possible distortions of sound by the instrument itself make careful enunciation mandatory. Furthermore, because the person at the other end of the line cannot see you or your facial expressions, he can draw his impressions only from what he hears. For best results in using the telephone, start by observing these rules.

1. Speak directly into the mouthpiece in your normal voice. Don't shout; don't murmur.

2. Speak in an alert, animated way, but not too fast to be understood clearly. A flat, monotonous tone adds to the distance between you and the listener.

3. Articulate clearly; the listener can't get any help from your facial gestures or lip movements. Because many letters sound alike over the telephone (for example, *N* and *M*, *F* and *S*), it is good practice to use key words when

A as in Alice	J as in James	R as in Robert
B " " Bertha	K " " Kate	S " " Samuel
C " " Charles	L " " Louis	T " " Thomas
D " " David	M " " Mary	U " " Utah
E " " Edward	N " " Nellie	V " " Victor
F " " Frank	O " " Oliver	W " " William
G " " George	P " " Paul	X " " X-ray
H " " Henry	Q " " Quaker	Y " " Young
I " " Ida		Z " " Zebra

Figure 1-3 Key words used in spelling names over the telephone.

giving initials or spelling a name; for example, "R. E. Morris—*R* as in *Robert, E* as in *Edward*, Morris—*M* as in *Mary-O-R-R-I-S*." A list of key words will be found in Figure 1-3. A guide to the phrasing of telephone numbers is given in Figure 1-4.

4. Converse naturally. Speak to the other party as if you were in the room with him. Use the tone and vocabulary that are most expressive of your own personality.

5. Be attentive, pleasant, sympathetic, patient, reassuring. The other party will appreciate it. He will also be a lot easier to handle when a difficult situation arises.

6. Say "please" and "thank you" often. Say "sorry" for even slight inconveniences.

Telephone Listings.   Obtaining a telephone number can be the most time-consuming part of making a telephone call. For that reason it is a good idea

---

SEVEN-DIGIT NUMBERS

674-1674 *Six seven four* (pause) one *six* (pause) seven four.

363-9500 *Three six three* (pause) nine *five* hundred.

555-6000 *Five five five* (pause) six thousand.

AREA CODE WITH NUMBER

212 393-4703 Area Code *two one two three nine three* (pause) four *seven* (pause) oh three.

919 232-4111 Area Code *nine one nine two three two* (pause) four *one* (pause) one one.

702 FA3-1256 Area Code *seven oh two F A three* (pause) one *two* (pause) five six.

Figure 1-4 Phrasing of telephone numbers.

to keep handy a list of frequently called numbers and to be able to find other numbers quickly in the telephone directory.

1. Have a small directory or file of the outside numbers frequently called. Keep the list up-to-date. Include such numbers as the following.

Accountant
Airlines
Attorney
Bank
Building manager or superintendent
Car rental agency
Express office
Family and friends
Garage
Hotels, motels, and restaurants used for company business
Insurance broker

Messenger service
Personal services: barber, dentist, doctor, stockbroker, clubs, stores, and so on
Post office
Repair services (typewriter and other machines)
Stationers
Telegraph office
Theater ticket agency
Trade association
Travel agency

2. Keep the company's internal telephone directory handy and make any necessary corrections and additions to keep it up-to-date. Note especially the extensions to call in emergencies and put the numbers on the cover.

3. Keep in a private place a list of the home phone numbers of executives and office employees.

4. Have up-to-date local telephone directories, and know how to use them. See the front of the directory for the following numbers.

Directory assistance
Emergencies: police, fire, ambulance
Long distance
Telephone company's business office
Time
Weather forecast

The following directory information may also be of help.

Federal government: all offices, including post offices, are listed under "United States Government."

State, county, and city offices: all are listed under the names of the state, county, and city respectively.

Consulates: listed under name of country and in the classified directory (yellow pages) under "Government—Foreign Representatives."

Office buildings: see "Office Buildings" in the classified directory.

Public libraries: listed under the name of the city or the name of the library.

Radio and television stations: alphabetically listed; also found in the classified directory under "Radio Stations and Broadcasting Companies."

Incoming Calls.   People are always sensitive to the way their calls are received. They appreciate courtesy and seldom conceal their irritation when it is lacking.

1. Answer the telephone promptly. At the first ring, if possible. A ringing telephone suggests that it is unattended. When you pick up the receiver, acknowledge the call immediately. Do not under any circumstances continue to talk to someone else while you hold the line open.

2. Identify yourself. The conversation cannot begin until the caller knows he has reached the right place or person. If you are working for a company that has no switchboard, give your firm's name, followed by your name, as "XYZ Corporation, Miss Johnson." In handling calls coming directly to your desk through Centrex, the direct-inward-dialing system, you should state your name only.

Miss Gates
Dora Bliss
Peterson

If your company has a switchboard, give your name when answering your own extension. When answering another's telephone, give his name, followed by your name, as, "Mr. Smith's office, Miss Porter speaking." When answering an office or factory extension, identify the office or department and give your name.

Personnel Department, Mrs. Drummond.
Assembly Station 14, Jenkins.

3. Take calls for others courteously. The person called may be in the office but unable to answer his own telephone. Because the caller cannot see what is happening, give a sufficient explanation, as, "I am sorry, Mr. Johnson is talking on another line." Offer a choice between waiting or being called back, as, "Do you wish to wait, or may I ask him to call you?" Unless you have instructions to the contrary, it is usually better *not* to say:

He's in conference and can't be disturbed.
He's out.
He's busy.
He's ill.
She hasn't come back from lunch yet.
He hasn't come in yet.
She's in the ladies' room.
He's in court.
He took the afternoon off.
I don't know where she is.

These reports are more acceptable.

Mr. Jones is not at his desk right now.
He is talking with someone in his office just now.
I expect him back in a few minutes.
He's in a meeting. It will probably last until two o'clock.
He's out of town on business this week.
He stepped out for a few minutes.
She's talking on another line.

Always offer some kind of assistance.

May I help you?
May I take a message for him?
May I have him call you?
Mr. Erhard is handling his calls while he is out of the city. Would you like to talk to him?

4. Screen calls tactfully. More and more executives are finding it good public relations to be easily accessible by telephone. The use of the Centrex system, which bypasses the switchboard, promotes this trend. If, however, your employer wishes to have his calls screened, you will have to use an extra measure of tact. By identifying yourself when answering, you may encourage the caller to do the same. If possible, a report should be given before you ask the identity of the caller.

If the person called is available, say,

Yes, he's in. May I tell him who is calling, please?

If the person called is not available, say,

He is out of the office just now. May I help you or may I tell him who called?

5. Don't keep the caller waiting. If the called person is busy, ask the caller if he wants to leave a message or be called back. Or, preferably, see if you can give him whatever help he needs. If he is a caller who should not be kept waiting, hand a note to the called person, if you can, or try to reach him on another extension. When the caller does wait, give him frequent reports, like these.

Mr. Smith's line is still busy. I'll connect you as soon as it is free.
Mr. Smith has not returned yet. Will you please wait a little longer?
Hello, still waiting.
Here's Mr. Smith now. Thank you for waiting.

When you leave the line temporarily, you might say,

Will you excuse me a moment while I answer another call?
Would you hold for a moment, please, while I look up that information?

If advisable, explain that you are putting the caller on hold, so that he won't think you have hung up when the hold button clicks.

6. Transfer calls carefully. When it is necessary to transfer an incoming call, tell the caller why a transfer is necessary. Also make sure that the caller is willing to be transferred. If he is not willing, offer to obtain the information and call back. If the caller agrees to the transfer, signal your PBX operator by depressing the plunger to the count of 1-2 pause, 1-2 pause. Give the operator enough information so that she can complete the transfer to the proper person or department. Wait for her to acknowledge your request, then hang up gently.

If you wish to show special deference to the caller and spare him the necessity of repeating to a second party information he has already given you, you should if possible brief the other party on the situation before the caller talks to him. For example:

Mr. Brown, this is Miss Elliott. I have a call from Mr. Brennan, who would like some information about our fall line. Will you speak to him please? He's on the phone now. . . . Mr. Brennan, here's Mr. Brown.

7. Take messages accurately. If the caller leaves a message, be sure to take it down carefully and note the date and time as well as the name of the caller and—if a return call is necessary—his telephone and extension numbers. Most companies provide a printed form for this information. In the interests of accuracy, repeat the information over the telephone, or ask the caller to repeat it and spell out names. When an incoming long distance, person-to-person call requires a call-back, be sure to get—in addition to the information already mentioned—the operator's number and the city and state in which the call originated.

8. Answer questions pleasantly—and cautiously. "I'll look it up" is better than "I don't know." If the caller asks for some information that you are not sure may be given out, say,

> Let me find out and call you back.
> I'll have to speak to Mr. Smith.
> I'll do what I can to get you that information.

Guard carefully information about the company's business operations, sales, finances, personnel, and credit. If there is some question about the legitimacy of the call, ask for the caller's name and telephone number, and offer to call back. Then check the number through the directory or your office records. In any case, the best advice is summed up in the phrase, "Don't give away the store." A great deal of business information is private even when it is the subject of common talk around the office.

9. Let the caller hang up first. This permits him to say all that he wishes to without being cut off. If he prolongs the call beyond a reasonable time, you may drop a hint, like, "Well, it was good to talk to you," or, "Do enjoy that trip. I'll talk to you again when you get back." If the caller persists, you may then offer an excuse for getting off the line. For example:

> Oh, I'm sorry, but I'm wanted on another phone.
> I'd love to talk with you some more, but I'm due at a meeting now.
> I'll have to say good-bye now. There's a letter I've got to get off in the next mail.

10. Be courteous in other ways, too. The telephone offers many other opportunities for tact and courtesy. By greeting the caller pleasantly and using his name, you'll make a friend for the company. Callers like to feel that they are receiving individual rather than routine consideration. Be especially tactful when handling complaints or refusing a request because of company policy. Be a good listener and remain calm even under provocation. When the situation calls for it, give a full and sympathetic explanation, and offer assistance. Apologize for mistakes, as, "I am sorry that happened." Avoid expressions such as "you have to" or "you must." A comment such as "If you'll come in Monday, we'll be happy to check that for you" is preferable to "You'll have to come in Monday if you want that checked."

11. Systematize the work. If you work for a busy executive, have him help you set up a priority list for telephone calls. The list will include:

Internal calls from his superiors.
Internal calls from others.
Calls from customers.
Calls from suppliers doing business with the company.
Calls from salesmen soliciting new business.
Calls from civic and trade organizations.
Personal calls.

Learn which calls your employer wishes to handle immediately by himself. Find out which calls can be handled by a return call from him personally and which can be handled by you. Even with such priorities set up in advance, however, there will be many occasions when you will have to use your own judgment. Every secretary learns that the less she disturbs her employer, the better he likes it, but that he won't easily forgive her for the one time when she should have asked him to take a call and didn't.

Many secretaries find it advantageous to keep a log, or list, of calls received, with a note as to the action that has been taken or has yet to be taken. The log can be put before the employer several times a day, when he can select the calls he will answer while he turns over to you any others that have not yet been attended to. In this way, the employer always knows what business is being transacted whether he handles it personally or not. The log is also useful for future reference, should a question about a telephone transaction arise.

Outgoing Calls.   The telephone is so handy that there is a great temptation to use it carelessly. It is better to recognize its potential and learn to use it to get good results every time.

1. Plan the call beforehand. Decide whom you want to speak to and what you are going to say. Then you won't have to flounder around and waste time after you are connected. Also have some alternatives ready in case you don't get the party you want or the answer you anticipated. In some instances, you will find it advisable to make some notes for reference before you place the call.

2. Dial correctly. If you are not sure of the number, check the telephone directory or your personal list of numbers. Listen for the dial tone before dialing. And allow time to answer. Give the person you are calling at least a minute to reach his telephone.

3. Identify yourself immediately. Your name and the name of the company or the person on whose behalf you are calling will get attention. At the same time, name the person you want to talk to.

Mrs. Smart calling Mr. Brown.
I'm Miss Anderson of the Acme Corporation. May I speak to Mr. Peet?
Good morning, Mr. Burns. This is Ann Maxwell.
This is Miss Jameson calling Mr. Bromley.
Mr. Happel? Mr. Somers would like to speak with you.

If you do not know what individual to talk to, you may ask for a particular department, though in many instances it is better to state your business and let the operator direct you to the proper party.

Adjustment Department, please.
I'd like to order a book, please.
This is Aiken and Company. We have a question about an invoice.

4. Arrange for a call-back. If you cannot be connected to the party you want, leave your name and number (or your employer's) and ask to be called back. If a special time is best, name it. If, however, it is going to be inconvenient to receive the return call, ask when it will be best for you to call back and set a definite time if possible.

5. Be sure your employer is ready to speak. If you place a call for your employer, wait until you are connected, then say to your party, "Mr. Smith? Here is Mr. Jones." Or have Mr. Jones ready to greet Mr. Smith without your intervention. In any case, Mr. Jones should be ready to speak. It is very rude to keep the other party waiting when you have called him.

6. Speak in your employer's name. When you call on behalf of your employer, give information or make a request in his name, not yours.

NOT: Will you please let me know . . .
BUT: Mr. Brown would like to know . . .

NOT: There'll be a luncheon on Thursday.
BUT: Mr. Brown asked me to tell you that there will be a luncheon on Thursday.

7. Be brief. The other party will appreciate it, and besides you'll free your phone for other calls. If your call is going to take more than a few minutes, you may find it advisable to state your business and then ask, "Is it convenient for you to talk to me now?" If the time is not convenient, you can arrange to call back at another time.

Out-of-Town Calls. Lower costs and vast improvements in telephone technology have made out-of-town calls commonplace. To save time and money, however, toll calls must be placed correctly. For example, you must be aware of differences in time in the United States and throughout the world. The map of the United States on page 449 includes the four time zones, the telephone rate zones, and the area codes for each state. International time is shown on page 455. Area codes for the most important cities in the United States and Canada are listed in the front of your local telephone directory. Your telephone directory also includes typical charges for out-of-town and overseas calls, with different rates for day and evening calls and for directly dialed, operator-assisted, and person-to-person calls.

Person-to-Person Calls. To place a long distance person-to-person call, dial *0,* then the area code and telephone number of the person you wish to reach. Before the connection is completed, the operator will interrupt to ask whom you wish to speak to. She will also ask for your telephone number.

Appointment and Sequence Calls. These two types of person-to-person calls enable one to specify a certain time he will talk with a party in another city or with a list of variously located parties in a specified order. The operator will try to put an appointment call through at the exact time you designate. Sequence calls are handled in rapid sequence by the operator from the pre-arranged list that you supply her. The charge is the same as for person-to-person calls.

Station-to-Station Calls.   Because charging begins when the called telephone is answered, be careful to dial the correct area code and correct telephone number. However, should you reach a wrong number, ask the person who answers for the name of his city. Then immediately dial the operator and give her this information so that you will not be charged for the call. Always report any difficulties to the operator.

To obtain a telephone number in a city outside your area, dial the area code for that city and *555-1212* and ask for the information. For example, if you want to obtain a number in Detroit, dial *313* (the area code), then *555-1212*. There is no charge for this service.

Rates for station-to-station calls are lower than for person-to-person calls. If the called person is the only one who answers the phone or if anyone at the phone may handle your call, use the less expensive station-to-station call.

Collect Calls.   A collect long distance call may be dialed in the same manner as a person-to-person call. Dial *0,* then the area code and telephone number. The operator will ask the called person if he wishes to accept the call. If the person refuses the call, it is canceled and no charge is made.

Inward WATS.   Station-to-station long distance calls may be made, without charge to the caller, to businesses that have wide area telephone service (WATS, described on page 443). This service is offered to customers dialing from certain locations. Dial area code *800* plus the special number of the company having this service. To determine whether the party you want offers this service, dial *800* plus *555-1212*.

Conference Calls.   Through the use of a conference call, an executive may be connected with a number of other telephones (up to ten) in different cities. All the connected parties are able to hear each other and to exchange information. A speech to a larger audience in another city may also be arranged if you ask the telephone company to install loudspeaker equipment appropriate for the size of the audience. If you wish to place such conference calls, dial the operator and she will connect you with the conference operator.

Mobile and Marine Service.   Local and long distance calls can be made to automobiles, trucks, and boats equipped for mobile telephone service. Ask the operator for the mobile service operator or the marine operator.

Overseas Calls.   Overseas calls can be made to practically any telephone in the world ("overseas" includes Alaska and Hawaii). Dial the operator (*0*) and give her the name of the country you are calling. If you wish, she will also give you an estimate of the charge before the call is placed, and the exact charge after the call is completed. Direct dialing to selected cities overseas is available to special subscribers.

WARNING: Before making any maritime or overseas call, be sure to check the time zone of the area you are calling. Two o'clock in the afternoon at your office might be two o'clock in the morning at your destination. (See international time chart, pp. 455–456.)

Long Distance Charges. If you wish to know the charges for a long distance call, dial *0,* then the area code and telephone number. Make your request to the operator when she interrupts. She will call you back after the completion of your call and give you the exact charges. Keep an accurate record of long distance calls and be sure to include in it (1) the name of the person calling, (2) the name of the person called, (3) the date and the time, (4) the location and the telephone number, and (5) the charges.

A flat charge is made for the first three minutes of a long distance call. After that, you are charged at another rate for each additional minute of conversation. Rates on a call depend on the distance between calling points, the kind of call you are making, and the time of day when the call is made. Reduced rates are in effect every evening between 5 p.m. and 8 a.m. and all day Saturday and Sunday.

See the front pages of your telephone directory for helpful information about domestic time zones, area codes, and rates.

1.4 TALKING TO GROUPS

A career in business offers many opportunities to attend conferences and participate in their proceedings. The nature of the participation varies with the kind of meeting and runs the gamut from attentive observance of the proceedings to selling the group on a new idea (Figure 1-5). This section deals with improving individual effectiveness at meetings, whether they are held on company premises or elsewhere.

For information on conference arrangements, parliamentary procedure, and minutes of meetings, see "Meetings," Chapter 2.

Responsibilities of Attendance. When you attend a conference, you have a duty to the sponsors and the chairman to be an active participant. Here are some ground rules.

1. Arrive on time. Lateness unfairly penalizes other members of the group.

2. Come prepared. Know the purpose of the meeting, familiarize yourself with any background material available to you, and have at least some tentative ideas and opinions.

3. Listen attentively. Be alert to what is going on. Instead of letting your eyes wander, look straight at those speaking and listen with interest. Because you can listen twice as fast as the speaker can talk, use the extra time to analyze the speaker's remarks by relating what you hear to what you already know.

BRAINSTORMING. A free-wheeling bull session in which all ideas, however wild, are listed and later examined more closely.

BRIEFING. A concise recital of all the facts needed to understand a situation; often a team of speakers, assisted by charts, slides, and other visual aids, is used.

BUZZ SESSION. One of a number of similar groups into which a larger, unwieldy group has been divided for a short discussion of a problem after a common briefing. Each buzz session consists of not more than six individuals who seat themselves in a circle, with one member acting as leader. When the allotted time has elapsed, the sub-groups come together again, reports from the leaders are heard, and general discussion leads to some conclusion.

PRESENTATION. A talk designed to influence a decision, often with the help of visual aids.

REPORT. A statement based on observation, investigation, or deliberation, often ending with a recommendation for action.

ROLE PLAYING. A technique employed in training, through which individuals act out roles assigned to them. The spontaneous nature of the performance (no rehearsal time is allowed) helps the participants understand the point of view of the persons they portray.

SENSITIVITY TRAINING. A technique in which several small groups (called T-groups) participate, spending as much as two weeks together in listening to lectures, seeing illustrative motion pictures, and engaging in experiments in group behavior. The purpose is to achieve a greater awareness of how the individual relates to others. It can be a corrosive experience.

Figure 1-5 Dictionary of terms for conference participants.

4. Take notes. Jot down information you want to retain and statements you may want to question, comment on, or rebut when you are given the opportunity. Do your writing, if possible, during pauses or interruptions in the speaker's presentation. Do not, under any circumstances, tune out the speaker while you take notes.

5. Enter into the discussion. Without monopolizing the meeting, comment on the ideas of others, provide what information you can, and express your own thoughts and feelings. If you see inconsistencies or errors, point them out tactfully. Do your part to keep the conference going toward a satisfactory conclusion.

6. Be tolerant of the views of others. Your fellow conferees have as much right to their views as you have to yours. If you listen without prejudice, you may actually change your mind. That's all right; just don't accept other people's views only because you are too lazy to analyze or promote your own.

7. Object tactfully. If you don't agree with a speaker, avoid attacking him head on. Instead, ask questions that will help clarify his position or expose the flaws. Never attack a speaker personally, but address your arguments solely to the issues.

8. Keep a cool head. Don't get emotional. Don't engage in debate with any individual. Talk to the whole group. The calmer and more reasonable you seem, the more persuasive you are likely to be.

9. Give in gracefully. If the discussion goes against you, accept your defeat in good humor. The group will respect you if you have held your view sincerely and maintained it even against great odds. And there is always a chance that their regard for you will help you at other meetings and in other ways.

Chairing a Meeting. If you chair a meeting, you will probably have no trouble in generating discussion. However, the meeting will be unproductive unless you direct the discussion into purposeful channels.

1. Be prepared. Why has the meeting been called? What background information must you provide? What specific issues are to be discussed? What are the views of the various participants likely to be? The better prepared you are with the answers to these questions, the better you can anticipate the course of the meeting and direct it to your purpose.

2. Lead, but don't push. You want to lead the group step by step to the solution of the problem the meeting is designed to solve. In performing that task, you will call on particular individuals to give information or state their views; you will also ask questions, summarize arguments, and in general lead the meeting to a conclusive end. On the other hand, don't try to impose your views on the group. Let them talk freely and at length, provided they don't get off on tangents. If you see that the business of the meeting cannot be completed within the time allowed, settle for some lesser objective or arrange to continue the discussion at another time.

3. Assign tasks beforehand. To help the group reach an informed conclusion, you may ask them to come prepared with ideas or information on the subject. Or you may direct your request only to particular individuals who have special information to impart. Obviously, much more can be accomplished when people are prepared to contribute than when they are not.

4. Don't show personal favoritism. Give everyone an equal chance to engage in the discussion and don't favor any one person with your attention and comments. If you see that some members of the group are not participating fully, or that the meeting is becoming a one-man show, draw out the shy ones by asking specific questions in their field of authority or by asking their opinions regarding the ideas expressed by others.

5. Follow through. When the group has formed its conclusions or come to some agreement, sum up the results. Then take whatever action is necessary to implement the decisions. Thus you may appoint committees or assign

individuals to specific tasks, or you yourself may take on such duties as writing letters and talking to people. You should also draw up memorandums to be sent to the individuals with assigned duties, confirming their assignments and setting a date for completion. If other meetings are necessary, you should also take the initiative in arranging those. Meetings of any kind almost invariably engender follow-up work, and if the work is not undertaken, the results of the meetings are unfortunately lost along with the time of everybody who had any part in them.

Giving a Talk.   Everyone with responsibility occasionally finds himself (or herself) in the position of having to talk to a group. He may be introducing a speaker or giving the principal talk himself. The subject may be as simple as instructions on the care of a typewriter or as complex as the effect of the new tariffs on imports. In such speaking situations, you usually know of your assignment in advance and have the time to prepare. Here are some suggestions.

1. Know your subject. If you are inclined to be nervous about the prospect of giving a talk, the best remedy is the knowledge that you know your subject thoroughly. The chances are that you were chosen to give the talk because of your special knowledge. If your subject needs advance preparation or investigation, come to your talk well armed with your data—then concentrate on what you want to say instead of on your personal feelings.

2. Look good. The audience will get their first impression of you from your dress and grooming. Make sure the impression is favorable. Look your best—but in a low-keyed way, so that the audience can concentrate on what you are saying.

3. Stand up straight and face the audience. Don't fidget with clothes or objects on the rostrum. If there is a table in front of you, come around to the side of the table to speak, unless the table holds papers to which you must refer. Gesture naturally with hands or head but avoid moving around unnecessarily. Shift your gaze to various members of the audience. Don't look down at the floor or up at the ceiling or out of a window while you are talking.

4. Speak up. Talk loudly enough so that everyone can hear you without difficulty, and enunciate clearly. Don't talk too fast or too slow, but pause now and then, slow up to stress an important word or phrase, and vary your pitch to give your speech color and interest. Flatness and lack of variety are always dull.

5. Never memorize a speech. Too much nervous energy is expended in committing a speech to memory, and there is too much danger of going blank if you forget any part of it. Instead, put an outline or the salient points on small cards, which you can hold in the palm of your hand and refer to inconspicuously when necessary. Although technical and official papers are often read from manuscript, reading a speech is likely to bore an audience

and should generally be avoided. Without a manuscript the phrases may not be as polished, but they carry far greater interest.

6. Organize your thoughts. Have a definite purpose, and work in an orderly way through the important points to your conclusion. Don't underestimate the advice often given to speakers: "Tell them what you are going to tell them, tell them, and then tell them what you've told them."

7. Get and keep the interest of the audience. Speaking is always easier and much more pleasurable when the audience is entertained. Begin with some *relevant* story or anecdote, some dramatic facts, or a challenging statement. During your talk, don't make generalizations without supporting them with specific facts, instances, and examples. Keep in mind, also, that the more narrative or personal experience you put into the talk, the more interesting it will be. Refer to actual people, places, and events. Engage the audience. Ask them questions and wait for a response. Also let them ask questions. Do all this without wandering from the purpose of your speech or using more time to make a point than it is worth.

8. Use visual aids intelligently. A chart or other visual aid can help to clarify a point and add considerable interest to the presentation. But be sure the chart is big enough to be seen. Also keep it out of sight until you are ready to use it; otherwise it will be distracting. When you do show it, see that there is an easel to hold it properly, and do not obscure it by getting in front of it. When you are through using it, put it out of sight again.

9. End conclusively. Sum up your main points, tell what action is needed, or relate an anecdote that brings your talk to a relevant close. Thanking the audience for their attention is gracious, but it is not necessary.

Introducing a Speaker.   When you are called on to introduce a speaker, find out what his subject will be and what his background or qualifications are. This information is best obtained from the speaker himself, either by mail or by phone before the day of the meeting, or by talking with him briefly just before he is scheduled to speak. In the absence of information from the speaker himself, the chairman may go to the speaker's secretary or use published biographical data such as may be found in *Who's Who in America,* newspaper files, or trade publications. In any case, it is best to make some notes, which you can refer to if necessary. Be sure you know the correct pronunciation of the speaker's name and his most recent official title, for example, assistant vice president, chairman of the executive committee, and so on.

The introduction itself may be very brief. For example:

As you no doubt know, we recently contracted with the Electrex Corporation of Cambridge, Massachusetts, to set up a system for computerizing our personnel records. I'm sure you'd like to know what the purpose of this system is and how it will work. There is no man better qualified to tell you about it than John Devers, vice president of the Electrex Corporation, who has been working out the details of the system for the past several weeks. Many of you already know him and have had an opportunity to talk to him. Mr. Devers is a graduate of M.I.T. He has installed systems similar to ours in a number of large banks and insurance companies. Mr. Devers.

Such a basic introduction could, of course, be expanded with more details about the speaker's education, background, and experience and, where appropriate, references to his origins, home, or family. Some cautions, however, are worth mentioning.

1. Don't go perfunctorily through the speaker's record as if you were reading a catalog. Select the few points that you consider most relevant and important and mention them with some feeling.

2. Don't extend the length of the introduction beyond what the speaker or his subject deserves. Also avoid fawning over the speaker or showing obvious flattery. If he is worth his salt, his record will speak for itself.

3. Don't raise the expectations of the audience unreasonably. When you go into raptures about how interesting or entertaining the speaker is going to be, you only make his job harder. It is usually enough to say, "I'm sure you'll be very much interested in what he has to tell you." If you want to give lavish praise to the performance of the speaker, the time to do it is after he has spoken, not before.

1.5   OFFICE SUPERVISION

The supervisor is a key figure in managing the office and seeing that the work gets done. Many secretaries and administrative assistants are given supervisory functions because they have performed so well the other duties assigned to them. They soon discover—sometimes to their chagrin—that the qualities that make good workers are not the same qualities that make good supervisors. Then a period of adjustment and the acquiring of new skills must begin.

Perhaps the most startling change in the new supervisor's position is that she (or he) is now on management's side, interpreting management's policies, and carrying out management's aims for greater efficiency. These aims are not necessarily contradictory to those of workers, but they require an extra measure of such qualities as orderliness, firmness, loyalty, patience, and fairness.

Although supervisory duties vary considerably, those described in this section may be taken as characteristic.

Employee Relations		*Office Routine*	
Interviewing	p. 26	Methods and Procedures	p. 38
Employment Interview	p. 27	Maintenance of Office	
Training	p. 28	Machines	p. 39
Communication	p. 32	Supplies	p. 40
Morale	p. 33	Housekeeping	p. 40
Motivation	p. 34		
Merit Rating	p. 34		
Grievances	p. 35		
Discipline	p. 37		
Exit Interview	p. 37		

EMPLOYEE RELATIONS

Interviewing. A large part of the supervisor's communication duties consists of talking individually to members of the staff. On a formal basis, the talks become interviews.

For specific types of interviews, see "Discipline," "Employment Interview," "Exit Interview," "Grievances," and "Merit Rating."

Consider these points relating to all interviews.

1. Planning the interview:

(a) Determine your objective. In that way you will be able to measure your success and benefit from your mistakes. In every case, you will want to accomplish your objective with a maximum of goodwill.

(b) Analyze the situation. What kind of person will you be talking to? What is his background? What attitudes can you expect to meet?

(c) Devise your strategy. Make a list of points you want to cover or questions you want to ask. Anticipate the objections that will arise, and be prepared to cope with them. Decide what alternative courses of action are open to you.

(d) Arrange the time and place. Try to conduct the interview when you are not pressed with other business and when the other party is likely to be relaxed also. Choose a place where you can be alone with your interviewee without telephone or other interruptions.

2. Conducting the interview:

(a) Establish rapport with the interviewee. Greet him pleasantly, show him to a chair, exchange friendly remarks.

(b) If a conflict is to be discussed, try to begin with unobjectionable statements. These may consist of expressions of praise or appreciation or a review of areas of agreement. The conflict will be resolved more easily if both parties find they have much in common.

(c) When the interviewee's help is desired, map out the problem, show where his interests are involved, and invite him to work with you toward a solution.

(d) Let the interview develop by making points and asking questions. Questions are better than flat statements whenever some difference in views is suspected. Leading questions—for example, "Don't you agree that . . . ?" —will get a prejudiced answer or arouse resentment. Questions calling for "yes" and "no" answers are sometimes helpful in establishing facts, but better questions usually ask "how?," "what?," or "why?"

(e) Make brief notes if there is danger that important details may be forgotten. However, it is usually better not to distract the interviewee.

(f) Listen carefully to what the interviewee is telling you (see "Communication"). Observe his behavior carefully and try to interpret the meaning and motives behind the words. Is he posing? Is he concealing information? Is he repressing his real feelings?

(g) Do not encourage conversation once the purpose of the meeting has been accomplished. You can close by summing up the gist of the interview, indicating the next step, if any, and expressing appreciation for the interviewee's time and help.

3. Following up the interview:

(a) If you have taken notes during the interview, go over them to make sure they are clear. If you have not taken notes, or if the notes are incomplete, make a record of the interview as soon as it is over, including all the information you think you will need for reference later on.

(b) Decisions resulting from the interview must often be communicated to others, for example, to your own superior, to the personnel department, to the payroll department, and so on.

(c) A letter or memorandum should be written when the interview has resulted in the delegation of a duty, the issuance of instructions, or an agreement on future action. In such a case, the letter provides a confirmation that can be rebutted if any of the details are contrary to the interviewee's understanding.

(d) A follow-up in person is also desirable to see that the consequences of the interview are working out satisfactorily.

Employment Interview.   The purpose of an employment interview is to determine the qualifications of an applicant for a particular job. Keep in mind that while you are sizing up the applicant, he is forming opinions about you and the desirability of working for your company. What he thinks has an important relation to your ability to attract good workers. Some suggestions:

1. Keep in mind the requirements of the job.

2. Study beforehand the applicant's letter, or the filled-in application form, or the employment test results if available. Use the letter of application as a point of departure for the interview; use the company's application form as a checklist of qualifications.

3. See the applicant in private. Put him at ease and be relaxed yourself.

4. Confine the discussion to matters related to the job. Seek information not given in the application or not given in sufficient detail.

5. Let the applicant do most of the talking, but direct his remarks by an occasional question.

6. Describe the job and the conditions of work specifically, and notice the applicant's interest or lack of interest. Do not oversell the job.

7. Invite questions and answer them, adapting always to the interests and needs of the applicant.

8. Observe the applicant's manner, posture, and nervous movements. Check on his personal habits by observing the condition of his clothing, hair, hands, and so on. However, don't make unwarranted inferences from

appearance. Errors in judgment are easily made when the applicant is stereotyped, or made to fit the interviewer's preconceived notions.

9. Avoid expressing or eliciting opinions about religion, politics, race, and other sensitive subjects.

10. Avoid general judgments about the applicant's personality. Try rather to judge such specific facets of personality as intelligence, ability, ambition, industry, and imagination.

11. Tell the applicant what the next step will be. For example, he is to return to the personnel department, or he may start on Monday, or he will hear from you shortly (you still have some applicants to interview), or you don't have anything quite suitable. Be tactful. Help preserve the applicant's self-esteem always.

12. No matter what the decision, end the interview pleasantly.

13. Make notes during the interview only of the facts you may not remember later. Write up the full report immediately after the interview, while the details are still fresh in your mind.

Training. The supervisor must see that proper training is given to an employee who is newly hired or transferred from another position in the company. The main kinds of training are (1) induction training and (2) on-the-job training. In addition, some provision must be made for instructing those recruited to fill in temporarily for ill or absent employees.

Induction Training. An employee needs to be acquainted with the duties he is expected to perform, as well as with those policies and practices that directly affect him. You can best break in a new employee by giving him work he can already do without special training and then adding duties as he gains experience. This procedure gives him confidence and makes him feel productive from the start.

Information about the company's policies and practices can be imparted briefly in an orientation interview before the new employee begins work. At that time, he should be given the company's employee manual and any other literature designed to acquaint employees with their obligations and benefits. He should also be encouraged to ask questions about his job and the conditions of his employment whenever such questions arise.

On-the-Job Training. Both new and seasoned employees must be given training on the job if they are to be able to handle tasks for which their experience does not fit them. Methods of training vary, and often a combination of methods is used. They include:

1. Personal observation and coaching.

2. Counseling sessions designed to point up the employee's strong points and deficiencies.

3. Understudying an experienced worker.

4. Self-instruction through the study of company manuals and programmed and conventional texts.

5. Formal instruction and practice, either individually or with a group (Figure 1-6).

You should be thoroughly acquainted with all the training programs your company has available so that you will be able to make recommendations to your subordinates. Also be familiar with pertinent courses given in the community. Many companies pay part or full tuition for evening study at local schools and colleges.

HOW TO GET READY TO INSTRUCT
1. Have a timetable.
    How much skill do you expect the worker to have?
    By what date?
2. Break down the job.
    List important steps.
    Pick out the key points.
3. Have everything ready: the right equipment, the right materials and supplies.
4. Have the workplace properly arranged just as the worker will be expected to keep it.

HOW TO INSTRUCT
1. Prepare the worker.
    Put him at ease.
    State the job and find out what he already knows about it.
    Get him interested in learning the job.
    Put him in the correct position.
2. Present the operation.
    Tell, show, and illustrate one important step at a time.
    Stress each key point.
    Instruct clearly, completely, and patiently but give him no more than he can master.
3. Try out performance.
    Have him do the job—correct his errors.
    Have him explain each key point to you as he does the job.
    Make sure he understands.
    Continue until you know he knows.
4. Follow up.
    Put him on his own.
    Designate a person to whom he goes for help.
    Check frequently. Encourage questions.
    Taper off extra coaching and close follow-up.

Figure 1-6 How to instruct on the job (adapted from Training Within Industry Foundation).

Because training is costly in time and money, it is important to assess its effectiveness. A check should be made both at the completion of a particular program and after a suitable interval, say, six months. These criteria may be used.

1. Has morale improved?
2. Has the quality of the work improved?
3. Has the number of errors been reduced?
4. Has there been a decrease in absenteeism? lateness? job turnover?

A determination may then be made as to whether the program was worthwhile, whether the instruction needs to be expanded or changed, and whether some kind of refresher is necessary.

Training for Back-Up Duties. A training problem calling for a somewhat different approach is that required to ensure temporary assistance in case of the illness or absence for other reasons of a regular employee.

---

1. GENERAL. What is the name of your office or department? What is the full name of your immediate superior? His title? Who may make decisions in his absence?

2. MAIL. At what times and from what station is outgoing mail picked up? What incoming mail do you open? Is there any special procedure for routing incoming mail? Does any incoming mail get special treatment? What letters do you answer yourself? Where are sample replies kept?

3. TELEPHONE. What extensions do you use? Whom does each extension serve and how do you answer it? How do you announce calls? Do you screen telephone calls? How? How do you place calls for your superior? Where are key telephone numbers kept?

4. FILES. What is the location of file units? Where are special items kept? What rules govern the filing and withdrawal of confidential material? What charge-out system is followed for general material? Where are keys and combinations kept? Is a tickler file maintained? Where is it?

5. DICTATION AND TYPING. What are your superior's dictation habits and preferences? Is any special stationery used? How many copies are usually made? Are there any special distribution lists? What is your superior's preferences in letter make-up? (Include samples.) What liberties does your superior encourage in editing his dictation?

Figure 1-7 Sample data to be included in workbook for guidance of back-up secretary. A similar pattern may be followed for other positions.

6. OFFICE. Who are your principal contacts? What directories and manuals are available? What equipment do you have charge of? Do any special rules govern its use? How do you call for repair service? What security measures must be taken to protect person and property?

7. SUPPLIES. Where are supplies kept? When and how do you order? What special items do you use?

8. MEETINGS AND APPOINTMENTS. How much initiative do you use in arranging appointments for your superior? How is your superior reminded of his appointments and daily schedule? Where is the calendar of meetings kept? What is your responsibility for sending out notices of meetings? What rooms are used? Are reservations necessary? Who takes minutes? To whom do copies go?

9. TRAVEL AND MEALS. How are advances, including petty cash, obtained? What are your superior's preferences in airlines, hotels, restaurants? What arrangements are made for car rental? What credit cards, if any, are used?

10. PERSONAL. When do you take lunch? Coffee breaks? Does your superior approve of your smoking at your desk? What is your superior's lunch schedule? What are his preferences regarding coffee service for him and his visitors? How does he like his coffee? What brand of cigarettes or cigars does he smoke? What organizations does he belong to? What positions in them does he hold? What duties must you perform in connection with them?

Figure 1-7   (continued).

Probably the best way to train a back-up is to assign certain duties to an assistant, who then assumes responsibility for them. There remain, however, many personal chores and special ways of doing things that such training will omit. There are also times when no suitable replacement is available for training and one must rely on temporary help from another department or an employment agency. For these situations, key employees should be encouraged to compile a workbook or manual in which they write out instructions to cover the many special facets of their jobs—those not covered by the existing written procedures. For a secretary such instructions would include the handling of her employer's mail, telephone calls, travel arrangements, and so on (Figure 1-7). If the information is arranged alphabetically, one subject to a page, and kept in loose-leaf form, the instructions can be updated regularly.

ONE-WAY COMMUNICATION

TWO-WAY COMMUNICATION

Figure 1-8   One-way versus two-way communication.

Communication.   Probably the chief difficulties of supervisory communication are (a) failing to let people know, (b) failing to adapt to people and circumstances, and (c) assuming understanding when no understanding exists. These difficulties can be avoided by strict adherence to good communication principles.

1. Develop two-way communication. This is the overriding principle. It is not enough to talk to people. It is also important for these same people to talk to you and for you to benefit from what you hear (Figure 1-8).

2. Ensure contact. Communication can take place only when a message is received. Make sure the other person hears you when you talk and that he fully understands you. Ask questions to find out. If there are special rules or instructions the worker is expected to follow, make sure he knows about them.

3. Use feedback. Note carefully the response to what you say, including your instructions and orders. The response, called *feedback,* will give you some idea of how well you are communicating. If necessary, repeat your instructions or try new approaches.

4. Invite feedback. Encourage your people to talk to you, to give you their opinions, and to ask questions. A lot of mistakes can be avoided that way, and rapport will be improved.

5. Practice empathy. Good communication requires that you develop expectations about the behavior of others. Project yourself into the feelings and thoughts of your workers, so that you can better anticipate their responses and adapt to them.

PAY ATTENTION. Look at the speaker, hear what he is saying, and shut out distractions. Nod occasionally, smile, or use some other expression to show you are getting the message. A verbal response such as "Yes" or "I understand" will perform the same function.

LEARN. From the speaker you can learn much about him: What kind of person is he? What does he want or need? How can you please him? How can you get him to cooperate with you? From the speaker's "feedback" you can also learn how well your message has been getting across to him. If his response suggests that you haven't succeeded, you can try again.

LISTEN WITHOUT BIAS. Regardless of your prejudices, listen with an open mind to what the speaker is saying. Don't twist his remarks to mean what he does not, and don't jump to conclusions he never intended. It's not just that your hostility will show and antagonize the speaker; if you filter his remarks through your prejudices, you'll never really hear what he is saying.

Figure 1-9   Some rules for effective listening.

6. Listen. When others talk, give them your full attention. You'll get your turn later (Figure 1-9).

7. Adapt your message. In framing your message, keep your language on the listener's level and adjust your content to his interests and motives. What you want isn't nearly so important to him as what he wants. If your interests clash, attempt a compromise.

8. Choose your time and place. It makes good sense to approach the other person when he is most likely to be receptive and to stay out of his way when you or your message is likely to irritate him. Also, a private room is better than an open office for some messages; other messages are best casually dropped in a washroom conversation or in a chance meeting in the hallway.

9. Follow up. Follow up on orders and instructions not only to see if they are being carried out, but also to make sure they have been accurately understood in the first place.

Morale.   The morale of subordinates depends on many factors outside the supervisor's competence, but you can contribute in these ways.

1. Distribute work fairly. Show no favoritism of any kind.

2. Give clear and specific instructions for each job. Invite questions and answer them to the employee's satisfaction.

3. Take a personal interest in each subordinate's performance. Offer encouragement and express appreciation frequently.

4. Follow through to see that the work is done—and done properly.

5. Insist on the observance of all office rules. Set an example yourself.

6. Plan work carefully to keep rush work and overtime to a minimum. Pitch in yourself when an emergency arises.

7. Listen sympathetically to subordinates' complaints and do what you can to take care of those that are justified.

8. Keep subordinates up-to-date on changes in company policies and rules.

9. Keep your own employer informed of your supervisory activities. You need his backing to be effective yourself.

Motivation. Every worker has certain emotional needs that he seeks to satisfy through his job. If he cannot satisfy them, his performance will suffer and he will eventually seek satisfaction elsewhere. Through proper supervision you can help any worker find the job satisfactions outlined below.

1. The need to feel that the work is important. Let the employee know how the work he does ties in with the work of others and serves the needs of the whole organization. In that way he will develop pride in a completed task, maintain interest, and improve performance.

2. The desire for recognition. Show interest in the employee's work, thank him for his cooperation, praise him for the things he does well, and see that he is recommended for the raises and promotions he deserves. Find opportunities to mention his good performance to others.

3. The desire to know what is expected. Never leave any doubt as to what an employee is to do, what standards are to be maintained, and what your attitude is toward lateness, absenteeism, and other aspects of personal behavior on the job.

4. The desire for direction. This point is closely related to the preceding ones. Prove by your actions that you have authority in your particular sphere and that you intend to exercise it firmly and beneficially. Know every job under your jurisdiction, and take the initiative in promoting improvements in performance.

5. The desire for responsibility. As far as possible, let the employee work out problems for himself. When instructions are given, make sure he understands them and then leave him alone to carry them out. Give him the opportunity to do a job from start to finish instead of just a small part of it.

6. The desire for dignity and self-esteem. Never reprimand an employee in the presence of others. When an error is made, concentrate on correcting not the individual, but the way the work is done. That keeps your criticism objective. Don't say, "This is wrong," but rather, "Do you think there might be a better way?" Encourage the worker to find the solution.

Merit Rating. To be properly motivated, an employee needs to know what management thinks of his work and he must be given incentives to improve. Merit rating helps fill this need. Usually twice a year, the supervisor reports on the performance of the employees under him. The report will indicate areas of strength and weakness, suggest means of improvement, and serve as a basis for a salary increase, promotion, or transfer.

Although several methods of evaluation are in use, the rating chart is common to most. Selected traits are listed, along with a scale indicating the degree to which the employee exhibits each trait. Factors rated include job knowledge, quality of work, cooperation, initiative, adaptability, and dependability. The scale may consist of such simple terms as (1) outstanding, (2) above average, (3) average, (4) below average, and (5) unsatisfactory; or a short description of each point on the scale may be provided.

The ratings should be as objective as possible. If they are, a small number of employees will probably score low on a single trait, an equal number will score high on the same trait, and a little more than half will score average. Rating nearly everyone "average" usually shows excessive timidity or poor judgment on the part of the evaluator.

Merit rating forms are supplied by the personnel department, which also oversees their use. It is up to the supervisor, however, to rate his own employees and to discuss the results with each one in a private counseling session (Figure 1-10).

Grievances.   Whenever people work together, frictions and dissatisfactions will occasionally arise. If you have gained the confidence of your employees, they will instinctively go to you with their complaints. You, on your part, should encourage frank discussion of complaints and should be ready to lend a sympathetic ear. A complaint should always be heard in private. These techniques are suggested.

1. If, as is usually the case, the complainant comes in angry or upset, your first task is to calm him. Offer a chair. Pour out a glass of water, presumably for yourself, and ask if he would also like some. If tea or coffee is available, offer that. Another device is to ask him to excuse you while you make a phone call at your desk; he should not be requested to leave the room.

2. Encourage the complainant to talk freely while you listen. At opportune times ask questions to establish the facts clearly and to elicit his views and opinions.

3. If the subject is one that requires further investigation, assure him of your sympathy and promise to look into the matter promptly.

4. If you can correct the trouble, do so without delay, but do not make any promises that you may not be able to fulfill. If the final decision must go to a higher level, say that you will take it there and report back as soon as possible.

5. If the trouble cannot be corrected, explain the prevailing conditions, or the appropriate policies and the uses they serve. Never refuse satisfaction because of personal prejudice.

6. If the satisfaction of a complainant requires concessions by other employees, talk to them also; then try to settle the matter on a cooperative basis. Never report to another employee any personal or negative remarks made about him by a complainant.

PERFORMANCE APPRAISAL

Name of Employee _____ Branch _____

Position _____ Department _____

Rated by _____ Date _____

Instructions: Carefully consider the definition of each quality and compare the employee with others doing the same or similar work in this company. Then place a check (✓) below the descriptive adjective that most nearly applies.

QUALITIES	REPORT				
	Out-standing	Above Average	Average	Below Average	Unsatis-factory
1. *Job Knowledge*. Understanding of work required and ability to perform it.					
2. *Ability to Learn*. Ability to learn new methods and follow instructions.					
3. *Industry*. Energy and application given regularly to each task.					
4. *Quality of Work*. Neatness, accuracy, thoroughness.					
5. *Initiative*. Ability to work without constant direction and contribute own ideas.					
6. *Cooperativeness*. Success in working together with others, including those with greater authority.					

Remarks:

Figure 1-10 Merit rating chart to be used by the supervisor in evaluating an employee's performance.

7. If there is no satisfactory alternative, you may offer to arrange a change in duties or a transfer to another office.

Discipline.   Work is best accomplished when every employee knows his responsibilities and takes pains to carry them out. Common disregard of rules can only lead to disorder and unhappiness. When infractions are detected, the supervisor should act promptly to correct the situation. This is best accomplished through an interview with the offender. A proper technique for this interview must be carefully observed to protect the rights of the employee and at the same time to bring about a positive change in his behavior. These suggestions have proved effective.

1. Get all the facts before the interview. Find out what you can about the individual from your personnel records. If another person is involved, talk to him.

2. Conduct the interview in complete privacy.

3. Begin with some favorable report or observation about the employee.

4. Make clear the nature of the dissatisfaction, not by direct confrontation but by questioning. For example, "Mary, is it true that . . . ?" or "Can you explain . . . ?" After all, your facts may be wrong, or you may have misinterpreted the situation.

5. Listen. Give the employee a fair chance to explain. Don't interrupt until he has spoken all that is on his mind. Look for emotional reactions, and respond sympathetically.

6. Don't be personal. Don't accuse. Examine the action rather than the individual. Search for the causes.

7. Suspend judgment until all the facts are in. You don't have to impose discipline at the interview.

8. When discipline is imposed, it should be with a view toward educating the employee rather than punishing him. Such a spirit will help to minimize ill will.

Whatever penalty is eventually imposed should be one that you as supervisor can take responsibility for, though you may first want to discuss the matter with your supervisor. Possible penalties take many forms: a simple reprimand, a notation on the employee's personnel record, the removal of some perquisite or privilege, an apology to an injured party, docking wages or imposing overtime for excessive latenesses and absences, and, finally, demotion, transfer, or dismissal.

Exit Interview.   It is customary to interview departing employees in order to obtain information that may be put to constructive use by the organization. The *exit interview,* as it is called, helps establish the causes of labor turnover and permits a check of morale, working conditions, and reactions to policies, jobs, and people. Because the employee who leaves has few of the inhibitions of those who stay, he may be counted on for a frank, if one-sided, report. Here are some special facets of the exit interview.

1. It may yet be possible to keep a desirable employee if the reason for his leaving can be ascertained and remedied. If there has been a quarrel or a misunderstanding, or a failure to adapt, perhaps a transfer to another department can be effected. If he feels he is not making sufficient progress, perhaps you can suggest additional training.

2. If the employee has a new job, try to find out why he finds it preferable to the job he is leaving. Is it because of better pay, better working conditions, more benefits, easier travel, closeness to friends? You may learn something you can put to use in hiring new personnel.

3. If the employee has been discharged, try to convince him that the action was taken with regret. Emphasize his positive qualities as you offer to suggest other sources of employment or vocational guidance. Tender a smile, a handshake, and your good wishes as he departs.

OFFICE ROUTINE

Methods and Procedures. Efficiency is improved when the supervisor eliminates unnecessary work and finds simpler, better ways to do the necessary work (Figure 1-11).

1. Ideas for improvement are always better when they come from the workers themselves than when they are imposed from above. For that reason you should encourage your assistants to come forward with suggestions. Furthermore, you should receive those suggestions with an open mind and, wherever feasible, permit them to be tried out. Also, those who offer work-saving suggestions must be rewarded with more interesting and more responsible work, not threatened with no work or more work of the same kind.

2. Recopying information is one of the biggest time wasters in the office. It also leads to error.

(a) When information comes in by phone, have it noted if possible on the form that will be used in processing it—calendar, card, memorandum, sales slip, and so on.

(b) Consider the use of carbon interleaved forms to prevent rewriting, with different parts of the form going to different locations for processing or information purposes.

---

1. Eliminate unnecessary procedures.
2. Shift jobs to those in the best position to perform them.
3. Find the most efficient time and place to perform the job.
4. Change the sequence in which a job is performed or combine steps to improve efficiency.
5. Simplify forms and reduce paperwork.

Figure 1-11 Five keys to job simplification.

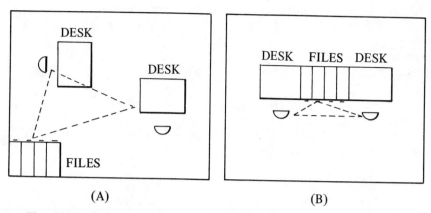

Figure 1-12   Saving steps through proper arrangement of furniture and equipment.

(c) Where copying must be done, machine copies are invariably cheaper than hand-typed copies.

3. Reduce unnecessary movement of persons and papers. For example, wait until you have several items before you call for a messenger; bring machines and operators close together; or try a simple rearrangement of files and desks to minimize walking (Figure 1-12).

4. Observe an orderly pattern in feeding work to subordinates. Don't panic an employee with huge amounts of work. Instead, hand out work at a reasonably steady rate and, except in emergencies, permit one job to be finished before another is begun. In that way an employee may experience the satisfaction of accomplishment. To provide work for slow periods, keep a backlog of secondary tasks.

5. Both your employer and your subordinates expect you to keep up to date on developments in office methods and machines. Browse through business periodicals regularly, read the literature provided by manufacturers of office machines and equipment, and go to office equipment trade shows when they come to your city.

See also "Improving Correspondence Procedures," Section 4.4, and "Data Processing," Section 5.1.

Maintenance of Office Machines.   The supervisor must see that office machines are in good working condition. Breakdowns in office machines cause disruption of work and dissatisfaction on the part of both the operators and the executives. Faulty and inoperative machines will of course be repaired as soon as a repairman and the necessary parts are available. Preventive maintenance, however, can reduce materially the number of breakdowns and keep machines running at maximum efficiency. The manufacturer's recommendations for cleaning, oiling, and periodic inspection should be followed.

Maintenance service contracts are available through the manufacturers or lessors of the machines or through independent contractors. These contracts usually provide for regular inspection, cleaning, oiling, adjusting, and replacement of worn parts. They also provide for emergency repairs in case of breakdowns. Large firms sometimes employ their own maintenance and repair crews.

The supervisor should always take seriously complaints about machine performance and see that faults are corrected as soon as possible. Operators should be thoroughly trained in the use and care of their machines so that breakdowns will not occur through mistreatment.

Supplies.   Adequate supplies of paper, printed forms, envelopes, file folders, stencils, typewriter ribbons, and other stationery items should be available at all times.

1. On the basis of experience and ordering cycles, establish maximum and minimum quantities for all items, and take an inventory at regular intervals. (In a small office it is sufficient to hang a pad inside the door of the supply closet, so that items in short supply can be noted.)

2. Reorder from the stationer or stockroom in ample time for delivery before the supply is depleted.

3. Let the stockroom know in advance when you anticipate the need for an especially large quantity of a particular item.

4. Look into any unusually heavy consumption of supplies.

5. Discourage the taking of office supplies for personal use.

6. If necessary, put one person in charge of the supply closet and require receipts for all items taken.

Housekeeping.   Work can be done efficiently only when all conditions contribute to the result. Comfort, cleanliness, and neatness are essential. Check for the following.

1. Windows, heat, or air conditioning adjusted for comfort. The ideal temperature is 68 to 70 degrees.

2. Blinds and shades uniformly drawn; adequate light for each work requirement.

3. Access to work space clear; desks uncluttered.

4. Walls cleared of all but authorized pictures and charts. No hammering of nails into the wall by any unauthorized personnel.

5. Clothing and personal belongings in lockers and wardrobes, inaccessible to intruders.

6. Plenty of wastebaskets, but out of sight.

7. Bookcases neat and frequently dusted.

8. Flowers and plants, if any, attended to regularly.

9. Typewriters covered and desks cleared of loose papers at the end of the day.

1.6 BUSINESS ETIQUETTE

Etiquette is no more than a decent regard for others. Good manners create harmonious working relationships, promote efficiency, and establish an atmosphere of friendliness and cooperation. Although formal rules are less important than good instincts and genuine consideration for others, the following may be regarded as a code of generally approved business conduct.

Absenteeism.   Large organizations often provide for an allowable number of days off. They are intended to be used for the normal emergencies caused by illness, death in the family, weather and road conditions, and transportation strikes. Extra days off, taken for frivolous reasons, almost invariably place an unfair burden on others and make a negative impression on the employer.

Borrowing.   Every worker should have his own tools and supplies. If he must borrow, the items should be returned promptly with thanks. A note on the calendar pad should serve as a reminder of the debt.

It is best not to borrow even small sums from co-workers. However, the lender is better off asking for the return of the money than nursing a grievance.

Some companies and unions have funds from which money can be borrowed for emergencies and capital purchases. No stigma is attached to such borrowing when the loan is repaid in the required manner.

Borrowing and lending money are personal matters. They should never be discussed with co-workers.

Cafeteria.   The diner should patiently wait his turn in line to be served; no urgency provides an excuse for breaking in ahead of others. Hovering over a diner to pressure him into vacating his seat is equally repugnant.

Tables are meant to be shared, and it is always gracious for a member of either sex to join in polite conversation with co-workers, even though they may be strangers.

If there is waiting for tables, diners who are through should leave promptly; they may continue their conversation in the lounge or recreation area.

Complaints.   Personal complaints should be kept under control. No one likes to work in an atmosphere of discontent. An employee with a legitimate complaint should see the person who is best able to deal with it. If the condition cannot be changed, the employee should try to adjust to it.

Many companies have regular grievance procedures to deal with complaints about work assignments, salary increases, promotions, benefits, and the like. Employees should learn the procedures and use them.

Confidential Information.   An employee should not mention confidential matters to his family or friends, and he should not discuss such matters with other employees who have no right to the information. He should also not tantalize his associates with the remark that he has information that he cannot reveal. The tight-lipped employee will certainly gain more respect and more confidences than the garrulous one.

Confidential papers should be put away in a desk or file drawer after use, so that they cannot be seen by inquisitive persons. If the nature of the papers requires, the drawer should be kept locked.

A person who asks for confidential information should be put off until his right to the information can be verified.

Telephone calls of a confidential nature should be handled discreetly. If a visitor is in the office at the time, he may be courteously dismissed or seated in another room before the telephone conversation proceeds; the call may be taken in another room; or the call may be returned later when the visitor is gone.

For treatment of confidential information in letters to the government and the military, see Section 3.2.

Cooperation.   If work cannot be accepted and done cheerfully and on time, the reason should be discussed with the employer or supervisor.

It is always correct to offer a helping hand to a fellow employee who is temporarily overloaded with work. And it is correct for the co-worker to reciprocate when the occasion permits.

When requests for cooperation are received from outside one's own department, cooperation should be given cheerfully, at least to the extent that one's own work or loyalty to his own group or organization is not impaired.

Counseling Female Subordinates.   When counseling a female subordinate, a man should handle only problems that influence the employee's work and should avoid getting into a discussion of personal problems. He should respond objectively to the employee's difficulties without seeming unsympathetic. All counseling should be done on the company's premises during regular business hours.

Courtesy.   The rules of courtesy in the office are sometimes altered but never suspended. Greetings should be pleasant, and brief social conversation should be engaged in when chance brings co-workers together in halls, lounges, and so on.

Kindnesses should be offered to those in need and kindnesses received should be reciprocated. A pleasant demeanor, sympathy, patience, and normal consideration for the feelings of others also help to make the office a more livable place for everyone.

Criticism.   It is rude and ego-damaging to criticize a subordinate in the presence of others. (See also "Office Supervision," Section 1.5.)

An employee should not criticize company policies before strangers, for he as well as the company loses esteem. If he believes a policy is wrong, he should speak to his superiors, but not before he has plenty of solid evidence to support his position.

The suggestion systems operating in many organizations provide an orderly way for all employees to voice criticism and offer constructive remedies.

Death.   The death of an employer, associate, or employee may be acknowledged by flowers and/or a personal note to the closest bereaved relative. (See "Condolence Letters," Section 4.5.)

In addition to the relatives, friends, and associates who attend the funeral, individuals or small groups may be sent as representatives of organizations to which the deceased belonged. A private funeral is of course confined to invited mourners only.

Dining Out.   An expense account lunch is accepted by the guest with thanks, but without the need to reciprocate.

A reservation should be made in advance if it will spare waiting for a table. State the number in the party, the time of arrival, and any special instructions for seating or service.

If business is to be discussed, the host should be permitted to introduce the subject. A guest who is pressed for time, however, may tactfully bring the conversation around to the business of the meeting.

In the matter of ordering, the guest takes his cues from the host. The considerate host will say, "The antipasto here makes a very good start for the meal," or, "The roast beef is a specialty here." The guest need not order what is suggested, but he knows that he is expected to have an appetizer and something as expensive as the roast beef.

The host will usually offer the guest a drink. The considerate guest who does not want a drink will say, "No, thanks, but you go ahead and order one for yourself." The host may then order one or not.

A female secretary or administrator should have no compunction about inviting a man to be her guest for a business lunch. A credit card, however, will save embarrassment when the check is presented. The male guest will thank his hostess, but should not offer to pay.

When two business associates arrange spontaneously to have a friendly lunch together, without embarrassment each may pay his own share of the bill. If several acquaintances are having a "dutch" lunch, the bill may be evenly divided to spare the detailed accounting procedure that would otherwise be necessary.

If one of the luncheon parties has an engagement to keep, he may find it advisable to mention it beforehand, so that he will not seem rude if he has to conclude the meal abruptly. Neither host nor guest, however, should schedule a meeting so early in the afternoon that a prior luncheon engagement must be rushed.

Dress (see "Grooming").

Elevator.   Where a few individuals are involved, it is polite for men to let women enter and leave the elevator first. If there is a crowd, it is best for the persons nearest the door to enter and leave first.

A gentleman need not remove his hat unless he is accompanied by a lady and there is sufficient elbow room to remove the hat without awkwardness.

Cigarettes and cigars should be extinguished before one enters the elevator. This is a matter of safety as well as etiquette.

In a crowded self-service elevator, the person nearest the signal board may be asked to press the button for the floor desired, and he should comply graciously.

Employer-Secretary Relations.   The secretary is expected to be polite, cheerful, and even enthusiastic in the presence of her employer. With exceptions for small talk, her conversation with him should be brief and limited to business matters. She should keep his confidences, but never encourage him to speak about private or personal matters. She should always give him reason to be proud of her.

The employer is expected to treat his secretary with the consideration due her position and her responsibilities. He finds occasions to compliment her on her work but tempers his criticism and accepts any blame that is his. He schedules his work, where possible, to free her of near-five panic and overtime. He makes sure his speech and personal habits never cause her any embarrassment. He is solicitous of her personal welfare but does not intrude in her private life.

Gifts.   An executive may give his secretary a gift at Christmastime, or at any time in appreciation for her interest in her work or for doing special favors for him, such as running errands during her lunch hour. Gifts on the order of candy, perfume, or two tickets to the theater are best. The secretary should acknowledge the gift graciously.

A secretary does not customarily give her employer a gift, though she may send him a holiday greeting card or birthday greeting, or some novelty that is in good taste and has little or no intrinsic value. An exception is a gift to the superior from the whole staff if it is the custom of the office.

Co-workers who exchange gifts should do so out of the office or at a time when others are not present.

Many organizations have strict rules about accepting gifts from suppliers and others whose gifts may be construed as a bribe. When in doubt, one's superior should be consulted. A gift that is considered improper should be graciously returned.

Grooming.   The best guide to dress and grooming for the office is one's own observations of current practice within the organization. Considerable individuality is often permitted in such professions as college teaching, science, and the arts. Commercial houses are likely to be somewhat more restrictive, especially in the instance of front-office personnel. In general, clothes should be clean, neat, and fashionable, but not eccentric. Business suits for men and tailored suits or skirt and sweater separates for women are almost always correct at work. Women going from the office directly to an evening engagement may wear a simple dress with a jacket that can be removed for the evening and dressed up with costume jewelry.

Hair should be combed and neat and conservatively styled for the office. In the matter of beards, sideburns, and hair length, men should cultivate some sensitivity to the feelings of employers and co-workers. Makeup on ladies should be understated. Perfumes and aftershave lotions should be subdued, if used at all.

Husband and Wife Working Together.   When husband and wife work for the same company, private feelings and personal problems are best kept outside the office. In addressing each other, the couple should follow the office custom, using either first or last names. Before the public, they should address each other as Mr. and Mrs., but otherwise behave as naturally as possible.

Introductions.   Business introductions differ from social introductions in that they are governed primarily by rank and importance rather than by sex or age. When one person is introduced to another, the person to whom greater deference is due is named first, for example, "Mr. Big, this is Mr. Little."

Introducing Individuals. The man is presented to the woman only when their ranks are equal or the woman has superior rank. Otherwise the woman is introduced to the man.

Subordinates are introduced to their superiors.

No special order of precedence is followed in introducing men of equal rank or status, though it is courteous to mention the older man first. The difference in women's ages, however, is tactfully ignored. The following forms are correct.

> Mrs. Jones, may I present Mr. Gordon?
> Mr. Ford, may I introduce Mrs. Jones?
> Mr. Parks, this is Mr. Gordon.

Introductions may give some helpful information about the persons being introduced. For example:

> Mr. Ford, this is Mr. Gordon. He's the new assistant manager of our data processing center.
> May Smith, I'd like you to meet Alan Gordon, who will give you the information you need.
> Mr. Jackson, may I introduce Fred Thomas, who will be working on sales contracts. Jim Jackson is in charge of production, Fred.

As the last two examples suggest, when the first name of one party is given, the first name of the other is given, too, though judicious exceptions may be made when there are wide disparities in age or status.

Group Introductions.   When a group is called together for a meeting, luncheon, or dinner, the host or hostess for that meeting should be the first to arrive and take charge of the introductions. Each person is introduced upon arrival to the assembled group, or to one of the subgroups if it is a large meeting. The basic rules of introductions are observed.

A man introduced to women:

Miss Brown, Mrs. Fletcher, this is Mr. Weber.

Men introduced to a woman or to women:

Miss Brown, Mrs. Fletcher, this is Mr. Weber . . . and Mr. Green.

A man or men introduced to a group of men:

Mr. Weber, this is Mr. Curtis . . . Mr. Pepper . . . and Mr. Ogden.
Mr. Weber, Mr. Clark, this is Mr. Curtis . . . Mr. Pepper . . . Mr. Ogden.

A group of men and women introduced to men:

Mr. Weber, Mr. Clark, this is Mrs. Fletcher, Miss Floyd . . . Mr. Curtis . . . and Mr. Ogden.

Introductions to a Large Group.   The introduction of an individual to a large group should be handled as easily and naturally as possible. Normally, the individual is introduced to the few people nearest him, and then to others as the situation permits. If there is a reason why the person must meet everyone present, the host introduces him to a few people at a time, moving from one group to the next after a few words of conversation.

A woman introduced for the first time at a committee meeting need not stand when introduced unless she wishes to do so. However, if a man is introducing her to the group, he will stand when making the introduction. If the woman is introduced before the meeting to men sitting in the immediate vicinity, they will rise to acknowledge the introduction.

Self-Introduction.   A person introducing himself should preferably address the other person by name first, if he knows it.

Mr. Atkins? I'm Mr. Porter (or John Porter or, simply, Porter). Please come in.
Mr. Atkins, I'm Miss Davis, Mr. Porter's secretary. Mr. Porter will return shortly. Please have a seat.

When the introducer does not know the other person's name, he gives his own name and may add his title or business connection.

My name's Jones.
I'm Miss Davis, Mr. Porter's secretary. May I help you.
Hello, I'm Dave Reeves. I'm in the Securities Administration Division.

In a social situation, the introducer always uses his full name and omits the title *Mr., Miss,* or *Mrs.*

Acknowledging an Introduction.   When the introduction is completed, it is acknowledged verbally and perhaps by handshake, depending on the circumstances and the wishes of the parties involved.

The proper response is, "How do you do?" or "How are you?" or "I'm glad to know you." The phrases "Pleased to meet you" and "I'm glad to make your acquaintance" are considered stilted and should be avoided.

When one is introduced to a group of people, he should vary his acknowledgments by saying, "How do you do, Mr. Gordon," "Mr. Smith," "Good to see you," "Hello," and so on.

Names.   The secretary should always address her employer as *Mr., Dr., Professor,* or whatever other title is appropriate. In speaking to his secretary, the employer may call her by her first name or nickname if both feel comfortable about it, but to those outside his immediate circle of intimates he should refer to her as *Miss* or *Mrs.*

In addressing co-workers, the secretary should take her cue from the practices she observes around her, but she should avoid using first names too fast. If in doubt, she should consult other employees about individual preferences.

Usage is generally more formal in public and in the presence of strangers. Thus the person addressed as *Judy* or *George* in private might better be addressed as *Mrs. Johnson* or *Mr. Morton* in special circumstances.

Neatness.   Tidiness should be observed in personal habits and appearance, in hallways and elevators, and in all areas where work, rest, recreation, or eating takes place.

When smoking is permitted, ash trays should be emptied frequently.

If cafeteria rules require, trays and dishes should be taken to the proper station when the diner leaves.

If coffee or meals are taken in one's office, crumbs should be removed, and paper cups and napkins discarded. Chinaware should be promptly rinsed and stored out of sight.

Parties.   When a party or social affair is held for employees, whether on the office premises or not, some of the rules of protocol are relaxed to the extent that sociability and freedom from snobbery become more important than the preservation of rank. This fact, however, should not lessen the deference normally shown to others because of sex, age, or position; and the familiarities developed during the party should be forgotten when the participants return to work.

Personal Habits.   Consideration for others dictates strict control over the application of makeup at one's desk and prohibits completely the cleaning of fingernails, the combing of hair, and the adjusting of clothing.

The feet-on-desk posture is acceptable only in a private office when there are no visitors and no secretary present.

The use of mouthwash or toothpaste in the washroom is better than the use of gum or a mint in the office.

The regular use of a deodorant by both sexes is absolutely necessary.

Personal Phone Calls. Business discourages the use of the telephone for personal calls, but realizes that some such calls are legitimate and necessary.

Long, intimate conversations on the company's time and in the presence of others are never in good taste.

Relatives and friends should be discouraged from telephoning.

Non-business-connected toll calls at the company's expense are larcenous.

Urgent calls that cannot properly be made from the office should be made, if possible, from a pay phone in the building lobby or in the employees' lounge.

Personal Visitors. Visits by friends or family are not encouraged, especially in the lower ranks. If a friend calls for lunch or at quitting time, the employee should be ready to leave promptly. If the friend is early, it is better for him to wait in the reception room than at the employee's desk.

Those with private offices can, of course, feel somewhat freer to see family and friends during office hours than those who share space with others, but even high executives prefer as little intrusion as possible during business hours.

Precedence. A secretary opens the door for visitors and permits them to enter her employer's office first.

The secretary follows her employer to his office, but he may permit her to enter first as he opens the door.

When a meeting breaks up, senior members are permitted to leave first, and the secretary follows her employer, unless he tarries.

See also "Elevators."

Private Dining Room. Part of a company's private dining room is usually set aside for random seating of the company's executives. The seats are filled in order; a lone diner does not take a place removed from others. Where meal times are assigned, the diner should arrive promptly and, in any case, leave as soon as he is through, so that someone else may have his place.

Reservations are usually required when an executive has guests. The reservation should be made at least a day in advance, if possible, and the time of the reservation should be observed by the host. If one of several guests is late, the others may start without him. In a crowded dining room, a specific period may be allowed for the meal, as between 12 and 1 o'clock. The host should tactfully close the luncheon meeting promptly. If necessary, the conversation can continue in his office.

The private dining room usually has a limited menu; however, a guest who is on a diet may feel free to ask for simple substitutes like tomato juice, eggs, and toast for other items on the menu that are not agreeable. The waiter will probably have some suggestions.

Ordering procedure varies. The waiter may take the order from each guest individually; the host may take the orders for all and write them on a card to be passed on to the waiter; or each guest may be given a menu with instructions to check the items he wants.

No tips are to be left for the waiter. However, depending on the custom in the particular company, an executive using the dining room regularly will pay a sum monthly into a pool for the waiters or have it added to the sum charged to him for his personal meals.

The guests' meals are always paid for by the company and except for the usual "thank you," no reciprocation is expected or necessary.

Punctuality.   The visitor should arrive promptly for all his appointments. If he is going to be even a little late, either he or his secretary should call ahead. If an appointment cannot be met, the host should be notified as long in advance as possible and a new date arranged.

Employees should arrive promptly at work and return promptly from luncheon and coffee breaks. This is not just a matter of giving the employer a full return for his hire, but of being considerate of fellow workers and helping to maintain everybody's morale.

Work promised, assigned, or contracted for should be completed on time, or the other party should be notified sufficiently in advance to permit him to adjust his plans accordingly.

Rising.   Common sense should alter the usual rules about the etiquette of rising to meet guests.

A secretary does not rise when her employer enters, and the employer does not rise when his secretary or associates enter.

The executive will rise as a special mark of courtesy for visitors of either sex and for women employees to whom he wishes to show special deference.

A male subordinate will rise for his employer.

Romance in the Office.   Couples who form legitimate romantic attachments in the office may have lunch together, but should avoid any emotional displays on the business premises. This does not mean that they must avoid each other; however, their contacts should be brief and confined to necessary company business. They are also well advised not to discuss their romance with others in the organization lest there be grave embarrassment to both.

Tipping. It is not necessary to tip porters, mail boys, and other service employees. However, an executive may offer a gift in cash or merchandise for special services rendered him personally; and a group of employees may take up a collection at Christmastime for service employees who have been helpful during the year.

An executive may offer a cash bonus from his own funds for any secretarial duties performed for him personally on the employee's own time. (See also "Gifts.")

It is not customary to tip outside messengers, repair men, and others who call at the office to render service.

Traveling with Secretary. Hotel reservations made for a male executive traveling with his female secretary should specify two rooms and mention both names and the relationship. If the hotel has not provided rooms on separate floors, the person who registers (executive or secretary) should see that this is done.

Separate registration cards should be made out for each party (not "John Brown and secretary").

Work that must be done together should be done in the executive's room after it has been made up. The best accommodations for this purpose are a studio bedroom or a parlor suite.

Meals may be ordered to be served in the room if it is impractical to go out.

2

Meetings

This chapter deals with the preparations for organized meetings and the formalities of minutes and parliamentary procedure.

CONTENTS

2.1 Conference Arrangements   p. 52
2.2 Parliamentary Procedure   p. 60
2.3 Minutes   p. 68
2.4 Conventions and Large-Scale Meetings   p. 78

For further information on participation in meetings, see "Talking to Groups," Section 1.4.

For arrangements covering private meetings, see "Appointments and Visitors," Section 1.3.

Meetings provide a way of dealing with common problems by discussion and by the participation of all in the decisions of the group. This method has been found, in many instances, to be an improvement over the older process by which an individual unilaterally makes decisions and gives orders that they be carried out.

Common types of meetings are staff conferences and committee meetings. Another type is the task meeting, which brings together a number of individuals who do not ordinarily work as a unit, but who have been brought together to apply their particular skills to the solution of a problem. Corporate meetings include meetings of the directors and the annual meeting of stockholders. Other meetings are held for dealers and distributors, groups of consumers, civic leaders, and the press. Many companies and their personnel also lend their services to the running of meetings or conventions for the business or professional societies to which they belong.

Meetings may also be classified by the functions they perform or the nature of the business that takes place in them. These functions are easily identified.

1. Instructional. Attendees come to learn about new administrative procedures, changes in organizational personnel, and new developments in

their professional or technical specialty. All training sessions also come under this category.

2. Advisory. An administrator seeks the advice of his peers or subordinates before making a decision.

3. Deliberative. A committee or other group meets to make decisions for which the whole group is responsible.

4. Persuasive. Those who call the meeting hope to sell their ideas, services, or products in a usually one-sided presentation.

5. Negotiative. Two sides with opposing views get together to reach a settlement. Labor negotiations fall into this category.

In addition, each group usually has a self-perpetuating function that may involve (1) electing officers, (2) adopting rules for its own conduct, (3) maintaining records, and (4) giving recognition to those who serve it well, for example, a gift, a citation, a vote of thanks, or a testimonial dinner.

2.1   CONFERENCE ARRANGEMENTS

The term *conference* is here used to denote the meeting of a relatively small group of individuals for consultation and discussion. Ordinarily, the routine associated with a conference will include these steps.

1. Arranging for the meeting place.
2. Sending out meeting notices.
3. Preparing the agenda.
4. Taking the minutes.
5. Following up on meeting business.

Division of Responsibilities.   An executive is normally responsible for holding conferences in his area of authority, and he makes whatever plans are necessary to ensure their success. As staff director, he runs the staff meetings. If he is the chairman of any committee, it is his duty to call meetings of that committee, also, and to preside at them. A committee may have an elected secretary, though it is common in business for the chairman to ask his private secretary to assist in the routine planning and to take minutes or less formal notes of the proceedings. How much the private secretary does depends on the authority assigned her by her employer and on her own initiative and ability. Certainly, she can be of enormous help in practically every phase of conference planning and performance outside of the actual deliberations.

Informal Conferences.   In anticipation of a small, informal meeting, the executive will communicate to his secretary the extent to which her services are required. She will probably assist in performing the following basic routines.

```
                                        October 10, 19--


To Members of the Personnel Committee:

There will be a special meeting of the Personnel
Committee on Thursday, October 24, at 3 p.m. in the
14th floor conference room. The purpose of the meet-
ing is to discuss several proposals for disability
insurance.

Please notify the Secretary or Miss Farmer (Ext.
3201) if you are unable to attend.

                                        James Gary
                                        Secretary
```

Figure 2-1   Notice of a meeting.

1. Reserve the conference room. This is necessary if the executive's own office is not to be used. The room chosen should be large enough to accommodate the group comfortably. A check should be made of the seating, ventilation, lighting, and electrical outlets, if needed.

2. Invite the participants. This is done by telephone or mail. Those who cannot attend are usually asked to give notice to that effect. In some instances the participants are consulted beforehand so that a mutually convenient time may be set. The notification should tell the nature or purpose of the meeting and what contributions any individual participant is expected to make as, for example, to give a report or explain a procedure (Figure 2-1).

3. Prepare conference material. The secretary may be required to type the order of business and obtain or prepare data for her employer's presentation. She may also have to have reports duplicated for distribution at the meeting.

4. Check the room. The secretary should arrive shortly before the time set for the meeting and see that the room is in order. At the start of the meeting she will take the attendance and, if feasible, remind the absentees by telephone that the meeting is starting.

5. Take notes. The secretary may be required to keep notes of the course of the discussion and provide an oral summary from time to time during the meeting.

6. Follow through. When the meeting is over, a summary is usually typed and distributed to the participants (Figure 2-2). Either by the underlining of the applicable passages or by separate memorandums, the attention of individuals is drawn to tasks assigned to them at the meeting.

November 14, 19--

Memorandum to: B. C. Farnum   R. B. Sterling
                    M. Greggson   H. S. Timmons
                    C. T. Madow   G. Wanderly

A meeting of the Education Committee was held on
Monday, November 10, 19--, in Mr. Madow's office.
Present were Messrs. Madow, Sterling, Timmons, and
Wanderly.

Mr. Madow began by saying that fringe benefits were
becoming increasingly important in attracting and
holding ambitious young people and that unless we
liberalized our tuition refund plan, we would be
placing our future development in jeopardy.

Mr. Sterling said he hoped we wouldn't tamper with
the present policy of not refunding tuition for
courses in which D and F grades were received. He
said that part of the merit of the present plan was
that it offered a strong incentive for good work.
Mr. Wanderly said that such an incentive was built
into the grading system and that making an employee
pay tuition for a course in which he got a low grade
simply encouraged employees to take the easiest
courses.

Mr. Wanderly said that with the rising cost of text-
books, the company could most help its student employees by offering to pay up to $50 a term for
books.

Mr. Madow asked that Mr. Timmons and Mr. Wanderly
pool their information and design a new tuition refund package that would reflect the soundest modern
practices. This could then be presented at the next
meeting of the Education Committee, scheduled for
December 12.

Eleanor Drier
Secretary to Mr. Madow

Figure 2-2   Memorandum embodying notes of an informal meeting.

Formal Conferences. Many formally constituted groups meet to make decisions that are binding on the participants or their constituents, and they must therefore follow very orderly procedures to ensure the validity of their decisions. Even when the legal aspects of the meeting are minimal, there may be need for systematic planning, observance of rules, and careful record-keeping.

Preliminaries. The secretary is expected to assist with the following preparations.

1. Calendar. Formal conferences should be and usually are scheduled well in advance. Regular meetings of a committee or similar body may be announced for a full year ahead. Mark the dates on your calendar as soon as they are known; then, allowing the needed time for preparation, schedule the work on your calendar or in your tickler file.

2. Meeting file. Set up a folder for each scheduled meeting and put into it all the correspondence, notices, and other documents relating to it. A planning schedule should be included in the folder or stapled to the cover for easy reference (Figure 2-3).

3. List of conferees. Obtain a list of those who are to be invited to the meeting. If some people are to attend several meetings, keep their names and addresses on cards or put them on stencils for machine addressing. Sheets of gummed labels interleaved with carbon paper may be used for the same purpose. Keep the mailing list up-to-date by making changes in names and addresses as soon as they are known. Also make careful inquiry regarding special guests for each meeting and add their names to the list.

4. Room facilities. Reserve the room for the meeting as far ahead as possible. At the same time arrange for a tape recorder, a projector, or other equipment, if necessary. Remember to check the location of an electrical outlet and the possible need for an extension cord, and make a note to have an extra bulb for the projector handy in case of emergency. If an operator is needed, arrange for that, too. Just before the meeting, see that the equipment is in place and that the seats are arranged the way your superior wants them. Distribute pencils and pads. Have water pitchers and glasses strategically located, with such service available at least for the head table. Be sure there are enough ash trays. Check the air conditioning or ventilation.

5. Notices. Notice of the meeting should be sent out reasonably well in advance, the amount of time depending on the nature of the meeting, the business pressures on the participants, travel requirements, and other factors. When notices are sent out far in advance to ensure that busy recipients reserve the date, it is customary to follow up with a reminder close to the day of the meeting.

The meeting notice should include the name of the group or organization, and the date, time, and place of the meeting.

Unless only routine business is to be taken up, the notice should state the purpose of the meeting or the chief subject of discussion.

MEETING

Group _____ Date _____ Time _____ to _____

Room _____ Reservation made (date) _____ No. of persons _____

Seating Arrangements   ☐ Regular
                        ☐ Special (If special room layout is required, send
                                    diagram to Building Dept. and file copy
                                    in folder.)

Equipment Required	*Ordered*	Refreshments	*Ordered*
☐ Blackboard	_____	☐ Coffee ·	_____
☐ Pad and easel	_____		
☐ Lectern	_____	☐ Tea	_____
☐ Public address system	_____	☐ Soft drinks	_____
☐ Neck microphone	_____		
☐ Slide projector	_____	☐ Danish	_____
☐ Overhead projector	_____		
☐ Movie projector (__ mm.)	_____	☐ _____	_____
☐ Screen	_____		
☐ Place cards	_____	☐ _____	_____
☐ _____	_____	☐ _____	_____

Figure 2-3   Form used in planning meetings.

The notice may include a tentative agenda and copies of any reports or other documents that need to be studied in advance.

Conferees may be asked to send information on any reports they wish to make or items of new business they would like to have taken up at the meeting (Figure 2-4). Those from whom reports are expected should be reminded by telephone if they do not respond promptly.

If it will serve a useful purpose, all recipients should be asked to reply by mail or telephone within a time limit. A postcard form may be included to ensure an answer. Another follow-up arrangement is to call each member of the group a few days in advance of the meeting to find out if he will attend, a procedure that is always necessary when members of the group fail to respond as requested.

6. Food and refreshments. If coffee or food is to be served at the meeting, special arrangements must be made with the catering service, preferably a

```
                              July 24, 19--


Memorandum to Mr. Collier:

Mr. Huff is calling a staff meeting for Monday,
August 9. If you as chairman of the Work Measure-
ment Committee expect to have a report, please let
me know so that the item may be included on the
agenda.

It would also be appreciated if you would let me
have a copy of your report before the day of the
meeting.

                              Evelyn Pawling
                              Secretary to Mr. Huff
```

Figure 2-4   Request for a report.

week or two, or several weeks, in advance. The exact number of persons to be served can be relayed by telephone a few days before the meeting. (See also "Food Service," p. 84.)

7. Agenda. Whether it is called the agenda, or the order of business, or the calendar, the plan of the meeting must be carefully outlined beforehand. Unless the bylaws of the group indicate otherwise, the usual order of business is as follows.

Call to order
Approval of the minutes of the last meeting
Announcements
Reports of standing committees
Reports of special committees
Old business (carried over from previous meetings)
New business
Adjournment

With the information already in your meeting file and in the minutes of the last meeting, you should know what business has been held over and, to some extent, what reports are to be made and what new business is to come up. With the help of your employer, you can then incorporate these and other specifics into the agenda for the meeting. (See example in Figure 2-5.) It is customary to have copies of the agenda for distribution to everyone at the meeting, especially if changes have been made in a previously distributed tentative agenda.

COMMITTEE OF PROFESSIONAL WOMEN
FOR THE MUSIC CENTER

Board Meeting--October 8, 19--

AGENDA

I.   Call to Order

II.   Introductions
         New Board Member
         Guests

III. Minutes of the June 22 Board
         Meeting   Anita Reeves

IV.   Treasurer's Report   Carol MacGregor

V.   Old Business
         President's Advisory Board

         Bus-to-Bowl Event   Genevieve Carroll

         Membership Matters   Agnes Deringer

VI.   New Business
         Fall Event - November 19 Genevieve Carroll

         The Orchestra
            European Tour
            Series W
            Philharmonic Fund

         Annual General Meeting

         Publicity
            Events
            Officers
            Newsletter

VII. Adjournment

Figure 2-5 A sample agenda.

The Meeting. You should be in the room before the first conferees arrive. Bring with you a list of the persons expected, copies of the agenda, copies of any reports to be distributed, and your meeting file.

1. Attendance. Methods of taking attendance vary, but you should be sure to have a record of those who attend and be able to tell the chairman if there is a quorum. The quorum is the number of the group required to be present for business to be transacted—usually a simple majority. Latecomers should be recorded as present and in cases where individual voting records may later be needed, notations should be made of those who leave the room.

2. Notes. A careful record must be kept of the proceedings of the meeting. Notes taken at the meeting will later be edited and written up as the minutes of the meeting. (See "Minutes," Section 2.3.)

If you are asked to take notes at the meeting, you will find some of the information you need already available in the agenda and in the reports and resolutions submitted in advance. However, you will have to pay strict attention to motions as they are offered and record them on the spot. Skeletal forms prepared in advance will ease the task of recording (Figure 2-6). Additional notes will include summaries of announcements and oral reports, arguments made for and against motions on the floor, and a brief record of the other matters discussed.

Many times you will be asked to repeat the phrasing of a motion or of amendments to it, and to tell the chairman what the state of any particular motion is. A knowledge of parliamentary procedure is useful for this purpose (see "Parliamentary Procedure," Section 2.2).

The verbatim proceedings of a meeting taken by a stenographer or recorded on tape can be a valuable aid in the preparation of the minutes. However, it should be kept in mind that such records will not include many details, such as the date and time of the meeting, the time of adjournment, the attendance, the names of speakers, and individual voting records. You must be alert to fill in the gaps from your own notes.

Recorded proceedings of meetings are useful for purposes other than the writing of the minutes. They may be filed for the use of absent members and those who wish more details than the minutes provide. For convenience of reference, tapes should be transcribed, a task that may be turned over to the typing pool.

Post-Meeting Functions. After a meeting, there is always a considerable amount of follow-up work. Here is a quick checklist.

1. Prepare the minutes for the signature of the chairman or the organizational secretary.

2. Enter corrections of minutes of the previous meeting in the official minutes book (see "Minutes," Section 2.3).

3. Prepare vouchers to pay for any fees or expenses.

4. Send copies of resolutions of appreciation, condolence, and so on, to the affected parties, with a covering letter.

Motion no. _____

Proposed by:

Seconded by:

  Voted for: Voted against:

Discussion:

Figure 2-6 Form to aid in taking of minutes.

5. Notify affected individuals of election, appointment, or special assignment growing out of the meeting.

6. Remind the chairman or organizational secretary to write letters authorized by the meeting; or draft the letters and offer them for approval and signature.

2.2 PARLIAMENTARY PROCEDURE

In order to ensure the orderly conduct of business and the observance of democratic principles, formally constituted committees, clubs, and other organizations observe to some degree the rules of parliamentary procedure. The rules are so named because they have their origins in the practices of the British Parliament.

Basic Principles

1. All members of the group have equal rights and obligations. Any member may offer motions and take part in the debate.

2. All officers of the group are elected by a majority vote, and majority rule prevails.

3. Meetings are conducted in an orderly fashion. The agenda shows what business will be taken up and in what order, and one item must be disposed of before another can be considered.

4. Personalities are avoided. The discussion is addressed to ideas rather than individuals. In keeping with the aim of objectivity, members are addressed not as "you," but as "the chairman," "Mr. Simmons," "the gentleman," "the previous speaker," and so on.

5. Full discussion is permitted as long as it relates to properly presented motions and resolutions.

6. Every member has the right to know the exact language and status of any motion being discussed, and it is up to the chairman to see that this right is preserved.

7. Impartiality requires that the chairman take no sides and that he give all members an equal opportunity to speak. The chairman never makes a motion while in the chair, nor does he debate a motion without having first called the next ranking officer to preside in his place. In such an event, he does not return to the chair until the vote has been announced.

Order of Business.   Unless otherwise stated in the bylaws of the organization, the usual order of business is as follows.

Call to Order.   The chairman says, "The meeting will come to order." He may add any opening remarks.

Approval of Minutes.   The chairman calls on the organizational secretary to read the minutes of the last meeting, then asks, "Are there any corrections?" If the minutes have been distributed before the meeting, the reading can be dispensed with. No motion is needed for approval of the minutes. The chairman says, "The minutes stand approved," or "The minutes stand approved as corrected."

Reports.   The chairman asks for reports from officers, standing committees, and special committees, in that order. After a report is presented by the officer or committee chairman, the meeting chairman asks if there are any questions or discussion. If not, he orders the report filed. No motion is needed for the adoption of a committee report unless recommendations for action are made.

Unfinished Business.   The chairman announces that unfinished business is in order, and either he or others he designates present facts relating to matters held over from other meetings and included on the current agenda. At the conclusion, a member wishing to take up any other matter not concluded at an earlier meeting rises to be recognized, refers to the matter, and makes a motion.

New Business.   The chairman asks, "Is there any new business?" Motions relating to new business can now be made.

Announcements.   The chairman asks, "Are there any announcements?" He may add any announcements of his own.

Adjournment. The chairman says, "If there is no further business, the meeting will stand adjourned." When the business of the meeting is not finished, however, the chairman must ask for a motion to adjourn, and the motion must be seconded, voted on, and passed.

Conduct of Business. The business of a formal meeting is transacted by means of motions and resolutions (Figure 2-7). A *motion* is a proposal for a specific course of action. It may be stated, for example, as "I move that group life insurance benefits be extended to part-time consultants." A *resolution* is an expression of the views of a group. It usually consists of a preamble beginning "Whereas," followed by "Be It Resolved," and the resolution.

A *main motion* is one placed before the group when no other business is under consideration. Amendments to the main motion may be proposed, but they must be discussed and voted on before a vote is taken on the main motion. A very urgent or important motion takes precedence over other motions. All motions must have a single objective and must be presented in accordance with the rules of order.

Presenting a Motion. To present a motion, a member stands and addresses the chair by his title, for instance, "Mr. President." The chairman recognizes the speaker by nodding to him or speaking his name. The presenter then says, "I move that," or "I move the adoption of the following resolution." In some instances, it is helpful to offer some explanation before the motion is made. In that case, the speaker may say, "I have a motion to make, but first I would like to say a few words by way of introduction."

After presentation of the motion, the chairman says, "You have heard the motion. Is it seconded?" Any member may, without rising, second the motion. If the motion is not seconded, the chairman says, "There being no second, the motion is not before the meeting." If the motion is seconded, the chairman states the question: "It has been moved and seconded that . . ." There can be no discussion or vote until the motion is so stated, at which time the motion becomes the *question* and is so referred to. The chairman now calls for discussion or vote, as the group wishes.

The Motion Considered. Except for some motions relating to parliamentary procedure, all principal motions are subject to debate. The presenter should be given the opportunity to speak first if he claims the right promptly. Others should be given their turn, and no one should be permitted to speak twice when others desiring to speak have not yet been given the opportunity. Discussion must be confined to the question, and the chairman should be sure the assembly knows at all times what the issue is.

At the end of the discussion, a member may shout, "Question." Or the chairman may ask, "Are you ready for the question?" If some members still want to debate, a vote may be taken on a motion to close debate. This motion, which is not debatable, requires a two-thirds vote. When

Motion	Inter-rupt Speaker	Second Needed	Amend-able	Debate-able	Vote Required
Privileged Motions[1]					
Adjourn	No	Yes	Yes	Yes	Majority
Recess	No	Yes	Yes[2]	No	Majority
Question of privilege	Yes	No	No	No	No vote
Orders of the day	Yes	No	No	No	Majority
Subsidiary Motions[1]					
Lay on the table	No	Yes	No	No	Majority
Close debate	No	Yes	No	No	Two-thirds
Limit debate	No	Yes	Yes	No	Two-thirds
Postpone to a specified time	No	Yes	Yes	Yes[3]	Majority
Refer to committee	No	Yes	Yes	Yes	Majority
Amend	No	Yes	Yes	Yes[4]	Majority
Postpone indefinitely	No	Yes	No	Yes	Majority
Main Motions[5]					
General	No	Yes	Yes	Yes	Majority
Specific					
Reconsider	Yes	Yes	No	Yes[4]	Majority
Rescind	No	Yes	Yes	Yes	Majority
Take from the table	No	Yes	No	No	Majority
Change order of business	No	Yes	Yes	Yes	Two-thirds
Incidental Motions[5]					
Point of order	Yes	No	No	No	Chair
Appeal from decision of chair	Yes	Yes	No	Yes[4]	Tie or majority
Parliamentary inquiry	Yes	No	No	No	Chair
Request for information	Yes	No	No	No	Chair
Withdraw a motion	No	No	No	No	Chair[6]
Division of a question	No	No	Yes	No	Chair[6]
Division of the assembly	Yes	No	No	No	Chair[6]
Suspend rules	No	Yes	No	No	Two-thirds
Object to consideration	Yes	No	No	No	Two-thirds negative

[1] Arranged in order of precedence.

[2] Only length of recess is amendable.

[3] Only propriety of postponement is debatable.

[4] Only when specific motion to which it applies is debatable.

[5] No order of preference among themselves. Incidental motions rank above subsidiary motions and take precedence over the motions from which they rise.

[6] If an objection is raised, a majority vote is required.

Figure 2-7   Table of motions.

it passes, a vote is taken first on any amendments, and then on the main motion.

The chairman is required to repeat a motion before a vote is called for. In putting the motion to a vote, the chairman says, "All in favor, say 'Aye.'" The members cast their vote. Then the chairman says, "All opposed, say 'No.'" If the voice response is clear-cut, the chairman will say, "The aye's [or no's] have it. The motion is carried [or is defeated]." If the voice vote is questioned, the vote may be taken by a show of hands, by having members stand, by ballot, or by roll call. The last is used when a record of the vote is desired.

All main motions are decided by a majority vote. The chairman may cast his vote in a tie or whenever the vote is taken by ballot or roll call.

Other Actions. In addition to simple discussion and vote on the main motions, motions may be altered, delayed, or killed, and previous actions may be modified.

1. Amendments. A member of the group may change a motion by amending it or by dividing the question. An amendment may consist of an addition, a deletion, or the substitution of words, or any combination of these methods. The amender says, "I move to amend the motion to read *may* instead of *shall*." Like the main motion, the amendment must be seconded, opened to discussion, and voted by a majority. The initial or primary amendment may itself be amended by a secondary amendment, but no more than two amendments to the main motion are permitted. The secondary and primary amendments must be disposed of in that order before discussion of the main motion, as amended, can be resumed.

2. Division. Consideration of a complex question may be aided by a division into its parts, with discussion and a vote on each part separately. A motion to divide may be decided by the chairman without a vote.

3. Lay on the table. To postpone action on a motion, a member may move to "lay it on the table." The latter motion, which takes precedence over all others, is not debatable and is passed by a majority vote. A tabled motion must be offered again later at the same meeting or at the following meeting; otherwise it is considered dead. A motion to "take from the table" may be made when new or unfinished business is in order and no question is pending.

4. Postpone. A specified time for consideration may not be incorporated into a motion to lay on the table. If resumption of consideration is desired at a specific time, a motion to postpone until that time is in order. Such a motion may be amended and debated.

5. Commit. A motion requiring further investigation or discussion may be referred to a committee. A member says, "I move that the question be referred to a committee of three appointed by the chairman." If the number, composition, and method of selection of the committee are not stated in the motion, the decision must be made by the chair or on further motion by the assembled group. After consideration by his group, the committee chairman reports to the assembly and recommends the action to be taken.

6. Object to consideration. An objection may be raised to consideration of a motion, provided it is done before the first speaker is through talking. The chair responds by calling for a vote.

7. Postpone indefinitely. A vote to postpone a motion indefinitely has the same effect as a vote to defeat it.

8. Withdraw. A member may ask to withdraw his motion. The chairman responds by asking if there is any objection. If there is no objection, the motion is withdrawn. If there is objection, a vote must be taken.

9. Reconsider. Any action already taken may be reconsidered provided a member moves reconsideration on the same day as the main motion was adopted or defeated. The motion to reconsider is entered in the minutes for consideration at the next meeting.

10. Rescind. A member may move that an action already taken be rescinded.

Rights of Members.   Some questions affecting the rights of members are so urgent that they may be raised even at the cost of interrupting a speaker.

1. Question of privilege. A member may get immediate attention to a request affecting comfort, heating, or the like, by rising to a "question of privilege." On action by the chairman, the regular business of the meeting is resumed.

2. Point of order. A member may call attention to a violation of procedure by saying, "I rise to a point of order." The chairman will ask him to state his point and then declare that it is either well taken or not.

3. Appeal. The decision of a chairman may be appealed. The chairman then puts the question to the assembly. "Shall the decision of the chair be sustained?" Debate is permitted, and a majority rules.

4. Inquiry. The chairman may be asked to rule whether a parliamentary procedure is in order or to explain the meaning of a motion.

5. Point of information. A member may interrupt a speaker to ask for clarification of a point, but not to offer information.

6. Division of assembly. When the tally of a vote is uncertain, a member may call out, "Division." The "aye's" and "no's" may then be asked to rise and be counted.

7. Orders of the day. When the scheduled order of business is not being followed, a motion for "the orders of the day" may be offered to ensure proper treatment of a measure. No vote is required.

Adjournment.   A motion to adjourn is in order at any time except when a speaker has the floor or the assembly is occupied with important business. Forms of the motion include, "Mr. Chairman, I move that we adjourn," "I move that we adjourn at three o'clock," and "I move that we adjourn until Thursday, September 22, at four o'clock." The last type of motion is made to ensure another meeting when a regular meeting has not been

QUARTER CENTURY CLUB

Minutes of the Meeting of the Board of Directors

September 2, 19--

The regular quarterly meeting of the Board of Directors of the Quarter Century Club was held in the 14th floor conference room on Wednesday, September 2, 19-- at 4:00 p.m.

The meeting was called to order promptly by the President, Eugene Kane. Present, in addition to Mr. Kane, were Mary Blair, Marvin Denny, Eleanor Farber, Roy Gilston, William Harrison, Burt Reynolds, and Teddy Walhovic. Absent were Gloria Porter and Stephen Simon. Miss Farber acted as secretary in the absence of Mrs. Porter.

The minutes of the previous meeting, June 14, 19--, were read and approved without correction.

Mr. Kane announced that Jerome Daly, an active member of the Board, had died after a short illness on August 8. All stood for a moment of silence. Mr. Kane asked Miss Farber to prepare a suitable letter of condolence to be sent to Mrs. Daly on behalf of the Board.

Treasurer's Report. Mr. Denny reported on the statement of income and expenses as follows:

Income	$5,703.00
Expenses	8,672.78
Excess of Expenses Over Income	2,969.78
Credit Balance, June 30, 19--	4,963.52
Credit Balance, June 30, 19--	$1,993.74

The report was accepted as read.

Membership Committee. Mr. Harrison reported that, as of September 1, four additional members of the staff were eligible for membership in the Quarter Century Club. They are Neil Goldberg, Henry T. Grady, Lillian S. Harrison, and Benjamin Stromberg.

Upon motion of Mr. Harrison and duly seconded, the four employees named were admitted to membership. Mr. Kane asked that the Secretary so notify them.

Figure 2-8 Minutes of a formal meeting.

Jack - Transleft.
Master Cylinder - On Order -
        In next couple days -

4 6
            5 deposit
791.36   80.00

                    1227.24
            1350   90.00
                            Paid

J,

Don't forget to Bill Arc Rubber the frieght from Tucker when ~~they~~ Tucker returned to lifts of 7102 Assy & Rubber

T/,

Annual Dinner Committee. Mr. Reynolds reported
that plans for the annual dinner were well under way.
The affair is set for January 25 at the Ambassador
Hotel. In response to a question, he said that complaints about slow service, heard frequently at the
last dinner, would be avoided; the hotel has promised to provide an extra staff of waiters.

Education Committee. Miss Walhovic said that
because of the increase in the cost of living,
tuition, and other expenses, the $500 scholarships
offered annually to sons and daughters of employees
now seemed inadequate. She therefore proposed the
following resolution:

> RESOLVED, That the value of the
> annual Quarter Century Scholarships be
> increased to $1,000 and that members be
> assessed $5 a year in order to cover the
> increased expense.

The motion was seconded and, after some discussion, carried.

President's Remarks. Mr. Kane noted that there
was general concern about the increasing cost of
living and the consequent erosion of the purchasing
power of anticipated pensions. He said the consequences would be felt particularly by those who, for
some reason, were not participating in the profit-
sharing plan or who had subscribed to the plan only
lately. He thought that if members were properly informed, they could still make adjustments in the
amount of their participation in the profit-sharing
plan in order to improve their retirement income.

After some discussion, Mr. Gilston introduced
a resolution asking the Treasurer to look into the
merits of Mr. Kane's proposal and report back to
Board at its next meeting, January 6, 19--.

There being no further business, the meeting
was declared adjourned at 4:50 p.m.

Eleanor Farber, Acting Secretary

September 5, 19--

Figure 2-8 (continued).

scheduled. A break in any meeting can be obtained with a motion calling for a recess. Such a motion must state the length of the recess or the time the meeting will resume.

2.3 MINUTES

The minutes are the official records of the meetings of all kinds of groups (Figure 2-8). The more formal the group's organization and the greater the legal implications of its actions, the greater the necessity for formal and complete minutes. (See also "Conference Arrangements," Section 2.1.)

Mechanics.   A distinction should be made between the minutes duplicated and sent to members of a group and the minutes kept as the official record.

1. The official minutes should always be the original typed copy, on plain white paper of good quality.

2. Minutes may be single- or double-spaced. However, double spacing makes it easier to write in corrections voted by the group at the following

-3-

9.   In regard to the new production and backlog reports, Mr. Moses stated that the GRI 265 *255* Unit's cut-off dates are not consistent with the schedule. Mr. Davis said that each unit should use the actual cut-off dates for the runs reported on. He added that he will issue a schedule showing these dates.

10.   ~~Miss Knight asked if the Group Dept. would include the dollar amount for semi-private room and board benefit on the Group Issue Summary.~~ ~~Mr. Packer said he would look into it.~~   *Corrected statement on page 4. following*

11.   Miss Knight asked if the underwriters would forward any questions on the renewal rate memo through Mr. Packer. He *Mr. Greenfield* said he would try to get them to do this.

12.   The next meeting will be held on Monday, January 28, at 9:30 a.m. in the 16th floor conference room.

S. Berman

S. Berman
Secretary

Figure 2-9 Portion of official minutes showing use of numbered paragraphs and corrections ordered at the following meeting.

meeting. The use of marginal heads makes reference convenient. Numbered paragraphs may be used for the same purpose (Figure 2-9).

3. Number pages consecutively for each meeting or for the entire year. The latter practice is preferable when an index of the business of meetings is to be kept. Minutes of corporations follow separate rules (see pp. 71–78).

4. Type the name of the group in all capital letters, centered at the top of the first sheet. Below it, also centered, state the nature of the meeting and then the date of the meeting in upper- and lower-case letters (Figure 2-8).

5. In the body of the minutes, capitalize the titles of officers and such words as *Committee, Company, Corporation,* and *Board of Directors* whenever they relate to the assembly or the organization of which the assembly is a part.

6. Record each item of business or each separate action of the group in a separate paragraph. Indent motions and resolutions an extra five spaces at right and left.

7. The words *WHEREAS* and *RESOLVED* in resolutions should always (a) be typed all in caps, (b) begin a paragraph, and (c) be followed by a comma. The word *That* following *RESOLVED* should be capitalized (Figure 2-10).

Content.   Minutes vary in form from group to group, but the following content and order are fairly standard.

1. Name of the group.

2. Date, time, and place of meeting.

3. Regular or special meeting. If special, for what purpose.

4. Attendance: names of members present and absent; specially invited guests.

5. Name of the presiding officer and secretary.

6. Proceedings: a record of all announcements, reports, motions, and resolutions.

(a) Include only the *main motions* on which action has been taken (see "Parliamentary Procedure," Section 2.2), and the names of the proposers, if desired, but not of the seconders.

(b) Preserve the exact language of motions and resolutions, as passed.

(c) Reports may be summarized, or appended or filed elsewhere, with a proper reference in the minutes.

(d) A summary of the discussion is optional. It is especially helpful to absent members.

7. Date of the next meeting.

8. The time of adjournment.

9. The signature of the secretary and the date of signing. The close *Respectfully submitted* is not necessary.

Language.   The minutes should be expressed in an objective, businesslike way.

1. Exclude your personal opinions and interpretations.

1.

RESOLVED, That . . . .
. . . .
. . . .

2.

WHEREAS, the   . . . .
. . . ., be it

RESOLVED, That . . . .
. . . .

3.

WHEREAS, it . . . .
. . . . ; and

WHEREAS, the   . . . .
. . . . ; it is

RESOLVED, That   . . . .
. . . . ; and it is

FURTHER RESOLVED, That . . . .
. . . .

Figure 2-10   Forms of resolutions.

2. Avoid qualifying adjectives like *enthusiastic, interesting,* and *well received.*

3. Avoid any suggestion of bias. In reporting a discussion, do not favor one side over the other.

4. Adopt a formaˡ but not necessarily legalistic tone, with emphasis on clarity and precision.

5. Use ordinary memorandum or report style for minutes of groups that are informally constituted or conducted (Figure 2-2).

Corrections.   When corrections of the minutes of a previous meeting are approved, the secretary enters the corrections in red ink on the original copy (Figure 2-9).

1. Draw a line through the words to be deleted and write the substituted words directly above.

2. If a whole paragraph or section must be recast, draw a line through each line of copy to be deleted and append the new paragraph or section. A note in red ink on the original should make reference to the addition to the minutes.

Indexing.   An index is helpful whenever the number of actions taken at meetings is so great as to present difficulties in finding the references desired. The index is kept on file cards, with one topic or subtopic to a card. References are then listed chronologically with the date of the meeting and the page number. The cards are brought up-to-date after each new set of minutes is approved (Figure 2-11).

Corporation Minutes.   The bylaws of a corporation prescribe the rules for meetings and tell for what purpose and at what times they will be held. The annual meeting of stockholders is traditional. Other meetings, held more frequently, are those of the board of directors and various committees of the board.

The corporate secretary, a high company officer, is required to see that the meetings are held and that the minutes are kept in good order. The private secretary, however, may assist in the actual preparations for the meetings, take notes at the meetings, and write up the minutes afterward. Her job will be easier if she studies the bylaws carefully and reviews the minutes taken by her predecessor. Tape recordings of the proceedings are near-necessary safeguards against omissions and errors.

```
Minutes of Personnel Committee

    Tuition Refund Plan

            April 12, 1969, p.  3
            May 7, 1969, p.  2
            October 15, 1969, p.  5
            September 8, 1970, p.  3
            October 19, 1971, p.  4
```

Figure 2-11   Indexed references to minutes.

METRO CORPORATION

Meeting of Shareholders

May 1, 19--

CALL TO
ORDER

NOTICE OF
MEETING

LIST OF
STOCKHOLDERS

APPROVAL OF
MINUTES

The annual meeting of the shareholders of the Metro Corporation was held at the office of the Corporation, 320 Park Avenue, New York City, on May 1, 19--, at 10:00 a.m.

The meeting was called to order by Mr. David Brown, President of the Corporation, who presided. Mr. Henry Green, Secretary of the Corporation, acted as Secretary of the meeting as provided in the bylaws.

The Secretary presented the order pursuant to which the meeting had been called, together with his affidavit showing that a notice of the meeting had been mailed to each shareholder of record, addressed to him as of the close of business April 10, 19-- at the address as it appeared on the books of the Corporation. Upon motion, the affidavit was approved and ordered to be appended to the minutes of the meeting.

The Secretary presented a certified list of shareholders, and upon a call of the list and inspection of the proxies, it was found that there were present in person or by proxy shareholders representing 48,325 shares.

The Secretary then read the minutes of the annual meeting of shareholders held on May 2, 19--,

Figure 2-12 Minutes of a meeting of stockholders.

whereupon a motion approving the minutes was made and seconded and unanimously approved.

PRESIDENT'S REPORT

The President then read his annual report. Following questions from the floor, the report was duly approved and ordered placed on file.

INSPECTORS OF ELECTION

Upon motion, Messrs. Thomas Wright and James Stacy were nominated and elected Inspectors of Election. Thereupon they subscribed their oaths, which were ordered to be appended to the minutes.

NOMINATIONS FOR DIRECTOR

The President then called for nominations for six directors to hold office for a term of two years and until their successors should be elected and qualify.

The following were nominated:
(Names of nominees are listed.)

BALLOTING

The ballots were cast and then tabulated by the Inspectors of Election who reported the results as follows:

(List of names and number of votes for each.)

ELECTION

The President thereupon declared that Messrs. (names), having received the highest number of votes, were the duly elected directors of the Corporation for the ensuing two years.

ADJOURNMENT

There being no further business, the meeting was adjourned on motion properly presented, seconded, and approved.

David Brown, President   Henry Green, Secretary

Figure 2-12 (continued).

SIGMA INDUSTRIES, INC.

Report of Stockholders Meeting

June 12, 19--

The Special Meeting in lieu of the Annual Meeting of Stockholders of Sigma Industries, Inc., was called to order by Bernard Foy, Chairman of the Board and President, promptly at 2:30 p.m. on June 12, 19-- at the Statler Hilton Hotel, Buffalo, New York.

There were 84,884 shares of stock present at the meeting, in person or by proxy, representing more than 80 per cent of the total outstanding shares.

After the nomination of the nine Directors, Louis Brody, a stockholder, inquired as to the number of meetings held by the Board during the previous year and whether employee members received directors' fees. The Chairman advised Mr. Brody that ten meetings were held, lasting an average of two hours each, and employee Board members did not receive directors' fees.

The Company's proposals to amend the Certificate of Incorporation to increase authorized common stock from 200,000 to 500,000 shares and amend the Company's Qualified Stock Option Plan were acted upon favorably by the stockholders.

Mr. Brody's proposal for cumulative voting by stockholders in the election of directors was not carried.

Mr. Foy briefly reviewed the Company's activities during the year and plans for the future. Recalling that just four years ago the Company was in a weak financial position until present management took over, he described steps that had been taken to bring it into its present positive position. Mr. Foy

Figure 2-13 Minutes of a stockholders' meeting as reported to stockholders.

enumerated the companies which had been acquired since then and the roles they were playing in its growth.

In response to a stockholder's inquiry about the progress in the Datalab division, Mr. Foy explained that it was running well and "definitely on target." Mr. Foy concluded the question and answer period by stating that earnings increases in the near future would be attributed to acquisitions as well as to internal growth.

The inspectors of election reported the following results of stockholder votes:

(1) Election of Directors:

80 per cent of the outstanding stock voted in favor (84,515).

(2) Proposal Increasing Common Stock from 200,000 to 500,000 Shares:

For 81,373; Against 1,225—77 per cent of the outstanding stock voting in favor.

(3) Proposal to Amend the 19-- Qualified Stock Option Plan to Increase the Number of Shares issuable thereunder to 6,500:

For 78,915; Against 2,405—75 per cent of the outstanding stock voting in favor.

The meeting was adjourned at 3:15 p.m.

Respectfully submitted

Thomas E. Carson
Secretary

June 12, 19--
Buffalo, New York

Figure 2-13 (continued).

Minute Book. The minutes of stockholder meetings, directors' meetings, and committee meetings may be bound separately or not, but the minutes for each group should be kept together in chronological order.

1. Consecutive numbering of pages through the year helps prevent the loss of pages. In some instances, each sheet is also signed by the corporate secretary to ensure that no unauthorized substitutions are made.

2. The minutes are kept in a loose-leaf binder, often with a lock for security. The loose-leaf pages may be bound permanently at intervals of one or several years.

3. The minute book of a corporation may include a certified copy of its charter and bylaws. Other documents, referred to in the minutes, should be pasted in or bound in, or appropriate notes in the minute book should indicate where the documents are kept.

Minutes of Stockholders' Meetings. The minutes of the meetings of stockholders are generally characterized by the following details (Figure 2-12).

1. The place, date, and hour of the meeting; also the kind of meeting, for example, annual or special.

2. The names of the chairman and the secretary.

3. Reference to the proof of call and notice of the meeting. The proof of call is the legal authorization for the meeting, usually in the form of an order from the president of the company. The proof of notice of the meeting is an affidavit affirming that a notice was sent to every stockholder. Both documents are presented by the secretary of the meeting for inclusion in or as an appendage to the minutes.

4. The number of shares represented in person and the number represented by proxy. (If the number of stockholders is small, the names of those present may also be given.) A quorum is a majority of the number of shares outstanding and entitled to vote. Voting is by number of shares rather than by number of shareholders.

5. The names of inspectors of election, if any, and how they were chosen.

6. A record of all actions taken, including those on motions, resolutions, and reports duly moved and seconded. The discussion preceding a vote is not legally significant and need not be included except in the interests of good corporate relations with absent stockholders to whom the minutes are sent. (Minutes sent to stockholders may be written as a report, with any changes in language and order that may be needed to maintain interest. See Figure 2-13.)

The names of persons making and seconding motions should be omitted except on special request; sometimes a stockholder wishes his dissent to be recorded.

7. Record of adjournment.

8. Signatures of the secretary and the president.

METRO CORPORATION

Meeting of the Board of Directors

April 1, 19--

PRESENT

A regular meeting of the Board of Directors was held at the office of the Corporation, 320 Park Avenue, New York City, on Tuesday, April 1, 19--, at 2:30 p.m.

There were present the following directors:

(Names are listed.)

Messrs. Ralph Day and Emmett C. Dorp were absent.

PRESIDING

Mr. David Brown, President of the Corporation, presided as Chairman of the meeting. Mr. Henry Green, Secretary of the Corporation, acted as Secretary of the meeting.

NOTICE OF MEETING

The Secretary presented the notice pursuant to which the meeting had been called, together with a certificate showing that a copy of the notice had been mailed to each director, as required by the bylaws; and, on motion, the notice and certificate were ordered filed.

READING OF MINUTES

The Secretary then read the minutes of the previous quarterly meeting held on December 31, 19--. The minutes were approved as read.

FINANCIAL STATEMENT

The President submitted to the Board a financial statement prepared by Joseph Blank & Co., certified public accountants, covering the operations of the Corporation for the quarter January 1, 19-- to March 31, 19-- and also showing the condition of the Corporation as of the close of business on March 31, 19--. Upon

Figure 2-14 Minutes of a meeting of corporation directors.

                              motion duly made and seconded, the
                              following resolution was approved:

DIVIDEND   RESOLVED, That a regular quar-
DECLARED   terly divident of $1.00 per
                              share is hereby declared, pay-
                              able April 15, 19--, to all
                              shareholders of record at the
                              close of business on March 31,
                              19--.

REPORT OF   Mr. Donald E. Finley, Chairman
CHMN OF   of the Finance Committee, offered a
FINANCE COMM.   report on the prospects for bene-
                              ficial legislation affecting the
                              Corporation's financial plans. The
                              report was accepted and ordered
                              placed on file.

ADJOURNMENT   No other business having come
                              before the meeting, it was on motion
                              adjourned.

                              _____

                              Henry Green, Secretary

Figure 2-14   (continued).

Minutes of Directors' Meetings.   The minutes of directors' meetings follow
the general pattern and style of those of stockholders' meetings, but these
specific comments may be added.

1. The minutes should show the names of the directors present and the
names of those absent.

2. All actions are taken on the basis of one-man–one-vote, not on the
basis of the number of shares held.

3. It is not proper for a director to vote on a matter involving his personal
interests (for example, a motion to compensate him for special services
rendered), and the minutes should show that he abstained.

4. It is not necessary to include the names of directors making or seconding
motions. However, a director making a dissenting or protesting motion may
want his name on the record, and his request should be honored.

See Figure 2-14 for an example of the minutes of a meeting of corporation
directors.

2.4   CONVENTIONS AND LARGE-SCALE MEETINGS

One of the most hectic and demanding experiences for an executive and his
secretary is to take charge of the details of a major meeting or convention.
Such an event may come about when the company decides to have a regional

or national meeting of its staff or its distributors. Or it may occur when the executive is selected to organize a meeting of some trade or professional society of which he is a member. In either case, there are usually months of planning, followed by active duty at the convention site.

The major administrative work and decisions are usually made by the convention chairman, but his secretary is always close by to see to the particulars. Normally, the planning for a convention will begin a year or more before the actual event, and the person in charge will have to perform these tasks:

Choose the convention site.
Engage hotel facilities.
Set up the program.
Invite speakers and guests.
Provide for off-hour activities.
Contract for displays and exhibits.
Arrange for hotel accommodations and transportation for VIP's.
Prepare and send out announcements.
Answer inquiries.
Take advance registrations.
Order printed programs, tickets, badges, and so on.
Contact the local Visitors' Bureau or Chamber of Commerce for maps and folders
  describing places of interest.
Ask local firms to contribute samples, souvenirs, useful product data, and so on.
Plan for personnel, supplies, and equipment for the office and for the registration
  desk at local headquarters.

A good convention chairman can often farm out many of these tasks to committees, but it still takes a great deal of energy to appoint the committees or their chairmen and to follow up to see that they perform their functions. Major help of another sort can be provided by the convention offices of hotels and airlines that serve the convention city as well as by the local chambers of commerce and visitors' bureaus. Early consultation will elicit planning guides, literature, and advice, as well as actual assistance in booking transportation and hotel rooms and running the meeting. For assistance in planning meal functions, a close working arrangement with the hotel's banquet office is indispensable. Early in the planning stage, the secretary should obtain the names of key people in every functional area, and then go directly to them when problems arise.

Some days in advance of the opening date, the convention chairman and his secretary and staff move to the convention site and set themselves up for the actual business of running the meeting. Figure 2-15 provides a facilities checklist that should be useful to anyone with responsibilities for the administration of a large conference.

Location.   Large meetings are held in locations that offer the greatest attractions for the participants. In many instances, the host organization has a plant or other facility in the area and is prepared to offer its hospitality and

Acoustics	Maitre d'
Air conditioning (noisy?)	Master switch location
Air Freight carrier	Meeting headquarters
Blackboard, easels, etc.	Piano availability (type)
Buses, taxis, limousines	Platforms
Capacity	Projection equipment
Carpenter	Reception and registration
Ceiling height	Rehearsal space
Chairs available	Rest room availability
Check cashing clearance	Room availability dates
Checkroom facilities	Room size and decor
Display area (room name)	Security
Door sizes (interior)	Sleeping rooms needed
Dressing rooms	Sound facilities
Electrician	Sound man
First-aid room	Special decoration
Floor plans	Special lighting equipment
Florist	Stage area
Food area (room name)	Storage space
Freight elevators	Tables available
Hotel representative	Traffic pattern
Lecterns	Traffic restrictions
Loading platforms	Transfer company (trucking)
Local model and talent agency	Union requirements (if any)

Figure 2-15 Checklist of convention facilities. (From American Airlines)

attend to many of the local arrangements. Be sure to check the meeting site for

> Distance from airports and railroad stations.
> Taxi, bus, and other local transportation facilities.
> Parking facilities.
> Restaurants, stores, and recreational facilities.

Hotel Liaison.   Arrangements must be made in advance for office space, hospitality suites, and meeting rooms, for which there is generally no extra charge.

> Know the names of the people in the hotel convention office who have a direct interest in your meeting.
> Request that confirmation of all reservations be sent directly to attendees.
> Ask the desk for the room numbers of VIP's and others you may need to call frequently.
> Get the numbers, names, and locations of the rooms to be used for all convention functions.

Supply a daily program for listing on the hotel bulletin board.
See that there are adequate checking facilities.

Meeting Rooms.   Preferably, meeting rooms should be just large enough for the purpose—neither too small nor too large. However, a little crowding is usually better than a sea of empty chairs. If a room is too large, the use of screens can effectively reduce the seating area. Other considerations:

Check air conditioning, lighting, and acoustics.
Avoid a location subject to noise interference from the outside, for example, the kitchen, construction work, main passageways, and so on.
If you need several rooms, see that they are close together, if possible, and easily accessible to each other.
Before engaging the rooms, try to inspect them while they are in use to see how well they meet the demands made on them.
See that the chairs are sturdy and comfortable.
Make sure posts don't interfere with the line of vision.
Check the availability of electrical outlets for audio-visual or other equipment.
Make provision in advance for the handling of an overflow. It may be possible to bring in extra chairs, open a partition to an adjoining room, or pipe the program into another location, using closed-circuit television or loud speakers alone.

Office Arrangements.   The hotel will usually provide a complimentary room or suite to serve as office headquarters for the meeting. The convention correspondence should be placed in transfer files and moved to this office several days before the meeting begins. In addition to telephone service, desks, chairs, and wardrobes for clothing, have the following supplies and equipment, or know where you can get them in a hurry.

Pencils, pens, erasers.
Letterheads with envelopes, plain paper, carbon paper, file folders, gummed labels, manila envelopes in several sizes, steno notebooks.
Staple machine with staples; paper clips, Scotch tape.
Stiff paper for signs, felt marking pens.
Typewriters; adding machine; Ditto or other duplicating machine.

Printing and Duplicating.   Programs, agendas, ballots, signs, and as many other forms as possible should be printed beforehand and shipped to the convention site in ample time for distribution.

On-the-spot printing needs, including bulletins and announcements, may be met in the convention office on a borrowed or rented duplicating machine. Be sure to arrange with the hotel in advance for such equipment and have the necessary supplies: paper, stencils, ink, and so on.

Registration.   Much of the secretarial detail centers on the registration desk. This must be set up as much as a day in advance of the meeting and staffed by at least a couple of shifts from early morning until the beginning of the last meeting each day.

Arrange with the hotel for phone service during registration hours.
Check the need for the following equipment:
Enough tables and chairs—for registrants and office help.

Typewriters (hotel can supply, usually without cost).

Notepaper, pens, pencils, ash trays, wastepaper baskets.

Cash box, with change, if fees are charged; receipts for fees received.

Badges or other identification, with provision for filling in names with large-type typewriter or felt-tip pen.

Registration cards, preprinted with space for name, title, business affiliation, fee paid, and so on.

Tickets of admission to various meetings and events.

Signs to instruct registrants and direct them to correct locations

Bulletin boards for emergency notices and last-minute instructions.

Set out programs and give-away materials for self-service, or prepackage sets of material.

In case of advance registration, have all materials for each individual in an envelope marked with his name, and arrange envelopes alphabetically for distribution at convention time.

Hospitality (Speakers and Guests).

Speakers and guests of honor always get special consideration. Check the following services.

Arrange for travel and hotel accommodations.

Provide necessary tickets for convention events.

Meet dignitaries at airport or send company car.

Assign some individual to look after the needs of each guest.

Arrange for reception and seating of dignitaries at the meeting.

Obtain in advance from each speaker a personal data sheet for use in publicity and in his introduction to the audience. If you will need a photo, ask for it at the same time.

Have flowers or fruit in VIP's room on arrival; corsages for the ladies.

Hospitality (Conferees)

1. A local hospitality committee is best equipped to arrange for the ordinary amenities expected by convention visitors. Printed literature or a mimeographed bulletin prepared for distribution at the registration desk should give such information as the following.

Hotel directory.

Parking facilities.

Dining facilities in the area.

Entertainment available.

Points of interest.

2. Sometimes an interested organization or special group will provide a social hour or other special event for all attendees or for selected guests. Proper notice should be included with the registration materials or placed in the guest's mailbox or under his door.

3. Guest hospitality includes obtaining and distributing free literature and souvenirs not directly connected with the meeting. For example:

Complimentary notebook.

Pencil, ballpoint pen.

Key ring.

Small samples of locally grown or manufactured products.

Literature or products contributed by interested or participating companies.

Large envelopes or shopping bags for carrying such gifts.

Platform.   For a group of 20 or less, a round-table, oval, square, or U-shaped arrangement is usually most satisfactory. For larger groups, auditorium-style seating becomes necessary, with a raised platform for the speakers. A platform raised about a foot is usually better than a higher one, which gives the impression of a stage and removes the speakers too far from the audience.

Place the platform away from the entrances and exits so that latecomers and early leavers will not disturb the others.

Drape platform tables to the floor, especially if women are to be seated there.

Provide a public address system, if necessary, with the choice of a neck or a standing microphone.

Check with the speakers in advance to determine the need for a blackboard, an easel, or other equipment.

For a panel session, provide a name card in front of each speaker and a table large enough for all speakers to be seated comfortably.

See that there is plenty of ice water and that there are enough glasses.

Audio-Visual Equipment

1. After the program has been arranged, the speakers should be asked to indicate (a) what kind of equipment they need, (b) whether they will bring their own equipment or want the convention management to supply it, and (c) whether they will need an operator. In large cities, union rules prohibit the operation of motion picture and other audio-visual equipment by any but union operators; the hotel can advise on this point.

2. Some additional suggestions:

Before bringing in equipment from the outside, check with the hotel to find out what is available there.

Ask the hotel to provide a lectern for the speakers and make sure the light on it works.

Check into the need for sound amplification and ask the hotel to provide any necessary equipment. Make the hotel responsible for the performance of any equipment it provides, but personally test it a half-hour before the meeting.

See that the room can be darkened for film presentations. Find out where the light switch is and have someone stationed there when needed.

Check the location of the wall outlets. Have the necessary extension cords and provide for emergencies with extra bulbs for the projection equipment. Make sure the power is adequate.

If talks are to be recorded, make proper arrangements for a microphone, a tape recorder, and an operator.

3. Now for a quick check of equipment needs.

Amplification system (necessary for large and noisy rooms).

Blackboard (provide chalk and eraser).

Easel for charts; large flip pads and felt marking pens.

Flannel board.

Lectern.

Microphones (stationary and lavaliere).

Motion-picture projector (for sound or silent films).

Opaque projector (projects original documents, but noisy and hot).

Overhead projector (requires transparencies).

Slide, sound-slide, or film-strip projector (have extension cord and extra bulb).

Tape recorder (with plenty of tape).

Videotape recorder (check lighting).

Program Assistance. Although the program content must be left to those in charge, staff assistance is needed to ensure the program's success.

> Make sure session chairmen are provided with speakers' biographies well in advance.
>
> Advise chairmen of the exact time for the beginning and end of each session, and impress on them the necessity of keeping speakers within the limits set.
>
> See that the meeting rooms are set up as planned and that all equipment is in place and in good working order. After each session have the rooms cleared of the equipment no longer necessary.
>
> Be sure that the signs at the entrances clearly identify the meeting rooms and the current programs.
>
> Have ushers, if necessary, to collect tickets, distribute session programs, and assist in seating.
>
> Check with the session chairmen to be sure their speakers are present and that their other needs are met. Use house telephone to round up tardy participants.
>
> Advertise changes in program as promptly as possible through lobby posters, handbills, signs outside meeting rooms, and announcements at the beginning of meetings.

Food Service. A large meeting may require coffee breaks, luncheons, and dinner banquets. Except for coffee breaks, it is always best if separate rooms can be obtained for food service. If this is not possible, have tables set up in advance and screened off to avoid disturbance while the meeting is in session.

Coffee Breaks. Coffee is usually served between breaks in the morning and afternoon sessions (about 10:30 and 3:30). Doughnuts or Danish pastry may be served with it. If the Danish pastry is cut in advance, there is no need for plates or knives and fewer pastries are needed. In small meetings a coffee brewer may be kept standing for self-service at any time. Paper cups prevent the nuisance of rattling china.

Bar Service. If a bar is to be available, it is best opened for socializing after the day's sessions or before dinner.

> Drinks may be prepaid by the host or the guests.
>
> A pay bar collects from the guest for each drink served.
>
> An open bar permits guests to serve themselves.
>
> For convenience or quick service, selection of drinks may be limited and prepared in advance.

Meal Service. Arrange details with the hotel or caterer. Personally check table arrangements before every meal, and review special requirements with the maître d'hôtel. Give attention to these considerations:

> Times of service.
>
> Service or self-service.
>
> Menu.
>
> Special beverages.
>
> Guaranteed price, including tips and taxes (based on guaranteed minimum number of persons).
>
> General table positions and seating plan.
>
> Desired set-up for dais, including lectern and microphone.
>
> Table decorations, candles, flowers, and so on.
>
> Place cards.
>
> Elapsed time for service (the more waiters, the quicker the service).
>
> Music, if desired, with instructions to leader on start and stop times.

Exhibits

1. Many meetings are enhanced by exhibits put up by the sponsors or participating organizations. Adequate space should be set aside for these exhibits, preferably outside the meeting rooms.

2. Make provision for receiving, storing, setting up, dismantling, and returning exhibits. Most exhibitors provide their own personnel to staff the exhibits.

3. Protect valuable exhibits against damage or loss. Provide guards, operators, or attendants, if required. Check with your attorney or insurance company to determine your liability and means of protection.

4. Check facilities and equipment needs:

Tables with flannel tops.
Vertical display boards.
Room dividers.
Shelves.
Adequate lighting (including spotlights).
Moldings or hooks for wall hangings.
Outlets and sufficient power for electrically operated exhibits.

Publicity.   Wherever possible, the publicity chores should be put in the hands of the company's public relations department or a special publicity committee. These are the jobs that need to be done.

Obtain biographies and glossy photos from principals at the time the program is arranged.
Send advance press releases to editors of company publications, trade press, and daily newspapers, radio, and television. (See "The Press Release," Section 7.1.)
Make arrangements with a professional photographer for convention pictures and prints. These may be used for current news stories and for release to principals and participating organizations.
Obtain advance copies of principal talks.
Release photos, news stories, and copies of talks to local newspapers, news magazines, trade press, and company publications.
Set up a press room at the convention; have someone meet reporters, arrange interviews with principals, and provide food and beverages. Consider the need for telephones, typewriters, and writing supplies.
Put organization's name on lectern, so that it will be included in news photos of platform speakers.

Post-Meeting Duties.   For those in charge, the end of the meeting signals another burst of activity. Here are some things that usually have to be done.

Check meeting rooms to make sure nothing has been left behind.
Return borrowed and rented equipment.
Dismantle and return exhibits.
Pack records and ship them to home base. (Exception: put untranscribed steno notes in personal luggage.)
Verify and pay bills.
Write "thank you" notes.
Write report of experience to guide those who take over convention duties the next time around.

3

Letter Make-Up

The initial impression created by an attractive letter is a key to its effectiveness. Not only must the typing be neat and accurate, but such parts as the date, the inside address, and the complimentary close must also conform to the standards of effective usage. Special problems arise in handling classified correspondence and correspondence to government agencies. This chapter shows modern ways to frame the letter, set up its principal parts in a variety of circumstances, and prepare it for mailing. Information on setting up inter-office memorandums and typing envelopes is included.

CONTENTS

3.1   Letter Form and Style   p. 86
3.2   Letters to Government and the Military:
         Format and Security Precautions   p. 115
3.3   Forms of Address   p. 134

The actual composition and phrasing of the letter are taken up in Chapter 4.

3.1 LETTER FORM AND STYLE

The rules for the mechanical form of business letters have their roots in custom and etiquette, as well as in the more practical considerations of convenience, effectiveness, and the necessities of recordkeeping. Departures from approved forms are sometimes made for good cause in individual instances but, on the whole, conformance to the guidelines in this section should relieve any uncertainty about correctness.

Placement of the Message	p. 87	Firm Name	p. 99
Letter Formats	p. 87	Signature Line	p. 100
Punctuation Patterns	p. 91	Title of Addressor	p. 100
Principal Parts of a Letter	p. 93	Identification Initials	p. 101
Date Line	p. 93	Miscellaneous Parts of a Letter	p. 101
Inside Address	p. 93	Personal or Confidential	p. 101
Salutation	p. 95	Attention Line	p. 101
Body of the Letter	p. 96	Subject Line	p. 102
Complimentary Close	p. 98	Reference Line	p. 102

Enclosure Reminder	p. 104	Addressing Envelopes	p. 106
Mailing Notation	p. 104	ZIP Code Addressing	p. 109
Carbon Copy Notation	p. 104	Steps to Take Before Folding	
Blind Carbon Copy Notation	p. 105	and Inserting	p. 110
Postscript	p. 105	Folding Letters	p. 111
Second and Subsequent pages		Ascertaining Correct Postage	p. 112
of a Letter	p. 105	Chain-Feeding Envelopes	p. 112
Personal or Diplomatic Letters	p. 105	Internal Communications	p. 112

Placement of the Message. Center the letter on the page. In modern business practices, equal left, right, and bottom margins are used. Whether the message is to be typed on standard $8\frac{1}{2}'' \times 11''$, executive $7\frac{1}{4}'' \times 10\frac{1}{2}''$, or any other size stationery, the margins should be carefully worked out. Before starting to type, judge the approximate number of words or the length of the message. You can make your estimate from your shorthand notes, from the length of dictated tape, from the used portion of the dictation disc, or from the rough copy. If necessary, reset the right and left margin stops for each letter. Margins can be changed in seconds on either manual or electric machines once you are familiar with the stops for short, average, and long letters.

The letter placement guide (Figure 3-1) shows the correct placement of short, average, and long messages. The right and left margin stops for both pica (10 pitch) and elite (12 pitch) type are given. Before setting them, be sure that the left edge of the paper is at *0* on the paper guide scale. The term *10 pitch* means that there are 10 spaces per inch across the typing line; 12-pitch machines have 12 horizontal spaces to an inch.

Vertical spacing is also important because the bottom margin should be approximately the same as the left and right margins. In planning for the bottom margin, remember that there are 6 vertical lines to an inch on all typewriters. For instance, to have a one-and-a-half-inch bottom margin, leave 9 blank lines. Place a light pencil line near the bottom before inserting the paper to remind you to leave space for the margin. On the second and succeeding pages of a long letter, leave 6 blank lines, or one inch, at the top and start typing on line 7. The date is typed from 2 to 4 lines below the letterhead.

Letter Formats. Most companies choose one letter style or format for all outgoing correspondence. Others allow each typist to use the style she prefers. Approximately 95 percent of business letters use a variation of the block style. The following forms are generally accepted.

1. Block. All lines except the date and the complimentary close begin at the left margin. The date and the complimentary close are indented. This is probably the most popular letter style (Figure 3-2).

2. Semiblock. Along with the block style, the semiblock has won wide acceptance. This style has indented paragraphs in addition to the indented date and complimentary close. A 5-space paragraph indention is usual, although the paragraph may be indented as many as 10 spaces (Figure 3-3).

In General. Side and bottom margins at least 1" to 2". The shorter the letter the wider the margins and the more space between the date and inside address.

Short.	up to 100 words
Length of line:	50 spaces
Margin stops: Pica	17-67
Elite	25-75
Side margins:	2"

Average.	100-300 words
Length of line:	60 spaces
Margin stops: Pica	12-72
Elite	20-80
Side margins:	1½"

Long.	over 300 words
Length of line:	65 (pica)
	78 (elite)
Margin stops: Pica	10-75
Elite	12-90
Side margins:	1"

Figure 3-1 Letter placement guide.

WOODS BROTHERS
662 North Euclid Avenue
Anaheim, California 92806

February 1, 19--

Mr. James A. Jones
12205 Sunnybrook Street
Anaheim, California   92813

Dear Mr. Jones:

In answer to frequent requests we have had for a
conservative suit which would incorporate the important new styling trends, Woods Brothers is introducing the Executive Model.

This new model sharkskin suit is made of fine quality imported worsted (feel the swatches). It has
softly padded shoulders, three buttons, flap pockets,
and the increasingly popular plain front trousers.
The suit is available in a wide range of colors and
sizes including medium gray, dark gray, navy, olive,
and dark brown.

Come in soon and see our new Executive Model. You
would expect to pay much more than our low price of
$110 for a suit of this quality.

                          Sincerely yours,

                          Stephen C. Shulheimer
                          President

SCS:mt

Enclosure

Figure 3-2   Block style. Mixed punctuation.

Full block style. Open punctuation   Semiblock style. Mixed punctuation

Indented style. Close punctuation   Hanging-indented style. Mixed punctuation

Figure 3-3 Four letter formats.

3. Full block. All lines in the letter begin flush with the left margin. The advantage of this style is its simplicity for the typist. However, there is some objection to the imbalance on the left side (Figure 3-3).

4. Indented. In this style, all principal lines are indented: the date, second and succeeding lines of the address (five spaces more than the preceding line). first line of each paragraph, complimentary close, each line of the signature (three spaces more than the preceding line). The indented style is used infrequently in modern correspondence (Figure 3-3).

5. Hanging-indented. The block style is sometimes modified for advertising letters in order to attract the reader's attention. The date and the complimentary close are indented as usual. The paragraphs begin with the first line blocked at the margin, and the second and succeeding lines indented five spaces. This style is not used for ordinary correspondence (Figure 3-3).

6. Simplified. This variation of the full block style uses a subject line in place of the salutation. The complimentary close and the dictator's initials are omitted. The typist's initials, *cc* (carbon copy), and *Enclosure* may be omitted or used as preferred. This style is recommended by the Administrative Management Society (formerly the National Office Management Association) (Figure 3-4).

Punctuation Patterns.   Three accepted punctuation patterns (*open, mixed,* and *close*) may be used with the letter styles already described. Most business letters are typed with mixed punctuation, but the open style is gaining in popularity in the United States.

Open.   No punctuation mark is added at the ends of lines in the date, address, salutation, complimentary close, and signature. If a line, however, ends with an abbreviation, a period follows the abbreviation as usual. Any punctuation marks within the lines themselves are retained. Many companies are adopting the open punctuation style, as it saves time and does not detract from the clarity of the letter. Open punctuation is always used with the simplified letter style and is often used with the full block style (Figures 3-3 and 3-4).

Mixed.   The popular mixed punctuation pattern uses two marks of punctuation. A colon follows the salutation and a comma follows the complimentary close (Figure 3-2).

Close. With this pattern, punctuation marks are used with all principal parts of the letter. A period follows the date line. Commas are placed at the end of each line of the address except the last, which ends with a period. A colon follows the salutation. Commas are placed after the complimentary close, after the firm name (if used), and after the typed signature if a title is to follow. Periods are used after the typed signature if no title follows or after the title of the person signing the letter. No punctuation mark is used after the identification initials or the enclosure notation. Close punctuation is often used with the indented style and seems to be preferred in Great Britain. Fewer and

FIRST NATIONAL BANK
201 South Main Street
Butte, Montana 59701

March 15, 19--

Mr. John H. Willow
896 Fletcher Avenue
Butte, Montana 59701

APPLICATION FOR EXTENDED CREDIT

Your application for extended credit has been referred to this
department for processing. As you know this new plan guarantees
a checking account additional funds during times of heavy spending or in case of an emergency.

Extra funds from $300 to $1,000 are made available to our customers upon approval of the evaluation committee. In order to
determine the amount of extended credit we may offer you, the
following information is needed:

1. A copy of last year's income tax form.
2. Verification of present employment and your employment from
    1968 to date.
3. The names and addresses of five credit or character refer-
    ences.
4. A list of places of residence during the past ten years plus
    an indication whether rented or owned.

To take advantage of a protected checking account as soon as possible, please send us the requested information within the week.

Herbert A. Downie

HERBERT A. DOWNIE - Manager, Accounts Department

mt

cc: J. A. Smith, Frances Humes

Figure 3-4 Simplified style. Open punctuation.

fewer letters written in the United States use these extra punctuation marks (Figure 3-3).

Principal Parts of a Letter.   The principal parts of a letter are the date line, the inside address, the salutation, the body or message, the complimentary close, the signature line(s), the reference initials, and the carbon copy or enclosure notation.

Date Line.   The date line is typed two to four spaces below the letterhead. If the date is not blocked at the left margin as in the full block and simplified styles, many companies prefer to block it at the right margin (Figure 3-2). To do this, move the typewriter carriage to the right margin and depress the back-space key once for every letter, number, punctuation mark, and space in the date. Set a tabular stop for the date when you type the first of several short, average, or long letters.

Abbreviations are never used in the date line. No punctuation is needed at the end of the line unless close punctuation is used with the other principal parts. The military-style date line (e.g., 10 November 1971) is used by the U.S. military and in Great Britain.

Some companies prefer the date line to be a part of the design of the letterhead; others begin the date at the center point and use this same place-ment for the complimentary close to speed typing. Attractive placement is the criterion to use in deciding where to place the date in the block, semiblock, and indented business-letter styles (Figure 3-5).

Inside Address.   Begin the inside address at the left margin, approximately four to eight lines below the date line. Additional blank lines may be left after the date when needed to place the message more attractively on the page. If possible, always use the street address or post office box number with the city and state. If no street address is available, type the city on the second line and the state on the third. Avoid using more than five typed lines for an address. No line in the address should extend beyond the middle of the page. Long company names may be typed on two lines; indent the second line two spaces. All inside addresses are single-spaced, even though a short message in the same letter is double-spaced.

AEROSPACE CORPORATION

Post Office Box 95085, Los Angeles, California 90045, Telephone 648-5000

2641-122
January 15, 1972

Figure 3-5   Positioning the date and reference number in harmony with the letterhead design.

Mr. Robert R. Smith
The Smith, Needham, Walters and Clark Corporation
6289 Spruce Street
Philadelphia, Pennsylvania 19142

Individual and company names are both used in the inside address of the majority of letters written today. To ensure prompt and proper handling, address the letter to an individual in the company. Type the person's name on the first line and the company's on the second. Be sure to use the correct first name and/or initials of the addressee. The company name should be typed exactly as printed on its letterhead or on one of its official publications.

Department names are often used in the inside address when the writer does not know the name of the person who handles the matter discussed in the letter. In such instances, type the company name on the first line and the department name on the second.

Union Carbide Corporation   S. M. Roth & Company
Public Relations Department   Accounting Department

Special titles, such as *Dr., Professor, Reverend,* or *Senator,* may precede the addressee's name. If not, *Mr., Mrs.,* or *Miss* should always accompany an individual's name. Some authorities suggest the use of *Ms.* if you do not know the marital status of the woman addressed.

Business titles are not used in the address block today unless needed for identification. If one is included, however, use the placement that gives the best balance. The title may be placed as follows.

1. On the second line of the address block:

Mr. F. O. Morehead
Vice President and Manager
Burnham Associates, Inc.
1212 Olive Street
Des Moines, Iowa 50324

2. On the first line after the addressee's name:

Mr. B. B. Birch, Director
Technical Research Corporation
804 Orange Grove Avenue
Pasadena, California 91107

3. On the second line preceding the company name:

Mrs. Leslie K. Corrothers
President, Fashion Fair, Inc.
101 Fifth Avenue
New York, New York 10006

Do not abbreviate business titles or positions, and do not hyphenate a civil or military title denoting a single office.

NOT: Sec'y   BUT: Secretary
       Bus. Mgr.   Business Manager
       Vice-president   Vice President
       Brigadier-General   Brigadier General

CORRECT: Secretary-Treasurer (two positions)
           or
           Secretary and Treasurer

When addressing a person who holds several offices in his company, use the same title from the signature line in his letter or the title of the highest office he holds if you originate the correspondence. If you can ascertain his preference (possibly from previous correspondence), use the title the addressee prefers. See Section 3.3 for additional information on titles.

Street addresses should not contain abbreviations. Use figures for house numbers (except *one*) and numbered street names beginning with thirteen. Spell out number *one* if it is a house number and *one* through *twelve* if they are street names. When a numbered street name follows the house number, put a spaced hyphen between them.

1824 North Vine Street	208 West 42 Street
One West Eighth Street	2945 - 29 Street
2310 H Street NW	5 Boulevard Place

Cities and states should be spelled out, unless the official spelling is abbreviated as in *St. Louis. D.C.,* the only exception, is always abbreviated. The ZIP Code, a five-digit coding system that identifies each post office and each delivery unit at large post offices, follows the name of the state. The first three digits identify the sectional center or major city, and the last two identify the post office or other delivery unit. The ZIP Code need not be included in the address box on the letter but *must* be typed as part of the address on the envelope. The preferred place is two spaces after the state name.

Salutation.   The salutation is typed flush with the left margin, two spaces below the inside address or the attention line if there is one. Capitalize only the first word, title, and surname or special title.

Dear Mr. Grant
My dear Senator Anderson
My dear Madam Mayor

Although most business letters use a colon after the salutation, a growing number of companies are adopting open punctuation, which omits the colon. A comma may follow the salutation in personal and social letters, and must be used if they are handwritten.

The form of salutation may vary with the tone of the letter and the degree of acquaintanceship between the writer and the addressee. The current emphasis on the personal, friendly approach in business writing calls for the use of the addressee's name instead of the formal *Sir, Dear Sir, Dear Madam,* and the like.

1. If the letter is addressed to an individual, use his title and surname only.

Right	Wrong
Dear Dean Jacoby	Dear Dean
My dear Dean Jacoby	My dear Dean Jacoby, Ph.D.
Dear Mrs. Hughes	Dear Treasurer
Dear Dr. Wanous	Dear Doctor

A personal acquaintance of the writer may be addressed by his first name.

Dear Bob
My dear Frank
Dear Mildred

If in doubt about the marital status of the woman being addressed, use either *Miss* or *Ms.*

2. A letter addressed to two persons with the same or different names will have one of the following salutations.

Dear Messrs. Tyler (two men with same name)
Dear Mesdames Smith (two married women with same name)
My dear Misses Smith (two unmarried women with same name)
Dear Mr. Jones and Mr. Wilson
My dear Mrs. Heath and Miss Heath
Dear Miss Smith and Miss Herbert
My dear Mrs. Carlson and Mrs. Stahl

3. Use *Gentlemen* as the salutation in a letter addressed to a company, even though it contains an attention line naming an individual.

4. When writing to a women's organization, either of these two salutations is acceptable: *Ladies* or *Mesdames.*

5. In a letter addressed to a group of men and women, use *Gentlemen* or *Ladies and Gentlemen.* In a letter addressed to a man and a woman, use *Dear Miss Hunt and Mr. Morgan.* The salutation for a married couple reads *Dear Mr. and Mrs. Cetner.*

6. Use the salutation appropriate for a man when in doubt as to the sex of the addressee.

7. The salutation *To Whom It May Concern* is written in capitals and lower case. Where this salutation is used, the complimentary close is omitted.

8. The correct salutations to use for people in official or honorary positions are given in Section 3.3.

9. A subject or catchline may replace the salutation. The simplified letter style (Figure 3-4) uses a subject line typed flush with the left margin. Three blank lines are left before and after the subject. Examples of catchlines used in advertising or form letters are these.

$7 is little to pay
for one new concept . . .
        a solution to a problem . . .
                even a useful fact!

May we help you
help your students?

But First, Ask Yourself
If This Is an Invitation
You Should Accept . . .

Body of the Letter.   Business letters are single-spaced unless they are unusually short. Double-space between paragraphs. In double-spaced letters, paragraphs should be indented or set off by triple spacing. Begin each line flush with the left margin in full block, block, and simplified letter styles. First lines of paragraphs may be indented five to ten spaces in semiblock and indented styles. Five-space indention is preferred.

Tabular inserts, such as lists, quoted matter, addresses, and short tables, are usually indented five to ten spaces from the left and right margins in order to set them off from the message. Double-space before and after the insert. If the insert contains several items, these may be single-spaced if each item may be typed on one line. Items that take several lines should have a double space before and after them for clarity. In enumerated material, the number may be followed by a period or enclosed in parentheses. Space twice after the period or the right parenthesis before typing the information.

Dear Mr. _____.

    _____
    _____ .
    _____.
    _____ :

    1. _____
          _____
          _____..

    2. _____ .
    3. _____
          _____ .

    _____
    _____..

                                      Yours very truly,

Enumerated items that are complete sentences should end with a period. Those that are not sentences but that are words or phrases that complete the sentence may be followed by commas and the last one by a period. Other enumerated items that are merely lists used as an illustration or definition need no punctuation after the last word (Figure 3-4).

Quoted matter may be preceded and ended by quotation marks, but common practice omits these marks if it is obvious from the previous paragraph that the material is a quotation.

> The letter we received from the Los Angeles Civic Light Opera Association gave the following reason why guarantors are being contacted:
>> Because some very promising prospects will need aid to cover cost of tuition, and some out-of-town students may be worthy of help in dormitory living on the campus, it occurred to us that some of our guarantors might enjoy undertaking the sponsorship of a full or partial scholarship.
>
> If you desire to help these talented young people, please fill in and mail the enclosed form to us as soon as possible.

In order to make special information stand out, such as an address for the reply or a source to contact, indent the information in block style.

Please contact our local retail outlet in your city:
　　Jones & Jones
　　515 Perkins Street
　　Memphis, Tennessee 38103

Your reply to this letter should be addressed to:
　　Mr. John H. McIlroy
　　Engineering Sales
　　General Electric Company
　　Penn Square
　　Philadelphia, Pennsylvania 19102

A table should be centered on the page in a manner similar to the format of tabulated material in reports. (See Section 11.2 for suggestions on arranging tables.)

Dear Mr. _____:

_____
_____..

_____
_____:

Europe	April 22	41 days	$985
West Indies	Weekly	11 days	$270
Alaska	July 9, 23	20 days	$575
Mexico	Weekly	13 days	$325
South America	July 10	38 days	$995

_____
_____
_____.

When using the simplified letter style, begin each line of the tabulated material at the left margin. If an item takes more than one line, type to the right margin and then start the second line under the first word of the preceding line. If the letter itself is long, you need not double-space between items (Figure 3-4).

It is sometimes necessary to divide a word at the end of a line in order to keep the right margin as even as possible. Check the rules for hyphenating words in Section 10.5 to be sure that you divide each word correctly. In order to speed up your production and make reading easier, avoid dividing words at the end of lines. Do not divide words at the ends of more than two consecutive lines. Do not divide the last word on a page or the last word in a paragraph.

Complimentary Close. A courteous business phrase, called the complimentary close, is used to end the writer's conversation with the reader. Reflecting the tone of the letter, it may be the fairly conventional *Very truly yours,* or a more personal phrase, such as *With all good wishes.* Always write the close dictated by the writer. If the close is not dictated, use one that fits the message or the person addressed (see Section 3.3).

Capitalize the first word of the close and use lower case for all other words. Use a comma after it if a colon is used with the salutation. In most business letters the close is typed two spaces below the last line in the message. Sometimes three or four spaces are left in order to frame the letter more attractively on the page. Here is a list of the positions usually occupied by the close:

1. In the full block style, the close is typed flush with the left margin.

2. In block, semiblock, indented, and personal styles, the close may be typed (a) five spaces to the left of page center to allow ample space for long signature lines, (b) at center or five spaces to the right of center, (c) at a predetermined spot that assures the ending of the longest line in the signature block at the right margin, or (d) in direct line with the date or some portion of the letterhead.

The following complimentary closings are used most frequently in business.

1. For formal situations and diplomatic correspondence.

Respectfully
Respectfully yours

2. For less formal situations.

Yours truly
Very truly yours
Yours very truly

3. For friendly situations.

Sincerely
Sincerely yours
Very sincerely
Very sincerely yours
Most sincerely
Cordially
Cordially yours
Most cordially
Yours cordially

4. For special situations.

Best wishes
Best regards
Kindest regards
Kindest personal regards
With all good wishes
With kindest wishes
With the season's greetings
With best wishes to you and Mrs. _____

Firm Name.   Ordinarily, a letter on the firm's printed letterhead should *not* have the firm name typed below the complimentary close. Its omission saves time and space. If the letter is considered a formal document or a contract, or if it contains professional advice, the firm name may be typed in all capitals or written by hand after the complimentary close. If a business letter is typed on blank paper, the firm name in all capitals is typed two spaces below the complimentary close.

Signature Line. The name of the person signing the letter is typed four spaces below the complimentary close (or below the firm name). In capitals and lower case, type the signature exactly as the writer signs his name and, if necessary, include any degrees or titles that indicate how he wishes to be addressed in the reply.

TYPED SIGNATURE:	IN REPLY:
George P. Tucker, M.D.	Dear Dr. Tucker
L. W. Erickson, Associate Dean	Dear Dean Erickson

If the signer's name and his title are part of his personal company letterhead, they need not be typed again. The *only* titles that may precede the typed signature are *Miss* or *Mrs.,* even though they are not included in the hand-written signature.

Women's signatures may be written as follows.

1. An unmarried woman or a married woman using her maiden name may precede her typed signature with *Miss* or omit it. If no title is included, the assumption is that she should be addressed as *Miss* in reply.

2. A married woman should precede her typed signature with *Mrs.* She may use either her first name and/or initial(s), or her husband's name and/or initials. In social correspondence she should always use her husband's name.

	Business	Social
Preferred:	Mrs. Ruth J. Barrons	Mrs. Donald A. Barrons

3. A widow may use either her first name and/or initials or her deceased husband's name with *Mrs.*

4. A divorcee may sign her maiden name if regained, may sign her first name with or without the initial of her maiden name and her former husband's surname, may use her maiden name and former husband's surname.

Right (divorcee)	Wrong (divorcee)
Ruth R. Jones	
Miss Ruth R. Jones	
Mrs. Ruth J. Jenkins	*Miss* Ruth J. Jenkins
Mrs. Jones Jenkins	Mrs. *Frank K.* Jenkins
Mrs. Ruth Jones Jenkins	

When signing a letter for someone else, you may sign his name followed by your initials immediately below. When signing a letter in your own name for someone else, include the other person's title and surname only below your typed signature.

Right	Wrong
Robert T. Levin	Robert T. Levin
Assistant to Mr. Berkowitz	Assistant to Mr. O. L. Berkowitz
Eleanor M. Doan	Eleanor M. Doan
Secretary to Mr. Wagner	Secretary to T. J. Wagner

Title of Addressor. It is customary to place the title and/or department of the person signing a business letter on the line below the typed signature. The title indicates that the person is acting in his official capacity for the company.

On personal letters written on company letterhead, the title is usually omitted. If the signer's title is included in the letter, it may be omitted in the signature block.

U. C. Bruin, Supervisor   Paul L. Thomas
General Offices Services   Secretary-Treasurer

There appears to be a definite trend toward the omission of the typed title, especially in large companies. It should be apparent, however, in the message, letterhead, or reference numbers where the signer may be reached in reply.

Identification Initials.   Initials of the dictator and the transcriber are placed two spaces below the last line in the signature block at the left margin. They indicate the persons responsible for the information in the letter. The dictator's initials are written first followed by two initials of the transcriber. The easiest setup is all caps with a colon, which requires only one shift of the typewriter.

EMD:JK

Some companies prefer that the dictator's initials be in caps and the transcriber's in lower case.

EMD:jk   DB/mo

A letter dictated by one person and signed by another may use the following style of identification—the signer's initials, followed by the dictator's, and then the transcriber's.

DDC:TRW:bb

Or, if the signer prefers, the identification may use only the initials of the dictator and the transcriber.

There appears to be a trend to omit the dictator's initials if his name is typed in the signature block. Ordinarily, when the typist's initials appear alone, it means that the letter or telegram was composed by her or that it is a form letter. The latest accepted business practice is to show identification initials on the carbon copy only. If the dictator signs the letter, only the typist's initials are shown. The dictator's initials are shown if someone else signs the letter.

Miscellaneous Parts of a Letter (Figure 3-6).   *Personal or Confidential.*   The *personal* notation is used in cases where the message should be seen by the addressee and no one else. The *confidential* notation applies to the information in the message; the confidential letter may be seen by others who have been approved to handle such matters. Type the personal or confidential notation in all caps approximately four lines above the inside address at the left margin.

Attention Line.   Use the attention line only when the letter is addressed to the company and contains information concerning the company's business that you want acted upon should the person named be absent. In modern practice, the majority of letters are addressed to individuals within the company.

If it is necessary to use the attention line, type *Attention* followed by the name two spaces below the address at the left margin for all letter styles. Do not underline *Attention* nor write it in all caps, nor follow it with a punctuation mark. Use *Gentlemen* as the salutation with an attention line because the letter is addressed to a firm. Use the person's given name or initials, if known (Figure 3-6). Type the attention line on the envelope in the lower left corner (Figure 3-10).

Subject Line. A subject line briefly summarizes the message. Most business letters contain a subject line to alert the reader to the message that follows and to assist in routing and filing the letter in both the sender's and receiver's offices. The Federal Government asks that all incoming and outgoing letters contain subject lines.

Type the subject line in capitals and lower case two spaces below the salutation at the left margin or centered on the typing line. Auxiliary words are not used with the subject line except for *In re* or *Re* which are used in legal correspondence. A few companies prefer to use *Subject* or *Reference* followed by a colon. Other companies feel that the position of the line clearly indicates its nature.

PREFERRED: Marketing Plans for the XB100
ACCEPTABLE: Subject: Marketing Plans for the XB100

Letters prepared in the simplified format use a subject line in place of the salutation. In these letters the subject is preceded and followed by three blank lines (Figure 3-4).

A letter should cover only one subject. If two or more subjects are included, sideheadings may be substituted for the subject line. Be sure to make sufficient carbon copies for each subject file.

Reference Line. Often a file, correspondence, order, invoice, or policy number is placed on the letter for control and ease of handling. The preferred position of a reference line is from one to four spaces below the date line. A few companies prefer to type the reference line immediately above the date line (Figure 3-5). If the date line ends at the right margin, type the reference line to end at the right margin also.

PREFERRED: October 10, 1972
                   L-123-2
OR: October 10, 1972
                   Policy No. C18972
ALSO USED: 71G0641-122A
                   October 10, 1972

Many large companies, in order to process correspondence and reports more efficiently, assign control numbers, such as the ones illustrated above, to all incoming and outgoing letters, memorandums, and reports. The mailroom or file department usually assigns the number based on the following

AMCO AIRCRAFT CORPORATION

10789 Space Park

Seattle, Washington 98119

September 22, 19--

CONFIDENTIAL

General Corporation
1121 Lincoln Boulevard
Chicago, Illinois

Attention Mr. John J. Jones

Gentlemen:

Conditions of Sub-Contract for XYZ Project

In awarding your company the sub-contract to manufacture Part No. 145WK, we are sending you specific

If you have any questions regarding these operating
procedures, please write us and we will do our best
to clarify them.

Yours very truly,

AMCO AIRCRAFT CORPORATION

Frank A. Patton Hwk

Frank A. Patton, Administrator
Sub-Contracts Department

FAP:mt

Enclosure

cc: James T. Pierce
     Elwin O. Slaughter

Figure 3-6 Placement of miscellaneous parts of a letter.

information: addressee, author, subject, date, and classification. On outgoing correspondence, the typist uses the date the number is assigned and not the date the letter or memorandum is prepared. For example, if the number is obtained on Monday, May 1, but for some reason the correspondence is not typed until Wednesday, May 3, the date of May 1 is still used. The control number usually expires after five calendar days. The typist notifies the proper person to cancel the number and obtains a new one.

Enclosure Reminder. Letters accompanied by an enclosure or an attachment should have the word *Enclosure* (or the abbreviation *Enc.*) typed flush with the left margin one or two spaces beneath the identification line. For more than one, indicate the number of items enclosed, for example, *Enclosures 4.* If the enclosures are of special importance, list and describe each one individually. The word *enclosures* may be followed by a colon.

    Enclosures: 1.   Annual Report (1971), 2 copies
                       2.   Vendor List
                       3.   Profit and Loss Statement 1/1/72–6/30/72

It is recommended that a notation such as the following appear in the upper right corner on each page of each enclosure:

    Enclosure (1) to (*Company name*) letter No. L-2645, dated
    May 17, 19—, page 1 of 5 (if enclosure has several pages).

Such a notation will ensure that the addressee can locate the letter to which a particular enclosure was attached. If the enclosure is a bound item and too bulky to insert in the typewriter, place a handwritten notation in the upper right corner of the first page only. See Section 3.2 for special information on how to list enclosures to the military.

Mailing Notation. If the letter is to be sent by any method other than regular mail, type the mailing notations—for example, *Air Mail, Special Delivery,* or *Certified Mail*—flush with the left margin two spaces below the enclosure reminder. Some companies prefer this notation to appear on all copies of the letter, and others type it on the carbon copies only. See Figure 3-10 for placement of the mailing notation on envelopes.

Carbon Copy Notation. The distribution of carbon copies should be typed at the left margin below all other notations. If space permits, double space after the last notation. The preferred carbon copy notation is *cc:*, except in the simplified letter style, which omits the *c*'s before the distribution list.

    All recipients of a carbon copy should be listed alphabetically. Include addresses if there is a possibility the addressee might need this information. If the person receiving a copy of the letter is also receiving an enclosure, indicate which enclosure and how many copies.

    cc: Mrs. Carlton Howes (2 copies Training Questionnaire)
          Houghton School
          123 South River Street
          Portland, Oregon 97214
          B. A. Morningfield

T. B. Shaw
L. T. Woods

To save space, the address of a recipient of a carbon copy may be typed across the page instead of in block form as shown above.

Blind Carbon Copy Notation. If the addressor wishes to distribute carbon copies without indicating the distribution to the addressee, the blind carbon copy notation *bcc:* together with the alphabetical list of names is placed on internal copies only. It may be placed in the upper left corner of internal carbon copies or in the usual position at the bottom of the page.

Postscript. A postscript may be added to a letter two spaces below the last notation. Indent five spaces and type the message single-spaced. Be sure to use the same margins as in the body of the letter. If the paragraphs of the letter are blocked, block the postscript. If the paragraphs are indented, indent the first line of the postscript. The abbreviations *P.S.* and *P.P.S.* (second postscript) may precede the message, but the present trend is to omit these abbreviations because placement indicates the addition of another thought.

Second and Subsequent Pages of a Letter. When a letter has two or more pages, type the second and subsequent pages on a plain sheet of bond paper of the same size and quality as the letterhead. At least three typewritten lines of the message must be carried over to the second page. Never place the complimentary close and signature lines by themselves on the second page. The heading for additional pages of a letter may be written in either of the two styles shown in Figure 3-7.

Type the heading for the second and subsequent pages approximately one inch, or six lines, from the top of the page. Space down four to six lines after the heading and continue the message. Be consistent and use the same heading and spacing for each additional page. To be sure that the pages of a letter do not become separated, you may staple them together in the upper left corner.

Personal or Diplomatic Letters. Personal and diplomatic letters use the same format to distinguish them from ordinary business correspondence. The address block is moved to the bottom of the page; and identification initials, if used, are double-spaced below the address. The date, salutation, and complimentary close are typed in their regular positions. Usually, the typed signature line and the identification initials are omitted. They may be typed on the carbon copy, however. If the writer's signature is difficult to read or if he is not well known to the reader, type his name beneath his signature as usual (Figure 3-8).

These letters are usually typed on executive stationery. If this stationery does not include a street address in the letterhead or if the message is typed on plain bond paper, the name and address of the writer may be typed immediately above the date or below his signature (Figure 3-9).

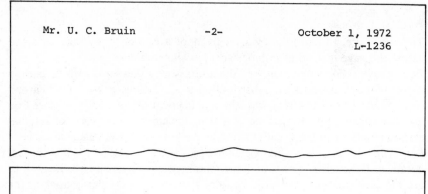

Figure 3-7 Two styles of second-page headings.

Addressing Envelopes.   The addressee's address is typed in the approximate vertical and horizontal centers of the envelope. Most address blocks are placed a little to the left (five spaces) of horizontal center in order to allow for exceptionally long lines. If the address block contains only three lines, double-space it on the envelope. If it has four or five lines, single-space it. Block form should be used on the envelope (Figure 3-10).

The ZIP Code, required by post office regulations, should appear two spaces after the state name in both the address of destination and the return address. A comma should not be inserted between the state name and the ZIP Code (Figure 3-10). The *National ZIP Code Directory* lists ZIP Codes for all post office addresses. It may be secured from the Superintendent of Documents, Washington, D.C. Special rules for ZIP Code addressing, including authorized state abbreviations, will be found on pp. 109–110.

The information on the envelope may include the class of mail or special service you wish the correspondence to receive. This type of information should be typed in all capitals below the stamp so that post office personnel will see it immediately.

Class of mail:	*Special service:*
FIRST	SPECIAL DELIVERY
SECOND	REGISTERED
THIRD	CERTIFIED
FOURTH	COLLECT-ON-DELIVERY
	AIR MAIL

THE NATIONAL HISTORICAL SOCIETY
78 Constitution Avenue
Washington, DC 20016

December 15, 1972

My dear Ambassador Manos

You and your wife are cordially invited to a reception on January 27, from six to eight in the evening, in honor of The President and The Vice President of the United States.

We look forward to greeting you at this festive occasion.

Respectfully

James A. Miller
Chairman of the Board

R.S.V.P.

His Excellency Alberto P. Manos
Ambassador of Honduras
332 Ambassador Row
Washington, DC   20005

Figure 3-8 Personal and diplomatic style.

See Chapter 15 for an explanation of classes of mail, special services, rates, and other postal information.

The *personal* notation should be written in all capitals to the left and one line above the address block (Figure 3-10). The *attention* line is written in the lower left corner of the envelope. Any other special handling instructions to

210 Spring Street
Des Moines, Iowa   50322
March 22, 19--

Dear David

_____

OR

_____

Cordially

James A. Dillon
210 Spring Street
Des Moines, Iowa   50322

Mr. David A. Peters
3150 Sunset Plaza
Washington, DC   20022

Figure 3-9 Position of return address on unprinted executive stationery.

be followed when the letter reaches its destination should also be typed in the lower left corner. For instance, *holding* or *forwarding* instructions may need to be given. Another notation to be included is the sender's name and possibly his department name immediately above or below the printed return address of the company. If the letter is undeliverable, it can be returned quickly to the person who sent it.

Window envelopes permit the inside address on the letter to be used for the

```
Thomas R. Jones
North American Van Lines
700 East Imperial Highway
El Segundo, CA   90241

                                                 SPECIAL DELIVERY
                                                 REGISTERED


                         PERSONAL
                              Mr. T. W. Platt
                              Harrison Manufacturing, Inc.
                              2500 North Hanson Road
                              Dallas, TX   75204

     HOLD FOR ARRIVAL
```

```
Thomas R. Jones
North American Van Lines
700 East Imperial Highway
El Segundo, CA   90241

                                                      AIR MAIL



                         Harrison Manufacturing, Inc.
                         2500 North Hanson Road
                         Dallas, TX   75204


     Attention Mr. T. W. Platt
```

Figure 3-10 Envelope address styles.

mailing address. Additional information to be included on the envelope, however, must be typed before the letter and/or its enclosures are inserted.

ZIP Code Addressing.   Advancements in the electronic processing of mail have prompted the Postal Service to issue updated rules governing envelope addresses.

1. The following state abbreviations are recommended on envelope addresses showing destination. The name of the state should *not* be spelled out. However, the full name of the state and conventional abbreviations may be used in the return address, as well as in the inside address and other parts of the letter.

Alabama	AL	Kentucky	KY	Ohio	OH
Alaska	AK	Louisiana	LA	Oklahoma	OK
Arizona	AZ	Maine	ME	Oregon	OR
Arkansas	AR	Maryland	MD	Pennsylvania	PA
California	CA	Massachusetts	MA	Puerto Rico	PR
Colorado	CO	Michigan	MI	Rhode Island	RI
Connecticut	CT	Minnesota	MN	South Carolina	SC
Delaware	DE	Mississippi	MS	South Dakota	SD
District of Columbia	DC	Missouri	MO	Tennessee	TN
Florida	FL	Montana	MT	Texas	TX
Georgia	GA	Nebraska	NE	Utah	UT
Guam	GU	Nevada	NV	Vermont	VT
Hawaii	HI	New Hampshire	NH	Virginia	VA
Idaho	ID	New Jersey	NJ	Virgin Islands	VI
Illinois	IL	New Mexico	NM	Washington	WA
Indiana	IN	New York	NY	West Virginia	WV
Iowa	IA	North Carolina	NC	Wisconsin	WI
Kansas	KS	North Dakota	ND	Wyoming	WY

2. The last line of the envelope address should consist of the name of the city, the recommended two-letter state abbreviation, and the ZIP Code number (Figure 3-10). The city and state names should not be put on separate lines.

3. A room, suite, or apartment number should be typed immediately after the street address on the same line.

Example: 2344 Courtland Place, Apt. 2B

4. The address should cover an area no larger than $1\frac{1}{2}$ by $3\frac{3}{4}$ inches and leave at least a half inch of space from the right and bottom margins. Where a window envelope is used, nothing but the address should appear in the window space, and there should be at least a quarter of an inch between the address and the right, left, and bottom edges of the window space.

Steps to Take Before Folding and Inserting

1. Proofread the letter carefully to be sure it is correct and has been signed.

2. Check to see that all enclosures mentioned in the letter are noted in the enclosure notation. Verify that the right enclosures have been collected and duplicated, if necessary. If the enclosures are to be a permanent part of the letter, staple them to it in the upper left corner. Do not use pins. If the enclosures are to be returned, or are to be circulated by the addressee, or are bulky, clip them to the letter with a paper clip. Be sure to fold the clip inside the letter and insert the papers into the envelope so that the clip is underneath the return address on the envelope. If the clip is underneath the stamp, it will interfere with the stamp-canceling machine.

3. Check to see that the address on the letter corresponds to the address on the envelope. Now, you may insert the material into the envelope and seal it.

Folding Letters.   To fold a one-page $8\frac{1}{2}'' \times 11''$ letter to fit the small or short business envelope (No. $6\frac{3}{4}$, $6\frac{1}{2}'' \times 3\frac{5}{8}''$), follow these steps.

1. Place the letter flat on the desk, face up.

2. Bring the bottom edge to within one-fourth inch of the top edge and crease.

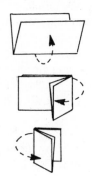

3. Fold the right edge a little less than a third of the width toward the left edge and crease.

4. Fold the left edge within one-half inch of the now creased right edge.

5. Place this last fold in the envelope first.

A one-page letter with enclosures or a letter of two or more pages should be placed in a No. 10 envelope, $9\frac{1}{2}'' \times 4\frac{1}{8}''$. To fold an $8\frac{1}{2}'' \times 11''$ letter to fit the large or long business envelope, follow these steps.

1. Place the letter on the desk, face up.

2. Fold a little less than a third of the sheet from the bottom toward the top and crease.

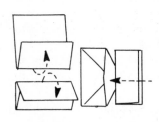

3. Fold the top third down to one-fourth inch from the first crease.

4. Insert the last fold into the envelope first.

A letter to be mailed in a window envelope should initially be folded the same way for either a small or a large envelope.

1. Place the letter face up on the desk.

2. Fold up the bottom third of the letter and crease.

3. Turn the letter over and fold the top third down even with the first crease. The inside address is now visible, upside down on the right.

4. Insert this last crease into a large window envelope so that the address is visible.

For a small window envelope, make one additional fold of approximately two inches opposite the address to make the folded letter a little smaller than the envelope.

Ascertaining Correct Postage. Each piece of mail that contains three or more pages should be weighed to determine the correct postage to use. Be especially careful of air mail letters. Office postal scales should be checked for accuracy before you weigh the piece you are sending. An adjustment screw at either the top or the side will allow you to balance them. The post office counts every ounce or fraction of an ounce for regular postage. Every half ounce or fraction of a half ounce is counted in figuring air mail postage. Do not estimate weights. Mail may be delayed because of insufficient postage, or the addressee may resent receiving postage-due mail. See Chapter 15 for postal rates.

Chain-Feeding Envelopes. Approximately 150 envelopes an hour may be addressed if they are fed continuously into the machine. Place a stack of envelopes with flaps up and toward you on the left of the typewriter. Next, position the first envelope to be addressed in the machine about two inches (12 lines) from the top edge. Insert the second envelope on top of the disappearing portion of the first envelope and next to the platen or roller. Space down to type the address at the middle and slightly to the left of center. Be sure to set a margin stop instead of a tabular stop at this point in order to save carriage return time. As the address is typed on the first envelope, the second will move into position. The left hand should be used to feed a new envelope into the machine as the addressed envelope is removed from the machine with the right hand. Stack the finished envelopes face down at the right of the typewriter.

Use a chain of two if you must add information to the printed return address on the envelope. Use a chain of three if mailing instructions, *personal* or *attention,* are the only extra items to be included on the envelope. Practice the steps slowly at first as you build speed and economy of movement. You should not have to turn the envelope over or twist the hand around to place it properly in the machine; the left and right hands work together.

Internal Communications. Information transmitted within a company is set up as a memorandum on either blank paper or a printed form, preferably in a color other than white. The form may include the company name or symbol together with a caption such as *MEMORANDUM* or *INTEROFFICE CORRESPONDENCE* and essential headings such as *To, From, Date, Memo No., Subject,* and *Copies to.* These headings may be arranged at the discretion of the designer of forms within the company. Three examples of typical memorandum forms are shown in Figure 3-11.

If a printed memorandum form is not available, type *MEMORANDUM, INTERDEPARTMENTAL COMMUNICATION,* or *INTEROFFICE CORRESPONDENCE* in capital letters on the seventh line from the top of the page. The heading may be centered or typed at the left margin. Triple-space and type the address information. Spacing between the headings *To* and

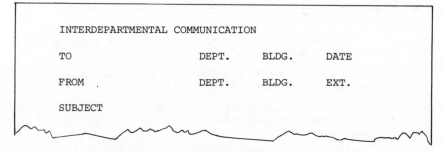

Figure 3-11   Examples of internal correspondence forms.

From may be expanded to permit the typing of a number of names. It is good practice to use a man's first name and initial or both his initials, and the full first name of a woman, so that the memorandum reaches the right person. Margins may be set where desired and single- or double-spacing used depending on the length of the memo. A half sheet is used for short messages.

In a large company, it is good practice to note the addressee's and the writer's locations, such as department, room, and building numbers (Figure 3-11).

The carbon copy distribution list may be typed at the top of the page. Arrange the names alphabetically in one or two columns in both the *copies to* list and the addressee list. If there is not enough room on the printed form for either the addressee list or the *copies to* list, these lists may be placed at the bottom of the page (Figure 3-12).

Interdepartmental communications may or may not show reference initials, and most of them are not signed. If the originator feels that the message would carry more weight or its instructions would be followed more carefully if a personal signature were included, he may place his initials or complete signature by his name on the *from* line or at the end of the message.

MEMORANDUM

```
                                                        71-54
TO:         Distribution List           DATE:  April 10, 19--

FROM:       John R. Drew, 82-01

SUBJECT:    Memorandum Format

COPIES TO:  Distribution List


xxxxxxxxxxxxxxxxxxxxxxxxxxxxxxxxxxxxxxxxxxxxxxxxxxxxxxxxxxxxxxxxxxxxxx
xxxxxxxxxxxxxxxxxxxxxxxxxxxxxxxxxxxxxxxxxxxxxxxxxxxxxxxxxxxxxxxxxxxxxx
xxxxxxxxxxxxxxxxxxxxxxxxxxxxxx.

xxxxxxxxxxxxxxxxxxxxxxxxxxxxxxxxxxxxxxxxxxxxxxxxxxxxxxxxxxxxxxxxxxxxxx
xxxxxxxxxxxxxxxxxxxxxxxxxxxxx:

   1.   xxxxxxxxxxxxxxxxxxxxxxxxxxxxxxxxxxxxxxxxxxxxxxxxxxxxxxxxx
        xxxxxxxxxxxxxxxxxxxxxxxxxxxx

   2.   xxxxxxxxxxxxxxxxxxxxxxxxxxxxxxxxxxxxxxxxxxxxxxxxxxxxxxxxx
        xxxxxxxxxxxxxxxxxxxxxxxxxx

xxxxxxxxxxxxxxxxxxxxxxxxxxxxxxxxxxxxxxxxxxxxxxxxxxxxxxxxxxxxxxxxxxxxxx
xxxxxxxxxxxxxxxxxxxxxxxxxxxxxxxxxxxxxxxxxxxxxxxxxxxxxxxxxxxxxx.

JRD:mt

Enc. (3)

To:  J. B. Adams, 25-02          Copies to:  P. W. Anderson, 11-2
     S. Booth, 25-02                         J. K. Johnson, 25-02
     J. D. Davis, 102-5                      Susan Parsons, 82-01
     Janet Dunn, 82-01                       Security
     B. W. Perkins, 82-01                    D. A. Weaver, 11-4
     D. J. West, Customer Sales
```

Figure 3-12 Sample memorandum form showing distribution and "Copies to" lists.

Second and subsequent pages are typed on a plain sheet the same size, weight, color, and texture as the first page. The format for these pages is the same as that of the second page of a letter (Figure 3-7).

Classified memorandums require proper classification stampings and usually an accompanying receipt form. A declassification stamp or downgrade notation should be used when appropriate. See the discussion on marking classified information in Section 3.2.

File copies must be prepared for memorandums also. Carbon pack memorandum forms can be secured from your stationer in a variety of sizes and numbers of carbon copies. The use of these printed packs saves time in assembling copies and typing introductory headings.

3.2 LETTERS TO GOVERNMENT AND THE MILITARY: FORMAT AND SECURITY PRECAUTIONS

Of concern to the government and the military, as well as private business, is the security of letters and other documents. The main problem is safeguarding confidential information from those who might misuse it. A related problem, especially acute in large bureaucracies, is ensuring that all documents, whether confidential or not, are marked in a way that ensures their delivery into the right hands and, subsequently, their prompt and efficient attention.

All correspondence to any agency or department of the U.S. government should conform to the requirements of the agency addressed. Communications incorrectly prepared or addressed may be misplaced and delayed or may be rejected and returned. Because the return of a letter for correction would result in loss of time and perhaps interfere with a company's production schedule, care must be taken to prepare each letter as requested by the agency.

Nonmilitary Government Correspondence	p. 115	Enclosures	p. 124
Military Government		Carbon Copies	p. 124
Correspondence	p. 116	Approval Line	p. 125
Importance of Security	p. 116	Second-Page Heading	p. 125
Company Control Numbers	p. 116	Copies of Military	
Classification	p. 117	Correspondence	p. 125
Marking Correspondence	p. 117	Transmission of Classified	
Format of Military		Correspondence	p. 125
Correspondence	p. 120	Mailing Classified Material	p. 127
Subject Lines	p. 120	Handling of Classified	
Address Lines	p. 120	Material	p. 128
Reference Line	p. 123	Security of Company	
Salutation	p. 123	Documents	p. 129
Body of the Letter	p. 123	Proprietary Information	p. 129
Closing Lines	p. 124	Sensitive	p. 129
Identification Initials	p. 124	Limited	p. 129

Nonmilitary Government Correspondence. Most letters to departments of the government follow the business-letter format used in the business world.

Also, the same informal conversational tone is used in correspondence to government officials as you would use with business associates. A letter should be as clear and concise as possible, yet maintain a friendly, courteous approach. It is important to use a comprehensive subject and a reference number when initiating the correspondence. The government agency or department will then be able to route your message correctly and refer to it specifically in reply. It is also important to address elected and appointed officials correctly as illustrated in Section 3.3.

Military Government Correspondence. Letters to various agencies of the Department of Defense, however, are set up in special formats, designed by the agency involved. The military letter styles are similar in the order of introductory parts. The differences in format will be pointed out in the discussion that follows. Of more importance than format, however, is compliance with military security regulations established by the Department of Defense.

Importance of Security. Much of the correspondence between a firm and the government concerns unclassified information that in no way jeopardizes the security of this nation. It is the security of classified information that is important. The security of classified information that passes between the U.S. government and business firms must be ensured by both the government and the firm involved. The Department of Defense has established a security program for handling classified information. This program provides that certain security measures be taken to preserve and maintain the security of the United States through the prevention of improper disclosure of classified information, sabotage, or any other act detrimental to the security of the United States. Every employee of a firm who handles or has knowledge of classified information is responsible for protecting and accounting for it. This responsibility extends to the safeguarding of classified information against unlawful or unauthorized dissemination, duplication, or observation. Classified information is released to persons on the basis of security clearance and need to know.

Company Control Numbers. In order to ensure the maximum security of documents, companies that have been granted government contracts set up a system of control numbers that are assigned to:

1. All classified documents that have been so designated by the government agency.

2. All communications concerning the negotiation or administration of contracts covering projects for the Department of Defense.

3. All communications from their engineering department relating to military procurement and projects.

A control number may be any arrangement of digits and letters that a company wishes to use. Generally, the year, department initials, and a numerical count number make up the control number. For example, *71ENG124* is the number given to the one-hundred-twenty-fourth incoming or outgoing document from/to the engineering department in 1971.

Responsibility for classified documents is vested in a classified-documents office. This office keeps records of the receipt, dispatch, and internal account-ability of all classified documents. It is also responsible for the destruction of these documents and the maintenance of related records for a specified period of time. In order to keep adequate records, the following information should be gathered before a control number is assigned.

1. Date (date that will appear on document).

2. Type (e.g., letter, report, interdepartmental communication, photo-graph, and so on).

3. Destination.

4. Company cross-reference (e.g., previous company correspondence and enclosures, if any, to which this document refers).

5. Subject.

6. *Signed by/Dictated by*.

7. Classification (e.g., confidential, secret, top secret, and so on).

8. Control station number.

9. Name of person asking for the control number.

10. Number of copies to be made (e.g., original and five copies, ditto master and twenty-five copies, and so on).

11. Where document is to be duplicated.

Classification.   Classified information is official information that requires protection in the interest of national defense. Materials bearing the following designations are safeguarded according to prescribed rules and regulations set up by the Department of Defense.

1. Top secret. Information or material that, if disclosed without authoriza-tion, could cause exceptionally grave damage to the nation.

2. Secret. Information or material that, if disclosed without authorization, could cause serious damage to the nation.

3. Confidential. Information or material that, if disclosed without author-ization, could be prejudicial to the defense interest of the nation.

4. Restricted data. In addition to classification markings, this designation is applicable to any information or material subject to the provisions of the Atomic Energy Act of 1954. It may be used with top secret, secret, or confi-dential classifications.

Marking Correspondence.   The security classification is always stamped in letters not less than one-fourth inch in height at the top and bottom of each page (Figure 3-13). In addition, each document is grouped in one of four categories as required by the automatic downgrading system and is stamped accordingly. Department of Defense security regulations determine the assignment of specific information to one of the four categories (Figure 3-14).

The espionage clause must appear on all classified correspondence to companies, organizations, and agencies other than the military (Figure 3-16).

TOP SECRET   CONFIDENTIAL

SECRET   CONFIDENTIAL
                                MODIFIED HANDLING AUTHORIZED

| TOP SECRET |

RESTRICTED DATA
ATOMIC ENERGY ACT — 1954
SPECIFIC AUTHORIZATION FOR ACCESS REQUIRED

| SECRET | | CONFIDENTIAL |

RESTRICTED DATA   RESTRICTED DATA
ATOMIC ENERGY ACT — 1954   ATOMIC ENERGY ACT — 1954
SPECIFIC AUTHORIZATION FOR ACCESS REQUIRED   SPECIFIC AUTHORIZATION FOR ACCESS REQUIRED

Figure 3-13   Security classification stamps.

On classified letters, interdepartmental communications, and similar correspondence not having covers and title pages, the espionage clause is placed on the first page in the lower right corner. It need not appear on any other pages. On classified reports, proposals, and other bound documents, the espionage clause should be typed or stamped on the outside front cover (if one is used), the first page, and the title page. If a stamp is not available, the following may be typed on the appropriate pages in the lower right corner.

THIS DOCUMENT CONTAINS INFORMATION AFFECTING THE NATIONAL DEFENSE OF THE UNITED STATES WITHIN THE MEANING OF THE ESPIONAGE LAWS, TITLE 18 U.S.C., SECTIONS 793 AND 794. ITS TRANSMISSION OR THE REVELATION OF ITS CONTENTS IN ANY MANNER TO AN UNAUTHORIZED PERSON IS PROHIBITED BY LAW.

All classified material must bear a classification marking at least as high as the highest class of its contents. All classified documents must be accompanied by a transmittal or covering letter stamped with the appropriate classification. Unclassified correspondence that is attached to or enclosed with other data that are classified must be marked with the highest classification of the attached or enclosed material. It should be marked to indicate that it becomes declassified when removed from the attachments or enclosures.

GROUP 1
Excluded from automatic downgrading
and declassification

GROUP 2
Exempted from automatic downgrading

GROUP 3
Downgraded at 12-year intervals;
not automatically declassified

GROUP 3 (Optional)
SECRET -
CONFIDENTIAL -
NOT AUTOMATICALLY DECLASSIFIED

GROUP 4
Downgraded at 3-year intervals;
declassified after 12 years

GROUP 4 (Optional)
DOWNGRADED TO:
SECRET on -
CONFIDENTIAL on -
DECLASSIFY on -

Figure 3-14   Automatic timephased downgrading and declassification stamps.

The following declassification stamp should be placed in the lower left corner of the letter.

IF ENCLOSURES ARE WITHDRAWN OR NOT ATTACHED, THE CLASSI-
FICATION OF THIS CORRESPONDENCE WILL BE CANCELED IN
ACCORDANCE WITH THE INDUSTRIAL SECURITY MANUAL FOR
SAFEGUARDING CLASSIFIED INFORMATION.

A classified letter or memorandum transmitting enclosures that bear a higher classification than the letter or memorandum itself is marked with the following stamp placed in the lower left corner of the letter.

DOWNGRADE TO _____ WHEN DETACHED FROM ENCLOSURES.

Figure 3-15 indicates the markings that should be placed on military letters according to their classification and the classification of their enclosures.

Format of Military Correspondence. Letters to the U.S. Army, Navy, and Air Force use the same general format. The *subject* and *to* lines are required on all formal military letters. Letters to the Air Force should list the subject first whereas letters to the Army and Navy start first with the *to* address and the *via* routing information (if needed). The full block or block letter styles are used. The date is written in the military style—25 October 19—. Control numbers are assigned to assure proper handling of these important messages. A model form is shown in Figure 3-16.

Subject Lines. In a letter to the U.S. Air Force, the subject lines follow the date and control number, at least three to six lines below depending on the length of the letter. The appropriate contract number, when applicable, is typed on the first line after *Subject:* (or abbreviation *Subj.:*). The project or program name, when applicable, is typed on the second line. The subject of the message is placed directly below and should be limited to two typewritten lines, if possible. Military letters are designated by the originating agency as either classified or unclassified. On a *classified* letter, the subject itself must bear a security designation. The parenthetical abbreviations *(U), (C-MHA), (C), (S),* and *(TS)* should be used, respectively, for unclassified, confidential-modified handling authorized, confidential, secret, and top secret.

18 September 1971
71G0987
Subject: Contract AF 13(108)-1125
           Air Defense Command Program
           Computer Programs for SQUID (U)

In letters to the Army and Navy, the subject lines come after the address and the routing instructions.

Address Lines. The inside address begins two spaces below the subject in letters to the U.S. Air Force or four to six spaces after the date in letters to the Army and Navy. The word *to* followed by a colon is typed at the left margin, and the lines in the address are blocked at the same point as the subject information and other preliminary parts of the letter. If the correspondence must be directed to a specific person within the office addressed, the attention line is typed after the name of the office.

To: BSD (BSRR)
      Attention John H. Jones
      Air Force Unit Post Office
      Los Angeles, California 90045

Classification of Letter	Classification of Enclosures	Markings on Letter			
Unclassified	Unclassified	None			
Unclassified	Confidential	Confidential	Declassification		
Unclassified	Secret	Secret	Declassification		
Unclassified	Confidential and Secret	Secret	Declassification		
Confidential	None or Unclassified	Confidential		Espionage	Timephase
Confidential	Confidential	Confidential		Espionage	Timephase
Confidential	Secret	Secret	Downgrade to Confidential	Espionage	Timephase
Confidential	Confidential and Secret	Secret	Downgrade to Confidential	Espionage	Timephase
Secret	None or Unclassified	Secret		Espionage	Timephase
Secret	Confidential	Secret		Espionage	Timephase
Secret	Secret	Secret		Espionage	Timephase
Secret	Confidential and Secret	Secret		Espionage	Timephase

Figure 3-15 Guide to classification and marking of letters to the military.

121

SECRET

T H O M P S O N   M A N U F A C T U R I N G,   I N C.
12456 Arizona Highway, Phoenix, Arizona

Date
Control number   OR In reply refer to:
                                      (Control number)

Subject: xxxxxxxxxxxxxxxxxxxxxxxxxxxx

To: xxxxxxxxxxxxxxxxxxxxxxxxxxxx
           xxxxxxxxxxxxxxxx

Through: xxxxxxxxxxxxxxxxxxxxxxxxxxxx
           xxxxxxxxxxxxxxxxxxxxxxxxxxxx
           xxxxxxxxxxxxxxxxxxxxx

Reference: (a)   xxxxxxxxxxxxxxxxxxxxxxxxxxxxxxxxxxxx
            (b)   xxxxxxxxxxxxxxxxxxxxxxxxxxxx

1. xxxxxxxxxxxxxxxxxxxxxxxxxxxxxxxxxxxxxxxxxxxxxxxxxxxx
xxxxxxxxxxxxxxxxxxxxxxxxxxxxxxxxxxxxxxxxxxxxxxxxxxx

    a.   xxxxxxxxxxxxxxxxxxxxxxxxxxxxxxxxxxxxxxxxxx

    b.   xxxxxxxxxxxxxxxxxxxxxxxxxxxxxxxxxxxxxxxxxx
         xxxxxxxxxxxxxxxxxxxxxxxxxxxxxxxxxxxxx

2. xxxxxxxxxxxxxxxxxxxxxxxxxxxxxxxxxxxxxxxxxxxxxxxxxxxx
xxxxxxxxxxxxxxxxxxxxxxxxxxxxxxxxxxxxx

THOMPSON MANUFACTURING, INC.

Signer's name, Title
Department

(Initials, optional)

Enclosures: (1)xxxxxxxxxxxxxxxxxxxxxxxxxxxx
              (2)xxxxxxxxxxxxxxxxxxxxxxxxxxxx

cc: xxxxxxxxxxxxxxxxxxxxxxxxxxxxxxxxxxxxxxxx

SECRET

Figure 3-16   Form of classified correspondence to the Air Force.

If the correspondence must be sent through another office or agency before transmittal to the addressee (for information, approval, or other reasons), the office name, initials, or symbol (in parentheses) is typed two spaces below the inside address. Use the word *through* in letters to the Air Force: use *via* in letters to the Army and Navy. A colon follows the word. If the correspondence must be handled by a specific person or section in that office, the attention line is the second line of the block.

Through: Chief, U.S. Air Force Liaison Office
           Attention John H. Jones
           c/o System Development Corpora:ion
           Santa Monica, California 90312
                           OR
Through: SSD (SSKMA) Mr. A. M. Rossbo

Reference Line.   The reference line (when required) is two lines below the inside address (or coordination office, if applicable)—or two lines below the subject block in letters to the Army and Navy. The designation *Reference* or the abbreviation *Ref.* is followed by a colon. Referenced items should be listed chronologically.

Reference: (a) AFLC letter MCFD/AJ dated 4 May 1971
             (b) AFLC letter MCFD/AL dated 22 October 1971
             (c) NavAirSysCom ltr (add complete file code, serial, and date)

Salutation.   Salutations are *not* used in letters to the military.
Body of the Letter.   Start the body of the letter two spaces below the inside address, the coordination office, or the last line of the reference, as applicable. Each paragraph is usually numbered consecutively. The numbers are flush with the left margin. In a one-page letter, you have the option of omitting paragraph numbers; however, it is a good idea to identify subparagraphs. To facilitate the referencing of letters over one page in length, number the main paragraphs (*1., 2., 3.,* and so on) and identify subparagraphs (*a., b., c.,* and so on).

1. xxxxxxxxxxxxxxxxxxxxxxxxxxxxxxxxxxxxxxxxxxxxxxxxxxxxxxxxxxxxxxxxxxx
xxxxxxxxxxxxxxxxxxxxxxxxxxxxxxxxxxxxxxxxxxxxxxxxxxxxxxxxxxxxxxxxxxxxxxxx
xxxxxxxxxxxxxxxxxxxxxxxxxxxxxxxxxxxxxxxxxxx:

    a. xxxxxxxxxxxxxxxxxxxxxxxxxxxxxxxxxxxxxxxxxxxxxxxxxxxxxxxxxxxxxxxx
       xxxxxxxxxxxxxxxxxxxxxxxxxxxxxx

    b. xxxxxxxxxxxxxxxxxxxxxxxxxxxxxxxxxxxxxxxxxxxxxxxxxxxxxxxxxxxxxxxx
       xxxxxxxxxxxxxxxxxxxxxxxxxxxxxxxxxxxxxxxxxxxxxxxx

       (1) xxxxxxxxxxxxxxxxxxxxxxxxxxxxxxxxxxxxxxxxxxxxxxxxxxxxxxxxxx
          xxxxxxxxxxxxxxxxxxxxxxxxxxxxxxxx
       (2) xxxxxxxxxxxxxxxxxxxxxxxxxxxxxxxxxxxxxxxxxxxxxxxxxxxxxxxx

2. xxxxxxxxxxxxxxxxxxxxxxxxxxxxxxxxxxxxxxxxxxxxxxxxxxxxxxxxxxxxxxxxxxx
xxxxxxxxxxxxxxxxxxxxxxxxxxxxxxxxxxxxxxxxxxxxxxxxxxxxxxxxxxxxxxxxxxxxxxxx

Closing Lines. The complimentary close is omitted on letters to the U.S. Army, Navy, and Air Force. The company name, however, is typed in all capitals two spaces below the last line in the body of the letter. The addressor's name is typed four spaces below the company name. His title may be typed on the same line as his name or one space below with the department title, if used. Use the placement that gives the best balance. The addressor on letters to the military is a person officially authorized by the company to sign on its behalf.

xxxxxxxxxxxxxxxxxxxxxxxxxxxxxxxxxxxxxxxxxxxxxxxxxxxxxxxxxxxxxxxxxxxxxxxx
xxxxxxxxxxxxxxxxxxxxxxxxxxxxxxxxxxxxxxx.

LOCKHEED-CALIFORNIA COMPANY

C. C. Jones, Manager
Contracts and Proposals

DDD:CCJ:aa

Identification Initials. Initials may appear on the original copy of a letter to the U.S. Army, Navy, or Air Force; or they may appear solely on the internal copies of the letter. The signer's, dictator's, and typist's initials should be shown. Some companies omit the dictator's initials on the carbon copy if he also signs the letter. In these cases the typist's initials are the only ones that appear on the copies of the correspondence.

Enclosures. In military correspondence, all enclosures should be listed and identified carefully. Arabic numerals, followed by a period or enclosed in parentheses, are used to list two or more enclosures (or groups of enclosures). Use *Enclosure* or the abbreviations *Encl.* or *Enc.* in letters to the Navy and Air Force; use *Inclosure* or *Inc.* in letters to the Army. Each enclosure should be identified on each page either in the upper right corner or centered one inch from the bottom of the page. The notation should be "Enclosure (1) to (your company name) letter (control or file number, if any), dated _____, page 1 of 5."

Enc: (1) 3 copies of Report XXxx dated 27 December 19—
       (2) 2 copies of Contract 12345 (Copies 12 and 14)
       (3) (SC) 1/c ea. photographs listed in paragraph __

Enclosures sent under separate cover should be listed and identified by (*SC*) immediately preceding the description. Be sure that the information given in the body of the letter agrees with the manner in which the enclosures are described in the enclosure block. The enclosure block may be double-spaced below the identification initials, or it may appear immediately after the reference information at the beginning of the letter.

Carbon Copies. Following the abbreviation *cc:* or *Copy to:* list alphabetically all persons or agencies receiving carbon copies, with addresses if necessary. The *copy to* line is placed at the left margin two spaces below the last line in the signature block or the last line in the enclosure block. On military letters, the list on the original contains only the names of persons or agencies outside the company receiving copies. Internal copies of the correspondence contain both external and internal distribution lists. Those addresses (both external and internal) receiving one or more of the listed enclosures should show the following information—*cc: Col. J. K. Patrick, Edwards AFB (w/enc. (1)—2 copies).*

Approval Line.   An approval line may be added as the last item on the page when it is necessary for the correspondence to be returned to the originator with an approval signature and date. Two copies of the letter should be sent to the addressee if one is to be returned with the approval signature.

APPROVED:

_____

Date   (Type in addressee's title)

Second-Page Heading.   Headings for the second and succeeding pages of letters to the military should include all pertinent information. The control number, subject, abbreviated inside address, date, and page number should be included. The security classification, if any, must be stamped at the top and the bottom of each page. Several ways to head second pages are shown in Figure 3-17.

Copies of Military Correspondence.   Because most government agencies require several copies of each piece of correspondence, it is usually economical to type the communication on an original company letterhead and make a vellum or ditto master as the carbon copy of the original for reproduction purposes. No tissue copies are needed unless specifically requested. Ditto masters with appropriate security classifications imprinted on them can be secured. If a blank ditto master is used, all copies made from it must be stamped with the appropriate classification. The originator of a communication should carefully determine the number of copies required. Care should be taken to reproduce no more copies than are absolutely necessary. An original and four copies are usually asked for by the U.S. Army, Navy, Air Force, and Space Agency. The external distribution list for government agencies and other companies appears on both the original letterhead and the master ditto. The identifying initials and the company internal distribution list, however, appear on the master ditto only.

Transmission of Classified Correspondence.   Most companies handling classified government material require a receipt for the transmittal of secret material within or outside the company. They also require a receipt for the transmittal outside the company of confidential material. A receipt for the transmittal of confidential material within the company is not necessary. Top secret material is never sent by mail but is handled according to special instructions issued by the Department of Defense.

The transmittal and receipt form should contain the following information, as shown in Figure 3-18.

```
(Subject line(s))                          15 January 19--
(Abbreviated address)                          70ENG-445
                                                Page 2
```

```
To:       AFLC Plans Office, Dir. Plans & Programs       Page 2
          Hq., AFLC, Wright-Patterson AFB, Ohio       6 June 19--
          Attn.:  Colonel J. Jensen, MCFD               70G0-1111

From:     North American Aviation, Inc., General Offices
Subject:  Customer Letter Format (Air Force) (U)
```

```
                        S E C R E T

NASA, ASPO, MSC, Houston, Texas
Attention Mr. C. D. Sword
6 June 1970
70G0-1112
Page 2
```

```
To:       Chief, BuWeps, Washington, D. C.               Page 2
          Attention:  WEPS                             6 June 19--
From:     North American Aviation, Inc.                 70G0-1113
          General Offices
Subject:  Customer Letter Format (Navy) (U)
```

Figure 3-17 Styles of second-page headings for military correspondence.

Addressor's name and complete address
Addressee's name and complete address
Project or contract number
Unclassified subject or brief description of material being transmitted
Identification or control number
Copy number
Security classification
Date of material
Originator's name and department or room number
Mailing or delivery instructions
Acknowledgment section for signature and date
Postal registry number, if applicable

Mailing Classified Material.   Government security regulations require that classified material be enclosed in two opaque envelopes before it is mailed through the facilities of the U.S. Postal Service or before delivery by a commercial carrier. Both envelopes should bear the names and addresses of the

TRANSMITTAL AND RECEIPT FOR CLASSIFIED MATERIAL S 1001		CLASSIFICATION SECRET	Log. No. Out ____ In
Date	Page of Pages	Postal Registry No.	
From		To	
Originator Room No.		☐ Airmail ☐ First Class	

Material listed below is being transmitted as enclosures _____

Classification	Copy No.	Identification Number and/or Title

If enclosures are withdrawn or not attached the classification of this correspondence will be cancelled in accordance with industrial security manual.	RECEIPT OF THE ABOVE IS HEREBY ACKNOWLEDGED
Classification SECRET	Signature Date

Figure 3-18   Transmittal and receipt form for classified material.

addressor and the addressee. The inner envelope must be marked with the security classification of the documents and the restricted data stamp, when applicable. The classified document should be protected from direct contact with the inner envelope by a cover sheet or by being folded inward. Check to see that the classification stamp is not visible through the outer envelope. The inner envelope must contain a classified-material receipt and must be sealed and inserted into the outer envelope, which is also sealed.

Security regulations require that confidential material be sent by certified mail and that secret material be sent by registered mail. The outer envelope must be stamped "Certified Mail No. ____" or "Register No. ____" before it is placed in the outgoing mail basket or taken to the post office.

For *material that cannot be folded,* use two manila envelopes, one slightly larger than the other (sizes $8\frac{3}{8}'' \times 11\frac{1}{2}''$, $9'' \times 12''$, $10'' \times 12''$, or $12'' \times 16''$) and type two identical mailing labels. Then follow the steps outlined above.

For *material too bulky for manila envelopes,* prepare two mailing labels. Double-wrap the documents, enclose the receipt, affix the labels, stamp the proper classification on the inner wrapping, register or certify the package, and mail it.

Handling of Classified Material. The transmission, destruction, accountability, storage, and marking of classified material follow certain specific procedures. Figure 3-19 is a chart of recommended procedures for handling top secret, secret, and confidential material. Anyone who has clearance to work with classified information must be familiar with these procedures.

Security regulations require also that all secret and confidential waste generated during the preparation, typing, or reproduction of classified information be destroyed. Usually the classified-documents control office is responsible for the destruction. Classified waste includes preliminary drafts; carbon sheets; carbon typewriter ribbons; plates; stencils; Azograph, ditto, vellum, and other masters; composition recording tapes; stenographic notes; work sheets; and similar items containing classified information.

Safeguarding classified material during use, storing and filing it carefully, and seeing that only authorized personnel have access to it are security controls that must be exercised by everyone cleared to handle these documents. Tips on how to avoid security infractions are listed below.

1. Never leave classified material exposed or unattended.
2. Use a cover sheet with each classified document.
3. Use file markers on all classified files and containers.
4. Do not take classified material home to work on.
5. Be certain of three facts before discussing classified information with anyone: the person's identity, his or her level of clearance, and whether or not the person "needs to know" the information.
6. Commit your safe combination to memory.

7. Erase all classified information from blackboards.

8. Never store classified material in a desk or table drawer.

9. Know that your area is secure with all files locked, whenever it is unattended during the day or night.

10. Do not discuss classified material over the telephone, at home, or in public.

11. Store, handle, and destroy typewriter ribbons, steno pads, rough drafts, and other classified waste with the same precautions as you would the finished documents.

12. Perform classified work only in classified facilities.

13. Don't pry into classified projects that are not your direct concern.

14. Don't leave classified documents or unopened mail in your mail trays overnight.

15. Use the facilities of a classified-documents control office for recording incoming and outgoing documents, and for mailing classified material; or keep complete records yourself if such an office has not been established.

Security of Company Documents.   Certain information circulated within the company is of a private nature. The disclosure of this type of information to unauthorized persons would be contrary to the best interests of your company. Company private information includes, but is not limited to, certain financial records, payroll records, employee investigation records, personnel records, minutes of executive- and policy-committee meetings, proprietary information, and any other information judged to be private in nature.

The corporate designations used to limit and control access to specific information follow.

Proprietary Information.   Information or material that, if disclosed without authorization, could be prejudicial to the interests of the corporation. This designation is used to protect patentable information and information concerning the competitive technological processes of private organizations.

Sensitive.   Information or material that, if disclosed without authorization, could be detrimental to the interests of the corporation or an individual. Both the reproduction and the distribution of copies are controlled by the author.

Limited.   This designation allows control of the distribution of a document by the author. It does not control the handling or the safeguarding of the document copy itself.

Many companies prefer to use either *Private Data* or *Private Information* on all material in the nature of private company business. The terms *confidential, secret, top secret,* and *restricted* are reserved for classified government material. A company's security designation is never stamped on a document having a military or government security classification. Private information of a company should be handled in much the same way as government classified material.

	Top Secret	Secret	Confidential	All Classifications
T R A N S M I S S I O N	Distribution and transmittal handled by a corporate officer or his representative. Special instructions issued by the Department of Defense.	*Inside Company:* 1. Use red-bordered interoffice envelope; send via interoffice mail or deliver personally. 2. Double wrap if hand-carried between buildings. 3. Include receipt. *Outside Company:* 1. Double wrap. Address inner wrapping and stamp both sides with classification. 2. Include transmittal and receipt form. 3. Send only by U.S. registered mail. 4. Do not send classified material marked *Personal*. 5. All materials must be sent through a control station. 6. Special instructions are issued for courier authorization.	*Inside Company:* Same as for Secret but no receipt required. *Outside Company:* Same as for Secret	1. Classified information may not be transmitted via telephone or telegram. 2. Follow instructions covering transmission of bulky classified material.

130

DESTRUCTION	All Top Secret material is destroyed by the responsible corporate officer.	1. Prepare a record of items being destroyed. 2. Destroy by burning or pulping in the presence of a witness. 3. Accountability records should be retained for ten years.	Same as for Secret.	Deposit in classified waste closets or containers all nonaccountable classified materials (notes, working papers, carbon paper and ribbons, etc.).

ACCOUNTABILITY	The responsible corporate officer receives, records, and is responsible for all accountable Top Secret material. He or his representative must authorize access to Top Secret material.	1. A corporate office should keep master records for company authored documents.
		2. The files or the library should keep master records for documents written and published outside the company.
		3. The mailroom and the files should keep master records for documents sent out of company and those sent to company via U.S. mail.
		4. An inventory should be made and an accounting submitted periodically.
		5. All classified mail should be logged in by the mailroom.
			Same as for Secret.	1. An employee is responsible for all documents for which he signed a receipt.
				2. Before releasing classified information make sure:
				  a. of recipient's identity.
				  b. of his need to know.
				  c. of his clearance level.
				  d. that he signs a receipt for the material.

Figure 3-19 Recommended procedures for handling classified material.

STORAGE	6. Maintenance of incoming and outgoing mail logs is recommended. Top Secret material should be returned to responsible corporate official or his representative at a specified time, such as 4:30 p.m., for overnight storage. No Top Secret items should be left in other offices or files overnight even though these may be securely locked.	1. Return material to filing cabinet for overnight storage or when person responsible leaves office during working hours. Use an approved combination-locked, steel file safe which has been recommended by the Defense Department. 2. Physical custody or surveillance by authorized personnel is required when not stored.	Same as for Secret.	1. When material is in use, protect it from being seen by an unauthorized person. 2. Return to locked file cabinet as soon as practical after use.
	1. Copy numbered in series. 2. Each page numbered in series. 3. Total number of copies in existence marked on each document. 4. Classification stamped on top and bottom of each page.	1. Bound documents: Classification stamped on top and bottom of front and back covers, title page, and first and last pages of the volume. 2. Unbound documents: Classification stamped on top and bottom of each page. 3. Charts, maps, drawings, and photographs: Classification shown on both top and	Same as for Secret.	Refer all technical questions to the corporate officer or his representative who is responsible for classified documents.

4. Films: Classification shown at beginning and end of each roll, and on film containers.

5. Letters of Transmittal:

a. Show same classification as material it accompanies.

b. Include notice of downgrading, if applicable: *If enclosures are withdrawn....*

6. Documents sent outside company: Stamp notice of espionage laws on cover: *Notice: This document contains information....*

7. Documents containing restricted data: Stamp *Restricted Data Atomic Energy Act 1954* in addition to Classification markings.

8. Records of recipients and copy numbers of authordelivered information should be filed in mailroom or some other control office.

9. Recommend stamping of classification, not typing.

Figure 3-19 (continued).

133

3.3 FORMS OF ADDRESS

Selection of the correct address for an American is a relatively simple matter for the businessman. In this country we tend to treat every citizen with the same respect. Therefore, the titles *Mr., Mrs.,* or *Miss* are correct for everyone when you are not sure of the recipient's official, appointive, honorary, or earned title. If you are familiar with a person's special title or his position in the government, the military, or the educational and religious fields, it is courteous to use the appropriate form of address for him. Correct statements of titles and their forms of address may be quickly checked in the alphabetical listing at the end of this chapter.

General Practices	p. 134
Special Titles	p. 135
Excellency	p. 135
Honorable	p. 135
Esquire	p. 135
Military	p. 135
Additional Pointers on Forms of Address	p. 137
Alphabetical List of Important Titles and Their Forms of Address	p. 137

General Practices. The inside address and the address on the envelope should be identical as to content and form, except that the ZIP Code may be omitted from the inside address. Ordinarily, a person's business title is omitted unless he holds an official or honorary position. With the emphasis in business communications on the informal, friendly tone in letters, the salutation should be one that uses the recipient's name. *Dear Sir* is rarely used today, and *Sir* is used only for a very formal situation or when the message is of an extremely serious nature. *Sir* establishes a cold atmosphere, whereas *Dear Mr. Blank, Dear General Blank,* or *My dear Ambassador Blank* establishes a warm relationship between the two correspondents.

A businessman should make every effort to locate the exact title and correct address of the person with whom he must correspond. Correct titles of United States officials may be verified in the *Congressional Directory,* the *United States Government Organization Manual,* the *Biographic Register of the Department of State,* and the military services registers. Titles of foreign dignitaries may be found in the monthly *Diplomatic List* published by the Department of State, in the quarterly *Foreign Consular Offices in the United States* also published by the Department of State, and in the *Congressional Directory.* Copies of these publications are in most public libraries and in the government publications sections of university libraries.

When addressing private individuals in a foreign country, it is common practice to use the appropriate American forms when the letter is worded in English. If the letter is written in a foreign language, appropriate foreign titles should be used. The *Department of State Correspondence Handbook, Part III* is a helpful guide for United Nations diplomats, who are also listed in the United Nations official directory. The correct forms of address for members of royalty and nobility in Great Britain may be found in the *Department of State Correspondence Handbook, Part III.*

Special Titles

Excellency.   This title is not used very often in America. *His Excellency* is the complimentary diplomatic title to use in addressing foreign presidents, foreign ambassadors, foreign cabinet officers, and foreign high and former high officials. *His Excellency* is used in the address; *Excellency* in the salutation; and *Your Excellency* in the body of the communication. In ecclesiastical correspondence, *Excellency* is used in addressing all Roman Catholic archbishops and bishops.

Honorable.   This title is used in addressing the following American officials: ex-Presidents, Presidents-elect, and all high ex-officials; governors, cabinet officers, senators, congressmen, American ambassadors, American ministers, secretaries or assistants to the President, under secretaries and assistant secretaries of the executive departments, judges, mayors. *Honorable* must be followed by initials or a first name and may be abbreviated (*Hon.*) when *the* is omitted.

Esquire. This title is used sometimes in the United States for professional men, such as architects and attorneys. The person's full name without a title, such as *Mr.,* is followed by a comma and *Esquire* or *Esq.* It may be used for foreign-service officers below the grade of career minister, for a clerk of the Supreme Court of the United States, and for officers in other courts.

In England, *Esquire* is often used after the names of persons prominent in the social, diplomatic, and business worlds.

Military. In official and formal correspondence, all military officers should be addressed on the envelope and letter by their complete titles. These titles may be abbreviated when followed by the given name, or initials, and the surname. In the salutation, brigadier generals, major generals, lieutenant generals, and generals are all addressed as *General;* lieutenant colonels and colonels, as *Colonel;* the fleet admiral, full admirals, vice admirals, and rear admirals of the U.S. Navy and Coast Guard, as *Admiral.* In conversation, officers of the U.S. Medical and Dental Corps may be addressed as *Doctor,* and officers of the Chaplain Corps as *Chaplain.*

When addressing correspondence to an enlisted man in any of the five services, use his abbreviated title plus his full name on the first line; and on the second indicate his branch of the service followed by the designation of the military division.

M. Sgt. John J. Jones
Company B, Headquarters Wing U.S.A.F.
Kelly Air Force Base
San Antonio, Texas 78200

The comparative ranks and abbreviations of the five services are shown in Figure 3-20.

	ARMY (U.S.A.)		NAVY (U.S.N.)		MARINE CORPS (U.S.M.C.)		AIR FORCE (U.S.A.F.)		COAST GUARD (U.S.C.G.)	
(1)	General of the Army (wartime)		Fleet Admiral (wartime)		No Equivalent		General of the Air Force (wartime)		No equivalent	
(2)	General	Gen.	Admiral	Adm.	General	Gen.	General	Gen.	Admiral	Adm.
(3)	Lieutenant General	Lt. Gen.	Vice Admiral	Vice Adm.	Lieutenant General	Lt. Gen.	Lieutenant General	Lt. Gen.	Vice Admiral	Vice Adm.
(4)	Major General	Maj. Gen.	Rear Admiral	Rear Adm.	Major General	Maj. Gen.	Major General	Maj. Gen.	Rear Admiral	Rear Adm.
(5)	Brigadier General	Brig. Gen.	Commodore (wartime)		Brigadier General	Brig. Gen.	Brigadier General	Brig. Gen.		
(6)	Colonel	Col.	Captain	Capt.	Colonel	Col.	Colonel	Col.	Captain	Capt.
(7)	Lieutenant Colonel	Lt. Col.	Commander	Comdr.	Lieutenant Colonel	Lt. Col.	Lieutenant Colonel	Lt. Col.	Commander	Comdr.
(8)	Major	Maj.	Lieutenant Commander	Lt. Comdr.	Major	Maj.	Major	Maj.	Lieutenant Commander	Lt. Comdr.
(9)	Captain	Capt.	Lieutenant	Lt.	Captain	Capt.	Captain	Capt.	Lieutenant	Lt.
(10)	1st Lieutenant	1st Lt.	Lieutenant (jg.)	Lt. (jg.)	1st Lieutenant	1st Lt.	1st Lieutenant	1st Lt.	Lieutenant (jg.)	Lt. (jg.)
(11)	2nd Lieutenant	2nd Lt.	Ensign	Ens.	2nd Lieutenant	2nd Lt.	2d Lieutenant	2d Lt.	Ensign	Ens.
(12)	Chief Warrant Officer	CWO	Chief Warrant Officer	CWO	Chief Warrant Officer	CWO	Chief Warrant Officer	CWO	Chief Warrant Officer	CWO
(13)	Warrant Officer	WO	Warrant Officer	WO	Warrant Officer	WO	Warrant Officer	WO	Warrant Officer	WO
(14)	Staff Sergeant Major or Specialist E9	S. Sgt. Maj. / Spec. 9	Master Chief Petty Officer	MCPO	Master Gunnery Sergeant	MGySgt.	Chief Master Sergeant	CMSgt.	Master Chief Petty Officer	MCPO
(15)	First Sergeant or Master Sergeant	M. Sgt.	Senior Chief Petty Officer	SCPO	Sergeant Major	Sgt. Maj.	Senior Master Sergeant	SMSgt.	Senior Chief Petty Officer	SCPO
(16)	Sergeant First Class or Specialist E7	Sfc. / Spec. 7	Chief Petty Officer	CPO	Master Sergeant	M. Sgt.	Master Sergeant	M. Sgt.	Chief Petty Officer	CPO
(17)	Staff Sergeant or Specialist E6	S. Sgt. / Spec. 6	Petty Officer First Class	PO1c	1st Sergeant	1st Sgt.	Technical Sergeant	T. Sgt.	Petty Officer First Class	PO1c
(18)	Sergeant or Specialist E5	Sgt. / Spec. 5	Petty Officer Second Class	PO2c	Gunnery Sergeant	Gy Sgt.	Staff Sergeant	S. Sgt.	Petty Officer Second Class	PO2c
(19)	Corporal or Specialist E4	Cpl. / Spec. 4	Petty Officer Third Class	PO3c	Staff Sergeant	S. Sgt.	Airman First Class	A1c.	Petty Officer Third Class	PO3c
(20)	Private First Class	Pfc.	Seaman	S1c.	Sergeant or Corporal	Sgt. / Cpl.	Airman Second Class	A2c.	Seaman First Class	S1c.
(21)	Private 2	Pvt.	Seaman Apprentice	SA	Lance Corporal	Lance Cpl.	Airman Third Class	A3c.	Seaman Apprentice	SA
(22)	Private 1	Pvt.	Seaman Recruit	SR	Private First Class	Pfc.	Airman	A.	Seaman Recruit	SR

Figure 3-20 Ranks and abbreviations of the five services.

Additional Pointers on Forms of Address

1. Retired officials and holders of honorary positions are extended the courtesy of *The Honorable* in the address but are called *Mr.* in the salutation. Even a former President of the United States reverts to *Mr.* unless he has a military title and is addressed by it.

2. Judges and persons holding officer rank in the military retain these titles for life.

3. When a person has been officially appointed to act for another, use the word *acting* preceding the title in the envelope and letter address but do not use *acting* in the salutation or in spoken address.

4. Address a person by his highest title.

5. Wives of officials do not share their husband's titles but are always addressed as *Mrs. Blank*. When husband and wife are addressed jointly, the envelope and inside address should read *The Honorable and Mrs. John C. Blank* and the salutation *Mayor and Mrs. Blank*.

6. Women are addressed just as men are in similar positions. The formal salutation is *Madam*.

7. The husband of a woman official does not share his wife's title. When addressed jointly, the address is *Mr. and Mrs. John C. Blank*.

8. The use of a formal or less formal salutation and complimentary close depends on (1) the nature of the message (official, routine, personal, civic) and (2) the relationship between the writer and the addressee.

Alphabetical List of Important Titles and Their Forms of Address

Inside Address	*Salutation and Complimentary Close*
Alderman	
Alderman John C. Blank	Dear Alderman Blank
	Dear Mr. Blank
The Honorable John C. Blank	
Alderman, City of Philadelphia	Yours very truly
	Sincerely yours
Ambassador	
*The Honorable John C. Blank	Sir
American Ambassador	Dear Mr. Ambassador
London, England	My dear Mr. Ambassador
	My dear Madam Ambassador
Central and South America:	
	Very truly yours
The Honorable John C. Blank	Sincerely yours
The Ambassador of the United States	
Bogotá, Columbia	

* If the ambassador holds a military rank, omit *The Honorable* and use his military rank.

Inside Address	*Salutation and Complimentary Close*
Archbishop The Most Reverend John C. Blank	Your Excellency Most Reverend Sir Dear Archbishop Blank Respectfully yours Respectfully Sincerely yours
Armed Forces Officers General John C. Blank, U.S.A. Admiral John C. Blank, U.S.N. General John C. Blank, U.S.M.C. Colonel John C. Blank, U.S.A.F. Captain John C. Blank, U.S.C.G.	Sir Dear General Blank My dear Admiral Blank
Chaplain: Lieutenant John C. Blank (Ch.C.), U.S.N.	My dear Chaplain
Chaplain John C. Blank Captain, U.S.A.	My dear Chaplain Blank
Retired Officers: Colonel John C. Blank, U.S.A., Retired	Dear Colonel Blank
Associate Justice of the U.S. Supreme Court Mr. Justice Blank The Supreme Court Washington, D.C. 20543	Sir My dear Mr. Justice Dear Mr. Justice Blank Very truly yours Sincerely yours
Bishop (Catholic) The Most Reverend Bishop Blank	Your Excellency Dear Bishop Blank Respectfully yours Sincerely
Bishop (Protestant) The Reverend Bishop Blank The Right Reverend Bishop Blank	Most Reverend Sir My dear Bishop Blank Respectfully yours Sincerely yours
Cabinet Member The Honorable John C. Blank Secretary of State Washington, D.C. 20520	Sir Dear Mr. Secretary Dear Madam Secretary Dear Mr. Blank Yours very truly Sincerely yours

Inside Address	*Salutation and Complimentary Close*
Cardinal (Catholic) His Eminence, John Cardinal Blank Archbishop of New York New York, New York 10022	Your Eminence My dear Cardinal Blank My Lord Cardinal (*to Cardinals of foreign countries*) Respectfully yours
Chaplain (See "Armed Forces Officers")	
Chief Justice of the United States The Chief Justice The Supreme Court Washington, D.C. 20543 The Honorable John C. Blank Chief Justice of the United States	Sir My dear Mr. Chief Justice Yours very truly Sincerely yours
City Attorney Hon. (or Mr.) John C. Blank City Attorney Denver, Colorado 80202	Dear Mr. Blank Very truly yours Sincerely yours
Commissioner, Director, or Chief of Government Bureau The Honorable John C. Blank Director, Bureau of the Budget Executive Office Building Washington, D.C. 20503 Mr. John C. Blank Commissioner of Labor Statistics Department of Labor Fourteenth Street and Constitution Avenue NW Washington, D.C. 20210	Dear Mr. Blank Very truly yours Sincerely yours
Commissioner (City) The Honorable John C. Blank Commissioner of the City of Buffalo New York 14202	My dear Mr. Blank Dear Mr. Blank Very truly yours Sincerely yours
Congressmen, Territorial Delegate, Resident Commissioner The Honorable John C. Blank House of Representatives Washington, D.C. 20515 The Honorable John C. Blank Representative in Congress 5312 Wilshire Boulevard Los Angeles, California 90036	Dear Representative Blank My dear Mr. Blank My dear Mrs. Blank Yours very truly Sincerely yours

Inside Address	*Salutation and* *Complimentary Close*

Consul
  Mr. John C. Blank
  *American Consul
  Moscow, Russia

Sir
Dear Mr. Blank

Respectfully yours
Sincerely

County Officials
  Hon. (or Mr.) John C. Blank
  Supervisor, Ventura County

Dear Mr. Blank

Very truly yours
Sincerely

Dean of a School
  Dean John C. Blank
  School of The Arts
  New York University
  Washington Square
  New York, New York 10003

Dear Dean Blank
Dear Dr. Blank

  Dr. John C. Blank
  Assistant Dean, School of Law
  Stanford University
  Palo Alto, California 94305

Dear Dr. Blank
Dear Dean Blank

Sincerely yours

District Attorney
  The Honorable John C. Blank
  District Attorney, Sunflower County
  County Courthouse
  Indianola, Mississippi 38751

Dear Mr. Blank

Very truly yours
Sincerely yours

Foreign Officials
  His Excellency
  The Ambassador of Germany
  Washington, D.C. 20035

Excellency
My dear Mr. Ambassador

  His Excellency
  Mr. John C. Blank
  Minister of Luxembourg
  Washington, D.C. 20046

Sir
My dear Mr. Minister
My dear Mr. Blank

Respectfully yours
Sincerely yours

  His Excellency
  Count John C. Blank
  Ambassador of Italy
  Washington, D.C. 20046

  The Right Honorable John C. Blank,
    C.M.G.
  Prime Minister of the Dominion
    of Canada
  Ottawa, Canada

Governor
  The Honorable John C. Blank
  Governor of North Dakota
  Bismarck, North Dakota 58501

Sir
Dear Governor Blank

Very truly yours
Sincerely yours

---

* In Central and South American countries: *Consul of the United States of America.*

Inside Address	*Salutation and* *Complimentary Close*

Judge
  The Honorable John C. Blank   Dear Judge Blank
  Judge of the Circuit Court
                                               Respectfully yours
  The Honorable Judy C. Blank   Sincerely
  Judge of the District Court

Lieutenant Governor
  The Honorable John C. Blank   Sir
  Lieutenant Governor of Ohio   Dear Mr. Blank
  Columbus, Ohio 43200   My dear Governor Blank

                                               Respectfully yours
                                               Very truly yours

Mayor
  The Honorable John C. Blank   My dear Mayor Blank
  Mayor of Los Angeles   Dear Mr. Mayor
  Los Angeles, California 90054
                                               Respectfully yours
                                               Very truly yours

Minister
  The Reverend John C. Blank   My dear Mr. Blank
                                               Dear Mr. Blank
  With Scholastic Degree:
  The Reverend John C. Blank, D.D.,   My dear Dr. Blank
    Litt.D.   Dear Mr. Blank
                                               My dear Dean Blank
  The Very Reverend John C. Blank, D.D.
  Dean of St. Luke's Cathedral   Respectfully yours
  New York, New York 10008   Sincerely yours

President of a School
  Dr. John C. Blank   Dear Dr. Blank
  President, University of California   Dear President Blank
  Berkeley, California 94700
                                               Very truly yours
                                               Sincerely

President of a Catholic College
  The Very Reverend John C. Blank,   Dear Father Blank
    S.J., D.D.
  President, Loyola University   Very truly yours
                                               Sincerely yours

President of the United States
  The President   Mr. President
  The White House   My dear Mr. President
  Washington, D.C. 20500
                                               Respectfully yours
  The Honorable John C. Blank   Faithfully yours (official)
  The White House   Very respectfully (private
  Washington, D.C. 20500   individual)

Inside Address	*Salutation and Complimentary Close*
Priest	
The Reverend John C. Blank St. John's Church	Dear Reverend Father Dear Father Blank
The Reverend John C. Blank, Ph.D. Notre Dame University	Dear Dr. Blank
	Sincerely yours
Professor	
Professor John C. Blank	Dear Mr. Blank Dear Professor Blank
Dr. John C. Blank Associate Professor, Department of Chemistry	Dear Dr. Blank
	Very truly yours Sincerely
Rabbi	
Rabbi John C. Blank, Ph.D. Dr. John C. Blank Rabbi John C. Blank	My dear Rabbi Blank My dear Dr. Blank My dear Rabbi Blank
	Sincerely yours
Secretary or Assistant to the **President of the United States** The Honorable John C. Blank Secretary to the President The White House Washington, D.C. 20500	My dear Mr. Blank
Major General John C. Blank The Assistant to the President The White House	My dear General Blank
	Very truly yours Sincerely yours
Senator	
The Honorable John C. Blank United States Senate Washington, D.C. 20510	My dear Senator Blank
	Very truly yours Sincerely yours
Retired Senator: The Honorable John C. Blank (home address)	My dear Mr. Blank
Speaker of the House The Honorable John C. Blank Speaker of the House of Representatives Washington, D.C. 20515	My dear Mr. Speaker
	Respectfully yours, Sincerely yours
State Legislator The Honorable John C. Blank State Senate Oklahoma City, Oklahoma 73100	Dear Senator Blank Dear Mr. Blank
	Very truly yours Sincerely yours
The Honorable John C. Blank House of Representatives Oklahoma City, Oklahoma 73100	

Inside Address	*Salutation and Complimentary Close*

State Officials
The Honorable John C. Blank
Secretary of State of Iowa
Des Moines 50300

Sir
My dear Mr. Secretary
Dear Mr. Blank

The Honorable John C. Blank
Superintendent of Banks
San Francisco, California 94100

Very truly yours
Sincerely yours

**Under Secretary and Assistant
Secretary of a Federal Department**
The Honorable John C. Blank
Under Secretary of the Treasury

My dear Mr. Blank

The Honorable John C. Blank
Assistant Secretary of Labor

Very truly yours
Sincerely yours

United Nations
His Excellency John C. Blank
Secretary General of the United Nations
United Nations, New York 10021

My dear Mr. Secretary General

Respectfully
Sincerely yours

The Honorable John C. Blank
Under Secretary of the United Nations
United Nations, New York 10021

My dear Mr. Blank

Very truly yours
Sincerely yours

His Excellency John C. Blank
Representative of Great Britain
    to the United Nations
United Nations, New York 10021

My dear Mr. Ambassador

Respectfully
Sincerely yours

The Honorable John C. Blank
United States Permanent Representative
    to the United Nations
United Nations, New York 10021

My dear Ambassador Blank

Respectfully
Sincerely yours

Vice President of the United States
The Vice President
United States Senate
Washington, D.C. 20510

My dear Mr. Vice President

Respectfully
Very truly yours
Sincerely yours

The Honorable John C. Blank
Vice President of the United States
Washington, D.C. 20501

4

Letter Writing

Over the years many improvements have been made in the typewriter and other means of letter production. Telephone dictation, with central transcription centers, provides great convenience for large and busy offices. The magnetic-tape typewriter makes it possible to correct typescripts to any extent without hand retyping. Other examples of mechanical progress can be cited. Basically, however, the business letter itself remains unchanged: it still poses a challenge to the writer (or dictator) to say the right things and find the right words. An understanding stenographer or transcriber can be of great help at such times. And a good sense of order and efficiency can help cut down the writing load. This chapter has a wealth of ideas for all who dictate letters, take dictation, or have an interest in the improvement of correspondence and correspondence procedures.

CONTENTS

4.1	Effective Letters	p. 144
4.2	Dictation Techniques	p. 155
4.3	Taking and Transcribing Dictation	p. 159
4.4	Improving Correspondence Procedures	p. 164
4.5	A Treasury of Model Letters	p. 174

4.1 Effective Letters

The test of an effective letter is the impression it makes on the reader. The letter is effective when (1) it moves the reader to take positive action, and (2) it leaves the reader with good feelings toward the writer and the organization he represents. Such results depend largely on the content of the letter and the controlling business policies. They also depend on the writer's ability to express ideas in ways that are acceptable to the reader. Here is a review of the writing techniques that influence the effectiveness of a letter.

For additional help with the style of business writing, see "Writing the Report," Section 6.2.

An effective letter is
1. Timely.
2. Reader-oriented.
3. Clear.
4. Well organized.
5. Courteous.
6. Tactful.
7. Natural (not stereotyped).
8. Positive (not negative).
9. Concise.
10. Persuasive.

Figure 4-1 Ten qualities of effective letters.

In General (Figure 4-1)

1. Before you write, learn as much as you can about the reader and the situation you are dealing with. Be sure you have examined previous correspondence and other pertinent records.

2. Recognize the importance of timeliness. Deal with situations as they arise and answer incoming letters promptly. If you don't have all the information you need for a prompt reply, send an interim letter to let the reader know he has not been forgotten (Figure 4-2).

3. Set a goal for each letter; for example, to build goodwill, to help the reader, to collect the debt, to sell the goods. Then carefully choose the content and language that will accomplish the goal.

Dear Mr. Farnum:

We're pleased that you want a copy of Mr. Leffler's speech before the Buffalo Chamber of Commerce last week.

Copies of the talk in an attractive format should be off the press in about ten days, and you may expect a copy shortly thereafter.

Sincerely,

Figure 4-2 An interim letter.

4. Use the "you" approach, that is, express ideas from the reader's point of view rather than yours. For example, don't say, "The new forms save *us* money," if you can say, "The new forms will save *you* time."

5. Use the language that sounds most natural, almost as if you were talking. There should be no special vocabulary for business letters.

6. Be concise, but use all the words you need to express yourself clearly and effectively. Avoid any suggestion of haste.

7. Put a full measure of tact and courtesy in every letter. Say "please" and "thank you" often. Be considerate of the reader's interests and feelings always.

Planning the Letter

1. Plan a long or formal letter in three parts: the beginning, the body, and the ending.

(a) The beginning introduces the subject and sets the mood.

(b) The body provides the necessary information. It may consist of one or several paragraphs.

(c) The ending is designed to produce a particular action or emotional response.

2. The body paragraphs are usually longer than the opening and closing paragraphs, but avoid paragraphs that run beyond 10 or 12 lines.

3. Arrange ideas in a logical and consistent way, for example, chronologically or in the order of interest or importance.

4. When details are numerous, list and number related ideas (such as reasons, steps, advantages) in order to simplify the organization of the letter and save time and space.

5. If a very short letter sounds abrupt, try adding a few pleasant words at the beginning or end (Figure 4-3).

6. Unrelated messages for a single addressee are best put in separate letters. In that way, each message gets individual attention at the reader's end. The reader is also spared needless recopying of parts of a letter for the attention of others in his organization.

The Beginning (Figure 4-4)

1. Try to introduce the subject in a pleasant and natural way. Avoid such lame beginnings as "In reply to your letter" and "We are in receipt of your letter." It is better to say:

Thank you for your letter
We appreciate your notifying us that
We are glad to send you

The phrases in Figure 4-4 suggest natural (unhackneyed) ways of beginning and ending many types of routine letters. They should not be used when individual circumstances require different treatment.

When the message can be expressed very
briefly, a pleasant opening or close will
remove abruptness.

Dear Mr. Seddon:

Nice   We are pleased to have your letter.

Necessary   Our representative, Mr. Thomas Coles,
             will be in your vicinity on April 21,
             and he will make it a point to call on
             you.

                              Sincerely,

Dear Mr. Ambrose:

Necessary   Your order of January 6 is now scheduled
             for shipment on March 11.

Nice   Thank you for your patience.

                              Sincerely,

Figure 4-3   Brevity without abruptness.

2. If, for any reason, you want to begin with a dry acknowledgment, these
forms are less stereotyped than others.

I have your letter of
I am replying to your letter of
Your letter of (date) asks

3. Instead of using the opening to acknowledge the incoming letter, try
using it to *answer* the letter. The reference to the incoming letter can be either
subordinated or implied.

The pamphlet you refer to in your recent letter has been out of print for several
    months.
The delay in shipping the binders to you has been caused by

BEGINNINGS

We are pleased to reply to your letter of (date) in which you ask

I am (sorry, glad) to learn from your letter of (date) that

We appreciate your telling us that

Your letter of (date) asks

As you requested, we are (tell what you are doing)

You will be glad to know that

Thank you for your prompt reply to our letter of

I have your letter of (date) in which

In the absence of Mr. Jones, who is away on business, I am pleased to answer your letter of

Mr. Jones has asked me to reply to your letter of (date) regarding

I am enclosing—Enclosed is—You will find enclosed

I wish it were possible to

We appreciate your request for

We have given careful consideration to your request for

ENDINGS

(For Action)

May we hear from you soon?

Will you please give this matter your (prompt, urgent) attention.

We shall appreciate your writing and telling us your wishes.

Please send us your answer as soon as you can.

We shall appreciate your prompt answer.

I am looking forward to hearing from you soon.

Will you please let us know what action you want us to take.

Your promptness in replying will be much appreciated.

I'm looking forward to your reply.

(For Goodwill)

We appreciate your interest.

It is a pleasure to be of help.

Thank you for giving us the opportunity to be of service.

I hope this information will be helpful to you.

We look forward to the opportunity of serving you again.

Thank you again for writing.

If we can be of any (further) help, be sure to let us know.

Please tell us if there is anything more we can do.

It was nice to hear from you. Please call on us again.

Thank you for your courtesy.

You may be sure that we appreciate your efforts on our behalf.

Figure 4-4   Useful letter beginnings and endings.

4. When the situation requires, sympathize with the reader, or even apologize.

> We are sorry to learn that
> We regret that we were not able to
> Please accept our apologies for

5. Don't put a negative decision in the opening. If you have to say "no," say it later.

> NOT: We regret to inform you that your suggestion is not acceptable.
> BUT: We appreciate the suggestion you made.
> OR: We have carefully considered your suggestion.

6. When you are initiating the correspondence, use the opening to tell why you are writing.

> In looking over our records, we find that it is some months since you last called on
>   us for service.
> Can you help us locate a nozzle for a Dietrich Blower, Model 3206?
> We have recently received a request for credit from the Superior Frame and Door
>   Company, Racine, Wisconsin, who gave us your name as a reference.

The Ending (Figure 4-4)

1. A formal ending is often not necessary. Just stop after you've given the last piece of information.

2. In any case, avoid such hackneyed phrases as, "Hoping this is satisfactory, I remain." If that's all you want to express, it would sound more natural if you said, "I hope this is satisfactory."

3. The ending is usually the best place to tell the reader what you want him to do. You can be as mild or as forceful as the situation requires.

> If you will give me a call, we can arrange a mutually satisfactory date.
> Please return the card at your convenience.
> Don't delay another minute. You must send your check now to avoid serious trouble.

4. Whether or not the close seeks action, it can often be used to express your goodwill or otherwise leave a pleasant feeling.

> We appreciate your writing to us.
> Thank you for giving us the opportunity to serve you.
> If I can be of any further help, please let me know.
> We'll most certainly keep you in mind.
> Again, many thanks for your letter. I hope I've been of some help.

5. If you have been at fault, try to smooth things over with some expression like the following, provided you have not already used a similar idea elsewhere in the letter.

> Thanks so much for your patience.
> We are sorry for the inconvenience caused you.
> I assure you that we will try to do better next time.
> Please accept our sincere apologies.

Language

1. Use the pronouns *I, we,* and *you* to help make your letters personal and interesting. However, don't overdo the *I* and *we. You* is better if the phrasing can be made to accommodate it.

Impersonal	Personal
Please communicate with the *undersigned*	Please write to *me*
As requested	As *you* requested
It is believed	*We* believe
This pamphlet deals with estate problems	*You* will find this pamphlet helpful in dealing with estate problems

2. Avoid business-letter clichés. They rob your letter of individuality (Figures 4-5 and 4-6).

Stereotyped	Natural
We wish to acknowledge receipt of your letter of recent date.	We have received your recent letter.
Please be advised that this charge was made by the collecting agency.	This charge was made by the collecting agency.
Replying to yours of the fourth, we are herewith sending you the form you requested.	We are pleased to send you the form you requested in your letter of August 4.
We have your order and thank you for same.	Thank you for your order.
Under date of February 10, we returned to your goodselves a check in the amount of $50.	On February 10 we returned to you a check for $50.
Thanking you for your courtesy in this matter, we are,	Thank you for your courtesy.

3. Use pleasant words as often as possible. For example:

thank you	promptly
please	benefit
appreciate	considerate
glad	generous
pleasure	happy
service	delighted

4. Keep to a minimum, or avoid altogether, unpleasant or tactless words.

Tactless	Softer
you claim	your letter states
your delinquency	your oversight
you failed to	you did not
your complaint	your letter
we must refuse	we are sorry we cannot
you must have misunderstood	apparently there was an oversight

NOT: We are sorry for the inconvenience caused by our mistake and hope there will be no recurrence of this unfortunate incident.

BUT: We are sorry for the inconvenience caused you.

NOT LIKE THIS
(stereotyped):

Dear Mrs. Pastor:

Pursuant to your communication of recent date, we
are enclosing herewith the Summary of the Annual
Stockholders' Meeting of the Excelsior Pictures Corporation. The empty envelope which you returned to
us should have contained same.

As advised by you, we are changing your address on
our records to read as this letter is directed.

Regretting the inconvenience caused in this matter,
we are

                              Very truly yours,

BUT LIKE THIS
(natural):

Dear Mrs. Pastor:

Here is the Summary of the Annual Stockholders'
Meeting of the Excelsior Pictures Corporation. It is
the report that should have been enclosed in the envelope you received from us. Please excuse the over-
sight.

We have changed your address as you requested.

                              Very truly yours,

Figure 4-5 Natural—simple—friendly. The way a good letter should sound.

RECOGNIZE THESE EXPRESSIONS?

Do you use any of the following expressions in your letters? They usually indicate a lack of freshness and should be replaced with expressions that are more original or more natural. Some exceptions may be made in legal and other very formal documents.

in reply to, replying to, with reference to (at the start of the letter)
contents carefully noted
hand you herewith
enclosed herewith
attached hereto
pursuant to
deem it advisable
at your earliest convenience
thereto, therefor, therein, thereunder
per, as per
in lieu of
hereinbelow set forth
re, in re
reference is made to
relative to
wish to say, wish to state, wish to advise
advise you further, please be advised,
in receipt of, receipt is acknowledged, pending receipt of
acknowledge receipt of
the undersigned
thanking you, we are
thanking you in advance
we remain, yours truly
your favor (for "letter")
esteemed favor
same (as in "please return same")
kindly (for "please"), kindly advise
in due course
hereby
above-captioned, above-mentioned
aforesaid, aforementioned
subject (as in "the subject policy")
duly
yours of the 23rd (for "your letter of the 23rd")
this day (for "today")
trusting, hoping (in the letter close)
your goodselves
and oblige

Figure 4-6 Stereotyped expressions.

5. Rephrase negative ideas to make them positive (Figure 4-7).

Negative	Positive
I cannot send you the information because you failed to give your account number.	I'll be glad to send you the information as soon as you give us your account number.
We hope there will be no further delay in shipping your order.	We're trying very hard to get your order to you promptly.
You'll have no reason to regret your decision.	This is a wise decision.
It is against our policy to sell direct to the consumer.	It is our policy to sell only through retailers.

6. Adapt the language to the reader.

TECHNICAL: Will you please acknowledge payment by receipting and returning to us the voucher accompanying the check.
NON-TECHNICAL: Will you please sign the blue slip accompanying the check and return it to us as our receipt.

Writing for the Employer's Signature. When you draft a letter for your employer's signature, write the letter in his style, not yours.

1. Go to the file for samples of similar letters your employer has written in the past.

2. If there are no guide letters, think of how your boss would dictate the letter himself. Use the language that is characteristic of him, not you. If you have any doubts, lean toward a simple, unaffected style.

3. Don't use the occasion to change your boss's or the company's way of dealing with the situation. If you think the traditional way is wrong, discuss it with your boss before you write the letter. Otherwise, he may resent your forwardness.

4. Don't let pride of authorship get in the way. After all, it's the person who signs the letter who takes the responsibility; he should have his letters done the way *he* wants them.

Polishing the Boss's Work. You not only *may*—you are *expected* to make any change in your employer's dictation that will save him embarrassment. That goes for errors in dates, amounts, and other facts; obvious errors in grammar and word use; and any faults in word order or sentence structure that distort the intended meaning.

On the other hand, don't pretty up the language to the point that it sounds artificial or uncharacteristic of the signer. The sound of the real man talking is far better than some sugary version of it. It's your job to help him preserve his individuality on paper.

Letters Signed by the Secretary. When the secretary writes for her own signature, she is expected to act to perfection the role of secretary to a busy man. The following suggestions should be helpful.

NOT LIKE THIS
(negative):

Dear Mr. Brown:

We regret that we cannot comply with your request
to withdraw $50 from your savings account and send
you a check for that amount.

It is a strict rule of the Bank that no withdrawals
can be made without presentation of the passbook.

We will have to hold up your request until this rule
is complied with.

Very truly yours,

BUT LIKE THIS
(positive):

Dear Mr. Brown:

We are looking forward to sending you a check for
the $50 you wish to withdraw from your savings
account.

Will you please fill out and sign the enclosed withdrawal slip and return it to us with your passbook.
Your check will be sent immediately.

Thank you for giving us this opportunity to serve
you.

Very truly yours,

Figure 4-7 Positive and negative. A contrast in tone.

1. Be as polite, considerate, and courteous in your letters as you would be
in person. Don't let any provocation (or flattery) ruffle you or cause you to
set aside your dignity.

2. Be correct in every detail, including your use of language. Any errors you make will reflect on your employer—a point he is apt to be very sensitive to.

3. Be brief. State your business, offer a pleasant word if the situation permits, and sign off. In that way, you'll give the impression of a busy, efficient secretary—isn't that the way you want it?

4. When you write to convey a message for your employer, be sure the message is so phrased that it seems to come from him, not you.

NOT: I am sorry that Mr. Dempsey will be out of town next week and will not be able to keep his appointment with you.

BUT: Mr. Dempsey regrets that he will be out of town next week and will not be able to keep his appointment with you.

NOT: I should be pleased if you would have lunch with Mr. Dempsey next Friday at noon at our Park Avenue headquarters.

BUT: Mr. Dempsey, who is out of town for a few days, has asked me to extend to you an invitation to be his guest at lunch next Friday at noon at our Park Avenue headquarters.

5. Try to sound as natural in your letters as you do in person or over the telephone. Too often the reader of a letter gets the impression that the secretary is cool or unfriendly when, in fact, she only has a mistaken idea of what a business letter should sound like.

This letter gives a bad impression.

Dear Mr. Kent:

In reference to your letter dated February 15, Mr. Downes would like to see you in your office at approximately 2:30 p.m. on Thursday, February 27.

Please mark your calendar accordingly.

> Yours very truly,
>
> Mrs. Alice Patterson
> Secretary to Mr. Downes

The following letter would be more favorably received.

Dear Mr. Kent:

Thank you for your letter of February 15. Mr. Downes has made plans to see you in your office at 2:30 p.m., Thursday, February 27.

Please let me know if this time is not convenient for you.

> Very truly yours,
>
> Mrs. Alice Patterson
> Secretary to Mr. Downes

4.2 DICTATION TECHNIQUES

Dictation is the modern way to "write" letters. Dictation gives the advantage of speed; it also helps letters sound natural because talking is a more natural process than writing.

Dictating Person to Person.   Although machine dictation is rapidly increasing, many executives still prefer to dictate in person to their secretaries and stenographers. Under the right conditions, this method can provide the maximum flexibility and personal attention to the dictator's needs. For those who use a stenographer, these suggestions are offered.

1. Organize your dictation beforehand, so that you do not waste the stenographer's time. Keep handy any records or correspondence needed for reference. Make brief outlines of long or involved letters. *Know* what you are going to say before you start dictating.

2. See that your stenographer has a comfortable place to work: preferably a straight chair and a desk top or pull-out shelf on which to rest her notebook.

3. When you start dictating, concentrate on the first idea, and express it as simply and clearly as you can. Then go on to the second idea, the third idea, and so on. The *think-then-speak* formula will ensure a logical progression throughout the letter, and it will help you avoid the stereotyped openings and closings that are largely the result of not thinking about content.

4. Speak distinctly, facing the stenographer. Do not walk around or chomp on a cigar while speaking. Maintain an even rate, and watch your speed when you dictate from printed material; you may be going too fast for the stenographer's ability to take notes.

5. Give the stenographer explicit instructions at the beginning with respect to the name, title, and address of the receiver, as well as enclosures, number of carbons, and special handling in the mail. If convenient, let the stenographer get names and addresses from past correspondence. Spell out other names and technical or unusual words.

6. If you have any special wishes regarding paragraphing, punctuation, underlining, and the like, indicate that to the stenographer. Otherwise she will paragraph and punctuate according to her understanding of the sense.

7. If you are dealing with a difficult situation or have trouble with a letter for any reason, ask the stenographer to type a double-spaced draft. That will give you a chance to make any corrections you want to on your own time before returning the draft for final typing.

8. If you are interrupted by a telephone call or a visit that may take some time, give the stenographer permission to leave until you are ready to dictate again.

9. Watch your personal habits when you dictate. If you behave like a lady or gentleman in the presence of a co-worker, you will get courtesy and better work in return.

10. Avoid overlong dictating sessions. Also dictate early in the day, if you can, so that the work can be ready for you later the same day without undue pressure. You will get better work that way and enjoy better relations with the stenographer—an important factor in your own efficiency.

11. When your typed letters are delivered to you, read them over carefully for content, form, spelling, and punctuation. If you find an error, mark the

correction on a file carbon or on another sheet of paper, not on the original. The stenographer may be able to correct the error without retyping the whole letter.

12. Take the blame for your own errors. Compliment your stenographer whenever she does an especially creditable job.

Machine Dictation.   Machine dictation imposes special responsibilities on the dictator. Especially when telephone dictation systems are used, there is no personal contact with the transcriber. Thus the instructions to her must be very explicit and follow a particular pattern. You can imagine the waste of time, for example, if you fail to tell her—before she starts typing—that you want extra carbons; or if you make a mistake in dictating and fail to tell her about it until she is well past the point where the correction can be made without a retyping of the whole letter.

To avoid these mistakes—and others—it is best to follow the instructions of the manufacturer, your employer, and others with experience in the use of the machines. Although machines and systems differ, the rules that follow may be considered generally applicable to all. Of course, they should be supplemented by the appropriate advice given in the preceding section on dictating to a stenographer.

1. Know your machine and follow the instructions for its use. It's disheartening to dictate a long letter only to discover that it has not been recorded. Other difficulties may be caused by your failing to stop the machine or to cover the mouthpiece when you interrupt your dictation to talk to someone else. Any extraneous noises or failure to speak directly into the mouthpiece may also interfere with clear reception.

2. Modulate your voice, so that it is neither too loud nor too soft, and articulate clearly. Talk directly into the mouthpiece, keeping it about three inches away from your lips. The speed of dictation is not important, one way or the other, because the transcriber can adjust the playback to suit herself.

3. If you want a particular letter or report to have priority, note the fact on the indicator slip that accompanies some types of machines. In other instances, tell the attendant or transcriber personally or by phone, or leave a note for her.

4. Start by giving such basic information as (a) your name, department, location, telephone extension; (b) type of message, for example, letter, memo, schedule; (c) number of carbons needed; (d) name and address of addressee, including attention line, if any; (e) salutation, for example, *Dear Mr. Dunn, Dear George, Gentlemen;* and (f) subject line, if desired.

5. Preface any corrections or special instructions with the word *correction* or *operator* (or *Miss Jones* or *Mary*), so that the words in the instructions won't be confused with those in the letter. For example:

Our tapes are packed six boxes *operator, make that eight boxes* to the carton.

It is also important to know that the operator types as she listens and is never more than a few words behind the record or tape. Thus, if you think of a correction more than a few words past the point where it is to be made, you may still dictate the correction, but the operator will have to be notified by a mark on the indicator slip, or by telephone, or in person. (See the special instructions provided by the manufacturer for the use of your machine.) Following are examples of delayed corrections, as dictated.

> A good sales correspondent was in 1953 worth about $75 per week and whereas today his salary is closer—correction, please—begin this paragraph again— Back in 1953 the average salary of a good sales correspondent was $75 a week. Today it is closer to $150 a week.

> —correction, please—insert the following after the first paragraph in the letter to Jones and Company—It was thoughtful of you to arrange for theater tickets for Mrs. Brown while we were at the sales banquet.

6. Indicate paragraphing and uncommon punctuation, such as semi-colons, colons, dashes, parentheses, and quotation marks. Be sure not to omit the "close parentheses." Voice inflection as in normal conversation may indicate commas and periods, but experience will tell you whether it is best to indicate these, too.

7. Dictate long or uneven figures by digits. For example, .0035 percent would be "point double-oh three five percent."

8. Spelling can be very troublesome unless you help.

(a) Spell out unfamiliar names unless they appear in the correspondence forwarded to the transcriber.

(b) Spell out technical and unfamiliar words. Indicate initial capital letters with instructions in the style of "Operator, cap J Jacksonville," or "Operator, initial caps Mary Jones."

(c) When sounds may be confusing, use a phonetic key, for example, "V, as in Victor." (For key words see p. 12.)

9. When you get to the end of the letter, indicate:

(a) the closing, for example, "Very truly yours," "Sincerely yours," and so on; (b) the signer's name and title; (c) enclosures, if any; and (d) instructions for marking carbons.

A Dictation Model.   The following model will give you an idea of how the recording of a dictated letter might sound to the transcriber. What it cannot convey is the voice inflection, which can be as valuable as the instructions themselves in guiding the operator.

> Operator, this is David Green of the Stock Transfer Department. My telephone extension is 3347. I have a letter requiring two carbons. Please address the letter to the United States Fidelity and Guaranty G-U-A-R-A-N-T-Y Company, 100 Maiden Lane, New York, New York, Zip Code one double-oh three eight. Attention Mr. Arno A-R-N-O Tauck T-A-U-C-K, Gentlemen, Subject National Foods Corporation.

We have your letter of September 6 regarding the issuance of a replacement certificate for—operator, cap C Certificate cap N oh period two nine eight five B—operator, B as in Bertha—for twenty shares of common stock registered in the name of Laurence L-A-U-R-E-N-C-E Nostrand N-O-S-T-R-A-N-D. Paragraph. Both the affidavits and the bond forms should be executed in three counterparts period—operator, counterparts is one word. They should include—operator, change they should include to the bond forms should include as obligees O-B-L-I-G-E-E-S —operator, initial caps National Foods Corporation comma Metropolitan Trust Company comma and the City Trust and Savings Bank of Geneva G-E-N-E-V-A New York. Paragraph. We will be glad to issue a replacement certificate as soon as these requirements are met. Very truly yours, David Green, Stock Transfer Department. Operator, please mark one carbon for Mr. D. R. Granger at our 60 Broad Street Office, third floor.

Here is a copy of the same letter, as transcribed:

September 9, 19—

United States Fidelity and Guaranty Company
100 Maiden Lane
New York, New York 10038

Attention Mr. Arno Tauck

Gentlemen:

National Foods Corporation

We have your letter of September 6 regarding the issuance of a replacement for Certificate No. 2985B for 20 shares of common stock registered in the name of Laurence Nostrand.

Both the affidavits and the bond forms should be executed in three counterparts. The bond forms should include as obligees National Foods Corporation, Metropolitan Trust Company, and the City Trust and Savings Bank of Geneva, New York.

We will be glad to issue the replacement certificates as soon as these requirements are met.

Very truly yours,

David Green
Stock Transfer Department

DG:rh
Copy to Mr. D. R. Granger

4.3   TAKING AND TRANSCRIBING DICTATION

As the person responsible for the transcription of dictation of company correspondence and other documents, the stenographer or secretary handles some of the most important tasks in the office. The following suggestions will assist you as one of these key employees to perform your activities in an effective and efficient manner.

Taking Dictation.

1. Establish harmonious working relationships. Whether you take dictation from one or several persons, you should build a friendly, courteous relationship between yourself and the dictator. A smile and a pleasant word upon entering his office for the dictation session establish a good climate in

which to work. Show that you are willing and eager to contribute your skills to making the company successful. You should be poised, confident, approving, alert, but unobtrusive. Control mannerisms and nervous habits that might distract the person who is concentrating on what must be said next. When the dictator pauses to think, keep alert while refraining from staring at him or daydreaming. Your eyes should be on your notebook, perhaps rereading the copy, and your pen should be ready to write. Do not supply a word when you sense that the executive is searching for one, but wait for him to ask for your help. Learn when to interrupt during dictation. Some men prefer to be interrupted immediately when a question occurs, others prefer to complete the thought before being interrupted, and still others prefer to wait until all dictation is completed. When the session is over, gather your materials quickly and indicate that you will get right to work on a task he has told you is a rush job or of particular importance to him. Or indicate in a helpful, courteous way the approximate time you will have his work transcribed.

2. Be available. Many times a dictator must send a telegram immediately or dictate before he leaves the building for an unexpected meeting elsewhere. Consequently, you should be at your desk the major part of the working day. When you must leave the immediate area, arrange for someone to cover your desk and contact you if you're needed. Or, if no one is available, leave a note in your typewriter indicating where you have gone and when you will return. If you will be gone for a considerable length of time, it is a good idea to tell the people from whom you take dictation the approximate amount of time that you'll be away from your desk. Then they will be able to give you dictation before you leave, if they plan to leave before you return. By being thoughtful in these ways, you can avoid much friction.

3. Be prepared. Preparation means that the supplies needed for taking dictation are immediately available. A separate spiral notebook should be kept for each dictator with his name and yours on the outside cover and with a rubber band securing the used pages to the stiff cover. When only a few unfilled pages are left, take a fresh notebook with you. Date each notebook on the cover with the beginning and ending dates of dictation. Several sharpened shorthand pencils or shorthand ball-point pens should be ready to be picked up as you leave your desk. Take at least two with you together with a sharpened colored pencil to mark insertions in the dictated copy, a point that will be discussed later. A good secretary must be flexible—able to drop one task and take hold of another.

Help the dictator prepare for dictating sessions by supplying him with the files and other information he will need in order to answer the correspondence. Many times the file is sent along with a letter or any other type of message when it first arrives. If this is not the procedure in your office, read the incoming correspondence as you prepare it for your superior and try to determine whether additional material will be needed when the answer is being composed. Collect what you can without overstepping your authority.

4. Be attentive. When taking dictation, listen carefully. Ideally, a secretary should face the dictator in order to hear clearly what is being said. Often, however, the executive will walk around or shift his chair, making this impossible. By being alert, you can hear every word. If a few words are missed or need clarifying, read back a few lines at the next pause so that your notes may be corrected if necessary. Listen for copy changes and directions. Be sure to write these also and leave nothing to memory.

5. Take notes efficiently. Your notebook should rest on the corner of the desk or on the extended arm rest. If this is not possible, learn how to support it firmly on your lap while maintaining businesslike posture. Enter the date and time on the first page of a day's dictation, preferably at the bottom so that you can see it when flipping through pages. Leave two or three lines before each message in which to write special instructions, such as number of copies, special mailing, or order of transcribing.

Take down the message exactly as dictated. Use shorthand symbols for most of the words, and when hearing a new word, don't panic. It might be wise to write the first few letters or the complete word in longhand. Abbreviations might also come to mind faster than the shorthand outline. It is permissible to write both longhand and shorthand in your notes. Accurate transcription is your goal. Names and initials should be written in longhand and numbers in figures. Be especially careful to write numbers as heard in order to avoid transpositions. If you are having difficulty recalling shorthand symbols, practice writing shorthand from materials in the files during slack periods of the day. Work out in advance the shorthand symbols for technical words used in your company. And take a refresher course at night, if your skill is not adequate for the dictator and the job.

Most dictators dictate at an uneven rate of speed, sometimes as fast as 150 words a minute but more often at an average of 70 words a minute. By concentrating on the message, you will be able to catch up during pauses. Because portions of previously dictated material are often changed, you are usually given time to find the place and cross out the unwanted words. Use the colored pencil to indicate where to place the insert, which will probably be further along in your notes. Number each insert and place the corresponding number at the place where the revision is to be made. At other times, the dictator will give you instructions to look up additional information and insert it at a particular place. Write as exact a description as possible of the needed material, and leave a few blank lines on which to write it when found. Pages containing rush work should be folded diagonally so that the edge protrudes from the notebook. Usually the dictator will hand you a piece of correspondence or file that concerns the message just dictated. Place each piece face down on top of the last one to keep the stack in the same order as the dictation. Use a second notebook for dictation of technical material, reports, and other work that extends over several days.

When interruptions occur, such as telephone calls or visitors, you should usually remain in the office and spend your time reading your notes; correcting shorthand outlines; and inserting punctuation, paragraphs, capitalization and other transcription aids. Your presence gives the dictator a reason for cutting the interruption short. If, however, you sense that the matter is private or will take considerable time, you may quietly leave and begin transcribing at your desk. Do not wait to be called back, but when the executive is again free, reenter his office and be seated ready to take dictation. Read back the last paragraph or a few sentences to refresh his memory after each interruption.

Transcribing Notes and Tapes

1. Set aside a portion of the day when interruptions are at a minimum. If this is not possible and interruptions do occur, mark your notes at the last typed word with a colored pencil so that you may find your place easily when you return to them. When you are using transcribing machines, there is no problem because the tape, disc, or belt remains at the point where the machine stops.

2. Clear your desk of the other tasks you might be working on and stack them in a neat pile in order of priority. Thus, you will be able to complete these tasks later with little need to review the work already finished.

3. Establish a system that you automatically follow each time you get ready to transcribe. A set routine makes for more efficiency. The next steps may be handled in any order that fits your work habits.

4. Assemble the correspondence to be answered in order of priority as indicated by the dictator or as determined by information you possess. For instance, if you know you will not be able to complete all the transcription before quitting time, you should first work on messages that should go out that day. Always transcribe rush jobs first and take them to the dictator for his approval and/or signature when they are ready.

5. Check the typewriter keys to see that they are clean, and be sure the ribbon is fresh and makes a strong, black copy.

6. Place your shorthand notebook in an upright position so that you may easily flip the pages when necessary. If a metal copyholder is not available, make your own support by attaching a button at each end of a six-inch length of string. Stand your steno book between the two buttons to keep it from slipping. If you are doing machine transcription, insert the tape or belt and place the paper strip on the machine. Put on the earphones.

7. Read your notes (or listen to the tape) to locate any special instructions and to decide on the number of copies to make. Be sure to check this number against the established company procedures regarding records retention with which you are familiar.

8. Arrange supplies so that a minimum of effort is necessary in collating the sheets of paper or in locating erasers, correction fluid, pencils, and other supplies. Assemble the paper pack and insert it into the machine.

9. Gauge the length of the message from the number of columns used in your shorthand notebook or by the marks on the transcription machine strip in order to set the margin stops. Be especially careful to pick out long letters or medium-to-long letters. These may take two pages or more. In deciding what margins to set, leave adequate left and right margins. A well-framed message is attractive to the reader. Recall that the closing parts of a letter usually take 10 to 12 lines, and that the bottom margin has at least six lines in it. Therefore, the last line of a message should end about three to three and a half inches from the bottom of the page. If the message is too long to allow sufficient space for the closing parts and the bottom margin, set the margin stops for wider margins, leave a one-and-a-half- to two-inch bottom margin, and carry at least three lines of the message to the second page. (See Chapter 3 for the correct placement of letter parts.)

10. Use the right date. Letters to be signed and mailed at the end of the day should bear that date. Letters that are to be signed the next day or when the dictator returns in several days, however, should bear the date of mailing.

11. Type the correct inside address. A check of the correspondence being answered or the file will reveal the recipient's name, its spelling, and the initials; the person's title; and the company name and address or box number.

12. Transcribe your shorthand notes by reading them rapidly in thought units, or by listening to the tape in thought units. Apply the rules of English composition as you read or listen. Check grammar, spelling, and punctuation in this reference book and in the dictionary. Be sure that all names, figures, dates, and addresses on finished copies are the same as those in your notes and on letters or memorandums that you are answering. When listening to dictation on tape, be especially sure that you hear names and figures accurately. A secretary is responsible for the correctness of all messages she transcribes. Most dictators expect her to reword awkward and ungrammatical passages. However, to avoid overstepping your authority, ask the dictator about your exact responsibilities when you are first assigned to him.

13. Type in rough form the transcription of technical or complicated messages and reports. It is also a good idea to make a rough draft the first time you transcribe work for a new dictator, and always type one if his dictation is on tape. Making a rough draft is good practice when you have questions about the copy and must wait for an opportune time to talk to the dictator. After you confer with him, you can type the final copy from the corrected rough draft quickly.

14. Proofread copy in the machine, and correct any errors as neatly as possible.

15. Type the correct size and kind of envelope. See "Letter Form and Style," Section 3.1.

16. Arrange in correct order the original copy, all enclosures, the envelope, and carbons of a distribution list that need to be signed in a folder for the dictator's signature. The flap of the envelope may be placed over the original

and/or enclosures and a paper clip affixed to the top left corner to hold the papers together. The folder keeps the pages neat and clean and offers a certain amount of privacy. Submit transcribed material to the dictator several times a day instead of taking him a large batch at the end of the day. When transcribing for several dictators, attempt to give the same service to each one. Transcribe rush jobs for all dictators before transcribing the regular correspondence for any one of them.

17. Draw a diagonal line through notes (or on the transcription machine strip) that have been transcribed.

18. After letters have been signed, fold them as explained in Section 3.1 and insert in envelopes. Place the sealed envelopes in the out or mail basket or deliver them to the mail room. You are responsible for seeing that important or rush messages leave the company in the next mail pickup. Therefore take the time to speed messages on their way by doing some of the messenger work yourself or by calling for company messenger service.

19. See that carbon copies and/or file folders are forwarded to the file department, if you have a centralized filing system. Or place the file copies and/or folders in your department files when convenient.

20. At the end of the day, check your shorthand notebook or the transcription tapes to make sure that you haven't overlooked something. This rechecking is particularly important if you have been transcribing material in a different order than it was dictated.

21. File filled notebooks (and tapes) for possible future reference. Place the dictator's and your own name plus the beginning and ending dates of use on the cover. Set up a realistic retention schedule for these notebooks and destroy the older ones when you file a new one. Often they need not be kept more than three to four months. Many transcription tapes, belts, and discs are reusable; therefore, they should not be stored very long but should be placed back in circulation as soon as they are not needed for reference.

22. Be gracious when asked to handle end-of-the-day dictation and transcription. Often the securing of a contract or the sale of a product depends on the correspondence reaching the client within a certain time period. Decisions regarding the matter may take all day to reach, and yet the executive still must close the deal that day. Hopefully your willingness to stay after closing will be rewarded by time off later, a commendation that will be noted at promotion time, or some other expression of appreciation.

4.4 IMPROVING CORRESPONDENCE PROCEDURES

Estimates put the cost of a single letter between $2 and $3. But the cost cannot be measured in dollars only. Inefficient correspondence procedures take up a disproportionate part of a company's energies, cause delay, and create dissatisfaction among the parties to the correspondence. In this section you will find a roundup of tested ideas that will save time and money, and at the same time promote good relations with the reader.

Acknowledgments	p. 165	Return Envelopes	p. 169
Copies	p. 165	Routing Slips	p. 169
Follow-Ups	p. 165	Sheet Size	p. 169
Form Letters	p. 166	"Speed Letters"	p. 171
Handwriting	p. 167	Telephone	p. 171
Printed Enclosures	p. 169	Training Aids	p. 172
Reply Copy	p. 169		
Return Address and Telephone			
Number	p. 169		

Acknowledgments. Distinguish between situations that require letter acknowledgments and those that do not.

1. Omit the letter acknowledgment when the acknowledgment is already taken care of satisfactorily by such documents as statements, credit slips, and receipts.

2. Omit the letter acknowledgment when the action you take itself provides the answer to a letter, order, request, and so on. Just be sure to act promptly; otherwise an interim acknowledgment might be needed.

3. When routine acknowledgments are necessary, consider a form letter or write the acknowledgment on the incoming letter and mail a machine copy to the sender.

4. Don't acknowledge an acknowledgment unless a discrepancy is discovered.

5. Continue to use personal letters or the telephone for acknowledgments in the instance of favors, complaints, and similar situations in which goodwill depends on your giving the matter your individual attention.

Copies. The distribution of needless copies clogs the mails, increases filing expenses, and wastes the time of recipients who have no need for them. Ingenious office machines make it so easy to produce copies that strict control must be exercised.

See also "Duplicating and Copying," Section 12.2.

1. Make as many copies as required, but not more.

2. Don't send anyone a copy of a letter or other document unless he needs it and will use it to advantage.

3. Destroy extra copies when they are no longer needed to prevent them from getting into the files.

4. Use a color code for carbon copies distributed internally. The color of the tissue will indicate which copy is to go into the permanent files and which copies can be thrown away after they have served their purpose. The color code is also helpful in the sorting and distributing of carbons.

Follow-Ups

1. When you anticipate the need to follow up a letter, make an extra carbon to use for this purpose. If an extra carbon is not available, a machine

copy of the file carbon will do. Then write or type at the top, "Did you receive this letter? A reply would be appreciated," or words on that order. An alternative is to attach to the copy a business card or note sheet with the same message. (Be sure the carbon or attachment bears your return address.)

2. To cut down on the need for follow-up correspondence, make it easy for the reader to respond. For suggestions, see "Reply Copy" and "Return Envelopes."

3. Use the telephone for local or toll-free calls when you don't receive an answer promptly. Before making a toll call, weigh the cost against the advantage to be gained.

Form Letters.   Probably the biggest savings in correspondence can be obtained through the use of form letters, guide letters, and form paragraphs.

The idea behind the use of these forms is that a great deal of routine correspondence is repetitive, and because the same situations arise time and again, the same or similar phrasing can be used at each occurrence. The advantages of form letters may be summed up as follows.

1. They can compensate for a staff inadequate in numbers or training.

2. They can often be expressed in better English and with less risk of offending than letters personally dictated by staff members.

3. They can provide a standard way of dealing with matters involving company policy.

4. They save time and money.

Two objections to the use of correspondence forms usually arise.

1. Form letters lack originality and spontaneity.

2. Form letters look impersonal.

There are answers to both objections. So-called original letters quickly lose their originality when they have to be dictated over and over again. Form letters can be made to sound less hackneyed because they have to be written only once, and more time can be given to their composition. Also, through the use of alternative phrasing and optional forms, they can be individually adapted to a particular reader.

The second objection—that form letters look impersonal—can be attacked in two ways. Form letters do not have to look impersonal. They can be personally typewritten from the standard phrasing provided, or they can be reproduced by an automatic typewriter or other machine to resemble a typed letter. But even if form letters are printed—and there are times when efficiency requires it—there is still something to be said for a printed letter that promptly, completely, and satisfactorily handles a situation, as against a typewritten letter that may be late in coming or indifferently written.

If a disadvantage is to be found in form letters, it is that they offer a correspondent the temptation to use them when they, in fact, do not accurately fit the situation. In those circumstances, the form letter must be altered or a new letter must be dictated.

Printed Form Letters.   The printed form letter (or card) is valuable in the handling of an especially large volume of correspondence of the same kind. For example, it may be used to answer complaints or inquiries, to acknowledge orders, to give notice of shipment or delivery, to notify customers of a change of address or telephone number, and the like.

Three kinds of printed form letters are common.

1. Printed without blanks for fill-in. In these, the same situation is handled without variation.

2. Printed with blanks for fill-in. These permit the insertion of names, dates, and other individual details.

3. Check-off form. These have a list of statements. When one or more of the statements are checked off, they constitute a notice to the reader, an inquiry, or the answer to an inquiry. Blank lines at the end permit the writing in of additional information.

Guide Letters.   Guide letters are precomposed to handle a variety of anticipated situations, but they are personally typewritten as the need arises. Changes in phrasing can be made at any time to adapt the letters to particular individuals and cases. Alternative forms can also be provided to prevent the necessity of sending the same letter in rapid succession to the same reader. When many guide letters are used, putting them in a loose-leaf binder with an index makes reference easy. Some companies suggest that their correspondents dictate guide letters to the typist or secretary instead of specifying them by name or number. In that way they are forced to read the letter and at the same time can make any changes necessary to fit it to the particular situation.

Form Paragraphs.   The greatest flexibility in mechanized correspondence is offered by form paragraphs. These paragraphs are written in advance to handle particular situations, they are carefully indexed, and then they are called forth by the correspondent in any combination that suits the letter requirements. Blank spaces in the form paragraphs afford the opportunity for individual details. The typing is done by hand or on an automatic typewriter that has the alternative paragraphs stored for retrieval when proper instructions are given to the machine. The machine can be set to stop at any point for the insertion of handtyped material. Even so, the uniform appearance of the letter is not disturbed because the same type and ribbon are used.

A sample page of a form paragraph manual is shown in Figure 4-8. An index to all the paragraphs is available to the correspondent. His instructions to the typist will look like this.

```
Calvin Dryer
  Cr 190   April 16, April 13, $8.93
  Cr 193   50 cents
  Cr 197
```

Handwriting.   Even in this electronic age, the human hand is sometimes more efficient than the machine. Handwriting is fairly standard for "Speed

Cr 100-200   INCORRECT REMITTANCES

    Cr 180-190   Error in Check

Openers

| Cr 181 | We have just received your check for $ - - - - sent us in payment of our invoice of __(date)__ . | Cr 181 |
| Cr 182 | Thank you for your check for $ - - - - sent us in payment of our invoice of __(date)__ . | Cr 182 |

Check Not Signed

| Cr 185 | We notice, however, that through an oversight your signature was omitted from the check. | Cr 185 |

Numerical and Written
Amounts Disagree

| Cr 186 | We notice, however, that the written amount does not agree with the amount in figures—the correct amount. | Cr 186 |

Closer

| Cr 188 | We are returning your check to you and ask that you send us a corrected check promptly. | Cr 188 |

    Cr 190-200   Follow-Ups to Secure Stamps or Check

Opener

| Cr 190 | On __(date)__ we wrote you about an error in your remittance of __(date)__ for $ - - - - . | Cr 190 |

Awaiting Stamps

| Cr 193 | We asked that you send us the balance of - - cents in stamps. | Cr 193 |

Awaiting Corrected Check

| Cr 194 | We returned your check in our letter and asked you to mail us a corrected check for $ - - - - . | Cr 194 |

Figure 4-8 A page from a form paragraph manual.

Letters" and routing slips. It is also permissible in business for short informal notes to people you know.

A typewritten letter containing errors should never knowingly be submitted for signature. When an error is discovered in a typewritten letter, however, the signer may wish to correct it by hand rather than wait for retyping. A postscript may also be added by hand. The personal touch shown by the handwriting often overrides any impression of carelessness. But, of course, individual circumstances should always control the decision.

Printed Enclosures.   Do not write long letters containing material that is already available in printed form. Where possible, answer an inquiry with a folder or booklet sent with a short covering letter. If the printed form is one of a kind, perhaps it can be photocopied. Another point: if you find yourself or your co-workers repeating the same data in letter after letter, why not suggest that the data be put into a printed leaflet for enclosure, or that a processed form letter be used.

Reply Copy.   When agreement is required, it is common practice to enclose a carbon copy of the original letter with the request that the reader sign and return it to signify his approval.

Return Address and Telephone Number.   Many company letterheads do not have adequate addresses, and some do not include telephone numbers. Delays in receiving mail and phone calls are the inevitable result, not to speak of the inconvenience to the other party. If the information on your company's letterhead is deficient, type in the building name or number, the room number, the street address, the ZIP Code, or your particular extension, as the need indicates. The information can be fitted neatly into the letterhead design or blocked above the date.

Return Envelopes.   When a reply is essential, the use of a prepaid envelope will materially increase the chance of response and cut down on the need for follow-up letters. This technique, however, is more successful in dealings with private individuals than with businessmen.

Routing Slips.   Routing slips are printed memorandum forms usually about $3\frac{1}{2}'' \times 5\frac{1}{2}''$ in size (Figure 4-9). Some have a checklist of instructions as well as space for a personal message. Routing slips are especially useful within the organization as a cover for letters, reports, clippings, and other attachments. But they serve just as well to carry attachments or independent messages—handwritten or typed—to friends outside the organization.

Sheet Size.   By a kind of Parkinson's Law, messages are expanded to fill the size of the sheet. Letters are shorter when limitations of space are kept in

From:
ROGER B. KELLETT, *Assistant Secretary*
350 Park Avenue - 14th Floor - 350-5109

Date _____

To: _____

Date _____

To _____

Of _____

From _____

Please

☐ Attend to
☐ Note and return
☐ Note and forward to files
☐ See (phone) me re attached
☐ Prepare reply for my signature

☐ For your information
☐ For your files
☐ As per conversation
☐ As requested .
☐ For your comments and suggestions
☐ Does attached meet with your approval?
☐ For signature, if you approve

Other remarks: _____

Figure 4-9 Routing slips.

mind. Use half-size letter sheets whenever possible for your own correspondence, and encourage others to use them, too. Also keep handy a small note pad and post cards for informal use, when copies are not needed. Like routing slips, they save time and free stenographic help for other chores.

Of course, once a long letter is dictated, there is no point in trying to crowd it into a small letter sheet if a larger one is available.

"Speed Letters."   Available from stationers are carbon-interleaved forms for internal correspondence or for correspondence with close members of your business family (vendors, for example). These forms, sometimes called "Speed Letters,"[1] have space for a reply and provide a copy for each party. Either handwriting or typing can be used. (Figure 4-10.)

Telephone.   Where telephone service is efficient, it's faster, and often cheaper and better, to call than to write. Here are some handy guidelines.

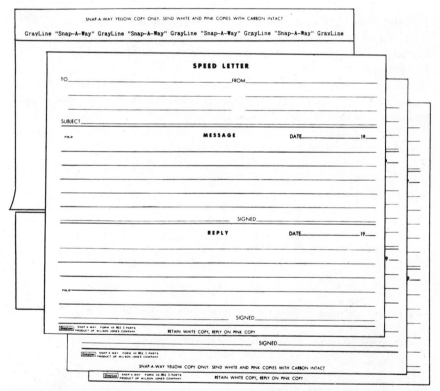

Figure 4-10   "Speed Letter"—message-and-reply form. (Reproduced by permission of Wilson Jones Company)

[1] "Speed Letter" is the registered name of forms printed by the Wilson Jones Company.

USE THE TELEPHONE:

1. When speed is of controlling importance.

2. When the situation has a number of uncertainties that can best be resolved by instant two-way communication.

3. When the nature of the information to be imparted makes it undesirable to put it in writing (unfavorable credit information, for example).

4. When voice communication will help the business relationship.

WRITE A LETTER OR MEMO:

1. When a telephone call requires confirmation.

2. When you must have a permanent record of the message.

3. When a phone call may embarrass the other party or reach him at an inconvenient time.

4. When the message can be expressed more tidily on paper.

5. When the difference in cost, or the difficulty of reaching the other party, favors writing.

Training Aids.   Manuals, bulletins, and other training aids are accepted ways by which a company sets standards for its letters and encourages good performance. The standards relate particularly to letter format, English usage, and phrasing.

Manuals.   Unless a company has special requirements or special rules it wishes its employees to follow, this handbook can serve as its official style manual for both stenographers and correspondents.

1. For stenographers. Subjects of principal interest to stenographers and typists may be located in this volume as follows.

Chapter
  or
Section

3.1   Letter Form and Style
3.2   Letters to Government and the Military
3.3   Forms of Address

4.3   Taking and Transcribing Dictation

8.1   Spelling Guide
8.2   Words Often Confused
8.5   Dictionary of English Usage

9.   Punctuation

10.1 Abbreviations
10.2 Capitals
10.3 Numbers
10.4 Underlining
10.5 Word Division

11.1 Improving Typing Efficiency
11.2 Typing Statistical Material
11.3 Typing Special Characters, Formulas, and Equations

12.3 Telephone and Wire Services

16.   Dictionary of Business Terms

17.   List of Standard Abbreviations

2. For correspondents. Subjects of principal interest to correspondents may be located in this volume as follows.

Chapter
   or
Section
   4.1   Effective Letters
   4.2   Dictation Techniques
   4.4   Improving Correspondence Procedures
   4.5   A Treasury of Model Letters

The Need to Know

The recent mail strike has made everyone more aware of the value of letters. Not to know—to be deprived of the comfort of words—is one of the cruelest predicaments to confront a citizen in a time that has been called "the age of communication."

If a lesson can be learned from our experience, it is that letters have a value beyond what they actually say. They give the reader a sense of community, of being in touch. To ask a question and not get an answer is to feel a loss of security. To suffer pain or experience pleasure without someone to share either increases the one and diminishes the other.

What you as a correspondent can do to help is fairly simple:

1.   Answer incoming letters promptly, courteously, and helpfully.

2.   Anticipate the customer's banking needs and problems, and let him know you are ready to assist in meeting them.

3.   Write the letters you don't <u>have</u> to write—the letter of condolence, the letter of congratulation, the letter of appreciation.

A recent issue of <u>Time</u> magazine says, "Nothing seems to work any more." We'd like to claim an exception. Letters work. Just use them and see.

Figure 4-11   A letter improvement bulletin for employees. (Manufacturers Hanover Trust Company)

6. Report Preparation
6.4 Memorandums
8. Correct English Usage
9. Punctuation

Bulletins. Many companies use bulletins to maintain the interest of their correspondents in effective writing. Consisting of a page of more and issued on a fairly regular basis, a bulletin usually concentrates on a single point or theme and offers examples from current letters (Figure 4-11). One of the most productive themes is the systematization of correspondence through the development of forms and guides. As discussed earlier under "Form Letters" (pp. 166–168), these offer the best route to saving time and money and improving the quality of correspondence as well.

4.5 A TREASURY OF MODEL LETTERS

Here is a collection of many different types of letters, accompanied by special instructions for the person who is called on to write letters similar to them.

Although the letters cannot cover every contingency, they have been selected for their general utility and can easily be adapted to a large number of similar situations. The content of the letters will usually indicate whether they are to be signed by the assistant, the secretary, or the employer. In some instances —with a slight change or none at all—the letters would be equally appropriate from any one of those sources.

Acknowledgments	p. 174	Invitations Answered	p. 186
Appointments	p. 177	Invitations Confirmed	p. 186
Appreciation	p. 178	Recommendations	p. 187
Complaints	p. 178	References	p. 188
Condolence Letters	p. 179	Refusals	p. 188
Confirmations	p. 180	Requests	p. 189
Congratulatory Letters	p. 181	Sympathy	p. 190
Follow-Up Letters	p. 183	Ticket Orders	p. 191
Introductions	p. 184	Transmittal Letters	p. 191
Invitations	p. 185	Travel Arrangements	p. 192

Acknowledgments. *Of Documents Received.* When valuable papers are received, an acknowledgment should be sent whether or not it is requested.

1. Acknowledge receipt.

2. Name the document.

3. If the situation requires, state the disposition of the document.

4. Unless the matter is strictly routine, express appreciation or offer some other personal comment.

Dear Mr. Stewart:

Thank you for sending us the will of Mr. Henry F. Connelley for safekeeping. It will be kept in our vaults, from which you may obtain it at any time

Sincerely yours,

Dear Mr. Hill:

We have received our copy of the contract putting into effect our participation in the 19— National Marketing Survey.

Many thanks for your efforts in our behalf.

Sincerely yours,

Dear Mr. Ryder:

Thank you very much for sending us a copy of your audited report as of December 31, 19—.

We have been most interested in reviewing these figures and wish to extend our congratulations on the way you have maintained your fine condition. I observed particularly the substantial increase in sales and profits and know how gratifying this must be to you.

Kindest regards,

Of Letters Addressed to Employer.   When the boss is away and letters are received that require his personal attention, they should be acknowledged immediately.

1. Identify the letter by date or subject.

2. Tell how long the addressee will be away or when he will return.

3. State that a reply can be expected.

4. If you wish, give the reason for your employer's absence ("away on business," "on a brief vacation," and so on); but if he is ill, he will probably appreciate it if you say only that he will be "away from the office" for a certain time.

5. Answer the letter yourself if you have the necessary information and know that you are following your employer's wishes.

Dear Mr. Rodney:

Mr. Read will be away from the office for the next ten days. I am sure he will answer your letter of February 14 as soon as he returns.

Very truly yours,

Dear Mr. Dorfman:

Your letter of November 8 about the Carpenter project will be brought to Mr. Farnum's attention as soon as he returns from a short business trip.

Very truly yours,

Dear Mr. Tyndall:

I am answering your letter of May 12 in the absence of Mr. Ryan, who will be out of the office for a few days.

Mr. Ryan customarily receives sales representatives on Thursday mornings from 9 to 12. If you would like to call on him any Thursday after May 20, I am sure he would be glad to talk with you. To arrange a definite appointment, please call me a day or two in advance.

Sincerely yours,

Dear Mr. Gulton:

Because Mr. Fisher is away on business, he is unable to answer personally your letter of August 18 regarding the error in the printing run he specified in our Purchase Order No. 3257.

I have, however, taken up the matter with Mr. Sampson in our advertising department, who assures me that the figure should be 200,000, just as you surmised. A corrected purchase order will be sent to you in a few days.

Sincerely,

Of Personal Letters. Many letters that have to be answered are those of a personal nature, for example, letters of condolence, sympathy, and congratulations. These require a special touch and are never as easy to write as they sometimes seem. They should always be signed personally by the person to whom the original message was sent.

1. Be brief.
2. Be personal.
3. Be gracious.
4. But don't gush.

Reply to Congratulatory Note

Dear Mr. Brown:

Thank you for your letter conveying the good wishes of your company and your own in particular. These anniversaries come rather frequently when one has had as many as I have. However, they will never come close enough together to make the good wishes of friends less appreciated than they were in my younger days.

Sincerely,

Dear Fred:

Thank you very much for your congratulatory note. I don't know how good the work has been, but I know that there has been plenty of it.

If and when you happen to be in Washington, please stop in, for Elwood and I would both be happy to see you.

Cordially yours,

Dear Raymond:

A nicer note I never received.

May I tell you how deeply I appreciate your good wishes and how fortunate I am to have a friend as thoughtful as you.

Sincerely,

Reply to Letter of Compliment

Dear Mr. Sadler:

Thank you for your kind comments on my talk. I would like you to know that your generous and encouraging words are very much appreciated.

Sincerely yours,

Replies to Letters of Condolence

Dear Mr. Stevens:

Your expression of sympathy on the death of our president, Mr. George C. Grady, is very much appreciated.

Sincerely,

Dear Mr. Fenton:

Thank you for your kind expression of sympathy. Mr. Durand often spoke of you with the affection he reserved for his most highly regarded friends.

Sincerely yours,

Gentlemen:

We are deeply touched by the fine tribute your organization paid to Ellen Fox at the time of her death.

Miss Fox always had a keen interest in your association and spoke enthusiastically of the inspiration she received from her fellow members.

Your kind words have been a source of consolation to all who knew her, and we thank you for them.

Sincerely,

Appointments. Letters and the telephone provide able assistance in making appointments. A good appointment letter will

1. Indicate the reason for the appointment (or for the inability to make it or keep it).

2. Seek to set the exact time and place and to obtain confirmation.

Dear Mr. Gray:

Mr. Sims would like to see you in his office on Monday morning, October 17, at 10 o'clock to discuss the reorganization plan you have suggested. He would like you to stay for lunch after the meeting.

Will you please let me know if the time is convenient to you. My telephone number is (212) 435-6666.

Very truly yours,

Dear Mr. Tomes:

Mr. George Howard, our treasurer, is going to be in your city on Tuesday, March 22, and would like the opportunity to chat with you for about a half hour in the morning. He believes that you may be of some help to him in working out a problem in connection with our company's employee pension plan. Mr. Howard will be staying at the Hilton Plaza Hotel and will be pleased to see you there or at your office. He is taking a one o'clock plane back to Chicago.

Will you please telephone me at the above number to let me know whether a meeting would be agreeable to you and when and where you would like it to take place?

Very truly yours,

Dear Mr. Ames:

I will be glad to see you about your job application in my office at 3 p.m. Monday, January 14. If this time is agreeable, please telephone my secretary, Miss Jane McGorry, collect. She will see that you receive your round-trip plane fare.

I am looking forward to our meeting.

Sincerely yours,

Dear Mr. Silver:

Mr. Downey regrets that he will be unable to see you on the date you suggested because he will be out of town on business. If you would find it convenient to drop in some morning during the week of February 10, please let me know. I am sure that Mr. Downey will be glad to make some time for you.

Very truly yours,

Appreciation (also see "Acknowledgments").
For Gift

Dear Mal:

You are indeed a very thoughtful person and I am a fortunate and grateful one. The package that was delivered to me yesterday came as a most pleasant surprise. I am very happy with the generous supply of Creston's excellent products and the container that housed them.

With my thanks, I send you the season's greetings and every good wish for a happy, healthful, and prosperous New Year.

Sincerely,

For Personal Favor

Dear Mr. Graham:

I appreciate very much your sending me the newspaper clipping containing the announcement of my promotion. It's very flattering that anyone so far away would take notice.

Best wishes.

Sincerely,

Dear Mr. Morrison:

I enjoyed the use of your office and the proximity to the many nice people in Room 1050. Carol Black was especially helpful in enabling me to produce a great deal of work I could not have done under other conditions.

Thanks very much for your kindness—and welcome back.

Sincerely,

Dear Mr. Crutchfield:

I have been intending for some time to write and express to you my appreciation for the consideration you have shown to Bob Ellison, whom you hired on my recommendation. He has often told me how much he enjoys working under you, how much he learns by being associated with you, and how many interesting opportunities are being afforded him.

I do hope that Bob is reciprocating in the best way—by doing his job well. Kindest regards.

Sincerely,

Complaints. Some complaint letters relate to office maintenance and services; others, to products bought and used in the office.

1. State clearly the nature of the complaint and any relevant facts.

2. Appeal to the reader's motives.

3. Ask for specific action to be taken.

4. Display cool determination, but avoid abuse. (An offended reader is not the most cooperative.)

Memorandum to the Office Maintenance Department:

I have called several times about the condition of the sofa in Mr. Platt's office. If the sofa cannot be satisfactorily cleaned or slip-covered, then it should be re-covered with new fabric or replaced. As things stand, this piece of furniture is an embarrassment to Mr. Platt and does not speak well for the company or your department.

Will you please send someone to examine the sofa and let me know promptly what action you propose, so that I can tell Mr. Platt?

Gentlemen:

For several weeks now we have been using your Super-X carbon paper in our Mogul Electric Typewriters. We find that it leaves a broad streak that we are unable to erase or eliminate. We still have a considerable supply of this carbon and are reluctant either to continue using it or to discard it and take the loss. Perhaps if your service representative could see your carbons in use, he would have some remedy to suggest. We certainly would not consider ordering any more carbon paper from you until the problem is solved.

Will you please have your man call on me personally as soon as possible.

Very truly yours,

Memorandum to the Purchasing Department:

The Bentley portable tape recorder you recently purchased for Mr. Wyler's use (Purchase Order No. 23–465) has been giving considerable trouble. It picks up too much extraneous sound and has a tendency to blur. Because the guarantee period of 60 days is still in effect, we suggest you have the vendor pick up the machine and either repair it or replace it with one that operates more satisfactorily. A temporary replacement would be helpful.

The messenger who calls should ask for me in Room 435.

Condolence Letters.   It is customary and thoughtful to send a letter of condolence to the family or close business associate of a deceased employee, customer, or other friend.

1. Keep it brief.

2. Include other members of your family or organization in the expression of sympathy.

3. Be sympathetic but not maudlin.

4. Recall the achievements or character of the deceased, or a particular episode in your relations with him.

5. In writing to the family, offer your assistance if appropriate.

Dear Jim:

I do not need to tell you of our profound sorrow at the news of Al Bowen's death. He was a banker of great quality and left a heritage and tradition at First National that will long be remembered. I count it a privilege to have known him as a friend.

I want to express to you and your associates and to his family my very deep sympathy.

Sincerely,

Dear Bill:

We are deeply grieved this morning to learn that Phil Greene passed away so suddenly yesterday. No doubt it was his wish to go the way he did, while in the service of one of the numerous activities to which he was devoted. He was a splendid gentleman and a warm good friend of mine, always inspiring confidence and respect from those with whom he had contact.

My deepest sympathy to all of his associates and to the members of Phil's family.

Sincerely,

Dear Harold:

You and your family have been very much in our thoughts these days, and I want to express to you this very sincere word of sympathy. I am sure that you will always remember with great pride what your father stood for and what he accomplished, and the high regard in which he was held by all who knew him.

Sincerely,

Dear Mrs. Fellow:

It was with sincere regret and surprise that I read in this morning's paper of Jim's passing. I had spoken with him only last Friday, at which time we had tentatively arranged for a get-together yesterday. His friendship will be sorely missed.

My staff joins me in extending our deepest sympathy. If we can be helpful in any way, please be sure to call on us.

Sincerely,

Dear Harry:

All of us here at National are deeply saddened this morning on learning of Colonel Farr's passing.

He was a staunch friend of ours and an executive whose achievements and personal qualities have left their mark on the American scene.

Our deepest sympathy to all of the Tyler organization and to all members of the family.

Sincerely,

Dear Mrs. Mayer:

It is with deep sorrow that we have received the sad news of your loss. We, in some measure, share your loss, for your father was a charter member of our club.

The officers and members of the Quarter Century Club extend to you their deepest sympathy in your bereavement.

Sincerely yours,

Dear Mr. Troy:

I am extremely sorry to learn of the recent passing of your president, Mr. George S. Farmer, and on behalf of the officers and directors of the Steele Manufacturing Company, I wish to extend to you and your associates our deepest sympathy.

Sincerely yours,

Confirmations. When a personal conversation or telephone call results in some understanding, it is usually wise to confirm the agreement by mail. If the other party obtained a different impression from the conversation, he then has the opportunity to correct it before any serious damage is done.

1. Tell how and when the agreement was reached.

2. Tell specifically what the agreement covered.

3. Add any details necessary to carrying out the agreement.

4. Express your goodwill or, more specifically, your desire to carry out your part of the arrangement. In some circumstances, you may thank the reader for his part in the arrangement.

Dear Mr. Greer:

This will confirm the arrangements we agreed on today pertaining to the Community Chest Drive. If you will send us the printed circulars, we will enclose them in our weekly payroll envelopes to be distributed on January 3. We will need 3,500 of the circulars, and they will have to be in our hands by December 30.

We're very glad that we can offer this kind of cooperation, and we hope our employees will respond generously.

Sincerely yours,

Dear Mr. Saxe:

As Mr. Sattler mentioned to you today when you visited him, our messenger will pick up the framed portrait of John Applegate on Friday morning in Room 1011, 660 Fifth Avenue. I will appreciate your leaving the necessary instructions with your public relations department for the release of the painting.

The portrait will be well cared for while in our possession and will be returned to you as soon as the photoengraver is through with it, probably in a week or ten days. Thank you for lending it to us.

Sincerely,

(The letter that follows, signed by the secretary, is somewhat informal because of the informal nature of the "agreement.")

Dear Mr. Traube:

Just a reminder that you are going to be Mr. Field's guest at the Finance Club's monthly luncheon at the Waldorf on Tuesday, March 20, at 12:30 p.m.

Very truly yours,

Congratulatory Letters. Business anniversaries, elections and appointments to office, and personal achievement of any sort provide the opportunity for writing congratulatory letters. These are most effective when they are warm, personal, and concise, with a minimum of the customary clichés.
Business Anniversary

Dear Jack:

I am pleased to learn that on Tuesday you will have completed 25 years with the company. May I extend my best wishes to you on this anniversary and congratulate you on your eligibility for membership in our Quarter Century Club.

This is an occasion of great significance to both you and the company. I am sure you can look back with a great deal of satisfaction to your record of accomplishment and to the lasting friends you have made among your associates.

My best wishes for your happiness now and through the years to come.

Sincerely yours,

Dear Mr. Caine:

We're very proud to note that tomorrow, December 9, will mark the tenth anniversary of the opening of your account with us.

I do not want to let this occasion pass without again thanking you for the business with which you have favored us and telling you how highly we value a relationship extending over so many years. In looking forward to the next ten years of our association, I hope you will continue to prosper while calling on us to be increasingly helpful to you.

To you and Mr. Cornell I send my very kind regards and best wishes.

Sincerely,

New Job

Dear Mr. Marston:

My warm congratulations and best wishes to you as you assume the vice presidency of Clinton Manufacturing Company. You bring to this high post a splendid background of achievement and I am happy to join your many friends in every best wish for the years ahead.

I hope you will be coming our way soon. It will be a privilege to welcome you at 10 Wall Street.

Sincerely,

Dear Jim:

I am sorry that an out-of-town engagement prevented my joining in the toast to you at the Metropolitan Club last night.

I should have liked to tell you how much your association has meant to us and how much we are going to miss you. Please know that you carry with you to your new assignment my best wishes for your success and the hope that it will give you every bit of personal satisfaction you ever wanted from your work.

Cordially,

Dear Tom:

How nice to be an executive vice president! I can imagine how proud Elsie and the children must be. And how fortunate for Clark and Company.

Please accept my congratulations and best wishes for your success.

Cordially,

Promotion

Dear Charlie:

I couldn't have wished for any better news this morning than the report of your promotion. Once again the management of the Standard Tool Corporation have proved how astute they are, and they as well as you are to be congratulated.

For you and your family, I wish the best of everything in the years ahead.

As ever,

Dear Rod:

I am pleased to read in this morning's news of your election as Treasurer of the Bliss Lighting Corporation. This is most assuredly a well-merited promotion and one that must give you a great deal of personal satisfaction.

Congratulations and my very best wishes for the future.

Cordially,

My dear Mr. Hall:

Congratulations on your promotion.

The penalty for doing good work is more good work to do.

Sincerely,

Dear Mr. Sampson:

The good news of your recent promotion has just reached us here. My associates and I want to join your many friends in extending our heartiest congratulations and sincerest wishes for your continued success.

Cordially yours,

Special Honors

Dear Stanley:

I learn from the *Alumni News* that you have won the Alumni Meritorious Service Award.

As one who has been privileged to work with you for a long time, I want to add my congratulations to the many you will receive. I hope your period of usefulness to the university has only begun and that you and your family will enjoy the benefits of your good health and good works for many years to come.

As ever,

Dear Mr. Legrand:

It was indeed a pleasure to learn that you have been made a Knight of the Legion of Honor, a tribute bestowed only on those who have attained the greatest achievement.

Allow me to extend my heartiest congratulations on this recognition.

Sincerely yours,

Dear Mr. Plimpett:

Just a note to express my congratulations and best wishes on your election as President of the Commerce Club. You have a fine opportunity for public service, and I know you will make the most of it.

Sincerely yours,

Speech, Article, and So On

Dear George:

I enjoyed your talk the other night, as did the rest of the audience. Your remarks on the businessman's responsibility to his employees couldn't have been more apt or more interestingly put.

In the weeks and months ahead, I hope you will be given other opportunities to express your views. Everybody would benefit. Again, my most sincere congratulations.

Cordially,

Dear Mr. Winston:

I have just had the pleasure of reviewing the report that you have made to the stockholders of the Chambers Corporation for the fiscal year recently ended, and I compliment you on this informative and attractive document. The results clearly reflect the vigor and foresight of Chambers' management.

My congratulations to you and your associates and best wishes for the years ahead.

Cordially yours,

Follow-Up Letters. When a reply to a letter is expected but is not received, you should follow up the matter by phone or mail. If you signed the original letter, you should also sign the follow-up letter. If your employer signed the original letter, you may prepare the letter for his signature or for your own, if he prefers. Sometimes it is less embarrassing to both principals if the secretary takes over the follow-up.

1. State the purpose of the letter.
2. Describe the letter to which an answer is wanted.

3. If the situation requires, ask the reader to investigate the matter.

4. Request a reply.

Signed by Secretary

Gentlemen:

On July 12 Mr. Henry Flint sent you his subscription to the *Standard Business Review* and enclosed his check for $10 in payment. Although more than two months have now passed, he has yet to receive his first issue.

Will you please look into this matter and see what you can do to put the subscription in force. A prompt answer will be appreciated.

Sincerely yours,

Signed by Employer

Dear Mr. Felton:

Some time ago, responding to your request, I filled out a long questionnaire on the subject of hiring sales personnel. Your letter indicated that a copy of your study, when completed, would be sent to all respondents.

The subject of your investigation is one of great interest to me. If the results are available and have somehow been sidetracked, will you please send me a copy. If your report is not yet completed, perhaps you can tell me when I may expect it.

Sincerely yours,

Dear Mrs. Dawson:

May we have a reply to our letter of September 4 asking for approval of our purchase of stocks for your account. A copy of the letter is enclosed. Please sign it in the space marked and return it in the envelope we have provided.

We look forward to hearing from you by return mail.

Very truly yours,

Introductions. A letter of introduction is written to a business acquaintance on behalf of an employee, customer, or other person who desires some help from the addressee.

1. State the business connection of the person introduced.

2. Give the reason for the introduction.

3. Ask the reader to provide such assistance as may be required.

The following letters are intended to be presented personally by the individual who is being introduced.

Dear Mr. Mornet:

May I introduce Mr. William Haley, chairman of the Haley Manufacturing Company, Akron, Ohio.

As I write this letter, Mr. Haley is preparing to leave on a trip to Europe. While he is in your city, he may have occasion to call on you for some information or advice.

Any courtesy you may be in a position to extend to Mr. Haley will be very much appreciated.

Sincerely,

Dear Mr. Rose:

This letter will serve to introduce its bearer, Mr. Philip Denton, a Detroit businessman with whom we have had the pleasure of doing business for the past seventeen years.

Mr. Denton is President of Denton Plastics, Inc., a leader in the design and production of molded plastic containers for prepackaged liquid consumer products. He is now visiting the Southwest for a purpose that he will explain to you in person. I am sure you will receive him cordially and give him, to the best of your ability, the help he is seeking.

Sincerely,

A copy of the letter of introduction with a covering letter is customarily sent ahead to the person addressed.

Dear Mr. Rose:

Early next month you will receive a visit from Mr. Philip Denton, a very good customer of ours, who would like to establish business connections in your part of the country. Enclosed is a copy of a letter with which we have provided him.

As the letter indicates, we have a high regard for Mr. Denton, and we believe that his plans will be of considerable business interest to you. We will be grateful for any help you give him.

Sincerely,

Invitations. Invitations may be classified as formal or informal. The formal invitation is either printed or typewritten on an engraved letterhead in a series of centered short lines. The informal invitation is set up as a letter, but usually on small engraved stationery, with the inside address at the bottom. (See Figure 3-8.) The invitations below are arranged in order of descending formality.

Formal

Mr. James S. Patterson
cordially invites you to attend
a reception in honor of
Chancellor Carl V. Kronenberg
on Monday, the tenth of February,
from 5:00 to 6:30 p.m.
at the University Club
50 West 54th Street
R.S.V.P.

Informal

Dear Hobart:

The pleasure of your company is requested at the Annual Reports Awards Banquet to be held at the Statler Hilton Hotel on Monday, October 25, at 7:00 p.m.

I hope you can be with us and shall look forward with pleasure to your acceptance.

Cordially yours,

Dear Fred:

I am arranging a small luncheon on April 23 to mark the retirement of our Executive Vice President, Mr. Samuel Treadwell. We'll be meeting in our Executive Dining Room on the 44th floor at 12:30 p.m.

Will you please let me know if you are free to join us.

Sincerely,

Invitations Answered.   All written invitations of a personal nature require an answer. If time permits, the answer is best given by letter. As a precaution against error, it is usually a good idea to repeat the time and place.

Answer to Formal Invitation.   The answer to a formal invitation takes the same form as the invitation. For example:

Mr. and Mrs. Charles S. Stratton
are pleased to accept
(or) regret that they are unable to accept
your kind invitation to
the reception in honor of
Chancellor Carl V. Kronenberg
on Monday, the tenth of February,
at the University Club

Answer to Informal Invitation (Accepted)

Dear Gary:
I am pleased to accept your invitation to attend the Annual Reports Awards Banquet to be held at the Statler Hilton Hotel on Monday, October 25, at 7:00 p.m. It was nice of you to think of me.

Sincerely,

Dear Arthur:
I'll be very happy to join you at the luncheon for Mr. Treadwell on April 23, at 12:30 p.m. in your Executive Dining Room.
Thank you for the invitation.

Cordially,

Answer to Informal Invitation (Declined)

1. Give a tactful reason for being unable to accept.
2. Express appreciation for the invitation.

Dear Gary:

Because I will be away on business on the evening of October 25, I am sorry that I will not be able to accept your kind invitation to attend the Annual Reports Awards Banquet.
Thank you anyway. It was nice of you to think of me.

Sincerely,

Dear Arthur:

Another engagement, made some time ago, will prevent me from attending the luncheon for Mr. Treadwell on April 23.
I'm especially sorry because I have the highest regard for your executive vice president and would like to join in honoring him.
Thanks for inviting me. I'll convey my good wishes to Mr. Treadwell separately.

Sincerely,

Invitations Confirmed.   When a luncheon or dinner involves several different parties, and especially when such arrangements have been made by telephone, a confirming letter is helpful in preventing misunderstandings.

Dear Mr. Bliss:

I am very glad that Mr. Carroll Dennis will be able to join us for dinner next Monday, November 1, and that you and Mrs. Bliss as well as Mr. R. M. Clouder will also be with us on this occasion.

As I have confirmed separately with Mr. Dennis, we will meet at the Maisonette Russe at the St. Regis Hotel, Fifth Avenue at Fifty-fifth Street, where I have made dinner reservations for 8 p.m.

Mr. and Mrs. Hartman and my wife and I are very much looking forward to seeing you all then.

With kindest personal regards.

Sincerely,

Recommendations.   A letter of recommendation is an endorsement usually given to an employee or friend who is seeking other employment or preferment. The letter may be addressed to a particular individual or "To Whom It May Concern." If addressed to an individual, it should be mailed directly to him; otherwise, it is given to the subject, who may show it or send copies at his discretion.

1. State the reason for the letter.
2. Indicate the relation of the subject to the writer.
3. Describe the qualifications of the subject.
4. Offer your endorsement.

Dear Mr. Crawford:

Mr. Nelson F. Connelley informs us that he has applied to your company for the position of trainee in your management development program.

We know Mr. Connelley as a former employee who worked in our plans department from the time of his graduation from Bard College in June of last year until he left us about a month ago. Although his duties were mainly clerical, we learned to respect his accuracy, his thoroughness, and his capacity for hard work. We particularly liked his pleasant personality and his ability to get along well with others. We were sorry to see him go, but we understood his desire for a position in a business that could offer more rapid advancement.

We have no hesitation in recommending Mr. Connelley for any responsibility you may see fit to assign him in the position you have open.

Very truly yours,

To Whom It May Concern:

To our great regret, the bearer of this letter, Mr. Alfred Cummings, has tendered his resignation as he is terminating his Wall Street career to enter industry, where he believes there is a broader field for knowledge and advancement open to him.

Mr. Cummings entered our employ in April 19— and became a registered representative in October 19—. During the entire period of his association with us, we knew him as a gentleman of the highest integrity and of most pleasing personality. He is intelligent, intuitive in grasping ideas, and most enthusiastic in everything he undertakes. For these reasons we believe he will be a success in any enterprise in which he is engaged.

Dear Mr. Sabin:

As an alumnus of Excelsior University, may I add a personal word to the application of Mr. Ernest S. Carr for admission to the Graduate School.

I have been a friend of Mr. Carr's family for more than twenty years, and I can recommend Ernest for your consideration, confident that his character and scholarship measure up to the University's high standards. Ernest's father, Dr. Ralph M. Carr, is himself an outstanding alumnus of our College of Medicine.

Any consideration you give to Mr. Carr's application will be most appreciated.

Sincerely yours,

References.   A letter of reference is different from a letter of recommendation in that it reports rather than recommends. It is useful in answering routine inquiries about former employees who have applied for work elsewhere.

Dear Mr. Clark:

Mrs. Jane Dammler, about whom you inquire in your letter of September 21, was employed by us from June 26, 19— until May 18, 19—, when she resigned to remain at home.

Mrs. Dammler served as a typist-clerk and performed her duties in a satisfactory manner.

We found no reason to question her honesty or integrity.

Very truly yours,

A more complimentary letter of reference follows.

Dear Mrs. Graves:

Your letter of April 10 asks about our experience with Mr. Oscar Welford, who has applied for a position in your advertising department.

Mr. Welford was employed as a production assistant in our advertising department from November 19— to January 19—, when he left to go into military service. We liked Mr. Welford personally and considered his work to be of superior quality. He was offered the opportunity to return to work with us when his military service was completed.

Our experience with Mr. Welford suggests that he will be an asset to your company.

Very truly yours,

Refusals.   Turning down a request represents one of the most difficult of all writing jobs. It is best to follow these rules.

1. Keep the refusal out of the opening.
2. Be sympathetic.
3. Give a reason.
4. Say "no" tactfully.
5. Close on an affirmative note.

Charity Solicitation Turned Down

Gentlemen:

Your invitation to take advertising space in the souvenir program of the annual dinner of the League for the Underprivileged has been given our careful consideration.

Much as we are in sympathy with the aims of your organization, we regret that our advertising budget does not include funds for such a purpose. As a corporation we regularly contribute to a list of charities approved by our Board of Directors.

On their own, our executives and other employees also contribute to a large number of worthy causes, and we don't doubt that the League shares in their benevolence.

With all good wishes, we are

Sincerely yours,

Job Refused

Dear Mr. Williams:

It was good to talk with you the other day about the possibility of a job in our operations department.

We have now seen a number of candidates for the job and we are impressed with the qualifications they offer. The choice was especially difficult, but we had to make it. We are sorry that you missed out by a small margin.

We believe, however, that you have much to offer an organization and wish you much success in achieving your career goals.

Sincerely,

Employee's Suggestion Turned Down

Dear Mr. Conway:

The Suggestion Committee acknowledges your proposed plan for a consolidation of our "Weekly Management Bulletin" and the biweekly "RDC Review," which also reaches management personnel.

After careful weighing of both the advantages and the disadvantages, we came to the conclusion that the need to retain the double forum for management views outweighed all considerations of economy and efficiency. We have therefore decided to retain the publications in their present form.

Although your suggestion did not win you an award, we compliment you on the thought you gave it and hope you will continue to give us your ideas for improvements in any area of the company's operations.

Sincerely yours,

Customer's Suggestion Turned Down

Dear Mrs. Belmar:

Thank you for your suggestion for improving the package of Gordon's Wheat Nibbles.

We have tried a number of ways, including the method you suggest, for making the package easier to open, but we have found no way that would keep the product as fresh in use as the present package.

We are pleased to know that we have such a loyal and interested customer and hope you will continue to enjoy the freshness that every package of Gordon's Wheat Nibbles affords.

Sincerely yours,

Requests. A request for information, copies of printed materials, samples, and the like, represents an imposition on the reader and therefore requires special courtesy and tact.

1. Tell what provided the impetus for the request.

2. State specifically what you want. Keep the request within reasonable limits. Obviously, you can ask more from a reader who is in some way dependent on you than you can from one who has no ties with you at all.

3. If you think it will help, tell how you will use the material you are requesting.

4. If what you want has a monetary value, offer to pay for it or to reciprocate in some other way.

5. Express your appreciation.

Gentlemen:

Yesterday's *Times* reported a speech by Mr. William Rathbone before the Foreign Trade Association. If a copy of the full talk is available, I would appreciate your sending it to me, so that it may be circulated among some of our export people here.

Thank you for your trouble.

Sincerely,

Gentlemen:

I have learned through trade sources that your company has initiated a programmed course in customer relations. We have been thinking of doing the same and would welcome any ideas from a company we regard as well as we do yours.

Could we impose on you to send us a copy of your manual and any instructions that go with it? Also, is there anything you can add in the way of advice to a company contemplating a similar program?

If you prefer, we could arrange to send one of our training personnel to see you and discuss the matter with you. In any case, we hope you will give us the opportunity to reciprocate in some way soon.

Sincerely yours,

Sympathy.   A letter of sympathy may be sent to a friend or colleague who has suffered through illness or accident.

1. Express regret.

2. Tell how much he is missed and in the thoughts of his friends.

3. Offer encouragement.

4. If the situation permits, try a little quiet humor or facetiousness.

Dear Doug:

I received encouraging news about you in the last few days and hope to hear soon of your complete recovery.

Many of your friends have been asking about you. Only the other day Miss Feller and Mrs. Corrigan were reminiscing about the "old days" when your work frequently brought you to their department. Your many kindnesses are still very affectionately remembered.

We all send our regards and good wishes.

Sincerely,

Dear Morris:

I was sorry to hear about your accident and hope this letter finds you much improved.

At first I thought the whole incident was part of a well-conceived plot to obtain an extra vacation, but on sober consideration, I decided that you wouldn't voluntarily patronize any place that didn't offer golf and fishing.

Do hurry and get back soon. We miss you.

Cordially,

Letters Ordering Tickets. Tickets to theatrical presentations and sporting events may be obtained directly from the box office or from a ticket broker with whom your employer may already have a charge account. The broker charges a premium for his service but is often able to get better seats and on shorter notice than the box-office customer.

Letter to Box Office

1. Order well in advance.
2. State the preferred location, date, and whether it is for a matinee or an evening.
3. Give alternative dates, if possible.
4. Enclose payment and a return envelope stamped and addressed.
5. Address the letter to the theater or stadium box office.

Gentlemen:

Please send to Mr. Walter Field two orchestra seats for Friday evening, November 12. Mr. Field prefers a center location. Alternative dates are November 10 and 11 in that order. Mr. Field's check for $21.00 and a stamped return envelope are enclosed.

Very truly yours,

Letter to Ticket Broker

1. Give the name of the attraction.
2. State the preferred location and date—alternative dates for a very popular show.
3. State an alternative attraction if tickets for the first are not available.
4. Ask for a bill or direct that the amount be charged to the individual or to the company account.

Gentlemen:

Mr. Walter Field would like two orchestra seats for *The Misanthrope* for Saturday evening, February 16. Please mail the tickets directly to him and charge his account.

If tickets are not available, please try *Pygmalion* or *Roman Holiday* in that order.

Very truly yours,

Transmittal Letters. Do not send documents or other material without a covering letter. If the letter cannot feasibly be enclosed with the material, send it separately.

Letter with Documents

1. Tell what is enclosed.
2. Tell why it is being sent.
3. Ask for acknowledgment, if desired.

Dear Mr. Grimes:

Mr. Fields thought you would be interested in the enclosed copy of the talk he gave to the Aurora Merchants Association about a week ago. He thinks you will be especially interested in the underlined portions, which touch on political activity by business organizations—a topic on which you and he have had some discussion.

Sincerely yours,

Dear Mr. Somers:

I am enclosing a suggested draft for the press of a statement relating to our joint participation in the purchase of the stock of the Mercer Company, Inc. I think this will be more satisfactory than separate statements, which may lead to some misunderstanding about our mutual interests.

Please return the statement as soon as you can with your corrections, amendments, or comments. We'll aim for a November 25 release date.

Sincerely,

Letter Sent Separately. Send the letter separately when (1) it might be overlooked in a bulky or odd-shaped package, (2) when you want it to be received before the material to which it refers, or (3) when postage costs would be considerable if the letter, requiring first-class postage, accompanied material that could otherwise qualify for third-class or parcel post rates.

NOTE: Postal rules permit fastening a first-class letter to the outside of a package sent by third- or fourth-class mail (Figure 15-5).

Dear Mr. Hammond:

I am sending you separately a copy of our new "Employees Handbook." In past discussions you have mentioned the need for such a manual in your own business, and I thought you might like to see what we have done.

Sincerely,

Travel Arrangements. Hotel accommodations and transportation may be obtained through the employer's travel agent or directly from hotels and transportation companies. There is no charge for the services of the travel agent, who is often able to command scarce accommodations for his clients. When arrangements are made directly with hotels and airlines, the telephone is often more satisfactory than writing because confirmation can be obtained immediately. Further, if desired accommodations are not to be had, there is no waiting to learn the available alternatives. Large hotels and hotel chains, like the airlines, have instant reservation services in many cities. Consult your local telephone directory. If you find it more convenient to write for hotel accommodations, follow these instructions.

1. State whom the reservation is for, including the number of persons.
2. Tell what type of accommodation is desired.
3. Give arrival date (also time, if later than 6 p.m.) and date of departure.
4. Ask for confirmation—by wire if time is too short for a mail response. See also "Travel Arrangements," Section 12.4.

Gentlemen:

Please reserve for Mr. John Regan a suite consisting of living room, bedroom, and bath for two nights beginning Thursday, July 17. Mr. Regan, who is traveling alone, expects to arrive about 9 p.m.

A confirmation of this reservation is requested.

Very truly yours,

Gentlemen:

Please reserve for Mr. and Mrs. John Regan and their two young children two twin-bedded rooms for arrival on Monday, April 14. Connecting rooms with separate baths are desired. Mr. Regan and his family expect to stay until 5 p.m. Thursday, April 17. May I have your prompt confirmation.

Very truly yours,

5

Handling Business
Information

The office exists to collect and process data. Different kinds of data require different kinds of treatment. This chapter gives some insight into the data-processing revolution and provides assistance in finding, documenting, and displaying information for business reporting needs.

For assistance in writing reports, see "Report Preparation," Chapter 6.

CONTENTS

5.1	Data Processing	p. 194
5.2	Information Sources	p. 210
5.3	Footnotes and Bibliographies	p. 219
5.4	Tabular Presentation	p. 228
5.5	Graphic Presentation	p. 231

5.1 DATA PROCESSING

Anyone who works in a modern office is aware of the data-processing revolution. What used to be known as "paperwork" and "recordkeeping" —an incidental part of any business operation—has in only a short span of years emerged as a prime business function. Machines, at first rudimentary in design, have grown in sophistication and capacity. The number of applications to business problems keeps increasing, too, so that machines now impinge on almost every aspect of office work.

Although data processing employs computers and other machines, the term refers in fact to any operation by which data is obtained, stored, manipulated, retrieved, and transmitted. Large businesses operate their own computer installations. Smaller businesses may use smaller, less advanced machines, as well as manual methods; or they may farm out their work to central data-processing centers that serve a number of companies. In any case, however, there has been a dramatic recognition of the need for fast, systematic methods of dealing with paperwork problems.

194

The Need for Data Processing.   The potential of data processing for any organization is directly related to the needs of the times.

1. The number of business transactions and the records needed to support them have increased at a phenomenal rate. Some indication of this increase may be seen in the fact that in the last ten years alone, the gross national product—the value of all goods and services produced in this country—has more than tripled. To cite a single industry, the average number of shares sold on the New York Stock Exchange has almost quadrupled in the same period. Only modern data-processing methods can now save the back offices from catastrophe during heavy selling periods. In many instances, the computer itself may be cited as a cause of the increasing paperwork. The banks and oil companies are able to offer credit cards to tens of millions of customers only because the computer is able to process credit transactions quickly and economically. The need for data processing is also fed by the demands of the government. Income taxes, sales taxes, and Social Security records alone account for billions of document entries annually. Without modern data-processing methods, it would not be possible for businesses or governments to handle the required paperwork.

2. Clerical costs are increasing rapidly. Today one out of six persons is engaged in clerical work. Thirty years ago it was one in ten. With the increasing number of clerical workers has come a marked increase in wage rates and fringe benefits. It is thus easy to see why business seeks to cut down on clerical costs. Lest anyone envision an army of the technologically unemployed, it is estimated that over the years the number of new clerical jobs created by the growth of business and government will more than offset the loss of clerical jobs through automation.

3. Increases in the number of clerical transactions required by modern business put a severe strain on human accuracy. Clerks tire and grow careless, and they seek freedom from the boredom of repetitive effort. Errors and waste of time are the inevitable result. Machines make mistakes, too, of course, but they are easier to control and will work any number of hours at the same tasks without appreciable loss of efficiency.

4. The swift pace of modern business makes severe demands for up-to-date reporting. With current information, businesses can correct mistakes before irreparable damage is done, and they can also compete more successfully in the marketplace. Whereas reports of sales, inventory, or expenses might take weeks to prepare by hand, computers can prepare them almost instantaneously. The same machines can make projections, or predictions, of future trends.

What Data Processing Can Do.   As a way of helping businessmen decide how data processing can help them, the National Cash Register Company proposes six questions.

1. What new information can be secured through data processing to help in managing the business better?

2. Can the needed information be developed by organizing available data? In other words, is this a problem that data processing can solve?

3. Is the volume of data to be processed into the needed reports too great for manual handling and is it sufficient to justify machine processing?

4. How frequently is the information required?

5. Can the data to be processed be readily accumulated?

6. Can savings be generated by automating the present system? Or, to phrase it differently, will a better system increase profits?

The answers to these questions need not necessarily lead to a decision to automate every phase of the clerical work, but they will help to uncover opportunities to improve systems and reduce costs. In fact, data processing is useful in any situation in which there is the necessity to perform repetitive clerical operations, store large amounts of information in a form that makes it instantly available, and manipulate data in a way that brings out significant relationships for decision-making purposes (Figure 5-1).

A common application of data processing is seen in the preparation of payroll records and checks. The computer, given a list of employees, hours worked, rates of pay, and deductions, can prepare an earnings statement and a check for each employee. At the same time it can store and accumulate the information and, when needed, produce records for Social Security, unemployment insurance, and income tax purposes. It also has built into it the capacity to recognize errors and inconsistencies.

A more inclusive application is that used by a large sales department. Orders from customers are fed directly from the sales office to the computer, which prepares customers' invoices and at the same time transmits shipping

Accounts payable	Job costing
Accounts receivable	Market analyses
Addressing	Payroll processing
Balance sheet	Personnel recordkeeping
Bid estimating	Production scheduling
Billing	Productivity reports
Breakeven analyses	Programmed instruction
Calculating and summarizing	Purchase order processing
Collections	Quarterly payroll reports
Credit management	Record retrieval
Data storage	Sales forecasting
Income statement	Sales order processing
Inventory control	Sales reports
Inventory management reports	Tax reports

Figure 5-1 Some tasks for the computer.

instructions to the appropriate warehouse. The computer also keeps track of the stock at the warehouse, so that requisitions for replenishment can be sent to the factory. The same computer can determine the factory's needs for the materials of production and, on cue, issue the proper orders to the suppliers. Meanwhile, at any stage, executives have available current information about sales and inventory and can use the machine to help with decisions about future strategy.

Many office machines that are not classified as computers nevertheless perform computer functions. One machine—the IBM Magnetic Tape Selectric Typewriter—applies computer principles to permit the correction of typewritten copy without the necessity of hand retyping.[1] A second machine will locate and extract any one of 200,000 microfilmed engineering drawings and print an enlargement—all in a little more than six seconds. Another machine, for use in the mailroom, electronically reads preprinted marks or prepunched holes to match related paper items and insert them into their envelopes—a process ideally suited to credit card companies that must insert transaction cards and printed notices of various kinds with the monthly statement. A device is also available for automatically sorting the envelopes by weight.

Steps in Data Processing.   Although details differ in specific instances, all data processing encompasses essentially the same steps.

1. There must be a body of source documents from which data can be taken. These documents may be in the nature of sales slips, invoices, purchase orders, time cards, and the like.

2. The data on the source document must be converted into a form acceptable by the machine as *input*. Thus the information or any part of it may be transferred to punched cards, punched paper tape, or magnetic tape by using a code, which will be explained later. Some machines are also capable of taking data directly from documents by scanning or optical means.

3. The machine performs the desired operation on the data. It may sort the data alphabetically, numerically, or in some other sequence; it may perform all kinds of mathematical computations; it may provide totals, summaries, and comparisons, and show other relationships.

4. The *output,* or information delivered by the machine, may be in the form of (a) a typewritten document, such as a pay check, invoice, or report; (b) a voice response, as in the talking typewriter used in the teaching of children; (c) a visual response, as on a screen; or (d) punched cards, paper tape, or magnetic tape compatible with other machines.

5. Information entered into the system or developed by the system is stored for further use. The storage unit also retains the programs, which serve as instructions for the various manipulations of data.

[1] The IBM Mag Card Selectric Typewriter, performs similar duties on a more limited scale.

Manual Processing. Of the many methods available for processing data, manual processing is the oldest and most time-consuming, though for reasons of cost or other necessity, there may be no satisfactory substitute.

Improvements in manual processing are designed to eliminate recopying, speed the classification and sorting of data, and aid in filing, storing, and retrieving documents. Accounting, even when done by hand, may be viewed as a means of classifying monetary transactions. With the help of ledgerless bookkeeping, which eliminates the need for posting, or the use of an accounting board or pegboard, much recopying can be avoided. Carbon-interleaved forms and document-control registers such as those used by store clerks provide similar savings in time and effort. The sorting of documents is speeded by pigeonhole techniques, as well as by the use of cards with notched edges. Any coding of documents by number will also make filing, reference, and retrieval easier. Visible record files and open-shelf files are other aids for rapid retrieval.

Mechanical Processing.   One of the earliest office machines was the typewriter. It has been followed by a number of other machines designed for recording, calculating, and transmitting data. The electric typewriter is rapidly replacing the manual machine and further refinements, IBM's magnetic tape typewriter and Mag Card Selectric, have already been mentioned. Other typewriters, reading instructions on punched tape, produce documents automatically, stopping only for the insertion by hand of such variable data as names, addresses, quantities, and prices. The Varityper and other machines in its class prepare copy for offset printing in the office, with professional results. The Graphotype is used in the preparation of embossed plates in metal or plastic for addressing and credit card identification.

Machines used for recording data also include a number of addressing and imprinting devices, such as signature machines, check protectors, time stamps, numbering machines, and postage meters. To these may be added duplicating and copying machines of all kinds. (For a full description, see "Duplicating and Copying," Section 12.2.) Adding, calculating, and accounting machines—not excluding cash registers—constitute another group of data-processing devices that operate on mechanical or electronic principles. The calculators add, subtract, multiply and divide; and they print or display the results. Many of the accounting machines are equipped with typewriter keyboards, which make them suitable for billing and other duties requiring the typing of names, addresses, and descriptive data. Another valuable feature of most accounting machines is the ability to print and add several rows of columns horizontally as well as vertically, so that amounts totaled in the columns can be accumulated and totaled again.

Mechanical methods of transmitting data inside the office include dumbwaiters, conveyor belts, facsimile reproduction by wire, and closed-circuit television, by which documents displayed in one part of an office can be read in another. For the external transmission of data the telegraph and teletypewriter are probably the most common media (see "Telephone and Wire Services," Section 12.3). The telephone system also permits facsimile transmission of documents, and data transmission by wire from a central computer is now commonplace.

Punched-Card Processing. Between the mechanical processing of data already described and electronic data processing, there stands an intermediate method that is best described as electromechanical. The basis of this system is the punched card and its associated machines. Developed by Dr. Herman Hollerith for tabulating and sorting data, the punched card was first used on a large scale in processing the United States Census of 1890.

Coding. Standard cards measure $7\frac{3}{8}'' \times 3\frac{1}{4}''$, and the most common of these, developed for IBM systems, has 12 rows and 80 columns per card (Figure 5-2). The cards are made with corners cut at the upper right or left for convenience in handling (a jutting corner signifies a card out of place). Data is represented on the cards by punched holes coded to signify digits, letters of the alphabet, and such symbols as an asterisk, an ampersand, and plus and minus signs. A single-hole punch on one of ten positions in a column designates a digit. Two punches in a column (a punch in one of the lower nine positions and another in one of the upper three positions) designate a letter of the alphabet or a symbol. The upper two rows (11th and 12th), known as the *X-* and *Y-punch* respectively, are also used to activate special operations and machine functions, such as adding or subtracting. Instructions for processing data may specify whether cards are to be fed into the processing machine from the top or the bottom edge and face up or face down.

When the punched cards go through the machine, electrical contact is made through the cards at the point where the holes are punched. A reading brush senses the position of the contact and translates this information into instructions for the machine.

Advantages. A big advantage of punched-card processing over older methods is that it reduces all documents to a single shape and size. The cards are easy to store and retrieve manually and can be handled uniformly by machine. Another advantage is that all of the data is uniformly recorded in a way that the machine can read it. Finally, in contrast to written records, each punched card contains only a single type of data. For example, a single sales slip might bear the name of the salesman, the name of the customer, the name of the department, and a list of products sold. Thus it would be difficult by conventional means to separate and summarize the data by individual salesman, customer, department, or product without an enormous amount of manual work. The use of the punched card solves this problem, however, because a separate card is used for each unit of information, and sorting by any desired classification can be made automatically. Any part of the data can also be removed at will and additions can conveniently be entered on the cards.

Figure 5-2 IBM punched card showing code of punches for numerals, letters of the alphabet, and special characters.

Punched-Card Machines.   A number of machine processes are involved in the recording of information on the punched cards and in the processing of punched cards to obtain the desired results. A card-punch machine (sometimes called a *key punch*) is necessary for punching the holes. The operator takes information from source documents and transfers it to the cards by depressing keys similar to those on a typewriter. Records already obtainable on punched cards may be transferred to other punched cards by an automatic punch machine. Such a machine is also used to punch repetitive data into any number of cards. Because punched cards are hard to read, a machine called an interpreter may be used to translate the punched holes and print the information on the same card or on another one. Most cards have some data printed on them for easy reference.

A sorting machine is used to arrange cards in a particular sequence. In numeric sorting a separate pass will be required for each digit in a column. Thus a three-digit column will require three runs through the machine. In alphabetic sorting, two passes are required for each column because, as has been explained, each alphabetic character consists of two punches. The sorter may also be adjusted to select and classify only certain cards from the whole group.

Complex sorting problems not suited to the sorter are handled by the collator. With this machine it is possible to match cards from separate files and to reject those cards for which there is no matching card. At income tax time, for example, it is used to match a name-and-address card with another card on which tax withholdings for the same period are recorded; then both cards are combined to complete the Treasury Department's Form W-2.

Arithmetic functions are performed on still another machine, called the *calculating punch*. This machine is designed to read the data on a card and perform any necessary addition, subtraction, multiplication, or division. The results are then punched on the same or the following card. Such a machine is used, for example, to compute wages and add overtime, compute and deduct Social Security and income taxes, and perform other arithmetic functions.

The last stage of punched-card data processing is converting the data on the punched cards into printed reports and documents. This function is performed by the accounting machine, which is capable of printing a line for each card at 80 to 150 lines a minute and faster. The accounting machine may be programmed to select only certain data from the cards, rearrange the data for the print-out, and combine and summarize data. By hooking up an automatic punch machine to the accounting machine, it is also possible to transfer the summary data to new punched cards for further processing.

Integrated Data Processing.   An important aim of any data-processing system is to reduce the amount of manual copying. Considerable savings are achieved, for example, when an accounting machine, cash register, or typewriter can not only prepare original documents, but also produce punched cards or punched paper tape that can be inserted into other machines for further processing. These other machines may be any of the various punched-card machines or computers. When manual and machine functions are combined in the manner indicated, the result is called *integrated data processing* (*IDP*).

Common Language Media.   Essential to integrated data-processing is the use of certain media through which data and instructions can be transmitted from one machine to another. One medium for such communication is the punched card, which has already been described. Other media, described below, are punched tape, edge-punched cards, magnetic tape, magnetic-ink characters, and optical characters. When the "language" of documents that must be processed is not compatible with the machine that must do the processing, a conversion machine can be used to convert from one medium to another as, for example, magnetic tape to punched card or punched tape, paper tape to magnetic tape or punched card, and punched card to magnetic tape or paper tape (Figure 5-3).

Punched Tape.   Originally used to transmit written data by telegraph, punched tape now finds a wide variety of uses on other office machines as well. Data is recorded by the positioning of punched holes in the paper (Figure 5-4). Tapes have an advantage over cards in that the tapes are continuous and a single length can therefore store a complete record. A great number of cards may be needed to hold the same information. On the other hand, cards have an advantage in that the individual units of data can be easily separated, recombined, and otherwise manipulated.

Data is recorded on paper tape by an arrangement of punched holes, running in parallel channels along the length of the tape. The number of channels varies from five to eight. By coding the punches, it is possible to produce any numbers, letters, and signs up to the capacity of the tape.

Edge-Punched Cards.   Tape coding can be used with cards as well as with paper tape. The cards are punched along the bottom in five or eight channels. A print-out of the punched data may be gummed to the upper portion of the card for easy manual reference. The cards are joined in seven-inch sections and folded accordion-like. They are more durable than tape and are easier to handle and store (Figure 5-5).

Magnetic Tape.   Coding on magnetic tape is similar to that on paper tape except that plastic tape is used, like that in sound-tape recorders, and the coding is accomplished not by punched holes, but by invisible magnetized spots or bits, that create electrical impulses. Seven parallel channels are commonly used, and each character is represented by the configuration of bits in a single column across the width of the tape (Figure 5-6).

Magnetic Ink Characters.   Such documents as checks and deposit slips are

(A)

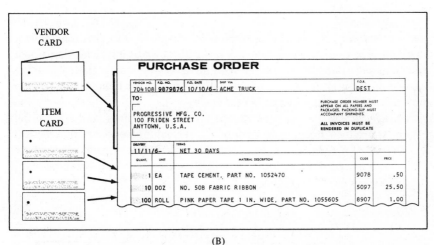

(B)

Figure 5-3   A purchase order writing system. (The Singer Company, Friden Division)

Figure 5-4   Punched paper tape (1-inch wide) showing use of 8-channel code. (International Business Machines Corporation)

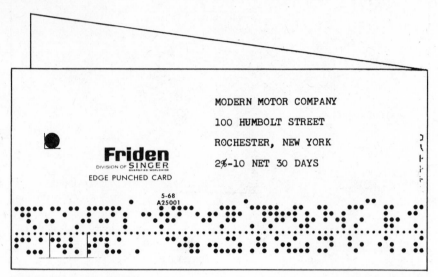

MODERN MOTOR COMPANY

100 HUMBOLT STREET

ROCHESTER, NEW YORK

2%-10 NET 30 DAYS

Friden
DIVISION OF **SINGER**
DIVERSIFIED WORLDWIDE
EDGE PUNCHED CARD

5-68
A25001

Figure 5-5 Sectioned edge-punched cards showing print-out of punches. (The Singer Company, Friden Division)

encoded by means of characters preprinted in magnetic ink. These characters, which must be of distinctive style, are picked up by reading heads that translate them into machine language without a key-punching step. Thus the documents themselves "talk" to the computer without human intervention and the attendant risk of error (Figure 5-7).

Optical Characters.   Some cash registers, adding machines, and accounting machines produce documents printed in special numeric or alphabetical characters that may be read photoelectrically by an optical scanner. Magnetic ink is not required. Because of its simplicity, increasing use is being made of this processing medium (Figure 5-8).

Figure 5-6 Symbolic representation of half-inch wide, 7-channel magnetic tape with each mark representing a magnetized spot. (International Business Machines Corporation)

FOR CREDIT TO THE ACCOUNT OF

J. HAROLD JANIS

DATE_____19 _____

DEPOSITED WITH

CHEMICAL BANK NEW YORK TRUST COMPANY

⑆0 59⑈ 20 9 49 6⑈

		DOLLARS	CENTS
CASH (INCLUDE COUPONS)			
CHECKS List Separately	1		
	2		
	3		
	4		
	5		
	6		
BANK USE ONLY	7		
UNITS	8		
TOTAL			

Figure 5-7   Bank deposit slip imprinted with numerals in MICR (Magnetic Ink Character Recognition) format which can be read by machine. The figures (bottom) represent the branch number and the account number.

Electronic Data Processing.   The most recent stage and the most important advance in the development of data processing is represented by the electronic computer. An important feature of the computer is that the machine does its work by electrical impulses rather than by the movement of mechanical parts. The result is speeds measured in the thousandths, millionths, and

Figure 5-8   Optical-printing adding machine. The characters, produced on paper tape, can be read photoelectrically. (National Cash Register Company)

even billionths of a second. A second distinctive feature of the computer is that is has an internal memory—that is, it can store vast quantities of data as well as instructions, or programs, for its use. Then, properly activated, the machine can apply the instructions repetitively to the data and even modify the instructions under certain conditions. Because the necessary data is stored in the machine, processing is continuous; there is no need to move data from one operation to the next.

Figure 5-9   Organization of a computer system.

A Computer Configuration. A computer installation consists of input devices, a central processing unit (CPU), and output devices. It also has supplemental equipment for storing data outside the CPU (Figures 5-9 and 5-10). *Input Devices.* The input consists of information and instructions that have been converted into a form that the machine can assimilate. The data is fed to the computer by means of a console typewriter, a punched-card reader, a magnetic- or punched-tape reader, an optical scanner, or some other device.

1. CONTROL. The control console is the primary control interface between the computer operator and the machine. Here, the operator can start or shut down the system and keep a running check on machine operation.
2. INPUT/OUTPUT. The console terminal can be used by the operator to type instructions and enter them into the system. It also can automatically type out programmed messages for the operator (for example, to alert him to prepare a magnetic tape drive for an upcoming job).
3. PROCESSING AND MAIN STORAGE. The central processing unit contains main core memory for storage of programs and data during processing and arithmetic/logic circuits which process calculations and logic operations.
4. INPUT/OUTPUT/STORAGE. Magnetic tape can be used as input or output or as temporary storage during processing.
5. INPUT. Card read-punches convert the hole-code in punched cards to a code of electrical impulses for entry into the central processing unit. They also punch output results into cards. In many large systems, card-read punches are used to transfer information to magnetic tape, from which it can be entered into the central processing unit at higher speed.
6. OUTPUT. High-speed printers are used to prepare reports, analyses, invoices, tabulations, at speeds of more than 1,000 lines per minute.

Figure 5-10 A wide-angle view of a computer installation. (International Business Machines Corporation)

Central Processing Unit.   The CPU consists of a console, or control unit; an arithmetic unit, which manipulates the data in response to signals from the control unit; and an internal memory unit, which stores the instructions and data for use when needed. At the console terminal, the operator can type instructions for the computer to follow, and the same machine can automatically type out instructions to guide the operator.

The CPU's arithmetic unit performs all the steps required for calculating and decision making. Here devices called *registers* store data, instructions, or results of computations until directed by the control unit to transfer them to another part of the system or until new data instructions or results are brought into the registers. The computer can be programmed to add, subtract, multiply, divide, move and compare data, write, and stop. It can also be instructed to break a sequence, repeat it, or change to another. The number of different operations any computer can perform depends on its design.

Output Devices.   Data produced by the computer is delivered to the user in a number of ways. The same console typewriter that is used for input may also be used for output. Because it is too slow for most computer needs, however, its use is often limited to typing out special messages concerning the status of the computer job. The heavy printing is done by a line printer, which prints a line at a time after the characters have been assembled in the memory unit. Consistent with the speed of the computer itself, the line printer operates at speeds up to twenty-four hundred lines per minute.

Other output devices may consist of machines that convert the information to punched cards, punched paper tape, and magnetic tape. The data may also be relayed by a voice-response unit or a cathode-ray display unit.

Computer Programming.   The machines that constitute the electronic data-processing system can operate only in response to instructions that tell what data is to be used and what operations are to be performed with it. Programs in the computer are activated by a source language that the computer can translate and act upon. The first source languages, using a binary code of ones and zeros (for example, 001, 100, 110), were long and cumbersome.

An early breakthrough in programming occurred with the development of the computer language known as *FORTRAN* (for *FOR*mula *TRAN*slation). This is still widely used for the solution of mathematical problems, but it would present difficulties to all but highly trained personnel. A more recently developed language, better suited to general business uses, is *COBOL* (for *CO*mmon *B*usiness *O*riented *L*anguage). Expressed in terms very similar to English, a COBOL statement looks like this:

COMPUTE STOCK VALUE =
UNIT PRICE* (STOCK ON HAND
+ RECEIPTS − SHIPMENTS).

This particular program is designed to find the value of present stock on hand in an inventory. The asterisk is a multiplication sign. A translation program stored in the computer converts the statement into a sequence of instructions the machine can follow.

Still more recent languages for general use are *PL/1* (for "Programming Language") and *RPG* (for "Report Program Generator"). These and other languages, together with the necessary programs for making them intelligible to the computer, are usually provided by the manufacturer. They are simple enough to be used by office workers, who need no technical knowledge of the computer and can concentrate exclusively on the job to be done.

Job-oriented computer programs are either custom designed for particular users or ready-made to serve the needs of a number of users whose information needs are reasonably similar. In the latter instance, the programs offered range from specific routines for such functions as inventory control, payroll processing, billing, and accounts receivable to extensive packages for management information systems. Program repertoires are also available for the growing number of machines that bridge the gap between conventional calculators and full-scale computers (Figure 5-11).

Operating Systems.   A number of systems have been developed to use the computer as efficiently as possible. *Time sharing* permits a number of users, each with his own terminal, to use the same computer during the same time span. By dividing time into thousandths of seconds, interlayering the slices in a scheduled sequence, and operating at incredible speeds, the computer gives each user uninterrupted use of the machine.

Through *real-time processing,* the computer performs its work as it receives its instructions. An airline computer used for passenger reservations works on this principle. A clerk at any reservation console can find out immediately what seats on any flight are available and stand by while a central computer books reservations and withdraws the seats from the available pool. Through *batch processing,* information is accumulated over a period of time before being entered into the computer. Thus, if withdrawals and additions to inventory are accumulated for processing each night, the figures available from the computer would be up-to-date only as of the previous night. This is a relatively slow method of processing, but it permits concentrated use of the computer during otherwise slow or idle hours.

Batch processing lends itself to the use of magnetic tape, on which transactions are registered in sequence as the reel unwinds. Real-time applications, on the other hand, use random-access memories, such as those stored on revolving discs or drums. These permit the location of any address directly and instantly.

Users who are physically removed from the computer require some means of data transmission. This is usually accomplished through regular telephone or telegraph lines, with terminal equipment capable of sending and receiving data. Smaller users may also accumulate punched or optical-font tapes and send them by mail or messenger to the data computer center for processing.

1. GENERAL APPLICATIONS

Invoicing
Payroll
Depreciation
Proration and distribution
Conversions

2. STATISTICS

Analysis of variance
Chi square distribution
Correlation analysis
Sampling means and differences
Moving averages
Trend analysis
Sampling distribution
Central tendencies
Measures of dispersion

3. INSURANCE

Life insurance
Casualty insurance
Automobile liability
Premium adjustments
Long-term investments
Fund projections

4. FINANCE

Interest
Installment loans
Mortgages
Trust accounting
Savings accounts
Amortization

5. MATHEMATICS

Elementary functions
Vectors, determinants, and matrices
Solutions of equations
Analytic geometry
Calculations in number theory

6. ENGINEERING

Differential equations
Numerical integration
Bessel functions
Kinematics
Circuit design
Stress analysis
Hydrodynamics
Process control
Estimating

Figure 5-11 Some basic categories contained in the program library for the Olivetti Underwood Programma 101, a desk-top calculator-computer.

An encouraging development is that, through local banks and other service companies, the use of the computer is now available on a part-time basis to doctors, dentists, and small businessmen. Thus the computerization of billing, bookkeeping, payroll processing, and other routine functions becomes economically feasible for a class of user that has hitherto been excluded.

5.2 INFORMATION SOURCES

Knowing where to go for information and how to extract it is a valuable business asset. The occasions for collecting data are many.
1. You are researching a problem on your own.
2. You are obtaining data for your employer's information.
3. You are checking the facts in the draft of an employer's report.
4. You are writing a report for your employer.

5. You are preparing a background paper for use by your employer in making a presentation or speech.

Personal Inquiry.   A most useful way to get certain kinds of information is to go directly to people. You may use the telephone, see people in person, or write for information. You may go to co-workers in your own organization or to persons in other organizations who may have the answers you seek. You may also observe certain processes, procedures, conditions, and human activities in order to report on them. Another method is to make up a questionnaire in order to get the experiences and views of others in a form that permits the tabulation of results.

Here are some points to keep in mind as you make personal inquiries.

1. Don't pry or arouse suspicion of your motives in other ways. State frankly and clearly what your purpose is and what use will be made of the information you obtain.

2. Be courteous and attentive always. And brief. It's you who are asking the favor.

3. Take notes of points you may forget, but try not to make the other person self-conscious.

4. Don't argue, but don't accept at face value all you hear, either. Consider the motives of your informant.

5. Don't arouse resentment by asking personal questions; for instance, about salary or religion.

6. If you want confidential information, be sure your authority or your right to it is well established. Use the name of your employer if you are acting on his behalf.

7. If you are going outside your organization for information, offer to reciprocate.

See also "Interviewing," in Section 1.5.

Company Files.   There is no point in developing from scratch information that already exists in the company's files. Care should be taken, however, to distinguish between the public and private records of the organization.

Public Records.   The information you need may be found in readily available published documents such as these:

The annual report and quarterly reports to stockholders
Reports of annual meetings of stockholders
SEC registration applications
Proxy statements
Company newspapers and magazines
Catalogs
Advertisements
Handbooks and manuals
Press releases
Public speeches of company officers

An important advantage of material from these sources is that it is both official and public and does not have to be cleared with anyone before it can be used. Watch for the exception, however, in published bulletins intended for private circulation among top executives.

Private Records. Other information originating in the company may be obtained from the files. Such materials include:

Letters	Bookkeeping records
Memorandums	Personnel records
Reports	Purchase orders
Estimates	Sales slips
Proposals	Appointment books
Instructions	Diaries
Procedures	Contracts
Minutes	Leases

Most of these documents are private and should be obtained through regular channels. Documents removed from the files should be promptly returned. Any copies made should be kept securely and destroyed when they are no longer needed. Confidential information in the documents should never be communicated to unauthorized persons.

Library Sources. The number and variety of books, pamphlets, and periodicals is so vast that any researcher must be prepared to set aside some time just to discover what is available. You may already have on your desk that most useful of reference books, a dictionary, and possibly an atlas of the world, a trade directory, and an all-purpose book of facts. Your company's library, if there is one, should have these and other reference books and periodicals, especially those relating to trade and economic matters (Figure 5-12). The reference division of your public library will have an even more comprehensive collection of publications and information as to where and how any published data may be obtained.

Many trade associations and other business, philanthropic, and professional organizations maintain libraries containing valuable printed materials in their own area of interest. For lists of such libraries consult publications of the Special Libraries Association as well as Anthony T. Kruzas' *Directory of Special Libraries and Information Centers,* 2d ed. (Detroit: Gale Publishing Co., 1968) and *Subject Collections* by Lee Ash and Denis Lorenz (New York: R. R. Bowker, 1967). Colleges and universities are also known to extend library privileges to alumni and community organizations. Consult the librarian.

At least two cautions are necessary in connection with all published sources of information.

1. Note carefully the publisher and the author. Some sources are more reliable than others. Government publications and the publications of university presses and research bureaus are usually highly authoritative. Commercial publishers and other enterprises should be judged individually.

BOOKS

The New York Times Encyclopedic Almanac
Statistical Abstract of the United States
Rand McNally Commercial Atlas and Marketing Guide
H. Webster Johnson, *How to Use the Business Library, with Sources of Business Information* (Cincinnati: South-Western Publishing Co.)

PERIODICALS

Monthly Economic Letter of the First National City Bank of New York (free)
Newsweek, *Time*, or *U.S. News and World Report*
Business Week
The Wall Street Journal
The New York Times

MISCELLANEOUS

A trade or professional directory in your organization's product or service area
Publications of your trade or professional association
Government publications touching on your organization's interests
A dictionary of business or technical terms in your specialty
A handbook covering your special field of interest (e.g., accounting, management, foreign trade)
Business and technical periodicals in your subject area
Your company's annual report, catalogs, and other published data

Figure 5-12   A basic business research library.

Facts issued by individual businesses and industries must be expected to be biased.

2. Note the date of publication. Old information may have historic value, but it may be worse than useless as an indicator of present conditions. Many printed works are issued periodically or in revised and updated editions. Try to find the latest editions available.

Library Tools.   To tap the library's riches, you must know how to use the tools the library provides.

1. The General Catalog. All the printed works in the library are listed in its catalog. Books are listed by author, by title, and by subject. If you want to see if the library has a particular book, you will look for it in the catalog by author or title. A book issued by a "corporate author"—that is, a government body, a corporation, an institution, or a society—will be listed under the name of the organization. For example:

U.S. Department of Commerce
American Management Association
Museum of Modern Art

If you have no particular book in mind, but want to know what the library has to offer in a particular subject area, you will look up the subject. The card file will also tell you what periodicals the library stocks and, in some instances, what issues are available.

2. *Cumulative Book Index.* All books published in English are listed in the *Cumulative Book Index* (CBI), which is published monthly and cumulated twice a year. Periodically volumes are published covering a number of years. Books are listed alphabetically by author, title, and subject. For titles published before 1928, the *U.S. Catalog of Books* should be consulted.

3. *Books in Print.* This annual publication is a handy reference to all books currently published. One volume lists books by title, and another by author. Two additional volumes, *Subject Guide to Books in Print,* complete the set. For a list of soft-cover editions, see *Paperbound Books in Print.*

4. *Vertical File Index.* Because much material is published in monographs, pamphlets, or leaflets, rather than in books or periodicals, it is good to know that you can go to the *Vertical File Index* for information on the availability of such materials. Many of the pamphlets listed in the *Index* will probably be found in the library. Because of the difficulty of handling them, they are filed in boxes, which are stored vertically on the shelves.

5. Indexes to periodicals. If you want to know what materials are available in newspapers and magazines, you will look up the subject in any of a number of indexes that are available. The *New York Times Index* and the *Wall Street Journal Index* are guides to the articles printed in those publications. They will tell you in what issue an article appears and on what page. A similar index to articles in general periodicals will be found in the *Reader's Guide to Periodical Literature.* Articles in business publications are indexed in the *Business Periodicals Index.* Other specialized indexes include the *Accountant's Index,* the *Index of Economic Journals,* the *Management Index,* and the *Public Affairs Information Service.*

6. General guides. Every library has a number of volumes that are, in fact, directories to books and other publications in particular subject areas. Some of the most useful for businessmen are the following.

Comans, Edward T., Jr. *Sources of Business Information,* rev. ed. Berkeley: University of California Press, 1964.

Johnson, H. Webster. *How to Use the Business Library, with Sources of Business Information,* 3d ed. Cincinnati: South-Western Publishing Co., 1964.

Management Information Guide Series. Detroit: Gale Research Co., 1963–. The 20-odd volumes so far published cover information sources in real estate, building construction, public finance, the textile industry, the developing nations, standards and specifications, public utilities, transportation, business trends and forecasting, investments, and other business fields.

Another useful bibliography of a more general sort is Constance M. Winchell's *Guide to Reference Books,* 8th ed. (Chicago: American Library Association, 1967).

Reporting Services. Some publishers specialize in providing businessmen with digests and analyses of legislation, court decisions, and the rulings of regulatory bodies. They also provide guidelines for dealing with problems of taxation, accounting, personnel, and communications. The most prominent publishers in this field are Prentice-Hall (P-H), the Commerce Clearing House (CCH), and the Bureau of National Affairs (BNA). The following list of publications represents only a small fraction of the output of these organizations.

Prentice-Hall (Englewood Cliffs, N.J.)

Federal Tax Service
State and Local Tax Service
Insurance Service
Labor Relations
Personnel Policies and Practices
Union Contracts and Collective Bargaining
Real Estate Service
Securities Regulation Service
Wills, Estates, and Trust Service
Prentice-Hall Management Letter
Lawyer's Weekly Report

Commerce Clearing House (Chicago, Ill.)

Federal Banking Law Reports
Stock Transfer Guide
New York Stock Exchange Guide
American Stock Exchange Guide
Food, Drug, Cosmetic Law Reports
Government Contracts Report
Federal Carriers' Report
Utilities Law Reports
Insurance Law Reports
Workmen's Compensation Law Reports
Legislative Reporting Service
Federal Tax Guide Reports
All-State Sales Tax Reports
State Tax Guide
Unemployment Insurance Reports

Bureau of National Affairs (Washington, D.C.)

Antitrust and Trade Regulation Report
Government Security and Loyalty
Tax Management
Construction Labor Report
Labor Arbitration
Labor Relations Reporter
Retail Labor Report
Union Labor Report
Executive Library Service
United States Patents Quarterly
Standard EDP Reports
International Trade Reporter
Collective Bargaining Negotiations and Contracts

Government Publications. Information on almost any subject, including valuable statistics, is published by the Federal Government, but it is not always easy to find out about the availability of the material. Depository libraries are maintained in a number of cities, and most libraries have lists of the publications available as well as guides to their use. Most current publications are offered for sale through the Government Printing Office at prices ranging from a few cents upward.

For a general survey of government publications, the following books are recommended.

Schmeckebier, Lawrence F., and Roy B. Eastin. *Government Publications and Their Use,* rev. ed. Washington, D.C.: The Brookings Institution, 1969.
Andriot, John L. *U.S. Government Serials and Periodicals,* 3 vols. McLean, Va.: Documents Index, 1969.
Andriot, John L. *Guide to U.S. Government Statistics.* Arlington, Va.: Documents Index, 1961.

Valuable government bibliographies are *United States Department of Commerce Publications* (supplemented annually), and the *Catalog of United States Census Publications.* A comprehensive list of all government publications will be found in the *Monthly Catalog of U.S. Government Publications;* a yearly subscription is approximately $6. If you write to the Superintendent of Documents, Washington, DC 20402, you will be put on the mailing list to receive free the semimonthly list of *Selected United States Government Publications.*

The Small Business Administration (SBA) of the U.S. Department of Commerce publishes a large number of management and technical aids, many of them free, for small businesses. To receive lists of available publications, write to the SBA office nearest you or to the Small Business Administration, Washington, DC 20230. SBA's *Survey of Federal Publications,* also for owners of small businesses, can be obtained for 45 cents from the Superintendent of Documents, Washington, DC 20402.

Probably the most useful of all statistical compilations is the *Statistical Abstract of the United States,* which gives information on population, vital statistics, education, employment, military affairs, Social Security, income and prices, manufactures, commerce, and other topics. The *Cities Supplement to the Statistical Abstracts* gives special data for cities with a population of more than twenty-five thousand.

Other popular sources of business data are the *Survey of Current Business* (monthly) and the *Foreign Commerce Weekly,* both published by the U.S. Department of Commerce, and the *Monthly Labor Review,* published by the Department of Labor. The President's Council of Economic Advisers publishes the monthly *Economic Indicators,* which gives current statistics and forecasts trends and indications of government action.

The *Congressional Record* gives in full the daily proceedings in both houses of Congress. The *Federal Register,* published daily by the National Archives, contains the official pronouncements of the many government agencies and regulatory bodies. The *Congressional Directory* is the official guide to the

Senate and the House of Representatives; congressional committees; government agencies, departments, and commissions; the diplomatic corps; and foreign diplomatic representatives in the United States. Names, positions, and official duties are given.

Directories.   Information about individuals and organizations can be obtained from directories. *Who's Who in America* gives biographical information about distinguished living men and women. Regional biographical sources include *Who's Who in the East, Who's Who in the West,* and *Who's Who in the South.* The *Directory of the American Medical Association* is only the best known of the many directories of members of professional organizations. The professional and academic community are also represented in the *Directory of American Scholars* and *American Men of Science.*

The most complete and up-to-date listing of associations is contained in the *Encyclopedia of Associations* (6th ed., 1970) published by the Gale Research Co., Detroit.

Some of the most useful directories of individuals in business are *World's Who's Who in Commerce and Industry, Poor's Register of Corporations, Directors and Executives of the United States and Canada, Rand McNally's Bankers Directory,* and the *Directory of Directors in the City of New York.* Other directories, not always up-to-date, of leaders in particular fields include *Who's Who in Advertising, Who's Who in Banking, Who's Who in Labor, Who's Who in Insurance, Who's Who in the Public Utilities Industry,* and *Who's Who in Transportation and Communication.*

Leading directories in publishing and advertising are *Ayer's Directory of Newspapers and Periodicals,* the *Standard Directory of Advertisers,* the *Standard Directory of Advertising Agencies,* and the *Standard Rate and Data Service,* whose numerous directories cover all advertising media.

General business and industrial directories include the following.

Thomas Register of American Manufacturers, 7 vols. A useful guide to products, trade names, and manufacturers.

MacRae's Blue Book. Some of the same information as in the *Thomas Register.*

Kelly's Directory of Merchants, Manufacturers and Shippers. Covers companies in the British Isles, the British Commonwealth overseas, and other countries.

The Fortune Directory of the 500 Largest Industrial Corporations. Also includes companies in merchandising, banking, transportation, life insurance, and public utilities.

Million Dollar Directory. A Dun & Bradstreet publication that lists all firms with net worth of over $1,000,000.

Middle Market Directory. Another Dun & Bradstreet publication that lists twenty-four thousand American business enterprises having total assets of $500,000 to $1,000,000.

Economic and Financial Services.   Information for investors is provided by Moody's Investors Service and Standard & Poor's Corporation Services. Moody's *Manual of Investments* is issued in five parts, kept current with weekly and semiweekly supplements. The components are the *Bank and*

Finance Manual, the *Public Utility Manual,* the *Industrial Manual,* the *Transportation Manual,* and the *Municipal and Government Manual.* For each company listed there is detailed information on its financial condition and descriptions of its corporate history, organization, and activities. Standard & Poor's *Corporation Records* consists of a number of loose-leaf volumes, alphabetically arranged by company and continually revised. The information is similar to that in Moody's, with detailed data on financial structure, securities, and corporate background. Both guides are usually available for inspection in stockbrokers' offices.

Other subscription services supplying current information on business, economics, and finance, include the following.

The National Industrial Conference Board (New York)
Babson's Business Service (Babson Park, Mass.)
Bureau of National Affairs, Inc. (Washington, D.C.)
The Kiplinger Washington Letter (Washington, D.C.)
Research Institute of America (New York)
Dun & Bradstreet, Inc. (New York)

Dictionaries, Encyclopedias, Atlases, and so on.   In addition to the standard dictionaries of the English language, the researcher has access to special dictionaries of various kinds. Examples are *Black's Law Dictionary,* the *Dictionary of Business and Scientific Terms* (David F. Tver), the *Encyclopedic Dictionary of Business and Finance,* the *New Dictionary of Economics* (Philip A. S. Taylor), *Thomson's Dictionary of Banking,* the *Dictionary of Foreign Trade* (Frank Henius), and the *Dictionary for Accountants* (Eric Kohler).

Good sources of encyclopedic information are the *Encyclopaedia Britannica,* the *New International Encyclopedia,* and the *Encyclopedia Americana.* The one-volume *Columbia Encyclopedia* is handy, but its brevity limits its usefulness. The *New York Times Encyclopedic Almanac,* the *Information Please Almanac,* and the *World Almanac and Book of Facts* are annual compendiums of miscellaneous data. The *Economic Almanac,* published by the National Industrial Conference Board, is strong on business statistics.

Among the atlases, the *Rand McNally Commercial Atlas and Marketing Guide* ranks high for business use. Others are the *Rand McNally International Atlas, Hammond's Ambassador World Atlas,* and *Odyssey World Atlas.* Good geographical dictionaries are the *Columbia-Lippincott Gazetteer of the World* and *Webster's Geographical Dictionary.*

Handbooks of information relating to particular business functions are published in profusion. Examples are the *Accountants Handbook,* the *Dartnell Public Relations Handbook,* the *Encyclopedia of Banking and Finance,* the *Encyclopedia of Management,* the *Data Processing Handbook,* the *Handbook of Personnel and Labor Relations,* the *Marketing Handbook,* the *Public Relations Handbook,* the *Production Handbook,* the *Sales Executives' Handbook,* and the *AMA Handbook of Wage and Salary Administration.*

Useful in the preparation of speeches and articles are Bartlett's *Familiar Quotations* and the Burton Stevenson *Home Book of Quotations.*

International Reference Works.   Many of the kinds of information available about the United States are also available about foreign countries, industries, and individuals. Some representative publications follow.

Statesman's Year-Book. Information about nations, governments, and diplomatic representatives.
Worldmark Encyclopedia of the Nations, 5 vols.
United Nations Statistical Yearbook.
Yearbook of Labour Statistics (Geneva).
Europa Yearbook, 2 vols.
Who's Who (British).
Whitaker's Almanack. The British parallel to the American *World Almanac and Book of Facts.*
Whitaker's Cumulative Book Index. The British parallel to the American *Cumulative Book Index.*
Kelly's Directory of Merchants and Manufacturers, 3 vols. (British).
The Canada Yearbook.
Year Book Australia.
New Zealand Official Yearbook.
The South American Handbook.
Japan Register of Merchants, Manufacturers and Shippers.

For reference to U.S. Department of Commerce publications on foreign countries and foreign trade, see "International Trade," Chapter 14.

5.3   FOOTNOTES AND BIBLIOGRAPHIES

Printed sources of information are often listed for reference in the form of a bibliography. They also appear individually as footnotes at the bottom of a page to identify the source of a statement or quotation.

Footnotes and a bibliography are indispensable in research reports based at least partly on the printed word. They show from what sources the author has received help, they establish the authority for the author's statements, and they guide the reader to sources that he may wish to consult for himself. Footnotes and bibliographies should never be used for pretension, however, and should be kept to a minimum or avoided completely. In many instances, the reference to a source can be woven into the text, so that a footnote is not needed. Also, when only a few works are acknowledged in a report, they can be mentioned in the letter of transmittal or the introduction instead of in a formal bibliography.

Where footnotes and bibliography are used, they should conform to accepted rules of style to ensure that they are complete, clear, and consistent.

Footnotes. Footnotes are of two kinds. An *explanatory footnote* gives a cross-reference to another part of the same report or contains some incidental remarks of the author. Examples:

¹ For a fuller discussion of this point, see page 23.

² The situation is analogous to that frequently encountered in officer candidate schools during World War II.

A *reference footnote* gives credit for a quotation or other borrowed material (Figure 5-13).

General Style. Footnotes are separated from the text by two blank lines. A rule of one and a half inches (15 pica spaces or 18 elite spaces) is typed after the first blank line, beginning at the margin.

1. Identify footnotes by arabic numbers raised a half space above the line. Similarly identify the corresponding reference points in the text. If possible, the number in the text should be placed at the end of a sentence or paragraph, but in any case it should immediately follow the point the footnote refers to (Figure 5-13).

2. Number footnotes successively throughout the report or throughout a chapter or section.

3. Indent the first line of each footnote five spaces. Use single-spacing, with preferably a double space between entries.

4. Use standard abbreviations to save space (Figure 5-14).

5. See that footnotes end even with the bottom margin—at least one inch above the edge of the paper.

6. A footnote should appear on the page on which the reference is made.

---

internal auditors will acquire a conviction as to
the overall adequacy, application, consistency, compliance, and effectiveness of company policies as
they have been established by management.²

There are many descriptions applied to various
forms and kinds of internal audits, e.g., functional

---

¹Bradford Cadmus, "Selling Modern Internal
Auditing," The Internal Auditor, Vol. 18 (Winter
1961), p. 55.

²Herbert Elwood, "Audit Programs in Internal
Control," Journal of Accountancy, Vol. 128 (September 1969), pp. 37-43.

Figure 5-13 Placement of footnotes.

ca. (*circa*)	about. Used where the exact date is unknown, as in "ca. 1918."
cf. (*confer*)	compare.
ch., chs.	chapter, chapters.
ed.	edition, editor, edited by.
e.g. (*exempli gratia*)	for example.
et al. (*et alii*)	and others, as in "Carl I. Hovland et al." to signify other authors.
f., ff.	and the following page, pages, as in "pp. 28ff."
fn., fns.	footnote, footnotes.
ibid. (*ibidem*)	in the same work. Refers to the immediately preceding footnote.
i.e. (*id est*)	that is.
infra	below.
l., ll.	line, lines.
loc. cit. (*loco citato*)	in the place cited. Used with the author's name to refer to the same passage cited in an earlier footnote.
MS., MSS. ms., mss.	manuscript, manuscripts, as in "Biddle MSS."
n.d.	no date of publication given.
op. cit. (*opere citato*)	in the work cited. Usually superfluous.
p., pp.	page, pages.
passim	here and there. Denotes scattered references, as in "pp. 35-52 passim."
rev.	revised by, revision.
ser.	series.
supra	above.
trans.	translated by, translator, translation.
viz. (*videlicet*)	namely.
vol., vols.	volume, volumes.

Figure 5-14 Abbreviations and Latin terms commonly used in documenting reports. The English terms are almost invariably preferred in business usage.

Content. A footnote consists of the following information arranged to form a single sentence.

1. Number.

2. Name of author or authors as given in the work.

3. Title of the work. Underline the titles of books, magazines, and other self-contained works. Put in quotation marks the titles of chapters, articles, and other parts of longer works. The edition of a book, other than the first, and the volume number follow the title.

4. Facts of publication. For a book, show in parentheses the place of publication, the name of the publisher, and the date of publication (last copyright date). For an article in a periodical, give only the date of the issue, but if the periodical is a scholarly journal, give the volume number followed by the date in parentheses.

5. Page reference.

The correct form of footnotes is shown in Fig. 5-15.

NOTE: Material underlined in typewritten work is ordinarily set in italics by the printer. In the text examples that follow, the italicized material would be underlined if typewritten.

Subsequent References. When additional references are made to works already footnoted, highly abbreviated forms are used. Although Latin terms are still preferred for this purpose in scholarly works, business reports tend to use plain English. The following examples show the alternative Latin and English forms.

[1] Peter F. Drucker, *The Age of Discontinuity* (New York: Harper & Row, 1969), p. 17.

[2] Ibid., p. 25. [Same work as above.]

OR   [2] Drucker, p. 25.

[3] James B. Conant, *Slums and Suburbs* (New York: McGraw-Hill Book Company, 1961), p. 77.

[4] Drucker, op. cit., p. 235. [In the work cited in an earlier footnote.]

OR   [4] Drucker, p. 235.

[5] Conant, loc. cit. [Same passage as before.]

OR   [5] Conant, same reference as footnote 3.

Footnoting Public Documents.[1]   The form of citation for public documents varies with the kind of document and the traditions governing references to them. Generally, however, the aim is to give enough information to permit the reader to gain access to the documents if he so desires.

Agency Publications.   Books and pamphlets issued by government agencies are cited with the name of the corporate author first, followed by the name of the work, the place and date in parentheses, and the page reference. If

[1] Reprinted by permission from J. Harold Janis, *The Business Research Paper: A Manual of Style* (New York: Hobbs, Dorman & Co., 1967), pp. 27–31.

BOOK (ONE AUTHOR)	[1]Carl Heyel, Computers, Office Machines, and the New Information Technology (New York: The Macmillan Company, 1969), p. 97.
BOOK (TWO AUTHORS)	[2]C. Orville Elliott and Robert S. Wasley, Business Information Processing Systems (Homewood, Ill.: Richard D. Irwin, Inc., 1968, p. 47.
BOOK (MORE THAN THREE AUTHORS; ONE OF SEVERAL VOLUMES)	[3]Bruno Klopper and others, Developments in the Rorschach Technique, vol. 2 (Yonkers-on-Hudson, New York: World Book Company, 1956), pp. 34-38.
BOOK WITH SUBTITLE; SECOND EDITION	[4]Herbert A. Simon, A Study of Decision-Making: Administrative Behavior in the Organization, 2d ed. (New York: The Macmillan Company, 1957) pp. 145-147.
EDITED WORK	[5]Monroe R. Lazere, ed., Commercial Financing (New York: Ronald Press Company, 1968), p. 268.
CHAPTER OR ARTICLE IN COLLECTIVE WORK	[6]Theos A. Langlie, "Performance Appraisal," in the Encyclopedia of Management, ed. Carl Heyel (New York: Reinhold Publishing Corp., 1960), pp. 654-663.
ARTICLE IN ENCYCLOPEDIA	[9]"Scientific Management," Encyclopaedia Britannica (Chicago: 1968), vol. 14, pp. 747-750.
VOLUME IN SERIES	[10]Norman E. Pflomm, Managing Company Cash (New York: National Industrial Conference Board, 1961), Studies in Business Policy No. 99, p. 83.
PAMPHLET (NO DATE OR AUTHOR)	[11]Speakers Guide (Washington, D.C.: Department of the Navy, n.d.) p. 35.
SIGNED MAGAZINE ARTICLE	[12]Conrad Berenson, "Marketing Information Systems," Marketing, vol. 33 (October 1969), pp. 16-23.
UNSIGNED MAGAZINE ARTICLE	[13]"Keeping up Steam," Sales Management, November 15, 1969, p. 36.
UNSIGNED NEWSPAPER ARTICLE	[14]"Patience Called a Key to Mediation," New York Times, Dec. 4, 1969, p. 106.
UNPUBLISHED WORK	[15]Minutes of the Summer Meeting of the International Communication Association, May 6-9, 1970 (in the files of the Association).

Figure 5-15 Correct form of footnotes.

the work carries the name of an individual author, the word *by* and the name of the author may follow the name of the work. The alternative is to give the name of the individual author first, followed by the name of the work and the name of the issuing agency.

¹ U.S. Department of Commerce, Bureau of International Commerce, *Establishing Business in Nigeria* (Washington, D.C.: April 1965), p. 12.

² U.S. Bureau of Labor Statistics, *Employment and Earnings* (Washington, D.C.: March 1964), p. 35.

³ David Lindley Clark, *Labor Laws That Have Been Declared Unconstitutional*, U.S. Bureau of Labor Statistics Bulletin No. 321 (Washington, D.C.: 1922), p. 14.

Congressional Bills, Hearings, and Reports.   References to congressional bills give the number of the Congress, the name of the house (House or Senate), the session number, and the number of the bill. In the instance of congressional testimony and reports, reference is also made to the name of the document, the volume or part, and the page number. Usage is divided on the inclusion of the facts of publication, although it is generally desirable to provide whatever information is necessary for locating the document. Because the titles of hearings often run quite long, the researcher may conveniently abbreviate them provided the essential identifying details are given. Underlining (italics, in printing) may be confined to the distinctive name given a legislative report or hearing. Such abbreviations as *H.R.* (House of Representatives, *S.* (Senate), and *J. Res.* (Joint Resolution) are common. A variety of styles is shown below.

¹ 88th Cong., 2d Sess., H.R. 6143.

² 88th Cong., 1st Sess., S. 2228.

³ 85th Cong., 2d Sess. (1958), J. Res. 335.

⁴ Hearings Before the Senate Finance Committee on H.R. 10650, 87th Cong., 2d Sess. (1962), Part I, p. 196.

⁵ *Monetary Policy, 1955–56.* Hearings Before the House Subcommittee on Economic Stabilization, 84th Cong., 2d Sess., Dec. 10 and 11, 1956 (Washington, D.C.: U.S. Government Printing Office, 1957), p. 76. [Date of hearings is included because year of publication is different.]

⁶ U.S. Congress, Joint Economic Committee, *Report on the Variability of Private Investment*, Part II, 87th Cong., 1st Sess. (Washington, D.C.: U.S. Government Printing Office, 1961), p. 327.

⁷ *Report on Practices and Procedures of Governmental Control of Transportation*, H. R. Doc. 678, 78th Cong., 2d Sess. (1944), p. 96.

⁸ Council of Economic Advisers, *Economic Report of the President*, transmitted to Congress, Jan. 23, 1957, p. 11.

⁹ *Report of the New York Joint Legislative Committee to Revise the Banking Law* (Albany, 1959), p. 22.

Laws and Regulations.   References to federal and state constitutions, statutes, and regulations give such information as the name of the document, the volume number, date, chapter, article, section, and pages—the exact data depending on the document. The name of the document is underlined or italicized.

[1] *United States Code,* Vol. 28, Sec. 2201. (Suppl. IV, 1957).

[2] *New York State Constitution,* Art. III, Sec. 14.

[3] *Louisiana Civil Code* (1870), Book 3, Title II, Ch. 1, Art. 1468.

[4] *Bank Holding Act* (1956), Sec. 7.

[5] *Internal Revenue Code* (1954), Sec. 46.

[6] *Public Utility Holding Company Act* (1964), Sec. 3(b)(2).

NOTE: A subsequent reference to a law or statute is abbreviated in the following fashion:

[7] *Code,* Sec. 7

Cases at Law.[2] Legal cases, including those tried before regulatory bodies, are cited by reference to the official reports or transcripts of those records by volume number, initial page number, and date. Except for such Latin words as *in re,* the name of the case is not underlined or italicized. The terse abbreviations (see the following examples) are designed to save space in legal briefs, but the same forms are used in documenting a thesis or dissertation.

1. Whenever possible, cases should be cited to the official reports and, except in U.S. Supreme Court and administrative cases, to one or more unofficial reports. Thus a tax case may be cited to both the *Tax Court of the United States Reports* (T.C.) and the *Prentice-Hall Tax Court Memorandum Decisions* (P-H Tax Ct. Mem.). If a U.S. Supreme Court decision has not yet been officially published, it may be cited to the *Supreme Court Reporter* (Sup. Ct.) or, if not in that, to *United States Law Week* (U.S.L.WEEK).

[1] Benedict v. Ratner, 268 U.S. 353 (1924). [The reference here is to Volume 268 of the official records of the U.S. Supreme Court, page 353.]

[2] Pittsburgh v. Public Utility Commission, 169 Pa. Sup. Ct. 400, 82 A. 2d. 515 (1951). [The references here are to the volume and page numbers in the official records of the Pennsylvania Supreme Court and in the unofficial *Atlantic Reports, Second Series.*]

[3] *In re* Ratner 35 C.C.P.A. (Patents) 682, 109 F. 2d 270 (1947). [The references here are to the *Court of Customs and Patent Appeal Reports* and to the *Federal Reporter, Second Series.*]

2. Unreported cases, including those yet to be compiled and published in series, should be cited by docket number, court, and full date.

[4] Connecticut Light & Power Co. v. Commissioner of Internal Revenue No. 49321, T.C., June 26, 1963.

3. Federal courts of appeals and district court cases are cited only to the *Federal Reporter Series,* currently in the Second Series (F. 2d) or the *Federal*

[2] Because of the many technicalities of legal citations, the reader is referred to *A Uniform System of Citation,* 10th ed. (Cambridge, Mass.: Harvard Law Review Association, 1958), the authoritative work in this field.

Supplement (F. Supp.). In addition to the volume and page number in the *Reporter,* the circuit or district should be noted, and the date.

⁵ Amazon Cotton Mill Co. v. Textile Workers Union, 167 F. 2d 183 (4th Cir. 1948).

⁶ Int'l Longshoremen's Union v. Sunset Line & Twine Co., F. Supp. 119 (D. C. Calif. 1948).

4. State court cases are cited from both the official and the unofficial reports, if both are available.

⁷ Nichols v. Somerville Savings Bank, 333 Mass. 488, 132 N.E. 2d 158 (1956). [The reference is the official report of the Massachusetts Supreme Court and the unofficial *North Eastern Reporter,* Second Series.]

5. Administrative cases (those involving regulatory bodies) are preferably cited to the official report only or to the official document number and full date. If neither is available, the unofficial report may be cited.

⁸ Lone Star Gas Corp. et al., 12 S.E.C. 287 (1942).

⁹ General Chemical Division, Allied Chemical & Dye Corp. v. Atlantic Coast Line Railroad et al., 298 I.C.C. 422 (1956).

¹⁰ Jaspan v. Philadelphia Electric Co., Docket No. IT-5461, Opinion No. 35, Federal Power Commission, December 3, 1938.

¹¹ New York State Electric Co., 21 P.U.R. 3d 276 (N.Y. Pub. Serv. Comm'n 1961). [The reference is to the unofficial *Public Utility Reports,* Third Series.]

6. When a case has gone to a higher court, the lower court decision is given first, followed by the subsequent history. The disposition of the case (e.g., affirmed, appeal dismissed, certiorari denied) is abbreviated and italicized or underlined.

¹² Otis & Co. v. Pennsylvania R.R. Co. et al., 61 F. Supp. 905 (E.D. Pa. 1945) *aff'd,* 155 F. 2d 522 (3d Cir. 1946).

¹³ A. P. Smith Manufacturing Co. v. Barlow, 13 N.J. 145, 98 A. 2d 581 (1953), *appeal dismissed,* 346 U.S. 861.

¹⁴ *In re* Lake's Laundry, Inc., 79 F. 2d 326 (2d Cir. 1935), *cert. denied,* 296 U.S. 622.

7. A subsequent reference to a citation already given in full should be abbreviated. Reference to a specific page may be given as in footnote 16 below.

¹⁵ Marcy v. Union Oil Co., *supra.*

¹⁶ Columbia Broadcasting Co. v. FCC *supra* at 77.

Bibliographies.   A bibliography lists works alphabetically by author and title (Figure 5-16). A long list is divided according to the type of materials as, for example, books, periodicals, government documents, and miscellaneous sources. For the style of bibliographical entries, follow these rules.

1. Give the last name of the author first. If there is more than one author,

BIBLIOGRAPHY

American Management Association. Changing Patterns
    and Concepts in Management. General Management
    Series No. 182. New York: American Management
    Association, 1956.

Brightman, Richard W., Bernard J. Luskin, and Theo-
    dore Tilton. Data Processing and Decision-Making.
    New York: The Macmillan Company, 1968.

Dennison Zip Code Directory. Washington, D.C.: Nor-
    man Publishing Co., 1968.

"Fortune Directory of the 500 Largest Industrial Cor-
    porations." Fortune, May 15, 1971.

Heyel, Carl. Computers, Office Machines, and the New
    Information Technology. New York: The Macmillan
    Company, 1969.

Pacter, Paul. "Reporting Discontinued Operations."
    Journal of Accountancy, Vol. 128 (November 1969),
    pp. 63-67.

Thayer, Lee. Administrative Communication. Homewood,
    Ill.: Richard D. Irwin, Inc., 1961.

_____, ed. Communication-Spectrum '7. Proceedings
    of the 15th Annual Conference of the National
    Society for the Study of Communication, 1968.

"Turmoil in the Capital Markets." Time, December 5,
    1969, p. 96.

U.S. House of Representatives, Committee of Ways and
    Means. Hearings on the Investment Tax Credit.
    87th Cong., 2d Sess. (1962).

U.S. Securities and Exchange Commission. Accounting
    Series. Release No. 96 (January 10, 1963).

Figure 5-16 Correct form of a bibliography.

the names of the other authors are usually written with the given names first.

2. Start each entry at the margin, but indent succeeding lines several spaces. Single-space the individual entries, but double-space between entries.

3. When an author is represented by more than one work, use an underscore line of ten spaces to denote the author's name in the second and succeeding entries.

4. Where no individual is credited for a work, list as author the name of the sponsoring organization or, if none is given, the title of the work in the correct alphabetical sequence.

5. Give the facts of publication as in footnotes, but set them off with periods instead of parentheses. You may use parentheses, however, to enclose an isolated date.

6. Give the inclusive pages of an article or chapter in a work that contains other material, but omit page references otherwise.

For additional examples of bibliographical listings, see "Authorities Consulted" in the front of this book.

5.4   TABULAR PRESENTATION

A collection of figures can best be communicated by means of a table. A table saves many words of description and permits easy reading and comparison.

See also "Typing Statistical Material," Section 11.2.

For information on positioning tables in a report, see "The Report in Finished Form," Section 6.3.

General Design.   Tables are often classified as spot tables or reference tables. *Spot tables* are integrated into the text of a report; they usually serve a very limited purpose (Figure 5-17). The more comprehensive *reference tables* are independent of the text of a report and bear a number and title (Figure 5-18).

The design of a table requires much thought and care. The main objective is to show relationships among the data in the rows and columns.

1. Data may be arranged geographically, numerically, alphabetically, chronologically, or by class, rank, or size.

2. When arranged by size, magnitudes usually diminish from left to right or top to bottom.

3. A table is better read across than down and is better long than wide.

4. In general, quantities should occupy the columns, whereas the things being studied (the *variables*) are named in the stubs on the right side of the table.

5. A column containing percentages, averages, ratios, and the like should be placed to the right of a column containing the base figures.

A survey of 127 typical plants and offices in the
East showed that companies paid their employees' tuition
as follows:

	Plants	Offices
In advance	16.8%	26.9%
After completion of courses	71.2%	57.7%
In installments	12.0%	15.4%

Most companies (about two-thirds of the firms having
percentage formulas) specified a flat percentage for
all reimbursements. Fifty per cent is the most frequently mentioned figure; seventy-five per cent is the
next.

Figure 5-17   Sample of text showing spot table.

6. Coordinate columns—that is, columns containing the same kinds of
information—should be the same width.

7. Horizontal rules are used to separate the column heads from the body

Table 8
Discounted Cash-Flow Technique

Year	Cash Return	(7.5 Percent) Present Value of Future Cash Flows
0	\$ 0	\$ 0
1	300	279.00
2	300	258.00
3	300	241.00
4	300	222.00
Total	\$1,200	\$1,000.00

Figure 5-18   Reference table.

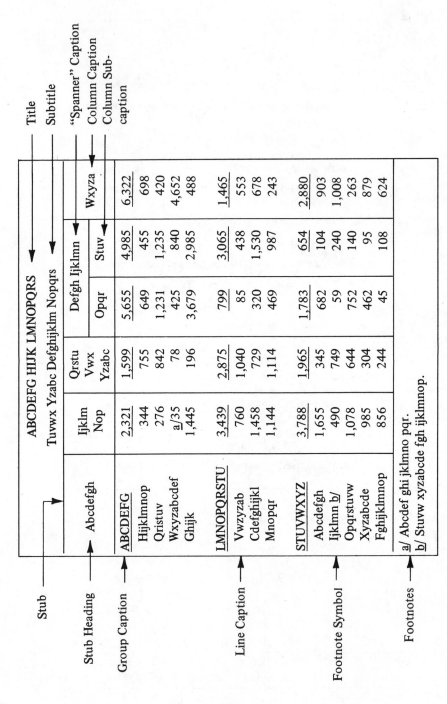

Figure 5-19 The parts of a table.

of the table, but other horizontal rules and vertical rules between columns are used only to improve display or prevent the confusion of figures. In any case, the sides are usually left open.

Parts of the Table.   The parts of a reference table are shown in Figure 5-19. The following is a description of the parts, with additional commentary on tabular techniques.

Title.   The title and number of a reference table are centered in one or several lines. Roman numerals may be used for the table number. Unit values, if applicable, are placed in parentheses below the title.

Columns.   Each column has a descriptive heading or caption centered in one or several lines to fit the width of the column. A caption may also span several columns, each with its own subcaption. Unit values applicable to any of the columns should be included tersely in parentheses, as, for example, *(000's)*, where three ciphers are to be added to the figures given.

Column totals should be placed at the top or bottom to suit the convenience of the reader. Subtotals within a column should be underlined.

Column spaces should not be left blank. If there are no figures to be supplied, the fact should be indicated by a long dash (—) or by the abbreviation n.a. ("not available").

Stubs.   The headings in the left-hand column are called *stubs*. The stub caption is the descriptive word or phrase at the top of the column. When stubs are subdivided, the main entry is the line caption; the subentries, indented two spaces, are the group captions. A space is left above the line caption. If a space cannot be left below the line caption, it may be underlined to separate it from the group captions. In a closely packed table, a space should be left between every five rows to make reading easier. Leaders, or spaced periods, may also be used to carry the eye from the stub to the column data. The periods should be aligned vertically.

End Data.   A single footnote reference in a table may be marked by an asterisk (*). If there are several footnote references, alphabetical symbols are more practical (numbers would be confusing). The alphabetical symbols are usually placed to the left of column figures to avoid disturbing the column alignment. All of the following styles are correct, but a single style should be adopted for use throughout a table or set of tables.

1,956[a]	a/1,956	(A) 1,956
560[b]	b/ 560	(B) 560

The symbols are repeated at the bottom of the table before the respective footnotes.

5.5 GRAPHIC PRESENTATION

Graphs and other types of charts are often used in reports as well as for independent use and presentation at meetings. Although some companies have specialists prepare these materials, the preparation of the drafts—if not the finished charts—may be assigned to a secretary or administrative assistant.

Graphs and charts cannot present the detailed information found in tables, even though tables provide the source data. The graphic exhibits do have an advantage, however, in their dramatic appeal to the eye.

Chart-Making Materials. The following materials are useful for making simple charts.

Graph paper
Ruler
Protractor
Compass
Ruling pen
Speedball pens
Black India ink
Lettering guide
Drawing board
T-square
Triangle

Printed graph paper is available in a variety of rulings, principally 5, 6, 8, 10, and 12 to the inch. The 6 ruling corresponds to the vertical spacing on the typewriter; the 10 and 12 correspond to the horizontal spaces of pica and elite type.

Other chart-making aids include colored cellophane tapes for use in making lines and bars, acetate film for use in shading, and alphabet packs with transferable letters and symbols. Some of the trade names under which these materials are available are Chart-Pak, Pretype, Formatt, and Letraset.

Materials for making transparencies for overhead projectors can be obtained from the 3M Company, St. Paul, Minnesota. The 3M Company also runs a training program in chart making in the larger cities.

General Techniques

1. Draw the graph in pencil on graph paper; then copy the draft on plain white paper. Keep grid lines to a minimum. Intermediate values can be shown, where necessary, by ticks along the horizontal or vertical axis.

2. The use of color for lines and bars helps to emphasize distinctions, but is impractical if the graphs are going to be reproduced in black and white.

3. Typewrite the title and other data on the graph or hand-draw them in block letters.

4. Explain distinctions in color, shading, or line quality by a legend on a convenient part of the chart (Figure 5-22).

5. Generally, time is indicated by the horizontal scale of a line or column graph, and quantity by the vertical scale. Clearly mark the points on both scales and place the index or unit of measure (examples: "1960 = 100"; "Thousands of Dollars") above the vertical scale or below the horizontal scale, as the chart requires.

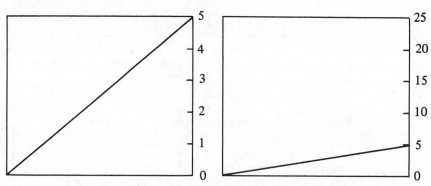

Figure 5-20   Visual effect of differences in scale.

6. Choose the scale range to represent conditions accurately. Figure 5-20 shows how the choice of range may accentuate a rise or drop.

7. Be consistent in your scale. Don't, for example, show five-year intervals at the beginning of the scale and one-year intervals at the end. All the measures must be uniform.

DISTRIBUTION OF ADVERTISING DOLLAR

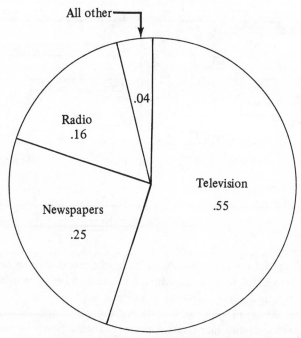

Figure 5-21   Pie chart.

NUMBER OF EMPLOYEES

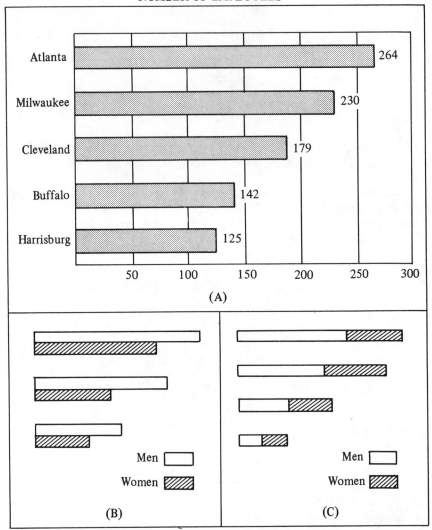

Figure 5-22   Bar charts.

8. Don't crowd the chart. Select carefully the few details to be shown and the few relationships to be established. Cut the number of words and figures to a minimum and make sure they are clearly visible.

The most common types of charts are the pie chart, the bar chart, the column chart, and the line chart, or curve. Instructions for drawing these types of charts follow.

FIVE-YEAR SALES RECORD

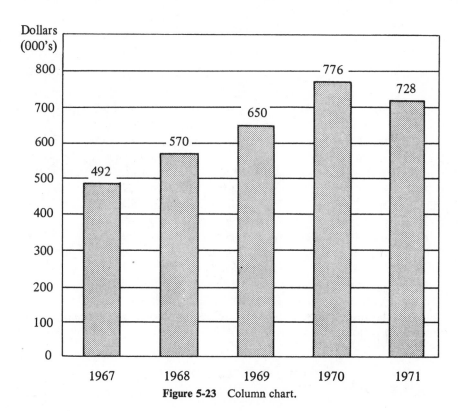

Figure 5-23   Column chart.

Pie Charts (Figure 5-21). A pie chart is a full circle that divides a whole quantity into its parts. Thus it might show the distribution of a dollar of income, the proportion of men to women in the employ of an organization, or the relative sales of a company's several product lines. To make a pie chart:

1. Convert all figures into percentages.

2. Beginning at "12 o'clock," mark off the required segments, going from the largest to the smallest, unless emphasis requires some other arrangement.

3. In allocating space, consider the circumference of the circle as 100 per-cent and determine the size of each segment by using a protractor or by making a close estimate. Reasonable accuracy is possible if the circle is quartered, then each quarter halved, and each half quarter halved again. Each of the 16 segments is then equal to 6.25 percent. If you use a protractor, keep in mind that the circumference of the circle is 360°; so 10 percent would be 36°, 20 percent 72°, and so on.

4. Place the segment captions and the percentages inside or outside the circle, depending on the space available. Segments may be shaded for contrast.

5. Type all captions horizontally. Draw arrows, if necessary, to the segments to which they apply.

Bar and Column Charts. The bar chart shows the magnitude, or quantities, of different things. A sequence of dates or amounts is marked off on the horizontal axis, and the things being compared are represented by the bars extending from the vertical axis. The bars may be subdivided to show their components, or they may be clustered in groups of two or three (Figure 5-22).

Although the bar chart may be set upright to form a column chart, the column chart is technically reserved for two-scale representations, that is, those that permit measuring both horizontally and vertically (Figure 5-23). As in bar charts, the columns may be subdivided or grouped.

The following suggestions apply to both bar and column charts.

1. Space the bars from one-half to a full bar width apart. Use narrower spaces or none at all between grouped bars.

2. Arrange the bars in ascending or descending order, or any other order consistent with the purpose of the chart or the emphasis you desire. A time sequence, however, must be plotted in chronological order, beginning with the earliest period.

```
              EMPLOYMENT OF TEMPORARY HELP

                  October-November, 19--

     OCT. ))))
     NOV. ####

                              Man-Hours

          0      50     100     150     200     250
          |       |      |       |       |       |

34th Street   120   )))))))))))))))))))
    Store     179   ##########################

59th Street    96   )))))))))))))))
    Store     168   ########################

86th Street    39   )))))))
    Store     109   ################
```

Figure 5-24 A typewritten bar chart. The upper bars are made of superimposed parentheses.

LAUNDRY DIVISION PRODUCTION

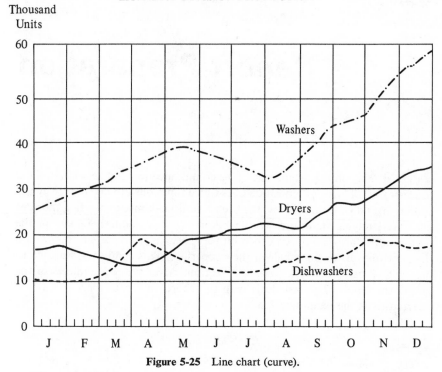

Figure 5-25   Line chart (curve).

3. Use a consistent shading scheme for the parts of divided bars and the members of grouped bars. For simple bars and columns, draw outlines or solids.

4. If you prefer, you may typewrite the charts instead of drawing them, using ordinary symbols to make the bars or columns (Figure 5-24).

Line Charts (Curves). When points along a horizontal scale are too close for a column chart to be feasible, the points may be connected to form a curve (Figure 5-25). Two or three curves may also be overlaid on the same grid to show other variations in quantity over the same period. Points applicable to line charts are listed here.

1. Plan the chart so that it is about half again as wide as it is high; this will prevent visual distortion.

2. Begin quantity scales at zero; otherwise a rise or fall will seem steeper than it is. If the curves begin somewhat high on the chart, the chart may be broken near the bottom to show the omission of part of the scale.

3. When several curves are superimposed, separate them by color or use a solid line for one, and broken and dotted lines for the others.

6

Report Preparation

Reports play an important part in the communication and decision-making processes of all large organizations. As office functions are taken over by the computer and other machines, the executive finds himself spending more of his time studying data and writing reports on his findings. Others in the organization, also, are often called on to write, assemble, or edit reports on their own behalf or on behalf of their superiors. This chapter is designed to help with those tasks. The first three sections cover the requirements of the long-form report. The last deals with the short, internal report commonly referred to as the memorandum.

CONTENTS

6.1 Planning the Report — p. 238
6.2 Writing the Report — p. 246
6.3 The Report in Finished Form — p. 250
6.4 Memorandums — p. 261

Information regarding other aspects of reports will be found in Chapter 5 as follows: "Information Sources," Section 5.2; "Footnotes and Bibliographies," Section 5.3; "Tabular Presentation," Section 5.4; and "Graphic Presentation," Section 5.5.

6.1 PLANNING THE REPORT

A report can be only as good as the planning behind it. The planning requires a specific objective, a search for the relevant data, and logical organization of the content. For all but the shortest reports, some form of working outline is indispensable. Fleshed out with suitable language, supporting exhibits, and attractive typographical display, the outline is transformed into an effective report. (Figure 6-1.)

Report Objectives. The chief criterion for judging reports is "Does it do its job?" (Figure 6-2). For that reason the report objective should be clearly

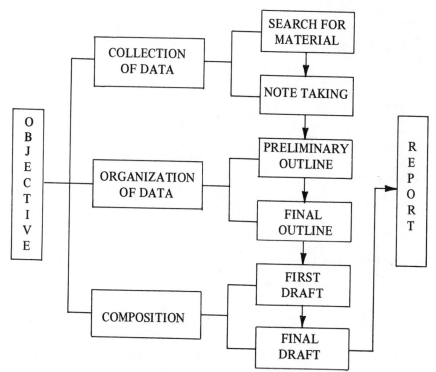

Figure 6-1   The report-writing process.

defined in the first place. Several of the following objectives may be combined in a single report.

1. To preserve information for legal or reference purposes.
2. To provide information for high-level decisions.
3. To evaluate performance.
4. To record individual, group, or machine performance for later evaluation.
5. To analyze current procedures.
6. To make recommendations.
7. To predict future results.

Developing Report Data.   The heart of any report is the information it contains. A reader may disagree with the writer's conclusions or recommendations, but the data should be complete, specific, and incontestable. Generally, two kinds of data are used: primary and secondary.

Primary Data.   This type of information is most desirable because it comes from an examination of original documents and the writer's own research and personal experience. Primary data includes the following.

Company records and files
Original letters, estimates, and proposals
Public records
Legal documents
Personal interviews
Questionnaires
Personal observation
Experimentation
On-the-job experience

Secondary Data. In many cases, the writer does not have access to original sources, or the research work has already been done by the government or other reliable sources outside his control. The following may be classified as secondary sources.

Government documents and statistics
Books
Newspapers and periodicals
Records and reports of private agencies
Business services (e.g., Standard & Poor's)
Published reports of surveys, interviews, and questionnaires

See also "Information Sources," Section 5.2.

---

1. UTILITY
   (a) The report serves the purpose for which it was prepared.
   (b) It provides information in a convenient form.
   (c) It is helpful to the reader.

2. RELIABILITY
   (a) The information is specific, accurate, and dependable.
   (b) The report includes all data that would affect the conclusion.
   (c) Unimportant data are not given undue weight.

3. PERSUASIVENESS
   (a) The conclusions and recommendations are adequately supported by the data presented.
   (b) The reasoning is logical.
   (c) Adequate consideration is given to contrary evidence and conclusions.

4. READABILITY
   (a) The report is organized for easy comprehension.
   (b) The language is as clear and simple as the subject permits.
   (c) The technical vocabulary, if any, is suited to the reader.
   (d) Ideas are expressed concisely.
   (e) Tables and charts are used where applicable.

Figure 6-2 Criteria of good reports.

Organization of Data.   Generally, the thinking that goes into a report is inductive; that is, it proceeds from an examination of the facts to the formation of conclusions based on those facts. The same method may be followed in the actual writing. However, for reasons of emphasis or convenience to the reader, the conclusions and recommendations are often placed ahead of the

METHOD	*EXAMPLES*
Time	Chronology of events. Conditions before—conditions after. Present system—proposed system.
Space	First floor—second floor. Eastern sales—western sales. North America—South America.
Classes	Kinds of accounts. Classes of products.
Parts	Parts of a machine. Steps in a process.
Support	General statement or conclusion followed by specific details (deductive order). Specific details followed by general statement or conclusion (inductive order).
Balance	Cause—effect. Need—fulfillment. Problem—solution. Question—answer. Point-by-point comparison of two or more things.
Importance	Most important to least important. Least important to most important (climax).
Interest	Most interesting points to least interesting.
Familiarity	Most familiar material to least familiar. Simple to complex.
Acceptance	Most acceptable ideas to least acceptable.

Figure 6-3   Methods of organizing data.

supporting data, and sometimes the supporting data is either omitted or put in an appendix to form a subordinate part of the report.

The most important steps in organizing a report are dividing or classifying the data and arranging the parts in logical order. The following patterns, though very general, should prove useful in a great variety of situations.

Useful Report Patterns

I. Introduction
II. Data

I. Introduction
II. Data
III. Conclusions and/or
　　Recommendations

I. Introduction
II. Conclusions and/or
　　Recommendations
III. Supporting Data

I. Abstract or Summary
II. Background (Introduction)
III. Discussion of Data
IV. Conclusions and/or
　　Recommendations

I. Statement of problem
II. Proposed solution(s)
III. Anticipated results
IV. Recommendations

I. Background
II. Faults of Present System
III. Alternatives
　　A. Advantages
　　B. Disadvantages
IV. Conclusions
V. Recommendations

Within the various parts of the report, data may be arranged also in a number of different ways for order and consistency (Figure 6-3).

Suggestions for Content.　Once the general outline is conceived, the particulars of the report can be distributed through the various parts. The following lists suggest not only the allocation of details, but also some of the kinds of information the report may contain.

1. Introduction
   (a) Authorization for the report.
   (b) Purpose of the report.
   (c) Scope and limits.
   (d) Statement of the problem.
   (e) Organization of the report.
   (f) History or background.
   (g) Methods of investigation.
   (h) Sources of information.
   (i) Definition of terms.
   (j) Acknowledgments.
   (k) Abstract or synopsis.
   (l) Summary of findings (conclusions).
   (m) Summary of recommendations.
2. Discussion (main body of data).
   (a) Analysis of present conditions; strengths and weaknesses
   (b) Details of structure, functions, methods.
   (c) Proposals.
   (d) Evidence, reasoning, and other forms of proof.
   (e) Use of models: mathematical or graphic.
   (f) Narrative or chronology.
   (g) Procedures: past, present, proposed.

(h) Causes and effects.
(i) Comparison of data.
(j) Alternatives.
(k) Advantages and disadvantages.
(l) Summary tables and charts.
3. Conclusion.
(a) Summary of purpose and main points.
(b) Detailed conclusions.
(c) Detailed recommendations.
(d) Anticipated results.
4. Appendix(es).
(a) Original documents (or copies).
(b) Reference tables and charts.
(c) Pictures and diagrams.

Outline Techniques.   Except for the most simple report, it makes good sense to prepare an outline before writing the report proper. The outline serves a number of purposes: (1) it provides a step-by-step plan for the presentation of

---

THE NEED FOR WORK MEASUREMENT
IN THE OFFICE

I. Evolution of work measurement

II. Purposes of work measurement

    A. Provide basis for evaluating and appraising performance

    B. Permit more efficient scheduling of work

    C. Allow for more effective cost control

        1. Screening of projects

        2. Budgeting

III. Work measurement techniques

    A. Subjective method

    B. Observation time study

    C. Historical records

    D. Stop watch studies

    E. Work sampling

    F. Standard time data

    G. Predetermined time data

IV. Conclusions

    A. Work measurement aids productivity

    B. Techniques must be carefully weighed

    C. Timing, personnel resources, and cost play important roles

V. Recommendation

Figure 6-4   A topic outline.

data; (2) it can be submitted for approval before time is spent (and perhaps wasted) on the finished report; and (3) it is useful in coordinating data when parts of the report are assigned to different persons to prepare.

An outline may consist of a few informal jottings on a scrap of paper or of a list of topics carefully phrased, arranged, and numbered. The exact form will depend on the length and complexity of the report and the use that will be made of the outline. The suggestions that follow should prove helpful in the framing of a formal outline but, in general, it should be kept in mind that a good outline is one in which the organization of ideas is logical, simple, and readily apparent.

1. Decide whether you want the outline to be in complete sentences (sentence outline) or phrases (topic outline); then be consistent in sticking to one or the other (Figures 6-4 and 6-5). The topic outline is usually preferred because of its simplicity and convenience, but the sentence outline gives more information and may therefore be preferred if it is to be submitted to others for examination.

2. Use roman numerals for identifying first-degree headings, capital letters for second-degree heads, arabic numbers for third-degree heads, and small letters with or without parentheses for fourth-degree heads. A further subdivision of material is usually not desirable. If only two levels of heads are used, you may prefer a combination of arabic numbers and small letters, or capital letters and arabic numbers, in the order named.

THE POST OFFICE BOX COLLECTION PLAN

I. The present method of handling cash receipts is far from efficient.
    A. Handling incoming checks takes three to five days.
    B. Steps taken to shorten time have not succeeded.
    C. The Post Office collection box plan offers a possible solution.

II. The proposed method has been in use for the past eight years.
    A. Mail is picked up by the company's trucks at local post offices.
    B. A cash report is prepared for the cashier by the mail department.
    C. The cashier examines each check for
        1. Post-dating.
        2. Name of payee.
        3. Signature
        4. Agreement of written and figure amounts.
    D. Verified checks are deposited, with each check listed on the deposit slip.

Figure 6-5 Part of a sentence outline.

NOTE: In outlining technical and scientific papers, it is customary to use a decimal numbering system or pure number code (Figure 6-6).

3. Avoid the use of a single subhead. If a second subhead cannot be created, the single subhead can be absorbed into the immediately preceding head. An exception can be made when a single subhead is used to denote the use of an example.

NOT: A. Number of employees   BUT: A. Number of employees: 60
         1. 60   B. Volume of mail
      B. Volume of mail   1. 100–150 pieces daily
         1. 100–150 pieces daily   2. 1,500 pieces at end of month
ACCEPTABLE: A. Public-service advertising
                1. Example: Georgia-Pacific

4. Show the logical relationship of ideas by the ranking you give them in the outline. Instead of giving unequal ideas the same rank, try to combine related ideas under suitable headings. The outline on the left is confusing because it does not equate the present system with the proposed system

TITLE

1. _____
    1.1 _____
    1.2 _____
    1.3 _____

2. _____
    2.1 _____
        2.1.1 _____
        2.1.2 _____
    2.2 _____

3. _____
    3.1 _____
        3.1.1 _____
        3.1.2 _____
    3.2 _____
        3.2.1 _____
        3.2.2 _____
        3.2.3 _____

Figure 6-6 Outline using pure number code.

signified in the title. It also lists the parts of the subject as if all were of equal rank. The outline to the right corrects these faults.

Poor	*Improved*
Proposed Mechanization of Bakery Order Procedure	Mechanization of Bakery Order Procedure
I. Present method described	I. Present method
II. Need for change	A. Description
III. Store processing	B. Need for change
IV. Office procedure	II. Proposed method
V. Bakery platform handling	A. Daily processing
VI. Weekly processing	1. At store
VII. Cost comparisons	2. At bakery
VIII. Other considerations	a. Office
	b. Shipping platform
	B. Weekly processing
	III. Cost comparisons
	IV. Other considerations

5. Apportion space in the outline about as you would in the report. Don't exaggerate minor ideas by giving them a long string of subtopics. Save the details for the report proper.

6.2 WRITING THE REPORT

When all the information has been gathered and assessed, and at least a rough outline has been made, the next step in the preparation of the report is writing the first draft. In the instance of a short, simple report, the first draft will probably be the final draft also. In a long report, however, there will probably be further editing and rewriting.

Report Language (General)

1. Title or subject. The title should be short and specific. If a short title does not identify the subject sufficiently, a subtitle should be added. Examples:

Space Requirements of the Legal Department

Investigation of the Delay in Shipments of R-200

Proposed Difference Procedure in the Sorting and Counting Division: Interim Report No. 1

Excelsior Electronic Calculator, Model 320S: Evaluation for Use in Domestic Research Division

2. References to author. In a short report that takes the form of a letter or memorandum, the author refers to himself as *I* (*we* if he wants to include others). In a more formal report the author who wishes to avoid the first person may use such terms as *the writer, the analyst,* and *the investigator.* With a little editing, however, it is possible to avoid references to the author altogether, as the following illustrations show:

Informal: I found . . .
Formal: An inspection showed . . .
Informal: I recommend . . .
Formal: It is recommended . . .
Informal: We propose three flexible alternatives.
Formal: Three flexible alternatives are proposed.

NOTE 1: A person of high position or unquestioned authority in his field of investigation should not hesitate to use the first-person ("I") style, even in a formal report.

NOTE 2: A formal report written in the name of an official group will refer to the signers as *we, the Committee, the Commission, the Board,* and so on.

We have stated on many occasions that we would not impair safety, or reduce standards of service, or cut service merely to keep down operating costs.
The Committee is unanimously of the opinion that all concessions should be let as the result of competitive bidding.

3. Objectivity.   The value of a report is in the facts it presents, rather than in the writer's personal opinions or unsupported conclusions. If opinions are offered, they should be backed by convincing evidence and stated in temperate language.

NOT: The conditions we found were disgraceful.
BUT: We found that 60 percent of the orders received during May were unattended to for periods ranging from nine days to three weeks.

NOT: Mr. Smith proved himself to be thoroughly incompetent in the new job.
BUT: Mr. Smith was charged with four errors last month. One of them involved a difference of $2,800. In another instance. . . . All in all, Mr. Smith's performance is well below that which we expect from an employee in his position.

4. Adaptation to the Reader.   Technical language is necessary and desirable in a report written for someone familiar with the writer's special subject, but it should be modified for the less knowledgeable reader. Reports originating in technical departments often have to be rephrased when they go to management. There is usually some loss of meaning in the transition.

TECHNICAL: Most refractory coatings to date exhibit a lack of reliability when subjected to the impingement of entrained particulate matter in the propellant stream under extended firing conditions.
NONTECHNICAL: The exhaust gas eventually chews the coating off existing ceramics.

Connecting Ideas.   The interconnection of ideas should be shown by sentence and paragraph structure and the repetition of key words. More specifically:

1. Let the heads and subheads give the reader clues to the relation between the parts of the report. For example, do not give two heads equal position and weight when one is actually subordinate to the other.

2. List and enumerate coordinate ideas, such as points, conditions, advantages, and so on. This technique saves words and shows clearly that all the listed units are part of the same category of information. As an example, note the list of points, of which this paragraph is a part.

3. Use topic, or summary, sentences to alert the reader to what follows. The repetition of key words will emphasize the connection. Example:

TOPIC SENTENCE:	The application of electronics to banking falls into two distinct areas: (1) *deposit accounting,* and (2) *all other bank recordkeeping functions,* including general accounting, loans, trusts, and mortgage activities.
FIRST POINT REPEATED AND DEVELOPED:	The problems involved in *deposit accounting* . . .
SECOND POINT REPEATED AND DEVELOPED:*	The problems incident to *all other bank recordkeeping functions* . . .

* Repetition of the word *problems* also helps to link the points and show their relation to each other.

4. Now and then use a connecting sentence or paragraph to sum up what you have said and to pave the way for what you are going to say. Example:

(reference to preceding point)
↓
In addition to *a decrease in telegraphic traffic volume,* the new system would also require *a substantial reduction in clerical time.*
↑
(reference to following point)

5. Use connecting words and phrases to signal the relation between ideas.

Relationship	Connectives
ADDITION	*and, also, too,* *besides, furthermore, moreover,* *first, second, third,* *one, another,* *finally, in conclusion*
EXAMPLE	*for example, for instance,* *to illustrate*
CAUSE AND EFFECT	*because, since, thus,* *for this reason,* *therefore, consequently, accordingly*
COMPARISON	*similarly, in the same way,* *likewise, in a like manner*
CONTRAST	*but, however, in contrast,* *on the other hand,* *in spite of*

Paragraphs

1. For reading ease, try to avoid paragraphs of more than 120 words (about 12 lines). Exceptions may be made in highly technical discussions, where the separation of qualifying details may adversely affect the sense.

2. Vary paragraph length, when possible, to make the page look interesting. An occasional paragraph of only a few lines provides a welcome break in a series of long paragraphs. However, except in an enumeration or for emphasis, avoid a series of very short paragraphs; they suggest a lack of development.

3. Ideally, each paragraph should develop a single idea or several closely related ones. A good method of development is to start with a general statement, or topic sentence, and then expand the statement in an orderly fashion. For an example, see "Connecting Ideas," point 3, in this chapter.

Sentences

1. Keep sentences reasonably short. An average of twenty to twenty-two words per sentence would be considered fair for most subjects.

NOT: The four-part continuous "Advice of Charge" forms were placed in the Flexowriter while the punched tape containing the consolidated shortages of the previous day's differences was placed in the auxiliary tape reader, which mechanically sensed codes punched in the tape and automatically typed "Advice of Charge" forms without an operator. (One sentence of 51 words)

BUT: The four-part continuous "Advice of Charge" forms were placed in the Flexowriter. Then the punched tape, containing the consolidated shortages of the previous day's differences, was loaded in the auxiliary tape reader. The reader mechanically sensed codes punched in the tape and automatically typed "Advice of Charge" forms without operator attention. (Three sentences of 13, 20, and 19 words respectively)

2. Rework sentences to simplify the structure.

NOT: The information collected from all branch offices as to actions taken to cope with short-run disruptions will be summarized and distributed in the form of a "Guidelines for Action."

BUT: The actions taken by all branch offices to cope with short-run disruptions will be summarized in the report, "Guidelines for Action."

NOT: Our report to the manufacturer will incorporate a request that they inform us of any product improvements they have made relevant to several serious shortcomings in their central dictation system.

BUT: We will ask the manufacturer what they have done to correct the serious shortcomings in their central dictation system.

3. Use similar grammatical patterns (parallel structure) to express parallel ideas in the simplest, most readable form.

NOT: The lack of training of the personnel, often too few to carry out their functions efficiently, coupled with an indifference toward enforcement policies, indicates the need for a reorganization of the office.

BUT: The office should be reorganized. The employees are *insufficient in number, improperly trained,* and *indifferent toward enforcement policies.* [Series of adjective phrases]

4. Express ideas concisely.

Wordy	*Concise*
The policy of the company . . .	The company's policy . . .
We are of the belief that . . .	We believe that . . .
The procedure is in the process of being reviewed.	The procedure is being reviewed.
The work that is of greatest interest to them . . .	The work of greatest interest to them . . .
During the course of their research in connection with the feasibility of . . .	During their research on the feasibility of . . .

Words

1. Use the simplest words consistent with precise expression and easy reading.

Compare		*Compare*	
aggregate	total	inadvertency	slip-up
approximately	about	modification	change
assistance	help	substantiation	proof
causative factor	cause	remuneration	pay
commence	begin	subsequently	later
converse	talk	termination	end
demonstrate	show	utilization	use

2. Use strong verbs. In each of the following examples, note how the meaning of the noun is transferred to the verb, with resulting force and conciseness.

Compare	
made a decision	decided
came to a conclusion	concluded
placed an order for	ordered
sending the enclosed	enclosing
be of service	serve
showed an increase	increased
for the conservation of	to conserve

3. Keep to a minimum expressions containing "it is," a common sign of official jargon.

NOT: It is the intention of the Budget and Expense Committee to . . .
BUT: The Budget and Expense Committee intends to . . .
NOT: It is realized that numeric codes can be supplied in all messages originating in the clearing banks.
BUT: Numeric codes can be supplied . . .

4. Avoid stilted language. If you wouldn't use an expression in speaking, don't use it in writing.

Stilted	*Natural*
per their request	at their request, *or*
	as they requested
as per company policy	in accordance with bank policy
the cost of said repairs	the cost of the repairs
in view of the above	in view of these facts
the subject study	this study

Also avoid *thereof, thereto, therefor, therefrom, therein, further to the above, under date of, same* (as in "have received *same*"), *deem, pursuant to, aforesaid.*

6.3 THE REPORT IN FINISHED FORM

Close attention to the final typing and assembly of the report returns extra dividends in the strong impression it makes. The instructions that follow apply chiefly to the long formal report. Moderate variations are always permissible, provided the results are clear and consistent.

General Considerations. *Binding.* A heavy paper cover protects the report and adds to its attractiveness. If your company does not have a standard report cover, use one that is commercially available. It should be heavy enough to support the weight of the report, but simple in construction and conservative in texture and color. It should call attention to the report, not to itself.

Margins. The typed pages should have a margin of at least one inch at the top, right side, and bottom, and one-and-one-half inches at the left side to allow for the binding. Leave two inches at the top of the first page and of every other page that marks the beginning of an independently titled major section.

Headings. The main title of a report or chapter is usually typed in all capitals and the subtitle is typed in capitals and lower case.

MARKETING INFORMATION SYSTEMS

A New Era in Marketing Research

Chapter headings and subheadings should follow a consistent pattern to show the reader the organization of the subject and the relative importance of each topic. Several systems are in use. Probably the most common system uses five degrees of headings as shown below.

FIRST-DEGREE HEADING

Second-Degree Heading

Third-Degree Heading

    Xxxxxxx xxxxxx xxx xxxxxxxxxx xxxxxxx xxx xxxxxxx xxx xxxx xxxx xx. Xxxx xxxx xxx xxxxxxxxxxxxx xx xxxxxxxxx.

    Fourth-Degree Heading. Xxx xxxxxxx xxxxxxxxxx xxx xxxxxxxx xxx xxxx xxx xxx xxxxxxxxxx xx xxxxxx xxx.

      The Fifth-Degree Heading is set up, with additional indention, as the first few words of a subdivision of the fourth-degree topic.

Another system omits the second-degree heading and goes directly to the third-degree heading. Still another starts with the second-degree heading. Considerable latitude is permitted provided consistency is observed throughout.

Generally, two blank lines (triple spacing) are left before and after the first- and second-degree headings. Two blank lines are usually left before a third-degree heading within the copy. Because all other copy is double-spaced, the extra line alerts the reader to the start of another major topic.

Underscoring of headings is optional but should be used whenever necessary for emphasis or attention, but again consistency of use is required. When a long heading is broken into two or more lines, the underscoring is placed only under the last line to preserve the neat appearance. However, the underscoring extends to the limits of the longest line.

This Is a Second-Degree Heading
Underscored for Emphasis

This Is a Third-Degree Heading
Underscored for Emphasis

     Xxxx xxxxxxxxxxx xxx xxxxxxxxxxx xxxx xxxxxxxxx xxxx xxxxxx xxxxxxxx xx xxxxx xx xxxxxxxx xxxxxx xxxx xxxxxxxxxxxx.

Spacing.   Double-spacing produces the most readable pages. However, good reading qualities may also be achieved with single spacing if lines are kept short and double-spacing is used to set off paragraphs and heads. Even when double-spacing is used in the report proper, single-spacing is conventional in these parts: the letter of transmittal, the abstract, the footnotes, the bibliography, and the appendixes.

Page Numbers.   A report containing a number of preliminary features (like a title page, an introduction, and a table of contents) is best numbered in the following way.

1. Beginning with the title page, allot a number to each page, and type the number on each page except the title page.

2. Center the small roman numeral *ii* a half inch from the bottom edge of the page following the title page, and number consecutively in the same manner all the pages up to the first page of the report text.

3. Number with arabic numerals all pages of the text of the report continuing through the exhibits, the bibliography, and the index, if such parts are included. Center the number of the first page of every independently titled major division (for example, section, chapter, bibliography, index) a half inch from the bottom edge. Type all other page numbers a half inch from the top at the right margin.

Quotations.   Set off from the text, by indention and single-spacing, a quotation of more than three or four lines unless it is closely interwoven with the narrative. An example is shown in Figure 9-1.

Footnotes.   The customary place of footnotes is at the bottom of the page. (See "Footnotes and Bibliographies," Section 5.3.) In the draft of a report, however, a footnote may be placed immediately following the line in which the footnote reference appears. A solid rule above and below the footnote will mark it off from the text.

Exhibits.   Follow these rules for positioning and labeling exhibits.

1. The position of reference tables and charts should serve the convenience of the reader.[1] The best place is usually as close as possible to the reference in the text. On the other hand, either custom or convenience may require that

---

[1] Spot tables and charts are always placed with the text. See Figure 5-17.

PROPOSED USE OF

REGIONAL BANK DEPOSITORIES

Dorothea R. Jordan

Administrative Assistant
Finance Department

Ace Chemical Company
Stamford, Connecticut

October 9, 19--

Figure 6-7 Title page.

HARBOR TRANSPORTATION CO.
785 Front Street
New York, New York 10005

July 8, 19--

Mr. George A. Fenton, President
Harbor Transportation Company
New York, New York

Dear Mr. Fenton:

At your request, contained in your memorandum of May 15, 19--,
I have made a survey of the office operations of our Routing
Department. My findings and recommendations are embodied in
the accompanying report.

During my study I directed my attention to these specific aims:

    1.   Improvement of service to customers.

    2.   Cost reductions wherever possible.

    3.   Adequate supervision and controls.

    4.   Improved personnel relations.

The adoption of my recommendations should do much to reduce
complaints and improve the overall efficiency of our operations.

I should like to thank Mr. Morton Fairbanks and Miss Arlene
Brody for their assistance in research and writing.

Should any questions arise concerning the content of this
report or the implementation of my recommendations, I will
be glad to discuss these matters with you.

                        Sincerely yours,

                        Egbert H. Grayson

                        Egbert H. Grayson
                        Vice President-Operations

Figure 6-8   A letter of transmittal.

they be placed at the end of the report. In some instances, special-purpose exhibits are put with the text, whereas general-purpose exhibits are put in an appendix. The difference is largely one of relevancy; the more pertinent the exhibit, the more reason for placing it close to the corresponding text.

2. "Close to the text" means immediately following the text or, if it cannot be fitted on the same page as the text, then at the top of the next page. Exhibits occupying a page without text should be positioned right after the reference page. If you want the exhibit page to face the text page, cut off the top left corner of the exhibit page at a right angle, so that the number of the reference page shows through. In this arrangement, the exhibit page is referred to by the same number as the reference page.

3. Other considerations aside, it is more efficient to put exhibits on separate pages from the text. The reasons are (a) it is often hard to estimate the exact amount of space that will be needed for an exhibit, and (b) an error in drawing an exhibit would otherwise require the retyping of the page.

4. If it is necessary to place a table or drawing sidewise to fit the page, the top should be at the bound edge.

5. If necessary, an extra-wide sheet may be used to accommodate an exhibit, provided the sheet is folded forward eight-and-a-half inches from the

TABLE OF CONTENTS

I. THE PROBLEM DEFINED   1

II. PRESENT METHODS OF HANDLING WRITTEN COMMUNICATIONS   3

III. DEFICIENCIES IN THE PRESENT SYSTEM   6

IV. OPERATION OF THE MAGNETIC TAPE TYPEWRITER   8

V. INSTALLATION COST   10

VI. ANTICIPATED RESULTS   11

VII. CONCLUSIONS AND RECOMMENDATIONS   12

EXHIBITS

A. ILLUSTRATION OF MAGNETIC TAPE TYPEWRITER   14

B. SAMPLES OF WORK PRODUCED   15

Figure 6-9 Table of contents.

TABLE OF CONTENTS

Preface

I. Control Division Tabulating Department 1

    Equipment Requirements 2
    Clerical Requirements 2
    Space Requirements and Miscellaneous Costs . . 3
    Personnel Displacement Resulting from Adoption
      of Tabulating Procedures 4
    Advantages of Tabulating Procedures 5

II. General Bookkeeping 6

    Standardization of Proof Procedures 6
    Preparation of Daily Statements 7
    Treasury Tax and Loan and Federal Tax Accounts 9
    Time Deposits 10
    Account Classification 11

III. Accounts Payable 12

    Application of Tabulating Procedures 12
    Signing Expense Checks 14
    Miscellaneous Recommendations 15

Figure 6-10 Table of contents in another style.

left edge. The sheet can be folded back again, accordian-style, to keep it free from the binding.

6. When only a few miscellaneous exhibits are included in a report, label them Exhibit 1, Exhibit 2, and so on; or Figure 1, Figure 2, and so on. Otherwise, use a different series for each class of exhibit; for example, Table 1, Table 2, and so on; Chart 1, Chart 2, and so on; Map 1, Map 2, and so on. Roman numerals may be used for a single series, preferably tables, but arabic numbers should be used for all others. The number and title of a table are always placed above it, but the numbers and titles of other exhibits may be placed above or below, as long as consistency is observed.

Assembling the Report. The following report features, with notes on their content and use, are discussed here in the order in which they are generally to be found.

Cover   Summary
Title page   Report body
Letter of transmittal   Appendix
Preface   Bibliography
Table of contents   Index
List of exhibits

I.

The Problem and Its Significance

    Several months ago the Ace Chemical Company found that under the
present method of handling cash receipts it was taking from three to
five days to list checks, reconcile the cash report, prepare the checks
for deposit, and deposit the checks to its account at the bank.

    Immediate steps were taken to correct the situation, and the delay
was cut somewhat. It is a fundamental fact that money from receivables
cannot begin earning until it becomes a deposit in the bank. For that
reason, float time and clerical time must be held to an absolute
minimum.

    The system now in use is the result of several refinements put into
effect during the past few months, but it is essentially the same as it
has been for the past 25 years. Lengthy delays have been eliminated,
but money is still kept out of the banks one or two days longer than
necessary. Since it will be difficult to achieve further speed in
handling the present methods, an alternate method of handling should be
examined.

    The system recommended is a banking service known as the lock box or
post office collection box plan. Though not a new concept, lock box
operations have only in recent years come into their own and are today
accepted as an excellent means of speeding up the collection of checks,
providing additional working cash, and reducing clerical work in the
preparation of deposits.

1

Figure 6-11 The introduction to a report.

Cover and Title Page (*Figure 6-7*). The cover gives at least the title of the report. It may also include the date, the name and title of the author, the name of the author's organization, and the client or company for whom the report was prepared. Some of the latter details, however, are usually reserved for the title page. The title is typed in capital letters a little above the center. The other details, in caps and lower-case letters, are arranged in one or two spots below it.

2

       At the start, some firms designated a single bank, often in or near the city in which the home office was located. The single-bank method has two great disadvantages. First, little or no time was saved in the process, so that the speed-up in cash flow was negligible. About all that was gained was the convenience of having the bank receive and process the customer's remittances. Second, a single bank handling all the receivables found itself so burdened with volume that the company was required to carry heavy compensating balances, offsetting any tangible gains in availability of funds.

       Experience has demonstrated that best results can be obtained from the lock box plan only when it is employed on a <u>regional</u> basis. Should Ace adopt a regional plan for handling deposits?

       That is the problem toward which this report is directed. The purpose is to examine the present method of handling cash and explore the alternate method of using regional depositories. Specific recommendations will be offered.

       Information for this report was obtained from several banks in each region, which were able to describe the plans they offered. Through questionnaires and personal visits, companies already using the plan gave the benefit of their experience with the system.

Figure 6-12   The introduction concluded.

10

department, and the local bank. The entire procedure
can be followed through an examination of the work
done by each group in turn.

Mail Department
    All mail is picked up at intervals during the
day by Company trucks at the local post office. The
mail is brought to the mail room and sorted. Any envelope which is marked to the attention of an individual is sent to him unopened. All mail addressed
to the Company is opened and the contents are
scanned.
    Any check contained in an envelope addressed to
the Company is removed and placed in an alphabetical
sorting bin and set up in strict alphabetical order.
Any check reaching an individual is sent back to the
mail room to be recorded on the cash report.
    After the checks have been set up, they are
then listed by typewriter on a cash report showing
the date of check, company name, detail, if any, and
amount of check (Figure 2). An adding machine tape
is run on both the checks and the listing to verify
the total. Copies of the cash report are given to
the accounting department, accounts receivable, the
cashier, and credit departments. The cashier is
given all the checks with his copy of the report.

Cashier
    On receipt of the cash report and accompanying
checks, the cashier must look at each check for the
following:

    1.   Is the check postdated?
    2.   Who is the payee?
    3.   Is the check signed?
    4.   Do the written and figure amounts agree?

The amount of each check is then compared against

Figure 6-13   A report page showing use of single spacing with side heads.

```
1.

          Subject:   Computer Rental Charges
                     Your memorandum of July 8


2.

In a conversation last week you asked me to look in-
to the need for an additional typist to assist Mr.
Greer with his year-end report.


3.

At the request of the Control Division, I have con-
ducted a study on the General Ledger area. The ob-
jectives of the study were twofold:

     1.   To find ways of speeding the filing of cur-
          rent material.
     2.   To devise an improved system for putting
          dated file material into storage.


4.

Yesterday I received a visit from Mr. William Hopper,
the local representative of the 3M Company. He made
some suggestions for handling our copying needs, and
they were so interesting I would like to pass them
on to you.
```

Figure 6-14 Examples of memorandum beginnings.

Letter of Transmittal.   The letter of transmittal, if bound into the report, should be placed right after the title page. It is usually typewritten on the company's letterhead with full mechanical treatment, including date, inside address, and signature. The contents of the letter of transmittal may include:
1. Notice of submission of report
2. Authorization for report
3. Purpose and scope of report
4. Sources of information
5. Acknowledgment of help received from others
6. Offer of further assistance

Figure 6-8 shows a sample letter of transmittal.

Preface.   A preface may be used as an alternative to the letter of transmittal. It may also be used when the letter of transmittal is merely a notice of submission.

Table of Contents (Figures 6-9 and 6-10).   A table of contents is helpful in a report consisting of numerous sections and subsections. The table should list all the features of the report, including the main heads and, optionally, the second-degree heads.

List of Exhibits (Figure 6-9).   Reference tables, charts, and other illustrations should be listed immediately after the table of contents, either on the same page or on the next page.

Summary.   Paralleling the abstract in scientific and technical reports, a summary of a business report is helpful when the report is long or complex. A common substitute for a summary of the whole report is the "Summary of Findings" or "Summary of Conclusions and Recommendations" at the beginning of the report body.

Report Body (Figures 6-11, 6-12, and 6-13).   Here is the main part of the report, complete with introduction, discussion, and conclusions and recommendations.

Appendix.   The appendix (or appendixes) should include any documents, details, summary tables, illustrations, or other materials not included with the text. Each item should be clearly identified and a reference to it should be made somewhere in the report discussion.

Bibliography.   The bibliography is more useful in academic papers than in business reports, but if a number of books and articles have been consulted, they should be listed at the end of the report. (See "Footnotes and Bibliographies," Section 5.3.)

Index.   The index is an alphabetical list, with page references, of all the topics covered in the report. It is usually reserved for published reports of some length and complexity. Subtopics in the index are listed alphabetically under the main headings, and cross-references are frequent.

6.4   MEMORANDUMS

A memorandum is a short report intended usually for readers within the organization. It satisfies a number of important needs.

1. It permits continuing communication between subordinates and their superiors.

2. It provides a medium for communication between departments and between individuals on similar levels of authority.

3. It records data for permanent reference, and guides and controls staff activities.

4. It records temporarily information to be included in a broader study and report.

Subjects Treated. Memorandums are versatile. Some of the uses to which they can be put include:

Report of a meeting or conference
Report of a visit
Credit report
Instructions
Policy statement
Official procedure
Change in policy or procedure
Notice or announcement
Inquiry and follow-up
Analysis of a job or procedure
Analysis of human or machine performance
Analysis of organizational structure
Results of a test or questionnaire
Suggestion
Proposal
Recommendation

Mechanical Form. The format of memorandums is treated in "Letter Form and Style," Section 3.1. These additional points are relevant.

1. The readability of a memorandum may be improved by (a) wide margins, (b) paragraphs of varied length, (c) occasional lists and enumerations, and (d) in a long memorandum, centered or side heads to mark the major divisions of the content.

2. Tables and other exhibits that are part of a memorandum may be positioned, labeled, and numbered in the same way as if they were part of a long-form report. (See "The Report in Finished Form," Section 6.3.)

3. The memorandum has no cover; its pages are stapled in the upper left corner.

Organization of Data. A memorandum is organized in the same way as a longer report (see "Planning the Report," Section 6.1). It has an introduction, a body, and, more often than not, a conclusion.

Introduction. The subject line in the heading may provide all the introduction that is necessary. If not, the opening lines should include such data as (1) the purpose of the memorandum, (2) the authorization for the memorandum, and (3) the background history or data. Figure 6-14 shows several ways of handling the introduction. If no introduction is necessary, the memorandum begins with the discussion or body of the report.

Body. The body paragraphs give the writer's findings. Even a short memorandum requires an orderly arrangement of the data in order to prevent wordiness and confusion. For tight organization, try these simplified techniques (see also "Planning the Report," Section 6.1).

1. Arrange discussion in chronological order, for example:

(a) History   (Past)
(b) Current status   (Present)
(c) Recommendation
(d) Anticipated results   (Future)

1.

Please let me know if there is any further information you need.

2.

I'd appreciate your following this practice in the future.

3.

My investigation showed a definite lapse in our service to the Farmhill district agencies. I suggest this matter be discussed at our next monthly meeting.

4.

The next report from Mr. Kenny is due on the 15th of this month. I'll let you know then whether there has been any change in the picture.

5.

From the evidence it would appear that a few simple changes in procedure would help us meet our publication schedule without difficulty:

1. Advance the initial planning of the catalog to August 1 of each year.
2. Use a second printer for the color insert and send the printed inserts to the primary printer for binding into the catalog.
3. Employ a mailing house for addressing, wrapping, and mailing.

I'll be glad to discuss these proposals with you any time.

Figure 6-15 Examples of memorandum endings.

STILTED (BAD)

Pursuant to your memorandum re above, notice has been taken of the faulty carbon ribbons and said supplies will be returned forthwith to the stationer. Upon due receipt of a satisfactory explanation and replacement of same, the undersigned will contact you and advise.

INFORMAL (BETTER)

I am returning to the stationer the faulty carbon ribbons you mentioned in your memorandum of October 8, and I am asking for an explanation and satisfactory replacement.

I'll let you know the results.

- -

FORMAL (ACCEPTABLE)

According to the Manual of Procedures governing the operation of the cafeteria, bids on meat and poultry are to be obtained on a quarterly basis.

During the recent three-months' absence of the unit head, his duties were taken over by the chief of the Services Division. The chief, on his own authority, asked for bids on a weekly basis. When the cook prepared the weekly menu to determine the quantities needed, she submitted the list to the chief. He then telephoned three vendors and received quotations on the items. This method resulted in a saving of $1,775 over food costs for the same three-month period (January-March) last year.

In view of the indicated savings, it is recommended that the Service Division continue the practice of obtaining bids on meat and poultry on a weekly, rather than quarterly, basis.

Figure 6-16   Memorandums written in different styles.

2. Work for a simple balance of elements. For example:

(a) Problem—Solution
(b) Cause—Effect
(c) Fault—Remedy
(d) Need—Fulfillment
(e) Question—Answer
(f) Plan A—Plan B
(g) Old Way—New Way

3. Treat parallel points in parallel fashion, as in this list.

A good system for organizing the company's publication needs should have a threefold objective:
   A. Service to the company
   B. Economy of production
   C. Coordination among designer, user, and producer

Conclusion.   Whether or not there is a formal conclusion, the memorandum should have some significance that is expressed or implied.

1. The information may speak for itself and require no conclusion.

2. The conclusion (or recommendation) may have been stated at the beginning of the report so that restatement at the end is unnecessary.

3. Most likely, however, the memorandum will end with some conclusive statement like (a) a bid for cooperation, (b) an assurance of action, (c) a summary of the main points, or (d) a recommendation. Some examples appear in Figure 6-15.

Language.   Ordinarily, the memorandum uses informal or conversational language with normal contractions (*I'll, can't, won't*) and the personal pronouns *I* and *you*. In no circumstances, though, is it considered good form to use the stilted and outworn expressions that have already been so discredited in letter writing. The best style is always a natural one, though it may be pitched on a lower or higher level of dignity depending on the circumstances (Figure 6-16).

See also "Writing the Report," Section 6.2.

7

Publicity and Editorial Work

Office duties often entail a variety of editorial tasks. These may include editing manuscript, preparing copy for the printer, reading proof, and—on occasion—writing press releases and other material for publication. Work of this kind requires a good command of English and some special reserves of creativity, resourcefulness, and mental discipline. This chapter is designed to give office editors the basic information they need to carry on their work with confidence and proficiency.

CONTENTS

7.1 The Press Release   p. 266
7.2 Editing   p. 271
7.3 Preparing Copy for the Printer   p. 275
7.4 Proofreading   p. 278

7.1 THE PRESS RELEASE

A press release is information sent to the press in the hope that it will be published as news. The "press" may be the company's own newspaper or magazine, local daily or weekly newspapers, trade or professional publications, or the official organs of social and fraternal organizations. Many publications look to press releases for much of their news and publish them as received or with some editing to conform to their space and style requirements. For the source, the press release means valuable free publicity and often the difference between success and failure when a meeting or other event is announced.

Press releases for use outside the organization should always be cleared by the organization's public relations department or by the official in charge. This procedure permits control over the number, content, and timing of stories and ensures conformance with company policies. The control of stories sent to the editors of company publications usually rests with the individual departments in which the news originates. In any case, the chances of acceptance are increased when the story is prepared in a form suitable for publication.

Subjects of Press Releases.   In a dynamic organization, there is so much activity that an alert reporter has more trouble in choosing his stories than in finding them. Besides the news of sales, earnings, appointments, and organizational changes that show up in the company's official records, additional news is made all the time in the peripheral activities of employees and of all who sell and use the company's products. The following topics will only suggest the range.

Election of officers
New appointments
Promotions
Transfer of personnel
Organizational changes
Property and plant improvements
Mergers and acquisitions
New plants, stores, and offices
Ground-breaking and cornerstone-laying ceremonies
New lines, products, and services
Reports on sales, earnings, and dividends
Government contracts
New stock issues
Unusual product displays and sales stories
Unusual uses of the company's products and services
Prominent visitors
Honors, awards, and prizes
Contests
Company philanthropies
Charity and community work by employees
Professional and educational attainments of employees
Speeches and reports

Mechanical Form (Figure 7-1).   The form of the press release should serve the convenience of news editors.

1. Use white paper, size $8\frac{1}{2}$ by 11 inches, with a heading consisting of the name, address, and telephone number of the news source. Preferably include the name and telephone number of the individual to be called if more information is wanted. There is no advantage in using the regular company letterhead.

2. Type the release directly on the sheet or mimeograph it, but do not send carbons.

3. Double- or triple-space copy, with margins of at least an inch. The editor can be expected to do a lot of revising and cutting.

4. Type the release date under the heading in such form as "For Immediate Release," "For Release Wednesday, April 24," or "For Release at Will." A story sent to out-of-town newspapers usually carries a dateline at the beginning of the first paragraph, for example, "Athens, Ohio, March 16." The

AMERICAN FAMILY INSTITUTE
5200 Sunset Boulevard
Los Angeles, California 90027

FOR IMMEDIATE RELEASE

For further information:

September 7, 19--

Mrs. Leslie M. Peters
(213) 461-2345

NEW HOMEMAKING COURSE

"Less Work, More Fun in Homemaking" is the
title of a five-week series to be presented each
Tuesday afternoon from 1:30 to 3:00, beginning September 18, at the American Family Institute, 5200
Sunset Boulevard, Los Angeles. Designed for the
young wife and mother who is beset by dishes, diapers, and dirt, the course will have as its motto,
"Run your house; don't let your house run you."

The informal lectures and discussions will
deal with such problems as fatigue, the common
enemy of homemakers, and how to prevent it; making
a work schedule that is flexible yet efficient; and
teaching children to enjoy helping around the house.

Reservations for the course may be made by
writing or telephoning the Institute, 461-2345.

\# \# \# \# \#

Figure 7-1   Form of the press release.

place named is that of the story source, and the date is the anticipated date of release, not the date of mailing.

5. Number at the top all pages after the first. At the bottom of all pages except the last write the word *more* to indicate that there is additional copy. Mark the end of the story by a series of *x*'s or number signs (# # #) several spaces below the last line. Clip or staple pages together in the upper left-hand corner.

Writing the Release. A press release is written in the same style as a story in a good newspaper. It presents the facts in an interesting way, but without expressing the writer's opinions or judgments. The news values are achieved by giving the reader the answers to the questions *Who? What? Where? When?* and *Why?* or *How?* For example:

WHO is the central participant in the event?
WHO is making the announcement?
WHO is the authority for the statement?

WHAT is the title or other identification of the persons named?
WHAT happened (or will happen)?
WHAT are the details?
WHAT is the significance of the event?

WHERE did (or will) the event take place?
WHERE does the central participant live or work?
WHERE does the announcement originate?

WHEN did (or will) the event take place?
WHEN was the announcement of the event made?

WHY is the event taking place—what are the reasons or causes?

HOW will the event or proposal be accomplished?

The Lead. The nub of the story is stated in the headline, if one is supplied, and in the *lead,* or first sentence or two.

> Richmond, Va.—Allen G. McCabe, Jr., office manager and assistant treasurer, Crawford Manufacturing Co., has been elected president of the Richmond Chapter of the Administrative Management Society. He succeeds J. W. Montgomery, assistant controller, Southern States Cooperative, Inc.

The stories an editor is most likely to print are those specifically adapted to his publication and its readers. Although the following story originated in Boston, the lead capitalizes on the home address of the subject in order to appeal to East Orange residents.

> John S. Talbert of 200 Grove Street, East Orange, an associate of the David Marks, Jr., agency in New York City of the New England Life Insurance Company, has qualified for the company's Hall of Fame.
> The honor is awarded to the company's field representatives who, in the course of giving outstanding service to their clients, have placed with New England Life at least one million dollars' worth of life insurance protection on their policyholders during the preceding calendar year.
> Portraits of those honored are displayed in a special hall at the company's home office in Boston.

In sending this story to the subject's college alumni newspaper, the writer added the following sentence to the first paragraph.

Mr. Talbert is a graduate of New York University, Class of '62.

The following brief story ran in the monthly house organ of the subject's company. The interest for Mr. Berger's co-workers is self-evident.

PROTESTANT COUNCIL HONORS BERGER

Philip H. Berger, executive vice president, was honored at a testimonial luncheon held in the Regency Hotel by the Factors and Finance Division of the Protestant Council of New York.

Additional Details.   When paragraphs are added, it is good practice to put the most important details first and to make each paragraph self-contained. This permits an editor to cut off a story at the end of any paragraph without serious loss.

Details suitable for the expansion of a story include the following.

1. Biographical details.

Mr. Astor is with the Metropolitan Division and supervises the development and promotion of retail banking and special corporate services.

He is a 1970 graduate of the Stonier Graduate School of Banking at Rutgers University and has been with the bank since 1965.

2. Historical details.

Put together six years ago as an advertising promotion for the April auto loan campaign, the "sponge on wheels" has led to a number of awards. These include the Town Crier Award for the best ad by a commercial bank and trust company and the SCB Award for the best magazine ad by a commercial bank.

3. Description.

The new facility has a number of features to recommend it over the old quarters. It has a total of 7,500 square feet as opposed to the old quarters' 5,700 square feet. The building is constructed of poured concrete, with exposed concrete as part of the interior design.

4. Quotation.

Lawrence Ross, sales training coordinator, emphasizes that the primary objective of the program is fact finding, but he notes that collateral advantages add to the success of the program.

"Naturally," he says, "during the week that a management trainee is assigned to the program, he absorbs an invaluable amount of on-the-job training in the highly developed skill of customer contact. He can thus broaden his knowledge of business and businessmen in the greater Los Angeles area."

Special Suggestions.   Press releases that do not meet the requirements of the publications they are intended for are a waste of time and may even antagonize the editors. Follow these rules to avoid some common mistakes.

1. Study the publication carefully to discover what kinds of material are suitable for it.

2. Check every statement and every name and date for correctness. The editor must be able to rely on your accuracy.

3. Send out the story in time for publication on the release date. If possible, let newspapers have it several days in advance, but in no case later than several hours before press time. Magazines need more time—sometimes several weeks—to plan their editorial content.

4. When words like *today, tomorrow,* or *next Wednesday* appear in the story, prevent confusion by putting the actual date in parentheses immediately after them. For example: "The annual meeting of the D. M. Kirby Corporation will be held tomorrow (March 15) at its national headquarters, 60 Wall Street, New York."

5. Adapt your language to the reader. Use the simplest language for most stories, but be sure to write to technical and professional people on their own level.

6. Avoid puffery. Let the facts speak for themselves.

7. See that all photographs carry suitable captions. Typewrite each caption on a separate sheet of paper; then tape or paste the top to the back of the photograph so that the caption can be read at the bottom when the photograph is held face up. Never write on the back of the photograph.

7.2 EDITING

An editor is a person who reviews and revises or corrects reports, speeches, articles, and other manuscripts prepared by others. One reason an editor is needed is that while the office writer is an expert in his particular subject area, he often lacks proficiency in written expression. Another reason is that even with a mastery of written expression, the writer is usually too pressed for time to be able to give his writing the careful review it requires. A third reason is that with many people in an organization turning out manuscripts of different sorts, only an editor can ensure that uniform standards and a consistent style will be maintained.

The Editor's Functions.   A good editor is a genuine friend of the author. Essentially, he performs two functions.

1. He examines the manuscript for content and organization, and either suggests changes to the author or makes the changes himself contingent on the author's approval.

2. He copy-edits the manuscript to ensure consistency in style and correctness in names, facts, punctuation, grammar, and the like.

Some editors perform one function or the other; some perform both. In either case, an important asset for the editor is tact. Assuming that you have been chosen for the role of editor, you should not try to impose your ideas on the author, for he is likely to resent it and your job will become untenable. A better approach is to make suggestions of such a kind and in such a manner that the author will recognize the improvement and will be grateful for the assistance offered. Of course many, if not most, of the errors you find will be so obvious that clearance with the author is not necessary; he expects you to find them and he will be disappointed if you do not.

Editing for Content and Structure. You should not attempt to make suggestions about the content of a manuscript unless you have some familiarity with the subject area and the audience. If you feel insecure in these matters, you may consult with the author to resolve any doubts you may have or, with the author's permission, seek the opinion and advice of some other person with the necessary qualifications. Taking the latter course is no reflection on the editor, who is not expected to be an expert in every field.

JUDGING A MANUSCRIPT

The Beginning
>   Does it spark the reader's interest?
>   Does it adequately suggest the content of the paper?
>   Does it lead quickly to the main point?

The Body
>   Is the organization logical and consistent?
>   Is the relation between the parts readily apparent?
>   Is the text clear and convincing?
>   Is enough use made of detail, example, comparison, and the like?
>   Can anything be left out, with resultant improvement?
>   Is interest maintained throughout?

The End
>   By summary or otherwise, does the end pull together the whole piece?
>   Is the end conclusive?
>   Is the conclusion warranted by the evidence presented in the body?

General
>   Is the title reasonably short, and does it accurately describe the tone and content of the text?
>   Is reasonable use made of tables, charts, and other illustrations to support and clarify the text?
>   Where appropriate, has the author made adequate use of headings and enumerations to add to the attractiveness of the text and make reading easy?

Figure 7-2   An editor's guide.

Questions you should be able to answer (or find the answers to) with respect to the content of any manuscript are these.

Does the author have a worthy subject?
Is the author competent to write on the subject?
Is the paper factually correct?
Is the subject matter up-to-date?
Is the treatment of the subject on a level suited to the reader?

Even without a great deal of expertise in a technical field, you should be able to judge the structure of a paper and make suggestions for improvement. An editor's guide to the organization of a manuscript—which may be equally useful to the writer—will be found in Figure 7-2. (See also "Report Preparation," Chapter 6.)

Copy Editing.   In most instances your editing chores will probably be confined to copy editing. In this task, you will correct errors and inconsistencies, but you will not attempt to evaluate the content or organization of the material.

Reference Tools.   You should have a good dictionary (preferably unabridged), a handbook of English, and a thesaurus. Some specific titles are suggested in Figure 7-3. If you are working in a specialized area (like accounting or insurance), you should also have a handbook on the subject, if one is available, and a dictionary or glossary of the technical terms used. (See the book lists in "Information Sources," Section 5.2, and the "Dictionary of

---

AN EDITOR'S REFERENCE SHELF

Bartlett, John. *Familiar Quotations*. 14th rev. ed. Boston: Little, Brown & Co., 1968.

Fowler, H. W. *A Dictionary of Modern English Usage*. 2d ed. revised by Sir Ernest Gowers. New York: Oxford University Press, 1965.

GPO Style Manual. Rev. ed. Washington, D.C.: U.S. Government Printing Office, 1967.

Manual of Style. 12th ed. Chicago: University of Chicago Press, 1968.

New American Roget's College Thesaurus. New York: World Publishing Co., 1969.

Perrin, Porter G., and others. *Writer's Guide and Index to English*. 4th ed. Chicago: Scott, Foresman & Co., 1966.

Random House Dictionary of the English Language (Unabridged). New York: Random House, 1966.

Webster's Dictionary of Synonyms. Springfield, Mass.: G. & C. Merriam Co., 1968.

Figure 7-3 Standard reference works for the copy editor.

ADVANCEMENT

General. The Bank ~~recognizes that the~~ 's success ~~of the organization is entirely~~ dependent ~~upon~~ on the

competence and character of ~~the men and women who~~ ~~comprise it's~~ its staff. (For that reason it has designed) (1) Policies ~~relating to advancement, as other personnel~~ policies, ~~are designed~~ to

attract and retain an able staff; (2) to ~~utilize fully~~ use their

~~the~~ knowledge, ~~skill, ability, and~~ interests ~~of each~~, and abilities to the fullest; (3) ~~individual,~~ to provide the incentive for excellence; (4) to maintain stable employment; and (5) to recognize the

dignity of each staff member, ~~as a person.~~ filled in the Bank are

~~It is the bank's policy to fill~~ Vacancies, when-

ever possible by reassigning members of the ~~present~~

staff. Only when qualified candidates are not avail-

able in its own ranks does the Bank ~~do we~~ recruit employees elsewhere.

In considering candidates for advancement, the

are: an objective?

supervisor must make a personal selection based on

merit. Included in this judgment ~~is~~ are the ~~staff mem-ber's competence in~~ individuals' past ~~assignments~~ performance, ~~relevant~~ apti-

tudes, ~~individual~~ and interests, ~~and constructive attitudes,~~ as well as his educational and work experi-

ence. The choice of one candidate over another

Figure 7-4   Example of an edited manuscript.

Business Terms," Chapter 16.) Other reference materials you should have are any instructions on style published by your own company for the guidance of its writers, secretaries, or typists. Unless there are good reasons for doing otherwise, you should adhere to the rules prescribed in those instructions.

Making Corrections.   Working with a lead pencil, rather than a pen, gives you the opportunity to change your mind without messing up the manuscript. You should indicate small corrections by drawing a line through a word or punctuation mark and inserting the replacement between the lines, using a caret (∧) to show where the insertion belongs. If more room is needed, you may use the top or bottom margins. Queries for the author should be put in the side margins next to the copy to which they apply, and they should be circled to prevent confusion with actual corrections. If changes are heavy, retype pages or parts of pages to make the amended version.

Editing Procedure.   The following steps are recommended.

1. Correct typographical errors.

2. Correct dates, proper names, and obvious errors in fact. If you think the author has to be persuaded, note the source of your information in the margin.

3. Correct errors in spelling, punctuation, grammar, and word usage. If a usage is optional, be guided first by the need for clarity, then by consistency with your standards. If there is some question, give the author the benefit of the doubt.

4. Take out or rearrange words to achieve conciseness and relieve awkwardness of expression, but be sure you preserve the sense and general tone of the manuscript. If in doubt, query the author on the proposed change.

5. Keep an alphabetical list of stylistic peculiarities. For example, *May 23rd* (as opposed to *May 23*), *advisor* (as opposed to *adviser*), *COD* (as opposed to *C.O.D.*). When you come across a question relating to these forms later in the manuscript, you will be able to choose the style you chose earlier. Otherwise, disturbing inconsistencies will result.

6. Question, in the margin, apparent inconsistencies in reasoning, seeming omissions, and dubious assertions. Unilaterally changing the author's statements can lead you into serious error.

An example of an edited manuscript is shown in Figure 7-4.

7.3 PREPARING COPY FOR THE PRINTER

Manuscripts of reports, speeches, and other documents need special attention if they are to be sent to a commercial printer for typesetting. Similar attention must be given to any manuscript prepared for publication in a book or magazine. The principal objective is to ensure accuracy, but another aim is to obtain a printed appearance that accords with the wishes of the author and the editor.

It is assumed that the printer has some model to follow or that he or a by setting forth the responsibilities and authori-

ties delegated to particular positions, the rela-

tionships that exist among positions, and the ac-

countabilities of the incumbent managers.[1]

---

[1]For a fuller discussion see "What's in a Posi-

tion Guide?" <u>Management Record</u>, September 1969.

If there is confusion about accountability, a

manager may fulfill only part of his responsibilities

under the impression that other parts of the job are

in another bailiwick. He may . . .

Figure 7-5   Placement of footnote in printer's copy.

designer has planned the printed product with regard to form, paper, page size, and typographical treatment. The editor's attention may then be confined to the manuscript itself. For best results, the following suggestions should be followed.

1. See that the copy is typed on one side of plain white 8½ by 11 inch paper, heavy and strong enough to withstand rough treatment.

This is set in Roman.
This is set in italic.
THIS IS SET IN ALL CAPS.
This Is Set in Caps and Lower Case.
THIS IS SET IN CAPS AND SMALL CAPS.
This is set in boldface.

Figure 7-6   Type styles.

(A) Cropping

Extraneous background on photographs and drawings may be eliminated by cropping. Draw arrows in margin to show what portions are to be retained. Mark size desired along one dimension and the other dimension will be reduced in proportion.

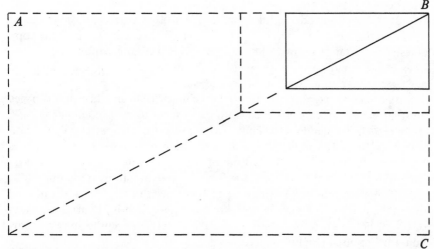

(B) Scaling

Pictures always reduce or enlarge along their diagonal. To scale a picture to fit a given space, draw a rectangle the size of the space to be filled; then draw a diagonal line from the upper right corner to the lower left corner and extending for some distance beyond. Any rectangle formed by angle *ABC* along the diagonal will have the same proportions. If it is desired to retain the proportion of the original drawing or photograph, the size of the reduction or enlargement may be ascertained in the same way.

Figure 7-7 Instructions for cropping and scaling pictures.

2. Leave at least a one-inch margin all around, and preferably an inch and a half at the left.

3. If several persons type the manuscript, see that the same style and size of type are used throughout; otherwise it is difficult to estimate the number of words—a matter of some importance to the typesetter.

4. Use double-spacing throughout.

(a) If the copy includes a long quotation that is to be set off from the text by indentation or a smaller type-face, draw a pencil line down the left-hand margin for the entire length of the quotation. This will call the printer's attention to it.

(b) Start a footnote directly following the line in which the reference to it appears; double-space the footnote and separate it from the text by a rule above and below the note (Figure 7-5).

5. Use upper and lower case (capitals and small letters) throughout the manuscript, including titles and heads. That leaves the typographer free to style the copy in any way he desires. If your mind is made up, however, you may use the standard printers' marks to specify bold face, italics, all caps, caps and small caps (Figure 7-6).

6. Underline on the typewriter all words in the text that should be set in italics (see "Underlining," Section 10.4).

7. If the copy includes printed matter from other sources, paste the copy neatly on the regular manuscript paper with rubber cement. (Typing the copy takes time, requires proofreading, and involves the danger of error.) If both sides of a printed page are to be used, obtain two copies of the original or make a photographic copy of the second side.

8. Number all pages consecutively in the upper right-hand corner. If pages must later be inserted, mark them with the number of the preceding page and the letters *A, B, C,* and so on. Thus, if you insert two pages after page 12, you will mark them *12A* and *12B.* Also, at the bottom of page 12 write "Pages 12A and 12B follow"; at the bottom of page 12B write, "Page 13 follows." Handwriting in dark pencil or ink will make these notations stand out.

9. If photographs or drawings are to be reduced in size, mark the desired size in the margin. If a photograph is to be *cropped,* that is, if part of the sides or top or bottom is to be cut off, draw arrows in the margin to show the part you want omitted (Figure 7-7).

10. Do not write on the back of a photograph. Type the caption on a separate slip of paper and paste it to the back of the photograph so that it hangs from the bottom edge.

7.4   PROOFREADING

Except when typewritten copy is photographed directly for reproduction, the printer will set the copy and submit proofs for correction before the work is put on the press.

Two kinds of proofs are offered: galley proofs, which are long sheets containing about three pages of material, and page proofs, which include the corrections made in the galleys and represent the final submission before printing. Unless you ask for more, the printer will submit two sets of both galley and page proofs. One set will contain his queries. These are marginal notations that may question a word or spelling or alert the proofreader to the possibility that some copy has been omitted. The queried set should be returned, corrected, to the printer. The other set, with all the corrections carefully copied, should be kept for reference. The original manuscript always accompanies the galley proofs. It should be used for checking the proof and returned to the printer with the corrected galleys, but no marks should ever be added to it.

Proofreader's Marks

1. Use a sharp black pencil, but one that will not smudge. Ink or crayon is also acceptable if the color is different from that used in the printer's queries. Pencil corrections can of course be changed more easily.

2. Answer every query by (a) striking out the query if it does not apply and writing "O.K. as set"; (b) striking out only the question mark if the printer's correction is valid; or (c) striking out the query and writing in the copy correction.

3. Draw a line through the incorrect material, insert a caret, and use other standard proofreading marks to call attention to an error; then write the correction in the nearer margin. Do not squeeze corrections between the lines, as you do in correcting manuscript (Figures 7-8 and 7-9).

4. If only a letter requires correction, write only the letter, not the whole word in the margin; but if you think the correction may be misunderstood, write the whole word as well, and circle it.

5. When a line contains more than one error, place corrections in the margin in the same order as they occur in the line, and separate them by a slant (/).

Galley Proofs

1. Read galley proofs for content, and then again for typographical errors. The first reading will ensure against inadvertent omissions, misplacement of material, and perpetuation of substantive errors in the original copy. The second reading will uncover errors in spelling, punctuation, numbers, spacing, type style, and so on.

2. Make only necessary changes. Because the pages have not yet been made up when the galleys are submitted, there is some leeway permitted in changing copy and making additions to the original. The author and the proofreader should be aware, however, that these changes may be costly, and that it is always preferable to make changes before the copy goes to the printer. Changes in format also require expensive resetting of copy. A way to

Mark	Explanation	Sample of Marked Proof	Corrected Proof
Punctuation Marks			
ˇ	Apostrophe	The authorˇs work.	The author's work.
[/]	Brackets	He∧the author]wrote.	He [the author] wrote.
: /	Colon	The author wrote∧	The author wrote:
⌃	Comma	The author wrote∧	The author wrote,
|—|	Dash	The author∧John Smith.	The author—John Smith.
. . . /	Ellipsis	The author∧wrote.	The author . . . wrote.
= /	Exclamation point	He has style∧	He has style!
= /	Hyphen	The author∧editor relationship.	The author-editor relationship.
⟨2⟩	Inferior letter or figure	CO∧	CO_2
(/)	Parentheses	The author∧John Smith∧ wrote.	The author (John Smith) wrote.
⊙	Period	The author wrote∧	The author wrote.
? /	Question mark	Is he the author∧	Is he the author?
⟨⟨ ⟩⟩	Quotation marks	He wrote∨Fantasy in F∨	He wrote "Fantasy in F."
; /	Semicolon	He wrote∧he spoke.	He wrote; he spoke.
⟨1⟩	Superior letter or figure	The author∧wrote.	The author[1] wrote.
Type Style			
ital	Set in italic	The author wrote.	The *author* wrote.
rom	Change from italic to roman	The (author) wrote.	The author wrote.
l.c.	Set in lower case	The Author wrote.	The author wrote.
caps	Set in capitals	the author wrote.	The author wrote.
c. & l.c.	Set in capitals and lower case	THE AUTHOR SPEAKS	The Author Speaks.
s.c.	Set in small caps	The author wrote.	THE AUTHOR SPEAKS.
c. & s.c.	Set in caps and small caps	The author speaks.	THE AUTHOR SPEAKS.
b.f.	Set in boldface	The author wrote.	The **author** wrote.
l.f.	Set in lightface (not boldface)	The author wrote.	The author wrote.

Other Marks

Mark	Meaning	Marked copy	Corrected copy
ℰ	Delete; take out	The author wrote.	The author wrote.
( )	Close up; no space	The aut hor wrote.	The author wrote.
℘	Delete and close up	The author wrrote.	The author wrote.
⋏	Insert	The auth wrote.	The author wrote.
𝟫	Turn inverted letter	The author wrote.	The author wrote.
stet	Let it stand; change made was wrong	The author wrote.	The author wrote.
sp	Spell out	23¢	23 cents
tr	Transpose	The wrote author.	The author wrote.
¶	Start new paragraph	in this manner. The author wrote.	in this manner. The author wrote.
No ¶	No paragraph; run in	manner. The author wrote.	manner. The author wrote.
↧	Push down unwanted type slug	The author wrote.	The author wrote.
#	Make a space	The authorwrote.	The author wrote.
eq #	Equalize space	The author wrote.	The author wrote.
⊗	Broken letter	The author wrote.	The author wrote.
w.f.	Wrong font (type style)	The author wrote.	The author wrote.
□	Indent one em	The author wrote.	The author wrote.
Center	Center copy on line	The Author Speaks	The Author Speaks
⌐┐	Raise the word or letter	The author wrote.	The author wrote.
⌐⌐	Lower the word or letter	The author wrote.	The author wrote.
⌐	Bring matter to the right	The author wrote.	The author wrote.
=	Align type	in this manner. The author wrote.	in this manner. The author wrote.
=	Straighten line	The author wrote.	The author wrote.

Figure 7-8 Proofreader's marks.

281

PRODUCTION

flush right
c. + l.c.

no ¶/s.c. From the day the manuscript is turned over to the production division to the day the finished book is published, usually nine to twelve months will elapse. In the first few weeks of

this time, a final check is made on the length of the manuscript and the cost of production, including composition, printing and binding of the text and the engraving of the illustrations. At the same time, sample pages, which show the typography and format chosen for the book by the designer, are prepared.

b.f. Sample Pages

Indent 1 em The material for sample pages is carefully chosen to show all typographical examples to appear in a book: sections of the body of the text, sections of extract material, footnotes, bibliography, mathematical, chemical and phonetic symbols, running heads, tables, etc.

run in On approval of the ~~the~~ sample pages by the department, they are forwarded to the author for his examination and checking. It is essential that the author make his suggestions for changes at this time. It is too late to make changes after the compositor has started setting the book.

b.f. Copyediting

Before composition is ordered, a copyeditor indicates in the manuscript the typography for each section of the text and corrects errors in grammar, spelling and punctuation, and the

OK as set? (major) inconsistencies that invariably occur. As a result of his work, the manuscript may be more accurate technically and

rom. more consistent, but the (quality) of writing will not be significantly improved. It is the author's responsibility to present his work clearly and effectively. If in the opinion of the copyeditor

stet ~~and the department,~~ the manuscript needs further work, it may be returned to the author, but only after the editor has discussed the problem with the author.

The copyedited manuscript is returned to the author for final checking, along with a list of the stylistic standards which were followed by the copyeditor. The copyeditor / may query the author on points of style or fact that the author may need to reconsider; these queries may be indicated in the margins of the manuscript, flagged, or listed on a separate sheet. All such queries must be answered before the manuscript is returned.

As will be noted later under Corrections, an author's alterations in proof can be expensive to him.

l.c.

tr.

∂#

b.f./ˇ

Figure 7-9 A typeset page after proofreading.

avoid such changes is to consult with the printer beforehand on the typographical design, even to the extent of having sample pages set.

3. Plan changes for minimum resetting of type. When copy changes or additions are to be made in the galleys, it is better if they occur toward the end of a paragraph. If a change is made near the beginning of a paragraph, the whole paragraph may have to be reset. When a phrase must be changed, it is desirable that the substitute copy occupy the same amount of space. In that way, resetting can be restricted to a line or two. The best way to measure space in a line of set copy is to count the number of type characters, including the spaces between words.

4. When lengthy additions are to be made, type each addition on a separate slip of paper, marking the slips with the galley number and the letters *A, B, C,* and so on. Then, using paste or Scotch Tape (not clips or staples), attach each slip to the appropriate place in the margin of the galley, and mark the proof to show where the copy is to be added.

Page Proofs

1. Check to see that the corrections in the galleys have been made as marked.

2. Proofread carefully any parts that have been added (for example, titles, running heads, and page numbers).

3. Read the end and the beginning of each page to make sure that the sequence is correct and that no lines have been omitted. (If the galleys have been read carefully in the first place, it is not necessary to reread the whole proof, although that may be done as a precaution.)

4. Make small copy changes, if necessary, for typographic reasons. For example, a very short top line ending a paragraph (called a *widow*) should if possible be filled out a bit with additional words, and copy that overruns the bottom margin by a line or two should be shortened. (Discretion must be used here; obviously a speech or article that is being reprinted verbatim cannot be altered without the consent of the author.)

8

Correct English Usage

Because business is always sensitive to its image—or what others think of it—it places a high value on the use of good English in its communications. A misspelled word, an incorrect word, or a grammatical error is bad not only because it may distort the sense, but also because it gives a bad impression of the organization and of the writer and the typist. Conversely, good English helps to build trust and confidence.

For anyone who cares about good English, a good dictionary is the one indispensable tool (Figure 8-1). To get the most out of it, study the introductory notes, acquaint yourself with the pronunciation key, and note the meanings of the many symbols that explain the forms, definitions, and usages of the words (Figure 8-2).

Unabridged Dictionaries

Random House Dictionary of the English Language (Unabridged Edition)
Webster's Third New International Dictionary of the English Language

Abridged Dictionaries

American College Dictionary
American Heritage Dictionary of the English Language
Funk & Wagnalls Standard College Dictionary
Random House Dictionary of the English Language (College Edition)
Webster's Seventh New Collegiate Dictionary
Webster's New World Dictionary (Second College Edition)

Figure 8-1 Dictionaries suitable for office use.

Collected in this chapter are some quick guides to the questions of usage that are most likely to arise in the business office.

CONTENTS ·

8.1 Spelling Guide   p. 285
8.2 Words Often Confused   p. 293

8.3   Glossary of Common Grammatical Terms   p. 303
8.4   Grammar Review   p. 308
8.5   Dictionary of English Usage   p. 323

For "Punctuation," see Chapter 9. For guides to "Mechanical Style" (abbreviations, capitals, numbers, underlining, and word division), see Chapter 10.

8.1 SPELLING GUIDE

Although English spelling is difficult, business people generally manage to cope with it. At any rate, it is comforting to know that some of the most troublesome words do conform to a few reasonably simple rules, and the others can at least be isolated and identified. An occasional review helps to fix the correct forms in mind.

Useful Rules.   *Words Ending in Silent* E.   A silent *e* at the end of a word is usually dropped before a suffix beginning with a vowel, but retained before a suffix beginning with a consonant.

advise, advisable	advise, advisement
continue, continuous	bare, barely
imagine, imaginary	care, careless
make, making	judge, judgment (exception)
sale, salable	hope, hopeful

Words ending in *ce* or *ge* retain the silent *e* before a suffix beginning with *a* or *o*.

advantageous	enforceable
changeable	manageable
courageous	noticeable

The silent *e* is also retained when mispronunciation or confusion with other words might result.

eyeing (*not* eying)	lineage (ancestry)
mileage (*not* milage)	linage (number of lines)
dyeing (changing the color)	
dying (expiring)	

Final Consonant.   Before adding a suffix to a word ending in a single final consonant following a single vowel, double the consonant if (1) the accent is on the last syllable, and (2) the suffix begins with a vowel.

allot, allotted, allotting
begin, beginning
control, controlled, controlling
occur, occurred, occurring
refer, referred, referring

provender

Catchword

Vocabulary entry

Etymology

Syllabication dots

Pronunciation

Loan phrase

Variant plural pronounced

Diagram and caption

Definition

Variant principal parts

Grammatical information

Variant spelling

Homograph number (separates words spelled identically but of different derivation)

Syntactic information

Example sentence

Alternate pronunciation

Capitalization style

Synonym list

Geographical entry (location, population and date, foreign name)

Verb inflected forms (past tense and past participle; present participle)

Cross reference to multiple-word entry

Usage label

Cross reference to one-word entry

Adjective inflected forms (comparative, superlative)

Idiomatic phrase

Example phrase

Mythological entry

Abbreviation

---

per·cept (pûr′sept), n. 1. the mental result or product of perceiving, as distinguished from the act of perceiving. 2. that which is perceived, the object of perception. [< L perceptum) something perceived, n. use of neut. of perceptus. pp. of percipere to PERCEIVE]

per·cep·ti·ble (pər sep′tə bəl) adj. capable of being perceived; recognizable; appreciable. [< LL perceptibil(is)] —per·cep′ti·bil′i·ty, per·cep′ti·ble·ness, n. —per·cep′ti·bly, adv. —Syn. discernible, apparent.

per di·em (pər dē′əm, dī′əm), 1. by the day. 2. a daily allowance, usually for living expenses while traveling in connection with one's work. [< L]

per·i·car·di·um (per′ə kär′dē əm), n., pl. -di·a (-dē ə). Anat. the membranous sac enclosing the heart. [< NL < Gk perikárdion, n. use of neut. of perikárdios heart-surrounding. See PERI-, CARDI-, -OUS] —per′i·car′di·al, adj.

per·i·carp (per′ə kärp′), n. 1. Bot. the walls of a ripened ovary or fruit, sometimes consisting of three layers, the epicarp, mesocarp, and endocarp. 2. a membranous envelope around the cystocarp of red algae. 3. a seed vessel. [< NL pericarp(ium) < Gk perikárpion pod] —per′i·car′pi·al, per′i·car′pic, adj. —per′i·car·poi′dal, adj.

ABC, Pericarp; of fruit of peach; A, Epicarp; B, Mesocarp; C, Endocarp

per·il (per′əl), n., v., -iled, -il·ing or (esp. Brit.) -illed, -il·ling. —n. 1. exposure to injury, loss, or destruction; risk; jeopardy; danger. —v.t. 2. to expose to danger; imperil; risk. [ME < OF < L perícul(um) trial, test, danger] —Syn. 1. See danger.

per·i·o·don·tics (per′ē ə don′tiks), n. (construed as sing.) the branch of dentistry dealing with the study and treatment of diseases of the bone, connective tissue, and gum surrounding and supporting a tooth. Also, per·i·o·don·tia (per′ē ə don′sha, -shē ə). [< NL; see PERI-, -ODONT, -UM, -ICS] —per′i·o·don′tic, adj.

perk[1] (pûrk), v.i. 1. to act, or carry oneself, in a jaunty manner. 2. to become lively or vigorous, as after depression or sickness (usually fol. by up): She began to perk up during dinner. 3. to put oneself forward briskly or presumptuously. —v.t. 4. to raise smartly or briskly (often fol. by up or out): to perk one's head up. 5. to dress smartly; make trim or jaunty (sometimes fol. by up or out): to perk up a suit with a new blouse. [ME perke(n)? ? akin to PEER?] —adj. 6. perky; jaunty. —perk′ing·ly, adv. —perk′ish, adj.

perk[2] (pûrk), v.t., v.i. Informal. to percolate: Is the coffee perking yet? [by shortening]

pil·grim (pil′grim, -grəm), n. 1. a person who journeys, esp. a long distance, to some sacred place as an act of devotion. 2. a traveler or wanderer. 3. (cap.) one of the Pilgrim Fathers. [early ME pilegrim, pelegrim, < OFrs pilegrim, MLG pelegrim, OHG piligrīm, Icel pīlagrīmr, all < ML pelegrīnus, dissimilated var. of L peregrīnus alien < peregrē abroad = per- PER- + -egr- (comb. form of ager field; see ACRE) + -ē adv. suffix] —Syn. 2. wayfarer, sojourner.

Pil·sen (pil′zən), n. a city in Bohemia, in W Czechoslovakia. 141,736 (1963). Czech, Plzeň.

pin (pin), n., v., pinned, pin·ning. —n. 1. a short, slender piece of metal with a point at one end and a head at the other, for fastening things together. 2. a small, slender, often pointed piece of wood, metal, etc., used to fasten, support, or attach things. 3. any of various forms of fasteners, ornaments, or badges consisting essentially or partly of a pointed or penetrating wire or shaft (often used in combination): a fraternity pin; a tiepin. 4. a short metal rod, as a linchpin, driven through the holes of adjacent parts, as a hub and an axle, to keep them together. 5. a short cylindrical rod or tube, as a wristpin or crankpin, joining two parts so as to permit them to move in one plane relative to each other. 6. the part of a cylindrical key stem that enters a lock. 7. a clothespin. 8. a hairpin. 9. See rolling pin. 10. a peg, nail, or stud marking the center of a target. 11. Bowling. one of the rounded wooden clubs set up as the target in tenpins, duckpins, etc. 12. Golf. the flagstaff that identifies a hole. 13. Usually, pins. Informal. the legs. 14. Music. peg (def. 2). 15. Wrestling. a fall. 16. Naut. See belaying pin. 17. a very small amount; a trifle. —v.t. 18. to fasten or attach with or as with a pin or pins. 19. to hold fast in a spot or position. 20. to give one's fraternity pin to (a girl) as a pledge of one's fondness or attachment. 21. Wrestling. to obtain a fall over one's opponent. 22. pin down, a. to bind or hold to a course of action, a promise, etc. b. to define with clarity and precision; to pin down some vague intuition. 23. pin something on someone, Slang. to blame someone for something on the basis of real or manufactured evidence. [ME pinne, OE pinn peg; c. D pin, G Pinne, Icel pinni; ? akin to MIr benn (for *bend), now beann peak, steeple, gable, etc.]

pin·y (pī′nē), adj. pin·i·er, pin·i·est. 1. abounding in, covered with, or consisting of pine trees. 2. pertaining to or suggestive of pine trees: a piny fragrance. Also, piney.

Pi·rith·o·üs (pi rith′ō əs), n. Class. Myth. a prince of the Lapithae and friend of Theseus, in whose company he attempted to abduct Persephone from Hades.

pk. pl. pks. (in dry measure) peck.

Figure 8-2 A page from a desk dictionary, with explanatory notes. (From the Student Guide of the Random House Dictionary, College Edition, Copyright 1969, 1968, by Random House, Inc. Reprinted by permission.)

Annotation labels (left column):

- Italicized entry
- Language label
- Historical entry
- Archaic label
- Antonym list
- Cross reference to hidden entry
- Symbol
- Hyphenated entry
- Subject label
- Comparison
- Combining form
- Illustration and caption (taxonomic name and size)
- Regional label
- Chemical formula
- Hidden entry
- Variant form
- Pronunciation key

Annotation labels (right column):

- Parts of speech
- Consecutive definition numbers
- Etymological cross reference to foreign word
- Synonym study
- Example in synonym study
- Usage study
- Example in usage study
- Stressed multiple-word entry
- Run-on entry
- Biographical entry (dates, nationality, profession)
- Foreign pronunciation
- Lower-case style
- Spot map
- Etymological cross reference to dictionary entry
- Cross reference to synonym study

Dictionary entries (first column):

per·manent press', (of a fabric) wrinkle-resistant and requiring little or no ironing after washing.

per men·sem (per men'səm; *Eng.* pər men'səm), *Latin* by the month.

Per·sia (pûr'zhə, -shə), n. 1. Also called **Per'sian Em'pire.** an ancient empire located in W and SW Asia: at its height it extended from Egypt and the Aegean to India; conquered by Alexander the Great 334–331 B.C. 2. former official name (until 1935) of **Iran.** [< L. var. of *Persis* < Gk < OPers *Pârsa*]

per·spi·ca·cious (pûr'spə kā'shəs), adj. 1. having keen mental perception; discerning. 2. (Arch.) having keen sight. [PERSPICAC(ITY) +-OUS] —**per·spi·ca'cious·ly,** adv. —**per·spi·ca'cious·ness,** n. —Syn. 1. perceptive, acute, penetrating. —Ant. 1. dull, stupid.

Pe·ru'vian rhat'a·ny [See under rhatany (def. 1)]

Ph, *Chem.* phenyl.

phase-out (fāz'out'), n. the act or an instance of phasing out: *A phase-out of obsolete production methods is essential.*

phase' rule', *Physical Chem.* a law that the number of degrees of freedom in a system in equilibrium is equal to two plus the number of components less the number of phases. Thus, a system of ice, melted ice, and water vapor, being one component and three phases, has no degrees of freedom. Cf. variance (def. 4).

-phasia a learned borrowing from Greek, used in the formation of compound words to refer to speech disorders: *aphasia.* Also, **-phasy.** [< Gk, comb. form akin to *phánai* to speak]

Ph.D., See **Doctor of Phi·losophy.** [< L *Philosophiae Doctor*]

pheas·ant (fez'ənt), n. 1. any of numerous large, usually long-tailed, gallinaceous birds of the family Phasianidae, of the Old World. 2. [*Southern U.S.*] the ruffed grouse. 3. any of various other birds that resemble or suggest a pheasant. [ME *fesaunt* < AF, OF *fesan* < L *phāsiānus* < Gk *phāsiānós (órnis)* (bird) of the Phasis River]

Ring-necked pheasant, *Phasianus colchicus* (Length to 3 ft.)

phe·no·bar·bi·tal (fē'nō bär'bi tal', -tôl', -nə-), n. Pharm. a white powder, used as a sedative, a hypnotic, and as an antispasmodic in epilepsy. Also called **phenylethylmalonylurea**

act, āble, dâre, ärt; ebb, ēqual; if, īce; hot, ōver, ôrder; oil; bŏŏk, ōōze; out; up, ûrge; ə = a as in alone; chief; sing; shoe; thin; that; zh as in measure; ə as in button. [See feed]

Dictionary entries (second column):

plan (plan), n., v., **planned, plan·ning.** —n. 1. a method of action or procedure. 2. a design or scheme of arrangement: *an elaborate plan for seating guests.* 3. a project or definite purpose: *plans for the future.* 4. a drawing made to scale to represent the top view or a horizontal section of a structure or a machine. 5. a map or diagram: *a plan of the dock area.* 6. (in perspective drawing) one of several planes in front of a represented object, and perpendicular to the line between the object and the eye. —v.t. 7. to arrange or project a plan or scheme for (any work, enterprise, or proceeding); *to plan a new recreation center; to plan one's vacation.* 8. to draw or make a plan of, as a building; design. —v.i. 9. to make a plan: *to plan for one's retirement.* [< L *plân(us)* level. See PLANE¹, PLAIN¹]

—Syn. 1. plot, formula, system. PLAN, PROJECT, DESIGN, SCHEME imply a formulated method of doing something. PLAN refers to any method of thinking out acts and purposes beforehand: *What are your plans for today?* A PROJECT is a proposed or tentative plan, often elaborate or extensive: *an irrigation project.* DESIGN suggests art, dexterity, or craft (sometimes evil and selfish) in the elaboration or execution of a plan, and often tends to emphasize the purpose in view (*a disturbance brought about by design*) A SCHEME is apt to be either a speculative, possibly impractical, plan, or a selfish or dishonest one: *a scheme to swindle someone.*

4. Unabr. Many teachers object to the phrase PLAN ON (followed by a gerund) considering its poor style for PLAN TO (followed by an infinitive): *I had planned to go to the movies tonight* (not *I had planned on going to the movies tonight*).

pop' art', a style in the fine arts characterized chiefly by forms and images derived from comic strips and advertising posters. —**pop' art'ist.**

Pow·ys (pō'is), n. **John Cowper,** 1872–1963, and his brother, **Theodore Francis,** 1875–1953, English authors.

Pro·ven·çale (prō'vän säl', prô'van-; *Fr.* prô vän säl'), *adj.* *Cookery.* (*sometimes l.c.*) prepared with garlic or garlic and tomato. [< F; fem. of PROVENÇAL]

Pro·vence (prô väns'; *Eng.* prə väns'), n. a region in SE France, bordering on the Mediterranean: formerly a province; famous for medieval poetry and courtly traditions.

prov·en·der (prov'ən dər), n. 1. dry food for livestock or other domestic animals. 2. food; provisions. [ME *prov·endre* < OF, var. of *provende, provende* < ML *prōbenda,* L *praebenda* what is to be supplied, prob. orig. neut. pl. of *praebendus,* ger. of *praebere, prēbere* to supply, var. of *praehibēre;* see PREBEND, PROVIDE] —Syn. See feed.

Province (spot map): DAUPHINÉ, LANGUEDOC, ITALY, Nice, Marseilles, MEDITERRANEAN SEA, SPAIN.

But no doubling of the consonant occurs when the accent is *not* on the last syllable.

    benefited
    canceling
    profited

If the accent shifts to an earlier syllable when the suffix is added, do not double the final consonant.

    prefer, preferred, preference

  Some exceptions:

    write, writing, BUT written (change in pronunciation)
    train, trained, training, trainee (final consonant preceded by two vowels)
    tax, taxes (NOT taxxes; word ending in *x* excepted from rule)

Final Y.   When a final *y* is preceded by a consonant, change the *y* to *i* before adding any suffix except one beginning with *i*. When the final *y* is preceded by a vowel, keep the *y*.

    carry, carries, carrying   *y preceded by vowel:*
    happy, happier, happiness   dismay, dismayed, dismaying
    likely, likelihood   employ, employer, employing
    marry, marriage, marrying   stay, stayed, staying
    plenty, plentiful   survey, surveyed, surveying
    worry, worrisome

  Some exceptions:

    day, daily   lay, laid   say, said
    dry, dryly,   pay, paid   wry wryly

The Rule of Addition.   When you add a prefix or suffix, or combine two words, and the last letter of the first part of the word is the same as the first letter of the second part, be sure that you retain both letters.

    dissatisfied   barrenness
    illiterate   meanness
    immaterial   soulless
    irresponsible   universally
    misspelling   woolly
    transship
    underrated   bathhouse
    unnamed   bookkeeper
    withholding   roommate

  Exceptions:

    eighteen (NOT eightteen)
    cross-section (NOT crosssection; never put three identical consonants together)

Ei *and* Ie.   When *ei* and *ie* are pronounced *ee,* place the *i* before the *e,* except after *c,* when the order is *ei.*

    achieve   ceiling
    believe   perceive
    field   receipt
    series

Some exceptions:

neither, species, leisure, seize, eight, weight (*ei* pronounced *ay*)

-Able, -Ible.   There is no fast rule for choosing between these word endings, but it may help to know that *-able* is much more common than *-ible*. Furthermore, the *-able* ending usually follows a full word or a full word minus the final *e*.

acceptable	dispensable	credible
believable	likeable	deductible
changeable	questionable	intelligible
considerable	valuable	irresponsible

-Ance, -Ence.   A *verb* ending in *er, or,* or *ur* and accented on the last syllable forms its noun by the addition of *-ence*. There is no other reliable guide to distinguishing between *-ance* and *-ence*, except your dictionary.

abhorrence	deference	allowance
concurrence	preference	guidance
conference	recurrence	performance

-Cede, -Ceed, -Sede.   The only word ending in *-sede* is *supersede*. The only words ending in *-ceed* are *exceed, proceed,* and *succeed*. That leaves just eight words ending in *-cede:*

accede	intercede
antecede	precede
cede	recede
concede	secede

-Ic.   When a suffix beginning with *e, i,* or *y* is added to a word ending in *ic,* a *k* is usually inserted to prevent mispronunciation.

mimic, mimicked, mimicking (*but* mimicry)
panic, panicked, panicky
picnic, picnicked, picnicking
politic, politicking
traffic, trafficked, trafficking

Plurals.   Many questions of spelling arise because of uncertainty about ending plural nouns. For example, is it *tomatos* or *tomatoes, editor-in-chiefs* or *editors-in-chief?*

Most nouns form their plurals by the addition of *s* or *es* to the singular (*books, taxis; sashes, taxes*). However, there are many exceptions and divided usages, as explained below.

Final Y.   When a final *y* follows a consonant, change the *y* to *i* and add *es*.

blueberries	ferries	plies
countries	Januaries	twenties

When a final *y* follows a vowel, just add *s*.

attorneys	displays	moneys (*also* monies)
buys (purchases)	keys	parleys

Final O.   When a final *o* follows another vowel, add *s* to form the plural.

cameos   duos   folios   patios   radios

When the final *o* follows a consonant, practice is divided between adding *s* and *es*.

dittos	mottoes (*or* mottos)
dynamos	noes (*plural of* no)
mementos	potatoes
pianos	tomatoes

Final F.   To form the plural of many words ending in *f* or *fe* (but not *ff*), change the *f* to *v* and add *es*.

calves   halves   knives   leaves   selves   wives
BUT: briefs   chefs   proofs   roofs   tiffs   whiffs

Compound Words.   When a term consists of two or more words, with or without hyphens, only the significant word takes the plural form. If both words are equally significant, both take the plural; and if no word is particularly significant, the plural form is placed on the last word.

Significant word first:

adjutants general	mothers-in-law
attorneys-at-law	notaries public
attorneys general	rights-of-way
commanders in chief	sergeants at arms

Significant word in middle:

assistant attorneys general   deputy chiefs of staff

Significant word last:

assistant directors	provost marshal generals
assistant secretaries	trade unions
brigadier generals	under secretaries

Both words equally significant:

coats of arms	secretaries-treasurers
menservants	women buyers

No word especially significant:

forget-me-nots	pick-me-ups
hand-me-downs	will-o'-the-wisps

NOTE 1:   When a noun is hyphenated with a preposition or adverb, the noun takes the plural.

droppers-in	hangers-on	passers-by
goings-on	listeners-in	runners-up

NOTE 2:   When neither word of a compound is a noun, the last word takes the plural.

also-rans   fill-ins   higher-ups
come-ons   go-betweens   tie-ins

NOTE 3:   Single words ending in *ful* are pluralized at the end.

armfuls   bucketfuls   cupfuls   pailfuls   spoonfuls

BUT: Separating the parts and pluralizing the initial word changes the meaning.

2 cupfuls (an amount equal to the content of two cups)
2 cups full of (two cups filled with)

Common Singular and Plural.   Some nouns, many with a final *s* sound, have the same form in the singular and the plural.

gladiolus   Chinese   deer
series   Japanese   salmon
species   Portuguese   sheep

NOTE 1:   Words ending in silent *s* have the same form in the singular and plural, though the *s* may be sounded in the plural.

chassis   faux pas   Bracques
corps   patios   Dumas

NOTE 2:   Some nouns ending in *s* are used only in the plural.

goods   means   proceeds   scissors   thanks

NOTE 3:   Other words ending in *s* are regularly construed as singular.

aeronautics   economics   news

NOTE 4:   Still other words ending in *s* are either singular or plural, depending on the sense.

Acoustics [the study] is a modern science.
The acoustics [the sound qualities] of Philharmonic Hall have been improved.

Other words in the same class include:

athletics   physics   statistics
ethics   politics   tactics

Proper Names.   Proper names, including those ending in *y* form their plurals by the addition of *s* and *es.*

Mr. Daly   the Dalys   Prof. Haney   the Haneys
Dr. March   the Marches   Mr. and Mrs. Kelly   the Kellys
Frank Vance   the Vances   Mrs. Prentis   the Prentises
ALSO: the Drs. March (two or more doctors by that name)
        Professors Haney and Carvell (two professors)
        the Messrs. Daly (two or more men by that name)
        the Mesdames (or Mmes.) Prentis (two or more women by that name,
           married or single)
        the Misses Hopkins and Joyce (two single women)

NOTE: When a name ends in Jr., II, III, and so on, add the plural ending to either the last name or the suffix. The first practice is considered somewhat more formal than the second.

Martin J. Beckley II
the Martin J. Beckleys II (*or* the Martin J. Beckley II's)
Henry Fairfield, Jr.
the Henry Fairfields, Jr. (*or* the Henry Fairfield, Jrs.)
John H. Marks, Jr.
the John H. Marks, Jrs. (*less awkward than* the John H. Markses, Jr.)

Words Used as Words.   In referring to words as words, form their plural by adding *s* (*es* if the word ends in *s*). If there is a chance that the word may be misread, add an apostrophe and *s,* or use quotation marks. Add the *s* alone to words that already have an apostrophe.

ands	the or's and nor's	the don'ts (*not* the dont's *or*
ifs, ands, and buts	the who's and which's	the don't's)
whereases	the "why nots"	the mustn'ts

Letters, Figures, Signs, Abbreviations.   Form the plural of letters by adding an apostrophe and *s*. However, there is a trend toward the omission of the apostrophe where no misreading would result. (See also "Abbreviations— Plurals," Section 10.1.)

p's	2's (*or* 2s)	*X*'s (*or X*s)
q's	Ph.D.'s (*or* Ph.D.s)	CPA's *or* CPAs
s's (*not s*s)	BTU's (*not* BTUs)	Mfrs. (*not* Mfr's)

Foreign Words.   The plurals of some words of foreign origin often cause difficulty. As the list below indicates, some of these words have both an Anglicized and a foreign plural.

Singular	*Plural*
addendum	addenda
adieu	adieus
agendum	agenda
alumna	alumnae
alumnus	alumni
analysis	analyses
antenna	antennas (*also, in zoology,* antennae)
appendix	appendixes (*also* appendices)
automaton	automatons (*also* automata)
axis	axes
bacterium	bacteria
basis	bases
beau	beaus (*also* beaux)
cactus	cactuses (*also* cacti)
crisis	crises
criterion	criteria
curriculum	curriculums (*also* curricula)
datum	data
dilettante	dilettantes (*also* dilettanti)
erratum	errata
executrix	executrices
focus	foci

Singular	*Plural*
formula	formulas (*also* formulae)
fungus	fungi
genius	geniuses (*also in sense of guardian spirit,* genii, *often capitalized*)
genus	genera (*also* genuses)
hypothesis	hypotheses
index	indexes (*also, in science,* indices)
insigne	insignia
larva	larvae
lira	lire
locus	loci
madam, madame	mesdames
matrix	matrices (*also* matrixes)
maximum	maximums (*also* maxima)
medium	mediums (*also, esp. in advertising,* media)
memorandum	memorandums (*also* memoranda)
minimum	minimums (*also* minima)
minutia	minutiae
monsieur	messieurs
nucleus	nuclei (*also* nucleuses)
oasis	oases
opus	opera
parenthesis	parentheses
phenomenon	phenomena
plateau	plateaus
podium	podiums
radius	radii (*also* radiuses)
radix	radices (*also* radixes)
referendum	referendums (*also* referenda)
residuum	residua (*also* residuums)
stadium	stadiums (*also* stadia)
stimulus	stimuli
stratum	strata
syllabus	syllabuses (*also* syllabi)
symposium	symposiums (*also* symposia)
synopsis	synopses
tableau	tableaus
terminus	termini (*also* terminuses)
testatrix	testatrices
thesaurus	thesauri (*also* thesauruses)
thesis	theses
ultimatum	ultimatums (*also* ultimata)
vertebra	vertebras (*also, in zoology,* vertebrae)
virtuoso	virtuosos (*also* virtuosi)

8.2 WORDS OFTEN CONFUSED

Many words in English sound alike, and even look alike, but mean different things. The chance of confusion is likely to increase when the secretary is transcribing from dictation. The following list contains the words most likely to cause "double trouble."

Key to Abbreviations
adj   adjective
adv   adverb
conj   conjunction

n	noun
part	participle
prep	preposition
pron	pronoun
v	verb

Key to Pronunciation

a	mat	ē	eat	ō	loaf	th	then
ā	day	er	mother	ô	bought	u	up
â	air	i	sir	oo	tool	û	urge
ä	arms	ī	bite	ou	loud	uh	data, alone
e	set	o	on	<u>th</u>	thin		

accept	(v) Receive. "I *accept* the honor."
except	(v) Leave out. "Only Jones was *excepted*."
	(prep) With the exclusion of, but. "All came *except* him."
access	(n) Means of approach. "*Access* to the files."
excess	(n) Immoderate quantity. "*Excess* baggage."
ad	(n) Advertisement (shortened form).
add	(v) To make a sum. "Let's *add* the figures."
adapt	(v) Modify. "One must *adapt* to conditions."
adopt	(v) Take. "They *adopted* a new name."
admittance	(n) Permission to enter. "They gained *admittance*."
admission	(n) 1. Right of entry, as by paying. "*Admission* is free."
	2. A point conceded. "A damaging *admission*."
advice	(n) 1. Counsel. "We gave our *advice* freely."
ad vīs′	(n) 2. Notice or communication. "Our *advice* is enclosed."
	"*Advice* from abroad."
advise	(v) To counsel, to inform. "Please *advise* us."
ad vīz′	
affect	(v) To influence. "The weather *affected* sales."
effect	(v) To bring about. "They will *effect* a change in strategy."
	(n) Result. "The *effect* of the change was noticeable."
all ready	All prepared. "We are *all ready* to leave."
already	(adv) Previously. "He had *already* offered his apologies."
all together	In a group. "They arrived *all together*."
altogether	(adv) Entirely. "The fuss was *altogether* unnecessary."
allusion	(n) A reference. "An *allusion* to Shakespeare."
illusion	(n) A deceiving appearance. "Easy profits are an *illusion*."
all ways	In every way. "He is in *all ways* a gentleman."
always	(adv) At all times. "He is *always* a gentleman."
ante-	Before, as in *antedate* (to put an earlier date on).
an′tē	
anti-	Against, as in *antisocial*.
an′tē, an′tī	
any way	In any one way. "*Any way* you look at it."
anyway	(adv) At least, nevertheless, in any manner. "*Anyway*, he tried."
a piece	(n) A thing or part. "*A piece* of pie is 50 cents."
apiece	(adv) For each. "We had one slice *apiece*."
appraise	(v) To put a value on. "He was asked to *appraise* the ring."
apprise	(v) To inform. "They were *apprised* of their rights."
arraign	(v) To bring before a court of law. "The prisoner was *arraigned*."
uh rān′	
arrange	(v) To put in order. "His lawyer *arranged* the transaction."
uh rānj′	

assay	(v) To make a test. "They *assayed* the situation."
	(n) An analysis. "An *assay* of the metal showed. . . ."
essay	(v) To try. "Only Smith would *essay* the difficult feat."
	(n) An attempt, a composition. "The *essay* was brief."
assistance	(n) Aid. "We need *assistance*."
assistants	(n) Helpers. "We had many *assistants*."
baring	(part) Exposing. "The witness is *baring* the details."
bâr′ing	
barring	(part) Excluding. "*Barring* an upset, we expect to win."
bär′ring	
bearing	(part) Carrying. "Kevin is *bearing* a difficult responsibility."
bâr′ing	
beside	(prep) Next to. "He sat *beside* us."
besides	(adv) In addition, furthermore. (See Section 8.5)
biannual	(adj) Occurring twice a year.
biennial	(adj) Occurring every two years. (See Section 8.5.)
born	(part) Brought into being. "He was *born* into a good family."
borne	(part) Carried. "The burden was *borne* by the treasurer."
breath	(n) Air inhaled and exhaled. "A *breath* of air."
breth	
breathe	(v) To inhale and exhale. "*Breathe* deeply."
brēth	
breadth	(n) Width, extent. "I admired the *breadth* of his interests."
Britain	(n) Great Britain (England, Northern Ireland, Wales, and Scotland).
Briton	(n) An inhabitant of Great Britain.
calendar	(n) A table showing the days, weeks, months, and so on.
calender	(n) A smoothing machine used in paper manufacture.
	(v) To press in a calender.
canvas	(n) A coarse cloth.
canvass	(n) A solicitation or inquiry. "A *canvass* showed. . . ."
	(v) To solicit. "He *canvassed* the district for votes."
capital	(adj) Of primary importance. "A *capital* idea."
	(n) 1. Principal city. "The *capital* of New York is Albany."
	2. Wealth invested in a business. "Started with $100,000 *capital*."
capitol	(n) Statehouse. "The legislature meets in the *capitol*."
Capitol	(n) The building in which Congress meets, in Washington, D.C.
censor	(v) To review for purposes of changing or expurgating.
sen′ser	(n) A person who censors or censures.
censure	(v) To blame or condemn. "I will not *censure* him."
sen′sher	
click	(n) A slight, sharp sound.
klik	
clique	(n) A small exclusive group. "He belonged to a *clique*."
klēk, klik	
climactic	(adj) Constituting the climax. "A *climactic* event."
klī mak′tik	
climatic	(adj) Relating to the climate. "*Climatic* conditions."
klī ma′tik	
clothes	(n) Apparel.
klōz	
cloths	(n) Pieces of cloth.
klôths	

coarse	(adj) Common, vulgar, rough, or harsh. "A *coarse* remark."
course	(n) Path, progress. "Followed an even *course*."
complement	(n) That which completes. "The scarf is a *complement* to her dress."
compliment	(n) An expression of courtesy or praise. "He paid her a *compliment*."
compose	(v) Constitute.
comprise	(v) Consist of. (See Section 8.5.)
comptroller kun trō′ler	(n) A person in charge of expenditures and receipts (finance).
controller kun trō′ler	(n) Another (but preferred) form of *comptroller*.
confidant kon fi dänt′	(n) A person in whom one confides.
confident kon′fi dent	(adj) Full of confidence, assured.
contemptible	(adj) Deserving of contempt, despicable. "A *contemptible* slander."
contemptuous	(adj) Showing contempt, disdainful. "*Contemptuous* of authority."
correspondence	(n) An exchange of letters. "A secretary handles her employer's *correspondence*."
correspondents	(n) Writers of letters.
costumer ko stoo′mer	(n) 1. A clothes rack. 2. One who makes costumes.
customer kus′tuh mer	(n) A patron.
council	(n) A body of advisers. "The *council* meets on Thursdays."
counsel	(n) 1. Advice. "We sought his *counsel*." 2. A person or persons giving advice, a lawyer. "Our *counsel* is Mr. Brown."
consul	(n) A government representative in a foreign country.
credible	(adj) Believable. "He told a *credible* story."
creditable	(adj) Deserving of credit. "His action was entirely *creditable*."
credulous	(adj) Easily convinced. "Only a *credulous* person would believe that story."
credit	(v) To put confidence in, to give credit. "They *credit* him for the savings." "We'll *credit* your account for $20."
accredit	(v) To authorize, to give credentials to. "An *accredited* agent."
critic kri′tik	(n) One who forms judgments. "The *critic* was severe."
critique kri tēk′	(n) A judgment or evaluation. "His *critique* was very perceptive."
cue	(n) A signal. "The bell was a *cue* to begin the performance." (v) To signal, give an indication to. "We *cued* him on his answers."
queue	(n) A line. "The patrons formed a *queue* at the box office." (v) To form a line. "The patrons *queued* up at the box office."
decease di sēs′	(n) Death.
disease di zēz′	(n) Illness.
decent dē′sent	(adj) Proper, respectable. "He came from a *decent* family."
descent di sent′	(n) 1. Downward motion. "The *descent* was steep." 2. Ancestry. "Of English *descent*."
dissent di sent′	(n) Disagreement. "He expressed his *dissent*." (v) To disagree. "He *dissented*."

decree	(n) An official order.
	(v) To issue such an order.
degree	(n) A step, stage, or rank.
depository	(n) A place for the safekeeping of money, jewels, and other valuables.
depositary	(n) 1. A person or organization entrusted with something for safekeeping.
	2. A synonym for *depository*.
deprecate	(v) To express disapproval of. "He *deprecated* the action."
depreciate	(v) 1. To lessen in value. "The stock *depreciates*."
	2. To disparage. "He *depreciated* his own achievements."

desert
  dez′ert,
  de zert′
	(n) A dry, sandy area.
	(v) To abandon. "We will not *desert* our friends."

dessert di zurt′	(n) A course at the end of a meal.
deserts di zurts′	(n) Deserved reward or punishment. "He got his *deserts*."
device	(n) 1. A mechanical instrument.
	2. A plan. "It was just a *device* for stimulating sales."
devise	(v) To contrive or plan. "They will *devise* a substitute for the broken part."
die (died, dying)	(v) To stop living.
dye (dyed, dyeing)	(v) To color. "The fur was *dyed* muskrat." (n) A coloring agent. "The *dye* ran."
disapprove	(v) To express an unfavorable opinion of. "I *disapprove* of such conduct."
disprove	(v) To prove something false. "The theory has been *disproved*."
disassociate	(v) To separate. "You should *disassociate* yourself from him."
dissociate	(v) Same as *disassociate*, but preferred.
disburse	(v) Pay out. "Window 9 *disburses* petty cash."
disperse	(v) Scatter. "The crowd *dispersed*."
discomfit	(v) To embarrass. "We did not intend to *discomfit* him."
discomfort	(v) To cause discomfort. "A tight shoe would *discomfort* anyone."
	(n) Lack of comfort. "Tight shoes cause *discomfort*."
discreet	(adj) Tactful. "A *discreet* inquiry."
discrete	(adj) Separate and distinct. "*Discrete* symbols.
done	(part) Finished, accomplished. "The job was *done*."
dun	(v) To ask for payment. "We *dun* delinquent accounts on the first of every month."
dual	(adj) Double. "He played a *dual* role in the merger."
duel	(n) A fight, contest. "They fought a *duel*."
egoist	(n) A person who is self-centered (not necessarily a term of reproach).
egotist	(n) A conceited person (usually signifies disapproval).
elder, eldest	(adj) Refer to the seniority of members of a family. "The *eldest* son."
older, oldest	(adj) More general terms relating to seniority to age, rank, and so on. "We could use an *older* man for the job."
emigrate	(v) To leave one's country and settle in another. "*Emigrate* from Ireland."
immigrate	(v) To come into a country. "*Immigrate* to Canada."
migrate	(v) A more general term meaning to move from one place to another; used of animals as well as people. "They *migrate* every spring."

eminent	(adj) Outstanding, distinguished. "An *eminent* surgeon."
immanent	(adj) Remaining within, inherent. "He had an *immanent* faith in the power of good works."
imminent	(adj) Threatening. "He was in *imminent* danger of bankruptcy."
enormity	(n) Great wickedness. "The public was appalled by the *enormity* of the crime."
enormousness	(n) Great size. "Visitors are astonished by the *enormousness* of the Pan Am Building."
envelop en vel'up	(v) To cover completely. "In this test the flames *envelop* the car."
envelope en'vuh lōp	(n) A container for letters.
equable ek'wuh bul, ē'kwuh bul	(adj) Uniform, serene. "An *equable* temperament." "An *equable* climate."
equitable ek'wi tuh bul	(adj) Equal, fair. "An *equitable* division of the profits."
exceptional	(adj) Unusual. "It is an *exceptional* example."
exceptionable	(adj) Open to objection. "An *exceptionable* remark."
exercise ek'ser sīz	(n) Physical activity. (v) To engage in such activity.
exorcise ek'sôr sīz	(v) To drive away, usually some evil spirit. "The masks are intended to *exorcize* the devil."
exhausting	(adj) Tiring. "An *exhausting* job."
exhaustive	(adj) Thorough. "An *exhaustive* search."
farther	(adv) Used in expressions of distance. "*Farther* down the road."
further	(adv) 1. Used in expressions of degree. "You can carry that reasoning even *further*." 2. Used as a synonym for *farther*. (See Section 8.5.)
fete fāt, fet	(n) A festival. "A *fete* marked the end of Lent."
feat fēt	(n) A remarkable accomplishment. "Lindbergh's *feat* was marked by wild acclaim."
feet fēt	(n) Plural of *foot*.
flaunt flônt	(v) To display ostentatiously. "He *flaunted* his wealth."
flout	(v) To show contempt for. "He *flouted* the law."
flounder	(v) To struggle awkwardly. "He *floundered* around on the slippery floor."
founder	(v) To sink, said of a ship; to collapse or fail. "The business *foundered*."
forbear fôr bâr' fôr'bâr	(v) To refrain from. "We will *forbear* criticism." (n) A *forebear*, ancestor, same as below.
forebear fôr'bâr	(n) An ancestor. "His *forebears* came from Sweden."
forcefully	(adv) Vigorously. "He spoke *forcefully*."
forcibly	(adv) By means of force. "The thief entered the premises *forcibly*."
forgo	(v) To do without. "Let's *forgo* the long introductions."
forego	(v) 1. To go before, usually found in such expressions as "a *foregone* conclusion" and "the *foregoing* statement." 2. Used as a synonym for *forgo*.
formally	(adv) In a formal manner. "The mayor *formally* takes office on January 1."

formerly	(adv) In the past. "Mr. Cain was *formerly* a salesman."
forth	(adv) Forward.
fourth	(adj) Next after third.
gourmet goor′–mā	(n) A person who likes fine foods. "He fancies himself a *gourmet*."
gourmand goor′–mand	(n) Also a person who likes fine foods, but often used in the sense of *glutton*.
guarantee gar un tē′	(n) A pledge of assurance that something meets specifications. "The maker's *guarantee* accompanies every purchase." (v) To give such a pledge. "The company *guaranteed* the article."
guaranty gar′un tē	(n) 1. A pledge to pay another's debt in case of default. "Mr. Dawson's *guaranty* of the loan will be accepted." 2. An agreement that gives assurance of performance, same as *guarantee*. (v) To guarantee. NOTE: *Guaranty* is used as a synonym for *guarantee* in all senses.
hardy	(adj) Bold, durable, robust. "A *hardy* traveler."
hearty	(adj) Vigorous ("a *hearty* laugh"); satisfying ("a *hearty* meal"); sincere ("a *hearty* welcome").
healthy	(adj) Having good health. "A *healthy* man."
healthful	(adj) Helping to promote health. "A *healthful* diet."
holy	(adj) Consecrated, sacred.
wholly	(adv) Entirely, as in "*wholly* fitting."
hypocritical hip uh krit′i kul	(adj) Not sincere. "He engages in *hypocritical* doubletalk."
hypercritical hī per krit′i kul	(adj) Too critical. "The *hypercritical* review seemed undeserved."
immanent **imminent**	See **eminent.**
inapt	(adj) Not suitable, lacking skill, awkward. "If he proves *inapt,* we will transfer him to another job."
inept	(adj) Same meaning, but usually in the sense of foolish, absurd, or clumsy. "The performance was so *inept,* we were embarrassed."
incidence	(n) Degree of occurrence. "The *incidence* of lung cancer is increasing."
incidents	(n) Occurrences. "The number of traffic *incidents* involving taxis is increasing."
incredible	(adj) Unbelievable. "An *incredible* number of errors."
incredulous	(adj) Unbelieving, skeptical. "You must be wary of the *incredulous* reader."
indention **indentation**	(n) A notch or recess. The words are used synonymously.
ingenious in jēn′yus	(adj) Clever, resourceful. "They devised an *ingenious* plan."
ingenuous in jen′yoo us	(adj) Frank, artless, naïve. "His *ingenuous* remarks were not amusing."
interstate	(adj) Between states. "The federal government controls *interstate* commerce."
intrastate	(adj) Within a state. "He thought the governor should concentrate on *intrastate* affairs."
isle	(n) A small island.
aisle	(n) A passageway.

its
(pron) Possessive of *it*. "We've seen the rise of railroad passenger traffic, and we've seen *its* decline."

it's
Contraction of "it is" or "it has." "*It's* no longer true." "*It's* been so long since we've seen you."

jibe
jīb
(v) Colloquial for "being in agreement." "Our views *jibe*."

gibe
jīb
(n) A jeer or taunt. "We ignored his *gibes*."
(v) To jeer or taunt. "He *gibed* at us constantly." Sometimes spelled *jibe*.

karat or carat
(n) A unit of weight for diamonds and other precious stones.

caret
(n) An inverted *v* (∧) to show where something is to be added.

later
lāt′er
(adj, adv) Occurring after, relating to time. "We'll call you *later*."

latter
lat′er
(n, adj) The last mentioned. (See *former, latter,* Section 8.5.)

lead led
lēd
led
(n) 1. A metal. "*Lead* is heavier than aluminum."
2. Front place. "We plan to take the *lead*."
(v) To show the way. "This staircase will *lead* you to the shelter."

led
(v) Past tense of *lead* (v). "We *led* the way to the shelter."

leased
(v) Given by lease. "*Leased* to the Jones Company."

least
(adj) The smallest in size, degree, or amount. "The *least* trouble."
(n) The smallest amount. "The *least* you can give is $10."

lessen
(v) To make less. "The insulation will *lessen* the noise."

lesson
(n) Something to be learned.

liable
li′uh bul
(adj) Exposure to some disadvantage. (See *apt, likely, liable,* Section 8.5.)

libel
(n) A written or printed defamation. "A suit for *libel*."

liqueur
li kûr′
(n) A sweet, syrupy, alcoholic drink. "We'll have a *liqueur* after dinner."

liquor
lik′er
(n) Any distilled alcoholic drink. "Prices for *liquor* have gone up."

loath
lōth
(adj) Reluctant. "I am *loath* to do it."

loathe
lōth
(v) To detest. "I *loathe* the new fashions."

local
lō′kul
(adj) Confined to a certain place. "The condition is *local*."

locale
lō kal′
(n) A place. "The *locale* of the story is Monte Carlo."

lose
looz
(v) To be unable to find. "Try not to *lose* the key."

loose
loos
(adj) Not tight. "The knot was *loose*."

luxuriant
(adj) Fertile, lush. "A *luxuriant* garden."

luxurious
(adj) Rich. "*Luxurious* surroundings."

material
muh tēr′ē ul
(n) Substance. "Have you ordered enough *material* to redo the entire roof?"

materiel
muh tēr ē el′
(n) Equipment, supplies, especially those used by the armed forces. "War requires men and *materiel*."

militate
(v) To work (against). "His quick temper will *militate* against his success."

mitigate
(v) To make less severe. "The loan will help to *mitigate* the effects of the flood."

moral mor'ul	(adj) Good, right. "The employer viewed the raise as a *moral* necessity."
morale muh ral'	(n) Mental condition, spirit. "The *morale* of the work force was high."
motif mō tēf'	(n) Theme. "The *motif* of the party was the gold rush of 1849."
motive mō'tiv	(n) Inner drive, incentive. "Money has always provided a strong *motive* for work."
ordinance	(n) A statute law. "The *ordinance* called for a $50 fine."
ordnance	(n) Artillery and ammunition.
past	(adj) Gone by. "The *past* president introduced his successor."
passed	(v) Moved forward, went through. "Mr. Dee *passed* here a moment ago."
personal	(adj) Private, individual. "It is a *personal* decision."
personnel	(n) Employees. "All *personnel* were affected by the decision."
perspective	(n) Objects "in *perspective*" are drawn to show their relation in space; also used in the sense of "mental view or prospect." "Seen in *perspective*, the decision was a wise one."
prospective	(adj) Expected, likely. "A *prospective* customer."
plaintiff	(n) A complainant, one who brings a suit.
plaintive	(adj) Mournful. "A *plaintive* voice."
post card	(n) A private mailing card.
postal card	(n) A mailing card issued by the Post Office, with imprinted stamp.
practical	(adj) Not governed by theory. "A *practical* solution." "A *practical* man."
practicable	(adj) Capable of being done, feasible. "The plan is *practicable*."
practice	(v) To perform; (n) a performance or exercise.
practise	(v) Another form for *practice;* not to be used as a noun.
precedence pres'i dens, pri sēd'ens	(n) Preceding in time; priority. "The law takes *precedence* over company regulations."
precedents pres'i dents	(n) Acts that establish rules or serve as justification. "The *precedents* for his action are many."
prescribe	(v) To give rules or directions. "Doctors *prescribe* rest in bed for flu patients."
proscribe	(v) To forbid. "The laws *proscribe* campaign contributions by government employees."
presentiment	(n) A premonition. "He had a *presentiment* of impending catastrophe."
presentment	(n) A presentation, especially the report of a grand jury, in the phrase, "handed up a *presentment*."
principal	(adj) First in rank. "Mr. Gray is the *principal* partner." (n) 1. The head person. "He is the *principal* in the transaction." 2. An amount invested or bearing interest. "Your *principal* earns 5 percent a year."
principle	(n) A rule or doctrine. "I am against the transaction on *principle*."
prophecy prof'i sē	(n) A prediction. "Your *prophecy* came true."
prophesy prof'i sī	(v) To make a prediction. "What do you *prophesy* for 1990?"
proportional	(adj) In proportion to, relative; used with reference to a number of related things. "*Proportional* representation." "*Proportional* shares."

proportionate	(adj) 1. In proportion to; used with reference to the relation between two things. "The effort was *proportionate* to the salary." 2. Same as *proportional*.
queue	See **cue**.
quiet	(adj) Still, not noisy.
quite	(adv) Entirely, truly, very. "*Quite* warm."
receipt ri sēt′	(n) 1. The receiving of something. "We are in *receipt* of your letter." 2. The acknowledgment of something received. "We will send you a *receipt* for your payment."
recipe res′uh pē	(n) A formula, instructions for preparing food or drink. "Follow the *recipe* carefully."
residence **residents**	(n) A dwelling place. (n) People who live in a place.
respectfully **respectively**	(adv) Showing respect. "*Respectfully* yours." (adv) Relating to two or more in the order named. "Mr. and Mrs. Reese opened their individual accounts in the amounts of $1,000 and $500 *respectively*."
rout rout **route** root, rout	(n) A disorderly flight. "Our competitors were put to *rout*." (v) To put to flight. "Our competitors were *routed*." (n) 1. A course traveled over. "Take the shortest *route*." 2. A newspaper delivery business. "He bought the *route* from his brother." (v) To send over a certain course. "We'll *route* the car through the turnpike."
sensual **sensuous**	(adj) Relating to the senses or appetites. "*Sensual* images." (adj) Affecting the senses aesthetically. "*Sensuous* rhythm."
sight **site** **cite**	(n) Something seen; (v) to see. (n) Location. "The *site* of the new building has not yet been chosen." (v) To refer to or quote. "We can *cite* the dictionary as our authority."
sometime **some time** **sometimes**	(adv) At some time or other in the future. "I'll see you *sometime*." (adj) Former. "Dr. King is a *sometime* professor of English." 1. A period of time. "*Some time* ago." 2. Same as *sometime*. (adv) (adv) Occasionally. "He is *sometimes* tardy."
special **especial**	(adj) 1. Particular, specific. "He wanted no *special* favor." 2. Outstanding. "This is a *special* treat." (adj) Not ordinary or common. Sometimes used as a synonym for *special*.
stable **staple**	(adj) Firm, steady. "The economy is now *stable*." (n) A place where animals are kept. (n) 1. A regularly stocked or used item. "Meat is a *staple*." 2. A wire fastener.
stationary **stationery**	(adj) Standing still; not movable. (n) Writing materials.
straight **strait**	(adj) Not crooked; upright, undeviating. (n) 1. Dilemma or predicament, usually *straits*. "Difficult *straits*." [Related usages include "strait-laced" (prudish), and "straitened circumstances" (financial difficulties).] 2. A narrow waterway connecting two larger bodies of water; also *straits* (construed as singular).

suit	(n) 1. A set of clothes or cards.
soot	2. A court action. "He promised to bring *suit* against our client."
suite	(n) 1. A set of matched furniture.
swēt (*or,*	2. A group of rooms.
for 1, soot)	3. An instrumental form.
than	(prep) Used in a comparison. "Taller *than* average."
then	(adv) At that time; next in order.
therefor	(adv) For it, for that. "Payment *therefor*."
thâr fôr′	
therefore	(adv) For that reason.
thâr′fôr	
through	(adj) Finished. "They're *through* with the painting."
	(prep) By way of, by means of, from one end to the other.
thru	Informal for *through* in prepositional sense.
threw	(v) Past tense of *throw*.
to	(prep) Used largely to indicate direction. "Walk *to* work."
too	(adv) 1. Also.
	2. Overly, as in "worked *too* hard."
two	(adj) A couple.
tortuous	(adj) Twisting. "A *tortuous* road led through the mountain."
torturous	(adj) Causing torture. "It was a *torturous* experience."
typography	(n) The use of type.
topography	(n) The surface features of a region. "The *topography* of the area includes a five-thousand-foot mountain."
use	(n) A way of using. "His *use* of the word *flustrated* raised some
yoos	eyebrows."
usage	(n) Customary use or practice. "The word *flustrated* is not in
yoo′sij	good *usage*."
waive	(v) To give up or forgo. "To *waive* immunity."
wave	(v) To move to and fro. "To *wave* the flag."
	(n) A moving ridge or swell, as in a lake or ocean.
weather	(n) Atmospheric conditions.
whether	(conj) If it be the case that. "He asked *whether*. . . ."
who's	Contraction of "who is" or "who has." " *Who's* going with you?" " *Who's* got the keys?"
whose	(pron) Possessive of who. " *Whose* keys are they?"
your	(pron) Possessive of you. " *Your* order will be filled promptly."
you're	Contraction of "you are." " *You're* paid up until June 1."

8.3 GLOSSARY OF COMMON GRAMMATICAL TERMS

Terms in boldface are defined in this glossary. Starred items (*) are discussed more fully in "Grammar Review," Section 8.4,

active verb A verb whose subject performs the action indicated by the verb. Example: We *mailed* the check yesterday. (*Mailed* is an active verb because its subject, *we,* did the mailing.) See also **passive verb.**

*****adjective** A word that describes or limits the meaning of a noun. An adjective usually precedes the noun it modifies (but see **predicate adjective.**) Example: *a large black* box (the italicized words are adjectives modifying *box*).

*adverb   A word that modifies or limits the meaning of a verb, adjective, or another adverb. It usually signifies time, place, degree, or manner. Example: The *heavily* overloaded truck arrived *very late*. (*Heavily* modifies the adjective *overloaded; very,* the adverb *late;* and *late,* the verb *arrived.*)

article   The articles are *a, an,* and *the.* They are adjectives.

case   An attribute of nouns and pronouns that shows their relation to the rest of the sentence. Thus the subject of a verb is in the *nominative case,* the object of a verb or preposition is in the *objective case,* and a noun or pronoun showing ownership is in the *possessive case.* Nouns have the same form for the nominative and objective cases, but pronouns often have different forms. For example, *I* and *he* are nominative, but *me* and *him* are objective.

clause   Any part of a sentence containing a subject and predicate. If the clause can stand alone as a sentence, it is a *main* (or *independent*) *clause;* if it cannot stand alone as a sentence, it is a *subordinate* (or *dependent*) *clause.* Main clauses are often introduced by coordinate conjunctions or conjunctive adverbs; subordinate clauses are introduced by subordinate conjunctions. See **conjunction.**

> We would appreciate it if you raised the discount.
> ←—— Main clause ——→ ←—— Subordinate clause ——→
> We asked for the first edition; we got the second.
> We asked for the first edition, but we got the second.
> We asked for the first edition; however, we got the second.
> ←——— Main clause ———→ ←——— Main clause ———→
> Although we asked for the first edition, we got the second.
> ←———Subordinate clause ———→ ←—— Main clause——→

collective noun   A noun that stands for all the members of a group, for example, *company, management, team, herd, flock.* Use of a collective noun often raises the question of whether it is to be treated as singular or plural. For the answer, see "Subject-Verb Agreement" and "Pronouns," in Section 8.4.

common noun   The generic or class name for persons, places, or things. See also **noun, pronoun,** and **proper noun.**

> The *spirit* of the *workers* is high.
> The *books* were a *shambles.*
> No *stencil* is needed.

complement   Any word or group of words that completes the meaning of a verb. It may be **object, predicate adjective,** or **predicate noun.** The italicized portions of the following sentences are complements.

> He signed *the letter.* (Object)
> The machine is *inoperable.* (Predicate adjective)
> It was *a beautiful performance.* (Predicate noun)

compound sentence   A sentence having two or more main clauses. For examples, see **clause.**

compound subject   Two or more subjects having the same verb. The verb is usually plural. For exceptions, see "Pronouns" and "Subject-Verb Agreement," in Section 8.4.

> Both the *employer* and the *employee* benefit from this plan.
> A *hammer* and a *screw driver* are all the tools you need.

compound predicate   Two or more verbs having the same subject.

> He *stopped* the truck and *asked* for directions.

conjunction   A word that connects words, phrases, or clauses. Coordinate conjunctions connect units of equal rank; subordinate conjunctions introduce subordinate clauses; conjunctive adverbs introduce main clauses. See **clause.**

> Coordinate conjunctions: *and, but, for, or, nor*
> Subordinate conjunctions: *since, because, after, that, if,* and so on.
> Conjunctive adverbs: *however, therefore, accordingly, furthermore, so,* and so on.

exclamation   A grammatically independent word or phrase expressing feeling, often followed by an exclamation mark, sometimes by a period or comma.

> *Ouch!*
> *My goodness!*
> *Yes,* I am in accord.
> *No.* I did not agree.

*gerund   A form of the verb ending in *-ing,* for example, *writing, comparing, asking.* A gerund is always used as a noun, that is, it performs the function of a subject or object.

> *Hiring* is the function of the personnel department. (Subject of verb *is*)
> Let's see what comes of *talking* with him. (Object of preposition *of*)

indirect object   A noun or pronoun that answers the question to whom? or to what?, for whom? or for what? after the verb. It is not preceded by a preposition. See **object.**

> We will allow *them* the discount. (*Them* is the indirect object, *discount* the direct object.)

*infinitive   A form of the verb usually preceded by *to* (the sign of the infinitive). It may perform the function of a noun, an adjective, or an adverb.

> He asked *to see* the new models. (Noun)
> She hadn't a thing *to wear.* (Adjective)
> Having fought *to win,* he was dejected in defeat. (Adverb)

nominative case   See **case.**

noun   The name of a person, place, thing, or abstract quality. A noun can be the subject or complement of a verb, or the object of a preposition.

> *Mr. Smith* rented a *home* in *Medwick.*

Nouns are singular or plural (*man, men; book, books*) and, as modifiers, may show possession (*men's* shoes, *ladies'* handbags, the *manager's* order). They are often preceded by *a, an,* or *the* (a *hat,* an *opening,* the *choice*).

object A *direct object* names the receiver of the action of a verb or verbal (participle, infinitive, or gerund).

> We sent the *invoice.*
> Selling *radios* is our business.

An *indirect object* tells to whom or to what or for whom or for what the action of the verb or verbal is performed, but is not preceded by a preposition.

> We sent them an invoice. (If the sentence were, "We sent an invoice to them," *them* would be the object of the preposition *to.*)
> Selling *dealers* radios is our business.

objective case See **case.**

*****participle** A verb form, usually ending in *-ing, -ed, -en,* or *-t,* which performs the function of an adjective.

> I noticed him *collating* the sheets. (Modifies *him*)
> *Bought* two years ago, the typewriter is still in excellent condition. (Modifies *typewriter*)

passive verb A verb whose subject is the receiver of the action of the verb. Active verbs are usually preferred. See also **active verb.**

> He *was given* a plaque by the Bowling Club. (Compare with, "The Bowling Club *gave* him a plaque.")
> The bill *was sent* by us. (Compare with, "We *sent* the bill.")

person An attribute of nouns and pronouns indicating the direction of discourse. The first-person pronoun is the speaker (*I, we*); the second-person pronoun is the person spoken to (*you*); the third-person pronoun is the person or thing spoken of (*he, it, they*). All nouns (*factory, book, chair*—anything) are regarded as in the third person. Verbs change their form to accommodate the person of the subject: I *am,* you *are,* he *is;* I *type,* you *type,* he *types.*

phrase Any group of related words without a subject and predicate. See also **clause.**

> Noun phrases: a suitable premium, the Multilith operator
> Verb phrases: have been tried, won't be able, has gone
> Prepositional phrases: in the room, from my desk, under the table
> Infinitive phrases: to fit the individual, to try my hand
> Participial phrases: walking across the aisle, working two nights

*****possessive case** A grammatical relationship usually, but not always, shown by the apostrophe (*Altman's, Max's; ours, theirs; a day's work*).

predicate That part of a sentence or clause that makes a statement about the subject. It consists of at least a verb, and usually of a verb and complement.

The letter *expresses our point of view fairly accurately.*
Although he *is still under 35,* he *seems certain to win a place on the Board.*

predicate adjective   An adjective following certain verbs, including *be, seem, appear, look, taste.* Its chief characteristic is that it describes the subject rather than a following noun.

The cartridge is *empty.* (Versus, "The *empty* cartridge.")
He seems *intelligent.*
The pie tastes *good.*

predicate noun   A noun (or pronoun) following a verb and representing the same thing as the subject. The predicate noun is in the nominative case. See **complement.**

He became *president* at 35.
It is *they.* (Not *them*)

*preposition   A preposition links a noun or pronoun with another word in the sentence. The noun or pronoun following a preposition is called the object of the preposition. Prepositions include *in, at, by, for, into, with, from, after, before, behind, toward, against, beyond, around, through, beside.*

at the desk   *behind* the counter   *with* great speed

*pronoun   A substitute for a noun. Some examples:

I, you, he, she, it, you, they; me, him, them (See **Case.**)
who, which, what
this, that, these, those
someone, somebody, anyone, anybody
myself, yourself, himself, oneself, themselves

Pronouns also have a possessive form:

mine, yours, his, hers, its, theirs, whose
anyone's, anybody's

proper adjective   An adjective form of a proper noun, usually capitalized.

American know-how
Victorian morality
Keynesian theories

proper noun   The distinctive name of a person, place, or thing; always capitalized.

David Kingsley
a tube of *Colgate* tooth paste
an office in *Rockefeller Center*

*sentence   A word or group of words that, in its context, can stand as a complete thought. It is followed by a period, a question mark, or an exclamation point. Customarily, a sentence has a subject and a verb; however, some sentences have neither a subject nor a verb, or have one or both understood.

I will write tomorrow.
Will I write? Of course. (Two sentences. "I will write" is understood to follow "Of course")
My goodness! How sales have risen! (Two sentences)

*subject   That part of a sentence, usually at the beginning, about which a statement is made. The complete subject may consist of a single noun or pronoun, a noun phrase, or a noun clause. See also **phrase** and **clause.**

Workers are getting scarce. (Noun)
Too many men fail to realize their full potential. (Noun phrase)
Eating on the job is prohibited. (Noun phrase)
To work for oneself is my idea of independence. (Noun phrase)
That he was capable was immediately apparent. (Noun clause)

subjunctive   A form of the verb used for special purposes, for example, in resolutions, requests, conditions, and wishes. See "Verbs," in Section 8.4.

I wish he *were* here. (Not *was*)

subordinate elements   Any phrase or clause that cannot stand alone as a sentence, as illustrated by the italicized word groups below.

If you order now, you will receive an extra 10 percent off.
I'll let you know *after I study the details.*
He did it *knowing that he would be criticized.*
To offer a commission only does not seem fair.

tense   The time (present, past, or future) shown by the verb, as I *write,* I *wrote,* I *will write.* See "Verbs," in Section 8.4.

*verb   A word or words, expressing action or state of being, through which an assertion is made about a noun or pronoun. With the complement, it forms the predicate.

The secretary *takes* dictation.
Free samples *will be distributed.*
The auditors *are* Brown, Henderson & Co.

verbal   A form of the verb: **infinitive, participle,** or **gerund.**

They propose *to sell* the entire stock. (Infinitive)
Having worked for the company for 40 years, he retired. (Participle)
He had some regrets after *signing* the letter. (Gerund)

8.4 GRAMMAR REVIEW

In grammar, as in word use, there is no absolute standard of correctness—only a general and sometimes highly disputed consensus of how people use the language. For that reason it would be a mistake to follow slavishly any given set of "rules." Still, the following review provides sensible norms for using language with clarity and precision—and some degree of formality—especially in writing.

For a "Glossary of Common Grammatical Terms," see Section 8.3.

For a "Dictionary of English Usage," see Section 8.5.

CONTENTS

Adjectives	p. 320	Prepositions	p. 322
Adverbs	p. 321	Pronouns	p. 313
Gerunds	p. 320	Sentence Completeness	p. 310
Infinitives	p. 319	Sentence Structure	p. 309
Participles	p. 319	Subject-Verb Agreement	p. 312
Possessive	p. 315	Verbs	p. 317

Sentence Structure

Sentence Fragment.   When an essential part of a sentence is missing, or when one part is incorrectly separated from another by a period, an incomplete sentence, or fragment, is created. Fragments are avoided by careful writers except in special cases.

FRAGMENT: Your letter of February 12 regarding our fall merchandising plans. (What about the letter?)
FRAGMENT (IN ITALICS):   I have your letter of February 12. *Regarding our fall merchandise plans.*
COMPLETE: I have your letter of February 12 regarding our fall merchandising plans.

NOTE: Fragments are sometimes used to save words or for stylistic effect, especially in advertising copy. Examples:

Over the calf hose. Cotton lisle. Four popular colors. $2.00.
Thunder and lightning. Zero to 60 in 9 seconds. What kind of family sedan is this?

See **sentence,** in Section 8.3.

Run-On Sentence.   Two independent clauses not joined by the words *and, but, for, or,* or *nor* should be separated by a period or a semicolon, not a comma.

RUN-ON: Mr. Jones will be in on Thursday, I suggest you call beforehand if you want to see him.
IMPROVED: Mr. Jones will be in on Thursday. I suggest you call beforehand if you want to see him.

And *as a Connective.*   Do not join ideas with *and* unless they are closely related. Either split the sentence, or find a more exact connective.

BAD: The company was founded in 1926 *and* manufactures steel furniture.
IMPROVED: The company was founded in 1926. It manufactures steel furniture.
BETTER STILL: The company, which was founded in 1926, manufactures steel furniture.

Ambiguous Connective.   If you use the connectives *as, since,* or *while,* be sure that they can be interpreted in only one way.

DOUBLE MEANING: *As* I was going to lunch, I took the letter with me to mail. (*As* could stand for *when* or *inasmuch as.*)
SINGLE MEANING: On my way to lunch, I took the letter with me to mail.

DOUBLE MEANING: *Since* we are without a sales manager, we have experienced a sharp drop in orders. (Does *since* mean *because* or *from the time that?*)
SINGLE MEANING: *Because* we are without a sales manager . . .

Point of View.   Hold to one point of view, as far as possible. Avoid switching from one subject to another.

FAULTY: *We* appreciate your order and *it* will be filled promptly.
IMPROVED: *We* appreciate your order and will fill it promptly. (*We* is also the subject of *fill.*)

FAULTY: After *you* enter all the amounts, *they* should be totaled in the last column.
IMPROVED: After *you* enter all the amounts, total them in the last column. (The *you* before *total* is understood.)

FAULTY: While [*we are*] not averse to the change, *the effects* will be felt for some time to come.
IMPROVED: While [*we are*] not averse to the change, *we* will feel the effects for some time to come.

Parallel Structure.   Coordinate ideas should be expressed in similar grammatical fashion. Have a sound reason if you change from one type of construction to another.

FAULTY: We will *accept* the funds, *send* receipts to the payers, and *crediting* your account at the same time.
IMPROVED: We will *accept* the funds, *send* receipts to the payers, and *credit* your account at the same time.

FAULTY: Sorting equipment would save *time, money,* and *provide greater control.*
IMPROVED: Sorting equipment would *save time, reduce costs,* and *provide greater control.*
OR: Sorting equipment would *save time and money* and *provide greater control.*

Position of Modifiers.   Words should be placed as close as possible to the words they restrict or modify.

AMBIGUOUS: We received a *letter* from your secretary, Miss Hinchley, *dated October 16.*
IMPROVED: We received a *letter dated October 16* from your secretary, Miss Hinchley.

AMBIGUOUS: He would be in bad straits if he *lost* what he now has *by improvident investments.*
IMPROVED: He would be in bad straits if he *lost by improvident investments* what he now has.

AMBIGUOUS: Audrey and I will see you at the horse show *in any event.*
IMPROVED: *In any event,* Audrey and I will see you at the horse show.

COMPARE: I would suggest that you go over each of the three plans we discussed with your attorney before making a final decision.
WITH: I would suggest that before making a final decision you go over with your attorney each of the three plans we discussed.

Sentence Completeness

Telegraphic Style.   Except in a telegram or informal note, the omission of words necessary for the completeness of a sentence is considered a mark of haste and is therefore discourteous.

NOT: Letter received.
BUT: *Your* letter *has been* received.

Omission of Other *and* Else. In making a comparison, use *other* or *else* when logic requires it. An exception to this rule may be made, however, in the interests of informality.

INFORMAL: This layout is better than any we've seen.
CORRECT: This layout is better than any *other* we've seen.

INFORMAL: We fly to more South American cities than anybody.
CORRECT: We fly to more South American cities than anybody *else*.

Omission of That *and* Those. In making a comparison, use *that* or *those* (or an equivalent expression) when logic requires it.

NOT: His qualifications are better than any other applicant we've seen.
BUT: His qualifications are better than *those* of any other applicant we've seen.
OR: His qualifications are better than any other *applicant's* we've seen.

NOT: The price is much lower than our competitor.
BUT: The price is much lower than *that charged by* our competitor.
OR: The price is much lower than our *competitor's*.

Mistaken Use of Other.   *Other* should not be used when it distorts the sense.

BAD: The special features of our generators justify a higher price than that charged
       for *other* inferior generators.
IMPROVED: ... justify a higher price than that charged for inferior generators.
OR: ... justify a higher price than that charged for *other* generators.

Completeness in Paired Expressions.   When two expressions are joined by *and* (or in some similar manner) be careful about making a single word do for both.

COMPARE: *The president and chief executive officer* arrived on Tuesday. (One man)
           The president and the chief executive officer arrived on Tuesday. (Two men)
FAULTY: *A Sheraton and Duncan Phyfe* chair ... (One chair? Not likely.)
BETTER: *A Sheraton and a Duncan Phyfe* chair ... (Two chairs)

FAULTY: We have no financial interest or other connection *with* that company.
BETTER: We have no financial interest *in* or other connection *with* that company.
OR: We have no financial interest *in* that company, or any other connection *with* it.

FAULTY: The truck needs *a new transmission and brakes*.
BETTER: The truck needs *a new transmission and new brakes*.

FAULTY: *The order was accepted and the goods placed* in the warehouse awaiting
          shipment.
BETTER: *The order was accepted and the goods were placed* in the warehouse awaiting
          shipment.

FAULTY: This is *one of the most popular numbers, if not the most popular*, in our line.
CORRECT: This is *one of the most popular numbers, if not the most popular number*,
           in our line.
BETTER: This is *one of the most popular numbers in our line, if not the most popular*.
          (Words may be omitted in a comparison at the end of a sentence. Here the omitted
          word is *number*. See rule below.)

Omissions in Comparisons.   Words may be omitted in expressions of comparison.

CORRECT: We are sure we can do the job as well as they ∧ . (*Can* is understood.)
CORRECT: Better that the business should benefit us than ∧ them. (*It should benefit*
           is understood.)

Subject-Verb Agreement. *Agreement in Number.* A verb agrees in number with its subject—singular subject, singular verb; plural subject, plural verb.

the customer says	our customers say
Mr. Teller works	our employees work
no one believes	we believe
a discount is given	discounts are given

Intervening Words. When words come between the subject and its verb, do not let the intervening words affect the number of the verb.

WRONG: *Mr. Farmer,* not the salesmen, *were* entitled to the commission.
RIGHT: *Mr. Farmer . . . was* entitled to the commission.

WRONG: The *full order,* consisting of an assortment of sizes and colors, *were shipped* by express.
RIGHT: The *full order . . . was shipped* by express.

Together with, as Well as, *and So On.* A singular subject followed by a phrase beginning with the words *with, together with, as well as,* and *in addition to* takes a singular verb.

Mr. Ray, with his two assistants, is expected to attend the hearing. (Compare: *Mr. Ray and his two assistants are expected* to attend the hearing.)
The Federal Government, as well as the state and city, has a stake in this measure.

Compound Subjects. Any subjects joined by *and* take a plural verb. (For exception, see "Plural Subjects as Singular Units," in this section.)

The three workers and their supervisor have been told . . .
The desk and the file are obstructing access to the door.

Plural Words Following Verb. A singular subject takes a singular verb even when the verb is followed by a plural complement.

The *limit was three boxes* per customer.
A good time to do it *is the first two weeks* in September.
A satisfactory proportion is two spoonfuls to a glass of water.

Collective Nouns as Subjects. A singular subject, representing a group of similar persons or things, takes either a singular or plural verb, depending on the sense. Collective nouns include such words as *company, committee, group, jury, staff, management, team, crowd,* and *faculty.*

The *committee has reported* favorably on the proposal. (Here the committee is acting as a unit.)
The *committee have submitted their reports.* (Here the individual members of the committee are acting separately.)
The *jury has been out* five hours.
The *jury are* hopelessly *divided.*

Subject Following Verb. When the subject follows the verb, be sure the two agree in number.

WRONG: There *is* still *three copies* to be accounted for. (*Copies,* not *there,* is the subject.)
RIGHT: There *are* still *three copies* to be accounted for.

WRONG: Attached to the table *was a price tag and instructions* for assembling.
RIGHT: Attached to the table *were a price tag and instructions* for assembling.

Alternative Subjects.   When two or more subjects are joined by *or* or *nor*, the verb should agree with the nearer subject.

> Neither Mr. Jones nor his *associates wish* to participate.
> Either you or *I am* in the lead. (But: "You and I are in the lead.")
> A catalogue or some descriptive *folders are needed*. (Preferred to "Some descriptive folders or a *catalogue is needed*.")

Singular with Each, Every, *and So On.*   Words like *each, every, someone, somebody, everyone, everybody, anyone, anybody, no one, either,* and *neither* are followed by singular verbs.

> *Each manager is* responsible for his own department.
> *Everybody* we invited *was* there.
> *Anyone is* eligible to enter the contest.
> *Either* of the models *is* acceptable.
> *No one was* more surprised than Mr. Lee.

NOTE: Although *no one* is always singular, *none* is singular or plural depending on the sense.

> Of all the clerks in his department, *none is* better able to do the job than Bob Loring. (Only one person is indicated.)
> *None of our customers live* outside Chicago. (More than one are indicated.)

A Number, the Number.   The subject *the number* takes a singular verb, but *a number* takes a plural verb.

> *The number* of exceptions *is* increasing.
> *A number* of good buys *are* currently available.

Subjects Expressing Part of a Whole.   Subjects like *some, part, half,* and so on are followed by either a singular or plural verb depending on the sense.

> *Part of the trouble is* that no one will take the responsibility.
> *Some of the rules are* not being followed.
> *Two thirds of our quota has* been met.
> *Two thirds of our sales force are* college graduates.

One of Those Who.   The verb following *who, which,* or *that* in a construction similar to "one of those who" is invariably plural.

> He is *one of those executives who are never satisfied* with things as they are.
> This is *one of the most beautiful properties that have come* our way.

Plural Subjects as Singular Units.   When a plural subject represents a singular concept, it takes a singular verb.

> *Fifty dollars seems* like a fair price.
> *Kellogg's Corn Flakes is* probably the most popular of the cold cereals.
> *Dip and dry is* all you do.

Pronouns

Nominative and Objective Forms.   Some pronouns have different forms for the nominative case and the objective case.

Nominative	Objective
I	me
he	him
she	her
we	us
they	them
who	whom

1. Use the nominative case pronouns as follows:
   (a) Subject of the verb.

We wanted to know *who* would be there.
We secretaries are in the best position to know.
They approved the plan.

   (b) Complement of forms of the verb *to be* (*is, am, are, was, were, been*).

It is *I.*
How would you feel if you were *he?*
It was *they* who should have taken the responsibility.
If I were *she,* I would not have permitted it.

NOTE: Rule (b) is ignored in speech and informal writing by many literate persons.

Acceptable: It's *me;* that's *her;* if I were *him.*

2. Use the objective case pronouns as follows.
   (a) Object of verb or verbal (infinitive, participle, or gerund).

He can have *whomever* he wants. (Object of *wants*)
I asked Mr. Day to give *me* the total cost. (Object of infinitive *to give*)

   (b) Object of preposition.

The quarrel is between *him* and *me.* (Objects of the preposition *between.*)
You can trust the information to Mr. Gray and *us.* (Object of preposition *to.*)

   (c) Subject of an infinitive.

You would expect *him* to respond promptly. (Subject of the infinitive *to respond;* the object of the verb *would expect* is the whole phrase, *him to respond promptly.*)

Pronoun After As *or* Than.   In a construction beginning with *as* or *than,* part of the sentence is often omitted. Determine the correct form of the pronoun by completing the sentence in your mind.

He is far more expert than *I* [am expert].   .
Better that we should get the credit than [that] *they* [should get it].
Please give it to me rather than [to] *him.*

Agreement in Number and Gender.   A pronoun agrees with its antecedent (the word or words it stands for) in number and gender (masculine, feminine, or neuter).

As soon as we know what *media* you have chosen, we will schedule our advertisements in *them*.

When *Miss Ray* calls, tell *her* I will be able to see *her* on Friday.

Please inspect the *shipment* carefully when *it* arrives.

Every worker should do the job for which *he is* (not *they are*) best suited.

1. When referring to a collective noun, a pronoun will be singular or plural depending on whether the noun is treated as singular or plural. An exception is occasionally made when consistency would be awkward.

CORRECT: The *management are doing* all *they* can.
CORRECT: The *management is doing* all *it* can.
ACCEPTABLE: Now that the *company is well established, they* have decided to limit *their* sales to authorized dealers.

2. A pronoun referring to two or more antecedents connected by *and* is usually plural.

CORRECT: The *foreman and the night watchman* took *their* break at the same time.
EXCEPTION: As *a father and a citizen, he* favored stricter control. (The antecedents *a father* and *a citizen* represent the same person.)

3. A pronoun referring to two antecedents connected by *or* or *nor* will be singular if both antecedents are singular, plural if one of the antecedents is plural.

Either *Bill or Joe* will have *his* car with *him*.
Neither *Mr. Jones nor his sisters* need worry about *their* lease.

See also "Subject-Verb Agreement," in this section.

Reference of Pronouns.   Be sure that the word or words the pronoun stands for are absolutely clear to the reader.

1. Do not use a pronoun—especially *it, this,* or *which*—unless it clearly refers to a specific word or idea.

BAD: Retooling is very expensive, *which* we will consider when designing a new model.
BETTER: Retooling is very expensive—a fact that we will consider when we design a new model.
ALSO GOOD: We will consider the expense of retooling before we design a new model.

2. Do not use a pronoun that may refer to more than one word or idea. If necessary, repeat the word or rephrase the sentence.

DOUBLE MEANING: Mr. Wells said that Mr. Carter would write the report after *he* had assembled the data. (Is *he* Mr. Wells or Mr. Carter?)
IMPROVED: Mr. Wells said Mr. Carter would write the report after assembling the data.
ALSO (ANOTHER MEANING):   Mr. Wells said that Mr. Carter would write the report after he, Mr. Wells, had assembled the data.

Possessive.   The possessive forms of nouns and pronouns are used to show ownership. They are usually, but not always, signified by the apostrophe ('). For example: *man's, Smith's, the company's.*

Possessive Pronouns.   The possessive form of personal pronouns is written without the apostrophe.

> my, mine   our, ours
> your, yours   their, theirs
> his, her, hers
> its (*it's* is the contraction of *it is* or *it has*)
> whose (*who's* is the contraction of *who is* or *who has*)

Other pronouns form their possessive with the apostrophe.

> one's
> someone's   somebody's
> anyone's   anybody's
> no one's   nobody's
> everyone's   everybody's

Possessive Nouns (Singular).   Singular nouns regularly form their possessive by the addition of the apostrophe and *s* (*'s*). When it would be awkward to add the *s* because the word already ends in *s* or the sound of *s*, only the apostrophe need be added.

> the President's advisers   the boss's daughter
> the bell captain's station   the *Times's* correspondent or
> an executive's privilege   the *Times'* correspondent
> the shipper's terms   Mr. Willis's office or
> the department's rules   Mr. Willis' office
> for his conscience' sake
> Los Angeles' airport
> Jesus' teachings

Possessive Nouns (Plural).   If a plural noun ends in *s*, add only the apostrophe. Otherwise, add the apostrophe and *s*.

> the Smiths' dinner party   our accountants' recommendation
> ladies' wear   men's clothing
> boys' camps   women's markets
> clients' problems   children's playthings

Double Possessive.   In certain constructions, especially after *this* and *that*, the word *of* and the possessive noun or pronoun are used together.

> CORRECT: that car of mine
>   a customer of ours
>   those photographs of Mr. Brown's (Compare with "those photographs
>   of Mr. Brown.")

Idiomatic Possessive.   In certain constructions, where possession is not involved, the possessive is nevertheless used.

> CORRECT: a day's pay, in a month's time, a week's delay

Compound Possessive.   When the expression showing possession consists of several words or a hyphenated word, the possessive is added to the last word only.

CORRECT: B. Altman & Co.'s Fifth Avenue store
            Bill Blake and Ed Conway's suggestion (Compare with "Bill Blake's
               and Ed Conway's suggestions.")
            General Motors' stock
            somebody else's responsibility
            his mother-in-law's heirs
            Fort Worth's centennial
            the branch office manager George Fry's records (But, "the branch
               office manager's, George Fry's, records.")

Possessive Before Understood Word.   The possessive is used even when the
thing possessed is not expressed.

CORRECT: at Macy's [department store]
            at your grocer's [shop]. (Also, "at your grocer")
            January's output exceeded February's [output].

Possessive Before Gerund.   When a verb form ending in *-ing* is used as a
noun (but not as an adjective), a noun or pronoun before it takes the possessive form.

CORRECT: Mr. *Gray's* coming was not anticipated.
            Their talking disturbed the operator.
            We were shocked at *his* leaving. (Not *him; leaving* is a noun, object of
               the preposition *at.*)
            We saw *him* leaving. (Correct because *leaving* is an adjective, describing
               the pronoun *him.*)

NOTE: The practice is growing of omitting the apostrophe in store and
company names. Follow the style adopted by the organization itself.

Gimbels   Mays   Broadstreets Wallachs
Sears   Harpers (magazine)   Merchants Bank

Verbs.   Verbs are words that help us make a statement about a person,
place, or thing. The italicized words in the following sentences are verbs.

We *sent* the order to you yesterday.
The two companies *were* not able to reach an agreement.
The package *was returned* because of insufficient postage.
Mr. Jones *will arrive* soon.
Miss Strum *is* forty-five years old.

Tense.   The form of the verb changes to show time. Note the forms of the
verb *walk.*

PRESENT: I walk, we walk (*also* am walking, does walk, do walk)
PAST: I walked, we walked, (*also* did walk)
FUTURE: I will (*or* shall) walk, we will (*or* shall) walk

PRESENT PERFECT: I have walked, we have walked
PAST PERFECT: I had walked, we had walked
FUTURE PERFECT: I will (*or* shall) have walked, we will (*or* shall) have walked

Irregular Verbs.   Verbs that follow the patterns shown directly above are
called *regular verbs.* Verbs that do not are called *irregular verbs.* The irregular
verb forms are given in the dictionary. Some examples:

(I) begin	began	have begun	am beginning
(it) bursts	burst	has burst	is bursting
(I) do	did	have done	am doing

Agreement with Subject.   The form of the verb must be consistent with the form of the subject. (See also "Subject-Verb Agreement" in this section.) Examples:

I go (BUT he goes)
I am (BUT you are, he is)
I have (BUT he has)
We say (BUT the customer says)

Time Relationships.   The various tense forms are used to show time relationships between verbs. Examples:

We *are shipping* your order today. (Present)
We *have shipped* your order. (Indefinite past)
We *shipped* your order on May 12. (Definite past)
We *will ship* your order promptly. (Future)
By August 1, we *will have completed* the shipment. (Time before some time in the future)
By August 1, *we had completed* the shipment. (Time before some time in the past)

Active and Passive Verbs.   Many statements can be made in two ways, depending on whether the active or passive form of the verb is used. Example:

ACTIVE: Mr. Benson signed the check.
PASSIVE: The check was signed by Mr. Benson.

When the active form of the verb is used, the subject invariably names the performer of the action of the verb—in this instance, Mr. Benson. When the passive form of the verb is used, the subject names the thing acted upon—in this instance, the check. The active form is generally preferred because it is simpler, more direct, and more concise, than the passive form. The passive form is useful, however, when the writer wants to stress the thing acted upon rather than the performer, especially for reasons of tact.

TACTLESS (ACTIVE):   You failed to sign the check.
IMPROVED (PASSIVE):   The check was not signed.

Subjunctive.   The subjunctive forms of the verb omit the *s* in the present tense (*he go,* not *he goes*) and substitute *be* for *am, is, was,* or *were,* and *were* for *was* in some constructions. Examples:

He asked that the case *be* dismissed. (Not *is*)
I wish I *were* going with you. (Not *was*)
I demand that Harry *go* with us. (Not *goes*)

Use the subjunctive:

(1) to express a request, command, motion, or resolution following the word *that.*

He requested that I *be* included on the committee.
Mr. Gordon insisted that Mr. Klein *withdraw* his petition.
I move that the meeting *be* adjourned.
Resolved, that the new training program *be* put into effect on September 1 of this year.

(2) to indicate an impossible condition following the word *if.*

He would be easier to deal with if he *were* not so stubborn. (He *is* stubborn.)
I would go if I *were* younger. (I am *not* younger.)
BUT: Mr. Starr wanted to know if I *was* coming. (I might come: so the condition is
not impossible.)

(3) to express a formal wish.

We wish he *were* able to handle the job.
I wish I *were* going with you.
BUT (informal): I wish I *was* going with you.

Words Formed from Verbs. Some words, called verbals, are formed from
verbs but have the characteristics of other parts of speech. For a description
of these forms, see "Infinitives," "Participles," and "Gerunds," following in
that order.

Infinitives. An infinitive is a verb form usually preceded by the word *to.*

He likes *to work.*
What are they going *to do* about it?
We would like *to have gone* with you.
We can help you *learn* a trade. (The *to* before *learn* is omitted.)

Split Infinitive. Splitting an infinitive is putting a word between the *to* and
the verb, for example, *to slowly walk, to eventually return.* When the split
infinitive is awkward, you should avoid it either by finding another place for
the intervening word or by recasting the sentence. In many instances, the
split infinitive is not awkward or is less awkward than the revised construction, and it should be retained.

AWKWARD: It is easy *to convincingly talk* about your own product.
IMPROVED: It is easy *to talk convincingly* about your own product.

AWKWARD: If you tried *to conscientiously apply yourself* to the problem, you would
undoubtedly be able to solve it.
IMPROVED: If you tried *to apply yourself conscientiously* . . .

NOT AWKWARD: The proposal was *to ultimately abandon* the old mine.

Tense of Infinitive. The infinitive changes its form to show time relationships.
However, the present infinitive (*to go, to be, to do, to see,* and so on) is used
whenever the action of the infinitive takes place at the same time as the action
of the verb.

I want *to go.* (Present)
I seem *to have misplaced* the key. (Time before present)
BUT: I wanted *to go.* (Past)
I would have liked *to go* with you. (Time before present)

Participles. A participle is a verb form that usually, but not always, ends in
-*ing* or -*ed,* and has the characteristics of an adjective, that is, it is used to
modify or describe a noun or pronoun.

Deprived of additional funds, he had to go out of business. (Modifies *he*)
The new man was seen *smoking* in the prohibited area. (Modifies *man*)

Dangling Participle.   A participle that does not logically relate to the word it modifies is called a dangling participle. To correct the error, recast the sentence.

> DANGLING: *Walking* across the aisle, *a hand truck* hit Mr. Haynes. (Seems as if the hand truck walked across the aisle)
> IMPROVED: *Walking* across the aisle, *Mr. Haynes* was hit by a hand truck.
> ALSO IMPROVED: A hand truck hit Mr. Haynes while he was walking across the aisle.

Gerunds.   A gerund is a verb form ending in *-ing* and having the characteristics of a noun, that is, it may be used as a subject or object.

> *Typing* is a valuable skill. (Subject)
> We objected to his *leaving* so early. (Object of preposition *to*)
> He liked *working* for us. (Object of verb *liked*)

Possessive with Gerund.   A pronoun modifying a gerund should be in the possessive form. (See also "Possessive," in this section.)

> We will appreciate *your* keeping a close watch on expenditures.
> *His* talking disturbed the others.

Clear Reference.   A prepositional phrase containing a gerund should clearly relate to some other word in the sentence. (See also "Dangling Participle," in this section.)

> AMBIGUOUS: You have been most helpful to us in advising our customer. (Who did the advising—"you" or "us"?)
> IMPROVED: The information you gave us helped us in advising our customer.

Adjectives.   Adjectives are words that describe nouns. They include the articles *a, an,* and *the* and can sometimes be identified by the endings *-able, -al, -ed, -ful, -ish, -less, -ous,* and *-y.*

a good day	*a large blue* box
the genuine article	*electronic filtering* system
working women	*leather* soles
used car	*a plentiful* supply
a harmless additive	*automatic* shift
stylish clothes	*callous* treatment

Use of Comparative and Superlative.   In formal English, the comparative is used when two units are being compared, and the superlative when the comparison involves more than two units.

> This is the *better* of the two.
> We make this shoe in a half dozen colors, but brown is the *most popular.*

> NOTE: In formal English, the superlative form is sometimes used in a comparison of two. Example:

> Between the sweet and the unsugared variety, our customers like the sweet *best.*

Comparison of Adjectives.   Adjectives change their degree of intensity by the addition of *-er* and *-est,* or by the words *more, most, less,* or *least* placed before them.

Simple	Comparative	Superlative
kind	kinder	kindest
	more kind	most kind
	less kind	least kind
early	earlier	earliest
competent	more competent	most competent

Irregular Adjectives.   Some adjectives do not follow the rules in their forms of comparison. When in doubt, consult the dictionary.

good	better	best
much	more	most
little	less	least

Adjectives After Certain Verbs.   Certain verbs, including *be,* (*is, was,* and so on), *feel, taste, smell,* and *turn* are followed by adjective complements that describe the subjects of the verbs.

The day was *hectic.*
The weather turned *warm.*
The new cream smells *good.*
I feel *great.*
I feel *good.**
I feel *well.**

*NOTE: In the last two examples, both *good* and *well* are adjectives, but *good* suggests a general state of well-being while *well* seems to refer to health alone.

Absolute Adjectives.   Some adjectives, like *unique, complete, perfect,* and *impossible,* already express the ultimate degree and therefore cannot logically be compared.

QUESTIONABLE: It has a *very unique* design.
CORRECT: It has a *unique* design.

QUESTIONABLE: The situation is becoming *more impossible* every day.
CORRECT: The situation is becoming *worse* every day.
OR: The situation is becoming *impossible.*

Adverbs.   Adverbs are words that limit or describe verbs, adjectives, or other adverbs. An identifying feature of many adverbs is the ending *-ly.* Some adverbs have two forms, for example, *slow* or *slowly, quick* or *quickly.*

worked *strenuously*	met *secretly*
a *very* likeable person	a *clearly* understood condition
very often mistaken	*too* soft
really unusual	*much* appreciated

Comparison of Adverbs.   Like adjectives, adverbs have degrees of comparison signified by the addition of *-er* and *-est,* or by the words *more* and *most* (or *less* and *least*) before them.

Simple	*Comparative*	*Superlative*
slow or	slower	slowest
slowly	more slowly	most slowly
	less slowly	least slowly
often	oftener	oftenest
	more often	most often
intelligently	more intelligently	most intelligently

Irregular Adverbs. Some adverbs form their degrees of comparison without regard to the rule above. When in doubt, consult your dictionary.

badly	worse	worst
well	better	best
far	farther, further	farthest, furthest

Double Negative. Using two negative adverbs to express a single negative idea is incorrect.

BAD: We can't see no advantage.
BETTER: We can't see any advantage.
OR: We can see no advantage.

BAD: We don't hardly go there.
BETTER: We hardly go there.

Prepositions. A preposition is a word that links a noun or pronoun with some other part of the sentence. Prepositions include such words as *in, at, to, by, for, after, before, above,* and *behind.*

Preposition at End of Sentence. There is some prejudice against the use of a preposition at the end of a sentence. However, a preposition may end a sentence when it would be awkward in another position.

AWKWARD AT END OF SENTENCE: Please let us know what conditions you will sell the property on Front Street *under.*
IMPROVED: Please let us know *under* what conditions you will sell the property on Front Street.

AWKWARD IN MIDDLE OF SENTENCE: It's a condition *with* which we will have to put up.
IMPROVED: It's a condition we will have to put up *with.*

Idiomatic Prepositions. Certain verbs characteristically take certain prepositions after them. Some verbs may be followed by one of several prepositions depending on the meaning.

We both *agree on* the need for improvement.
We *agree to* their stipulation.
I *agree with* you.

He *compared* the device *to* a thermostat. (Expresses similarity.)
The new model does not *compare with* the old in attractiveness. (Expresses dissimilarity.)

NOTE: If you are in doubt about the preposition following any verb look up the verb in your dictionary.

8.5 DICTIONARY OF ENGLISH USAGE

The correct use of words is determined by the consensus of educated people as revealed in their speech and writing. Some guidance is provided by dictionaries and books on usage, but even with these aids you have to depend to a great extent on your own judgment of what is appropriate in any given circumstance (Figure 8-3). In this listing you will find words about which

ACCEPTABLE

Formal. The language of documentary writing and of statements delivered on very dignified or state occasions.

General. The predominant language of the journalist, business writer, and public speaker.

Informal. The language characteristic of the everyday speech of educated persons and of writing that imitates such speech. Also called colloquial.

ACCEPTABLE WITH RESERVATIONS

Jargon. The specialized language of a particular trade or profession, useful in technical papers. Also, in an undesirable sense, unintelligible language or language marked by the use of pretentious words.

Slang. Language that has its origins in the streets and shops and often in the underworld. Many slang terms gain wide use and respectability and may, when used with discrimination, add color and force to otherwise dignified English.

UNDESIRABLE BUT TOLERATED

Archaic. Old-fashioned; outmoded. Occasionally found in legal writing and some business letters and memorandums.

Stilted. Stiff. Used especially to denote language that is too formal for the occasion.

Stereotyped. Applied especially to phrases that are fixed in form and have lost their vigor through overuse. Also called hackneyed.

NOT ACCEPTABLE

Illiterate. Characteristic of the uneducated. Includes distortions, misuses, and misspellings of acceptable words.

Obscene. Words that offend the sensibilities.

Figure 8-3 Levels of usage. This table is designed to help determine whether a word is acceptable and appropriate in business usage.

questions are most likely to be raised and some helpful advice on their proper use.

For questions of usage involving grammar, see "Glossary of Common Grammatical Terms," Section 8.3, and "Grammar Review," Section 8.4.

abeyance, as in "held in *abeyance"* Often used in legal papers, it is considered stilted in ordinary correspondence.

> NOT: We are holding our decision *in abeyance*
> BUT: We are holding *up* our decision.

above Correct as a noun ("the *above*") and adjective ("the *above* facts"), as well as in its traditional role as an adverb ("the date shown *above*," "the *above*-mentioned procedure"). However, more informality can be achieved with a substitute expression, for example, "these facts," "this date," "the procedure we mentioned."

above-captioned Because *captioned* refers to the heading or subject line, the word *above* seems superfluous. Thus, one might refer to "the captioned account" when the name of the account is shown as a subject line above the body of a letter. This language, however, is more suited to legal correspondence than to less formal letters and memorandums. (See also *subject*.)

administrate Misused for *administer*. Correct: Mr. Treadwell will *administer* the program.

advise Well used in the sense of "counsel," but stilted and overworked in the sense of "inform."

> GOOD: I would *advise* you to sell the property.
> STILTED: If you want us to go ahead with the order, please *advise*.
> BETTER: If you want us to go ahead with the order, please *let us know*.
> AVOID: kindly advise, please be advised, we wish to advise you.

affect, effect *Affect* is a verb meaning "to influence" or "to feign." *Effect*, as a verb, means "to bring about." As a noun, it means "result."

> His decision was *affected* by personal bias. (Influenced)
> How will the reorganization *affect* the workers. (Influence)
> He *affected* an English accent. (Feigned)
> He *effected* many changes in procedure. (Brought about)
> The *effect* of the price rise will not be known for some time. (Result)

aforementioned, aforesaid Except in legal papers, these expressions are somewhat stilted. If possible, use *this, that,* or some other expression. (See also **above**.)

> STILTED: the *aforesaid* company
> IMPROVED: *this* company, *that* company
>
> STILTED: the *aforementioned* circumstances
> IMPROVED: the circumstances *we mentioned earlier*

agenda   A list of topics to be taken up at a meeting, *agenda* is the plural of the Latin word *agendum*. However, it is usually construed as singular.

> CORRECT: The *agenda* for the meeting *has been drawn up.*

all-around, all-round   Use either word in the sense of versatile.

> CORRECT: He is a good *all-around* [or *all-round*] assistant.

alright.   Not in good usage. Use *all right* (two words).

> If Mr. Gross wants to come along, it's *all right* [not *alright*] with me.

among, between   Custom still favors the use of *between* when there are two alternatives; *among,* when the number of choices is more than two.

> We'll divide the luncheon tab *between* us. (The two of us)
> The estate was divided *between* the brother and the sister.
> The dispute *among* them was settled amicably. (More than two)

amongst   Better use *among.*

> NOT: We are looking for new markets *amongst* teen-agers.
> BUT: We are looking for new markets *among* teen-agers.

amount, number   Use *amount* to signify a sum or a quantity that cannot be measured in units; use *number* to refer to a quantity of units.

> The *amount* of the sale was $456.30.
> There is a negligible *amount* of waste in the process.
> A small *number* of passengers were stranded.

and etc.   Because *etc.* is the abbreviation for the Latin term *et cetera,* meaning "and the rest," the use of *and* with *etc.* is superfluous.

> NOT: booklets, pamphlets, circulars, *and etc.*
> BUT: booklets, pamphlets, circulars, *etc.*

anyways, anywheres   Misused for *anyway, anywhere.*

> CORRECT: We'll allow the discount *anyway.* (Not *anyways*)
>   He would be welcome *anywhere.* (Not *anywheres*)

and/or   Useful and correct in indicating "either of two, or both."

> CORRECT: The system employs videotape *and/or* film.

apt, liable, likely   *Apt* means suitable, tending (to), or quick to learn. *Liable* suggests exposure to something disadvantageous or responsibility for consequences. *Likely* refers simply to what is probable.

> It is an *apt* phrase. He is an *apt* pupil.
> If he breaks any more sales records, his success is *apt* to go to his head.
> It is *likely* that we will need more storage space soon.
> He is legally *liable* for his actions.
> If he insists on speculating, he is *liable* to get hurt.

as, that   Do not misuse *as* for *that* or *whether.*

> WRONG: We do not know for sure *as* we can meet the deadline.
> RIGHT: We do not know for sure *that* [or *whether*] we can meet the deadline.

as how   Do not misuse for *how* or *that.*

> NOT: We don't see *as how* our intervention will do any good.
> BUT: We don't see *that* [or *how*] our intervention will do any good.

as, like   *Like* is used for *as, as if,* or *as though* only in very informal English, and even then is often subject to criticism. *Like* is correctly used as a preposition.

> CORRECT: It looks *as if* [or *as though*] your prediction was right.
> QUESTIONABLE: It looks *like* your prediction was right.
>
> CORRECT: We shipped it in brown, *as* the order specified.
> QUESTIONABLE: We shipped it in brown, *like* the order specified.
>
> CORRECT: The report is bound *like* a book.

as per, per   Used in the sense of *as, in accordance with,* or *following,* these expressions are stilted and should be avoided in ordinary writing.

> STILTED: *As per* your request, we are sending you . . .
> BETTER: *In accordance with* your request, we are sending you . . .
> OR: *Following* your request, we are sending you . . .
>
> STILTED: We are sending you the booklet *per* your request.
> BETTER: We are sending you the booklet *as* you requested.

at about   The *at* is unnecessary.

> CORRECT: I'll call you *about* 10 o'clock. (Not *at about*)

awful, awfully   Although often used informally in speech, both words are best avoided in writing.

> QUESTIONABLE: He gave us an *awful* time.
> BETTER: He gave us a *hard* time.
>
> QUESTIONABLE: His performance was *awfully* good.
> BETTER: His performance was *very* good. (Or *first-rate, topnotch, lively, exciting,* and so on)

bad, badly   The correct expression is "looks *bad,*" "seems *bad,*" "feels *bad.*" It is also acceptable to say "feel *badly,*" as in "I feel *badly* (for *distressed, sorry*) about her misfortune." Otherwise *badly* is used in the sense of "in a faulty manner"; *bad,* in the sense of "faulty" or "not good."

> The copying machine is working *badly* again.
> The service is *bad.* (Not good)

balance, remainder   *Balance* is always correct in reference to accounts, but it is considered colloquial in the sense of *remainder.*

> CORRECT: We would appreciate receiving the *balance* of your account soon.
> CORRECT: We will ship the *remainder* (or *rest*) of the order on June 15.
> COLLOQUIAL: We will ship the *balance* of the order on June 15.

bank on   Colloquial for *depend on.*

based on   This construction is often used when *on the basis of* or *from* would be better. (See "Dangling Participle," in Section 8.3.)

CORRECT: Our estimate is *based* on last year's experience. (*Based* is used as an adjective modifying *estimate*.)

QUESTIONABLE: *Based on* last year's experience, we expect increasing foreign competition. (*Based on* is used as a preposition; this usage is not sanctioned in formal grammar, but is quite common in business.)

CORRECT: *On the basis of* [or *from*] last year's experience, we expect increasing foreign competition.

beg   Should never be used in such business-letter phrases as "*beg* to advise" and "*beg* to remain," in which it is considered stilted and antiquated.

being that   Incorrectly used for *since* or *because*.

NOT: *Being that* you are leaving for Los Angeles tomorrow . . .
BUT: [*Since*] you are leaving for Los Angeles tomorrow . . .

beside, besides   Often confused. *Beside* means "by the side of"; *besides* means "in addition to" or "furthermore."

Please put the carton *beside* the desk. (Not *besides*)
Who *besides* Mr. Grant and Mr. Fellows said they would come?
Besides, we didn't want to disturb the present arrangement.

NOTE: *Beside* is also used idiomatically in such expressions as "*beside* the point" and "*beside* oneself with fear."

best of any.   Used informally only. Expressions in better use are *best one* and *best of those*.

QUESTIONABLE: It's the *best of any* we've tried.
CORRECT: It's the *best one* we've tried.
CORRECT: It's the *best of those* we've tried.

between you and I   Common but ungrammatical. The correct expression is *between you and me*. (*Between* is a preposition and a pronoun that follows must be in the objective case.)

bi-, semi-   *Bi-* means "occurring every two" or "occurring twice." Thus *biweekly* means either "coming every two weeks," or "coming twice a week." To relieve the ambiguity, *semi-* is often used in the sense of "occurring twice," as in *semiweekly, semimonthly, semiannually* (every six months). *Biannual* means "occurring twice a year"; *biennial* means "occurring every two years."

bring, take   Careful writers and speakers use *bring* to indicate action toward them, and *take* to indicate action away from them.

Bring the report with you when you come.
Please *take* the finished copies back with you.

but   Like *and*, *but* may be used informally at the beginning of a sentence. *However* is generally preferred in more formal written work.

We tried to get Joe to work for us. *But* you know how temperamental plumbers are.

but what   Colloquial for *but that*.

COLLOQUIAL: I don't know *but what* you are right.
MORE FORMAL: I don't know *but that* you are right.

can, may In strict usage, *can* is used to denote ability, and *may* to indicate permission. In ordinary usage, however, *can* is almost invariably used in both senses.

> You *may* have both sizes if you want them. (Denotes permission)
> You *can* have both sizes if you want them. (Also denotes permission)
> Your application says you *can* write advertising copy. (Denotes ability)

can not, cannot Both forms are correct although the latter is generally preferred.

cannot help but In informal English, the better expression is *can't help;* in formal English, *cannot but.*

> QUESTIONABLE: You *can't help but* like a man like that.
> IMPROVED: You *can't help* liking a man like that.
> FORMAL: You *cannot but* like a man like that.

can't hardly Misused for *can hardly.*

> We *can hardly* wait for the spring fashion opening.

can't seem Informal for *doesn't seem able* or *seems unable.*

> INFORMAL: He *can't seem* to understand his responsibilities.
> FORMAL: He *seems unable* (or *doesn't seem able*) to understand his responsibilities.

compose, comprise These words are often confused. *Compose* means "to constitute"; *comprise* means "to include or consist of."

> The set *comprises* three leatherbound volumes.
> Three leatherbound volumes *compose* the set.

contact Although there are still some objections to the word in the sense of "get in touch with," *contact* is commonly and acceptably used in business when such words as *write, call on,* or *telephone* would be too specific.

> ACCEPTABLE: Please *contact* the customer as soon as you can.
> SOMETIMES PREFERRED: Please *get in touch with* the customer as soon as you can.

could of Illiterate for *could have.*

> He *could have* had any territory he wanted.

data Although it is the plural form of the Latin *datum, data* is acceptably used as a singular noun.

> CORRECT: the *data* show, or the *data* shows

deal Informal for such more specific words as *transaction, arrangement,* and *bargain.*

> INFORMAL: They offered a pretty good *deal.*
> FORMAL: They offered a *bargain.*
>
> INFORMAL: He refused to go through with the *deal.*
> FORMAL: He refused to complete the *transaction.*

deem Overformal for *think, believe,* or *consider.*

STIFF: We *deem* it advisable ...
BETTER: We *think* it advisable ...

different than   Now generally acceptable, although *different from* is sometimes preferred in formal usage.

> CORRECT: The present plan is much *different than* the one originally proposed.
> MORE FORMAL: The present plan is much *different from* the one originally proposed.

disinterested, uninterested   Although careful users of English still distinguish between *disinterested* (impartial) and *uninterested* (not interested), the former is commonly substituted for the latter.

> QUESTIONABLE: He seemed *disinterested* in our proposal.
> CORRECT: He seemed *uninterested* in our proposal.
> CORRECT: He was completely *disinterested* as to the outcome. (Impartial)

due to   There is some lingering objection to the use of *due to* in the sense of "because of," though not to its use in the sense of "caused by" or "owing to." Few businessmen would care to maintain the distinction.

> SANCTIONED BY USAGE: *Due to* a power failure, we were forced to suspend operations for a day. (Because of)
> CORRECT WITHOUT QUESTION: The shutdown was *due to* a power plant failure. (Caused by)

duly   This stilted expression, meaning "in a proper manner," should not be used except in legal writing.

> NOT: We have *duly* entered your order.
> BUT: We have entered your order.

effect   See **affect.**

enthuse   Little objection remains to the use of this word with *is, was,* and so on in the sense of "enthusiastic." It is better not used, however, when the meaning is "to express enthusiasm."

> CORRECT: Mr. Carmen was *enthusiastic* about the plan.
> GENERALLY APPROVED: Mr. Carmen *was enthused* about the plan.
> QUESTIONABLE: Mr. Carmen *enthused* about the plan.

Esq., Esquire   An archaic British expression still occasionally used in the United States to address attorneys; for example, Joseph Manners, *Esq.,* not *Mr.* Joseph Manners, *Esq.*

farther, further   In formal usage, *farther* is used to express distance; *further,* to express degree. In informal usage, including most business practice, *further* is used in both senses.

> FORMAL: The new plant should be located *farther* north.
> INFORMAL: The new plant should be located *further* north.
> CORRECT ON ALL LEVELS: The *further* you look into the story, the more convincing it is.
>   They must not go *further* into debt.

favor   Archaic when used in the sense of "letter."

NOT: We have your *favor* of February 16.
BUT: We have your *letter* of February 16.

NOTE: If you consider the letter a favor, say, "Thank you for your letter."

fewer, less   In strict usage, *fewer* refers to number, *less* to degree or amount.

He made *fewer* changes than we expected. (Not *less*)
They offered *less* than we asked.
The files contain *fewer* papers, *less* superfluous material, than they did a year ago.

figuratively   See **literally.**

finalize   Despite initial criticism, this word seems to have found a useful place for itself in the sense of "make final," "put the finishing touches on."

ACCEPTABLE: If you will let us hear from you, we will be able to *finalize* the language of the contract.

flammable   Correctly and advantageously used as a synonym of *inflammable,* which is sometimes mistaken for "not flammable." Both words mean "easily set on fire."

CORRECT: If we store *flammable* materials, we will have to pay higher insurance premiums.

focalize   Better say *focus.*

NOT: We will *focalize* all our attention on this campaign.
BUT: We will *focus* all our attention on this campaign.

former, first   Use *first,* not *former,* to indicate the first of more than two. (See also **latter, last.**)

NOT: We received bids from Allied, Murphy, and Consolidated, but we gave the order to the *former.*
BUT: . . . we gave the order to the *first.*
CORRECT: We received bids from Allied and Murphy, but we gave the order to the *former.* (Or, better, to "*Allied*")

forward   Strictly speaking, to *forward* a letter is to send it from an intermediate station to its destination. Thus if one receives a misaddressed letter, he may *forward* it to the addressee. In other circumstances, the word *send* is simpler and more common.

CORRECT: When the statement arrives, I will *forward* it to you.
CORRECT: We will *send* you the statement as soon as it is ready.
QUESTIONABLE: We will *forward* the statement to you as soon as it is ready.

forward on   *Forward* alone conveys the idea. The *on* is superfluous.

guess   Informal for *suppose.*

INFORMAL: If he asks for the day off, I *guess* we will have to let him have it.
FORMAL: . . . I *suppose* we will have to let him have it.

hand you herewith   To be used only when something is delivered with the letter in person. Otherwise, write "we are enclosing," "you will find enclosed," or "enclosed is."

hanged, hung   Criminals may be *hanged,* but pictures are *hung.*

happenstance   Informal for "accidental happening." In formal usage, the word should be *accident* or *circumstance.*

irregardless   Illiterate for *regardless.*

NOT: *Irregardless* of what you say ...
BUT: *Regardless* of what you say ...

kind of a, sort of a   The *a* is better omitted.

CORRECT: What *kind of* [or *sort of*] credit risk is he?
QUESTIONABLE: What *kind of a* credit risk is he?

NOTE 1:   In formal usage do not use *kind of* or *sort of* for *somewhat.*

INFORMAL: She acted *kind of* helpless.
FORMAL: She acted *somewhat* helpless.

NOTE 2:   Say *this kind* or *these kinds,* but not *these kind.*

NOT: I like *these kind* of finishes.
BUT: I like *this kind* of finish.
OR: I like *these kinds* of finishes.

kind enough to, so kind as to   The first expression is preferred, though both often imply some sarcasm.

NOT: Please be *so kind as to* return our deposit.
BUT: Please be *kind enough to* return our deposit.
USUALLY PREFERRED: We would appreciate it if you would return our deposit.

kindly   Correct when used in the sense of "with kindness," for example, "He *kindly* returned our deposit." It is a bit stiff when used in the sense of "please."

ACCEPTABLE: *Kindly* sign and return the carbon copy of this letter.
BETTER: *Please* sign and return ...

latter, last   Use *latter* to indicate the second of two; *last,* to indicate the last of three or more.

NOT: We received bids from Allied, Murphy, and Consolidated, but we gave the order to the *latter.*
BUT: ... we gave the order to the *last.*
CORRECT: We received bids from Allied and Murphy, but we gave the order to the *latter.* (Or, better, "to *Murphy*")

lay, lie   *Lay* means "to place" and always takes an object. *Lie* means "to recline" and does not take an object. Confusion occurs because *lay* is also the past tense of *lie,* whereas *laid* is the past tense of *lay.* Note these forms.

He always *lies* down in the afternoon.
He *lay* down yesterday afternoon.
He *has lain* down every afternoon this week.

Lay the carton on the floor.
He *laid* the carton on the floor.
He *has laid* the carton on the floor.

leave, let   Leave means "to allow to remain" ("He *left* the charts behind."); *let* means "to allow."

NOT: *Leave* the customer have the discount.
BUT: *Let* the customer have the discount.

NOT: *Leave* him go when he wants to.
BUT: *Let* him go when he wants to.

lieu, in lieu of   *In lieu of* means "in place of." It is sometimes mistakenly used for "in view of" or "because of."

NOT: *In lieu of* the defect, we are recalling all new models.
BUT: *In view of* [or *because of*] the defect, we are recalling all new models.
CORRECT: We'll take the discount *in lieu of* the bonus in merchandise.

like   See *as, like.*

literally, figuratively   *Literally* means "exactly what the words say"; *figuratively* means "not in the exact sense." Do not use one when you mean the other.

DO NOT SAY: When he objected, he was *literally* chewed up alive.
WHEN YOU MEAN: When he objected, he was *figuratively* chewed up alive.
OR (BETTER):   When he objected, he was violently shouted down.

meantime   Better say "in the meantime," or "meanwhile."

NOT: *Meantime,* we will look around for substitutes.
BUT: *Meanwhile,* we will look around for substitutes.
OR: *In the meantime,* we will look around for substitutes.

media   Plural of *medium* and should be treated as a plural.

NOT: The outdoor *media has* not been especially effective.
BUT: The outdoor *media have* not . . .
CORRECT: As a *medium* for classified advertising, newspapers cannot be equaled.

moneys, monies   The first appears to be preferred for currencies, the second for amounts of money.

CORRECT: The Chase Museum has a collection of *moneys* of the world.
CORRECT: The *monies* have yet to be collected. (Amounts from several sources)

most   Do not use for *almost.*

NOT: *Most* everybody came.
BUT: *Almost* everybody came.

NOT: *Most all* of us agreed.
BUT: *Almost all* of us agreed.

myself   Sometimes used incorrectly for *me. Myself* is correctly used as an intensifier of *I* or to refer reflexively to the subject *I.*

NOT: . . . between him and *myself.*
BUT: . . . between him and *me.*

CORRECT: I myself will do it. (Intensifier)
CORRECT: I bought one for *myself*. (Reflexive)

not as, not so In a negative comparison, the *not so* is more formal than *not as,* but both are correct.

CORRECT: The new design is *not so* simple as the old one.
CORRECT: The new design is *not as* simple as the old one.

noted Sometimes misused for *marked.*

NOT: We have *noted* our records accordingly.
BUT: We have *marked* our records accordingly.
CORRECT: We have *noted on* our records that . . .

of Illiterate when used for *have,* following *would, could,* or *should.*

NOT: He *could of* gone yesterday.
BUT: He *could have* gone yesterday.

off of The *of* is superfluous.

NOT: We'll try to keep them *off of* the property.
BUT: We'll try to keep them *off* the property.

only The position of *only* depends on the sense. Compare:

He *only* delivered the package. (He did not have anything else to do with it.)
He delivered *only* the package. (He delivered nothing else.)
Only he delivered the package. (He had no helper.)
He delivered the package *only*. (He delivered nothing else.)

NOTE: In informal use, when there is no chance of misunderstanding, the position of *only* is often shifted.

CORRECT: He *only talks* that way to customers. (For *only to customers*)

our, as in "*our* Miss Jones" Considered by some not to be in good taste. Better to say only "Miss Jones" or, if further identification is needed, use some phrase like "Miss Jones in our bookkeeping department."

party Correctly used in legal phrases and in reference to a telephone caller, but otherwise considered slang as a substitute for *person.*

QUESTIONABLE: Are you the *party* who called yesterday?
BETTER: Are you the *person* [or *lady* or *gentleman*] who called yesterday?
CORRECT: I have your *party* now. (Person telephoned to)
CORRECT: One of the *parties* to the contract raised a question about the language.

per Correctly used in such Latin expressions as *per* capita, *per* annum, and *per* diem, and in other formal expressions like "thirty hours *per* week," "$3.60 *per* hour," "ninety miles *per* hour." In informal expression, however, *a* or *an* seems more natural.

FORMAL: The rate of pay is now two dollars *per* hour for unskilled labor.
INFORMAL: We pay two dollars *an* hour for unskilled help.

per, as per   See **as per.**

percent, per cent   Both spellings are correct, but usage seems to favor the first.

percent, percentage   *Percent* means "per hundred"; *percentage* means "rate per hundred," or a share or portion.

> CORRECT: They pay 4 *percent* interest.
> The *percentage* of loss is really quite small.
> The producer receives a *percentage* of the gross.

percentage   Slang when used in the sense of "advantage."

> SLANG: There's no *percentage* in mistreating customers.
> MORE FORMAL: There's no *advantage* in mistreating customers.

practical, practicable   *Practical* means "useful," "not theoretical," or "experienced through practice"; *practicable* means "feasible" or "capable of being put into practice, but not yet tried." *Practical* may be used as descriptive of a person, but *practicable* may not.

> The plan you propose seems *practicable.*
> We are looking for a *practical* solution to the problem.
> A *practical* person is needed for the job.

prefer rather than   Better say *prefer to.*

> NOT: I *prefer* staying late *rather than* working on Saturday.
> BUT: I *prefer* staying late *to* working on Saturday.
> OR: I would *rather* stay late *than* work on Saturday.
>
> NOT: We *prefer* the rectangular model *rather than* the square one.
> BUT: We *prefer* the rectangular model *to* the square one.

prior to   Too formal for most uses. Say *before.*

> NOT: They are offering 10 per cent off *prior to* their official opening.
> BUT: . . . *before* their official opening.

proposition   Correctly used for *plan* or *proposal,* but slang in some other senses.

> SLANG: That's a pretty good *proposition you have on.* (Suit you're wearing)
> SLANG: She's a *neat proposition.* (Attractive girl)
> CORRECT: The *proposition* struck me as very fair. (Proposal)

proved, proven   Both are correct, though *proven* may sound better as a pure adjective (not part of a verb).

> He has *proved* [or *proven*] his point.
> The success of the device has yet to be *proved* [or *proven*].
> A *proven* fact (better than "a *proved* fact"); their *proven* ability (better than "their *proved* ability").

provided, providing   Both are correct as conjunctions, but the first is generally preferred.

> CORRECT: We will come into the plan *providing* we get a satisfactory advertising allowance.
> PREFERRED: We will come into the plan *provided* . . .

pursuant to   Very formal. Except in legal papers, it is better to use *in accordance with, following,* or a similar construction. (See also **as per, per.**)

> OVERFORMAL: *Pursuant to your request,* we are glad to send you . . .
> BETTER: *As you requested . . .*
>   *Following your request . . .*
>   *In accordance with your request . . .*
> BETTER STILL: We are glad to send you the booklet *you requested.*

raise, rise   To *raise* is to lift (something); to *rise* is to get up or to go up. Note these correct forms.

> We *raise* their pay every six months.
> We *have raised* their pay.
> We *raised* their pay.
> He *rises* at six in the morning.
> He *has risen* at six.
> He *rose* at six.
> Prices *are rising.*
> Prices *have risen.*
> Prices *rose.*

re, in re   Latin for "subject," "regarding," or "in the matter of," it is best avoided in ordinary correspondence.

> NOT: your letter *re* (or *in re*) the damaged carton
> BUT: your letter *about* the damaged carton

NOTE: When a subject line is used in a letter, the word *Subject* or no prefix at all is more modern than *Re.* Compare:

> *Re:* Your letter of October 14
> *Subject:* Your letter of October 14
> Your letter of October 14

reason is because   *Reason is that* is generally preferred.

> QUESTIONABLE: The *reason* he declined *was because* he had already committed himself to another company.
> BETTER: The *reason* he declined *was that* he had . . .

refer back to   The word *back* is superfluous.

> NOT: Please *refer back* to our order No. 16757.
> BUT: Please *refer* to our order No. 16757.

regard, regards   The correct expression is "in [or with] regard to," not "in [or with] regards to." *As regards* is somewhat stiff, but may be used correctly in the sense of "with regard to."

> NOT: your inquiry *in regards to*
> BUT: your inquiry *in regard to*
> CORRECT: *as regards* your inquiry

reimburse, reimbursement   These words refer to the repayment of money spent or compensation for damages, time lost, and so on. They should not be used in the simple sense of *pay* or *payment.*

NOT: We will *reimburse* you for the chairs.
BUT: We will *pay* you for the chairs.
CORRECT: The check enclosed is *reimbursement* for the expenses you incurred.
CORRECT: We expect to be *reimbursed* for the loss.

said   Except in legal writing, do not use *said* for *this* or *these*.

NOT: the *said* client, the *said* goods
BUT: *this* client, *these* goods

same   Considered stereotyped in the sense of *it* or *they*.

NOT: Please let us know the charges and we will send you a check for *same*.
BUT: . . . and we will send you a check to cover *them*.

NOT: We have your order and thank you for *same*.
BUT: We have your order and thank you for *it*.
BETTER STILL: Thank you for your order.

seldom ever, rarely ever   Informal for *seldom if ever, rarely if ever*.

INFORMAL: We *seldom ever* [or *rarely ever*] buy anything without getting a receipt.
USUALLY BETTER: We *seldom if ever* [or *rarely if ever*] buy anything without getting a receipt.
ALSO GOOD: We *seldom* [or *rarely*] buy anything without getting a receipt.

shall, will   The debate over *shall* and *will* never had much substance and has happily run its course. If in doubt, use *will* and don't worry about it. For a more precise guide to usage, follow these rules.

1. In formal statements, the following forms are correct:

Singular	*Plural*
I shall	we shall
you will	you will
he [she, it] will	they will

EXAMPLES:
I *shall* appreciate your prompt reply.
You *will*, of course, send us a confirmation.
The order *will* be ready when you call.

2. To express determination, the forms *shall* and *will* are reversed.

Singular	*Plural*
I will	we will
you shall	you shall
he [she, it] shall	they shall

EXAMPLES:
I will go. (That is, I am determined to go.)
You shall go. (That is, I am determined that you will go.)
He shall go. (That is, I am determined that he will go.)

3. In informal usage, *will* is used exclusively in all the instances already cited.

CORRECT: I *will* call you tomorrow.
          We will look forward to hearing from you.
          It will be good to hear from you.
          You will pay the bill; I'll see that you do. (Determination)

4. Use *shall* with *I* and *we* (but not with *you, he, she, it,* or *they*) in questions.

CORRECT: *Shall I* [or *we*] send you a copy?
CORRECT: *Will you* please send us a copy? *Will they* send us a copy?

5. Use *shall* in formally stated rules and regulations.

EXAMPLES:
The president *shall* be the chief executive officer.
Smoking *shall* not be permitted except in designated areas.
Tools *shc* . be returned to the supply room at the end of each day.

should, would   Most questions regarding *should* and *would* relate to their use with *I* or *we*. Both forms are correct, though *should* is considered more formal than *would*.

FORMAL: *I* [*we*] *should* be glad to fill your request.
INFORMAL: *I* [*we*] *would* be glad to fill your request.

1. Many writers prefer the *would* to *should* in the construction shown above because they feel the *should* implies obligation, although that is not the intent of the word.

2. Except to express obligation (see point 3), *would* is always used with all subjects other than *I* or *we*.

They would be glad to fill your request.
I am sure *you would* not object.

3. *Should* is correctly used in all constructions to express obligation. It is considered somewhat milder than *ought*.

We should follow the instructions.
They should try to meet their obligations more promptly.
It should be an interesting performance.

4. The difference between *shall* and *should* is that *should* expresses more hesitancy and is less emphatic and more polite. The same distinction holds for *will* and *would*. Compare:

Would you please let us have . . .
Will you please let us have . . .

I *should* [or *would*] be glad to . . .
I *shall* [or *will*] be glad to . . .

sick, ill   *Ill* is considered less crude than *sick,* which many people associate with nausea. Nevertheless, *sick* is a good informal word to denote any indisposition.

Mary was out *sick* yesterday.
Mr. Grimes has been *ill* for the past week.

-size, -sized   One may say "a *small-size* glass" or a "*a small-sized* glass." The latter is somewhat more formal.

someplace, somewhere, somewheres   *Somewhere* is preferred to *someplace*. *Somewheres* is incorrect.

BAD: We were looking for *somewheres* to go.
BETTER: We were looking for *someplace* to go.
MORE FORMAL: We were looking for *somewhere* to go.

subject   When a letter has a caption or subject line, references to the caption are sometimes made by such a phrase as "the *subject file*," "the *subject* account," "the *subject* letter," and so on. Such writing becomes rather stilted and is best avoided, except in fairly routine correspondence.

ROUTINE: The value of the *subject* account as of October 31, 19—, was as follows:
INFORMAL: The value of *this* (that is, the *subject*) account as of October 31, 19—, was as follows.

subsequent to   An overformal expression for *after* or *following*.

STIFF: *Subsequent to* his arrival . . .
BETTER: *Following* his arrival . . .
            After he arrived . . .

therefor, therein, thereon   Used in legal or other official papers, but considered stilted in ordinary letters and reports and should be avoided. *Therefor* means "for it" and should not be confused with *therefore*.

STIFF: The order is enclosed, with payment *therefor*.
BETTER: The order is enclosed with our check in payment.

STIFF: The drawings were kept *therein*.
BETTER: The drawings were kept *in it* [or *inside*].

STIFF: The electric coffee-maker consists of a separate heating element with a chrome urn *placed thereon*.
BETTER: The electric coffeemaker consists of a separate heating element with a chrome urn *on top of it*.

this here, these here   Omit the *here*.

NOT: *This here* style is the one we prefer.
BUT: *This* style is the one we prefer.

till, until   Both are correct, although the second often sounds better at the beginning of a sentence.

CORRECT: *Until* [or *till*] he came, we didn't know what to do.
CORRECT: Please don't do anything *till* [or *until*] you hear from us.

try and   Less formal than *try to*, but both are correct.

Try and stop me.
Try to find out when the shipment will arrive.

undersigned, the writer   Considered awkward and impersonal. Use the appropriate personal pronoun.

NOT: Please return it to *the undersigned*.
BUT: Please return it to *me* [or *us*].

unique   Because this is a superlative in a class with *most unusual*, it seems illogical to modify it with such words as *very* or *most*.

NOT: This is our *most unique* design.
BUT: This is our *most unusual* design.
OR: This design is *unique*. (The only one of its kind)

verbal This word means literally "in words," but is often used for *oral* (that is, not written) in such an expression as, "We had a *verbal* agreement." The word is now considered correct in this sense.

where Used informally for *that*.

QUESTIONABLE: I see *where* the Adams Company has moved again.
BETTER: I see *that* the Adams Company has moved again.

who, which, that *Who* usually refers to persons, *which* to things, and *that* to persons or things.

Anyone *who* is willing to pay the price can have it.
The table, *which* was more than six feet square, could not fit through the door.
It's a problem *that* [or *which*] calls for the most careful consideration.
The number of people *that* [or *who*] entered the contest was staggering.

who, whom *Who* is usually used as a subject, *whom* as an object. In speech, however, especially when the word comes at the beginning of a sentence, it is often difficult to figure out in advance what form is called for. In such circumstances, it is recommended that *who* be used in preference to *whom*.

CORRECT: *Who* will be responsible for the charges? (Subject)
CORRECT: He is not the man with *whom* we were dealing. (Object of preposition *with*)
CORRECT: I don't know *whom* he saw. (Object of verb *saw*)
ACCEPTABLE IN SPEECH: I don't know *who* he saw.
CORRECT: *Whom* shall I give the keys to? (Object of preposition *to*)
ACCEPTABLE IN SPEECH: *Who* shall I give the keys to?

whose Despite some minor objections, *whose* may be used for *of which*.

CORRECT BUT AWKWARD: We don't want a typewriter *of which* the type bars are made of plastic.
BETTER: We don't want a typewriter *whose* type bars are made of plastic.
BETTER STILL: We don't want a typewriter with plastic type bars.

-wise Somewhat overworked in such words as *sales-wise, budget-wise, profit-wise, construction-wise.*

QUESTIONABLE: We expect to show an increase *sales-wise*.
BETTER: We expect to show an increase *in sales*.

9

Punctuation

The purpose of punctuation is to help communicate clearly the sense intended in a particular passage. At the same time, the writer or typist is expected to be guided by established customs. The modern tendency is to use the fewest marks of punctuation consistent with clarity and reading ease.

Grammatical terms used in this chapter are defined in "Glossary of Common Grammatical Terms," Section 8.3.

CONTENTS

9.1	Apostrophe	p. 340
9.2	Brackets	p. 341
9.3	Colon	p. 341
9.4	Comma	p. 343
9.5	Dash	p. 347
9.6	Ellipsis	p. 348
9.7	Exclamation Point	p. 348
9.8	Hyphen	p. 349
9.9	Parentheses	p. 353
9.10	Period	p. 355
9.11	Question Mark	p. 356
9.12	Quotation Marks	p. 357
9.13	Semicolon	p. 360

9.1 APOSTROPHE   [']

To Form the Possessive. Use the apostrophe to indicate the possessive case of nouns and indefinite pronouns. (See also the section on the possessive in "Grammar Review," Section 8.4.)

Mr. David's proposal	everybody's business
Tom's arrival	a month's work
a sale at Altman's	the Smith's reception

For Omitted Letters. The apostrophe shows the omission of letters in contractions and shortened words. It is also used in abbreviated dates.

can't   I'll   we've
isn't   he's   you're (you are)

o'clock (of the clock)
M'Grath (McGrath)

'tis   Gifts 'n' Things   Class of '68

To Form Certain Plurals. The apostrophe is used to form the plural of letters of the alphabet, figures, and words named as words. (See also "Numbers," Section 10.3.)

dot the *i*'s
the *x*'s do not count
bundled in *10*'s and *20*'s
   (BUT: bundled in *tens* and *twenties*)
too many *and*'s and *but*'s

With Coined Verbs. The endings of some coined verbs are preceded by an apostrophe.

x'd out
O.K.'ing the copy (OR: *okaying* the copy)

9.2 BRACKETS   [ ]

Brackets are formed on the typewriter by the diagonal and the underline keys.

For Parentheses. Use brackets instead of parentheses within a passage already enclosed by parentheses.

In another work (*The Elements of Style* [Macmillan]), the point is treated . . .
According to the new law (Section IV [I-b]), the county . . .

Within Quotations. An editor or transcriber uses brackets, not parentheses, to explain, amplify, question, or correct copied or quoted material.

The contract says that "the vendor [Shepherd and Stern] agrees to bear 50 per cent of the advertising cost."
Part II applies these [principles] to the everyday realities of commercial life.
I quote: "Today [August 17] we fly to Brazil."
"In this contect [sic] it can be seen that . . . (*Sic,* meaning "thus," is used to show that the apparent misspelling was in the original material.)
OR: "In this contect [context?] it can be seen that . . ."

9.3 COLON   [:]

After a Formal Introduction. A colon may be used after a formal introduction to a quotation, enumeration, or explanation.

The telegram read: "Arrive Thursday . . ."

The following steps are involved:
1. Preparation of plate
2. Transfer of copy
3. Printing

Here is the plan we have adopted: Beginning April 2, the four o'clock shift will . . .

For Emphasis.   Use a colon in place of a comma (or of no punctuation) in order to emphasize the word or words that follow. Do not use the colon, however, unless the words to which the colon applies end the sentence.

In a word: No. (COMPARE: In a word, no.)
You can reach him by telephone at: (212) 588-7606.
BUT NOT: You can reach him by telephone at: (212) 588-7606 after 10 a.m. (Omit colon.)

Amplification.   Use a colon before a word, phrase, or sentence that interprets or amplifies. It is somewhat less emphatic than a dash, which may be used for the same purpose.

He was absent one day: Friday.
It's a popular plan: 98 percent of our employees elect it.
We have several models: manual, battery, and electric.
Two courses are open to you: to invest your savings or to fritter them away.

After a Salutation.   A colon is generally used after the salutation of a business letter, and after the salutation in any context in which the attention of the reader is desired.

Dear Mr. Jones:
Gourmets: Feast on passion fruit in the Arawak Dining Room.

Clock Time.   Use a colon to separate hours and minutes and minutes and seconds.

12:45 p.m.
He ran the mile in 4:3.5. (4 minutes, 3½ seconds)
The blast was registered at 4:16:23 a.m. EST.

Capital After Colon.   As a rule, capitalize the first word of a complete sentence following a colon. An exception may be made when the sentence is short and an informal effect is desired. When the words following a colon do not form a complete sentence, do not capitalize the first word unless it is a proper name.

Here is how we see the situation: The President is determined to have his tax increase.
You can't win: stock up for hot weather and you get snow.
Many types of businesses are affected: manufacturing, retail, service.

9.4   COMMA $\boxed{,}$

Comma Directory

Appositives	p. 345	Interrupting Elements	p. 344
Balanced statements	p. 346	Inverted names	p. 346
Clarity	p. 346	Name suffixes	p. 346
Connectives	p. 344	Nonrestrictive elements	p. 345
Contrasting elements	p. 345	Omitted words	p. 346
Dates	p. 346	Participial phrases	p. 343
Direct address	p. 345	Proper names	p. 346
Emphasis	p. 347	Quotations	p. 346
Geographical names	p. 346	Series	p. 344
Gerund phrases	p. 343	Subordinate clauses	p. 343
Independent clauses	p. 343	Verbal phrases	p. 343
Infinitive phrases	p. 343		

Between Independent Clauses.   A comma is usually used before *and, but, for, or,* or *nor* when they join independent clauses (complete statements).

> We are most impressed with the performance you describe, and we will include a reference to it in the report we make.
> The building was scheduled for completion in July, but shortages of material caused a two-month delay.

NOTE: The comma is often omitted when the clauses are short.

> Mail the tape to your secretary and she'll type it up before you return.
> You have to be satisfied or you won't owe us a cent.

After Introductory Subordinate Clauses.   A subordinate clause at the beginning of a sentence is followed by a comma. Usually, no comma is needed when the subordinate clause follows the main clause.

> If you want an extra supply, please let us know.
> Although we did not foresee the rise, we are prepared for it.
> After the floor is cleared, the carpenters can get to work.

BUT:

> The carpenters can get to work after the floor is cleared. (No comma because subordinate clause follows main clause.)

After Initial Verbal Phrases.   An introductory phrase containing part of a verb (participle, gerund, or infinitive) is followed by a comma.

> Having watched his performance, we feel he is well qualified for the job. (Participle)
> To ensure good condition of contents, store in cool place. (Infinitive)
> On learning what had happened, they immediately got in touch with their insurance agents. (Gerund)

1. No comma follows an infinitive or gerund phrase that is the subject of the sentence.

> To know him is a pleasure.
> Dealing in speculative stocks is risky.

2. No comma follows an introductory element consisting of a simple prepositional phrase closely related to the meaning of the rest of the sentence.

In many ways he was an excellent accountant.
For the next 12 months our hands will be tied.

After Initial Connectives.   Put a comma after an initial word or phrase used as a connective, a mild interjection, or a sentence modifier.

However, we are not prepared for the consequences.
For example, every stitch is sewn by hand.
Still, you should have foreseen the possibility of a price rise.
Naturally, we would be interested in such a plan.
In any event, Mr. Greer says his decision is final.
No, we couldn't think of it.
Well, what can we do?

In a Series of Words or Phrases.   Use commas to separate sentence elements arranged in a series. In journalistic practice, the comma is omitted before the *and* or *or* preceding the last member of the series. However, the comma is often included in other writing, especially when its omission may confuse the sense.

Procedures for preparing invoices, handling accounts receivable, and reporting balances will all need to be changed.
He wrote, he telephoned, he telegraphed—but he could get no answer.
The departments affected are Accounting, Marketing and Advertising, and Personnel. (Omission of last comma would cause confusion.)

NOTE: A series of adjectives modifying the same noun are separated by commas when each adjective has a direct reference to the noun. However, no comma is used when each adjective modifies the whole phrase that follows. *Hint:* Try substituting *and* for the comma. If the phrase makes sense, the comma is necessary; if not, the comma should be omitted.

The job required a strong, healthy, cheerful individual. (That is, "strong *and* healthy *and* cheerful.")
It was a cold, rainy April. (That is, "cold *and* rainy.")

But (no comma):

Featured in the sale was a short belted white coat.
They put up 24 two-story red brick houses.

To Set Off Interrupting Elements.   Use commas to set off words and phrases that interrupt the sense or the grammatical structure of the sentence. Do not use commas where no interruption exists.

1. Connecting words.

In these circumstances, therefore, we are waiving the deposit.
We are committed, nevertheless, to this course of action.
Every stitch, for example, was sewn by hand.
It was, in fact, the model we were looking for.

But (no interruption—no comma):

We are therefore waiving the deposit.
You are nevertheless entitled to the refund.

2. *Such as, namely, that is, e.g., i.e.*

Some energy fuels, such as wood and coal, have had sharp declines.
The prime contractor, that is, the company we are dealing with, could provide the
  specifications.
Use a street name or the equivalent, e.g., R.D. 4 or Box 45.

But (no interruption—no comma):

Such energy fuels as wood and coal have had sharp declines.

3. Appositives.

The old adding machine, an Addex 505, should be replaced.
Please address the letter to Mr. Grayson, the sales manager.
Bond & Co., their advertising agency, are now preparing the campaign.

But (no interruption—no comma):

My son George will enter the business next year.
The word *profit* sometimes has a negative connotation.
The call came from their Aunt Martha.
Thank the architect Gropius for the striking design.

4. Words in direct address.

Mr. Hanley, you are to be congratulated.
We are going to ask you, Mary, to order the flowers.

5. Contrasting elements.

The high interest rates, rather than the sales decline, caused our undoing.
I want an answer from the president, not his assistant.

To Set Off Nonrestrictive Elements.   Phrases and clauses that cannot be
separated from the rest of the sentence without changing the meaning are
called restrictive. Those that may be left out are called nonrestrictive. The
nonrestrictive elements are set off by commas; the others take no punctuation.
Compare:

Miss Thomas, *who has had some advanced mathematics,* is ideal for the job. (The
  italicized phrase is nonrestrictive because it can be left out without altering the
  sense.)
A girl *who has had some advanced mathematics* is ideal for the job. (The italicized
  phrase is restrictive because it cannot be left out without altering the sense.)
The Garry Duplicator, *with its strong guarantee,* should prove to be a good investment. (Nonrestrictive.)
A duplicator *with a strong guarantee* should prove to be a good investment. (Restrictive.)
The typewriter, which is now 10 years old, should be replaced. (Nonrestrictive.)
Any typewriter that is 10 years old should be replaced. (Restrictive.)

To Set Off Quotations.   A quotation is set off by commas from the words that introduce and follow it.

> He retorted, "What other motive could I have?"
> "Yes," he said, "we have just the size you want."
> "Staying another week," read the telegram.

See also "Quotation Marks," Section 9.12.

To Signal Omitted Words.   Use a comma as a substitute for words omitted.

> This is a stationary model; the other, a portable one.

To Separate Balanced Statements.   Use a comma between statements closely related in thought and structure.

> The more we pressed for the sale, the more he resisted.
> Once a deceiver, always a deceiver.

With Proper Names.   Use commas to set off the parts of dates and the names of persons and places.

1. Dates.

> On March 9, 197–, we brought suit against . . . (Also written with no comma after the year.)
> The record shows that March, 1970, marked the turning point. (Also, preferably, without the commas.)

2. *Jr., II., Inc., Ltd.,* and other name suffixes.

> Mr. David Green, Jr., is our executive secretary. (Also, preferably, without the second comma.)
> Robert Finch, Sr.'s account . . . (No comma after possessive.)
> Stephen Farnsworth II has accepted the invitation. (No comma if individual uses none.)
> We gave B. F. Hardy, Inc., a full line of credit. (Also, preferably, without the second comma.)

3. Inverted names.

> Smith, John A.
> Fairfield, William S., Jr.
> Deere, John, & Co.

4. Geographical names and addresses.

> He resides in London, Ontario.
> Our office in Paris, France, could be of great help to you.
> Please write to Dayton Forwarding Co., 765 South Third Street, Los Angeles, California 90028. (No comma before ZIP Code.)
> Mr. James McGrory of 1765 Creston Avenue, Bronx, New York, was one of the cosigners.

For Clarity or Emphasis.   Use a comma whenever it seems desirable to aid the reader's interpretation of a passage.

1. To prevent misreading.

NOT: Ever since we have refused to do business with them.
BUT: Ever since, we have refused to do business with them.

2. To break up a long passage.

Moreover, because smaller families are understandably reluctant to leave large, controlled apartments, these newer families, which tend to be fairly large, are denied access to the more spacious apartments they might find more easily in a free housing market.

3. To give emphasis. Compare:

We'll be glad to do it if that is your wish.
We'll be glad to do it, if that is your wish.

9.5 DASH   —

A dash is typewritten with the hyphen in any of the following ways:

This is a - dash.
This is a -- dash.
This is a--dash.

The last form is used in printers' copy and appears to be preferred for general office use.

To Show a Break in Thought.   A dash is used to show a sudden break in thought.

Our most recent experience—I can't remember the exact date—occurred within the last several months.
What would you do if—there's that *if* again.
More efficiency in production, a larger pool of manpower, and quicker delivery— these are the advantages of the new location.
You know, the bigger they are—.

In Quoted Speech.   The dash shows hesitation or unfinished thought in quoted remarks. It may also serve as a substitute for words too impolite or obscene to quote.

"Would you—would you consent to such a plan?"
"He didn't—?"
"I don't give a —!"

To Set Off a Parenthetical Remark.   Dashes may be used to give emphasis to a parenthetical remark for which commas or parentheses are considered too mild.

The Fair—which eventually grossed millions—attracted few backers.
If he understood the terms—and I'm sure he did—he'll live up to them.
He got out of the market—but not before he had seen a rise of ten points in his stock.

Between Parallel Elements.   Dashes may be used to emphasize parallel or balanced sentence elements.

You do your part—we'll do ours.
We waited—one hour—two hours—three hours—still no quotation appeared on the board.
That's our formula—win or lose—give or take a little.

To Emphasize Succeeding Words. A dash is sometimes used before a final word or phrase to give it emphasis. Phrases beginning with *for example, namely,* and *that is* are included in this rule.

If you're in doubt—ask.
Will you please mail your check now—before you forget.
It's yours and it's—free.
Three officers were elected—namely, the president, the secretary, and the treasurer. (The dash takes the place of a comma.)
A plan to suit you is available—for example, you can pay one third down and the balance in twelve monthly payments. (The dash takes the place of a comma, semicolon, or period.)

9.6 ELLIPSIS $\boxed{\,.\,.\,.\,}$

To Show Omissions. In quoted material, use *three* spaced periods to show an omission at the beginning or in the middle of a sentence. *Four* periods may be used when the omission occurs at the end of a sentence.

"... the proliferation of distinctly undervalued stocks ... can be expected to brighten the depressing investment climate during the next few months."

"The effectiveness of television is unchallenged. ... Even in Germany, where commercials are run in clusters of 20 minutes, there is a waiting line for time. ..."

For Stylistic Pauses. In establishing a mood, ellipses may be used in place of other punctuation to slow up reading. This device is common in advertising copy.

Chromacolor ... a revolutionary new color television system ... that outcolors ... outbrightens ... outdetails ... and outperforms ... every other giant-screen color TV.

To Mark an Unfinished Statement. Ellipses may be used instead of a dash after an unfinished statement.

I was wondering ... Oh, let me come back to this point later.

9.7 EXCLAMATION POINT $\boxed{\,!\,}$

To Show Strong Feeling. The exclamation point is placed after an expression of strong feeling. It should be used sparingly. (For punctuation after a mild exclamation, see "Comma," Section 9.4.)

Don't delay. Mail the order card at once!
How could they be so insensitive!
Sale! Bargains for Everyone! Come and Get Them!

9.8 HYPHEN |-|

General Usage.   The hyphen should be used only where required by custom or for reasons of clarity or consistency. Beyond these uses, variations in hyphenating are considerable. Dictionaries themselves do not always agree. The modern tendency, however, is to do with fewer hyphens, rather than more, and to join compounds into solid words, as *housewarming, sandpaper, tradespeople.* If in doubt about the hyphenation of a particular word or common compound, use the style recommended by your dictionary.

The principal uses of the hyphen are as follows.

1. To show the division of a word at the end of a line. (See "Word Division," Section 10.5.)

2. To separate the parts of certain compound words. A compound word is a combination of two or more words that form a single unit of thought. The words are sometimes hyphenated, sometimes separated, and sometimes written as one word.

even-tempered   census taker   bookseller

3. To avoid doubling a vowel or tripling a consonant, except after a short prefix.

anti-intellectual
shell-like BUT: preemptive
                   cooperative

4. As a substitute for *to* in such expressions as

1965–1970   pp. 21–23   2:30–3:30 p.m.
the Boston-Washington air corridor

5. To spell out a word.

spelled *d-e-s-i-c-c-a-t-e*

Improvised Compounds.   Hyphenate the parts of an improvised compound phrase.

a once-in-a-lifetime opportunity
a johnny-come-lately
blue-penciled copy
bread-and-butter merchandise
apple-pie order

Modifiers.   Hyphenate the elements of the compound expression modifying a following noun.

first-class service   built-in furniture
self-made man   would-be dictator
clear-cut issue   small-town business
well-known retailer   many-faceted career

1. The presence of three words in the compound, including especially a preposition, increases the probability that hyphens are to be used.

house-to-house salesman   happy-go-lucky attitude
portal-to-portal pay   rough-and-tumble tactics
up-to-date records   a five-day-a-week schedule
a pig-in-the-poke deal   no wage-and-hour provisions .

2. Hyphenate modifying phrases that might otherwise be misinterpreted.

former-partner's wife
common-stock holdings
terrible-tempered clerk
new-car buyer

3. Do not hyphenate a modifying foreign phrase.

per diem employees   laissez faire theory
ex officio member   per annum interest

4. Do not use hyphens when the first two words of a compound modifier are adverbs or when one of the words ends in *-ly*.

a very well developed plan
a not too obvious ploy
a highly regarded source
a necessarily risky adventure

5. Do not hyphenate a compound phrase when it follows the word it modifies.

The company is well known.
He thought the service was first class.
The gesture was heavy handed.

6. Noun phrases used as modifiers are generally not hyphenated as long as no confusion is likely.

a civil service job
family planning advice
Eastern District Headquarters

COMPARE: a personal loan service (confusing)
           a personal-loan service
           a personal loan-service

CONFUSING: blue gray walls
IMPROVED: blue-gray walls

Noun Compounds.   When two or more words form a noun expression:
  1. Hyphenate the expression when it has the force of a single word.

trade-in   close-up   right-of-way

NOTE: This rule is not consistently observed (for example, *makeup, setup, buildup*). When in doubt, consult your dictionary.
  2. Hyphenate the expression when the words show combined responsibility, participation, or constituency.

secretary-treasurer   AFL-CIO
plumber-electrician   Latin-American
artist-writer   Warner-7 Arts

NOTE: Ordinary compound titles are not hyphenated.

lieutenant colonel   BUT: president-elect
vice president   principal-in-charge
attorney general   minister-delegate

3. Hyphenate certain compounds showing family relationship.

mother-in-law   BUT: stepson
great-grandfather   foster mother
great-aunt   half brother

4. Do not hyphenate chemical and scientific terms.

sulfur dioxide   sodium chloride   methyl bromide
beta decay   angle of refraction photomicrograph

Numerals.   Hyphenate compound numerals as follows. (See also "Hyphenated Numbers" in Section 10.3.)

1. Compound numerals under one hundred.

eighty-four
one hundred and sixty-five
nineteen hundred and seventy-one

2. Numerals compounded with other words to form adjectives.

a 20-year-old building
easy 12-payment plan
fourth-grade pupil
280-page book
Twenty-third Street

3. Between the numerator and denominator of fractions written as words, unless either one is already hyphenated.

a one-third interest   twelve one-hundredths
one-half a point   twenty-one hundredths
two and seven-eighths   fourteen thirty-seconds

NOTE: When the fraction is used as a noun, the hyphen is sometimes omitted.

one half a point
three fourths of the total

4. Decades expressed in words.

the nineteen-twenties
the eighteen-forties

Prefix-Root Compounds.   Do not hyphenate a word beginning with a prefix except for a good reason.

1. To prevent confusion between similar words.

re-cover (cover again)   re-creation (creating again)
recover (regain)   recreation (play)

2. To prevent mispronunciation, especially when a vowel at the end of a prefix is the same as the vowel at the beginning of the root.

co-worker (not coworker)   semi-equal
intra-agency (not intraagency)   pro-urban
co-op (not coop)
  BUT: cooperate

3. When a capital letter follows the prefix.

pre-Revolutionary   pro-British
ex-President Johnson mid-Atlantic

4. When the prefix is a single letter.

T-square
L-shaped
U-turn

5. After *ex-, quasi-,* and *self-.*

ex-wife, ex-president, ex-councilman
quasi-judicial, quasi-public, quasi-military
self-made, self-incriminating, self-sealing

NOTE: Words beginning with the following prefixes are not usually hyphenated, for example:

ante-   antechamber, antedate, anteroom. BUT: ante-bellum
anti-   anticlimax, antiknock, antisocial. BUT: anti-intellectual
bi-   biennial, bifocal, bilateral, bivalve
circum-   circumnavigate, circumscribe, circumvent
co-   coauthor, coefficient, coexist, coinsurer
extra-   extramarital, extrasensory, extraterritorial
fore-   foreclose, foreknowledge, forerunner, foreshorten
hyper-   hypercorrect, hypersensitive, hyperthyroid
infra-   infrared, infrasonic, infrastructure
inter-   intercompany, interdependent, interurban
meta-   metaethics, metaphysical, metapsychology
micro-   microanalysis, microeconomics, microprint
mono-   monoculture, monomolecular, monosyllabic
multi-   multicolored, multilingual, multimedia, multivalve
neo-   neoclassic, neomycin. BUT: neo-Darwinism
non-   noncommunicative, noninterference, nonparticipation
over-   overanxious, overelaborate, overrun, oversubscribe
para-   paraesthesia, parasympathetic, paratyphoid
poly-   polyclinic, polystyrene, polyunsaturated
post-   postdate, posthaste, postnasal. BUT: post-impressionism
pre-   preassumption, predesignate, preinclination
pro-   prodemocratic, prounion, prowar. BUT: pro-American
pseudo-   pseudoclassical, pseudoliberal. BUT: pseudo-intellectual
semi-   semifinal, semimonthly, semiskilled
sub-   subcontractor, subfreezing, subparagraph

super- superconductivity, supermarket, supersaturate
trans- transcontinental, transoceanic, transatlantic. BUT: trans-Canadian
tri- tricornered, triennial, tripartite, triweekly
ultra- ultramodern, ultrahigh frequency, ultraviolet
under- underachieve, underemployed, underwrite

Suspension Hyphen.   When two or more compound words have a common base, put a hyphen after each "suspended" part of the compound.

20- and 30-year debentures
5- and 10-dollar bills
odd- and even-lot trades
8-, 12-, and 16-ounce bottles

9.9 PARENTHESES

Around Incidental Remarks.   Use parentheses to enclose explanatory or supplementary remarks. (See also "Brackets," Section 9.2.)

1. To set off parts of a sentence that might otherwise be punctuated by a colon, commas, or dashes.

The accident insurance provision is terminated upon retirement (age 65 for men, 62 for women).
Your kind remarks (especially your reference to Miss Greer) are very much appreciated.
The next step (I believe it's submitting copy for the client's approval) will have to be taken in my absence.

2. To enclose synonymous abbreviations and terms.

Magnetic ink character recognition (MICR) is part of all check processing.
Open-item accounts receivable procedures are usually followed by businesses that sell to other businesses (mercantile credit), whereas balance-forward procedures are usually followed by companies dealing with consumers (individual credit).

3. To show alternate terms and omissions in form letters.

Will you please verify the specimen signature(s) on the enclosed form(s) and return (it, them) to us.
On (date) we returned to you a check for (amount) drawn to your order by (name).

4. To enclose numeric amounts in some legal documents.

. . . declare a dividend of One Dollar ($1.00) per share

5. To enclose editorial references.

These functions are performed by the collator (Figure 4).

In Enumerations.   Use parentheses to set off the letters or numbers enumerating the items in a series.

The parties most concerned are (a) the manufacturer, (b) the supplier, and (c) the supplier's salesman.

Operating procedure
    (1) Location of units
    (2) Handling of invoices
    (3) Disbursement
    (4) Reconciliation

With Other Punctuation. For the use of other punctuation marks with parentheses, use these guidelines.

1. Put no punctuation before an opening parenthesis within a sentence. If the sentence requires punctuation at that point, put it after the closing parenthesis.

NOT: _____, (_____) _____.
BUT: _____ (_____), _____.

2. Put no mark inside the closing parenthesis within a sentence unless the sense calls for a quotation mark, an exclamation point, or a question mark. Any marks outside the closing parenthesis should belong to the rest of the sentence.

The rate paid on Systematic Savings Accounts is the same (5 percent).
We know what concessions he wants (he told us); however, we can't give in on every point.
The new heading ("Options")—it's at the top of page 4—has a penciled correction.
His continual promises (I'm so bored with them!) have been continually broken.
Do you care for the larger size (8″ by 14″)?

3. When a statement in parentheses is placed outside a sentence, the end punctuation (period, question mark, or exclamation point) belongs inside the closing parenthesis, not outside.

NOT: _____. (_____).
BUT: _____. (_____.)

Capitals with Parentheses. When parentheses are outside a sentence, capitalize the first word. When parentheses are inside a sentence, do not capitalize the first word unless it is a proper noun or begins a formal quotation.

Sale items are not returnable. (No exceptions.)
He agreed to the creditors' proposal (what else could he do?).
The free booklet (Professor Cramer recommends it highly) may be obtained by writing ...
The very first statement ("Men are interdependent") states the theme of the booklet.

Parentheses Within Parentheses. Parentheses may be used within parentheses, but it is better to use brackets within the parentheses or vice versa. (See "Brackets," Section 9.2.)

ACCEPTABLE: _____ (_____ (_____) _____).
BETTER: _____ [_____ (_____) _____].
OR: _____ (_____ [_____] _____).

9.10 PERIOD [.]

Sentence Stop. Use a period at the end of a declarative sentence, a mild command, an indirect question, or a request phrased as a question. (See also "Question Mark," Section 9.11, and "Exclamation Point," Section 9.7.)

1. Declarative sentence.

We will write for the catalogue.
The luncheon is planned for next Thursday.
You are to be congratulated on your enterprise.
Thank you for your check.

2. Mild command.

Please send your check at once.
Have a good time.
Order now and have the goods in time for Christmas.

3. Indirect question.

He asked what he should do.
The customer wanted to know if we would extend the guarantee two years.

4. Request phrased as question ("question of courtesy").

Will you please let us know your wishes.
May we ask you to return the application as soon as possible.

Abbreviations. The period is required after most abbreviations, but is optional after some and omitted after others. (See also "Abbreviations," Section 10.1.)

1. Period required.

Mr.   a.m.   St.   Sec.   A.D.   Calif.
Mrs.   p.m.   Ave.   Gen.   B.C.   U.K.

2. No period.

WNBC   SEATO   MOPAC   NAACP

3. Period optional.

r.p.m.   A.M.A.   A.F.L.-C.I.O.   U.S.C.
rpm   AMA   AFL-CIO   USC

Misuses. Do *not* use a period in the following instances.

1. After a signature.
2. After shortened words and contractions.

ad (*for* advertisement)
tab (*for* tabulator)
Sam or Sam'l (*But:* Jos.)
sec'y (*But:* secy.)
cont'd (*But:* contd.)
Phil (*for* Philip)

3. After words or phrases in a list or topical outline.

Be sure to include:
  Date
  Payee
  Amount

Preparation for canning
  (1) Cleaning
  (2) Sorting and grading
      (a) By quality
      (b) By size

4. After parenthesized letters or numbers forming an enumeration.

Checking accounts are classified as (1) regular, and (2) special.
The controller's major functions are (a) accounting, (b) credit, (c) systems and research, and (d) financial budgeting.

(See also the example of an outline in Rule 3 immediately preceding.)

9.11 QUESTION MARK $\boxed{?}$

After Direct Question.   Place a question mark at the end of a direct question.

Have you received our letter of March 13?
When did you wish delivery?
What trade-in allowance do you offer?

1. Sometimes the question mark comes inside the sentence instead of at the end.

Will we participate? is not the question.

2. A period, not a question mark, is used after an indirect question and after a question phrased as a command. (See "Period," Section 9.10.)

Rhetorical Question.   Place a question mark at the end of a question to which an answer is not expected ("rhetorical question").

How should we have known the truck had broken down?
Who could ask for a better deal?

To Express Doubt.   The question mark is used in parentheses to indicate doubt about a preceding figure or statement.

Last June (?) he came into the office to ask . . .

To Express Irony.   The question mark is sometimes used to express irony, but the practice is debatable.

We're expecting a message from the great man (?) momentarily.

9.12 QUOTATION MARKS   `" "`

Common Uses.   Use quotation marks to enclose:
  1. A direct quotation.

  The contract says, "The buyer will provide transportation from the warehouse to the destination."

  (a) Do not use quotation marks for words indirectly quoted.

  The contract says that the buyer will provide transportation from the warehouse to the destination.

  (b) Even in an indirect quotation, however, quotation marks may be used to enclose a fragment that is quoted exactly from the original.

  The contract said that the buyer must "provide transportation from the warehouse to the destination."

  2. Literary titles: article, chapter, short story, poem.

  Have you read "The New Elite" in this month's *Atlantic?*
  Chapter 3, "The Language of Business," should be of special interest.
  "Favorite Sons" is the first story in the collection.

  NOTE: Except in journalistic practice, which often prescribes the use of quotation marks, the names of books and magazines are underlined. (See "Underlining," Section 10.4.) In publishers' correspondence, the names of books are regularly set in full capitals.

  The quotation is from Peter Drucker's "The Practice of Management."
  The quotation is from Peter Drucker's *The Practice of Management.*
  The quotation is from Peter Drucker's THE PRACTICE OF MANAGEMENT.

  3. Distinctive names and technical terms, on first use only.

  Flip the "Conference" button and this portable will pick up normal voices 30 feet away. The Conference feature is exclusive with Stenotalk.
  A "check-credit" account is the answer. Check-credit enables you . . .

  4. Unusual word uses, especially when a word is not to be taken at face value.

  The result is that when the tire goes into service, the cord isn't forced to "grow" back to service dimensions.
  A distinction is made between telegraphic messages covering "free" deliveries of coupon bonds and those covering delivery against payment.
  Such "windfalls" could eventually lead to bankruptcy.

  5. Slang expressions in formal writing.

  FORMAL: The safety slogan was regarded by some officials as "corny," but it apparently contributed to the sharp drop in the accident rate.
  INFORMAL: Let's not have any corny slogans to embarrass us.

6. Words used as words. (See also "Underlining," Section 10.4.)

The word "convenience" was misspelled.
The now respectable musical term "rock and roll" had its beginning on the other side of the tracks.
By "gross" we mean what the exhibitors pay to the distributors.

Quotation Within Quotation.   Use single quotation marks (' ') to enclose a quotation within a quotation.

The chairman instructed, "Please answer 'Present' when your name is called."

Long Quotations.   A long quotation is one that exceeds four or five typed lines or contains the full text of a letter or telegram.

1. Separation from text. A long quotation is best set off from the unquoted text. This can be done by leaving a space before and after the quotation, single-spacing the quotation even when the rest of the copy is double-spaced, and indenting the whole quotation five spaces from the left margin and, if desired, an equal amount on the right. Quoted copy set off as indicated does not require quotation marks, although they may be used if there is likely to be some question that the material is quoted. (Figure 9-1.)

2. Paragraph punctuation. When quotation marks are used for quoted copy extending for more than a single paragraph, place a quotation mark at the beginning of each paragraph, but at the end of only the last paragraph. (Figure 9-1.)

3. Letters and telegrams. With modern copying methods, it is now seldom necessary to type quoted letters and telegrams in full. When a letter or telegram is retyped as an independent unit, however, the notation "Copy" at the top of each page makes the use of quotation marks unnecessary. When a letter or telegram is incorporated into a report, a legal brief, or another letter, the method of indention described in Rule 1 above is recommended. (See also "Incoming Wires," Section 12.3.)

Capitalization.   In a formal quotation, capitalize the first word and any other words that are capitalized in the original copy. If the quotation is run informally into the text, do not capitalize the first word unless it takes a capital anyway. (For capitalization in a broken quotation, see "Mixed Punctuation," in this section.)

As the advertisement says, "Let the man at Reynolds do the job."
In his own words, the statement caused "consternation among my friends and jubilation among my enemies."

Mixed Punctuation.   The prevailing practice is to put a comma or period inside a final quotation mark, a semicolon or colon outside the quotation mark, and other punctuation marks either inside or outside, depending on whether they belong to the quotation or to the whole sentence.

the safeguarding and profitable utilization of the

assets of the whole enterprise. The American Insti-

tute of Accountants defines internal control as

follows:

> Internal control comprises the plan of
> organization and all of the coordinate methods
> and measures adopted within a business to
> safeguard its assets, check the accuracy and
> reliability of its accounting data, promote
> additional efficiency, and encourage adherence
> to prescribed managerial policies.

A satisfactory system of internal control should

include (1) a plan of organization which provides ap-

propriate segregation of functional responsibilities;

Under the title, "Award of Merit Presented to
Ninth Street Office," the following story appeared in
MHT Topics:

"MHT's recently constructed Ninth Street Brooklyn
Office has been awarded the Award of Merit of the Concrete Industry Board, Inc. of N.Y.

"The award was given for excellence in design and
execution of materials.

"The architect for the building is William Milo
Barnum Associates. The exterior and the interior of
the building are constructed of reinforced and cast-
in-place concrete. Tellers' counter top is granite
as is the floor."

Figure 9-1   Two methods of handling long quotations.

"The Creative Revolution," an article by Grant Wilson, author also of "The
  Over-50 Job Hunter" . . .
From "The Creative Revolution": "You can't be brilliant in 30 seconds."
We resented his use of the term "sharp dealings"; still, there was little we could do
  but . . .
"Boom!" is the title of the movie.
He called us "victims"!
"What profits?" he wanted to know.
Did he say "profits"?
"Oh—," he blurted in frustration, "forget it."
"Beg pardon"—that's the term he used.

1. When a question is quoted within a question, use a single question mark
at the end.

Why did he say, "What's new"?

2. In legal work and other copy requiring the utmost accuracy, place any
necessary punctuation marks inside the final quotation mark when they are
part of the quoted matter; outside, when they are not.

The date should follow the style, "May, 1971,".
Please append the words "zealous" and "zither".

3. When quotations are used with expressions like "he said," use the
punctuation that the sentence structure would ordinarily require.

He wrote, "If this isn't the longest trip I've taken, it seems like it." (Comma following introduction to short formal quotation; see Section 9.4. Also see "Colon,"
  Section 9.3.)
"Please," he said, "I couldn't stand another 'favor' like that one." (Commas to
  enclose interrupting element; see Section 9.4.)
"We have been filling orders as they are received," the company replied; "however, we
  will consider giving priority on the basis of need." (Semicolon between two complete statements not joined by a simple conjunction. See "Semicolon," Section 9.13.)

OR:

"We have been filling orders as they are received," the company replied. "However,
  we will consider . . ." (Period used as sentence stop. See "Period," Section 9.10.)

9.13 SEMICOLON $\boxed{;}$

Instead of Period. A semicolon may be used instead of a period when two
complete statements, closely related in thought, are not joined by a simple
conjunction like *and, but, for, or,* or *nor.*

The colored seal on genuine bills has sharp sawtooth points; on bogus money the
  points are usually broken off.
The agent works on a contingent basis; he collects a fee only if the client is pleased.

Before Connecting Adverbs. Use a semicolon (or period) between main
clauses connected by words in the class of *therefore, however, nevertheless,
furthermore, accordingly, still, then, hence, thus,* and *consequently.*

The engine is made of aluminum; therefore it is very light.
His credit was excellent; still, he insisted on paying cash.
Our survey confirms the need for rented computer services; however, we disagree
that banks lack the flexibility to provide such services.

Instead of Comma.   Use a semicolon as a substitute for a comma to separate
coordinate (grammatically equivalent) elements within a sentence when they
are already broken up by commas. The semicolon will ease reading by signify-
ing a longer pause.

They will discuss such topics as labor-management relations and labor standards;
the importance of communication, consultation, and the resolution of problems;
the responsibility of labor, management, and the government to the public; and
the role of member countries, especially Canada, in external aid programs.
New electrode capacity was brought on-stream in Mobile, Alabama, as well as at
Welland, Ontario, and Liverpool and Sheffield, England; and construction was
planned or begun on facilities in Italy, Spain, and Sweden.

10

Mechanical Style[1]

In addition to the customary punctuation, writing employs other signs and devices to prevent the reader from stumbling and to help him interpret a particular word or passage. These signs and devices are dealt with in this chapter.

CONTENTS

10.1	Abbreviations	p. 362
10.2	Capitals	p. 365
10.3	Numbers	p. 372
10.4	Underlining	p. 379
10.5	Word Division	p. 380

10.1 ABBREVIATIONS

For a list of standard abbreviations see Chapter 17.

General Usage

1. Abbreviations are used to save space in technical documents and in footnotes, charts, and statistical work. They should be used sparingly in letters and the narrative parts of business reports.

2. As a rule, the greater the formality desired, the fewer the abbreviations.

3. When there are alternative abbreviations (*sec., sect.; m.p.h., mph; a.m., P.M.*) adopt a single form and use it throughout the manuscript.

---

[1] Additional material on mechanical style will be found elsewhere in this book as follows: "Letter Form and Style," Section 3.1; "Letters to Government and the Military," Section 3.2; "Forms of Address," Section 3.3; "Footnotes and Bibliographies," Section 5.3; "Tabular Presentation," Section 5.4; "Graphic Presentation," Section 5.5; "The Report in Finished Form," Section 6.3; "Memorandums," Section 6.4; "The Press Release," Section 7.1; "Editing," Section 7.2; "Preparing Copy for the Printer," Section 7.3; "Proofreading," Section 7.4; "Typing Pointers," Chapter 11.

4. In preparing copy for the printer, do not abbreviate any word that you want the printer to spell out.

5. Use the standard abbreviations that you will find in Chapter 17 or in any other approved list. Note carefully the use of capitals, spaces, and periods.

Capitalization.   Ordinarily, you do not capitalize an abbreviation unless the word it stands for would be capitalized. However, some abbreviations are customarily capitalized even though they stand for common nouns.

in.	agt.	Ill.	M.I.T.
ft.	cap.	CBS	Ger.

BUT: C (centigrade)
　　　EST (eastern standard time)
　　　CPA (certified public accountant)
　　　NE (northeast)

Spacing

1. Abbreviations are usually not spaced when all capitals are used or when periods are supplied.

a.m.	e.g.	HOLC	M.D.
sq.ft.	cpm	U.S.	B.W.I.

2. A space is usually observed in the following state abbreviations.

N. Dak.	N. Car.	N. Mex.
S. Dak.	S. Car.	W. Va.

3. The initials of persons are spaced, though an exception may be made when three initials are used.

F. S. Anderson   R.L.A. Perry

4. Put a space between the abbreviated parts of a title preceding a name.

Maj. Gen. Thomas S. Preston
Lt. Gov. David Haines

Periods

1. Though there are many exceptions, a period customarily follows each part of an abbreviation that stands for a word.

e.o.m.	B.C.	fl.oz.
i.e.	LL.D.	Br.

et al. (*et alii,* "and others"; no period after the *et* because it is not an abbreviation)

2. Periods and spaces are usually omitted from abbreviations used as the shortened names of organizations.

FBI	NLRB	ROTC	FHA	
WNBC	AFTRA	FDIC	RCA	(*but* A.T.&T.)

3. Shortened names of persons (as opposed to abbreviations) are generally not followed by a period.

Art (*but* Arth.)   Ed (*but* Edw.)
Ben (*but* Benj.)   Will (*but* Wm.)

4. Contractions are not considered abbreviations and are not followed by periods.

Int'l   Sam'l   Ass'n   Inc'd

Slant. A slant (diagonal line) is sometimes used to show the omission of a word like *of* or *per* in an abbreviation. At other times it takes the place of the period between two abbreviations.

C/D (certificate of deposit)
B/L (bill of lading)
n/o (in the name of)
bbls/day (barrels per day)
gal/min (gallons per minute)

Mr/Mrs.
M/Sgt.

Plurals

1. The plural of an abbreviation is usually formed by the addition of a small *s*.

qts.	yrs.	C.P.A.s
yds.	bbls.	Ph.D.s
mos.	rpms	YMCAs

2. An apostrophe is used in forming the plural of uncapitalized abbreviations internally punctuated by periods.

a.m.'s   r.s.v.p.'s (but RSVPs)   c.o.d.'s (*but* C.O.D.s)

3. Some abbreviations are the same in the singular and plural.

in. (inch or inches)   mi. (mile or miles)
ft. (foot or feet)   oz. (ounce or ounces)

4. Some plural abbreviations are formed by doubling a single letter.

v. (verse)   p. (page)   f. (folio)
vv. (verses)   pp. (pages)   ff. (folios)

Titles

1. Do not abbreviate a business title in the text or inside address of a letter.

the chairman of the board
Mr. Samuel Gore, Vice President

2. In formal usage, professional, religious, and military titles should always be spelled out, but in less formal usage, including letter addresses, the titles may be abbreviated if they are followed by a first name or initials.

the lieutenant colonel
Lieutenant Colonel Spanner
Lt. Col. Walter G. Spanner

professor of American history
Professor Jameson
Prof. H. R. Jameson

OR (MORE FORMAL):
Lieutenant Colonel Walter G. Spanner

OR (MORE FORMAL)
Professor Henry R. Jameson

NOT: Lt. Col. Spanner

NOT: Prof. Jameson

3. The titles *Reverend* and *Honorable* should be spelled out when they follow the article *the*.

the Honorable Lester T. Brooks (BUT: Hon. Lester T. Brooks)
the Reverend Mr. Chestnut (BUT: Rev. Paul Chestnut)

Company Names.   Follow the company's own style with respect to abbreviations in its name.

Tiffany & Co.
Empire Scientific Corp.
U.S. News & World Report
TAP Portuguese Airways

Names of Individuals.   In addressing an individual, use any initials or abbreviations he uses in his printed letterhead or official listing regardless of the style used in his signature. For example, a man who signs *Jno. F. Murphy* would still be addressed *John F. Murphy* if that is how his letterhead or company directory carries his name.

Misuses.   Except in telegrams and technical and reference matter, spell out:
1. Names of weights and dimensions.

NOT: 5 ft. 10 in.
8 × 10 ft.
10 ts.
weighed out in lbs. and oz.

BUT: 5 feet 10 inches
8 by 10 feet
10 tons
weighed out in pounds and ounces

2. Names of months and days.

NOT: Feb. 17
last Wed.
on Thurs. and Sats.

BUT: February 17
last Wednesday
on Thursdays and Saturdays

3. Names of streets, states, and other geographical divisions; also points of the compass except when they follow street names. (See also "Letter Form and Style," Section 3.1.)

1865 South Kensington Avenue, Delmar, New Jersey
Mount Royal, Montreal, Canada
1045 Fourteenth Street, NW

10.2   CAPITALS

General Usage.   Some capitalization is decreed by custom; other capitalization is a matter of individual or corporate preference. Avoid capitalization without good reason. Do capitalize:

The first word of every sentence.
The distinctive name of a person, place, or thing.
The first word of a formal quotation.
The first word of every line of verse, unless the author has done otherwise.
The important words in the title of a book, magazine, chapter, or heading.

These and other uses of capitalization are explained and illustrated in the sections that follow.

Calendar Periods.   Capitalization is necessary for the names of days and months, but not for other calendar periods. (See also "Historical Periods and Events" in this section.)

    the third Thursday in November
    Monday, May 16
    in July 1970

    BUT: spring, summer, autumn, winter
           in nineteen seventy-five
           the eighteen-eighties
           the mid-fifties
           first-quarter earnings

Compound Proper Names.   Capitalize a common noun or adjective forming an essential part of a proper name, but—with the exceptions noted in "Shortened Names" in this section—do not capitalize the common noun when it is used alone as a substitute for the whole name.

    George Washington Bridge   the bridge
    the Union Carbide Corporation   the corporation
    Jersey City   the city
    Allegheny County   the county
    Canal Street   the street
    Sinclair Building   the building

Departments in a Company.   The name of an organized group within a business need not be capitalized, though it is customary to capitalize the name if it applies to one's own organization. (See also "Shortened Names.")

    the sales department   OR   the Sales Department
    the computer section   OR   the Computer Section
    the legal division   OR   the Legal Division
    the executive committee   OR   the Executive Committee

Derivatives of Proper Names
   1. Capitalize the derivative of a proper name. (See also "Proper Names" in this section.)

    American   Orwellian   Elizabethan
    New Yorker   Christian   Asiatic
    Romanesque   Princetonian   Manhattanite

   2. Do not capitalize the derivative of a proper name when the derivative has acquired a common meaning.

pasteurize (after Pasteur)	china (porcelainware)
roman candle (after Rome)	morocco (leather)
macadam road (after J. L. McAdam)	utopia (after a fictional place)

Emphasis. A word or phrase that would otherwise not be capitalized may be capitalized for emphasis, especially in a sales or advertising presentation.

Every advertisement should have a Central Idea.
See your Travel Agent.
Your policy complies with the Financial Responsibility Laws in all states.
Only Mobil gives you an engine Detergent in Premium and Regular Blends.

Geographic Names

1. Capitalize the distinctive names of geographic subdivisions and topographical features.

the Western Hemisphere	Lake Michigan
the West	the Mississippi River
the Plains States	the Mojave Desert
the Rockies	the Isthmus of Panama
the Corn Belt	the Gulf of Mexico

2. Do not capitalize generic names, even when associated with specific places.

the western plains
the southern states
the California coast
the deepest South (But: the Deep South)

3. Do not capitalize points of the compass when used to signify direction.

travel north on Route 6
walking east
a southeast breeze
a northerly route

Governmental Units. The names of government departments, boards, commissions, judiciaries, and so on, are capitalized without exception.

the Civil Service Commission
the Board of Health
the Appellate Division
the President's Commission on Civil Disorders

Headings and Titles

1. Capitalize the important words (including always, the first and last) in titles of books, magazines, newspapers, reports, and the titles or headings naming the parts of such works. The important words consist of the first and last words and all other words *except* articles, the "to" before infinitives, and short prepositions and conjunctions (usually four letters or fewer). The abbreviations *etc.* and *et al.* are not capitalized even when they appear at the end of a title.

Comments on the Minutes of the Previous Meeting
The Facts About Employment with Con Edison
Suggestions for Using the Dictaphone

2. In a running text, do not capitalize the article *the* before the name of a newspaper or magazine. Exceptions to this rule may be made by publications in the use of their own name. Also do not capitalize the word *magazine* unless it is an official part of the title.

advertisement in the *Saturday Review*
a story in the *New York Times* (common usage)
a story in *The New York Times* (publisher's usage)
in *Life* magazine (or *Life*—not *Life Magazine*)
Time magazine (or *Time*)

NOTE: When the name of the periodical follows a quotation and a dash, the *the* is capitalized.

"Profits at Bank Show Increase"—*The New York Times*

3. When a title is split by a colon or dash, any word following the split should be capitalized.

The Business Research Paper: A Style Manual
Education for Today—And Tomorrow

Historical Periods and Events.   Capitalize the distinctive name of a period or event in history.

the Renaissance   the Crucifixion
the Second World War   the Panic of 1907
the Great Depression   the Era of Good Feeling
the Roaring Twenties   the Reign of Terror
the Ice Age   the Flood (biblical)

Hyphenated Words

1. Capitalize the parts of hyphenated words that would be capitalized anyway.

the Army-Navy game   the Lincoln-Douglas debates
Afro-American   Inter-American Industries, Inc.
anti-American slogan   Fifty-ninth Street
pre-Columbian art   the President-elect

2. In a title or heading, capitalize any part of a hyphenated word that would be capitalized anyway according to the rules for "Headings and Titles" in this section.

Fifty-Ninth Street Restaurant
"Chicken-in-a-Jiffy Is Infra-Red Triumph"
"Rules for Out-of-Pocket Expenses"
"Sit-In Workers Return to Jobs" (*In* is capitalized here because it is an adverb, not a preposition.)

Legal References.   Capitalize the important words in the names of laws, cases at law, statutes, and official reports. Do not capitalize *versus* or its abbreviations *vs.* and *v.*

United States Code, Vol. 28, Sec. 2201 (Suppl. IV, 1957)
Bank Holding Act
New York State Constitution
Economic Report of the President
Amazon Cotton Mill Co. v. Textile Workers Union

Letter Parts.   Only certain parts of the salutation and complimentary close of a letter are capitalized. (See also "Letter Form and Style," Section 3.1.)

Dear Mr. Henderson:
Dear Professor Marvin:
My dear Professor Marvin:
Dear Ray:

Very truly yours,
Sincerely yours,

Literary Usage.   A noun standing for some abstract quality is sometimes capitalized in literary usage.

He paid homage to Truth and Beauty.
. . . in his search for the Good Life.
No one has a monopoly on Wisdom.

Numerical and Alphabetical References.   Capitalize the descriptive word before a number or letter of the alphabet used for reference. Exceptions are commonly made in the instance of small literary subdivisions such as *page, line, paragraph, verse, note,* and so on. Do not capitalize the descriptive word when it is separated from the number or follows it.

page 4	Volume 2	Figure 3	Room 435
line 8	Chapter 6	Exhibit C	Conference Room F
note 1	Article IV	Appendix I	Public School 6
par. 2	Table VI	Form Y	Catalog No. 1238B

BUT: the third volume
the sixth chapter
the second part

The room number is 435.
The public school he went to is No. 12.
In the catalog the number is given as 1238B.

Prefixed Names
1. When a name begins with *de, du, della,* or the like, the prefix is not ordinarily capitalized unless it begins a sentence or stands without a first name or title. The German *von* and *van* are usually not capitalized except at the beginning of a sentence. As with the spelling and capitalization of all names, the usage of their owners should prevail.

E. I. du Pont de Nemours & Co.	Du Pont
Raimundo de Larrain	De Larrain
Jacques d'Arcy	D'Arcy
the Duke d'Uzes	D'Uzes
Werner von Braun	von Braun
Erich Von Stroheim (an exception)	Von Stroheim

2. When a prefixed name is set in all capitals, the prefix should also be in capitals unless there is no space between the prefix and the name. In that case, appearance is improved if only the initial letter of the prefix is capitalized.

MAC INTOSH but MacINTOSH	McKEE
McNAMARA	MacGREGOR

Proper Names. Capitalize the distinctive name of a person, place, or thing. (See also "Derivatives of Proper Names," in this section.)

Walter Bigelow	Seagram Building	Bufferin
Suffolk County	General Electric	Tide (the detergent)
Lake Michigan	Fifth Avenue	Chevrolet

Publications. Capitalize the names of books, newspapers, magazines, and technical and professional journals. (See "Titles and Headings" in this section.)

Quotations. Capitalize the first word of a formal quotation, but not of a quoted fragment unless it begins with a proper name.

In his testimony, he said, "The contract was made in good faith, but . . ."
When he said the contract was made in "good faith," he really meant . . .

Religious Names

1. Capitalize the names of the Deity, of the Holy Trinity, and of the Scriptures and other sacred writings of whatever religion. Also capitalize the names of religious figures and particular references to sacred works.

God (but godlike)	the Virgin Mary
the Messiah	the Son of Man
Moses	the Bible (but biblical)
the Almighty	the Talmud (but talmudic)
Muhammed	the Koran
Jesus	the Ten Commandments
Leviticus	the Psalms

2. Capitalize pronouns standing for the name of the Deity, but not if they occur within a few words of the name.

We believe in Him and all that He commands.
God is not dead, but he apparently does not show himself to everyone.

Shortened Names

1. It is customary to capitalize the shortened form for the name of one's own company or its departments. (See also "Departments in a Business" and "Titles" in this section.)

the Methods and Systems Department	the Department
Manufacturers Hanover Trust Company	the Bank
International Business Machines Corporation	the Company (*or* Corporation)
the Shipping Department	the Department*

*or Shipping, as in "We'll see that Shipping is notified."

2. Capitalize a common noun generally acknowledged as the short form of a specific proper noun.

Fifth Avenue	the Avenue
Wall Street	the Street
New York Stock Exchange	the Exchange
Lake Shore Drive	the Drive
West Point	the Point

3. Capitalize the shortened form of a specific government agency.

the Supreme Court	the Court
the Board of Standards and Appeals	the Board
the Commission on Human Rights	the Commission

The. Do not capitalize the article *the* before a company name unless it begins a sentence or is an official part of the title.

for The Texas Company
at The Custom Shop
from The White House (a department store)

BUT: the National Cash Register Company
       the Four Seasons (a restaurant)

Titles (Individuals)

1. Capitalize a title preceding a name.

Chairman Smith
Dean Harrison
General Westmoreland
Professor Edwards
Vice President Cluny

2. A title following a name or used alone is generally not capitalized unless it forms part of a letter address or belongs to an individual in one's own organization. (See also "Letter Form and Styles," Section 3.1.)

to Mr. Smith, chairman of the board, who
to Mr. Smith, Chairman of the Board, who (an official of the writer's company)
to Dr. Harrison, dean of the school, who
to Dr. Harrison, Dean of the School, who (dean of the writer's school)
the executive vice president of another company   .
our Executive Vice President

3. Capitalize any title to signify special distinction or deference.

William Westmoreland, Chief of Staff
the President of the United States (BUT: When a president is elected . . .)
the Chief Justice
the senior Senator from California (BUT: a senator's duty)
the Archbishop of London
the Mayor of Chicago

Trade Names. Capitalize the distinctive name of the product of a single manufacturer, but not of a trade name that has come into popular generic use.

Munsonwear	BUT:	nylon
Acrilon		dacron
Fritos		vaseline
Del Monte		mimeograph (but Mimeograph for the particular
Kodak Instamatic		machine of that name)

10.3 NUMBERS

General Usage. As a rule, spell out exact numbers of ten or less and use figures for higher numbers. However, in tabular and financial work, and whenever ready reference is desired, use figures for all numbers. (See also "Mixed Words and Figures" and "Round Numbers" in this section.)

three dozen	14 dozen
five dollars	$28
eight men	25 men
10 percent	16 percent

ALSO: priced at $2 each
           a three-year contract
           interest at 5 percent
           a six-months' delay

Abbreviations with Numbers. Always use figures with abbreviations.

3 doz. (*not* three doz.)
4 in. (*not* four in.)
Fig. 3 (*not* Fig. Three)

Alignment. Align whole numbers on the right and decimals on the decimal point. Fractions, ordinal endings, and parentheses are allowed to overhang. (See also "Typing Statistical Material," Section 11.2.)

23	$356	10.25	655	I	23rd
9½	5	4.00	(26)	II	24th
411	85	3.375	455	VIII	25th

Cents

1. Use the sign ¢, but not the abbreviation *cts.* for *cents*. For a more formal effect, especially in writing for publication, spell out *cents*.

CORRECT: 1¢   7¢   23¢   75¢
MORE FORMAL: one cent   seven cents (*or* 7 cents)
                 23 cents   75 cents

2. Do not use the $ sign with cents alone except (a) in a series of mixed amounts, (b) in a tabulation, and (c) before cents expressed in more than two figures. In a mixed series and whenever the possibility of error otherwise

exists, use a cipher and a decimal before amounts of less than one dollar. In a mixed series also add a decimal and two ciphers after even dollar amounts.

NOT: at $.49 each
BUT: at 49¢ (or 49 cents) each
CORRECT: earning $0.90, $1.50, and $2.00 an hour
            comes to a price of $0.375 each

3. Do not use the decimal and *cents* except to express hundredths of a cent. For example, *.40 cents* is not the same as *40 cents; .40 cents* means 40/100 (or two-fifths) of a cent.

Commas with Figures

1. Place a comma between each set of three figures counting from right to left, except for serial numbers, policy numbers, room numbers, dates, and the like (Figure 10-1).

23,465,322   BUT: Invoice No. 32258
    31,400   Policy No. 4526859
     2,655   Catalog No. 4302-S
                      Room 2305
                      projected for 1985

NOTE: Social Security numbers, credit card numbers, and the like employ spaces or hyphens between sets of numbers of varying length.

Social Security No. 085-26-4754
Credit Card No. 030 381 361 5

2. Numbers of four digits that would ordinarily be punctuated by a comma are often written without the comma.

sold 3600 shares
an order for 1200 dozen

3. Figures representing patent numbers customarily use commas.

U.S. Patents 2,278,731
             2,248,410
             2,244,845

Trillions	Hundred billions	Ten billions	Billions	Hundred millions	Ten millions	Millions	Hundred thousands	Ten thousands	Thousands	Hundreds	Tens	Units
1,	3	4	7,	2	8	9,	5	6	4,	1	2	4

Figure 10-1   Reading numbers.

Dates

1. Use the endings *-st, -nd, -rd, -d,* and *-th* only when the day precedes the month or month and year.

the 24th of January   the 24th of January, 1972
BUT: January 24   BUT: January 24, 1972

2. Spell out the date only in formal invitations and some legal documents.

FORMAL: on the fifth day of November, nineteen hundred and seventy-two
MORE FORMAL: on the fifth day of November, A.D. nineteen hundred and seventy-two
two
MOST FORMAL: on the fifth day of November, in the year of our Lord one thousand
nine hundred and seventy-two

3. When the abbreviated form of a year or period is written in words, use capital initials for emphasis, but no apostrophe.

back in Forty-eight   the Roaring Twenties
(NOT 'Forty-eight)   a Sixty-nine Buick (OR, CLEARER:
the Gay Nineties   a '69 Buick)

4. Note the following usages in representing dates.

back in '48
Class of 1975
the year 1975 (no capital)
1974–1975 or 1974–75 (*but not* 1974–5)

4/16/71 (American style) BUT: 16/4/71 (European style)
April 16, 1971 (American style)
16 April 1971 (U.S. military and British style)

the April, 1971, tax installment, *or*
the April 1971 tax installment

the April 15, 1971, tax installment, *or*
the April 15, 1971 tax installment

Decimals.   In the interests of precision, a cipher may be placed before a decimal point that is not preceded by a whole number, though there is a tendency to leave out the extra cipher when the decimal begins with a cipher. (See also "Cents" in this section.)

.12 milligrams
a specific gravity of 0.4325
.015 of an inch, *or* 0.015 of an inch

Dollars

1. Omit the decimal point and ciphers after even dollar amounts except (a) in bank practice or other writing requiring great exactness, and (b) in a series containing mixed amounts.

$29 $340 $12,000
A balance of $2,345.00 (*or* $2,345.) remained in the account.
available at $2.00, $4.50, and $6.25

2. Use the dollar sign before each figure amount; do not use the word *dollars* after a figure amount.

NOT: 76 dollars
BUT: $76 (*or* seventy-six dollars)

3. Repeat the dollar sign before each figure amount in a series.

three payments of $25, $50, and $100 respectively
a deposit of $25 or $50 (*not* of 25 or $50, *or* of $25 or 50)

Double Representation.   Except in legal documents and formal price quotations, where the practice is divided, do not spell out an amount that is also represented in figures.

LEGAL DOCUMENT: promise to pay the sum of Four Hundred Thirty-two and
    50/100ths dollars ($432.50) [Capitals are customary in this use.]
ORDINARY USE: my check for $432.50

Dual Sets of Numbers.   When two sets of numbers occur in the same passage, use figures for one set, words for the other, if convenient.

NOT: Three girls worked four hours, two worked seven hours, and twelve worked
    fourteen hours.
BUT: Three girls worked 4 hours, two worked 7 hours, and twelve worked 14 hours.

Fractions

1. Use full figures to express fractions. Use of the fractions on your typewriter keyboard is discouraged because they are sometimes illegible on multiple carbon copies. Note the styles below.

12 1/2   6 5/32   1/16   5/8 share (*not* 5/8ths share)
INCONSISTENT: $2\frac{1}{2} \times 5\frac{1}{2} \times 7$ 1/8
BETTER: 2 1/2 $\times$ 5 1/2 $\times$ 7 1/8

2. Isolated fractions may be spelled out. (See also "Numerals" in "Hyphens," Section 9.8.)

bought a one-half interest
you pay two thirds of the regular price

Hyphenated Numbers.   See also "Numerals" in Section 9.8.

1. Hyphenate spelled-out number compounds under one hundred, and hyphenate any number that becomes part of an adjective compound.

twenty-two   five hundred miles, *but*
thirty-five hundred   a five-hundred-mile trip
fourteen by twenty-six   thirty-two thousand, *but*
two and three-eighths   a thirty-two-thousand-dollar house

2. Use a hyphen to indicate the omission of intermediate figures, and carry over at least two digits of figures having two digits or more. Repeat the

initial digits, if necessary, for clarity. Telephone numbers are usually excepted from this rule.

1932–45 (*or* 1932–1945)
1900–09 (*not* 1900–9)
pp. 32–39 (*not* pp. 32–9)
pp. 126–132 (*or* pp. 126–32)

Nos. 36248–36253 (*better than* 36248–53)

in the period 1966–1970
from 1966 to 1970 (*not* from 1966–1970)
Telephone: 598-2231-2-3 (*but* 598-2208-09-10)

3. Repeat the symbols used with hyphenated figures.

32°–77°F. (*not*: 32–77°F.)
$10–$20 (*but*: 10 to 20 dollars)
3¢–5¢ (*but*: 3 to 5 cents)

Measurements. Use figures to express dimensions, weights, and capacities.

2′ × 3′	3 square miles	5 quarts
2 × 3 ft.	120 horsepower	16 barrels
2 by 3 feet	8 cylinders	26 tons

Ciphers and a decimal point are used in exact or scientific work.

a volume of 0.67 cubic inches

Mixed Words and Figures. When several coordinate numbers are used, do not mix words and figures.

NOT: maturities of five, 15, and 25 years
BUT: maturities of 5, 15, and 25 years

Ordinal Numbers

1. Ordinal numbers expressed in figures are written as follows.

1st, 2d or 2nd, 3d or 3rd, 4th, 5th, 6th, 7th, and so on.
2d and 3d are now generally preferred to 2nd and 3rd.

2. Ordinal figures are used with dates only when the day precedes the name of the month or when the name of the month is omitted.

on the 23d of May
on May 23 (*not* May 23d)
your letter of the 23d

BUT: May twenty-third (*not* May twenty-three)

3. Ordinal endings are generally omitted after street numbers expressed in figures, but are retained when the street number is spelled out.

220 West 45 Street
30 East Fourteenth Street
30 East 14 Street

ACCEPTABLE: 30 East 14th Street

Percentages

1. Percentage is written in the following styles.

% (use with figures only)
    6%   10%   25%   100%
per cent (use with words or figures)
    six per cent   6 per cent
percent (use with words or figures; now generally preferred to *per cent*)
    six percent   6 percent

2. Repeat the percent sign, but not the word *percent* (or *per cent*) after each figure in a series.

NOT: paying 4, 5, and 6% interest
BUT: paying 4%, 5%, and 6% interest
OR: paying 4, 5, and 6 percent interest

NOT: 10 to 25% off
BUT: 10% to 25% off
OR: 10 to 25 percent off

Plural Usage

1. The use of the singular and plural with numbers is demonstrated in this table.

Numbered amounts	two hundred, twelve thousand, five million 2 billion dollars, 2 billions of dollars 2.5 billion (*or* 2.5 billions) in foreign aid
With *several*	several hundred, several thousand several thousand dollars, several thousands of dollars
With *many*	many hundreds, many thousands, many millions many millions of people
With *by the*	by the yard (unit of measurement) Buy them by the dozen. (unit of sale) Buy them by the dozens. (in large numbers) Buy them by the hundred. (unit of sale) They came by the hundreds. (in large numbers)
With *by* or *in*	They come in pairs. sold by dozens multiplied by millions

2. Figures form their plurals by the addition of *s* or *'s;* the apostrophe is usually omitted in market quotations. When numbers are spelled out, the usual rules for plurals apply. (See "Spelling Guide," Section 8.1.)

in 2's and 3's	in 2s and 3s	in twos and threes
Treasury 4 3/4s	Alcoa 6s	Mexico 6 1/2s
the 5%'s	the 5%s	the five percents
the 1980's	the 1980s	the nineteen-eighties

the 2″ × 3″s are out of stock (*or* the 2″ by 3″s)
the two by three inches' are out of stock
the two by threes are out of stock

Roman Numerals (Figure 10-2). Roman numerals are currently used as follows.

1. To list important topics in an outline.

I. Causes
II. Effects

2. To number chapters and volumes of books.

Chapter XII
Volume III

3. To number the pages in prefaces and other material preceding the main text. Small Roman numerals are used for this purpose.

i iv x xiii xix xxii

4. To indicate the year on cornerstones and other architectural features.

MCMLXX (1970)

5. To identify individuals, historic and otherwise.

Louis XIV
Henry Ford II

Round Numbers

1. Round numbers should be expressed in words except where quick identification is desired.

about six hundred residents
not in a thousand years

employ 2,500 workers, *or*
employ twenty-five hundred workers (*not* two thousand five hundred)

1.	I	14.	XIV	90.	XC
2.	II	15.	XV	100.	C
3.	III	16.	XVI	200.	CC
4.	IV	17.	XVII	300.	CCC
5.	V	18.	XVIII	400.	CCCC or CD
6.	VI	19.	XIX	500.	D
7.	VII	20.	XX	600.	DC
8.	VIII	30.	XXX	700.	DCC
9.	IX	40.	XL	800.	DCCC
10.	X	50.	L	900.	CM
11.	XI	60.	LX	1,000.	M
12.	XII	70.	LXX	2,000.	MM
13.	XIII	80.	LXXX or XXC	1,000,000.	$\overline{\text{M}}$

Figure 10-2 Forming Roman numerals.

2. For ease of reading, use the words *million* and *billion* with figures.

$30 million for improvements
a $2 billion budget
spent 2 millions
a population of 200 million

Sentence Beginning.   Try to avoid using figures at the beginning of a sentence. If you cannot recast the sentence to put the figure inside, spell out the number.

BAD: 231 employees were added to our payroll last year.
BETTER: Two hundred and thirty-one employees were added to our payroll last year.
BETTER STILL: Last year 231 employees were added to our payroll.

Successive Numbers

1. Use a comma to separate two figures following each other. Or, if the numbers are not part of the same series, spell out one of the numbers. In other instances, rephrase the sentence to separate the figures.

BAD: In 1971, 250 new apprentices were hired.
BETTER: In 1971, two hundred and fifty new apprentices were hired.
BETTER STILL: In 1971 we hired 250 new apprentices.

2. When a number precedes a numeral adjective, spell out one of the numbers if it can be conveniently expressed in one or two words.

ten 5-pound boxes (*not* ten five-pound boxes)
three $100 bills (*not* three one-hundred-dollar bills)
twenty-five 50-cent cigars, *or*
25 fifty-cent cigars

BUT: a development consisting of 126 $30,500 homes (no comma)

10.4   UNDERLINING

General Usage.   Underlining is used to emphasize particular words or phrases and, in some instances, to take the place of quotation marks. Solid underlining (including spaces and punctuation marks) makes a better appearance than broken underlining, but the latter is better for emphasizing particular words. Do not underline punctuation marks at the beginning or end of an underline. (For exception, see "Italics" in this section.)

"Happy's" Almanac. or "Happy's" Almanac.

For the use of underlining in footnotes and bibliography, see Section 5.3.

Titles.   Underlining may be used for the titles of books and other long literary works, periodicals, newspapers, musical compositions, and the distinctive names of ships, trains, or planes; however, underlining is sometimes omitted altogether. Underlining is never used for the word *Bible* or for the books of the Bible.

the New York Times (*or* the New York Times)
the musical play South Pacific
copy of Time
the Golden Arrow flies to Chicago at 12 noon every day
sailed on Queen Elizabeth 2
BUT: the Bible, Proverbs xx, the Book of Job

Italics.   Use underlining to indicate any copy you wish the printer to set in italics. In copying printed matter, use underlining whenever you see italics.

NOTE: Because commas, semicolons, colons, exclamation points, and question marks following italics are also set in italics, these punctuation marks should be underlined in preparing printer's copy or in typewriting transcripts of such copy.

Words and Symbols.   In formal writing it is customary to underline words, numbers, letters, and other symbols when they are used for identification only.

the word receive was misspelled.
The 2 was written like a 7.
the % was missing after the figure.
There are two s's in misspelled.

Misuse.   It is bad form to underline words indiscriminately for emphasis. An occasional underlined word gets attention, but when many words are underlined, the attention is divided. The appearance of the page also suffers.

BAD: With your gift you will receive details of a plan that can help you achieve the financial security you want and need for your family.

10.5   WORD DIVISION

General Usage

1. Divide words at the ends of lines in order to avoid a jagged right-hand margin. Such division should be kept to a minimum. All word divisions must be made between syllables with due regard for appearance and pronunciation. If in doubt about where a syllable ends, consult your dictionary.

2. Do not divide a word of one syllable or one of less than six letters. Note that word endings do not always create extra syllables.

thought	exit	dropped	(one syllable)
made	refer	passed	(,, ,,)
freight	delay	warned	(,, ,,)

3. Do not divide after a single letter, and preferably not after two. Do not carry over less than three letters, and preferably not less than four.

BAD:	a/go	BETTER:	ed/itor	BEST:	con/sume
	e/merge		re/verse		nec/essary
	imprompt/u		nar/row		fore/cast
	want/ed		tun/nel		oppo/nent

Abbreviations. Do not divide an abbreviation.

UNICEF   m.p.h.   approx.   IC4A   entomol.

Affixes

1. Divide a word, if possible, after a prefix or before a suffix.

re/gain	ad/junct	discern/ible	happi/ness
pre/pare	dis/cuss	rebel/lion	astonish/ment

2. Do not divide a prefix or suffix.

under/lying (not un/derlying)
accept/able (not accepta/ble)

3. When a suffix is added to a word ending in two consónants, the division is usually made after the consonants.

tell/ing   impress/ive   remark/able   prevent/ive
BUT: instal/lation (*not* install/ation)

4. The word endings that follow form complete syllables and should not be divided except at the point indicated:

/cal	/cious	/gious	/tient
/cent	/cism	/nous	/tion
/ceous	/dant	/sion	/tious
/cial	/dure	/sive	/tive
/cian	/geon	/tent	/tude
/cient	/geous	/tial	/ture
/cion	/gion	/tian	

5. Do not divide a word before a suffix if a new syllable is not created.

dis/barred (*not* disbar/red)

Contractions. Do not divide a contraction.

wouldn't (*not* would/n't)
haven't (*not* have/n't)

Dates. Avoid dividing a date. If a division must be made, follow these styles:

June 27,/19—
September 6,/19—
Septem/ber 6,/19—
Sep/tember 6, 19—

Double Consonants.   A word containing a double consonant or two adjoining consonants flanked by vowels can usually be divided between the consonants if the division preserves the normal syllabication.

begin/ning	accom/modate	occur/rence
construc/tion	conser/vatory	cul/tural

BUT: remark/able (*not* remar/kable)

Figures.   Do not divide a figure or separate a figure from an accompanying word, symbol, abbreviation, or letter.

1975	page 36	23,455,865
$10 million	12 by 20 ft.	Sec. 255(b)(3)

Foreign Words.   Avoid dividing words that retain their foreign pronunciation.

mademoiselle (not mademoi/selle)
raconteur (not racon/teur)

Headings.   Do not divide a word in a title or heading.

NOT: Communication and Organi-
            zational Behavior
BUT: Communication and
            Organizational Behavior

Hyphenated Words.   Do not divide a hyphenated word anywhere but at the hyphen. Correct:

secretary-/treasurer   hard-/of-hearing,   *or*   hard-of-/hearing

Last Words.   Do not divide the last word in a paragraph or the last word on a page.

Mispronunciation.   Do not divide a word in such a way that mispronunciation may result.

BAD:	cauti/ous	moth/er	ear/nest	read/just
BETTER:	cau/tious	mother	earn/est	re/adjust

Proper Names

1. Avoid dividing a proper name. In any case, do not separate the title from the initials, or a middle initial from the first name. Correct:

Dr. R. T./Swanson	Lieutenant Colonel/Henderson
Mrs. Elsie D./Traynor	Lt. Col./John Henderson

2. Degrees and the designations *Jr., Sr., II,* and so on, should not be separated from the last name. Correct:

Frederick/Mason, D.D.S.   Mr. Samuel E./Krey, M.E.E.
                Mr. Irvin C./Hale, Jr.

Solid Compounds.   Do not divide a solid (unhyphenated) compound word anywhere but between the elements of the compound. Correct:

under/cover   multi/million   business/man

Successive Lines.   Avoid dividing words at the end of more than two successive lines.

BAD: .   .   .   .   .   .   work-
        .   .   .   .   .   debat-
        .   .   .   .   .   fore-

Vowels.   Divide a word after a single vowel forming a syllable or between vowels that are separately pronounced.

prevari/cate (*not* prevar/icate)   legi/bility (*not* leg/ibility)
innocu/ous (*not* innoc/uous)   notori/ety (*not* notor/iety)

11

Typing Pointers

The typewriter is one of the most important machines in the office. Properly used, it turns out good copy in an efficient manner. The following sections will help the typist become more expert in its use as she reviews the newer techniques for operating the machine and turning out clean, sophisticated copy.

CONTENTS

11.1 Improving Typing Efficiency   p. 384
11.2 Typing Statistical Material   p. 394
11.3 Typing Special Characters, Formulas, and Equations   p. 400

Of course, no amount of skill is going to produce good copy if the typewriter is not kept in excellent working condition. The following suggestions will assure proper care and maintenance.

1. Erasure crumbs and dust cause the majority of typewriter problems. Keep dirt out of the mechanism by covering the machine at night and by moving the carriage to the extreme right or left when you erase.

2. Dust the easy-to-reach parts with a soft brush and use a stiffer brush or a plastic cleaner to clean the keys at the beginning of each day.

3. Refrain from poking about in the parts with some makeshift tool or bending the key levers when trying to unhook jammed keys.

4. If the machine is not working properly, have it checked immediately. Continued use may cause costly damage.

5. Take advantage of a maintenance contract to have the machine checked and cleaned periodically, at least once a year. It is good insurance.

11.1 IMPROVING TYPING EFFICIENCY

A person who types several hours a day should first of all arrange the work station so that physical aches and tensions are minimized. Next, she should review techniques, experiment with new ways to handle repetitive

384

typing tasks, and practice more difficult copy work in preparation for advanced assignments. In fact, all typists should review typing techniques that indicate how to turn out copy more rapidly, how to set up copy accurately, or how to insert additional material in a finished document. The following topics are treated in this section.

Posture and Chair Height	p. 385	Word Substitutions	p. 389
Using a Copyholder	p. 385	Last-Line Corrections	p. 390
Writing Between Lines	p. 385	Typing Even Right Margins	p. 390
Correcting Originals and Carbon		Changing Ribbons	p. 390
Copies	p. 385	Using Special Keys and	
Correcting Bound Manuscripts	p. 386	Levers	p. 390
Locating the Original Typing		Selecting Carbon and Copy	
Line	p. 386	Paper	p. 391
Uniform Bottom Margin	p. 387	The Right Ribbon	p. 392
Ruled Lines	p. 387	Typing on Printed Forms	p. 392
Chain Feeding	p. 387	Proofreading Typewritten	
Typing Individual Labels	p. 388	Work	p. 394
Carbon Paper Hints	p. 388	Typing Two-Column Copy	p. 394

Posture and Chair Height.   For faster, easier typing at a considerable saving in energy, attempt to maintain a posture in which your arms are held parallel to the slope of the keyboard. For the average person, the typewriter should be about 28 to 30 inches from the floor. Chair seat height should be between 16 and 18 inches. If you feel eyestrain, back ache, or stiff neck, the typewriter is probably at the wrong height for you. Try experimenting with other heights.

Using a Copyholder.   A copyholder that supports the copy at eye level directly behind the typewriter permits fast, easy reading and reduces eye and neck strain. Most holders have a hand lever that raises the copy line by line to eye-level position. A ruler attachment helps you to keep the place and, if you are interrupted, to locate easily where you left off.

Writing Between Lines.   To type slightly above or below the original typing line, for example, when double-underscoring ($145.82) or writing subscripts (H_2O) and exponents ($90°$), use the automatic line-finder. This lever, at the left of the platen, releases the platen so that it may be rotated to the desired position. The platen will return to the exact typing line when the line finder is back in place. Move the line-finder lever forward *before* leaving the writing line. Rotate the platen to the new typing position and type in the information. To return to the original typing line, slide the line finder back to its stationary position and rotate the platen to lock it at the typing line.

Correcting Originals and Carbon Copies.   *With a Typewriter Eraser.*   Before making an erasure, move the typewriter carriage to the extreme right or left to prevent crumbs from falling into the mechanism. Use a good eraser, such as Rubacore by Dixon, and an erasing shield, such as the metal Norco Steno-Shield or a stiff card. Place the erasing shield behind the original copy and on top of the first carbon. A light circular motion of the white eraser on the letter(s) to be corrected will remove the ink. Be careful not to scrape off any paper fibers. Next, move the shield or card to the back of the first carbon copy and, with the pink eraser, carefully remove the error on this copy. Correct succeeding carbon copies in the same manner. Then return the carriage to typing position and insert the correct letter(s), being careful to match the intensity of the stroke in the other words. A skillful correction will not be noticeable.

With Special Carbon Papers.   The use of special carbon papers, such as Ko-Rec-Type products or Dixon Taperaser, eliminates erasing. Special carbons are available for correcting errors on originals, carbon copies, mylar-poly-paper, and colored and light-weight bond papers. Simply place these carbons *face down* on all copies over the word(s) to be corrected and *retype the error.* This process covers the black ink with white or another color, and leaves a blank space to be filled with the correct letter(s). Now, remove the correction carbons from *all* copies and strike the correct key(s). This procedure usually makes a neat, clean correction, but you may have to strike the keys harder in order to match the intensity of the other words.

With a Correction Fluid.   An opaquing fluid, such as Snopake, may be painted over the typographical error on the original and all carbons. After it dries, the correction is typed over a smooth, hard, white surface. Be careful to wait a few seconds for the fluid to dry before typing over it. If the liquid dries on carbon paper, that area of the carbon will not print when used the next time. Do not allow the liquid in the bottle to become too thick; a thin coat, merely enough to cover the error, should be used. A thinner is available for use with the correction fluid.

Correction fluid is especially effective for correcting material for photo-copying, photo-offset, xerography, and similar copying and reproducing processes. These undetectable corrections are also excellent for blocking out large areas and for use in graphic art work because the fluid may be ruled, drawn on, or lettered over.

Correcting Bound Manuscripts.   You need not take apart a manuscript bound at the top to make corrections on inside pages. Insert a sheet of blank paper into the typewriter until approximately one-quarter inch of the top page appears above the writing point. Next, make the erasure(s) or apply correction fluid to the pages in the manuscript to be retyped. Then slip the *bottom* edge of the page to be corrected *under* the *top* edge of the blank sheet (against the platen). Now roll the manuscript page down to the correct line and type.

Locating the Original Typing Line.   Once a paper is removed from the type-writer it is difficult to align the letters perfectly when you make corrections or insertions. Because all machines are slightly different in alignment, become familiar with the construction of your own machine by practicing the following technique. Insert the typed page and disengage the ratchet release or paper release lever, permitting the paper to move freely. Align the typed line to be corrected with the aligning scale. The aligning scale is behind the ribbon at the point where the keys strike the paper. See that the typed line is parallel to and immediately above (or sitting on) the aligning scale. Engage the ratchet release lever and examine the typed line clear across the page. If the typed line has shifted anywhere across the page and is not parallel to or is too far above or below the scale, disengage the lever and reposition. Next, find an *I, i, t,* or *l* in one of the words and move the carriage so that one of the white lines on the aligning scale bisects the letter. You may have to release the ratchet lever again to move the letter directly over the line. Be sure to recheck the typed line to see that it is parallel to the scale. Place the color control lever on *stencil* or disengage the ribbon and type over a few letters or a word to ascertain whether you have perfect alignment. If not, reposition and test. If you have, proceed to erase and make the correction or insert the additional copy.

Uniform Bottom Margin.   There are several ways to assure that each page will end on the same line. One method is to type vertically the numbers 1 through 66 (or 66 through 1) on the right edge of an $8\frac{1}{2}''$ × 11″ sheet of bond. Place this page behind the sheets to be typed so that the numbers extend beyond the right edge. Using the scale of six lines to a vertical inch, stop typing at line 59 (or line 7) for a one-inch bottom margin.

Some typewriters have an end-of-page indicator that is a vertical slide-up scale at the top of the typewriter to show how many lines remain on the page. As you type, the paper moves up the scale and you can easily read off the number of lines remaining.

Another common practice is to draw a light pencil line in the right margin slightly above the point where you want to stop typing, before inserting the paper into the machine. Your eye will see this line as you approach the bottom of the page, and warn you that you may type only one or two more lines. All copy should have at least a one-inch bottom margin. When adding footnotes, be sure to allow one-half inch for each one when marking the pencil line.

Ruled Lines.   You can make ruled lines on cards, stencils, ditto masters, or typing paper either vertically or horizontally by simply holding a sharply pointed pencil, ballpoint pen, or stylus at some notch or angle on the paper holder that allows you to hold the pencil or pen firmly. Rotate the platen forward for a vertical line, and move the carriage left to right for a horizontal one. The lines will be as straight as if drawn with a ruler.

Chain Feeding.   *From the Front of the Platen.*   When feeding small cards into the typewriter, chain-feed from the front of the platen. Position the first card and type the copy. Do not remove it, but backfeed it into the machine so that one-half inch of the top edge remains above the writing point. Insert the next card in front of the platen so that its bottom edge is underneath and held firmly by the top edge of the card still in the machine. Turn the platen back to position the new card. The completed cards will stack up against the paper rest in the order typed.

For an exceptionally small item, first make a pocket in a sheet of $8\frac{1}{2}'' \times 11''$ bond. To do this, make a 1/4- to 1/2-inch horizontal fold in the upper third of the sheet. Roll the pocketed sheet into the machine so that the pocket faces upward at the typing point. Drop each item into this pocket and type it.

From the Back of the Platen.   When addressing envelopes and other large items, such as $5'' \times 8''$ cards, chain feed from the back. Insert each new envelope or card so that its top edge is overlapped and held in place by the bottom edge of the preceding one. Put at least two or three envelopes or cards in position before starting to type. When the first item is typed, twirl the platen knob with the left hand and pick up with the right hand another envelope or card (stacked face up at the right of the machine) and insert it. A single twirl of the platen will release the completed item and bring the new one into typing position. With an electric typewriter, the left hand is used to remove completed items for stacking at the left of the machine. If items are not to be kept in a particular order, they may be allowed to flip over the back of the machine into a box.

Typing Individual Labels.   Small individual labels may be typed with the following backfeeding technique. First, insert a sheet of paper so that the edge is one-half inch above the aligning scale. Place the label behind the paper, and roll the cylinder toward you until the label is in typing position. When it has been typed, remove it and insert another one. Labels may also be purchased in perforated sheets with self-adhesive or in gummed rolls. These may be typed in the conventional manner.

Carbon Paper Hints.   *Feeding Carbon Packs.*   An envelope or short piece of paper folded over the top of several sheets of bond interleaved with carbons will help feed the pack evenly into the typewriter. Or a sheet of bond paper may be wrapped completely around the platen and the carbon pack slipped in between the platen and the open flap of this sheet of paper.

Removing Carbons.   Use carbon paper with the upper left corner cut off. Hold the original and all copies at this point and shake out the carbon papers. Carbon paper with an extended tissue edge also allows you to pull the carbons out of the pack easily.

Inserting Color.   To insert red figures or letters in the carbon copies without removing the pack from the typewriter, place a small piece of red carbon paper (red side down) in the desired position behind each one of the regular carbons. Type with the red ribbon, and then remove the red carbons before typing with black again.

Keeping Copies Clean.   To prevent onionskin paper from creasing or *treeing* with carbon lines, add a sheet of bond or heavy paper to the back of the carbon pack before inserting it in the typewriter.

Typing on Carbon Copies Only. You may place a special message only on the carbon copies by moving the original copy away from the typing line. If the message is to appear at the top of the carbons, use the ratchet or paper release lever to free the paper and move the carbon pack an inch or so *above* the original and the first sheet of carbon paper. If for some reason it is important that all material on the copies be in carbon, it will be necessary to type the message on the first sheet of carbon paper. Otherwise, type it on the first onionskin copy. After the message is inserted, realign all pages of the carbon pack by using the paper release lever. Be careful to lock the release lever in position before beginning to type. If typing on the first sheet of carbon paper, remember to position the machine at the spot for typing on the carbon copies *before* removing the original. It is your guide to the copy beneath the carbons.

If a message, such as a postscript or a notation about the distribution of carbon copies, is to go at the bottom of carbon copies only, first type in all the information that should appear on the original. Then release the paper by pulling the ratchet release lever toward you, and carefully slip the original out without disturbing the rest of the pack. Push the lever back to lock it, and type. If the message should appear on only one or two carbons, insert a small slip of paper behind each of the other carbons. These slips can be destroyed when the pack is removed from the machine.

Word Substitutions. *On Machines with Backspace Key Only.* To substitute a longer word (one or two letters longer) for a shorter word, such as *have* for *had,* first erase the incorrect word. Then position the carriage of a manual machine where the first letter of the word had been and press the backspacer halfway down while striking the first letter. Release it. After the machine spaces automatically, hold the key down halfway again and strike the next letter. Continue until the new word is typed. On an electric machine, the carriage must be held with the left hand and moved into position.

To substitute a shorter word for a longer word, position the machine where the first letter was and space forward once. Hold the backspacer halfway down and type the first letter of the shorter word. Spread the word to fill as much of the available space as possible. On an electric machine, use the carriage release button on the left to position the typing point to give the spread you want, as you hold the carriage firmly with the left hand.

On Machines with a Fractional Backspacer. After erasing the incorrect word, position the carriage where the first letter of the shorter word had been and press the fractional backspacer. Hold it down as you type the first letter of the new, longer word. Space forward once and again press the fractional backspacer. Hold it down as you type the second letter. Proceed in this way until the new, longer word has been typed.

To substitute a shorter for a longer word, return the carriage to where the first letter had been. Space forward once and then press the fractional back-spacer. Hold it down as you type the first letter of the new word. Forward space once again, press the special backspacer, and again hold it down as you type the second letter. Finish the word in the same manner.

Last-Line Corrections.　The following procedure will enable you to correct errors on the last few lines of a page without moving it out of line or having it slip from the feed rolls. Insert a sheet of bond paper between the feed roller and your last sheet of paper when the paper pack is within three inches of the bottom of the page. It will then be easy to reverse-feed the pack back into the typewriter to make erasures against the platen in the event any mistakes are made on the last few lines.

Typing Even Right Margins.　Make a copy of the text, using normal word breaks to end all lines at approximately the same place. Note the shortest and the longest lines. Determine the difference—usually from four to five char-acters. Add half the difference to the shortest line. Use this length for all lines in the text. As needed, contract and spread words, add extra spaces, or space once only after the period so that each line ends at the same point. If a line needs two characters to extend it, spread two words or spread one word and leave an extra space after a mark of punctuation. If another line is two spaces too long, contract one word near the beginning and one word near the end. If spreading and contracting are carefully done, the typing will appear uniform and the even right margin will make the copy more attractive.

Changing Ribbons.　Methods of changing typewriter ribbons vary for differ-ent makes of machines. Consult the manual that comes with your typewriter. In general, however, you should lift the top cover and study the course of travel of the old ribbon before removing it. Next, wind the remaining ribbon onto one spool and remove it. Set the new ribbon spool in place. Unreel 8 to 10 inches of the new ribbon and attach the end to the empty reel. Lock the carriage in upper case so as to lift the two ribbon guides at the typing point and make them more accessible. Thread the new ribbon through the guides. After unlocking the carriage, proceed to type. Check back to see that the ribbon is moving correctly.

Using Special Keys and Levers.　In addition to using the tabulator for statis-tical and columnar typing, use it for placing the date at the upper right side of letters; making paragraph indentations; placing the complimentary close and signature lines; typing addresses or other information on envelopes, cards, and labels; and adding other miscellaneous information, such as page num-bers. Learn to clear margin and tabulator stops and to reset them rapidly.

The following uses of special keys will speed up your output:

1. Use the paper release lever to remove paper rapidly.

2. Twirl (a faster motion than *turn*) paper into and out of the machine.

3. To type in the left margin or to add a letter or quotation mark to the first word on a line, press the margin release key and backspace.

4. Use the carriage release levers (not the space bar) to move the carriage to the extreme right of the paper.

5. Use both the upper and lower portions of an all-black ribbon by changing the color control lever so that the keys will strike the unused portion.

6. Plan each job in order to use as many special keys and levers of the typewriter as possible.

7. Arrange to type at one time all jobs using the same margin stops.

Selecting Carbon and Copy Paper. *General Types.* Carbon paper has been designed for each of the three kinds of typewriters—electric, standard, and noiseless. To determine whether your manual machine has standard or noiseless action, press one of the keys slowly and watch the movement of the type bar. If the bar swings like a golf club, you have a regular or standard-action machine. If it pushes forward like a billiard cue, it is a noiseless machine. The type on a standard-action machine hits fairly hard, whereas that on the noiseless hits lightly. Therefore, use electric carbon, regular carbon, or noiseless carbon, as the case may be.

Weight. To select the correct *carbon weight* for the number of copies to be made, follow these guides for an electric machine or a manual with standard action.

Number of Copies at a Time	Carbon Weight for the Job
1 to 5	Standard weight
1 to 10	Light weight
6 to 16	Extra-light weight

When using a noiseless-action machine, use standard weight for one to four copies, light weight for one to six copies, and extra-light weight for one to eight copies. The lighter-weight carbons produce many copies at a time, but they do not wear as long as the heavier-weight carbons. For economy, use the heaviest-weight carbon that will produce the desired number of copies.

Copy paper comes in several weights. With a standard-action or electric typewriter, use copy paper as follows.

Number of Copies at a Time	Copy Paper for the Job
1 to 3	20 lb.
1 to 6	16 lb.
1 to 12	13 lb.
6 to 20	9 lb.

When using a noiseless machine, use any weight copy paper for one copy and nine-pound copy paper for more than one copy.

Finish.   Type size affects the readability of copies. Pica type (10 characters to the inch) makes good readable copies with all kinds of carbon. Elite type (12 characters to the inch) and smaller type produce clearer carbon copies if the carbon paper used is extra-hard, hard, or medium finish. If intense or extra-intense-finish carbons are used, the *a*'s, *b*'s, *d*'s, *e*'s, *g*'s, *o*'s, *p*'s, *q*'s, and most *figures* fill in. These softer (intense or extra-intense) finishes should be used only with large type.

Carbon paper finishes give a range of impressions. Select the best weight and finish for each job. Hard or extra-hard-finish carbons (like hard pencils) produce a gray impression. Medium-finish carbons produce a medium tone. Intense and extra-intense carbons produce an extreme black. If the platen on your typewriter is new and soft, use a soft-finish (extra-intense, intense, or medium) carbon. Typing on a hard platen is like writing with a pencil on a paper laid over a hard surface, such as glass. Use medium-, hard-, or extra-hard-finish carbon with an old, hard platen. If your touch on the keys is strong and you hit them quite hard, use one of the harder finishes. If you hit the keys lightly, use a softer finish to get good, readable copies. When making a number of copies at a time, use a light-weight carbon with a softer finish so that the last copies will be distinct.

The Right Ribbon.   Be sure to select the correct ribbon for the make and model of your machine. For instance, electric machines use an extra-heavy fabric ribbon to withstand the heavy blow of the keys. A typewriter ribbon pads the type, thus reducing the sharpness of the imprint that has to carry through the entire paper pack. The thinner the ribbon, the less padding, and the sharper and more readable the copies. The use of nylon, silk, or fine cotton ribbons, which are tougher than plain cotton, will make better carbon copies. These ribbons wear longer, too. A typewriter equipped with both fabric and carbon-paper ribbons may be switched to carbon-paper ribbon when several copies are to be made.

The size of type is also important when you are choosing a ribbon. Larger type can use any inking on the ribbon, but smaller type should not be used with medium-heavy and heavy inkings because the type fills in and makes a blurred impression. The heavier the ribbon inking, the blacker the impression. Choices range from light, expert, and medium to medium-heavy and heavy inking. The harder the platen, the lighter the inked ribbon that is needed. If your touch is average, you should use a ribbon in medium inking. If your touch is light, swing toward heavier inking; and if heavy, swing toward lighter inking. Also, use the special touch-control setting on your machine to produce more readable copies.

Typing on Printed Forms.   Whether typing one copy or several of a printed form, first position it so that you will be typing slightly above lines and within boxes. Check the vertical line spacing also to find out if it corresponds to the single- or double-line spacing on your machine. If it does not, disengage the ratchet release lever and position each entry by hand.

When typing several copies of a printed form, check the alignment of these copies by holding them up to the light before inserting them in the machine. Attempt to use copies that are as closely aligned as possible. After aligning the copies, insert them in the typewriter *without* the carbons, just far enough

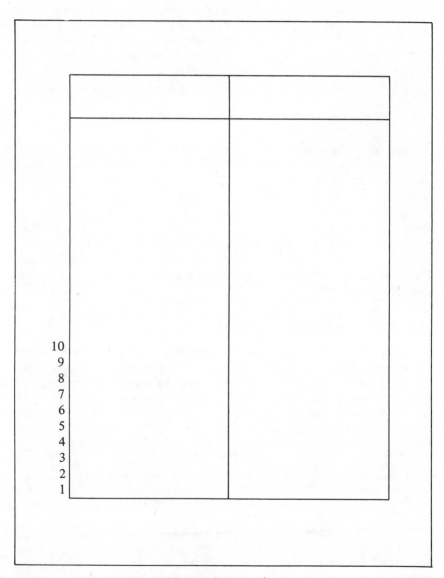

Figure 11-1   Guide sheet for two-column copy.

to hold them securely. Now place the carbons with the shiny side toward you between each one of the copies. Roll the pack into position and type.

Proofreading Typewritten Work.   Accurate proofreading is a skill. By being interested, alert, and particular, you can develop a high degree of skill in detecting errors in format and typography, including omissions and trans-positions. Proofread your own work before removing it from the machine. Always check the accuracy of numbers, especially addresses, amounts owed, estimates, bids, and dates. Two people other than the typist should proofread statistical work, if possible. When the typist must proofread her work with a second person, the typist should read the rough copy, phrase by phrase. If an error is discovered on the finished copy, place a small *pencil* mark in the margin opposite the error to allow the correction to be made without retyping the page.

See also "Proofreading," Section 7.4.

Typing Two-Column Copy.   To type a two-column page similar to newspaper or handbook copy, draw a guide sheet with India ink on your heaviest bond paper. A heavy black line should be drawn around the outer margins (one-inch margins on all sides except for one and one-half inches on the side to be bound). Next, draw a line down the center of the typing space. If heads are to be used over each column, draw a horizontal line at least one inch below the top margin line. Type the numbers 1 to 10 in reverse order at the bottom of the left column (Figure 11-1) to indicate the number of remaining lines. Place this guide sheet behind a lighter bond sheet or a stencil when typing the two-column material.

11.2   TYPING STATISTICAL MATERIAL

The centering of headings and the placement of material in rows and columns that are neat, attractive, and easy to read are important tasks of the typist. By preplanning the setup and following a few easy steps, anyone can turn out a good-looking table. Procedures for both the vertical and the horizontal spacing of tabulated data on single sheets or within paragraphs are described in the following order.

Headings	p. 394	Horizontal Placement	p. 397
Centering	p. 394	Centering Method	p. 397
Underscoring and Spacing	p. 395	Columnar Headings	p. 398
Vertical Placement	p. 396	Columnar Entries	p. 398
Spot Table	p. 396	Use of Leaders	p. 400
Reference Table	p. 396		

See also "Tabular Presentation," Section 5.4.

Headings.   *Centering.*   Table titles, subtitles, and columnar headings are easy to center by use of the backspace centering method. Find the *center of* *the typing line* and backspace *once* for every *two* letters, spaces, and marks of punctuation. For material bound at the left, allowance must be made for the wider left margin (usually one and one-half inches). Thus, by finding the *center of the typing line,* you need never be concerned with the differences in margin widths. For example, if the margin stops are at 30 and 100, the typing line is 70 spaces—one half that is 35, and added to the left margin stop at 30, places the *center of the typing line* at 65. Find the center of the typing line or the space allotted to the column in all instances.

Underscoring and Spacing. Underscoring is usually optional, but should be used when necessary to highlight headings or important columnar items that might be lost in the copy. When the main title of a table is typed in capitals and lower case, underscoring is optional. If the title is in all capitals, however, it is preferably not underscored because it has already been highlighted. A subtitle is always in capitals and lower case, and may be underscored if the main title is in capitals or has been underscored. Columnar heads are typed in capitals and lower case and should be underscored if the table is unruled. If the columnar heading is pyramided, only the bottom line need be underscored. The underscoring should extend the length of the longest line in the pyramid. A *total* line is a single underscore under the last item in an addition of numbers and must extend the same length as the longest item (including the $ sign) in the series. A double line may be used after the total to separate it from succeeding figures. (Figure 11-2.) Any other use of single or double underscoring with other representative figures, such as averages, percentages, or the last figure in the column, is at the discretion of the designer of the table, who may desire to call the attention of the reader to important figures.

Horizontal and vertical spacing depends mainly on the need to display the statistical material attractively. A slightly wider bottom than top margin and even left and right margins—except for the bound side, which is one-half inch wider on documents to be bound—are general rules to follow. Usually a subtitle is double-spaced after the main title, and columnar heads follow the subtitle after a triple space. The first column item is usually double-spaced after

	Number of Men		
	Present Work Force	Proposed Work Force	Reduction
Personnel reductions:			
Yard crews (five men to a crew)	40	35	5
Track maintenance gang	13	8	5
Locomotive maintenance:			
Shop men	6	5	1
Hostlers	3	1	2
Total	62	49	13

Figure 11-2   Spacing and underscoring in a typed table.

the head but may be singlespaced if it is necessary to compress a long table. Single- or double-spacing of items depends on the space available. Horizontal spacing must be carefully worked out to maintain adequate left and right margins and assure easy reading of the material in the columns. The following step-by-step directions should assist a typist to achieve attractive placement of statistical material.

Vertical Placement.　　Basic to the figuring of vertical placement is the fact that there are six line spaces to a vertical inch on most typewriters. For instance, if three inches or 18 line spaces are left on a page, you have 12 line spaces on which to type plus 6 for a one-inch bottom margin. If the table is longer than 12 lines, consider adding more paragraph material to that page and place the table on the next page. An $8\frac{1}{2} \times 11$ inch sheet of paper has 66 lines. When double-spacing, you leave one blank line and type on the second line. If triple-spacing, you leave two blank lines and type on the third line. To leave a one-inch top margin, space down seven times from the top edge of the paper so as to leave six blank lines and begin typing on the seventh line.

Spot Table.　　To place a short table attractively with paragraph material, determine first the number of vertical lines available. Then count the number of lines needed for the table.

　　1. Leave two or three line spaces between the last line in the paragraph and the main heading or the first line of the table.

　　2. Leave one line space between the main heading and the subhead.

　　3. Leave two lines between the main heading or subhead and the columnar headings.

　　4. Leave at least one line between the columnar heading and the first item in the column.

　　5. Keep all items in the table on one page. If space allows, you may double-space the items in a short table.

　　6. Triple-space, if space permits, before continuing paragraph typing.

Reference Table.　　To center a table vertically on a separate page, first determine the number of lines available—32 on a half sheet, 66 on an 11-inch sheet, 84 on a 14-inch sheet, 96 on a 16-inch sheet. Then follow these steps.

　　1. Add the number of lines in the tabulation. Watch for longer items that will need to be carried over to a second line.

　　2. Add to this total the number of blank lines. Be sure to count the headings and the blank lines between them. (See rules 2, 3, and 4 under "Spot Table" above.)

　　3. Subtract the total number of lines to be used from the total available.

　　4. Divide the answer by two for the number of line spaces for the top and bottom margins for exact centering. To have the table slightly above the center of the page, subtract three line spaces from the number of lines to be left at the top. In any case, be sure to leave at least a one-and-one-half-inch top margin and a one-inch bottom margin.

5. If the table continues to a second page, plan the first page so that four to six entries will be carried over. Always retype the columnar headings on the second page. A table of more than two pages should adhere to these general principles.

Horizontal Placement. It is necessary to know the number of horizontal spaces on a sheet of paper when planning the placement of columns. An easy way to learn the exact number is to determine the number of units your paper scans on the typewriter scale. If the left edge is at 12 on the scale and the right edge at 114, you have 102 spaces to work with. Another way is to know the type size. Pica type has 10 spaces to an inch and elite has 12. On paper $8\frac{1}{2}$ inches wide there are 85 pica and 102 elite spaces. Electric typewriters have a variety of special type faces with individual spacing characteristics. When using one of these, consult the operating manual.

Because all typed work should have at least one-inch margins on all sides, allow for these when figuring stops for tabulation. Also, remember that bound materials require a wider margin on the bound side.

Centering Method. To place a table attractively on the page, center it. Use the following five easy steps if your typewriter scale begins at zero at the left.

1. Count the number of strokes in the longest item in each column. Write these numbers on the rough copy or on a sheet of paper.

$$\boxed{12} \quad \boxed{8} \quad \boxed{19} \quad \boxed{14}$$

2. Determine the number of spaces to be allowed between columns, remembering that they are easier to read if close together—at least five and no more than ten spaces.

$$\boxed{12} \quad 7 \quad \boxed{8} \quad 7 \quad \boxed{19} \quad 7 \quad \boxed{14} \quad = 74$$

3. Clear all tabulator stops from the machine. Insert the paper with the left edge at zero and move the carriage so that the writing point is at the center of the paper. The center on pica machines is 42 and on elite 50. Or, if the left edge will be at some point other than zero, you may make a slight crease at the center of the paper before inserting it in the machine, and move the carriage to this spot.

4. Add the total number of strokes in the tabulation and backspace half the total. Set the left marginal stop at this point.

5. Now tap out on the space bar the number of strokes in the first column plus the number of spaces to be left between columns, and set a tab stop. Then space over the number of strokes in the second column plus the spaces between columns, and set a second tab stop. Proceed in a similar manner until all the necessary stops are in the machine.

If the typewriter has a zero-center scale, do steps 1 and 2 and set the left margin stop at half the total spaces. Now proceed with step 5.

Columnar Headings. A columnar heading that is shorter than the longest item in the column should be centered over the column. If it is longer, place it attractively on two or three lines and center each line. To do this, count the number of spaces in the heading, subtract from the number reserved for the column, divide by two, and space over or backspace that number before typing the heading. If the spaces between columns permit, a heading no more than eight spaces longer than the longest item in the column may be extended one half the difference into the spaces allowed between columns.

1971	1972	% Change 1971–1972
$24,358,635	$29,199,520	+19.9

Underline the last line of a heading unless the table is to be ruled. The last line of all columnar heads must be on the same plane no matter how many lines are pyramided in any one column.

A *spanner heading* is a primary columnar head that extends over two or more secondary columnar heads. If it is long, it may be placed on two or more lines. If it is shorter than the space needed by the secondary heads, it should be centered over them. The secondary head under the spanner may also take two (no more than three) lines. The spacing of these heads in relation to those of other columns calls for preplanning. The last line of the longest secondary head establishes the horizontal plane for all columns. For clarity, the underscoring of the last line of each spanner head should be extended to the full width of all columns covered by the heading.

	Actual Time		Number of Freight Cars	
Assignment	Start	Complete	Placed	Removed

Tables requiring elaborate headings are often ruled. Columnar headings are then centered vertically as well as horizontally in the space provided. (See "Tabular Presentation," Section 5.4, Figure 5-19.)

Columnar Entries. When the descriptive words in the first column (the stub) must be typed on two or three lines in order to fit the space given to the column, be sure to align the corresponding entries across all columns with the last line of the stub entry. Second and succeeding lines of a stub entry may be in block form (if double-spacing follows each entry) or may be indented one or two spaces. Subtopics under a stub entry are usually indented three to five spaces. The word *Total* after an addition of figures is indented five, ten, or more spaces, depending on the arrangement of the material or the preference of the typist (see Figure 11-2).

Plant and Equipment	$12,000	$14,000	$9,750	$11,950

Align columns of whole numbers on the right.

```
        15
       550
     3,500
   115,954
```

Figures with decimal points are aligned by the decimal point.

```
   .16
  1.4
 42.5
  5.498
   .7
```

Columns of dissimilar figures may be aligned on the left or centered.

```
515          $85
4231         35 ounces
39½          18 gross
$80          44.8%
55 lbs.      $1.95
```

Dollar signs, plus and minus signs, percent symbols, and the like are always aligned in a column. The dollar sign is placed in front of the first figure in the column and in front of totals and subtotals in columns containing only dollar figures. Align the dollar mark with the longest figure in the column, regardless of whether it is the first one.

```
$    24.00      −24.1%
    987.50      + 8.6
  1,032.24      +10.2
      7.98      − 3.0
  ─────────
$2,051.72
```

Place the dollar sign before the first number in the column when you have a column of dollar figures and the first spaces of the column are blank. Never put the dollar sign at the top of such a column.

```
        —              —
        —              —
        —          $  138.75
  $5,845.00            —
    462.58             —
        —          1,588.25
```

A double column of figures in a single money column has the dollar sign before both figures in the first line.

```
Repair Expense  .   .   .   .   .   .   .   .   .   .   $1,000–$1,500
Replacement Expense   .   .   .   .   .   .   .   .   .   2,200–  3,500
```

In a column of numbers in which some are monetary figures and some are not, place a dollar sign before each monetary figure. The dollar signs are aligned with the longest dollar figure.

$$
\begin{aligned}
&1,772 \\
\$\quad&11,100 \\
&69\% \\
&+10\% \\
&6,000 \\
\$&11,840,000
\end{aligned}
$$

In a mixed list of numbers in which there are percentages to a tenth or a hundredth and dollars and cents, the items should either be aligned at the left or centered. A guiding rule is to present the material as clearly as possible. *Use of Leaders.* Periods that connect the stub to the first column in the field are known as *leaders*. They are typed at *every other* space. In order to keep leaders vertically aligned, notice on the typewriter scale whether the first one starts on an odd or even number. In the first item of the stub, the initial period is placed immediately after the last letter. If the initial leader starts on an odd number, space to the first odd number after typing the second item and strike the first period for that row of leaders. If the initial leader begins at an even number, space over to the first even number.

All leaders end at the same point, at least two or three spaces before the start of the longest item in the next column. They are never used between columns of figures, but only between the stub and the first column in the field. When the first item in the stub takes more than one line, use leaders only after the last line in the item. Hyphens are never substituted for leaders because they can be mistaken for minus signs when figures are involved.

An index, however, may be set up as follows.

Abbott Smith Assoc., Inc.	60
Chartmakers, Inc.	54
Dale Carnegie & Assoc., Inc.	102
Eastman Kodak Co.	8
Methods Research Corp.	22
Readers Service Card	3, 4, 63, 64
Telex	18
Wilson Corp., H.	2nd Cover

11.3 TYPING SPECIAL CHARACTERS, FORMULAS, AND EQUATIONS

Special Characters.   The usual characters on standard typewriter keyboards may be used as they are or combined to form special characters. For example, the following symbols may be made by the use of two or three keys or a single key.

¶ Paragraph mark	Lower case *l* typed over capital *P*.
⌊ ⌋ Brackets	For left bracket: type diagonal, backspace *once,* type underscore, roll paper back one line, type underscore.

	For right bracket: type diagonal, backspace *twice,* type underscore, roll paper back one line, type underscore.
÷ Division sign	*Colon* and *hyphen* typed in same space.
= Equals sign	Two *hyphens*—one slightly below other.
≠ Plus sign	Type *diagonal,* backspace, strike *hyphen.*
x Multiplication sign	Use capital *X.*
Root or radical sign $\sqrt{}$	Type *diagonal,* roll platen back one line, strike underscore key as many times as necessary. Draw in first short line.
£ Pound Sterling sign	Either lower case *f* typed over lower case *t* or capital *L* typed over lower case *f.*
ç Cedilla beneath *c*	Lower case *c* and *comma* typed in same space.
' Accent mark	Use *apostrophe* one-half line above accented letter.
78°F Degree sign	Roll platen back one-half line and type lower case *o.*
o ' " Degrees, minutes, seconds	Roll platen back one-half line and type lower case *o*, apostrophe, and quotation mark.
! Exclamation point	*Apostrophe* and *period* in same space.

Equations and Formulas.   The typing of reports, speeches, manuscripts, and other material containing technical material is often difficult because of the presence of equations and formulas in the copy. Of first importance is a clear rough draft from which the typist may accurately copy the information. The typist should ask the mathematician, engineer, or scientist for a handwritten copy of frequently used symbols and the Greek alphabet in order to eliminate guesswork as she attempts to decipher his writing. It is also wise to type all equations or formulas on a practice sheet before placing them in the final copy. Because the position of each sign and symbol is of vital importance, this trial spacing will assure correct and meaningful placement.

Several aids for typing equations are available, such as the IBM Selectric typewriter with the Universal Element that contains the Greek alphabet and mathematical symbols. Technical keys are also obtainable for some machines either as interchangeable keys or as a bank of additional keys. Templates may be purchased at local stationery stores. Rapidesign No. 50 (Pocket Pal) and No. 17 with the Greek alphabet, mathematical symbols, and the chemist's triangle are especially useful. Adhesive transfers such as Prestype may also be used for time-saving and artistic application in the final copy. Hand-drawn symbols with pen and India ink should be made when the symbols cannot be typed or special aids are not available (Figure 11-3).

Spacing Rules.   In technical typing, equations and formulas are set up in two ways. Many times they are merely part of the sentence. At other times, they are set off and displayed in the copy. Displayed equations are usually complicated with numerous aggregates containing several superscripts (exponents) and subscripts (inferiors). The following format rules for typing both in-text and displayed equations give the horizontal and vertical spacing for standard typewriters and the IBM Executive with Bold Face No. 2 type. *Spacing for the IBM Executive is given in units in parentheses.*

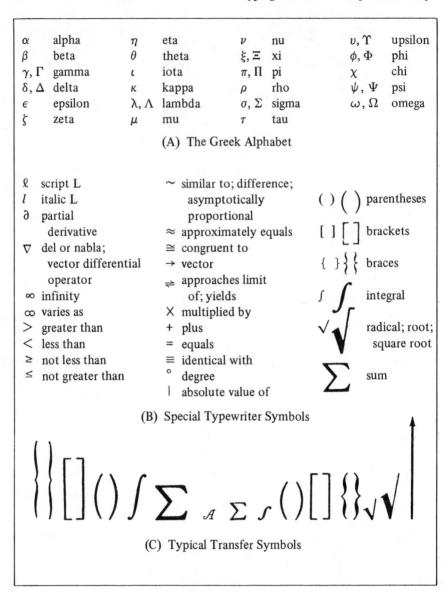

α	alpha	η	eta	ν	nu	υ, Υ	upsilon
β	beta	θ	theta	ξ, Ξ	xi	φ, Φ	phi
γ, Γ	gamma	ι	iota	π, Π	pi	χ	chi
δ, Δ	delta	κ	kappa	ρ	rho	ψ, Ψ	psi
ε	epsilon	λ, Λ	lambda	σ, Σ	sigma	ω, Ω	omega
ζ	zeta	μ	mu	τ	tau		

(A) The Greek Alphabet

ℓ	script L
l	italic L
∂	partial derivative
∇	del or nabla; vector differential operator
∞	infinity
∞	varies as
>	greater than
<	less than
≥	not less than
≤	not greater than

~	similar to; difference; asymptotically proportional
≈	approximately equals
≅	congruent to
→	vector
⇌	approaches limit of; yields
X	multiplied by
+	plus
=	equals
≡	identical with
°	degree
		absolute value of

( ) ( ) parentheses

[ ] [ ] brackets

{ } } { braces

∫ ∫ integral

√ √ radical; root; square root

Σ Σ sum

(B) Special Typewriter Symbols

} } [ ] ( ) ∫ Σ ₐ Σ ∫ ( ) [ ] { } √√ |

(C) Typical Transfer Symbols

Figure 11-3   Letters and symbols available for mathematical copy.

In-Text Equations and Formulas.   Read all the following suggestions before attempting to type any equations.

1. Leave 2 spaces (4 units) *before* and *after* a mathematical symbol, expression, equation, or formula that is part of a sentence.

2. Leave 1 space (2 units) *between* such symbols and expressions and a punctuation mark that follows.

3. Leave 2 spaces (4 units) between a comma (following a symbol or an expression) and whatever follows. Leave 2 spaces (6 units) between a period and the next sentence.

EXAMPLES ...corresponding to $\bar{k}^T$, which equals...
...the term $\bar{k}^T$. Then the ...

4. Leave 1 space (3 units) before and after $=$, $>$, $<$, $\geq$, and $\leq$.

EXAMPLE: ...in 2xy = b we find...

5. Leave 1 space (2 units) before and after $+$, $-$, $\pm$, $\times$, and $\cdot$ (a soft-rolled period).

6. Leave no space (1 unit) after $+$, $-$, and $\pm$ when these indicate the sign of a single term in the text.

EXAMPLE: ...within ± 4 cm ...

7. When a mathematical expression is followed by a unit of measurement, leave 1 space (2 units) between it and the unit of measurement.

EXAMPLE: ...the interval of $\Delta t = 0.04$ sec. used in the...

8. Fractions in the text should be typed with the diagonal (slash) fraction bar.

EXAMPLE: ...to the resultant $\underline{P}$ is $(1 \not= \bar{x})/2$ ...

9. Leave no space (1 unit) before, after, or between a group of three dots (ellipses) indicating an omission. Type the dots on the line as if they were periods.

10. Type chemical formulas without spaces (1 unit) between symbols and numbers.

EXAMPLES: $C_x(H_2O)_y$, $2C_2H_5OH$, $_nC_6H_{12}O_6$

11. Align reaction equations on the arrow or plus sign.

EXAMPLE: $C_6H_{12}O_6 \rightarrow 2\ CO_2 + 2\ C_2H_5OH$

Displayed Equations and Formulas.   These hints will be helpful when you are typing equations and formulas within paragraphs.

1. Center displayed equations or formulas on a line or lines by themselves.

2. Triple-space before and after the entire expression. A trial typing should be made in order to allow sufficient space for all superscripts, subscripts, and aggregates.

3. Use the horizontal bar (underscore) for most displayed fractions and the diagonal (slash) key occasionally where appropriate.

EXAMPLE: $s_t = \dfrac{10,000}{12} = 834$ lb./sq. in.

4. Leave 1 space (3 units) before and after the operational signs $+$, $-$, $\pm$, $\times$, and $\cdot$ (a soft-rolled period) when these signs indicate that a quantity

is being added to, subtracted from, added to or subtracted from, or multiplied by another quantity.

5. Leave 2 spaces (4 units) before and after $=$, $>$, $<$, $\geq$, and $\leq$.

6. Center material above and below a summation sign.

EXAMPLE: $\displaystyle\sum_{\infty-\circ}^{\circ}$

7. Make parallel lines long enough to extend to the top and bottom of the material between them.

EXAMPLE: $\left| E_{x_\circ}^2 \right|$.

8. Use signs of aggregation large enough to enclose all material. Center them relative to the equals sign. Leave no space (1 unit) between adjacent signs of aggregation. (Figure 11-4.)

$$\frac{1}{2\pi}\int_{-\infty}^{\infty}\frac{\exp\,(-itw_1)}{2\sigma_{11}\,\sigma_{12}\,\sin\theta_{12}}$$

$$\frac{dt}{\left\{\left[\frac{1}{4}\left(\frac{1}{\sigma_{11}^2\,\sin^2\theta_{12}}-\frac{1}{\sigma_{12}^2}\right)\right]^2+\left[\frac{1}{4}\left(\frac{1}{\sigma_{11}^2\,\sin^2\theta_{12}}+\frac{1}{\sigma_{12}^2}\right)-it\right]^2\right\}^{1/2}}$$

$$=\frac{1}{2\pi}\int_{-\infty}^{\infty}\exp\,(-itw_1)\left\{\frac{1}{2\sigma_{11}\,\sigma_{12}\,\sin\theta_{12}}\int_{0}^{\infty}\exp\left[-\frac{1}{4}\left(\frac{1}{\sigma_{11}^2\,\sin^2\theta_{12}}+\frac{1}{\sigma_{12}^2}\right)s\right]\right.$$

$$J_0\left[\frac{1}{4}\left(\frac{1}{\sigma_{11}^2\,\sin^2\theta_{12}}-\frac{1}{\sigma_{12}^2}\right)s\right]e^{ist}ds\left.\vphantom{\int}\right\}\,dt'$$

$$\frac{(-)^n}{n!}\,y^{2n}\left[(2+3+4\cdots+n)+2(3+4\cdots+n)\cdots+i(i+1+\cdots+n)\cdots\right.$$

$$\left.+(n-1)n\right]$$

$$=\frac{(-)^n}{n!}\,y^{2n}\left[\frac{(n-1)(n+2)}{2}+\frac{2(n-2)(n+3)}{2}\cdots+i\,\frac{(n-i)(n+i+1)}{2}\cdots\right]$$

$$=\frac{(-)^n}{n!}\,y^{2n}\sum_{i=1}^{n}\left[(n^2+n)\,i-i^2-i^3\right]$$

Figure 11-4   Examples of stacked right-hand and left-hand members and use of signs of aggregation.

9. Align the bar of a built-up fraction with the center of the equals sign. Center the numerator and denominator relative to the horizontal bar in a built-up fraction, allowing a small space above and below the bar.

EXAMPLE: I_o about $CD = \dfrac{1}{12}bh^3 = \dfrac{10 \times 6^3}{12} = 180$ in.

10. Leave no more than 1 space (1 unit) between the single-line elements of a product, and no space (1 unit) before punctuation within such material.

EXAMPLE: $I_o^2 \left(A_o^2, N \right)$

11. Leave 1 space (2 units) between double-line (built-up) elements of a product and 2 spaces (3 units) between elements of a product that exceed a double line.

EXAMPLES: $\dfrac{1}{2m} \dfrac{(j \neq m)!}{(j - m)!}$, $\dfrac{1 + \dfrac{\gamma - 1}{2} M_o^2}{\eta_c} \left[\zeta_{2,3}^{(\gamma-1)} \Big/ \gamma-1 \right]$

Placement of Subscripts and Superscripts.   The correct placement of these mathematical symbols follows a few general rules.

1. Type all superscripts and subscripts for a given line at one time so that they will be even.

2. Place subscripts and superscripts, respectively, half a line below and above the lowest and highest characters in the related material.

EXAMPLES: R_1 , $2\left(\dfrac{N\phi_1}{Eh}\right)^{1/2}$

3. Align subscripts with superscripts.

EXAMPLES: P_n^2 , $F^{(p,q)}$

4. Place sub-subscripts half a line below the subscript.

EXAMPLE: E_{x_o}

5. Use lowercase *o*'s for both subscript and superscript zeros, except in juxtaposition to other superscript or subscript numbers.

EXAMPLES: K_o^2 , $f_2(t_o) = f_2(t_1)$, $n^{0.15}$

6. Raise *th* to a superscript position.

EXAMPLES: n^{th} , i^{th}

7. Do not leave any spaces before and after $+$, $-$, $\pm$, $\times$, and $\cdot$ (a soft-rolled period) in subscripts and superscripts.

EXAMPLES: na^{n-1} , $\displaystyle\sum_{x=o}$

8. Leave no space (1 unit) before and after $=$, $>$, $<$, $\geq$, and $\leq$ in subscripts and superscripts.

9. Use the standard-size typewriter keys for aggregation signs when the material contains only simple superscripts or simple subscripts (but not both).

EXAMPLES: $(K^2 \neq A)$, $\left(K^2 \neq A_1 \neq K_2 \neq B^2 \right)$

10. Type the number preceding the sign for more than three plus or minus signs to a superscript.

EXAMPLE: P^{5+} (not P^{+++++})

11. Type the degree sign (lower case letter *o*) as the superscript and *zero* as the subscript when typing thermodynamic symbols.

EXAMPLE: S_0^o

Placement of Arrows. Horizontal arrows may be typed by the use of either the underscore or the hyphen. When using the underscore, raise the line almost two thirds of a space and type two underscores (or as many as needed). Draw the arrowhead with pen and ink using the *less than* or *more than* ($<$ $>$) signs, which can be found on a template, or finish freehand.

When using the hyphen, type two hyphens and backspace once. Then use the half-backspace key or hold the cylinder by hand to type a hyphen that fills the space between the other two. Draw the arrowhead.

To type double arrows, use the underscore. Type the bottom arrow a quarter line above the main-line character, backspace twice (or more if the arrows are to be longer), and roll the platen one-half line above the first arrow. Type the line. Make the arrowheads with pen and ink.

EXAMPLE: $SO_2 \neq H_2O \rightleftarrows H_2SO_3 \rightleftarrows H^+ \neq HSO_3^- \rightleftarrows 2H^+ \neq SO_3^=$

When explanatory material appears in equations above or below an arrow, make the arrow as long as necessary to fit the explanation.

General Spacing Rules. The following practices should be observed when you are setting up both in-text and displayed material.

1. Break an equation at the arrow or equals sign when it must be carried over to the next line. Do not break short equations. If there is no equals or arrow sign in the formula, you may break it at an operational sign. Type the arrow, equals, or operational sign as the last character on the line and indent the next line.

2. Use the sequence {[()]} for signs of aggregation, except where conventional notation specifies brackets or braces.

3. Use parentheses to enclose an argument that contains a plus or minus sign ($\ldots \cos (\omega t - \beta x)$).

4. Make a solidus extend from the top to the bottom of the values it separates.

EXAMPLE: $K^2/2c_1$

5. Type any required bar or dot immediately above the mathematical symbol so that it is obvious that either one and the symbol constitute a unit.

Make the bar over a capital letter by rolling the underscore back one line; roll up the hyphen for the bar over a lower case letter. For lower case *i,* roll the platen back one full line to raise the bar or the dot a little higher.

EXAMPLES: $\bar{\text{k}}$, $\bar{\text{k}}$, $\dot{\text{i}}$, $\dot{\text{r}}$

If bars are used over both capital and lower case letters in a report, the rolled-up underscore is used throughout.

6. Leave 1 space (2 units) before and after trigonometric, logarithmic, or exponential functions, and leave 1 space (2 units) between the parts of such functions. If these functions must be divided, divide them after an appropriate operational sign.

EXAMPLES: $\text{v} \cos \theta$, $\text{Y} \ln \text{x}$, $2 \log \text{y} \log \text{z}$, $\frac{1}{2} \exp \left(\text{a} \neq \frac{\text{h}}{2} \right)$

7. Leave 1 space (1 unit) before and after differentials and 1 space (1 unit) between differentials.

EXAMPLES: x dx , $(\text{x}^2 \neq \text{y}^2) \text{dx dy}$

8. Often symbols in an equation must be identified. The equation is centered on the next typing line, and each symbol is typed at the left margin in vertical alignment as illustrated here.

$$s = v_o t \pm \frac{1}{2} at^2$$

where

$$s = \text{distance}$$

$$v_o = \text{velocity}$$

$$t = \text{time}$$

$$a = \text{acceleration}$$

When only a few symbols are to be identified, the identifications may be given in horizontal alignment. For example,

$$E = mc^2$$

where E is the intrinsic energy, m the mass, and c the velocity of light.

Inserting Line Bonds.   Horizontal line bonds may be made by the typing of two underscores, raised one half a line. No space is left before or after the line.

$$\text{Na—Cl}$$

Vertical line bonds are drawn in by hand with pen and India ink, if interchangeable keys are not available.

To type a formula with vertical and horizontal line bonds, type the letters in the top line first, double-space and type the letters for the second and subsequent lines. Type all horizontal bonds. Remove the paper and draw in the vertical bonds.

$$
\begin{array}{c}
\text{H} \quad \text{H} \\
| \quad | \\
\text{H}\!-\!\text{C}\!-\!\text{C}\!-\!\text{H} \\
| \quad | \\
\text{H} \quad \text{H}
\end{array}
$$

To type a formula with diagonal line bonds, type the *central* letter on the *main* line first, then any other letters on that line. Space forward three times from the central letter, roll the platen back two lines, type the *upper right* bond. Return the carriage to the central letter, backspace three times plus one for each letter or number, roll the platen back two lines and type in the *upper left* bond. Return again to the central letter and type the lower left and right bonds, if necessary, in the same way. Draw diagonal line bonds with pen and ink.

$$
\left[
\begin{array}{cc}
\text{NH}_3 \quad & \quad \text{NH}_3 \\
& \text{Cu} \\
\text{NH}_3 \quad & \quad \text{NH}_3
\end{array}
\right]^{+2}
\qquad
\begin{array}{c}
\text{H} \quad \text{NH}_2 \\
\text{R}\!-\!\text{C}\!-\!\text{COOH}
\end{array}
$$

Double and triple horizontal line bonds may be typed with the underscore key when the ratchet lever is disengaged to allow the platen to move freely. Double and triple vertical and diagonal line bonds should be drawn with pen and ink.

Office Services

Skillful management of the office provides a solid foundation for the successful operation of any business. The person in charge, therefore, should possess practical knowledge of current office procedures and standards and should be familiar with office equipment and its efficient use. A person who is capable of managing people and who has had experience in handling the paperwork, using the office machines, and following the office routines would be a good choice. In some large companies, the office manager is hired mainly for his management skills, even though he has had little experience with the office routines and machines. In such cases, the manager will need to become familiar with office systems and procedures. Even managers who have been in the field for several years find it necessary to study new developments and to apply new techniques to old procedures when appropriate. Information on four important operating functions of the office is given in this section to assist the person in charge to initiate the functions, to perform or direct their performance, and to control them.

CONTENTS

12.1	Records Management	p. 409
12.2	Duplicating and Copying	p. 431
12.3	Telephone and Wire Services	p. 442
12.4	Travel Arrangements	p. 466

12.1 RECORDS MANAGEMENT

Because the creation, protection, storage, and disposition of records are vital functions in every office, information about these functions should be readily available for reference purposes. The application of the principles explained here will assist a department or a company in the systematic organization of its initial filing functions or in the reorganization of the existing system for greater efficiency. Administrative personnel and other workers who need a working knowledge of filing and the filing system in use in their company will find valuable information in this section on records management.

Storage of Records	p. 410
Alphabetical Filing Systems	p. 410
Nonalphabetical Filing Systems	p. 415
Filing Equipment Needs	p. 419
Planning the File System	p. 419
Steps in the Filing Process	p. 420
Indexing	p. 421
Charge-Out and Control of Records	p. 425
Centralized Versus Decentralized Files	p. 425
Importance of a Retention Schedule	p. 426
Transfer and Disposal of Records	p. 428
Microform	p. 428

Storage of Records.   The systematic arrangement of records so that they may be quickly found can be a simple problem. The first step is to determine the specific purposes of your files, the manner in which they are to be controlled, the equipment you have on hand, the different kinds of material to be filed, and the way the stored information is to be used by members of the organization. Often you find that your problem presents peculiarities that call for an individual application of a basic filing principle. Therefore, the next step is to combine the various methods of filing to fit the particular needs of your company for the retrieval of specific information.

The different methods may be illustrated in this way. Let us suppose you wish to file incoming orders. If you refer to these by the names of the people who order, use the *alphabetical* method. If the orders are numbered, you will want a duplicate file in which they are arranged numerically. On the other hand, your company may be interested primarily in the territories that generated the orders. In this case, the *geographical* method should be used. The *subject* method is used if you refer to orders by subject (the kind of goods ordered), and the *chronological* method if you refer to orders by the dates on which they were received or were filled. As can be seen, the material may be filed by a number of basic methods. Before deciding to adopt any one or a combination of methods, you should study the advantages of each.

Alphabetical Filing Systems (Figure 12-1)

1. Filing by name. The majority of firms file correspondence alphabetically according to the client's or supplier's name whether it be a firm or an individual. In card filing, the alphabetical method is used for cross-reference work and the indexing of names. In paper filing, it is best adapted to correspondence, invoices, purchase orders, and similar records. With this method, papers are found by direct reference; no card index is required as is true of some other systems. The method is flexible for small or large filing needs—any number of divisions can be created.

2. Filing by subject. Subject files are set up in much the same way as name files. Instead of the names of people or organizations, however, the captions

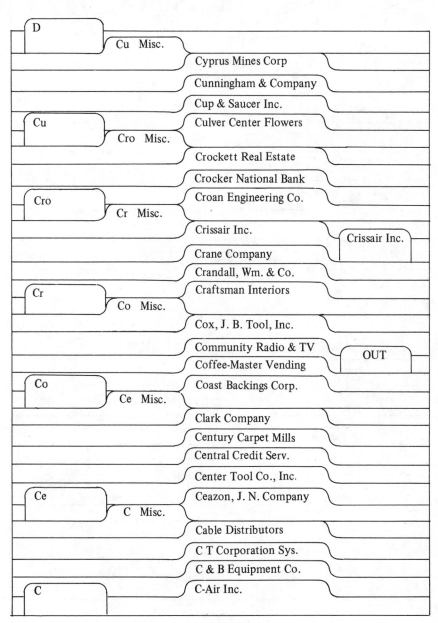

Alphabetic

Figure 12-1 Alphabetic, subject, geographic, and numeric filing systems. (Continued on pages 412–414.)

Subject

Figure 12-1 (continued).

Geographic

Figure 12-1   (continued).

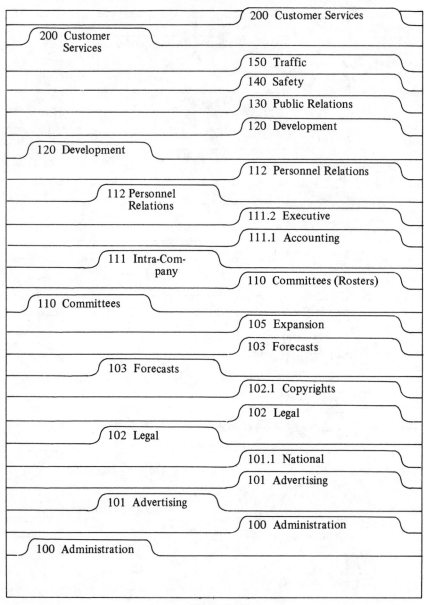

Numeric

Figure 12-1 (continued).

are concrete subjects. The subject method of filing meets a need in those offices that have a large quantity of related papers from different sources to file under one heading, for example, typewritten data, news clippings, catalogs, and so on. Records should be organized by subject in the following situations.

(a) When the records do not refer to the name of a person or an organization, e.g., inventory records.

(b) When it is likely that the records will be called for by subject.

(c) When all the records about one product or activity are likely to be needed at one time.

(d) When records might otherwise become unnecessarily subdivided.

Subject filing is accompanied by a card index that lists alphabetically all the headings, divisions, and subdivisions of the file. It should list also all topics related to the actual captions used. For instance, the subject of advertising might be subdivided into budget, 10-year plans, direct mail, sources of mailing lists, magazine, radio/TV, contests, promotional schemes, previous campaigns, competitors' campaigns, advertising agencies, and so forth. In this same case, budget information might be kept under the general headings of "Administration"; division: "Budgets"; subdivision: "Advertising Budget." Perhaps also under "Advertising Contests" there might be a subdivision for "Budget." Because individuals tend to differ in their selection of *the* filing subject for a piece of correspondence, all possible cross-references should be given in the card index to direct the search as quickly as possible to the needed document.

3. Filing by geographical area. Businesses that use *geographical* filing include sales organizations, mail-order houses, and public utilities. Where records are of a territorial nature, the geographical method is unquestionably the system of filing to adopt. The equipment consists of country guides in one color, state or province guides in another, county guides in a third, and city and town guides in a fourth color. If this system is used for a letter file in sales work, customers' folders may be tabbed on the left and prospects' folders on the right.

Nonalphabetical Filing Systems. *Numerical Index.* Records may be arranged according to serial numbers that are assigned arbitrarily and consecutively, or according to code numbers (Figure 12-1). The code number represents a topic or subject. Numerical filing systems are indirect. That is, the file clerk must first consult an alphabetical index to determine the code number of a record. Even though numerical filing may appear to require duplication of effort, many firms find that it has definite advantages over alphabetical filing.

1. Numerical systems make possible the quick sequential identification of records.

2. They aid efficient sorting and handling and result in fewer misfiles.

3. They provide for unlimited expansion.

4. They make possible permanent and extensive cross-referencing.

5. The card index for the numerical file provides a compact list of the names and addresses of correspondents and of subjects. It may also list various useful facts about clients.

Lawyers, architects, contractors, engineers, and scientists find a serial numbering system convenient for classifying cases and projects. The usual arrangement is in consecutive order from lowest to highest. The simplest system uses three-digit numbers in hundreds and tens. The first major alphabetical division is assigned 000 and each subdivision within the subject is assigned a ten, i.e., 010, 020, 030, 040, and so on. If more subdivisions are needed, the decimal-numeric system may be used. With the addition of more digits to the right of the decimal point, the subject may be divided into more and more parts, for example, 241 may be subdivided into 241.1, 241.2, 241.21, 241.22, and so on. The simple numerical system is limited to ten main headings 000 to 900 and nine main divisions under any one heading 010 to 090.

Public utilities find that the numerical system combined with letters allows them to use more headings and subheadings. One utility company, for instance, uses the letter *E* for "Equipment and Facilities" with numbered subdivisions as follows.

E7   Trunking
     E7.1   Assignments
     E7.2   Design Planning and Coordination
            E7.2A   Alternate Routing
            E7.2B   Extended Service
            E7.2C   Local
            E7.2D   Multimessage Unit
            E7.2E   Route Advance
            E7.2F   Special
            E7.2G   Tandem
            E7.2H   Toll
     E7.3   Leased Channels
     E7.4   Facility Relief
            E7.4A   Connecting Company
            E7.4B   Trunk Cable
     E7.5   Trunking Forecasts
            E7.5A   Interoffice Trunk Estimates
            E7.5B   Toll Circuit Estimates
     E7.6   Usage and Requirements

Bank checks, invoices, sales slips, and other prenumbered office forms are often filed by the terminal or the middle digit. Users of terminal-digit indexes claim a substantial reduction in misfiles, an unlimited expansion ability, and more efficient sorting and handling. In this system, numbers are read from right to left, and the end digits are considered in pairs or in groups of three:

Usual Sequence	Terminal-Digit Twos	Terminal-Digit Threes
10015	130 08	13 008
13008	100 15	10 015
22021	220 21	22 021
24589	357 21	24 589
35721	245 89	35 721

Those who use the middle-digit index find that it spreads items more evenly than does the terminal-digit system. The sequence in this system is based on the middle row of digits as follows.

> 1 00 15
> 2 20 21
> 1 30 08
> 2 45 89
> 3 57 21

Chronological Index. This method of filing is used mainly in connection with other basic methods. For instance, correspondence from a firm is placed in an alphabetical or subject folder by date with the latest date on top. When a folder becomes congested with letters, these are then subdivided according to years or months and placed in several folders. Chronological filing as a method in itself, however, is often used for daily reports, deposit tickets, freight bills, statements, order sheets, and other material that you may want to keep together by dates.

Another important use of chronological filing is for follow-up information in a card index. In the follow-up system, all cards that need attention on the 26th of January are filed behind the "26" guide, which in turn is behind the "January" guide. The card then turns up automatically on the proper date. After each card is given attention, it is refiled behind the guide that indicates the date on which it should again have attention—January 30, for example— or behind the monthly guide for the month in which it is to receive attention. At the beginning of the month, the cards are divided by days. Such a card file is an example of a follow-up system called a "tickler" file (Figure 12-2).

Phonetic Index. In this system, filing is done by sound rather than by actual spelling. Names that sound alike are grouped together. Such a system helps in the detection of duplications and minimizes the effects of transcribing and typing errors. In the several phonetic indexes, vowel sounds are omitted and the basic consonant sounds are stressed. The names are eventually filed by number. A phonetic index is most useful in large name files. One phonetic code is as follows.

Code numbers	Letter equivalents
1	b, f, p, v
2	c, g, j, k, q, s, x, z
3	d, t
4	l
5	m, n
6	r

Information-action card
(filed by month and then
by day action is to be taken)

Month guides (current
month in front)

Day guides (behind
current month only)

Subject	Tickler Date
MONTHLY INVENTORY	11/16
Action: Distribute tally sheets to	
stock clerks - Form #I-5a	
J. Bone-12-01, H. Thomas-33-10	
S. Smith-12-05, B. Williams-16-01	
Signed	

Figure 12-2 Tickler or follow-up file.

Each code is made up of the first letter of the name and three numbers from the code. Vowels and *w, h,* and *y* are not coded. Double key letters are treated as a single unit. A key letter and its equivalent, such as *ch* or *mn,* are coded as one unit. If a name cannot be coded into three numbers, zeros are added. To illustrate, Thomsen, Thompson, Tompson are all coded *T525.* Within each section of the file, names are arranged alphabetically by the second indexing unit—the given name or first initial.

Filing Equipment Needs. Careful consideration should be given to the extent of equipment necessary to carry out a filing plan. A sufficient amount of the correct supplies will eliminate congestion. The following guides are helpful in setting up efficient, orderly, and money-saving files.

1. A vertical 26-inch letter drawer holds approximately four thousand five hundred papers plus the average number of guides and folders.

2. No more than 50 papers should be placed in one folder. More papers will expand the folder until the tab is buried, and will cause mistakes in filing and lost time in hunting for misplaced papers.

3. When there are more than 50 papers for a folder, they should be subdivided into additional folders. This sorting may be done chronologically.

4. Folders marked "Miscellaneous" should be used sparingly. Inspect them periodically to see if there are enough papers on any one subject or from any one account to warrant a separate folder. When there are as many as five papers in a single group (for instance, five letters from one correspondent), they should be put in a separately labeled folder.

If the above guidelines are observed, one drawer for correspondence will need 25 alphabetical guides with a miscellaneous folder for each and about 75 separate folders. Then if you have approximately eighteen thousand papers in your current files, you will want four drawers or one four-drawer cabinet. Assuming that you are filing letters of a general run, you will need a 100-division set of alphabetical guides with accompanying folders. However, if your papers are confined to a few correspondents, you will want more folders, some of them subdivided perhaps, and a smaller division of guides.

Planning the File System. *Office-Planned.* Many offices set up their own filing system to fit their special needs. If the person in charge of records management knows exactly what arrangement of guides and folders is best for the filing procedures of the company, an office-planned system functions satisfactorily. But such systems are often found to be unsatisfactory because they are oversimplified and quickly become obsolete. Usually the advice of a records management expert should be sought early so that the firm's needs may be studied and a satisfactory system worked out.

Commercial. Most large file-supply companies manufacture patented filing systems that are complete with the exception of captions or individual folders. These systems represent the most modern thinking about record-keeping and may be tailored to meet any specific need. Special features of these systems include (1) use of color as a double check against misfiling, (2) numerical captions combined with alphabetical captions for a filing double-check, and (3) use of special guides to highlight important names or subdivide major alphabetical sections. Listed below are the names of a few commercial systems.

Filing System	Manufacturing Company
Varidex System	Remington Rand
Triple-Check Automatic Index	Remington Rand
Amberg Nual Alphabet Index	Amberg File & Index Company
F. E. Bee Line Filing System	Filing Equipment Bureau
Safeguard Index	Globe-Wernicke
Super-Ideal System	Shaw-Walker
Tell-I-Vision System	Smead Manufacturing Company
Director Line Filing System	Wabash Filing Supplies, Inc.

Steps in the Filing Process.   When material reaches the filing area, it should be scanned first for a release mark and/or date. Many firms use a *FILE* stamp with a line for the initials of the person authorizing release and the date of authorization. If a paper reaches the files without the release mark, it is customary to return it to the person to whom it was assigned. Having a document properly released to the files assures that any needed action has been taken.

Indexing.   The paper should be read quickly for determination of the name, subject, or other caption under which it is to be filed. In compliance with the indexing system(s) used by the firm, the paper may be classified by (1) the name in the letterhead, (2) the name of the person or organization addressed, (3) the signature name, (4) the subject discussed, (5) the project title, (6) the geographical location about which the correspondence is concerned, or (7) the date on the document. It should be determined at this point whether any other subordinate or related subjects should be cross-referenced. Because too many cross-references are a waste of time and file space, they should be limited to those absolutely essential to finding the paper.

Coding.   The paper should now be coded. The pinpointing of the captions (name, subject, geographical location, date, and so forth) selected for filing is called coding. Several methods may be used to highlight the main and secondary captions.

1. The main caption under which the paper is to be filed can be underlined with a colored pencil.

2. If the main caption is not identical to the one in the correspondence, as often occurs in subject or numerical filing, it should be written in the upper right-hand corner. The words in the correspondence that lead to the selection of the caption should be underlined.

3. If the correspondence is to be cross-referenced, the cross-reference caption should be underlined and followed by an *X* in the margin. It is helpful

to write the cross-reference caption in the upper right corner under the main reference.

4. Make follow-up notations if future action is needed. A simple method of doing this is to prepare a chronological file. Special folders (which bear across the top edge a printed range of dates from 1 to 31) may be used. To pinpoint the date on which action must be taken, metal clips or other signals are slipped over the date. This folder is then placed in the follow-up (tickler) file behind the correct month guide. When the date arrives, the folder is sent to the person responsible for taking action. Upon the folder's return, the material in it is placed in the regular files.

Sorting. After coding, the captions are arranged in alphabetical order. At this time, a cross-reference sheet, usually of a distinctive color, is made up under the subordinate subject to show where the original correspondence is filed. Sometimes a card index is preferable as the cross-reference index.

If a numerical filing system is used, numerical coding follows alphabetical sorting. The card index containing all the classifications in alphabetical order is consulted for the file number. The number is written in the upper right corner, and the papers are then placed in numerical sequence.

Storing. The papers are now ready to be placed in the files. Before being taken to the file cabinets, papers should be stapled together, if necessary, and torn ones mended. File carefully and accurately. Make a double check to see that each paper is filed in the correct folder. Besides checking the folder tab, check the caption on the paper to be filed against the caption on the latest paper already in the folder.

Indexing. The basic rules for indexing have been rather firmly established by business firms over the years. Each part of the name is an indexing unit; thus *Carlin, John G.* consists of three units, of which *Carlin* is the first. Generally, in determining the sequence of two or more names, you compare the first unit of each name, and if they are identical, proceed to compare the second unit to determine the alphabetical order. Another rule of thumb is that "nothing precedes something." For example, *Carlin* precedes *Carlins* because the *n* in *Carlin* is not followed by another letter whereas the *n* in *Carlins* is. Difficulty occurs, however, when you must determine what are the first, second, and third units. The following rules will help you solve all indexing problems.

1. Transpose and alphabetize the names of individuals by last, first, middle. For example, "Kayton, Elmer T."

2. Compare the first unit in each name, letter by letter. The second units are considered only when the first units are identical.

3. A surname prefix is NOT a separate indexing unit but is considered part of the surname (*d', D', Da, de, De, Del, Des, Di, Du, Le, M', Mc, O', Van, Von,* and so on). The prefix *St.* is indexed as though spelled out—*Saint.* *M', Mac,* and *Mc* should be alphabetized in regular order as part of the

complete surname, in spite of the existence of a *Mc* divider in many alphabetical card sets.

4. Titles or degrees are NOT units and are disregarded in indexing. Terms that designate seniority, such as *Jr., Sr.,* and *II,* ARE indexing units.

5. Firm names containing complete individual names are transposed as in names of individuals.

Clarkson	William	Securities	Incorporated
Williams	R.	J.	Co.

6. Firm names are considered in the same sequence as written when they do not contain the complete name of an individual. (See Rule 14 about the indexing of foreign company names.)

Abbott	Orthopedic	Supply
Burt	Plumbing	Co.

7. Articles *a, an, the,* and conjunctions and prepositions, such as *and, &, for, in,* and *of,* are not units and are disregarded in indexing, regardless of where they appear in the firm name or the caption.

8. Hyphenated words in firm names are indexed as *separate* units. Hyphenated surnames of individuals are considered as *one* indexing unit.

9. Abbreviations are indexed as though the represented words were spelled out in full. Single letters other than abbreviations are considered as separate indexing units.

AMB Carpet Co.	A	M	B	Carpet
Abbott Labs	Abbott	Laboratories		
Gen. Elec. Co.	General	Electric	Company	
Internat'l Trucking Inc.	International	Trucking	Incorporated	
St. George Hotel	Saint	George	Hotel	
Thomas Bros. Mfg. Co.	Thomas	Brothers	Manufacturing	Company
UP	United	Parcel		

10. Firm endings, such as *Bros., Co., Corp., Inc., Ltd., Mfg.,* and *Son,* are indexing units.

11. Names that may be written either as one or two words are indexed as one unit.

Inter State Bus Co.	Inter State	Bus	Company
Interstate Funding Co.	Interstate	Funding	Company

12. The parts of compound geographical names are separate units, except when the first part of the name is not an English word, such as *Los* in Los Angeles.

Des Moines	Tire	Company	
New	Jersey	Chemical	Company

13. Possessives. When a word ends with apostrophe *s*, the *s* is disregarded in indexing. When a word ends in *s* apostrophe, however, the *s* that is part

of the original word *is* considered. In other words, consider everything up to the apostrophe.

Nelson's	Management	Services
Nelson	Thomas	B.
Nelsons' (The)	Decorating	Shop

14. Names of foreign companies should be indexed exactly as written even though the words may be articles, conjunctions, or prepositions; foreign words for *company* or type of business; or names that are not distinguishable as either surnames or given names.

Banco	de	Acapulco (Mexico)	
Compania	Molinera	de	Alamos (Brazil)
Les	Parfums	Importers	

If the firm is engaged extensively in foreign trade, it may be more efficient to set up a geographical file by country, separate the folders by the type of business, and then alphabetize the companies by the name in the title most familiar to those working on the account.

15. Names pertaining to the Federal Government are indexed under "United States Government" and subdivided, first by department title, followed by bureau, division, commission, or board. For example, "Social Security Administration" would be

United States Government Social Security Administration

The U.S. Department of Commerce, Bureau of The Census, would be

United States Government Commerce Census
                                                (Dept. of)   (Bureau of)

16. Other political divisions are indexed under the name of the chief governing body, followed by its classification, such as *state, county,* or *city,* and then subdivided by the title of the department, bureau, division, commission, or board.

Board of Education, Atlanta Georgia:
Atlanta City Education
           (Board of)

Bureau of Weights and Measures, State of Wisconsin:
Wisconsin State Weights Measures
                   and   (Bureau of)

Water and Power Department, Austin, Texas:
Austin City Water Power
               and   (Department of)

17. A number in a name is considered as though it were written in words and is indexed as *one* unit. Numbers over 1,000, such as 1,435, should be indexed as *fourteen hundred thirty-five* and not as *one thousand four hundred thirty-five.*

18. When the same name appears with different addresses, it should be alphabetized according to city or town. The state is considered only when

there is a duplication of both individual or company name and city name. If the same correspondent is located at different addresses within the same city, then the correspondence should be alphabetized by streets. If the same correspondent is located at several addresses on the same street, the alphabetizing should be from the lowest to the highest street number.

Firestone	Stores	Newark	Delaware	
Firestone	Stores	Newark	Ohio	
Firestone	Stores	Providence	Main, 20	Street
			(20 Main St.)	
Firestone	Stores	Providence	Main, 520	Street
			(520 Main St.)	
Firestone	Stores	Providence	Maple	Avenue
Firestone	Stores	Tulsa		

19. Banks, churches, societies, associations, clubs, and so on, are indexed under the full name as written. If there are several branches, subalphabetize by the names of cities.

American Business Communication Association
American National Red Cross
    Albany Chapter, American National Red Cross
    Mobile Chapter, American National Red Cross
    New Orleans Chapter, American National Red Cross
    Pittsburgh Chapter, American National Red Cross
Bank of America
    Dallas, Bank of America
    Oakland, Bank of America
    Salinas, Bank of America
    Salt Lake City, Bank of America
    Tucson, Bank of America
English-Speaking Union
Society of Automotive Engineers, Inc.
United Presbyterian Church, USA
    Topeka, United Presbyterian Church
    Seattle, University Presbyterian Church
    Washington, D.C., Fourth Presbyterian Church
United Way
University Club (The)
    Chicago, University Club (The)
    St. Louis, University Club (The)

20. Universities, schools, and colleges are filed under the principal part of the name. A cross-index file may be kept under the full name, if needed.

California, University of (Berkeley)
John Marshall High School (Los Angeles)
New York University (New York City)
Notre Dame, University of (South Bend, Indiana)
Pennsylvania State University (University Park)
Stanford University (California)
Virginia, University of (Roanoke)
William and Mary, College of (Williamsburg, Virginia)

21. Married Women. The legal name of a married woman is the one used for indexing. Legally, the surname is the only part of a husband's name that

a woman assumes upon marriage. A married woman's legal name could be either (a) her own first and middle names together with her husband's surname, or (b) her first name and maiden surname together with her husband's surname. The name should be written on filing cards or folders as shown below:

Pollock, Lorna Jane (Mrs.)
(James G.)

McCarroll, Mary Parker (Mrs.)
(Neil C.)

Charge-Out and Control of Records. In order that file-section personnel have information at all times about the location of files, a record of all material loaned or removed should be maintained. Substitution cards with *Out* tabs at the top take the place of the folder or document in the file drawer. The card should contain the description of the document or the file caption or code, the date of removal, and the name and extension number of the borrower.

It is the responsibility of the file section to make periodic checks of charged-out records and, if they have been retained for more than 15 days, to contact the user and request the return of them. In some instances the user to whom records have been charged may need to send them to another person or department for action. Notification of the rerouting of records should be given the file section so that the *Out* card may be updated.

A valuable control, established by a majority of companies, is to dissuade everyone from removing papers or folders from the file cabinets or from placing any material in them, except for members of the file section.

Centralized Versus Decentralized Files. Records are usually located in (1) centralized files in which records for the entire organization are merged together and kept in a central location; (2) departmental files that are kept in the offices of the separate departments and contain only the records of those departments, such as corporate offices, sales, or advertising; and (3) a combination of centralized and departmental files.

Departmental files. Records should be located in the files of the various departments when:

1. They are confidential and should be available only to the department needing them.

2. Copies of the same records are filed differently according to how the using department calls for them.

3. Space for an adequate, well-staffed and well-equipped, centrally located file room is not available.

4. Fast, immediate reference to records is necessary.

5. It is more economical to locate records nearest the point of most frequent use.

Centralized file system. A centralized file system should be used when:

1. Records need to be well protected and controlled.

2. Records are used by more than one department and need to be easily accessible.

3. Duplication of records, space, equipment, and supplies must be eliminated in order to lower overhead.

4. Filing can be handled by full-time professional file clerks who can apply the latest filing techniques on a production basis.

5. Procedures can be standardized, making it easier to file, find, request, deliver, and return records to the files.

Combination of Decentralized and Centralized Files. Many large companies maintain a centralized file system for the protection of vital records. At the same time certain departments are permitted to maintain their own files under the supervision of the central file department or a records manager. Under this system departmental files are checked periodically to avoid costly duplication or proliferation of records.

Importance of a Retention Schedule. The needless filing of every piece of paper received by a company or generated within its doors should be scrupulously avoided. A records manager or another executive should determine the relative value of company records and establish a retention schedule which complies with State and Federal laws. The rules and regulations of the Federal Communications Commission regarding the preservation of the records of communication common carriers might be used as a guideline (Figure 12-3). Copies of FCC's *Rules and Regulations, Part 42, Preservation of Records of Communication Common Carriers* may be found in the government periodicals section of most libraries or may be secured from the Superintendent of Documents, who also has other excellent bulletins on records retention.

Vital records that are essential to the existence of the organization are kept permanently in a safe place because they are irreplaceable. Such documents as legal papers of incorporation, titles to ownership, deeds, major contracts, property plans, reports to stockholders, and insurance policies are considered vital records. Other important documents that should be kept permanently are

Accounting Records, such as ledgers, balance sheets, trial balances, and accountants' and auditors' reports.
Drafts, checks, and receipts for cash payments, plus the correspondence relating thereto.
Inventory records of plant facilities.
Invoices and related records.
Mortgages.
Payroll records.
Stock certificate records.
Tax records.
Vouchers.

Item No.	Description of records	Period to be retained
1	*Corporate and General* Corporate organization:	
	a. Charter or certificate of incorporation and amendments thereto	Permanently.
	b. Legal documents in connection with mergers, consolidations, reorganizations, receiverships, and similar actions which affect the identity or organization of the company.....	Do.
	c. By-laws	Do.
2	Corporate elections and stockholders' votes:	
	a. Notices of meetings, proxy statements, and proxy solicitation material	10 years.
	b. Voting lists	3 years.
	c. Proxies	Do.
	d. Ballots and tabulations of votes	Do.
	e. Judges' or inspectors' reports of results	Do.
3	Minutes of meetings:	
	a. Meetings of stockholders and directors	Permanently
	b. Meetings of executive committee and other directors' committees......................	Do.
	c Meetings of employees' benefit committee	Do.
4	Securities issued or assumed:	
	a. Applications to governmental bodies and authorizations therefrom to issue securities or assume debt issued by others.	Do.
	b. Registration statements and amend thereto ...	Do.
	c. Bids and contracts for sale of securities, including underwriting agreements, except as provided in item 4-1-(4).	Do.
	d. Agreements with trustees of security issues	Do.

Figure 12-3 Extract from FCC's 1961 *Preservation of Records of Communication Common Carriers, Rules and Regulations,* Part 42.

The following records may be kept for shorter periods of time.

Seven to Ten Years
Accounts receivable ledgers.
Contracts and agreements for other than purchase or sale of materials.
Deposit books and records of checks.
Documents substantiating claims.
Insurance records.
Inventories of merchandise, materials, and supplies.
Lists of proxies and voting stockholders.
Sales records.

Two to Three Years
Assignments, attachments, and garnishments.
Contracts for purchase or sale of materials.
Employees' fidelity bonds records.
Purchase orders.
Reconciliation papers.

Transfer and Disposal of Records. The systematic transfer of records that have future worth or value includes transfer from active to inactive files, and from inactive files to the storage area. At each move in the transfer process, the retention schedule should be checked and obsolete or useless records destroyed. Many times entire files are transferred to inactive status at some predetermined time, such as the beginning of the calendar year, the fiscal year, or the busy season. The material remains in the original folders and is moved intact to an adjacent file cabinet or to the bottom drawers of the cabinet. New folders are prepared for the new active files before transfer is made. *Periodic transfer,* as this method is called, operates most effectively if the inactive files are close to the new files for convenient reference. Transfer of these recent files to another floor or building would result in wasted time because of the frequent need to check past records at the beginning of the new period.

The *perpetual transfer* method places time limits on individual papers by appropriate marks on the folders. The files may be checked at intervals of two or three months or perpetually at irregular intervals for materials that should be placed in the inactive files, sent to storage, or destroyed. In situations where a transaction, such as a job or a case, is completed, all records generated by the transaction are transferred immediately.

Material in the inactive files is removed periodically and sorted by classification as either *important* or *vital. Important* material may be handled in three ways: (1) records placed in storage and eventually destroyed; (2) records microfilmed and then destroyed, films placed in storage and ultimately destroyed; (3) records destroyed, having outlived their span of importance. If the material is classified as *vital,* it is a permanent record and may either be placed in storage or be microfilmed, the record itself destroyed, and the film kept permanently. The destruction date of material should be placed on it at the time of transfer to storage. A separate card file should indicate the contents of transfer files and the destruction dates of papers.

Microform. The various methods of print-to-film transference are known by the generic term *microform.* Included in the group are microfilm, opaque microcard, and transparent microcard known as microfiche.

Microfilm. Through microfilming, documents may be photographed at reduced sizes with the developed film serving as the record. Companies using this method of storing documents find that it saves approximately 98 percent of storage space. One to two file cabinets of film hold the equivalent of hundreds of drawers of original records. The chances of losing a document are minimized because documents are photographed in sequence on a roll of film. The retained materials do not wear out, remain clean, and are easily handled. Because microfilm is of a noncombustible type, the hazard of fire is reduced. In addition to placing images on a roll of film, another microfilm process mounts a single frame on a punched card that carries the identification of the record. Even large engineering drawings, blueprints, specifications, and photographs may be reduced on film and, through a punched card system, quickly found and consulted.

A reading machine or viewer is used when there is need to consult a document. The document is magnified to readable size, or may even be enlarged further for projection on a screen. Some readers will make a full-sized photocopy of the filmed record. One machine, the FileSearch, automatically scans 6,400 microfilmed pages a minute in the search for a particular document.

A complete unit of microfilm equipment may be purchased or leased on an operational basis. The process of filming documents is relatively simple. The most difficult types of records to photograph, however, are green tissue carbon copies, faint hectograph and mimeograph material, negative photostats, deep shades of colored papers, and blurred carbon copies on white paper. Exposed film should be checked to see that every image is clearly legible; and, if not, the document should be rephotographed. Outside concerns that specialize in microfilm work will photograph a company's records either on its premises or at the company's plant. Usually the cost for this service, including film and developing, varies for each 1,000 pieces. A cost analysis should be made before a decision is made to purchase or lease equipment.

Microcard and Microfiche. *Microcard* is a flat sheet or film "card" that contains, on the average, sixty book pages. The cards can be opaque or transparent, the latter being known as *microfiche*. The advantage of this process is that the reader-printer that enlarges the card will also supply, at the press of a button, a copy of the page being read. (Figure 12-4.)

Microfiche reduces the original document from one fifth to one twentieth of its original size, enabling the equivalent of 10,000 pages to be stored in less than two inches of drawer space. It is especially valuable when one is filing and retrieving information in such documents as technical reports, scientific and research data, industrial catalogs, or maintenance manuals. Most standard systems of classification and indexing can be applied to microfiche. The standard fiche established by COSATI, the President's Committee on Scientific and Technical Information, measures approximately $4'' \times 6''$ (105 mm $\times$ 148 mm) and contains up to sixty $8\frac{1}{2}'' \times 11''$ pages (30 frames) filmed at $18 \times -20 \times$ reduction. An eye-legible heading on the fiche contains the classification or identifying number, the document title, its source, its author, and other basic information. For documents more than 60 pages in length, "trailer" fiche are used. These have an abbreviated heading and a maximum capacity of 72 pages. The exact method of filing is largely determined by the type of information, the frequency of updating, the frequency of reference, and related factors.

Companies engaged in providing tailor-made microfiche systems to businesses or in handling all production from master negative to hard copy at their own production sites are

National Cash Register
Bell & Howell
3M (Minneapolis)
Leasco Data Processing

Legality of Microform Documents.   Microform may cause some legal problems. Courts prefer original records. If these have been destroyed, the company must establish that the destruction was in the natural course of business. To be free from suspicion, the film of controversial records should be verified as to their authenticity by the insertion of a target on the film bearing the signature of an officer of the company. The Bureau of Internal Revenue advises against microfilming general books of account, such as cash books, journals, voucher registers, and ledgers. Taxpayers may, however, use microfilm reproductions for supporting records of details, such as payroll records, canceled checks, invoices, and vouchers, provided the following conditions are met: (1) microfilmed copies are retained as long as the contents may be needed as evidence in the administration of any internal revenue law; (2) appropriate

Figure 12-4   A typical microfiche system in operation. (Reproduced with permission from "Microfiche Fact File" published by the Industrial Products Division of the National Cash Register Company, Dayton, Ohio.)

facilities are provided for the safekeeping of the films and are open for inspection and review on a company machine at all times; and (3) transcriptions will be made from the microfilm when required.

12.2   DUPLICATING AND COPYING

Business papers are produced in quantity; rarely is a single copy adequate. The major need of a company is to produce as economically as possible the desired number of clear copies. Consequently, a knowledge of available processes will ensure selection of the right type of duplicating and copying equipment to meet reproduction needs. The following material includes information on the most popular and most modern reproduction equipment in use in today's business offices.

The Reproduction Department	p. 431
Duplicating Processes	p. 436
Copying Processes	p. 437
Auxiliary Equipment for Duplicating Work	p. 441

The Reproduction Department.   Most large firms establish a photographic and reproduction department in order to obtain more efficient use of special equipment and to capitalize on the skills of trained personnel. Some duplicating methods, however, can easily be handled by semiskilled operators. The most common of these methods are carbon paper, automatic typewriters, spirit and stencil duplicators, and copying machines such as Thermofax and Xerox.

The selection of a reproduction process should be based on cost, appearance, and reproduction time. (For a comparison of processes, see Figure 12-5.) *Cost* is determined by the number of copies needed and the process used. The *appearance* desired must be determined by ultimate use. *Reproduction time* may overrule other considerations because some processes are faster than others. If possible use the least expensive process that reconciles cost, appearance, and speed.

When a company has a graphic production department, requests for reproduction are made on a work order similar to the one in Figure 12-6. Fill in this form accurately and completely to get the quantity and quality of reproduction desired. Even page sequence should be stated on the work order. The originator, for instance, should specify whether page 1 is to be *backed up* with page 2, and so on, and whether the *backer* is to be *head-to-head* (the heading of the back copy directly opposite the heading of the front copy, so that the pages can be turned right to left) or *tumblehead* (the heading of the back copy at the bottom of the front copy, so that the pages can be turned bottom to top). Choice of *head-to-head* or *tumblehead* depends on whether copies will be bound on the left or along the top. If the job is complicated, it is advisable to prepare a dummy or mock-up.

PROCESS	Approximate Single-Copy Cost	Maximum Size (inches)	Economical Run	Remarks
Ditto. Black, purple, red, or green line on white or colored paper or on card stock. Fair appearance. Makes 50 to 60 copies a minute.	$.007–8½ x 11 $.012–11 x 17 $.03–Ditto master	11 x 17	10 to 150	Cheapest method up to 300 copies. Copies are of solid color becoming progressively fainter. Master may be reused once. Good for one-sided copy only. Not recommended when copy permanency is essential. Black ditto should not be used if runs of more than 100 copies are needed.
Mimeograph. Good copy appearance on white or colored 20# mimeograph paper or on card stock.	$.009	8½ x 13	50 to 5000	Typewritten or hand-drawn stencils produce a neat, sharp, legible copy. Both sides of paper may be used, if slipsheeted. Several colors of ink are available. Stencil may be rerun if properly stored.
Thermofax. Makes four copies a minute on lightweight paper. Several colors of paper are available.	$.05–8½ x 11 $.29–8½ x 11 transparency	11 x 17	Up to 10	Cannot enlarge or reduce. Extremely difficult to make additional copies from a Thermofax print. Will copy either opaque or translucent copy. Will not reproduce aniline dye inks, such as Ditto and ball point pen. Not recommended for filing.
Copytron. Black line on white background. Same size as original.	$.05–8½ x 11 $.10–11 x 17	11 by any length	15 copies	Reproduces any translucent or opaque copy.

Figure 12-5 Comparative features of reproduction processes.

Method	Cost	Size	Number of copies	Remarks
Xerography. Copies reproduced in 3 minutes; takes longer if cleanup needed after use of color. Produces finished copies from a paper plate in several colors or with an overlay of print, if desired.	Fraction of a cent to 5¢ a copy depending on type of material.	11 x 17	Subject to method used for subsequent reproduction. Usually 15-500.	Can make masters for offset printing or vellum copies for Diazo reproduction. Can enlarge and reduce. Reproduces opaque copy and/or originals printed on both sides. Quicker and less expensive than photo-offset printing. No negative needed. Both sides of paper may be used.
Xerox. Black line on white or colored stock. Same size as original. Books may be copied without being disassembled. Rapid process up to 40 copies a minute.	$.02 to $.10 Price based on sliding scale: $.86—100 $3.40—500	9 x 14		Will reproduce almost any original. Not good for half-tones. Reproduces from opaque and two-sided originals onto bond paper, cardstock, vellum, and a transparency.
Copyflo Xerox. Black line on white background. Reduction to 50 per cent from 22" maximum width. Produces 15 to 20 copies a minute.	$.09—8½ x 11 $.17—multilith plate	11 by any length		Will reproduce almost any original. Not good for half-tones. Least expensive way to make multilith plates and to reproduce opaque and two-sided originals. Quality not as good as flat Xerox equipment.
Blueline. Duplicates transparent or translucent material onto sensitized paper which produces a blue-on-white copy. Same size as original. A roll may be run at 12 feet a minute, and an 8½ x 11" sheet is produced in one minute.	$.03 sq. ft. —roll $.01—8½ x 11	36 by any length	Up to 15	Recommended for duplicates of drawings or layouts prepared on vellum. A fast, inexpensive method of reproducing large prints needing wide distribution.

Figure 12-5 (continued).

Process / Description	Cost	Size	Copies	Remarks
Ozalid or Diazo. Letter-size equipment produces 200 copies an hour. Other equipment takes copy up to 42″ wide, at speeds averaging 20 to 30 feet a minute. Makes a positive print from positive copy.	$.017 sq. ft. ½¢–8½ x 11	8½ to 42 in width by any length	1 to 25 originals, 25 copies each; 25 to 50 originals, 15 copies each; 50 to 100 originals, 10 copies each.	Masters can be prepared by pencil, ink, typing, printing, Xerography, etc., on translucent paper, cloth, or film. All prints are of equal clarity. Masters are good indefinitely. Fast, inexpensive method of reproducing large prints for small distribution. Economical method of reproducing half-tone prints where photo quality is not needed.
Multilith (Offset Printing). Black or colored ink on white or colored paper or on cardstock. Same size as image on offset plate, usually a paper per master.	$.82—20 copies $1.74—200 $3.27—500 $5.82—1000	Paper size 11 x 17 Printing area 10½ x 17	500 with paper masters	Used to produce forms, manuals, etc., when large volume is required. Makes better copies than other methods of reproduction. Since plates can be re-run, excellent process for repetitive work.
Photo Offset. Excellent appearance. Printing may be made in several colors on various grades and weights of white or colored paper, or on cardstock. Uses a metal master.	$.02—100 copies Fraction of a cent in longer runs.	3 x 5 to 17 x 22	50 to unlimited	Not recommended for one-time printing or short runs, except where excellent quality or exactness of reproduction is absolutely necessary.
Photostat. Black line on white background in positive. White line on black background in negative. May be reproduced in half scale or double size of copy.	$.20—18 x 24 negative $.40—18 x 24 positive	18 x 24 Sections can be spliced to make larger sizes.	Up to 5	Either negative or positive is an exact copy. Reasonable cost where few copies are needed. Recommended for legal documents. Advantage in being able to reproduce pages of bound books and magazines.

Note: Labor and equipment costs vary considerably and are not included in this table.

Figure 12-5 (continued).

SPECIAL INSTRUCTIONS		RUSH ☐	TITLE OF DOCUMENT # PAGES		NO.

PROCESS	QUANTITY	PRICE	PROCESS	QUANTITY	PRICE	INSTRUCTIONS BY: _____
Ditto			Set-up			# Copies _____
						Collate ☐ Dept. _____ Ext. _____
Stencil			Typeset			Staple ☐
						Punch ☐
Multilith			Photo print			Bind ☐ Date Submitted _____
Xerox			Vellum			Pad - 25 ☐
						50 ☐
Offset						100 ☐
			Collate			Cut ☐ Date Due _____
			Staple			Fold ☐ Distribution List: _____
			Punch			Covers ☐
			Bind			Color Paper: ☐
			Padding			Color Ink: _____
Covers			Cutting			Submitted Size _____
			Folding			X _____
						Finish Size _____
						X _____ # Copies to Author _____
						Rec. Order: _____
						DUPLICATING SECTION
Sub Total			Sub Total			Name _____ Date _____
						Dept. Costs $ _____
						Distribution Costs $ _____
						Date Distributed _____

Figure 12-6 Reproduction work order.

435

Duplicating Processes. *Carbon Paper.* When two to eight copies of a rough or final draft are needed, one typing with an original and carbon copies is the most economical process. Carbon paper is available in sheets (for insertion) and in rolls (for continuous feeding of forms). One-time carbon paper is used in snap-out forms and with second-sheet sets. Approximately 20 readable copies can be made on an electric typewriter with electric carbon paper. Eight to ten copies is the maximum that can be produced on a manual typewriter with the correct intensity of carbon, weight of paper, hardness of platen, and the right touch control on the machine.

Automatic Typewriters. Automatic typewriters rapidly reproduce stored information without error. A single operator can handle a bank of ten or more machines as she manually types the date, inside address, salutation, and any personalized fill-ins in the body of the message. These machines may be programmed to type certain portions of the message, stop, and continue when signaled to do so by the operator. Through the use of magnetic tape, stored information is located and combined automatically with material stored on a second tape to provide new combinations of typewritten material. Whenever changes are made in the copy or margins are reset, the machine respaces sentences, adjusts line lengths, even drops hyphens, and automatically checks itself to ensure accuracy of retyping. Any number of form letters and envelopes may be reproduced, depending on the number of machines and operators available.

Spirit Process. Ditto is the name commonly associated with the spirit process, but the terms *liquid* and *hectograph* are also used. Ditto is a quick, low-cost process and should be used when 10 to 150 copies are needed. It is possible to make up to 500 copies with a fresh, new Ditto master, freshly cleaned typewriter keys, and a plastic backing sheet, which provides a hard, even surface that sharpens the typewritten copy. With skilled operation to control the flow of the alcohol-base liquid that moistens the copy paper, a spirit duplicator can produce up to 500 copies. Ditto masters are reusable. The carbon backing, from which the impression is transferred to the master, comes in purple, blue, red, green, and black. Various sizes of masters and carbons, as well as single sheets or sets, are available. Lines and letters may be ruled on a Ditto master with a 6, 7, or 8H pencil or a stylus, provided the master is placed over a hard surface. Certain office forms are available on preprinted masters to which you may add your own data. Many stationers and specialized companies, such as Moore Business Forms, Inc., maintain a supply of these forms and will work with a company to develop new ones that meet individual needs.

Stencil Duplicating. The mimeograph process uses a stencil master on which the image may be cut by typewriter, stylus, or special machines. Lettering, handwriting, and art work can be imprinted on the stencil. Special pens, punches, and shaders are available for ruling, shading, drawing, and lettering. Tint plates and a shader are used to apply textures and patterns to drawings that have been made with the wheel or stylus pen. Preimprinted stencils of your letterhead or routine forms and art work may be obtained from stationers or manufacturers' outlets. Stencil duplicating is an inexpensive process when you are preparing more than 200 and up to 5,000 copies. Stencils may be filed, then altered or added to, and rerun. The copy may be produced in a wide color range that includes red, green, blue, brown, purple, yellow, and black.

A drawing and tracing desk is an important companion piece to the duplicator. The stencil is placed over a translucent, movable glass drawing surface, illuminated from beneath. A detachable lightweight T-square can be used either horizontally or vertically while the stencil is held firmly. A suspended stencil filing system is available to store, protect, and index up to 240 stencils in one unit. An electronic stencil cutter is a valuable addition to stencil duplicating. Such a machine automatically produces perfect stencils direct from line or wash drawings, heavy solids, half-tones or full-tone photographs. It cuts high definition stencils even when the original is in pastel colors or has very faint lines.

Copying Processes.   There are a variety of copying machines on the market today from the small table models to the large floor consoles. Some process single sheets only, whereas others are able to duplicate pages from bound books and periodicals. Some produce copy on thin white or beige paper, and others turn out copies on a heavier weight of white paper, which itself may be used to make additional copies. Usually the larger models may be leased from the supplier, who also provides maintenance service. The office manager must control the use of these machines. Most companies find that once a copying machine is installed, employees tend to copy material indiscriminately and to make too many copies without regard to the cost involved.

Thermofax and *Readyprint,* desk-model office copiers, use an exposure-by-heat process to reproduce single pages up to $8\frac{1}{2}'' \times 14''$. They are economical to use if five or less copies are needed. Copies are printed on opaque tissue or thin paper, usually light beige in color. Thermofax requires a strong carbon definition on the material to be copied, such as a clear, black typewritten or pencil copy. It is not capable of copying originals that have been written with a red or blue pencil or pen nor of copying Multilith masters or one of its own copies. The Readyprint produces exact copies of letters and other papers, including the letterhead and signature.

Copytron prints copies from any opaque or translucent master (bond, carbon copy, Ditto copy, and so on). The machine uses a dry, electrostatic process that places a charge on special Copytron paper as it enters the machine. The photosensitive image is then projected into a mirror, which, in turn, is reflected on sensitized paper. A developer is applied to the sheet to produce an image of the master, and finally the image is fused to the paper by heat. The finished print is highly legible and permanent. Use of Copytron is recommended when a few quick copies of important or complicated printed material are needed. The paper stock comes in several sizes $8\frac{1}{2}'' \times 11''$, $8\frac{1}{2}'' \times 14''$, and $11'' \times 17''$.

Xerography is a method of electrostatically reproducing an image directly on ordinary letter paper without the need for an intermediate master. Xerox office copying machines, which employ the xerographic process, can be operated by anyone in the office. The 720 and 914 reproduce written, printed, or typed originals up to $9'' \times 14''$ maximum size. The 2400, 3600, 813, and 660 reproduce originals up to $8\frac{1}{2}'' \times 14''$. All colors are copied with black-on-white fidelity; however, the larger solid black or colored areas fade to a light gray toward the center. Ditto or Thermofax originals do not reproduce satisfactorily. Photographs are copied with usable legibility. Either single sheets or pages from bound publications may be copied in their original size.

To operate the Xerox, you simply place the original document on the scanning glass, dial the number of copies desired, and push the button. The machine operates by itself, rapidly printing copies automatically, and turns itself off when the desired quantity is reached. The Xerox 2400 makes 40 copies a minute. The cost of reproduction by xerography is relatively high, especially for large quantities. Paper Multilith masters can be made on the Xerox, but the quality of printed material from the Xerox-produced masters is not generally equal to that produced by copy camera photography with subsequent printing from a metal master. Legibility is good to excellent.

Through adjustment of the Xerox camera, copy can be enlarged or reduced. The Xerox 7000 Reduction Duplicator, for instance, will reduce a $14'' \times 18''$ original to $8\frac{1}{2}'' \times 11''$, $8\frac{1}{2}'' \times 13''$, or $8\frac{1}{2}'' \times 14''$ size.

Copyflo Xerox is used to make full-scale copies of any original up to 11 inches wide by any length. Half-scale reproductions can be made of originals up to 22 inches wide by any length. The material to be copied must first be microfilmed, preferably on 35 mm film. Copies are made on bond paper, card stock, vellum, or any such material that comes on a roll. Multilith plates of adequate quality for internal use can also be made on this equipment at a cost saving over plates produced on flat Xerography equipment.

The *Blueline* process duplicates transparent or translucent material by exposing it onto sensitized paper. The sensitized paper then goes through an ammonia developing process that produces a blue-on-white copy. Blueline is recommended when you need duplicates of drawings or layouts prepared on vellum, or up to 15 copies of any transparent or translucent material. The master is typed or drawn on transparent or translucent paper (vellum, smooth onionskin, and so on) and backed with orange carbon or typewriter carbon for an especially dark, legible copy. The only corrections on the master that prove satisfactory are extremely neat erasures. Paper stock comes in several sizes: $8\frac{1}{2}'' \times 11''$, $11'' \times 14''$, $11'' \times 17''$, $17'' \times 22''$, and $22'' \times 34''$. The paper stock also comes in rolls $18''$ and $36''$ wide $\times 500'$ long. The maximum size of the original is $36''$ wide by any length. Yellow or blue writing will not reproduce, and cockled onionskin produces a fuzzy image because of irregularity of the paper surface.

Ozalid is a method of exact reproduction from an original of highly translucent or transparent material up to 42 inches wide and any length. This process, more expensive than Ditto, should be used only when the original is on translucent paper, and one or more of the following conditions prevail.

> Cost of retyping or copying to another form such as Direct Image Multilith master is excessive.
> Time is limited and copy of existing record or document must be obtained immediately.
> Handwritten notations or drawings must be reproduced exactly.
> Number of copies required is less than 25.
> Size of original exceeds maximum width and length of paper used on other processes.

The quality of reproduction is fairly good; however, the paper on which the final copy appears is sometimes slightly gray rather than pure white. Reproduction time on the machine is much longer than that of the Multilith process. Letter-size equipment produces copies at a rate of 200 copies per hour, whereas larger equipment produces copies up to 42 inches wide at a rate of 20 to 30 feet per minute. The preparation of the master consists of typing or drawing on highly translucent paper, such as vellum, which is backed with a piece of orange carbon paper for sharper copies. Overhead projection transparencies of $8'' \times 10''$ inches may be prepared by the Ozalid process. Masters may be rerun indefinitely with no decrease in quality of the copies and will last indefinitely providing they do not become damaged.

The *Direct Image Multilith* process, a simplified method of offset printing, may be used for production runs from 10 copies to as many as 5,000. Direct image plates can be procured in varying qualities, depending on the volume of the desired run—short-, medium-, or long-run plates. In this process typing, drawing, writing, or printing is placed directly onto the Multilith paper master, which reproduces the copies in the Multilith duplicating machine. The quality is less than, but nearly equal to, that of photo-offset reproduction. There is practically no decrease of image sharpness or density up to the recommended limit. Legibility is good to excellent if the master is carefully prepared. The following suggestions will assist you in preparing a good master.

1. Use an electric typewriter with any type face except a fine one that will not photograph well.

2. Use a ribbon suitable for Multilith duplication and a plastic backing sheet.

3. Locate the image properly on the master. Position the master in the machine so that the typewritten message will be in the same position as you would like to have it on the finished copies.

4. Select a paper master that is clean and in good condition without being cracked or dried because of long or improper storage. Handle the master on the edges to avoid the reproduction of smudges.

5. Make corrections carefully with a special Multilith eraser while the master is in the typewriter.

6. Use a Multilith reproducing pencil or pen for signatures, underscores, drawings, and sketches.

7. Allow an aging period of at least one-half hour for the image to set between typing and running.

Photographic Processes. The *photo-offset* process should be used when more than 500 high-quality copies are required. This process is basically the same as direct-image offset except that in the photo-offset method all typing, drawing, writing, or printing is on a piece of hard, smooth white paper that is then photographed. Ditto master paper produces excellent copy. Photo-offset allows enlargement or reduction in the finished copy. Paper or metal masters are then prepared for use on the Multilith duplicating machine. The quality is less than, but nearly equal to, that of typeset printing. It is superior to the direct-image process. There is no decrease in image sharpness or density, and practically no limit to the number of copies a Multilith metal master can reproduce. Reproduction time is short; copies may be reproduced at the rate of 4,500 to 6,000 an hour. In preparing the master it is important to make corrections carefully with Snopake correction fluid or with correction tape because a poor correction will show on the reproduction. A carbon typewriter ribbon should be used; or if a fabric ribbon is used, it should be new and bright. The maximum size of the original master may be $17'' \times 22''$ with the maximum finished size $11'' \times 17''$. Usually the original can be enlarged up to 10 percent or reduced by 50 percent.

Photostats are exact photographic reproductions of the original document. They may be the same size as the original, smaller, or larger. Either a negative photostat (white on black background) or a positive photostat (black on white background) may be obtained. This method is used only when an exact copy of an original document is needed; for example, for legal or tax purposes. If more than one copy is required, the first copy will be a photostat negative and the other copies will be made up as positives. Photostat negatives should be saved for reuse, if additional copies might be required, as this is a relatively expensive process. Use for up to five copies is considered economical. If more than five are necessary, another type of reproduction should be considered.

Microfilm is a process by which documents may be photographed in reduced size on 16 mm or 35 mm film. Usually the use of microfilm is confined to corporate records of such importance that destruction would prove a hardship on the company. However, the use of microfilming to conserve filing space is increasing rapidly, as explained in the records management section of this chapter.

Auxiliary Equipment for Duplicating Work. An *electric paper drill* can drill slits or holes either one-quarter inch or three-eighths inch in diameter. It usually accommodates any size paper and up to 500 sheets at one time.

An *electric collator* accommodates paper up to $8\frac{1}{2}'' \times 14''$. Approximately 20 pages can be collated at one time.

An *electric stapler* will staple up to 32 pages at one time.

A *paper cutter* may be purchased that accommodates paper up to 19 inches and can cut 500 sheets at one time.

A *padding machine* provides for the application of padding compound, which is an adhesive substance similar to that on scratch pads. It can accommodate up to $8\frac{1}{2}'' \times 11''$ paper.

A *binding machine* is useful, such as the kind that makes tubular plastic bindings one-quarter inch to one inch in diameter for $8\frac{1}{2}'' \times 11''$ paper.

An *electric folding machine* can fold a packet containing up to three or more pages. Paper $8\frac{1}{2}'' \times 14''$ can usually be accommodated and the following folds made: (1) single, (2) parallel, (3) double parallel, (4) accordion, (5) french (6) horizontal, and (7) double vertical.

Addressing machines make it possible to address envelopes rapidly for an active mailing list that is used periodically. The least expensive process appears to be the machine that uses stencil address plates. These stencil plates can be prepared by the typewriter on special fiber stencil masters designed for the addressing machine. The Addressograph machine uses metal plates prepared on a Graphotype, which embosses the names, addresses, dates, and any other needed information on the plates. These can also be notched or tabbed so that the Addressograph will select or reject plates automatically according to a predetermined pattern.

The *Vari-Typer,* with the usual typewriter keyboard plus six additional characters, prepares copy for reproduction by the offset process. The type is removable thus making it possible to use different sets of keys in various type styles and sizes on the same page. Type sizes vary from the small 6-point type to 16-point type; approximately 400 styles are available. The Vari-Typer makes it possible to vary spacing between lines and letters. The right-hand margin of copy can be justified or made even. Statistical material may be condensed into a small space by the use of very small type. All strokes of the keys are uniform, which guarantees sharp master copies resembling printing. The machine is especially useful in preparing newspapers, catalogs, and small booklets, such as employee handbooks.

The *Justowriter,* used to prepare material for offset or stencil duplicating, turns out even right margin copy. Two units, a recorder and a reproducer, are needed. As the copy is typed on the recorder, a punched paper tape is produced plus a visible copy for proofreading. Corrections may be made on the tape. The tape is inserted in the reproducer, which automatically types the justified copy at 100 words a minute on stencils, offset plates, or special paper for transfer by photographic processes.

12.3 TELEPHONE AND WIRE SERVICES

In a way, the organization's nervous system is its communication network. This includes its telephone and telegraph facilities. The administrator and the secretary are deeply involved in these systems not only because they use them, but also because they often have to decide, among the many alternatives available, which systems should be employed and in what manner. These vital links in the successful functioning of a company connect the home office with suppliers, customers, salesmen, branch offices, and the like. The office manager, therefore, should be aware of the types of available equipment and their advantages for the most efficient transfer of information between these groups.

Special Telephone Services	p. 442
Telephone Equipment	p. 443
Telegraph Service: Domestic	p. 447
Telegraph Service: International	p. 454
Incoming Wires	p. 460
Wires Concerning Government Information	p. 460
WUX, TWX, and TELEX	p. 463

Special Telephone Services. Besides the regular service whereby a company is assigned a single telephone number, there are other special telephone hookups for small and large companies.

Centrex. In many companies where the manual PBX switchboard is overloaded, it has been found to be more economical to install Centrex than to enlarge the switchboard. Through the use of Centrex, every person requiring outside service is assigned an individual telephone number from the city exchange. By dialing this number, an outside caller is connected to the inside party without the delay of going through an operator. One makes outgoing local and long-distance calls by simply dialing the desired number. In fact, only the calls to the listed company number go through the switchboard attendant. If the phone is manipulated correctly, one can have outside calls transferred quickly and easily by slowly depressing the cradle button all the way down once only to get a dial tone. Then the four digits of the station to which the call is being transferred are dialed. If the station number is not known, the call may be transferred to a company information four-digit number. One may also have a call transferred to a company building or unit serviced by a manual board by dialing "0" after receiving the dial tone. The call is then transferred manually within the company. As long as a call remains in the Centrex system, there is no limit to the number of times it may be transferred. One makes intercom calls by simply dialing a three- or four-digit number. Conference, consultation, and other automatic dial services are available.

A Centrex feature is individual number billing for long-distance calls.

The telephone company keeps an itemized statement that identifies and lists every long-distance call by the individual telephone number. Thus your company knows exactly what department or person to charge for the call.

Wide Area Telephone Service (WATS). WATS is a telephone service offered to companies having a high volume of station-to-station long-distance or toll calls. Only calls originated by the company use the WATS lines. Both intrastate and interstate (within the United States, but excluding Alaska and Hawaii) service is offered.

Interstate WATS users have a choice of two types of service, full-time and measured-time.

1. Full-time service enables the user to make an unlimited number of calls to all telephones within a designated calling area for a flat monthly charge.

2. Measured-time service enables the user to make calls totaling fifteen hours of conversation per month. If this usage time is exceeded, a fixed charge is assessed for each additional hour or major fraction of an hour.

A WATS user may subscribe to any of six calling areas or terminating zones across the United States. These zones are usually numbered consecutively from 1 through 6. Subscription to a higher numbered zone includes service to all lower numbered zones; for example, service to Zone 4 includes service to Zones 1, 2, and 3, as well. Assistance calls and calls to nondialable points are placed on a station basis by dialing "Operator" over a WATS line.

Intrastate WATS users have a choice of two types of measured-line services.

1. Measured time of 15 hours per month.
2. Measured time of 125 hours per month.

If usage time is exceeded on either of these, the user pays a fixed charge for each additional hour or major fraction of an hour. In states divided into two or more areas, an intrastate WATS customer may subscribe to any or all areas in his state, but is usually required to subscribe to the area in which the firm is located before he can have WATS service to another area of his state.

Because WATS service is offered only on a station-to-station basis, the operator will turn back all person-to-person, collect, and special instruction calls (e.g., bill to a third number, credit card, requests for time and charges, notify at a specific time). If a nondialable number has been placed with the operator and a busy, no answer, or out-of-order condition exists, she will request the customer to place the call later. The operator is not able to call back on a WATS service line.

Telephone Equipment. The telephone equipment manufacturers are continually improving their equipment. Your local telephone company representative will gladly demonstrate the latest models and will advise you on how to combine certain pieces in order to get the most efficient and economical system for your office or company. Some of the most useful and efficient pieces of equipment are described here.

Operator-Controlled PBX. The PBX system has been popular for many years because it provides control over all outgoing, incoming, and intercom calls. Calls are completed quickly with easy-to-handle cords and keys. In the latest models the writing shelf is completely free of equipment so that the operator can perform other office duties. Modern lowboy styling makes it ideal for a reception room. Formica-type cabinets match the office decor. When expansion is necessary, additional lines can be installed quickly and easily. A minimum of training is needed for efficient operation. The equipment allows for conference tie-lines, selected station night services, and connection to the company paging system.

The Electronic Secretary. The Electronic Secretary Telephone Answering Set is a fast, money-saving way to increase the efficiency of your telephone system. It answers the phone with your announcement message and then receives up to two hours of incoming messages with excellent fidelity. The announcement can be changed at any time. The machine may be used during the day to take customers' orders and, with a change of the announcement, to record out-of-town salesmen's reports in the evening.

Call Commander (or Director) Phone. The Call Commander is a key phone for larger offices. It provides up to 17 outside lines with a hold feature. Employees may answer and hold calls at the push of a button. They can pick up calls on other lines, transfer calls, and dial other phones in the key system. A pre-set conference service may be added to the Call Commander that allows groups of up to six preselected telephones to be called simultaneously by the dialing of an intercom code or by the push of a button. An add-on feature makes it possible to add another person (associated with your dial intercom) to an outside call.

Speakerphone. The Speakerphone frees both hands during a conversation. You may look up a file, check a blueprint, even write an order while you carry on a conversation with the called person. It is also usable during a conference if you need to call for additional information or have a question answered. The entire group in your office can listen and talk. It is also a private phone when the attached handset is used.

Executive Quick Call Service. If you have a P-A-B-X System (see the next paragraph), you may use an Executive Quick Call unit with 20 direct lines to the employees you call most often. On these inside calls, you merely press a button and the called party's telephone rings immediately. If the person you're calling is using his telephone, push another button and he hears a tone in the background of his conversation. Hearing it, he cuts short his conversation, presses the cradle button, and is connected to your line. An optional feature allows you to cut in on the busy line. This unit may be used with a Speakerphone for hands-free operation.

P-A-B-X (Private Automatic Branch Exchange).   This dial telephone system allows employees to dial both inside and outside calls without help from a switchboard attendant. Systems are available for 20, 40, or 80 telephones and include many versatile features. Inside calls are made by the dialing of three digits. An outside call is transferred to another inside party by the dialing of "1" and then the other party's number. You may consult another inside party while the outside call is placed on hold. You may set up a three-way conference with the outside party, yourself, and another inside party. All incoming calls may be handled by an attendant, or certain assigned telephones may be arranged to receive incoming calls, or anyone may pick up any phone and dial "8" to answer an incoming call.

Code Call Service.   The P-A-B-X system may include a Code Call Service that summons a person to answer a call at the nearest phone. Through the use of sound or light signals, you can reach any employee immediately by dialing the number of the Code Call unit and your party's code. When he hears his code or sees it flash in lights anywhere on the premises, he picks up the nearest telephone and dials an answering number. Paging is permitted from any telephone in the entire P-A-B-X system. A fire alarm feature is also included. The Code Call System can be arranged to signal only the building wanted for each call. Companies whose operations are spread out through a number of different buildings would find this service helpful. It may also be used to signal one or more departments in a single building.

Card Dialer Telephone.   The Card Dialer Telephone quickly, effortlessly, and automatically dials calls for you. Cards for frequently dialed numbers (maximum 40) are filed alphabetically right in the telephone. Additional cards may be coded and kept ready for use for such tasks as periodic calls at the end of the month or calls to groups of persons, such as salesmen. The machine is so flexible that it may be used for all kinds of calls—local, long distance, and intercom. You may add new numbers easily by merely punching the desired number on a new card with the point of a pencil or a ball-point pen.

Magicall *Electronic Dialer.*   The *Magicall* Electronic Dialer is a compact desktop companion to any telephone. It automatically dials up to 400 numbers with a standard tape cartridge or 1,000 with a special tape. You can record numbers quickly and accurately by writing or typing the names on tape and recording the numbers with the dial-in unit. Erase old numbers simply by dialing in new ones. Local, long-distance, and intercom calls—including access, area, and special codes—can be placed automatically. It is usable with any dial-telephone equipment. Such a machine saves time by eliminating a search for numbers, by cutting calling time, and by completing all calls quickly and accurately.

Electrowriter.   The Electrowriter Communication System transmits handwritten messages or sketches to any number of receiving stations—over any distance (50 yards, 5 miles, 5,000 miles). Messages are transmitted the instant you write them, exactly as you write them. Printed Electrowriter forms may be used to get specific needed information. The unit is powered by ordinary electrical outlets and operates over private wire, leased or company owned, as well as over regular local and long-distance telephone networks. An Electrowriter installed with a Data-Phone allows you to write and to receive any message, sketch, or graphic information and alternately talk as you write and receive. In addition, the flexibility of the Data-Phone permits you to call any third party to verify information.

Data-Phone. Besides providing direct communications between telewriting and facsimile business machines, the Data-Phone makes possible direct computer-to-computer operation. It accepts data signals from business machines that use punched cards, paper tape, or magnetic tape. Data-Phone service is provided on regular telephone lines for local or long-distance data communications at normal telephone rates, and operates in the same manner on private line service or WATS service at a fixed monthly charge. It offers automatic answering and appropriate terminating controls for unattended receiving stations. This tie-up with your computer offers an economical means of expanding data communications between the production plant and company headquarters, the warehouse and the distributing outlets, the regional sales offices and headquarters, and the purchasing department and production.

Dataspeed. The Bell System Dataspeed service is designed to meet the need for communicating information at high speed, high volume, and low cost. Information collected on paper tape by any of the coding schemes can be transmitted by Dataspeed equipment. A five-thousand-word message can be sent via the regular telephone network with accuracy and reliability in approximately five minutes. Transmission can be one-way or two-way at the same time over regular telephone lines (Data-Phone Service) or private line service. Units can be left unattended for automatic transmission. They can send and receive information at prearranged times, often at low-cost after-hours rates. Voice communications are usually an integral part of the service to allow voice contact with other stations and to check on transmissions.

Touch-Tone. With Touch-Tone telephone equipment, you can call your party much faster and easier than with the conventional dial phone. You merely depress electronic push buttons with the same letter and number designations as those on present dials. This service makes many new telephone options possible today and in the future. For instance, the Touch-Tone telephone can also function as an efficient data-input device. Today, many business and professional people use it to transmit billing information to a central billing and service organization to control inventories, purchasing, shipping, and a variety of other business activities. It is fast, economical, and simple to use. Its most efficient use is in situations in which there is a need to send small amounts of information on a frequent basis. The Card Dialer mentioned previously is available with Touch-Tone service.

Telegraph Service: Domestic. Before sending a message by telegraph, you should consider carefully the alternative ways to get a message to the receiver as quickly as possible at the least cost (Figure 12-7). A letter is definitely cheaper than a telegram and allows the sender to include a great deal more information. Will the time saved compensate for the extra cost of a telegram? Or will a telegram actually save time? If you are sending a message late Friday afternoon, it will not be delivered until the next business day—Monday morning. An airmail letter posted Friday afternoon should arrive on Monday also. Another question to ask yourself is "Would a telephone call be more economical?" A message that calls for an immediate answer might be cheaper if transmitted as one long-distance call than if two telegrams were exchanged. Besides saving money, the telephone call would save time.

To assure economy, companies having a large volume of wire messages assign one person or an office service department the task of determining the type of service to be used when sending wire messages. Thus, the burden of deciding on the most economical use of wire services is removed from the originator. The explanation of domestic and international wire services that follows will aid in setting up efficient practices for these special messages.

Classes of Service. Through the use of domestic telegraph service you can connect with all points served by wire in the continental United States, Mexico, Canada, Alaska, and Saint Pierre–Miquelon islands. It is possible to send three classes of telegrams, which differ in speed and cost. In all three classes, no charge is made for the first address and the signature, which may include the company name. Code may be used in the message.

Telegram. The telegram is the fastest and most expensive service available on a cost-per-word basis. A minimum flat rate is charged for the first 15 words or less, and you are charged extra for each word over 15.

Day Letter. The day letter costs less per word than the telegram and takes twice as long to reach its destination. A minimum flat rate is charged for the

---

Be Brief—Avoid "Rush" Teletype Service—Use the Mails

Eliminate wordiness; use simple, clear language and construction in the message.

Check time difference at destination.

Use Air Mail service when time permits.

Deliver teletype messages to company communication center early in day to avoid overloads in late afternoon.

Use "night letter" service on telegrams whenever possible.

Use standard teletype punctuation marks only—the period, slash, and dash.

Figure 12-7 Ways to cut telegram and teletype expense.

first 50 words, and an extra charge is made for each additional group of five or less words. A 63-word day letter would be counted as 65 words, or the minimum plus extra charges for three groups of five words each.

Night Letter. The night letter is the least expensive service, transmitted to its destination during the night and delivered in the morning of the next business day (no deliveries on Saturday or Sunday). A night letter may be filed with the telegraph office until 2 a.m. The minimum rate for 50 words is 15 to 25 cents less than a 15-word telegram and 70 cents to $1.20 less than a 50-word day letter. An extra charge is made for each group of five or less words over the minimum.

Factors to Be Considered. In choosing the class of domestic telegram to send, consider the factors of time, number of words, and cost.

1. Time. The four time zones in the United States—Eastern, Central, Mountain, and Pacific—are each separated by a one-hour time differential. If you are in New York City at twelve o'clock noon, the time in each of the zones is as follows.

Eastern Time	Noon
Central Time	11:00 a.m.
Mountain Time	10:00 a.m.
Pacific Time	9:00 a.m.

In other words, if you start at New York City and move west, the time is one hour earlier in Chicago, two hours earlier in Denver, and three hours earlier in Los Angeles. Or if you start at Los Angeles and move east, the time is one hour later in Denver, two hours later in Chicago, and three hours later in New York City. (See Figure 12-8 for a map of United States showing the time zones.)

Daylight Saving Time, as set forth in the Federal Uniform Time Act of 1967, is observed by all states, except for Kentucky and Alaska, who have temporary exclusion, and Hawaii. By this plan clocks are set ahead one hour on the last Sunday in April and set back one hour on the last Sunday in October.

2. Number of words. A clear message using the least number of words should be written. Because a telegram is expensive if many words are used, you may have to sacrifice speed for economy in a long message and consider the use of a day or night letter. When attempting to be as concise as possible, remember that common words not essential to the meaning may be omitted, for example, *I, we, the, a,* and *to.* The following message contains many unnecessary words.

AM ATTENDING AMERICAN MANAGEMENT ASSOCIATION CONFER-
ENCE UNTIL FRIDAY STOP WILL BE BACK IN THE OFFICE ON TUES-
DAY STOP PLEASE SET UP COMMITTEE MEETING WITH TAYLOR AND
JONES FOR TEN A.M. STOP   (Total words: 31)

Figure 12-8 Time zone map.

Now read the same message, which has been rewritten within the 15-word limit without any loss of meaning:

ATTENDING AMA CONFERENCE. RETURN TUESDAY FOR TEN A.M. MEETING WITH TAYLOR AND JONES. PLEASE ARRANGE

(Total words: 15)

Nouns, verbs, and adjectives are the important words in a message. Standard punctuation—period, comma, quotation marks, parentheses, hyphen—may be used without charge. Domestic wire messages should be punctuated. *Stop* is no longer necessary and a charge is made for it, if used.

3. Cost. The cost of a telegram may be determined with the aid of a rate chart supplied by Western Union. Clarification of the following points, however, is needed for an accurate estimate.

a. Addresses. No charge is made for essential material in the address. "Personal" and "Will Call" are free notations. You will be charged for additional or alternate names or addresses.

b. Signature and address of sender. No charge is made for the name of the sender and his city and state (included in the date line). The company name may accompany the name of the sender, but his department and title are charged for, if included. The telegraph company also charges for the sender's street address.

c. Word count. In general, each dictionary word up to and including fifteen characters counts as one word. Words of more than fifteen characters or combinations of dictionary words are divided and counted as two or more words. Hyphenated words are counted as one word for each part, unless the compound word is hyphenated in the dictionary. Words must be used in the same sense as conveyed by the definition in a standard dictionary.

The names of states, counties, and cities are counted according to the number of words they contain. For example, Las Vegas is two words; New York City is three. Running the names together as in *Newyorkcity* will not affect the count; it is still three words. Abbreviated city names, such as LA, NYC, and KC, count as one word.

Some abbreviations are permissible. Be sure before abbreviating that the result will be understandable. Do not abbreviate unless the length of the word is such that a shortening of the word count will result.

EXAMPLES:		
parts catalog	. . . .	2 words
parts cat	. . . .	2 words
District of Columbia	. . . .	3 words
D.C.	. . . .	1 word
Certified Public Accountant	. . . .	3 words
CPA	. . . .	1 word

Common combinations of abbreviations are permissible and are counted as five characters to a word. Arbitrary misuse of abbreviations and words is not permitted by the telegraph company.

EXAMPLES: National Association of Manufacturers . . 4 words
            NAM .   .   .   . 1 word
            Retel .   .   .   . 1 word (5 characters)
            Reurtel .   .   .   . 2 words (7 characters)
            Federal Bureau of Investigation .   .   .   . 4 words
            FBI .   .   .   . 1 word

Proper names are counted as they are normally written: Van de Kamp is three words.

A group of five figures or a combination of not more than five figures and letters will count as one word. Any more than five characters will add to the word count. Code numbers containing all figures or figures and letters may be hyphenated, because the hyphen is considered a mark of punctuation.

EXAMPLES: 72192 .   .   .   . 1 word (5 characters)
            T5437 .   .   .   . 1 word (5 characters)
            F-376-2 .   .   .   . 1 word (5 characters)
            AN-904 .   .   .   . 1 word (5 characters)
            P-129875 .   .   .   . 2 words (7 characters)

The diagonal (/) or slash mark with figures or letters is counted as one character.

EXAMPLES: T/5437 .   .   .   . 2 words (6 characters)
            1/2 .   .   .   . 1 word (3 characters)
            one-half .   .   .   . 2 words
            B/L .   .   .   . 1 word (3 characters)
            bill of lading .   .   .   . 3 words

The decimal point in figures is not counted, but the dollar sign ($) or the English pound sterling sign (£) counts as one character.

EXAMPLES: $22.50 .   .   .   . 1 word (5 characters)
            $220.50 .   .   .   . 2 words (6 characters)
            £118.50 .   .   .   . 2 words (6 characters)

The percent sign (%) is transmitted as 0/0 and counts as one word in the United States, Alaska, and Mexico and as three words in Canada and Saint Pierre–Miquelon islands. The symbol @ is not transmitted by wire; therefore, "at" should be used. The signs for pound, number, feet, inches, and minute are charged for as words. In a message to Canada or Saint Pierre–Miquelon islands, each figure or "other character" is counted as one word.

Special Telegraph Services.   In addition to the services mentioned, the telegraph company provides a variety of other useful business communication aids.

1. Telegraph money orders. These may be used to transmit money to any point in the United States. Two classes of service are available—the fast or full-rate daytime service, which is the most expensive, and the overnight or night letter service. Supplementary messages, either business or personal, may be included with the money order at the additional word rates, except that in an overnight money order no charge is made for the first ten words. The fee is determined by the distance and the amount of money being transferred.

The telegraph office provides a special form for telegraphic money orders. Besides including the name and address of the person who is to receive the money, you may indicate whether or not you waive identification when the recipient calls for the money. The usual practice is to ask for identification before relinquishing money.

2. Direct wire service. If you have a large volume of telegraphic messages, direct service between your company and a nearby telegraph office is possible through the use of Desk-Fax equipment, obtainable from Western Union. When sending and receiving messages with the Desk-Fax, you save delivery time and eliminate errors in verbal transmission over the telephone. Western Union allows a ten-cent discount on each direct wire after the first one-hundred sent in the month.

3. Errand service. Business errands may be handled by telegraph company messengers, who will pick up and deliver documents, blueprints, press releases, and any envelope or package. A messenger will call for personal articles at the home, office, cleaners, drug store, gift shop, and so on, and deliver them to a designated address. Gifts, such as flowers and candy, may be ordered and delivered through Western Union. A company may also hire messengers to act as temporary employees—parking attendants, guides, or couriers. Errand service is available in most cities on either a trip or an hourly basis.

4. In-transit service. Passengers on a train, plane, or bus can be reached by telegram. The message will be delivered to the passenger on his arrival at the station or airport. (See typing instructions in paragraphs 12 and 13 on page 454.)

5. Mailgram service. Western Union's computerized network speeds letters electronically to distant post offices. If the copy arrives at the receiving post office before 7 p.m., mailgrams are delivered the next business day in distinctively designed envelopes to any address in the 48 states. One text may be sent to as many as 100 addresses. The messages may be transmitted over a company's TELEX, TWX, and WUX teleprinter between 8 a.m. and 11 p.m. EST Monday through Friday.

Instructions for Typing Domestic Telegrams.   Telegraph blanks are provided free by Western Union. Regular office stationery may also be used (Figure 12-9).

1. Decide on the number of copies to make. Four copies of a telegraphic message are usual—the original for pickup by the messenger, a copy sent by mail to the recipient for confirmation purposes, a general file copy, and a copy for the telegraph account file for bookkeeping purposes.

Mail the confirmation copy immediately in case the addressee fails to receive the telegram and to ensure that he has an exact copy of the message for his records.

2. Double-space the message and triple-space between paragraphs. Paragraphs may or may not be indented, as desired.

Domestic Service - Day Letter   Charge: OMC 95

Report Delivery
Mr. James A. Webster
United Shippers
Pier 105B
New York, New York 10068   April 15, 19--   9:35 a.m.

Shipment 10578 of 86 two-by-three foot wooden boxes lost in tran-

sit. Tracer initiated. Word of whereabouts expected in 12 hours.

Request you hold space on African Star bound for Nigeria on

April 18. When shipment located will telegraph day and hour it

will reach docks.

                          H. T. Snyder

Oklahoma Manufacturing Co.
143 Factory Road
Oklahoma City, Oklahoma 73105

mt

Figure 12-9 Sample of typewritten telegram on company stationery.

3. Type in caps and lower case, allowing at least one-inch margins. Use caps for code words.

4. Type *Domestic Service* or *International Service* and the class of service *(Telegram, Day Letter, Night Letter)* at the left margin two spaces above the address. Single-space the address; be sure to use a street number and not a post office box. Addresses must be complete and accurate.

5. Type the date and hour at the right margin on the same line as city and state or on the appropriate line provided in a telegram blank.

6. Never divide a word at the end of a line.

7. Indicate in the appropriate space on the blank either *Paid* or *Collect*. If the telegram is to be charged, type the name of the charge account in the space provided on the blank.

8. Type the address and phone number of the sender in the lower left-hand corner of the blank. The reference initials may be placed one space below.

9. To indicate that an answer is requested, type *AR* in the space provided for payment information.

10. To confirm delivery, type the words *Report Delivery* for which you will be charged as part of the address. A collect telegram will be sent to your company indicating when and to whom the telegram was delivered.

11. To send the same message to a number of people, list the names and addresses on the special Western Union form for this purpose or type them on a separate sheet of paper. Usually, as many as four addressees may be typed in two columns on a telegraph form.

12. To send a telegram to a person on a train, include the following information: (a) name of the passenger, in care of the conductor; (b) train name and number and direction in which traveling; (c) car and reservation number; (d) station and arrival time; and (e) city and state.

13. To send a telegram to a person on a plane, give the following information: (a) name of passenger; (b) name of airline, flight number, and direction in which plane is traveling; (c) airport and arrival time; and (d) city and state.

Telegraph Service: International.   Messages to foreign countries are sent over cable or radio facilities. Basic procedures are similar to those for sending telegrams. You may file cablegrams and radiograms with your local Western Union office. Or you may file directly via your teletype equipment or a long-distance call to New York, San Francisco, or Washington, D.C., with ITT World Communications, RCA Communications, or Western Union International. To place a cable with Tropical Radio (TRT) for Bermuda or other points in the Caribbean, you may contact their offices in Miami or Fort Lauderdale. Because the four international carriers are not linked to the same cities overseas, it is helpful to check the routing chart *Pocket Guide to International Telecommunication,* distributed free of charge by ITT World Communications, for the most direct route.

Your cablegram will reach its destination faster if you indicate to Western Union the desired route. For instance, simply type *VIA WUI* after the destination in the address, if you find that Western Union International has a link to the city to which you are sending a message. If you do not indicate a routing, the domestic telegraph company cannot do it for you. Instead the message must go to a *pool* from which it is distributed to a carrier without regard to the most direct routing.

Classes of Service.   Two classes of international telegraph service are provided.

1. *Full rate cablegram (FR)* is the fastest service for international use. The distance traveled determines the rate per word. The FR charge per word from all points in the United States ranges from 21 cents for a cable to the Hawaiian Islands to 34 cents for one to Cambodia. A minimum charge is assessed for seven words. Any message wholly or partly in code must be sent FR.

2. *Cable letters (LT)* are an overnight service for longer messages. The minimum charge is for 22 words. An extra charge is made for each additional word. A cable letter of 22 words would cost approximately $2.31 to Hawaii and $3.74 to Cambodia, approximately half of the FR rate. It would be delivered after eight o'clock local time on the morning after the date of filing.

An LT telegram filed after midnight would be delivered the morning of the next calendar day, at least 32 hours later. An LT message sent from the Western Hemisphere to the Southwest Pacific and Far East might be delayed as long as two days because of the time differential.

Factors to Be Considered. As with domestic telegrams, international telegraph services are used more efficiently when one considers the time differences around the world and the cost per word. Of importance also is the need to specify delivery and handling instructions.

Time. Consider the time difference between the city of origin and the destination to decide whether a fast cable is justified. A message reaching its destination after 10 p.m. will not be delivered until the following morning unless special delivery is requested. Request night delivery by inserting the word *NUIT* before the name of the addressee. The ITT international time chart that follows will help you determine the approximate time at the destination of the cable. When using this chart, remember that it is based on Eastern Standard Time and that in crossing the International Dateline, your computation may take you into yesterday and tomorrow. Each new day starts at the International Dateline in the Pacific Ocean, and moves west across Auckland, Wake Island, Tokyo, Saigon, Moscow, Accra, London, Rio de Janeiro, New York, Lima, San Francisco, and Honolulu. Here is an example of how to use the chart.

At 10 a.m. in your office in Denver, you decide to cable Geneva, Switzerland. Because you are in the Mountain Time Zone, the time in New York (Eastern Time) is twelve noon. Opposite Switzerland on the chart you see +6, which means to add six hours to Eastern Standard Time. At 10 a.m. in Denver, the time is 6 p.m. in Geneva. A fast cable is transmitted in approximately one hour; therefore, your message would arrive about 7 p.m. It is doubtful that the office in Switzerland would still be open; therefore, a cable letter would be the more economical service to use.

To determine STANDARD TIME overseas, add (+) to or subtract (−) from EASTERN STANDARD TIME as indicated:

Afghanistan	$+ 9\frac{1}{2}$	Colombia	0	Haiti	0
Albania	+ 6	Congo, Rep. of	+ 6	Hawaii	− 5
Algeria	+ 6	Costa Rica	− 1	Hungary	+ 6
Argentina	+ 2	Cuba	0	Iceland	+ 4
Aruba	$+ \frac{1}{2}$	Curaçao	$+ \frac{1}{2}$	India	$+ 10\frac{1}{2}$
Australia	+ 15	Czechoslovakia	+ 6	Indonesia	$+ 12\frac{1}{2}$
Austria	+ 6	Denmark	+ 6	Iran	$+ 8\frac{1}{2}$
Azores	+ 3	Dominican Rep.	0	Iraq	+ 8
Belgium	+ 6	Ecuador	0	Ireland	+ 5
Bermuda	+ 1	Egypt	+ 7	Israel	+ 7
Bolivia	+ 1	Ethiopia	+ 8	Italy	+ 6
Borneo	+ 13	Finland	+ 7	Japan	+ 14
Brazil	+ 2	Formosa	+ 13	Korea	$+ 13\frac{1}{2}$
Bulgaria	+ 7	France	+ 6	Lebanon	+ 7
Burma	$+ 11\frac{1}{2}$	Germany	+ 6	Luxembourg	+ 6
Canal Zone	0	Ghana	+ 5	Madagascar	+ 8
Ceylon	$+ 10\frac{1}{2}$	Great Britain	+ 5	Malaya	$+ 12\frac{1}{2}$
Chile	+ 1	Greece	+ 7	Morocco	+ 5
China	+ 13	Guatemala	− 1	Netherlands	+ 6

Neth. Antilles	$+ \frac{1}{2}$	Portugal	$+ 5$	Switzerland	$+ 6$
Newfoundland	$+ 1\frac{1}{2}$	Puerto Rico	$+ 1$	Syria	$+ 7$
New Zealand	$+ 17$	Rhodesia	$+ 7$	Thailand	$+ 12$
Nicaragua	$- 1$	Romania	$+ 7$	Tunisia	$+ 6$
Norway	$+ 6$	Salvador, El	$- 1$	Turkey	$+ 7$
Pakistan	$+ 10$	Saudi Arabia	$+ 8$	USSR	$+ 8$
Panama	0	Singapore	$+ 12\frac{1}{2}$	Uruguay	$+ 2$
Paraguay	$+ 1$	So. Africa, Rep. of	$+ 7$	Venezuela	$+ \frac{1}{2}$
Peru	0	Spain	$+ 6$	Vietnam	$+ 12$
Philippines	$+ 13$	Surinam	$+ 1\frac{1}{2}$	Virgin Islands	$+ 1$
Poland	$+ 6$	Sweden	$+ 6$	Yugoslavia	$+ 6$

Other time factors must be considered, too. For instance, office hours move with the day and follow individual local patterns. Holidays vary from country to country. Almost every day is a holiday somewhere on earth. Midday closing in some cities may mean that afternoon office hours extend to 7 p.m., or offices may open at 7 a.m. and close for the day in the early afternoon. Working days do not coincide all around the world. As the day advances, weekends start and stop at different times; on Friday morning in New York the weekend has already begun in Manila. All weekends do not necessarily fall on Saturday and Sunday; the business week in Saudi Arabia and Egypt, for example, runs Saturday through Thursday. A telegram sent late Friday from Honolulu to Jidda could be acted upon within a few hours, whereas one sent the next day in the opposite direction could not. Telegraph offices themselves observe varying work weeks and business hours around the world, both for message delivery service and for the actual operation of the circuits. Major communication distribution points like Buenos Aires, London, New York, or Vienna operate seven days a week, 24 hours a day, but in smaller stations this is not so. If you are cabling Arica, Chile, for example, on September 18, it will help to know that September 18 and 19 are holidays in Chile and that on holidays the Arica telegraph office closes from 1 p.m. to 4 p.m. and from 8 p.m. to 9 a.m. Similar circumstances may hold true for a provincial French town or a holiday resort in Hawaii.

Cost. Determination of the cost of a cable may be made from a rate chart furnished by any one of the international carriers. Here are a few points to remember when estimating cable charges.

(1) Every word is charged for in a cable including name, address, and signature. Therefore, all unnecessary words should be omitted. The name of the country of destination, when enclosed in parentheses, is not included in the charges, but it must be part of the address. You may use a registered code address and a code signature.

(2) Punctuation marks are not transmitted in cables unless specifically requested by the sender. When punctuation is required to retain the meaning of the text, type at the beginning of the message *count punctuation*. Punctuation marks are counted as additional words except when used in groups of figures or letters. A punctuation mark used with figures is counted as one character. To give an example, 1,575 and 16/40 are each counted as one word.

The parentheses and quotation marks are counted as one word when used in pairs to enclose one or more words. Other acceptable marks counted as one word *each* are the period, comma, colon, question mark, apostrophe, dash, and diagonal. The percent sign (%) is transmitted as 0/0 (3 characters), and the ¢ sign, $ sign, and £ sign are spelled out—*cents, dollars, pounds*—and each letter is counted as one character. For example, $50 is transmitted as *dollars 50* (2 words); $98.50 and 87¢ are also two words each.

(3) Word count is based on dictionary words. Each dictionary word up to and including 15 letters is counted as one word. Words with more than 15 letters are divided and counted as one additional word for each group of 15 letters or less. The same general rules for abbreviations in other wire messages apply to cables except that charges will vary depending on the type of service (full-rate or cable-letter). Well-known commercial terms or trademarks that are familiar to the general public or are published in catalogs are counted in the same manner as figures (five characters per word). Word combinations are not allowed. If used they will be divided and counted separately, *except* as follows.

Compound words appearing in a standard dictionary of the admitted language (WU Tariff Book 5.501).
EXAMPLE: closefisted

Names of places, squares, streets, and other public roads.
EXAMPLES: Hollywoodway   for Hollywood Way
             Losangeles   for Los Angeles
             Ruedelapaix   for Rue de la Paix

Family names.
EXAMPLE: Vandegrift   for Van de Grift

Numbers written out as words. See paragraph 4, following.

Groups of figures and letters used as reference or identifying numbers. See paragraph 4, following.

(4) A group of five figures counts as one word. Each additional five characters or less count as another word. If more than one third of the text is in figures, full rates apply unless the figures are known to be reference or identifying numbers. Under this rule of counting, combinations of letters and figures are not permitted. When such information (figures plus letters) must be transmitted, the figures must be spelled out. Figures that require 15 or less characters when spelled are counted as one word.

EXAMPLES: *AN736* will be transmitted by the carrier as *AN seven thirty-six* (four words), unless the number is spelled or instructions are given that this is a reference number. You may write *AN seventhirtysix* (two words).
             sevenhundredthirtysix (21 characters): 2 words.
             eleventhousand (14 characters): 1 word.
             11,000 (6 characters): 2 words.

The exception to this rule of counting concerns reference or identifying numbers, such as file numbers or contract numbers. These numbers will be transmitted without spelling if you identify and list them on the original copy delivered to the international carrier or Western Union.

(5) Code may be used in the FR message and is usually counted as five characters or fraction thereof to the word.

Registered code addresses for overseas companies you contact may be secured from any regional office of the four international carriers. Because charges are assessed on each word in an address on wires sent to other countries, the use of one-word code addresses saves considerable money. Examples of code addresses are *BARCLADOM* for Barclay's Bank in London, *MENARDS* for Menards Custom Tailors in Hong Kong, *ORIENTRA* for Toyo International Corporation in Yokohama, and *BANKAMERICA* for Bank of America National Trust and Savings Association in San Francisco.

A code address for your company may be secured from the local Western Union Office, who will suggest a one-word address that is significantly different from other local code addresses. The registration fee is approximately $17.50 a year or almost half that for six months. Because the code address is a point-of-destination address, you should send it to your foreign contacts for their use in sending messages to your company.

Delivery and handling instructions. It is possible to specify exactly how you want your telegram handled. Instructions can cover details of payment, time or method of delivery, and forwarding or holding information. Operators experienced in handling international telegrams will code your verbal instructions, but domestic operators unfamiliar with international practice may not know how to forward your requests. The following coded instructions, which cost the price of one word each unless otherwise noted, will assist you in indicating exact international delivery instructions.

Specifying Place of Delivery

Instruction	Code	Example
Care of	CHEZ	JOHN SMITH CHEZ TURNER CHAMPS ELYSEES 117 PARIS FRANCE VIA ITT
Forward	FS (request of sender)	FS JOHN SMITH CHAMPS ELYSEES 117 PARIS FRANCE VIA ITT
		VIA VENETO 32 ROME ITALY VIA ITT
or	REEXPEDIE DE (request of addressee)	REEXPEDIE DE JOHN SMITH CHAMPS ELYSEES 117 PARIS FRANCE VIA ITT
		VIA VENETO 32 ROME ITALY VIA ITT
General delivery	GP	GP JOHN SMITH HELSINKI FINLAND VIA WUI
General delivery registered	GPR	GPR JOHN SMITH HELSINKI FINLAND VIA WUI

Hold for	TR	TR JOHN SMITH COPENHAGEN DENMARK VIA RCA
Personal delivery	MP	MP JOHN SMITH CUMBERLAND HOTEL LONDON ENGLAND VIA RCA
Post office box	BOITE POSTALE (2 words)	JOHN SMITH BOITE POSTALE 1098 BONN GERMANY VIA ITT

Specifying Time of Delivery

Daytime hours	JOUR	JOUR JOHN SMITH JONESMIT JOHORE MALAYSIA VIA RCA
Nighttime hours Specified date	NUIT REMETTRE (date)	REMETTRE 24 DEC. NUIT JOHN SMITH HOTEL OKURA TOYKO JAPAN VIA ITT
Shore/ship message (Number of days at sea-denoting when ship is to be called)	J(number)	J4 JOHN SMITH SS QUEEN ELIZABETH 2 NORTH ATLANTIC WSL VIA ITT

Specifying Method of Delivery

Airmail or Airmail, registered	PAV PAVR	PAV JOHN JONES 158 WILLIWAW SPRINGSIDE NEW SOUTH WALES AUSTRALIA VIA ITT
Mail	POSTE	POSTE JOHN SMITH 124 MADRID SPANISH TOWN, JAMAICA VIA TRT
Mail, registered	PR	PR JOHN SMITH 124 MADRID SPANISH TOWN, JAMAICA VIA TRT
Any method faster than mail	EXPRES (addressee pays delivery charges)	EXPRES JOHN SMITH PETITE ANSE HAITI VIA TRT
	XP (sender pays delivery charges)	XP JOHN SMITH MAMBALI TANGANYIKA VIA ITT
Telephone	TF (number)	TF PASSY 5283—JOHN SMITH PAULI PARIS VIA ITT
Telex	TLX (number)	TLX 84213465 JOHN SMITH LISBON PORTUGAL VIA RCA
Delivery confirmation	PC (sender pays for a seven-word minimum charge)	PC JOHN SMITH CALLE FLORIDA 194 BUENOS AIRES ARGENTINA VIA WUI

Specifying Rates and Other Details of Payment

Full Rate	FR (No charge for the symbol. FR service provided if no indication appears.)	
Letter Rate	LT	LT JOHN SMITH 215 CALLE JUAN LUNA MANILA PHILIPPINES VIA RCA
European Letter Rate	ELT	
Press Rate	PRESSE	⎫ Reserved for bona fide press representatives
Deferred Press	LCPS	⎬ sending messages to publishers.
Urgent Press	URGENT PRESSE	⎭
Reply prepaid	RP (Amount)	RP $4.50 JOHN SMITH 116 RUE DU RHONE GENEVA SWITZERLAND VIA ITT

The difference between LT and ELT is that LT service applies to traffic outside Europe or between Europe and another point. LT messages are delivered the day after the calendar date on which they are sent. ELT, Europe-to-Europe international deferred service, may be delivered five hours or more after being sent.

Payment for cables must be arranged for in advance with one or more of the international carriers. There is no blanket arrangement for collect service on international telegrams. It is covered by transferred and credit account agreements that differ according to the countries involved. Each carrier issues credit cards and is ready to handle credit applications and to furnish a credit card directory.

Incoming Wires.   Most companies establish a policy concerning receipt and opening of incoming wires. Often the wire is delivered to the mail room where it is logged in and then taken to the addressee. At other times the wire is delivered unopened to the addressee, who is responsible for noting the time of receipt and seeing that sufficient copies are made for the files and other personnel who need to know the contents of the wire. Copies may be made on a copying machine, or if one is not available, they may be typed on a printed form such as the one in Figure 12-10.

Wires Concerning Government Information.   Security regulations prohibit the transmittal of classified information by standard wire. Special facilities are available, however, for sending coded messages by wire as explained in the *Industrial Security Manual for Safeguarding Classified Information* and the *Cryptographic Supplement* to the manual, issued by the Department of Defense. In general, the same security measures are followed as for the preparation of classified letters (see Section 3.2). The message is given a classified control number, typed on a telegraph form with the correct number

COMPANY NAME

Copy of

INCOMING TELEGRAM (or CABLE)

Date and Time
of Receipt: 3:34 p.m.
                March 4, 1972

Copies to: B. B. Bias - for reply
            J. M. Sinson - for preparation
                           of quotation
            E. G. Timm - for information
            General Files

THIS FORM MAY BE USED WHEN COPYING INCOMING WIRES FOR DISTRIBUTION

UNLESS SO MANY COPIES ARE TO BE PREPARED THAT A DITTO MASTER WOULD

BE MORE PRACTICAL. IN SUCH EVENT USE DITTO MASTER IN PLACE OF

THIS FORM BUT USE SAME HEADING. THE WIRE SHOULD BE COPIED EXACTLY

AS RECEIVED WITH ALL DISTINGUISHING MARKS. IF MISTAKES ARE MADE

IN SPELLING, UNDERLINE THE ERROR.

                    SIGNATURE

rr (Initials of person who made the copy should be shown.)

Figure 12-10 Form used for copy of incoming wire.

461

of copies, labeled with the proper classification, signed by an authorized person, placed in the correct number of envelopes with an attached secret information receipt form, and delivered by the document control office to the proper communications message center. All copies and the supplies used in the preparation are safeguarded and destroyed in the same manner as for other classified material.

Unclassified teletypes and telegrams may contain either technical or administrative information. They may also contain statements of company policy, but most companies forbid the transmittal of proprietary or sensitive information by wire. Wires to federal agencies, such as NASA, the Air Force, or the Navy, use the format in Figure 12-11. The subject line in these wires may be omitted if its use will require an otherwise unclassified message to be classified or will noticeably increase the length of an otherwise brief message. A one-paragraph message need not be numbered, and where there are only one or two references, the identification may be included in the message. The wire to the Air Force in Figure 12-12 has no subject and lists the references

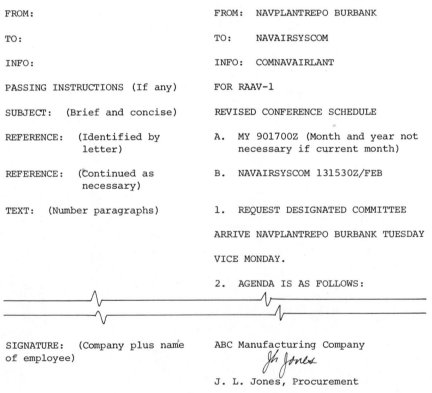

Figure 12-11   Recommended format for wires to Defense and other Federal service agencies.

---

21 February 1972

Dept. 898

Ext. 3456

TO: AIR FORCE PLANT REPRESENTATIVE, FORT WORTH

    IN TURN TO: AFLC PLANS OFFICE
                 DIRECTORATE OF PLANS AND PROGRAMS
                 HQ., AIR FORCE LOGISTICS COMMAND
                 WRIGHT-PATTERSON AIR FORCE BASE,
                 OHIO

                 ATTENTION: COLONEL J. JENSEN, MCFD

(Leave four blank spaces for insertion of reference number by teletype operator.)

AFLC LETTER MCFD/AJ, AF04(647)599, DATED 18 DECEMBER

1971. REURLETTER DATED 27 JANUARY 1972. REQUESTED

REPORTS WILL BE FORWARDED ON OR BEFORE 1 MARCH 1972.

PLATT-WHITNEY, INC.

C. C. Jones

C. C. JONES, MANAGER
CONTRACTS & PROPOSALS

aa

Figure 12-12   Modified format of short wire to Air Force.

with the text. If you send a wire of two or more pages, it is customary to head the second and subsequent pages with the complete address (Figure 12-13).

WUX, TWX, and TELEX.   WUX is the code name for wire service from the domestic telegraph company direct to the offices of a local firm. Desk-Fax is the name of the machine on which the message may be typed and transmitted over wires to the local telegraph office.

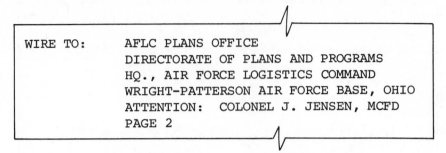

WIRE TO: AFLC PLANS OFFICE
                DIRECTORATE OF PLANS AND PROGRAMS
                HQ., AIR FORCE LOGISTICS COMMAND
                WRIGHT-PATTERSON AIR FORCE BASE, OHIO
                ATTENTION: COLONEL J. JENSEN, MCFD
                PAGE 2

Figure 12-13 Heading of second page of wire.

TWX is the code name for teletypewriter exchange service that permits the sending and receiving of *written* communication between two or more locations within the United States by use of telephone circuits. The teletypewriter used by the Bell System TWX is similar to an ordinary typewriter. Messages typed on one machine are instantly and exactly reproduced on any other teletypewriter to which it is connected. Each teletypewriter has its own number just as with telephones. All teletypewriter numbers and listings in the United States appear in one *Teletypewriter Directory*. The white-page section of the directory is arranged alphabetically by state, then cities within each state. The businesses are listed alphabetically by name under each city heading. The yellow-page section lists TWX users alphabetically by classified heading and by company name under each heading. To call another TWX give the teletypewriter operator the distant teletypewriter number. She then establishes the connection as rapidly as though it were a person-to-person call. Local and long-distance communications are two-way, and as many as six copies may be typed simultaneously. TWX charges are by the minute rather than by the word. A company may use its own business forms. Special equipment may be added to send pre-recorded messages automatically.

TELEX service connects a teleprinter with any one of thousands around the world. You pay for this direct subscriber-to-subscriber service by the minute instead of by the word. At the standard international speed of 66 words per minute you can transmit more information for less money than a telegram the same length will cost. Either tape or manual transmission is available. A teleprinter in your office may connect you directly with one of the international telegraph carriers, or may connect you with TELEX through a Bell System TWX station or a Western Union teleprinter. If your office is in New York City, San Francisco, or Washington, D.C., you may subscribe to a direct tie-line with an automatic switch to one of the international or marine traffic operations. The local representatives of the four international telegraph services will give you details.

Time and money are saved if you work your own international circuit, which delivers your message as fast as it can be typed and eliminates handling en route. Calling abroad by TELEX is as convenient as calling by phone: you type instead of talk, read instead of listen. Unfamiliar accents and languages are less important than when you use the spoken word. Also, you have immediate written confirmation of what transpired.

TELEX charges are based on minute-count, with either a one-minute or a three-minute charge in effect. For example, a 60-word telegram from New York to London costs $12.50 full rate (FR) or $6.30 night letter rate (LT), whereas a one-minute TELEX call from New York to London delivers 60 typewritten words for $3.00. Estimating transmission speed at 60 words per minute, you can send 180 words for a three-minute minimum charge of $6.00 to $12.60 (depending on destination). A telegram of 180 words would cost from $18.90 to $61.20, depending on destination and on rate (FR or LT). There is no simple formula for a break-even point between TELEX and message rates. The highest TELEX rates and the highest message rates do not always apply to the same countries, and the one- and three-minute minimum charges add another variable. In general, rates from the United States to Latin America, Europe, the Pacific, and the Far East are $3.00 per minute; to Africa and the Near East, $4.00 per minute. The few exceptions range from $2.00 (Hawaii, Bermuda, and Puerto Rico) to $4.20 (Rwanda and Burundi).

When making an international TELEX call, you are working with a circuit that can send and receive alternately at the standard international rate of 66 words per minute. A *word* is five characters and one space. No matter what time it is, the printer is ready to receive and hold transmission until the addressee's next business day begins. When there is peak demand, however, you may find a *no circuit* situation. Reaching an important commercial center at the close of its day or your own may be harder than at nonpeak hours. Automatic operation is available through the use of prepunched tapes. The cost of an ITT Worldcom automatic installation for 300 minutes of TELEX time annually is approximately $900. Manual operation, though slower, allows you to converse in writing with the person at the other end of the circuit. To determine whether to use the manual mode, you must balance the value of immediate conversational contact with the possibility of slower speeds, unused circuit time, and a higher cost per word. TELEX conversations are possible only when both ends of the circuit are manned, which limits their usefulness to coincidental office hours or to prearrangements. Calls to a public TELEX booth must be prearranged. Manual installations are available within the United States for an annual minimum billing of approximately $120, about 40 minutes of TELEX time. Both national and international installations will receive on an unattended basis so long as the teleprinter is plugged in and there is plenty of paper on the roll.

All of the international carriers have communication analysts who will study your total communications picture and recommend the right service for your firm. They offer guidance in the choice of proper terminal equipment, arrange for its installation, work out the necessary agreements with the foreign administration that handles the overseas portion of the circuit, see you through inauguration of service, and remain on call thereafter.

12.4 TRAVEL ARRANGEMENTS

Making arrangements for either business or personal travel involves collecting specific information about the type of transportation to use, time schedules, costs, the location of terminals, the availability of terminal transportation to parts of the city, baggage handling, insurance, hotel and motel accommodations, and many other features that contribute to the success of any trip. In some instances, companies maintain a transportation or travel reservation department that handles the details for business trips. A travel authorization form is filled out and approved before the trip is made (Figure 12-14). In other instances, the secretary or administrative assistant makes all arrangements or gathers the necessary information to pass on to the transportation department.

Use of Travel Agents	p. 466
Trip Information to Collect	p. 466
Itinerary	p. 467
Other Preparations for the Trip	p. 467
Expense Reports	p. 471
Classified Trip Requirements	p. 475
Attendance at Professional Meetings	p. 475
Use of Company or Personal Automobiles	p. 478
Travel Abroad	p. 480

Use of Travel Agents.   Because the travel industry today is highly specialized, a professional travel agent will provide expert guidance in the choice of transportation alternatives, accommodations, and other travel services. The 7,000 members of the American Society of Travel Agents, Inc., who display the ASTA insignia in their advertisements and offices, support high ethical standards of conduct in the sale of travel. There is no extra charge for their services, unless you ask for extraordinary service or cancel a trip after funds have been expended for long-distance calls or telegrams. An ASTA member will notify you in writing if you will be required to pay any charge in the event a booking is changed or canceled. The agent will help plan the itinerary, will secure the necessary tickets, make hotel and motel arrangements, arrange for car hire, and often extend credit for end-of-the-month billing. He receives a commission from airlines, railroads, steamship companies, hotels, motels, and car hire agencies. Some companies find it more efficient to work through a travel agent exclusively, especially for foreign travel.

Trip Information to Collect.   Before contacting the company travel reservations office, a travel agent, or the transportation carriers and hotels direct, compile the following information.

1. Destination plus any intermediate stops.

2. Probable date of departure, specific date(s) of arrival at business appointment(s), and date of return.

3. Desired method of travel.

(a) Type of service: by airplane, first-class or tourist; by train, roomette (one person), drawing room (up to three), compartment or bedroom (one or two); by ship, first-class or tourist and type of stateroom.

(b) Drive-yourself or chauffeur-driven car.

(c) Company-owned or chartered airplane.

4. Mode of transportation desired at each stop on the trip.

(a) Automobile rental: make of car, standard or automatic shift (especially important for one driving in a strange city or country), insurance coverage, credit cards available, need for maps of city or country, and desired delivery and return site(s).

(b) Local taxis, buses, or chauffeur-driven cars.

(c) Helicopter service, if available.

5. Overnight accommodations desired.

(a) Hotel: preference or location in city, type and number of rooms, floor preference, room location (proximity to conference attendees, travelers in same party, or exhibit rooms), special furnishings or telephones.

(b) Motel: location in or near city, type and number of rooms, floor and room location preference, special furnishings or telephones, motel facilities preferred (restaurant, bar, entertainment, swimming pool), proximity to other businesses (banks, telegraph office, pharmacy, and so on).

Itinerary. From the trip information compiled and from schedule and accommodation information received from the travel reservations office or some other source, a tentative itinerary is drawn up and approval secured, if necessary. The items and notes on the trip plans should be sorted in chronological sequence by the day and time each will occur. List and describe each item in order. The usual itinerary covers *when* the traveler will go, *where*, and *how*. It may also serve as a daily appointment calendar and contain helpful reminders. Include transportation and hotel reservations; appointments and personal appearances; and reminders of any details to be carried out by the traveler during the trip, such as last-minute ticket validations, confirmation of reservations, and appointments that must be reconfirmed on arrival. Sufficient copies of the approved itinerary should be made for supervision, the traveler's family, and any other person who might need to contact him while he is away. The itinerary format in Figure 12-15 is suggested.

Other Preparations for the Trip. To assure a pleasant trip, a travel package should be made that contains the following items.

1. Copy of ITINERARY.

2. TICKETS (check for conformance to itinerary).

TRAVEL ORDER

T.O. No. _____
Issued _____
Date _____

Employee no. _____ Name _____

Department _____

Is authorized to proceed from (origin) _____

to _____

via commercial air( ) rail( ) personal car( ) other( ) One way _____ Round trip _____

From _____ To _____ Per Diem Rate _____

Rented car authorized at _____

Travel advance

Cash $ _____ Checks _____ @ $ _____

Personal transportation costs _____
Company transportation costs _____
Estimated total advance _____
Estimated car rental _____
Total Estimated Trip Costs _____

	Distribution of Costs	
Dept.	Work %	W.O. & %

Total _____

Figure 12-14 Travel authorization form.

The form contains the following labeled fields:

Approved signatures

Traveler — Department — Administration

Places to Be Visited	Purpose of Visit	Dates	Persons to Be Visited

Miscellaneous Information

```
            Itinerary for Mr. Clarence C. Dotson
                      March 18-26, 19--
     Los Angeles--Dayton--Washington, D.C.--Los Angeles


     Monday, March 18 (Los Angeles to Dayton)

         8:45 a.m.      Leave Los Angeles on TWA, Flight 24
                        International Airport.

         3:35 p.m.      Arrive Dayton Airport. Hourly air-
                        port limousine service available
                        ($1.50). Reservations at Stratford
                        Motel. Single with bath, TV, and
                        typewriter. Address: 1012 Express-
                        way West.

                        Call Major Dodger (326-6666) to re-
                        confirm 8 a.m. Tuesday appointment
                        and pick-up by Government car at
                        7 a.m.

         6:30 p.m.      Dinner meeting with Mr. Alpha and
                        other officials of ABC Corporation
                        at Nikabob Restaurant. Company car
                        will call at motel at 6:10 p.m.

     Tuesday, March 19 (Dayton-Wright-Patterson)

         7:00 a.m.      Government car will arrive at motel
                        for trip to WPAFB.

     (Complete in detail)
```

Figure 12-15   Suggested form of itinerary.

3. MONEY (cash and/or traveler's checks).

4. Copies of WIRES OR LETTERS CONFIRMING HOTEL RESERVATIONS.

5. Blank TRAVEL EXPENSE WORK SHEETS.

6. Copies of PERTINENT CORRESPONDENCE and other material needed for the transaction of business, placed in clearly marked folders.

7. If applicable, INVENTORY OF HAND-CARRIED CLASSIFIED MATERIAL.

8. A briefcase or portfolio large enough to hold the material accompanying the traveler and additional items to be picked up during the trip.

9. Stamps and stationery items.

10. Company telephone directory or list of key personnel and company sales or product brochures and annual report, if needed for distribution.

Expense Reports. *Government Requirements.* The 1962 Revenue Act requires that complete and accurate records be submitted to support tax-deductible items in an expense account. Adequate records and substantiation are both necessary. For a full explanation of the U.S. Treasury Department laws, see the Internal Revenue Service Publication #463, "Rules for Deducting Travel, Entertainment and Gift Expenses." The following records must be collected by the business traveler.

1. A diary, account book, or similar summary of travel and entertainment expenses.

2. Receipts, itemized paid bills, and similar statements for single items exceeding $25. Exceptions:

(a) Receipts for travel expenses over $25 are required only when readily available, as for air travel.

(b) A canceled check is not acceptable. If a bill or voucher is not available, other evidence may have to be presented.

(c) Receipts for lodgings are required regardless of the amount unless their cost is covered by a per diem allowance of $25 or less.

Each receipted bill should contain the following data: (a) the amount of the expense; (b) the date the expense was incurred; (c) the place the expense was incurred; and (d) the nature of the expense. The diary and supporting records must be kept for three years after the due date for the tax return that the records support. Records must show the business reason for travel or the nature of the business benefit derived or expected as a result of the travel. The daily cost of breakfast, lunch, dinner, and other incidental travel expenses can be listed together as "meals, gasoline, and taxi fares." If the firm pays directly for transportation, such costs do not have to be included in the record. If the trip, however, is charged to the firm through a credit card, transportation costs must be reported.

Entertainment expense records for business or tax purposes should include the following information.

1. The cost of each entertainment.

2. The cost of incidental items, such as taxi fares and phone calls, which may be aggregated on a daily basis.

3. The date of entertainment. If it directly precedes or follows a business discussion, include the place, nature, and duration of the discussion.

4. The name, address or location, and description of the type of entertainment, such as dinner and/or theater, if these facts are not apparent.

5. The business reason or business benefit derived or expected.

6. The name, title, and occupation of the person entertained to establish his business relation to the host company.

7. When entertaining a group of associates, refer to the group as "five officials of ABC Corp." instead of listing each name.

The record of business gifts should include the cost of the gift to the taxpayer, the date of the gift, and the business reason for the gift or the nature of the business benefit derived or expected from it. The recipient's occupation, title, or other data showing his business relation to the donor must be given. Names are not needed for relatively inexpensive sports tickets given to many people—only a general description of the recipients. For season tickets, each use should be treated as a separate gift and the cost of the ticket prorated.

Company Travel Policies. Most companies establish travel policies for control purposes. Travel orders (Figure 12-14) are usually required as authorization for all business trips in excess of 100 miles from the traveler's work location, and for any trip that requires overnight accommodations. Other policies concern class of carrier or hotel accommodations, per diem allowance, reimbursable expenses, classified trips, removal of company property, attendance at professional meetings, and foreign travel.

Class of carrier or hotel accommodations policies are established partly to uphold the company image and partly to control costs. Usually a first-class flight is arranged if any part of the flight will be during nonworking hours. A tourist flight is normally arranged if the complete flight will take place between eight and five o'clock. When travel is by train, a first-class roomette accommodation is normally arranged. Many companies patronize hotels in cities around the nation with whom efficient working relationships have been established. In order to establish this long-term association, the hotels may offer special prices and services.

A per diem allowance is normally paid to the traveler on company business to cover expenses for hotels, meals, and tips. The traveler receives full per diem for all days between the first and the last day of the trip. On the day of departure and the day of return, per diem is figured by dividing the day into quarters. Figure 12-16 shows how to determine the amount of per diem to allow. A time allowance to and from the airport or terminal should be added to departure and arrival times. If the company prepays or charges the hotel accommodation, the per diem allowance ranges from $10 to $20. If not, the allowance may be as high as $40 a day.

All reimbursable expenses are entered on the expense report (Figure 12-17), which is normally due within five working days after the traveler returns. A statement of expenses incurred by the traveler is an authorization to credit those expenses to the travel funds advanced to him. The following expenses are normally allowed by most firms.

Day of Departure

Figure 12-16   Determining per diem allowance.

1. Excess hotel. Half of the traveler's per diem is allotted for the hotel. A reasonable hotel charge in excess of this amount is reimbursable, unless the room is shared by any member of the traveler's family.

2. Communications. Business phone calls or telegrams are reimbursable and are itemized if charges are $1 or more. Tolls less than $1 are noted without explanation.

3. Auto expenses. Parking fees, bridge or road tolls, and so on may be included on expense records.

4. Gas for a rented car. Normally receipts for gasoline are turned in to the car rental agency and a cash refund is obtained. If, however, they have not

TRAVEL EXPENSE REPORT

Audited by: _____
Approved by: _____

NAME _____ No. ___ Page _____

DEPARTMENT _____ Ext._____

Purpose of trip _____

Method of travel (be specific) _____

Transportation furnished by _____

Departures and arrivals (date and hour) _____

_____

Date								Total
Room plus tax (attach receipt)								
Breakfast plus tip								
Lunch plus tip								
Dinner plus tip								

Additional Expenses **TOTAL**

Date	Expense Description	Amount	Date	Expense Description	Amount
	Total Room and Meals			Total Forward	
	Total Forward			Total Expenses	

Traveler Account Balance

Due Co. from last report _____   Due Emp. from last report _____
Cash received _____   Expenses paid _____
Due Emp. at end of period _____   Cash returned to Co. _____
_____ _____   Due Co. at end of period _____
Total _____   Total _____

I Hereby Certify That All Expenditures Were Necessary Expenses.

Signature _____

Department _____

Employee No. _____

Accounting Department Use Account Distribution	Amount

Subject to Withholding Tax   Yes ☐   No ☐

Approved _____   _____

Department Head   Company Executive

Figure 12-17 Travel expense report.

been given to the car rental agency, the receipts are attached to the expense report and the amounts entered and itemized.

5. Excess baggage. Charges for excess baggage required for business are reimbursable.

6. Registration fees. Most companies pay the fees for attendance at professional meetings.

7. Traveler's checks. When traveler's checks are purchased by the traveler, reimbursement is allowed for the charge covering the amount of the original travel advance. Receipts are asked for.

8. Luncheon or banquet. Normally, the cost of a scheduled luncheon or banquet in connection with a professional meeting is reimbursable in the amount that exceeds the traveler's per diem allowance for that meal.

9. Valet and laundry service. Reasonable costs of laundry and valet service incurred on a trip are allowed by many companies. If the charges are not shown on the hotel bill, a separate receipt is required.

10. Purchase of technical material. Many times the purchase of technical material pertinent to the company's business is reimbursable.

11. Shipping documents. If it is not possible to use the mailing facilities of one of the company's offices, the cost of shipping documents or materials is reimbursable if a receipt is obtained.

12. Secretarial services. The costs of secretarial services are reimbursable.

13. Entertainment. The costs of entertainment are usually reimbursable only if prior approval has been obtained by the traveler. Social hours, cocktail parties, and so on are normally not reimbursable expenses.

Classified Trip Requirements.   Companies that work with classified government information usually construct a special form to be completed by a traveler to a secured facility to discuss classified information (Figure 12-18). The classified-trip-information form may include a space for the name of the originator of the trip as the person best informed about the nature of and need for the trip. Clearances must be obtained for the traveler to visit secured facilities. Permission is necessary for the removal of classified documents from the company premises, if the traveler needs to take these with him. Many companies, if possible, mail the classified material to the destination beforehand. If time does not permit mailing it ahead, an inventory of hand-carried classified material is prepared and special locked containers are used for its transport.

Attendance at Professional Meetings.   Most companies establish precise policies regarding the attendance of employees at professional meetings. A request form (Figure 12-19) is filled out and submitted well in advance of the meeting (three weeks to a month) for approval. After approval is obtained, the usual travel procedures are followed if the meeting is more than 100 miles from the company.

CLASSIFIED TRIP INFORMATION

Trip originator _____ Dept. _____ Date _____

Traveler(s) name in full	Emp. No.	Type of clearance	Clearance No.	Places to be visited		
				A	B	C
1.						
2.						
3.						
4.						
5.						

	Date of visit	Places to be visited (complete address)	Persons to be visited (name and title)	Purpose of visit and project number
A			Informed of visit?__	
B			Informed of visit?__	
C			Informed of visit?__	

Approved by _____ _____
Signature   Name and Title (Please type)

Figure 12-18 Form for trip involving discussion of classified information.

REQUEST FOR AUTHORIZATION TO ATTEND PROFESSIONAL MEETING

Name of professional organization _____ Date of request _____

Date(s) of meeting _____ Place of meeting _____

Date(s) of meeting _____ thru _____ Duration of visit at meeting, excluding travel time _____

It is requested that the following personnel be authorized to attend the above meeting for the reasons stated:

Name(s) of Personnel	Date Employed	Job Class	Emp. No.	Dept.	W.O. No.	Member?	Present Paper Yes	No	Business Trip Info. Dates, Incl. Travel Time	Location	Acct.	Cost per Person
1.												
2.												
3.												
4.												
											Total Cost	

Justification: Originating unit

Comments: Executive office

REQUEST SHOULD BE SUBMITTED THREE WEEKS IN ADVANCE. IF TRIP IS CANCELLED, NOTIFY THE EXECUTIVE OFFICE.

Requested by: _____   Approved, with exceptions as noted above:

         Department Head   Executive Office _____

Return copy to: _____   Date _____

Figure 12-19   Request form for attendance at professional meetings.

477

Use of Company or Personal Automobiles.　When an employee uses either a company car or his own on company business, authorization is secured before the trip is made. A special form requesting permission is completed and approved (Figure 12-20). A complete record of trip expenses is kept. For a single trip, a record of expenses is entered on the approved request form and presented to the cashier for reimbursement. An employee using his own car over an extended period submits itemized trip expenses at the end of a specified time or at the end of each month (Figure 12-21). When an employee

AUTOMOBILE TRAVEL ON COMPANY BUSINESS
(Single trip—personal car or company car)

Name	Dept. & Clk. No.	Date of trip	Approved by

IF A COMPANY CAR IS USED, MAKE ENTRIES HERE

Company Car No.	Time out	A.M. P.M.	Mileage in _____
Driver's License No.	Time in	A.M. P.M.	Mileage out _____
			Total miles _____

IF A PERSONAL CAR IS USED, MAKE ENTRIES HERE

Trip approval	From	To	Mileage only	Flat amount for specific trip
		☐ Round trip ☐ One way		

Other auto expense _____

PETTY CASH VOUCHER	Accounting distribution			
Received the sum of $ _____ as reimburse-ment for the trip shown above.	Dept.	Account	Order	Amount
Requested by _____				
Received by _____				
Approved by _____				

Figure 12-20　Reimbursement form for single trip using either company or personal car.

USE OF PERSONAL CAR EXPENSE RECORD

Use this form for more than one authorized trip a week by personal car. Use Form 000 for single authorized trips by personal or company car.

Name

Dept. &
Emp. No.   Date

Social Security No. _____

Trip approval	Date	From	To	Mileage only	Flat amounts for specific trips

Total Miles @ 8¢ | | $

Other auto expense:

$

*Withholding tax $

GRAND TOTAL $

Petty Cash Voucher	Accounting distribution			
	Dept.	Account	Order	Amount
Received the sum of $ _____ as payment for the amount shown above.				
Requested by _____				
Received by _____				
Approved by _____				
*Subject to withholding tax. Yes ☐ No ☐				

Figure 12-21 Example of form used to reimburse employee for use of his personal car on company business.

uses his own car, he is reimbursed at a flat rate, for example, ten cents a mile, plus other allowable expenses, such as parking fees and tolls. Some companies establish flat amounts for reimbursement of specific trips between company buildings and established points. Most policies state that there is no mileage reimbursement from the employee's home to his normal work place and return, or from his home to a closer destination than his normal work place and return. All mileage is paid for a trip from the normal work place to any destination (except home) and return, and partial mileage is paid for a trip to a farther destination than the normal work place and return. Compute partial mileage by subtracting the mileage between home and the normal work place from the actual mileage.

Travel Abroad. Foreign travel policies follow rather closely those established for travel within the United States. Employees who represent the company abroad are probably more carefully chosen, but the usual forms must be prepared and approved. A foreign travel form (Figure 12-22) is used to request authorization for business travel outside the continental United States (Alaska and Hawaii are usually included). After approval is received and the pertinent information gathered, the services of a travel agent are engaged because arrangements for a trip abroad are quite involved.

The travel agent can provide copies of three helpful Pan Am guide books, or they may be secured directly from Pan American Airways. The Pan Am *New Horizons World Guide* contains useful facts about countries all over the world—accommodations; holidays; customs regulations and the documents required; common courtesies and local customs; currency; laundry, cleaning, and medical facilities; entertainment and sightseeing. For those employees who are assigned to a foreign post, the *New Horizons Living Abroad* is a helpful guide to the living conditions in 88 countries. The minutiae concerning everyday living include information about shortages of items that Americans consider necessities and about items that can be bought more cheaply abroad than in the United States. Information may also be found on how to cope with local customs and the special documents to take with you, such as a police certificate of good standing, business letters of recommendation, and a medical certificate. Pan Am's *Passports and Profits* was written specifically for the businessman abroad. It contains up-to-the-minute factual information and authoritative advice on worldwide business customs. Such questions as the proper order of hand shaking after a business conference in Germany and the best time of day to make a business appointment in Paris are answered. More than 40 different categories of specific facts about each business center are included, together with illustrated maps and drawings.

The International Operations Division, Internal Revenue Service, Washington, DC 20025, supplies booklets explaining how to establish residence abroad and how to report income. Such booklets as *Tax Guide for U.S. Citizens Abroad, Fulbright Awards,* and *U.S. Income Tax: Tax Guide*

REQUEST FOR FOREIGN TRAVEL
(To be completed for all foreign visits whether classified or unclassified)

Date

1. Complete name of traveler	2. Is travel necessary and required according to terms of contract now in effect?
3. Job title	YES ☐ NO ☐
4. Current home address	(If yes, state contract no.) _____

5. Foreign languages (indicate whether you speak, read, or write)

6. Is travel for the sole or primary benefit of a foreign government?

Yes ☐   No ☐

7. Will foreign nationals be contacted? Yes ☐ No ☐	8. Will classified information be disclosed to foreign nationals? Yes ☐ No ☐

9. Mode of travel
☐ Commercial airline   Other _____

10. REMARKS. Include purpose of visit in detail indicating highest degree of classified discussion and additional information as required.

11. Departure date from United States:

12. Date(s) of visit.	13. Complete name and address of place(s) to be visited.	14. Person to be contacted.	15. Date appt. made.

Figure 12-22   Company form for travel abroad.

for Small Business are helpful. Any local book store also has a wealth of published material on foreign travel and living abroad.

Passport. A passport must be secured for foreign travel to all countries except Canada, Mexico, and the Caribbean islands, which usually waive the requirements for United States citizens who have a return ticket and some proof of citizenship. To secure a passport, take along a birth certificate (or notarized affidavit of birth vouched for by a relative or person who has known you for a long time), a baptismal certificate, or an expired passport. Two passport pictures should be obtained, front view, two and one-half to three inches square on a white background. A passport is valid for five years; the fee is $12. Application should be made in person at the Passport Division of the Department of State, Washington, D.C., or the Passport Agencies in Miami, New Orleans, Los Angeles, San Francisco, Seattle, Chicago, Boston, New York, and Honolulu. In other cities apply at the Office of the Clerk of a Federal Court. Many countries outside Western Europe require a visa or a tourist card. A travel agent, travel guidebooks, the consulate of the country to be visited, and the local State Department office can supply information about these. It saves time to get visas and tourist cards in the United States.

Health Documents. For reentry to the United States and for entry to most foreign countries, a smallpox vaccination certificate is needed if the traveler has visited a country at the time of a smallpox epidemic. Yellow fever and cholera certificates are required by most countries from travelers who have come from an infected area. The following periods of validity for vaccination certificates are accepted.

Smallpox—not less than eight days nor more than three years old.
Yellow fever—not less than ten days nor more than six years old.
Cholera—not less than six days nor more than six months old.

Typhus and typhoid-paratyphoid inoculation certificates are not required under the World Health Organization sanitary regulations as a prerequisite for admission to a country. They are recommended, however, for visits to some countries. Your physician or travel agent can advise you regarding the need for these shots. The record of inoculations must be entered by the local health authority in the official WHO certificate-of-vaccination form. Forms may be secured from a travel agent, an airline office, the steamship office, or from a doctor.

Travel Funds. Money may be carried in several ways. Traveler's checks may be purchased in $10, $20, $50, and $100 denominations from the American Express Company, and at banks, telegraph companies, some transportation companies, and most travel agencies. A business traveler may also apply for a credit card from the American Express and from U.S. banks that have established international credit. A traveler's letter of credit may be purchased before departure that will be honored at certain foreign banks of which the issuing bank is a correspondent. The traveler is furnished a list of these correspondent banks. Prearranged deposits may be made in foreign banks. Many foreign-based banks maintain local offices in major U.S. cities to facilitate international banking. Some of these are Barclay's Bank of London, Banco Nacional de Mexico S.A., Bank of Montreal, Royal Bank of Canada, Bank of Tokyo, Ltd., and Mitsubishi Bank, Ltd. Your local bank will also be able to help you transfer funds through its U.S. correspondent banks.

Foreign currency may be purchased before one leaves the United States, where frequently one may get a better rate of exchange. However, the traveler should note the total amount of foreign currencies that may be taken into each country. It is a good idea to familiarize oneself with the currency of countries in which one will be traveling. Most travel agencies and transportation companies can supply a currency converter that describes and pictures the various coins and paper used by other countries. A few one-dollar bills should be taken along so that it is not necessary to cash a traveler's check or exchange a large bill into local currency in order to make small purchases in those countries where one plans only a short stopover between planes. They also are convenient when one is paying for baggage handling and the taxi fare upon arrival at one's destination.

The U.S. government urges American citizens to purchase U.S.-owned foreign currency when traveling in Ceylon, Guinea, India, Israel, Pakistan, Tunisia, and the UAR (Egypt). Purchases may be made at the U.S. embassy or consulates in the above-mentioned countries. Sales are made at the official rate of exchange, and no conversion fee is charged. When local currencies are purchased in this way, the dollars stay in the U.S. government accounts, and there is no outflow of dollars to foreign holders. Additional information on doing business abroad may be found in Chapter 14, "International Trade."

13

Financial and Tax Considerations

Every business, large and small, has certain financial and tax matters to handle daily, to keep records on, and to report about to governmental agencies. In this chapter, those areas important to the smooth functioning of a business are presented to assist the businessman to establish reliable systems, to locate additional information, and to set up records that will produce adequate reports.

The material will be of help also to individuals in solving their personal financial and tax problems. And secretaries or assistants who maintain personal business records for an executive and handle minor business transactions for him will find the following sections invaluable.

CONTENTS

13.1	Banking	p. 484
13.2	Credit	p. 496
13.3	Insurance	p. 511
13.4	Securities Transactions	p. 521
13.5	Estate Planning—The Will	p. 536
13.6	Taxes	p. 543
13.7	Social Security	p. 556
13.8	Protection and Replacement of Important Documents	p. 571

13.1 BANKING

Most business men and women are familiar with banking procedures for savings and checking accounts and the need for adequate records of the in-and-out flow of funds. In this section, the services offered customers by most banks are explained, and attention is called to certain factors in savings and checking accounts of which an awareness will minimize losses. Additional information and definitions may be found in the "Dictionary of Business Terms," Section 16.2.

Checking Accounts   p. 485
Cashing Checks   p. 490
Deposits to Accounts   p. 490
Savings Accounts   p. 491
Banking Services   p. 494
Office Cash   p. 495

Checking Accounts.   A company may find it expedient to maintain several checking accounts for special purposes, departments, or subsidiaries. Individuals may also need two or more checking accounts, for example, personal, joint, household, travel, and so on. Accounts should be kept separate and carefully labeled so that monies in and out will not become intermingled. Besides careful labeling, the use of checks of different colors will help prevent errors in the handling of transactions.

Making Out Checks.   It is important that a check be correctly written from both the payer's and the payee's standpoints. The use of check-writers simplifies the writing because the words and figures are automatically entered in the appropriate blanks. There is no assurance, however, that the information on the check is correct; as with all other documents, the check will need to be proofread for accuracy against the original request. A variety of check-writing machines are available that supply automatic totals of the number and amounts of checks written for a specific period—daily, weekly, monthly. There is little chance of raising amounts on machine-written checks. The only opportunities for forgery occur in the signature and the endorsement. Access to the check-writing machine should be closely supervised, and it should be placed in the safe or vault each night and removed during the day only when checks are to be made out.

More care is needed when one is making out a check on the typewriter or by hand, and the following paragraphs point out areas of importance.

1. Date. The date of writing should be used on all checks. An earlier date may be put on a check, if necessary, but usually the date of receipt is the one established for payment, so little advantage is gained. Antedating over a week is frowned on. Postdating—putting a later date on a check—is possible, and the check cannot be cashed or deposited until the date arrives. If money is inadvertently paid on a postdated check, it may be recovered. Checks may be dated for any day of the year, holidays and Sundays included. If a check is received undated, fill in the date of receipt. Cash or deposit checks as soon as possible after receipt, or they may be refused by the bank if too old (stale), or the account may have insufficient funds at the later date.

2. Payee's name. The business or legal name of the payee should be used because this is the name to which the payment is credited and is the one that must be signed as the endorsement. If the check is made out to other than the legal signature, the payee then has to sign the name as written on the check followed by his legal signature. Companies with particularly long names should arrange with the bank for a shortened form and advise customers to use it. Most banks accept abbreviated commercial titles regardless of pre-arrangement, but it is wise to use the correct one in case there are several company names whose abbreviations could be confused.

Do not use titles preceding the name (Dr., Judge, and so on), but follow it with the title of an office (Treasurer, Secretary-Treasurer, and so on) if the person is acting in an official capacity for an organization. If the check is typed, it is recommended that the name be followed by three *** or hyphens, so that other names cannot be added.

3. Amount. The amount of the check should be in both figures and words. The figures after the dollar sign should be as close as possible to it and clearly written as to dollars and cents ($118.32). For even dollars be sure to fill in the zeros ($118.00). Spell out the amount on the next line in this manner.

One hundred eighteen and 32/100---------------Dollars

or

One hundred eighteen and thirty-two/100----Dollars

and

One hundred eighteen and no/100------------Dollars

As the examples illustrate, the line should be completely filled in to discourage the raising of the amount by a forger. The written words are considered correct, if there is a difference between them and the figures. It is also wise to spell out all cents up to nine or place a "0" before the number, e.g., "09/100" or "nine/100."

Large amounts should be written in the fewest words possible. For example, $3,256.22 may be written in the following ways.

Three thousand two hundred fifty-six and twenty-two/100---Dollars

Thirty-two hundred fifty-six and twenty-two/100-------------Dollars

Thirty-two hundred fifty-six and 22/100-------------------------Dollars

The last example is preferred.

4. Signature. The signature(s) should be authorized and on file at the bank. A good ink or ball-point pen should be used for a clear, legible signature. A lead or indelible pencil should never be used.

Changes on the Check. Corrections or changes on a check should be avoided. If a minor one must be made, erase carefully and correct; then ask the signer to initial the correction. Banks usually refuse to honor a check that has been changed, especially one in which the figures or spelled out words have been tampered with. A better practice is to cancel the incorrect check by writing "Void" across the face of both the check and the stub and filing the voided check in the check file.

Endorsements. A check presented for cash or deposit is signed by the payee on the reverse side, preferably at the opposite end from the figures.

The name as it appears on the face must be the one signed first. If it is not the person's legal name or the one on his own account at the bank where it is being cashed or deposited, he will need to follow the first endorsement with a second one. Several types of endorsements may be used.

1. Blank. In a blank endorsement, only the payee's signature is placed on the reverse side. This type of endorsement makes the check *payable to bearer;* therefore, it should be cashed or deposited immediately because if lost it may be cashed by whoever finds it.

2. Special or full. When the payee wishes to have a record of the company or person to whom he transferred the check, he may write "Pay to the order of (name of the recipient)" at the top left of the reverse side of the check. He then signs his name immediately after this special endorsement. The designated person or company must now endorse the check before cashing, depositing, or transferring it. Usually, a bank is the only institution that will accept a check with a third-party endorsement. Merchants and other business-men prefer to handle personal checks and occasionally might take one from the second endorser, if he is known as a good risk. The last endorser is the one who receives the amount shown on the face of the check if the maker's account has sufficient balance to cover it. If not, the last endorser might seek restitution from the endorser before him, to whom he gave credit or cash for the amount of the check.

3. Restrictive. To ensure that the money is paid to a designated person and no one else, the payee places a restrictive endorsement above his signature that states "Pay to (name of designee)".

4. Qualified. If the endorser desires to be relieved of any future liability on the check, he places the words "Without recourse" above his signature before passing it along to someone else. Attorneys frequently use this en-dorsement when transferring payments on judgments or claims to their clients. The client could expect payment only from the maker in such a case.

5. For deposit only. Checks sent through the mail for deposit should contain the words "For deposit only" above the payee's signature. Businesses are permitted to use a rubber stamp as the endorsement. The message in-cludes, besides the deposit statement, the name of the bank, the company, and the account number. The stamp may be obtained from the bank for a small fee.

To Stop Payment. Payment of a personal check may not be stopped by telephone or telegraph, but must be requested in writing by the maker, who also completes the bank's stop-order form. It may be secured by a telephone request but nothing will be done until the signed form is returned. If the stop order reaches the computer before the check is paid, the person who presented it will be notified that payment has been stopped. To speed matters, the check maker should go to the bank and fill out the form there.

Commercial accounts, however, may telephone a request for payment to be stopped. The bank will immediately initiate the necessary paperwork.

Record of Account Transactions. A daily balance of cash in the checking account ought to be maintained by businesses and individuals to avoid overdrawing. Therefore, it is important that a record be kept of all checks written and of deposits made. Maintaining a continuous balance on the check stubs or other forms supplied by the bank is an easy recordkeeping method.

Careful accounting of all legitimate transactions in and out of the account will uncover any irregularities more quickly. Unfortunately, there are a vast number of check forgers here and abroad and it is imperative that companies, and small businessmen in particular, be aware of problems in processing checks. Six principal types of check fraud are used: (1) raising the amount, (2) altering the payee's name, (3) altering the date, (4) counterfeiting existing checks, (5) concocting fictitious checks, and (6) forging signatures of either the drawer or the endorser. Usually, the proof of fraud rests with the person who drew the check. Checks, therefore, should be examined closely.

The Bank Reconciliation. When the bank statement is received after the end of the month, it should be compared with the record of deposits and checks drawn so that errors or omissions on either the depositor's or the bank's books can be corrected. The balance shown on the bank statement rarely corresponds to the balance on the check stubs or the cash-in-bank account. There are always outstanding checks or deposits. In a company, an employee other than the one who makes out checks should prepare the reconciliation as a control function.

Before beginning to reconcile the bank statement, gather these materials: the bank statement with the cancelled checks and other memoranda from the bank, last month's reconciliation statement, the check book or register, and the record of deposits as shown by duplicate deposit slips. The following steps should then be taken.

1. Check the canceled checks and other memoranda from the bank against the statement to ascertain that none are missing.

2. Arrange the checks in numerical order and compare them with the stubs or the entries in the check register to locate those that are still outstanding.

3. Compare deposits with the bank statement to locate any that have not been credited.

4. List the information from the bank memoranda: (a) corrections for errors in deposits; (b) bank charges; (c) automatic collections or payments made by the bank for the account; and (d) other items, such as notice of stop payments or uncollectable checks that have been deposited.

5. Prepare the reconciliation statement as illustrated in Figure 13-1.

(a) Copy the balance on the check book or register for the given date.

(b) List the adjustments to be made to the checkbook balance. When the reconciliation is complete and the bank statement balance agrees with the

ABC Corporation

Bank Reconciliation as of August 31, 19___

Checkbook Balance $6,225.56

Adjustments:
  Less: Bank charges . . . . $ 1.85
           Error in deposit 7/24 . . .   2.65
           Mortgage payment . . . .   375.20   –379.70
  Add: Automatic deposit—rentals
           from 2940 Garfield Bldg 472.50   92.80

Adjusted Checkbook Balance $6,318.36

Add: Outstanding checks #1472 . . .   25.00
                          #1503 . . .   78.90
                          #1504 . . .   10.95
                          #1505 . . .   115.08
                          #1507 . . .   34.00   263.93

Less: Outstanding deposit 8/30 . . . .   125.00   138.93

Adjusted Bank Balance $6,457.29

Balance on Bank Statement $6,457.29

Figure 13-1   Example of a bank reconciliation statement.

adjusted bank balance, these adjustments will need to be entered in the stub record and adjusting entries made, if accounting records are involved.

  (c) Find the adjusted checkbook balance.

  (d) List and add outstanding checks.

  (e) List and subtract outstanding deposits to determine the adjusted bank balance.

  (f) Copy the bank balance from the statement. If it is not the same as the adjusted bank balance, search for errors in the stubs or the register, such as additions, subtractions, items not listed or listed twice, transpositions, or items not picked up from the bank statement. The balance on the bank's statement should agree with the adjusted bank balance.

Cashing Checks.   According to law enforcement agencies, care should be taken when you cash a check for anyone. Most check swindlers appear to be respectable citizens. Here are some suggestions to follow.

Ask enough questions about the check to ascertain that it is genuine before cashing it, and don't let the check casher hurry you.

Get positive identification from the endorser, preferably several with his signature, because driver's licenses and Social Security cards are easily forged.

Refuse to cash checks that show signs of alteration. Recovery can be made only for the original amount of a raised check.

Ask that the check be endorsed in your presence and compare the endorsement with the person's signatures on his identification. Make sure the endorsement agrees exactly with the payee's name on the face of the check. If it is not the same name on the identification, ask the payee to sign his legal name below the first endorsement. Do not cash checks with second or third endorsements nor one with a rubber-stamp endorsement.

Investigate thoroughly if you are asked to cash a check outside of business hours or on Sunday. These are favorite times for the passers of bad checks.

Out-of-town checks should be cashed only for persons whose identity and character are known. Make sure the check is from an existing concern and is drawn on an actual bank.

Be just as careful about cashing what appears to be a bank cashier's or certified check as you would a personal check.

Cash checks for only a few dollars over the price of a purchase.

Because juveniles are not legally responsible, do not cash checks for them unless they and their parents are known to you.

Report to the police forged checks that the bank refuses, and supply all the facts possible to aid them in their search for the swindler.

Deposits to Accounts.   Almost any negotiable item may be deposited in checking and savings accounts. For instance, such items as the following are accepted by banking institutions.

Cash	Money orders
Checks	Promissory notes
Interest coupons	Unused portion of letters of credit
Traveler's checks	Foreign currency and checks
Drafts	

A deposit slip in duplicate listing each item should accompany the deposit. Usually, the totals of coins and currency are listed separately, then each check by its ABA bank number (see Section 16.2), and finally other items. A receipt is given upon request for hand-delivered deposits to checking accounts and to savings accounts if the depositor forgets to bring the passbook. Mail deposits to checking accounts are always acknowledged either by a receipt giving the total or a stamped acknowledgment on the duplicate list of deposits.

Deposits to checking accounts are usually not listed in a passbook but are recorded on the monthly bank statement. If a bank issues a passbook for checking accounts, the deposit is entered as a total only. Deposits to savings accounts are entered in a passbook and the account balance is adjusted to reflect the new total.

Checks to be deposited must be endorsed on the back. Either a rubber stamp or a handwritten "deposit only" endorsement should be used (see "Endorsements," in this section). Peruse checks carefully to see that they are properly drawn and signed. Figures and spelled-out amounts should agree; the date should be that day's date or one that is recently past. Postdated checks or ones with discrepancies are not acceptable to the bank. Before listing a check that indicates "paid in full," refer to the customer's account balance to ascertain that it is for the full amount due.

Interest coupons are collection items negotiable without endorsement and are not deposited to an account until payment is received. A collection teller handles them and they should be entrusted to the bank about a week or ten days before the due date. Often a coupon envelope and a certificate of ownership, supplied by the bank, must be completed for their records. Promissory notes and drafts drawn by a depositor on another person are also handled as collection items and are not credited until paid. The collection teller will handle these transactions and deposit the funds upon receipt.

Unused traveler's checks may be deposited after the owner inserts his name as payee and countersigns them. They are then endorsed on the back in the same manner as traveler's checks that have been accepted as payment on account. They are listed on the deposit slip with other items, such as bank drafts and money orders.

Deposits by mail should not include any negotiable items, such as cash or coupons. These should be taken to the bank or sent by a bonded messenger. The post office prefers not to handle letters with coins enclosed, but will register mail that carries paper money, coupons, or other negotiable paper.

Savings Accounts. Savings accounts, called time deposits, are interest-bearing accounts in which the depositor intends or agrees to maintain a certain balance. Banks, savings and loan associations, and mutual savings banks offer this service to customers.

Interest Paid. Interest rates on deposits tend to fluctuate with movements in the economy. Generally, commercial bank interest rates are from 4 percent on ordinary passbook accounts up to $5\frac{3}{4}$ percent on certificate accounts of less than $100,000 and as much as $7\frac{1}{2}$ percent on larger certificates. Interest rates paid by mutual savings banks range from 5 to 6 percent, depending on the maturity of the account. At savings and loan associations, the regular passbook account with no minimum deposit or term requirements pays an annual rate of 5 percent. Certificate accounts are available from a $100 minimum balance for 90 days to a $100,000 minimum balance for a term

Type	Term	Minimum Balance	Annual Rate	Annual Rate If Compounded Daily
Passbook	One day	$1.00	5.00%	5.18%
Certificate	90 Days	$100	5.25%	5.38%
Certificate	1-2 Years	$1,000	5.75%	5.92%
Certificate	2-5 Years	$5,000	6.00%	6.18%
Certificate	1 Year	$100,000	6.50%	6.79%

Figure 13-2   Interest rates paid by most savings and loan associations on passbook and certificate accounts.

of one or more years. Figure 13-2 lists the rates of interest, minimum balances, and term requirements for the several accounts offered by a typical savings and loan association.

Insurance of Savings Accounts.   The insurance provisions of the Federal Savings and Loan Insurance Corporation and the Federal Deposit Insurance Corporation (for commercial banks) are in substantial conformity as to the insurance of accounts. All types of savings accounts in an insured institution are insured, whether regular passbook, certificate or bonus, installment or systematic savings, or other forms of withdrawable accounts. The basic insured amount for each saver is $20,000. A person may, under certain circumstances, hold or have an interest in more than one separately insured account in the same institution. As illustrated in Figure 13-3, a family of two may maintain as much as $100,000 on a fully insured basis; a family of three, $200,000; and a family of four, $280,000. Legal title to the funds in the accounts is not the determining factor of insurance coverage, but it is the interrelations of individuals and joint account ownership. Of the nine possible ownership groups, four are basically personal account ownerships and five are entity account ownerships held by corporations, partnerships, and other entities. The nine ownership groups are as follows.

Single ownerships
Joint ownerships
Revocable trust ownerships
Irrevocable trust ownerships
Decedent estate ownerships
Corporation ownerships
Partnership ownerships
Unincorporated association ownerships
Public unit ownerships

Revocable and irrevocable trust accounts contain insurance provision for each beneficiary's interest to $20,000. The $20,000 maximum insurance for all other accounts listed above is applicable to each insured account in each

FOR A FAMILY OF TWO			
Individual accounts	Man (or child)	Individual	$ 20,000
	Wife (or child)	Individual	$ 20,000
Joint tenancy accounts	Man and wife (or child)	Joint	$ 20,000
Testamentary revocable trust accounts	Man	Trustee Wife	$ 20,000
	Wife	Trustee Man	$ 20,000
	Parent	Trustee Child	$ 20,000
		Total	$80,000 to $100,000

FOR A FAMILY OF THREE			
Individual accounts	Man	Individual	$ 20,000
	Wife	Individual	$ 20,000
	Child	Individual	$ 20,000
Joint tenancy accounts	Man and wife	Joint	$ 20,000
	Man and child	Joint	$ 20,000
	Wife and child	Joint	$ 20,000
Testamentary revocable trust accounts (for spouse-child-grandchild)	Man	Trustee Wife	$ 20,000
	Man	Trustee Child	$ 20,000
	Wife	Trustee Man	$ 20,000
	Wife	Trustee Child	$ 20,000
		Total	$200,000

FOR A FAMILY OF FOUR			
Individual accounts	Man	Individual	$ 20,000
	Wife	Individual	$ 20,000
	Child #1	Individual	$ 20,000
	Child #2	Individual	$ 20,000
Joint tenancy accounts	Man and wife	Joint	$ 20,000
	Man and child #1	Joint	$ 20,000
	Wife and child #2	Joint	$ 20,000
	Child #1 and #2	Joint	$ 20,000
Testamentary revocable trust accounts (for spouse-child-grandchild)	Man	Trustee Wife	$ 20,000
	Wife	Trustee Man	$ 20,000
	Man	Trustee Child #1	$ 20,000
	Wife	Trustee Child #1	$ 20,000
	Man	Trustee Child #2	$ 20,000
	Wife	Trustee Child #2	$ 20,000
		Total	$280,000

Figure 13-3 Savings account ownerships that qualify for maximum insured savings.

insured association without regard to the accounts in any other insured association. In the case of an association having one or more branches, the main office and all branch offices are considered as one association.

Banking Services.   Most banking institutions offer their customers the following services.

Appliance and furniture financing either through the dealer or with a personal loan.

Automobile financing for the purchase of a new or used car.

Automobile loans on a car to refinance an existing contract or to buy another one.

Boat financing for boats of all kinds, outboard motors, boat-carrying trailers, and other equipment.

Business loans for large or small businesses—with sound commercial, industrial, and agricultural purposes—on a secured or unsecured basis, for short- or long-term periods.

Checking accounts.

Check reserve accounts, which protect the checking account holder up to a predetermined sum in case the account is overdrawn.

Christmas club accounts.

Collateral loans on marketable stocks and bonds, warehouse and field warehouse receipts covering readily saleable merchandise, assigned accounts receivable, or other security.

Collection services, such as interest and principal collected for customers on notes and other obligations. Drafts collected for shippers, and documentary drafts discounted.

Data-processing services for small businesses and professional people, such as doctors, dentists, and lawyers. The data-processing department of the bank is able to take care of professional billing, customer billing, payroll, accounts payable, installment loans, and many other collection and accounting chores.

Escrow service, in which the bank acts as impartial intermediary between buyer and seller to hold funds and documents under instructions pending completion of a real estate or other transaction.

Farm loans, such as those for crop and livestock production and marketing, and the purchase of farm lands, buildings, machinery, and other equipment.

Insurance premium financing, which eliminates the paying of insurance premiums in a lump sum and enables one to take advantage of reduced premiums on longer-term policies. Monthly payments are arranged.

International banking services, which include the buying and selling of exchange, sending remittances abroad, issuing commercial and travelers' letters of credit, handling and financing of import and export transactions, and maintaining overseas offices to assist the American businessman.

Investment services, which include the buying and selling of federal, state, and municipal bonds; the executing of customers' orders for the purchase or sale of other securities; and the supplying of monthly records of transactions.

Mail banking for both savings and checking accounts with postage-paid envelopes provided.

Money orders made available up to $250 for a small fee and cashier's checks issued for larger amounts.

Personal loans arranged for depositors and nondepositors for almost any purpose, repayable in easy-to-budget monthly installments.

Property improvement loans to modernize, enlarge, or repair homes, apartment houses, stores, farm buildings, or any other property. Usually no collateral, endorsers, or down payment is required, and persons in all types of jobs are eligible. In many cases, repayment is extended to three years or longer.

Real estate loans for buying, building, or refinancing homes, apartment buildings, and other income property.

Safe-deposit boxes for the safekeeping of valuables in a guarded, fireproof vault. Only persons whose signatures are on file have access to the box. A yearly fee may be charged or the use may be a free service of the bank or association.

Savings accounts paying interest rates, which are compounded either daily or quarterly.

Traveler's checks available for purchase.

Trust services in which the bank acts as executor, guardian, trustee, transfer agent, registrar, and in other fiduciary capacities for individuals and corporations, and the management of securities and properties as required in estate matters.

Vacation club accounts.

Office Cash.   A petty cash fund is set up in most offices and entrusted to a cashier, a receptionist, or a secretary to administer. This fund allows for payments in cash for small items such as messenger service, stamps, postage-due mail, supplies, and other incidental expenses. A voucher system is used to process these transactions. A form such as the one in Figure 13-4 is prepared and signed by the person in the office who is authorized to approve the expenditure and the person receiving payment. Any bill, receipt, or other paper pertaining to the transaction is attached to the voucher. The petty cash fund also operates as an emergency loan fund for employees. Whenever cash is borrowed, an IOU for the amount should be placed in the petty cash box, and the keeper of the box should see that it is reclaimed within a reasonable time.

The worker handling petty cash should always have cash and vouchers totaling the amount of the fund for which he or she is responsible. In a small office the sum may be $10 and in large offices as much as $100. When the

```
┌──────────────────────────────────────────────────────────────────┐
│                   SAMUEL H. JONES COMPANY                          │
│                     Petty Cash Voucher                             │
│                                                                    │
│    Date  _____                      No.  _____             │
│                                                                    │
│    Paid to _____ , $ _____        │
│                                                                    │
│    For    _____       │
│                                                                    │
│           _____       │
│                                                                    │
│    Approved _____    _____       │
│                                       Payment Received             │
└──────────────────────────────────────────────────────────────────┘
```

Figure 13-4   Petty cash voucher.

cash is depleted, the worker takes the signed vouchers to the accounting department or the bookkeeper and receives in return for them a check or cash to replenish the fund to its maximum amount. The accounting records for the petty cash account are maintained by the accounting department from the vouchers.

13.2   CREDIT

Credit purchases by 50 million or more Americans using approximately 3,000 different types of credit cards present certain problems to both the consumer and the retailer. Each one should understand how the government attempts to protect the consumer by requiring a meaningful disclosure of credit terms. The following credit areas are discussed in this section.

Responsibility of Businesses Under the Consumer Credit Protection Act   p. 496
Business and Personal Use of Credit   p. 500
Credit Information   p. 507
Fair Credit Reporting Act   p. 509

Responsibility of Businesses Under the Consumer Credit Protection Act.   Any company or merchant that does not collect the full amount of a sale in cash is considered a lender. Thus he is required to comply with the law if he charges the customer for credit. However, he is excluded from compliance if payment in full is required in four or less installments and there is no finance or other charge for using the deferred payment plan. Under the Truth-in-Lending Act, the merchant must inform customers of all direct and indirect costs they have to pay when buying on credit. Also, customers are to be told the terms and conditions of credit arrangements. The customer will then be able to compare the cost of credit among different sources and shop more effectively for the best buy.

Truth-in-Lending Act.   A detailed explanation of the Truth-in-Lending Act and Regulation Z, which implements it and covers exactly what must be disclosed in writing to the customer when credit is extended, arranged, or just offered, may be found in *What You Ought to Know About Federal Reserve Regulation Z—Truth-in-Lending.* To secure a free copy, write to the Board of Governors of the Federal Reserve System, Washington, DC 20551. Additional references that should be consulted are

> *Understanding Truth in Lending.* Small Marketers Aids No. 139, Small Business Administration, November 1969. Free. Washington, DC 20416.
>
> *Truth in Lending, Regulation Z: Annual Percentage Rate Tables,* Vol. 1. 1969. $1.00. Board of Governors of the Federal Reserve System, Washington, DC 20551.
>
> *What You Ought to Know About Truth in Lending,* 1969. $2.00. International Consumer Credit Association, 375 Jackson Ave., St. Louis, MO 63130.
>
> *Truth in Lending: Understanding the New Consumer Credit Rules,* 1969. $2.00. Commerce Clearinghouse, Inc., 4025 W. Peterson Ave., Chicago, IL 60646.
>
> *Truth in Lending: Regulation Z: Annual Percentage Rate Tables,* 1969. $2.50. Commerce Clearinghouse, Inc., 4025 W. Peterson Ave., Chicago, IL 60646.

The two most important items to be disclosed to the consumer are the finance charge and the annual percentage rate. The finance charge is the total of all the costs that must be paid for obtaining credit, either direct or indirect. Included are interest, carrying charges, costs of insurance premiums (under certain circumstances), and the cost of the appraisal or investigation reports required to complete the sale, as well as similar fees. Costs that would be paid even if credit was not granted can be excluded. The annual percentage rate (APR) must be stated as a percentage to the nearest quarter of 1 percent. Figuring the APR for closed-end sales transactions may be greatly simplified by the use of the booklet published by the Federal Reserve Board, *Annual Percentage Rate Tables,* Volume 1. It contains four tables for closed-end credit sales with payment ranging from 1 to 60 months, 61 to 120 months, 121 to 480 months, and 1 to 104 weeks. It may be purchased for $1 from the nearest Federal Reserve Bank or by written request to the Federal Reserve System in Washington.

Open-End Accounts.   Purchases of relatively small value at such outlets as department stores and service stations are usually charged to an open-end account. A two-step disclosure procedure is involved. First, before the new account is opened, the customer is shown a written or printed form that states:

1. The conditions under which a finance charge may be made and the period within which, if payment is made, there is no finance charge (such as "30 days without interest").

2. The method of determining the balance upon which a finance charge may be imposed.

3. How the actual finance charge is calculated.

4. The periodic rates used and the range of balances to which each applies as well as the corresponding annual percentage rate—for instance, a monthly rate of 1 1/2 percent (APR, 18 percent) on the first $500, and 1 percent (APR, 12 percent) on amounts over $500.

5. The conditions under which additional charges may be made, along with the details of how they are calculated. (This applies to new purchases, when charges are added to the account.)

6. A description of any lien (secured interest) that may be acquired on the customer's property—for instance, rights to repossession of a household appliance.

7. The minimum periodic payment required.

Second, the periodic statement (usually monthly) on any account with an unpaid balance of more than $1.00, or one on which a finance charge is made, must include certain information as illustrated in Figure 13-5, a typical statement in use by department stores. It is possible to use other formats as shown in *What You Ought to Know About Federal Reserve Regulation Z.*

Closed-End Credit.   Installment contracts for the purchase of larger items, such as appliances, television sets, and furniture, must also provide the customer with written information. A typical retail installment contract as shown in Figure 13-5 must include certain information on the face of the sales contract above or adjacent to the customer's signature or on one side of a separate sheet that identifies the transaction. In particularly large sales, such as home improvements requiring installation, the customer has the right of rescission or cancellation of the sale within three days. He must notify the merchant by mail, telegram, or any other form of writing by midnight of the third business day following (1) the date the sale was made, or (2) the date the merchant supplied him the required disclosures, whichever is later. The businessman should give the customer along with the disclosure two copies of a notice of the right to rescission and should wait to start installation work, if required, until the cancellation period has expired.

Advertising Limitations and Penalties.   Under the Act, advertising is limited to such terms as "Use our easy payment plan" and "We welcome credit accounts." A specific down payment, installment plan, or amount of credit that can be arranged may be stated only when such terms are *usually* arranged. No specific credit terms may be spelled out unless *all* other terms are stated clearly and conspicuously. Such terms as "No money down" or "Thirty-six months to pay" may not be used unless all other related terms are given.

The Act provides for both civil and criminal penalties. The consumer has the right to sue a merchant who fails to disclose credit information. Anyone who willfully disregards the law is subject to criminal penalties of a maximum fine of $5,000 and maximum imprisonment of one year, or both.

ANY STORE U.S.A.
MAIN STREET–ANY CITY, U.S.A.

(Customer's name and address)

TO INSURE PROPER CREDIT RETURN THIS PORTION WITH YOUR PAYMENT   AMT. PAID $ _____

Transaction Date	Store	Reference Number	Dept. Number	Description	Purchases	Payments & Credits

Previous Balance	Minus Payments and Credits	Balance subject to FINANCE CHARGE	Plus FINANCE CHARGE	Plus Purchases	New Balance

Next Closing Date Is:

Regular account terms—Full payment is due upon receipt of statement.

YOU MAY ELECT TO PAY YOUR ACCOUNT IN FULL AT ANY TIME. THERE WILL BE NO FINANCE CHARGE IF THE NEW BALANCE IS RECEIVED BY YOUR NEXT CLOSING DATE. IF YOU ELECT TO PAY THE MINIMUM PAYMENT SHOWN ABOVE, A SMALL *FINANCE CHARGE* WILL BE ADDED, COMPUTED ON THE PREVIOUS BALANCE, AFTER DEDUCTING PAYMENTS AND CREDITS, AT PERIODIC RATES OF 1 1/2% (AN *ANNUAL PERCENTAGE RATE* OF 18%) ON BALANCES OF *$1000.00* OR LESS AND 1% PER MONTH (AN *ANNUAL PERCENTAGE RATE* OF 12%) ON THAT PORTION OF THE BALANCE OVER *$1000.00*.

Figure 13-5 Example of open-end account billing statement designed to conform with Truth-In-Lending Act.

499

Business and Personal Use of Credit. Sources of loan money are (1) banks, (2) savings and loan associations, (3) consumer finance and small loan companies, (4) credit unions, (5) pawnbrokers, (6) retail stores and automobile dealers when purchases are made, and (7) life insurance companies that make loans on life insurance policies. Most of these sources are readily available to the borrower, but some depend on a person's individual circumstances. Everyone, however, should know how they differ and be able to determine how much a loan from any one of these sources will cost him.

Determining the Cost of Credit. One method of identifying the cost of a loan is to compute the *dollar cost*—merely the difference between the total amount paid back and the amount borrowed or the original price of the purchased item.

Another method is to find the *true interest* rate. Under the Truth-in-Lending Act, lenders may no longer mislead the borrower when quoting interest rates or the conditions for borrowing or making purchases on time. Even so, the majority of borrowers generally underestimate finance costs by a large margin. For instance, if you borrow $100 at 6 percent, keep it a year and then repay $106, the true interest rate is 6 percent. But if finance charges are deducted immediately (discounted) and you receive $94 but pay back $100 at the end of the year, the actual annual interest rate is higher than 6 percent because you had the use of only $94 for the year. Or if, in addition, monthly payments are made on the discounted loan, the borrower has the use of only half the total amount over the course of the loan. In this latter case, the true interest rate would be almost double the quoted rate, or 12 percent instead of 6 percent.

The following formula may be used to compute true interest when one is checking the finance charges quoted by the lender. Most loans or purchases on time are presented as a total number of monthly payments of a specified sum of money. Suppose in shopping for a $1,000 loan, you are offered the following alternatives.

	Monthly Payments	Number of Payments
Loan 1	$89.40	12
Loan 2	52.75	24
Loan 3	38.40	36

Using the formula $R = \dfrac{2\,PC}{T(N + 1)}$ where R = the annual interest rate.

$\qquad\qquad\qquad\qquad\qquad\qquad$ P = the payment period in the *year*.

$\qquad\qquad\qquad\qquad\qquad\qquad$ C = the cost in dollars: the total in payments minus the amount borrowed. (In the case of a credit purchase, subtract the cash price of the merchandise from the total you pay—down payment plus all payments.)

T = the total amount borrowed or, on a
credit purchase, the *balance due*
after the down payment.

N = the total number of installments or
payment periods.

to compute the *true interest* rate for Loan 2 where, $1,000 is to be repaid in 24 months at $52.75 a month, P is 12; C is $266 (24 times $52.75 or $1,266 minus $1,000, leaving $266); T is $1,000, and N is 24.

$$R = \frac{2 \text{ times } 12 \text{ times } \$266}{\$1,000 \text{ times } (24 + 1)}$$

$$R = \frac{6,384}{25,000}$$

R = .255 or 25.5%

A borrower under Loan 2 would pay 25.5 percent annual interest. Of the three alternatives, Loan 1 offers the lowest interest rate (13.4 percent).

A helpful interest-calculating chart is available for twenty-five cents (coin or check) from *Changing Times* Reprint Service, 1729 H Street NW, Washington, DC 20006.

Banks and Savings and Loan Associations. Banks and savings and loan associations are anxious to loan to customers and other people who are good credit risks. Most personal loan departments collect their charges as discounts (a certain percentage of the amount collected in advance) or add-ons (a certain percentage added to the sum owed). A depositor of one of these institutions is usually not required to furnish references nor is a credit investigation made. A person not having an account would have to furnish references and his credit standing would be investigated. The minimum repayment period for other than a mortgage loan is usually six months, and the maximum five years. A monthly repayment plan is often used with the balance payable at any time without a prepayment penalty. Many institutions have eliminated late charges, fees or service charges, relying on the interest to cover the expenses of handling loans. Figure 13-6 shows a typical repayment schedule. True annual interest rates run between 8 percent and 18 percent, averaging about 12 percent.

Many banks offer preferred checking-account customers a ready-reserve account from which a predetermined sum may be drawn upon automatically in case the balance in the checking account is depleted. The loan terms for use of this ready credit are similar to the following.

1. A finance charge is imposed on the account consisting of (a) a transfer fee in the amount of 1 percent of each advance made to the account and added to the ready-reserve account balance at the time it is made, and (b) periodic interest as of each monthly statement date in an amount equal to $1\frac{1}{2}$ percent (annual rate, 18 percent) of the balance of the account at the end of the previous cycle date, less all payments made and credits applied during the statement period. Payments of the amount transferred and the 1 percent fee must be made within 25 days of the end of the statement period

Borrow	And repay this monthly amount		
up to	In 60 months	In 30 months	In 12 months
$ 300	$ 6.50	$ 11.50	$ 26.50
500	11.00	19.50	44.50
1,000	22.00	38.50	88.50
1,500	32.50	57.50	132.50
2,000	43.50	77.00	177.00
2,500	54.50	96.00	221.00
3,000	65.00	115.00	265.00
5,000	108.50	192.00	442.00
10,000	217.00	383.50	883.50

Figure 13-6   Typical repayment schedule for a loan from a savings and loan association.

if the borrower is to avoid the imposition of the finance charge mentioned in (b).

2. A minimum payment based on the balance of the account must be made within 10 days after the statement cycle date as follows.

Account Balance at Statement Cycle Date	Minimum Periodic Payment
$ 0.01 to $ 25.00	Balance due
$ 25.01 to $ 600.00	$ 25.00
$ 600.01 to $1200.00	$ 50.00
$1200.01 to $1800.00	$ 75.00
$1800.01 to $2400.00	$100.00

3. In the event the minimum payment is not paid prior to the next succeeding statement date, a late charge is made at the rate of five cents per dollar on the past-due amount, but not exceeding $5.00 per statement date.

4. As security for payment of the balance of the ready-reserve account, security interest, called a banker's lien, is acquired on any property which at any time is in the possession of the bank or on which the bank carries a mortgage or a loan.

Consumer Finance and Small Loan Companies.   Consumer finance companies specialize in small loans to the family. They generally want to know how the applicant for a loan pays his bills, how much he earns, and whether he has a steady income. The local credit exchange is contacted for the applicant's record for prompt payment, which follows a person from community to community. The applicant himself should gather the following information.

1. Is the loan agency licensed by the state?
2. What is the total amount to be repaid?
3. What is the total dollar cost or true annual percentage rate?
4. Are there penalties for late or missed payments? If so, how much are they?

5. What is the amount of the rebate for early repayment?

The contract should be read carefully, and amounts, dates, and terms checked for agreement with the applicant's understanding of the terms. Never sign a blank contract or one with any blank spaces. Obtain a copy of the contract and file it with personal papers for future reference.

Small loan companies are able to negotiate a loan quickly because most of them grant loans on a person's signature alone, not requiring collateral or a cosigner. True interest on the amount owed during the month is quoted. The range is from less than 2 percent a month to $3\frac{1}{2}$ percent, with the majority of companies charging $2\frac{1}{2}$ percent to 3 percent. Thus, the true interest rate varies from slightly less than 24 percent to over 36 percent a year, which must be stated according to Regulation Z. A sliding scale is used: the larger the loan, the lower the interest rate.

Credit Unions. If the employees at your company or the members of an organization to which you belong have formed a credit union, you may borrow from it. A credit union may loan to members only. Members deposit money, drawing interest in the form of dividends, and are eligible to borrow from the fund at a fixed rate, usually 1 percent a month. The highest rate that any credit union may charge according to the 1968 Truth-in-Lending Act is 1 percent a month, which under this regulation must be quoted as 12 percent per annum.

Pawnbrokers. A pawnbroker specializes in small loans that other loan sources wouldn't consider. An item of value, such as jewelry, a watch, or a musical instrument, is given as security until the loan is repaid. The borrower is charged a true interest rate from 2 percent to 10 percent a month (24 percent to 120 percent a year). These loans are not repayable in installments. Approximately, 20 cents to $1 a month is charged for each $10 owed. The pawnbroker has the right to sell the article left with him if the loan is not repaid with interest and charges within a certain time after the debt becomes due. The loan is limited to the resale value of the article, which is often considerably lower than its worth to the borrower.

Retail Stores. Sales or purchase credit is available at many retail outlets through several types of accounts. The regular charge account calls for payment on receipt of the monthly bill or, in a few cases, within 30 days of the date of the bill. If the customer fails to pay on time, service charges may be added (see the terms in Figure 13-5).

Budget accounts are available at some stores. Equal monthly payments are made of the total of the purchases plus finance or carrying charges. A similar type is the revolving purchase account, wherein the customer may make purchases each month up to a certain amount. A specific sum or percentage of the balance of the account plus carrying charges must be paid each month to keep the account revolving. No carrying charge is made if the account is paid in full each month.

Installment purchase contracts, such as conditional sales contracts, are also available for the purchase of appliances, television sets, and other expensive items (Figure 13-7). A down payment is required and the customer agrees to pay off the balance plus finance charges, usually in equal amounts, every month over a period of time. Chattel mortgages, bailment leases, and rental contracts are also available.

Department store revolving credit and revolving car-credit accounts cost approximately $1\frac{1}{2}$ percent a month or about 18 percent a year.

Automobile Dealers. Most automobile dealers prefer to sell cars on the installment purchase plan in order to take advantage of increased revenue through credit financing. Hidden costs in the purchase of automobiles on time should be assessed carefully. The true interest rate on the installment purchase of a new or used car has been known to be as high as 36 percent. The selling of automobiles at big-volume outlets is done on the *shuffle system* by a team made up of a *liner,* a salesman who meets the prospect, sizes him up, and gathers certain information; a *T-O man,* who builds up the deal with more extras, more insurance, longer terms, and so on; a *finance man,* who figures up the take on one deal as opposed to another and adjusts the terms to make up for the trade-in; and a *closer,* who winds up the deal. It may become so complicated that the prospective buyer is unable to assess clearly the terms and the actual cost to him over the life of the contract or the life of the car. The new disclosure laws ensure the customer the receipt of a written contract that he may take with him so that he can study the terms and compute the actual cost of the purchase before closing the deal. He may also decide to contact other sources for an automobile loan. Some insurance companies, some credit unions and most banks make automobile loans.

Insurance Companies. Cash loans to holders of certain types of insurance policies are available from insurance companies. These loans are based on the total or part of the cash value of the insurance, as explained in the policy. Many companies loan up to 95 percent of the cash value of a straight life policy. The true interest rates are from 5 percent to 7 percent and about 4 percent on GI policies. The advantages of a loan on an insurance policy are its low cost and the fact that as long as the policy remains in force the principal need not be repaid until the borrower desires to repay it. The disadvantage is that protection for the beneficiaries is seriously jeopardized while the loan is in effect. Borrowing against an insurance policy, until the loan is repaid, reduces the insurance protection unless term insurance is taken out to maintain the insurance program. Life insurance policies having cash or loan value may be used as security for cash loans from various agencies.

Additional Credit Charges. Many lenders make additional charges on loans for a variety of reasons. A borrower should recognize these as cost factors for the privilege of borrowing money.

1. Investigation fee. Many loan companies charge an investigation fee of $3 to $10. When a lender agrees to lend you $100 at 6 percent plus an investigation fee of $5, the cost of the loan is $11 or 11 percent, if the interest

Seller's Name _____ Contract # _____

RETAIL INSTALLMENT CONTRACT AND SECURITY AGREEMENT

The undersigned (herein called Purchaser, whether one or more) purchases from _____ (seller) and grants to _____ _____ a security interest, in, subject to the terms and conditions hereof, the following described property.

Purchaser's Name _____
Purchaser's Address _____
City _____
State _____ Zip _____

Quantity	Description	Amount

Description of Trade-in: _____

_____

_____

	Sales Tax	
	Total	

1. Cash Price $ _____
2. Less: Cash Down Payment $ _____
3.   Trade-in $ _____
4.   Total Down Payment $ _____ $ _____
5. Unpaid Balance of Cash Price $ _____
6. Other Charges:
   _____ $ _____
   _____ $ _____
7. Amount Financed $ _____
8. Finance Charge $ _____
9. Total of Payments $ _____
10. Deferred Payment Price (1 + 6 + 8) $ _____
11. Annual Percentage Rate _____ %

Insurance Agreement

The purchase of insurance coverage is voluntary and not required for credit. ____(Type of Ins.)____ insurance coverage is available at a cost of $_____ for the term of credit.

   I desire insurance coverage

Signed _____
Date _____

   I do not desire insurance coverage

Signed _____
Date _____

Purchaser hereby agrees to pay to
_____
at their offices shown above the "TOTAL OF PAYMENTS" shown above in _____ monthly installments of $_____ (final payment to be $ _____) the first installment being payable _____ 19__, and all subsequent installments on the same day of each consecutive month until paid in full. The finance charge applies from (date)
_____.

Signed _____

Notice to Buyer: You are entitled to a copy of the contract you sign. You have the right to pay in advance the unpaid balance of this contract and obtain a partial refund of the finance charge based on the "Actuarial Method." [Any other method of computation may be so identified, for example, "Rule of 78's," "Sum of the Digits," etc.]

Figure 13-7   Example of retail installment contract and security agreement.

is paid with the principal at the end of the year. If the interest is deducted in advance and the total principal is paid at the end of the year, the cost of the loan is slightly more than $11 or 11 + percent. If the loan is to be paid back in twelve monthly installments, the true interest rate is twice 11 percent or about 22 percent.

2. Delinquency charge. Another hidden cost when one borrows money involves penalties for failing to make payments within the required time. Credit unions rarely assess such penalties because payments are usually deducted from the member's paycheck. Some states have strict laws, which prohibit small loan companies from making such charges. In most states, however, lenders can exact penalties if payments are not made promptly.

3. Repayment allowance. Should a person repay a loan early, he may forfeit any prepaid interest he might have coming as a refund. Some states do not require lenders to refund any of the prepaid interest. Some banks will voluntarily make refunds; others do not. Some companies refund the prepaid interest but make a special charge for retiring a loan before its due date. Policies regarding repayment of a loan should be discovered before one signs any loan papers.

4. Insurance cost. Small loan companies and installment sales dealers, unless prohibited by law, may require the borrower to buy health, accident, or life insurance in order to secure a loan. A careful analysis of the insurance policy and its premiums should be made before one accepts the loan. It may be possible to arrange for the loan and/or insurance coverage at more favorable rates.

The use of credit life insurance is increasing, especially in connection with mortgages. Credit life insurance insures the life of the time purchaser or borrower for the unpaid balance in the event of death. Many states require that credit life insurance be described and listed separately with its cost in the contract. In some cases, lenders or creditors provide such insurance without extra charge. The person insured by credit life insurance should be the one whose income is paying for the mortgage, the credit purchase, or the loan.

Pointers on the Wise Use of Credit. Obtain a written statement of all terms and conditions of the credit transaction. Find out exactly what you are paying for the purchase or the loan in dollars and in true annual interest.

Before using credit make certain that the extra cost is offset by the advantages of that specific purchase or situation. Be sure that the immediate possession and use of what you acquire is worth the additional cost.

Report at once to your creditor if you are unable to make a payment on time, so that you may make arrangements to protect your credit rating and save penalty costs.

Make the use of credit a part of long-range financial planning in order to maintain a sound relationship between income, investments, and expenditures.

Consult a lawyer if the finance charges and interest rate are more than those stated on the contract. You have the right to sue.

Members of the legal profession, such as the Chicago Bar Association, suggest that a person using credit observe the following policies.

1. Read carefully every paper *before* you sign it.

2. Be sure *all* blank spaces are filled in before signing.

3. Total all the charges and compare them with the *cash* price.

4. Rely on the written word in the contract or note, not on sales talk.

5. Remember that a signed promissory note or conditional sales contract calls for prompt payment. Business reversals, sickness, accident, the loss of your job—these events do not excuse delay in payment.

6. Do not sign anything that is not clear. If the amount is substantial, consult a lawyer. He can be of more help *before* than *after* the document is signed.

7. Check monthly statements for errors, such as overcharges, uncredited payments, irregular finance charges. Computer errors do occur and when discovered should be reported in writing to the company with a clear explanation of the error. Overcharges may be the result of an unauthorized person's using the credit card or of a charge from another account with a similar name or account number. Arithmetical errors are not common, but often credits to the account arrive after the machine billing date and are not picked up by the computer until the next month. Sometimes interest charges are figured by a certain method when in reality another one should be used. For example, the count of the number of days for which interest is to be charged might not agree with the original terms. Any discrepancy between your figures and those on the statement should be checked immediately.

Credit Information.   *Collecting Credit Ratings.*   There are several sources of information regarding a person's or a firm's credit standing that should be consulted and their reports checked against each other before credit is advanced. The best known credit agency for company ratings is Dun & Bradstreet, Inc., which provides information to subscribers on businesses around the world. Dun & Bradstreet rates each firm, indicates the amount of working capital and the net worth, and supplies a credit rating of "High," "Good," "Fair," or "Limited," based on such things as experience of owners, pay record, and location. Depending on the service subscribed for, fees may be as high as $1,500 a year for the United States and Canada service, which includes four volumes listing over 3 million business firms by area, six complete revisions a year to update the information, and 100 credit reports, which provide more detailed credit information on individual companies. For regional service only, the fee of approximately $700 would include six complete revisions of the regional listings and 100 credit reports. In other words, a subscriber may choose a service to fit his needs. International credit information is also available for Latin America and Continental

Europe. For approximately $160 a subscriber to that service may secure 15 credit reports on foreign companies, or he may subscribe for the marketing guides, which list most companies in these areas for fees ranging from $225 to $300. Dun & Bradstreet also provides national and international collection services on past-due accounts as a separate service. For instance, international collection service may be had for $50 a year, plus 20 percent of the amount collected.

Many firms specialize in local credit reporting for subscribers on a yearly or case fee basis. Their addresses and telephone numbers may be found in the yellow pages of the telephone directory under "Credit Reporting Agencies." Other sources of local information are banks that give information on the credit standing of their customers; wholesale firms, which often supply information to competitors in return for similar favors; and the customer's own statement of assets and liabilities and sales for the past year. Credit agencies will secure for a client registered information of recent bankruptcies, assignments, compositions, mortgages and other preferential claims, and court judgments as they are recorded.

Several directories of manufacturers are available, and you should consult them to ascertain that the prospective creditor is actually a going concern and also to locate firms in certain trades with whom you desire to do business. One of the most complete is *Thomas' Register of American Manufacturers,* published annually by Thomas Publishing Company, New York. It contains a list of over 75,000 products with manufacturers' names under each product, arranged by state and city, and a list of the trade names and the trademarks of widely advertised products. *MacRae's Bluebook* (Chicago) is more complete as far as addresses of local distributors and branch offices are concerned than *Thomas' Register* but less complete in detailed information on the company. A classified-materials section and a list of trade names are part of the *Bluebook.* An international source of the names and addresses of merchants and manufacturers in each city within a country is *Kelley's Directory of Merchants, Manufacturers and Shippers of the World—A Guide to the Export, Import, Shipping and Manufacturing Industries,* published by Kelley's Directory, Ltd., London.

Supplying Credit Information. Policies regarding the supplying of customer credit information to other firms should be established by a company and certain personnel delegated to handle all such inquiries.

An employee's credit standing is a personal matter and any inquiries regarding it, including telephone requests, should be directed to the employee. If this is not possible, the personnel manager or someone else with delegated authority, possibly the employee's supervisor, should supply only certain routine facts, for instance, length of employment and job title, after first determining who the caller is and why he needs to know. In some cases, the request may have to be denied.

A secretary should never divulge personal information about her superior (or any other worker) unless she has been given permission to do so. She may indicate his title and approximate length of service with the company, if asked, but should refer the call to her superior for all other information.

Fair Credit Reporting Act. The Fair Credit Reporting Act guarantees the consumer certain rights in the reporting of credit information about him. He may see all the information in his credit file and be informed about the sources of the information. He may find out the names of those who have received employment reports within the past two years and the names of all others who have received credit reports within the past six months. He may review his credit record by visiting his local credit bureau(s) and furnishing proper identification, or he may write requesting a telephone interview. During a personal interview, he may be accompanied by another person of his choice (in addition to his spouse). This other person must furnish reasonable identification, and a signed statement may be required granting permission to the credit bureau to review the file in the presence of someone other than a husband or wife.

Contents of a Credit File. Information accumulated in a credit file includes identity facts (name, address, marital status, social security number), present employment (position held, length of employment, and salary), personal history (date of birth, number of dependents, previous address, previous employment record), credit history (credit experiences with credit granters), and other facts of public record.

Correction of Errors in a Credit File. A re-investigation of questionable items may be requested by a consumer. If an item is found to be inaccurate or can no longer be verified, it will be deleted. If the re-investigation does not resolve the question, a brief statement of about one hundred words may be filed that reports the consumer's side of the issue. The statement, or a summary of it, will be included in any future reports of the file. The credit bureau may be requested to notify those who have received employment reports within the past two years and all others who have received regular credit reports within the past six months of any deletions, changes, or additions of explanatory statements.

Cost to Review a Credit File. The Act provides that a consumer cannot be charged for an interview if within the past 30 days he has either been denied credit because of a credit report from a credit bureau or has received a notice from a collection department affiliated with the credit bureau. The bureau may, however, make a reasonable charge for a consumer interview (plus a charge not to exceed that which is charged to its own customers for furnishing notifications and statements) if a consumer has *not* been denied credit or received a notice from a collection department of the credit bureau. The amount of the charges must be stated in advance.

A consumer is not charged for notifications to previous recipients of a deleted item that is found to be inaccurate or can no longer be verified. Nor is he charged for notification to previous recipients of the addition of an explanatory statement if he has been denied credit within the past 30 days.

Locating a Credit File.   The credit granter who refuses credit must provide the name and address of the credit bureau supplying the report on which he based his decision. If he has contacted credit references directly, he must inform the consumer at the time the credit application is rejected that the consumer has the right to request in writing within 60 days the nature of the information on which the credit decision was based. The credit granter need not disclose the source of his information but must supply sufficient facts with which the accuracy of the information can be refuted or challenged.

File Life of Adverse Information.   Credit and employment records report adverse information on the following situations for a limit of seven or fourteen years:

7 years	*14 Years*
Suits and judgments (or until	Straight bankruptcies
statute of limitations expires)	
Wage earner plans	
Paid tax liens	
Collection accounts	
Accounts changed to bad debts	
Records of arrests, indictments,	
convictions, or other adverse	
information	

None of these limitations apply on credit reports in connection with credit or life insurance transactions over $50,000 or an employment report involving an annual salary over $20,000.

Qualified Recipients of Credit Reports.   A credit report on a consumer may be obtained if it is to be used in one of the following ways:

1. To consider a person for credit.
2. To review or to collect an account.
3. To consider a person for employment.
4. To consider a person for insurance.
5. To comply with a court order.
6. To fulfill a legitimate business need, such as a potential partnership, investment, or lease.
7. To comply with the written instructions of a consumer to a credit bureau to issue a credit report for a legitimate purpose.
8. To satisfy the requirements of a governmental agency that is proposing to extend credit, to collect or review an account, to employ or to insure a person, to make a military security clearance, or to comply with a law that states a person's financial responsibility must be checked.

In all other instances, individuals, companies, and governmental agencies may secure only identifying information from a credit bureau. Such information is limited to name, address, former addresses, place of employment, and former places of employment. Anyone who willfully obtains a credit report under false pretenses can be fined up to $5,000 or imprisoned for one year, or both.

13.3 INSURANCE

Insurance is a means of limiting economic losses by sharing risks with others who face similar risks. Today, one may insure himself and his property against almost any disaster or loss. A businessman should work with an insurance agent when attempting to select adequate coverage so that he will be fully insured at every possible moment. Shifts in inventory, merchandise on hand, construction in process, and the perils of doing business may change from day to day.

In this section the descriptive list of available insurance illustrates how extensive is the coverage. No attempt has been made, however, to present costs because premiums are based on the options selected when the policy is tailored to company or individual needs. Suggestions for safeguarding policies and maintaining records are included. An agent or broker will keep the businessman informed as to insurance needs, will check changes in company circumstances that require added or reduced coverage, will place insurance, will advise on renewals before expiration dates, will send bills for premiums, will cancel policies, will secure returns on prepaid premiums, and will report claims under the policies to the insurance company. But the businessman will need to maintain his own records of premium due-dates, expiration dates, and claims for loss; to receive and check policies for accuracy and safeguard them during their life; and to review the insurance program periodically to make certain that it includes recent changes in personnel, plant, equipment, or other conditions of doing business.

Treated in this section are the insurance topics listed below. Additional insurance options and terms can be found in the "Dictionary of Business Terms," Section 16.6.

Insurance Coverage for Businesses   p. 511
Protection of Policies   p. 514
Insurance Records   p. 514
Personal Insurance Coverage   p. 518

Insurance Coverage for Businesses. Practically any risk may be covered by insurance. Usually, a company purchases a general policy to cover common risks, and adds certain options according to the nature and location of the business. The newer types of policies are portfolio or package plans that extend basic protection against property damage losses on buildings and business personal property and include general liability coverage. Options are added as needed to complete the portfolio or package, which costs less than individual policies providing the same coverages. According to insurance companies, one agent, one company, one policy, and one premium mean better service with flexible premium payments either monthly or quarterly. The following list of business insurance illustrates the extent of available protection against risks.

The basic policy usually provides property coverage for loss or damage by:

Civil commotion
Explosion
Fire
Lightning
Riot
Smoke
Vehicles or aircraft
Windstorm and hail

Broader coverage that may be added as options to the basic policy includes:

Accounts receivable lost or damaged
Burglary, theft, or robbery while closed
Collapse of building
Expense of continuing normal operations
Falling objects
Glass breakage or damage
Interruption of business
Loss of rents
Malicious mischief
Premises burglary and robbery
Property being transported in motor vehicles leased or operated by the insured
Property temporarily off premises
Signs coverage
Sprinkler leakage
Valuable papers and records loss or damage
Water damage
Weight of ice, snow, sleet

The property coverage of buildings also applies to:

All additions and extensions attached to the insured buildings, except outdoor signs
Materials and supplies intended for use in the construction, alteration, or repair of the buildings
All permanent service equipment, machinery, and fixtures on the premises
Yard fixtures
Personal property of the insured used in maintaining or servicing the buildings, including floor coverings; fire extinguishing apparatus; refrigerating, ventilating, cooking, dishwashing, and laundering equipment; shades and outdoor furniture (but excluding other furnishings)

Business personal property coverage includes:

Furniture, fixtures, equipment, merchandise, and supplies on the premises and usual to occupancy of the buildings

Property belonging to others for which the insured is liable
Improvements and betterments to a rented office of the building

Basic general liability coverage insures against the following up to a policy limit.

Bodily injury to others
Damage to the property of others
Liability arising out of the operation of elevators, warehouses, parking areas, restaurants, swimming pools, gift shops, and private garages
The payment of expenses for defending the insured, including lawyer's fees and court costs, if a lawsuit results
The cost of premiums for appeal bonds and bonds to release attachment in such a suit
First aid expenses for others at the time of an accident
Any reasonable expense incurred at the request of the insurance company to attend hearings and trials

Any of the following liability options may be added to the basic general liability policy.

Cameras and musical instruments
Comprehensive general liability
Comprehensive personal liability
Contractual liability
Elevator collision
Employer's nonownership automobile liability
Fine arts
Garage keepers' legal liability
Guests' property–innkeeper's liability
Medical payments
Personal injury
Radium

Businesses may add the following comprehensive crime coverage to the insurance package.

Employee dishonesty—loss of money, securities, or other property.
Loss inside premises—loss of money and securities by destruction, disappearance, or wrongful abstraction within the premises, bank premises, or similar recognized places of safe deposit.
Loss outside the premises—destruction, disappearance, or wrongful abstraction of money and securities outside the premises while being conveyed by a messenger or armored car company, or while in the living quarters in the home of a messenger. Covers other property against loss or damage by robbery while being conveyed by a messenger or armored car company, and against robbery and theft while in the living quarters in the home of a messenger.
Loss due to counterfeit currency—covers counterfeit postal money orders, express money orders, and U.S. or Canadian paper currency.
Depositors' forgery—losses sustained through forgery or alteration of checks, drafts, notes, or similar written instruments drawn by or upon the insured. Coverage applies to the insured's instruments only—NOT incoming drafts, checks, and so on.

The following boiler and machinery coverage is available as an option.

Loss to property arising out of accidents to boilers and certain types of pressure vessels. After payment for damages to property, the remaining limit of liability is applied to expedite the repair and to pay for damages to the property of others. Extended coverage includes additional types of pressure vessels, machinery, electrical equipment, extra expense, use and occupancy (daily or weekly indemnity), consequential damage, and prevention of occupancy.

It is also possible to take out an umbrella liability policy. This is an extra-high, single-limit protection against catastrophe-type losses. It fills many coverage gaps in basic policies. Liability limits of $1 million or more are provided, subject to a deductible.

Protection of Policies. All insurance policies should be examined upon receipt to see that the names of the insured and the beneficiaries are correct. If the coverage is on jointly owned property, both owners' names must be listed. The face value, the terms, and any other typed information should be checked against the original application. The details of coverage and exclusions should be examined to determine that they meet the needs of the insured. Much of this checking can be handled by the secretary, but some of the finer points of coverage should be the responsibility of an officer of the company or the proprietor of the business.

After it is ascertained that all details are in order and that records have been made, the policy should be placed in a safe and readily accessible spot. A safe-deposit box at the bank is the safest storage for these valuable documents. The office safe or locked (fireproof) file cabinet, however, may be used, if the policies must be close at hand for frequent reference.

When the policy has expired or been canceled, it should be placed in storage according to a predetermined retention schedule (see Section 12.1). An old policy may be needed for reference or evidence if claims or possible claims covered by it are pending. Clip to the old policy the form on which a summary of the details of coverage was made when it was issued (Figure 13-8). The information on this sheet will save time when one is hunting for a particular policy; otherwise, each one might have to be unfolded and read.

Insurance Records. The keeping of insurance records cannot be left entirely in the hands of the insurance company or its agent. Even though an insurance agent can usually be counted on to handle most aspects of a client's business, a change in his office personnel, a breakdown in his billing system, or his own prolonged absence from the office due to illness, travel, or emergency could result in oversights and delays in the mailing out of important notices. Consequently, a businessman, company, or individual must keep his own records of payment and expiration dates. If a policy expires or is canceled on the last day of the grace period, insurance coverage ceases. Premiums

INSURANCE POLICY FOR (Name of company or person)

Type	Issuing Company	Amount	Date of Issue	Expiration Date	Details of Coverage	Beneficiary	Amount of Premium— Due Dates	Agent
				Cancellation date:	Exclusions:			

Figure 13-8 Form for recording information about insurance policies.

must be in the office of the insurance company or its agent prior to the due date for assurance of continuation of coverage. Even if a policy has been carried for years with the same company, that company has no obligation to underwrite a loss that occurs after the policy has expired or has lapsed because of nonpayment of the premium.

Tickler File Record.   When the policy is first received, a card for the tickler file should be prepared. The two important entries on it are the premium due dates and the expiration date. It should be placed in the file so that it automatically receives attention a week to ten days before the due date and approximately one month before the expiration date. It may be necessary for the insured to arrange a loan to cover the premium, or the company management might wish to discuss changes in the coverage, the agent, or the issuing company. One need not wait until the expiration date, however, to make an important change. There are many ways to modify an existing policy during its life, and it may be canceled at any time, with prepaid premiums being returned or applied to a new policy.

The card should also contain sufficient information to identify the policy—type, number, issuing company, insured, amount of premium, and where to pay. A typical setup for such a card may be seen in Figure 13-9.

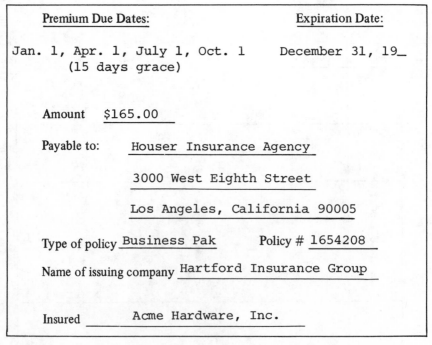

Figure 13-9 Tickler card for payment of company or personal insurance premiums.

Insurance File Record.   A record of each insurance policy should be maintained on a form similar to the one in Figure 13-8. All pertinent details regarding the policy and its coverage can be listed on an 8 1/2" × 11" sheet that will allow interested persons to review the total coverage for that policy. It is important to include a summary of the details of coverage and the exclusions. If the coverage is extensive and it is desired to restrict the information to one page, the executive responsible for the insurance program should indicate to the stenographer the features of the coverage that should be listed. These records should be separated in the files by the company, the subsidiary, or the person insured. Later, the sheet should be attached to the canceled, lapsed, or expired policy when it is placed in storage.

Claims Records.   A loss covered by an insurance policy should be reported immediately to the agent or the insurance company. A claim form or proof of loss will need to be filled out and a duplicate filed with the other insurance records. A detailed explanation of the events leading up to the loss and a description of the items damaged, lost, or whatever should be prepared. This record should be as detailed as possible and probably will contain more facts than the insurance company wants. But writing down this material when it is fresh means that the facts will be more accurate than if one waits until the insurance company requests the information. File the description of loss with the other insurance records and use it when filling out proof of loss and other required insurance forms.

Additional Insurance Records.   Often it is helpful to see the total insurance program at a glance. A list of policies according to type, amount, issuing company, policy number, and yearly premium should be compiled. It could be organized by the type of coverage with sufficient space left between types to allow the addition of new policies under their categories. Canceled, lapsed, or expired policies could be crossed out, and a new list typed only when necessary, such as for a special meeting or when the sheet becomes hard to read.

Another worthwhile grouping of insurance information is a yearly schedule of premiums due. It may be a list by the month or a calendar chart. With many companies and individuals carrying several policies, premiums might all become due within a few weeks or be scattered unrealistically throughout the year. Perhaps the seasonal flow of cash does not coincide with the required cash premium payments. If the payment of premiums as they automatically fall due results in hardship or the need to borrow, the insured should arrange with his agent for a distribution of payments that fits his ability to meet the due dates.

Other records may be compiled, but as the executive, the secretary, or an individual works with the insurance program, he will know best the kinds that should be designed to fit the company's or his own needs. It is important mainly that policy records be kept separate by the name of the insured so that confusion will not arise.

Personal Insurance Coverage.   Insurance on an individual, his family, and his personal property is available for almost every conceivable purpose.

Personal Insurance to Cover Business Risks.   Coverage may be purchased by a professional or prominent person to protect himself against major lawsuits. An excess indemnity policy written around coverage in primary policies provides high-limit personal (and professional, where applicable) liability insurance up to $1 million, $2 million, or $5 million. Merchants, office building owners, processing and servicing firms, doctors, lawyers, and motel and apartment house owners are a few of the types of people who might find such coverage worthwhile.

Corporations, individual businessmen, and partnerships have found it profitable to insure themselves or key members of the firm when death or prolonged illness would create hardships for the firm. For instance, if one of two partners dies, the surviving partner would need funds to buy his partner's share of the business, or he might have to hire someone to take over the duties of the man who died. The death of a key man could be a major problem for a small company, and a life insurance policy would provide money while a new man is being trained.

Business health insurance benefits business and professional men who are unable to work because of illness or accident. Called business overhead or professional overhead insurance, the policy pays overhead expenses, such as salaries, rent, utilities, and other expenses, for a year or more, until the insured is able to return to his practice or arrange to close the office.

Types of Life Insurance.   Straight life insurance is the most widely used of all the types of ordinary life insurance because it provides lifetime protection. Its low annual cost results from the payment of premiums throughout the policyholder's life. A cash value is accumulated on which the insured may borrow in an emergency.

Limited payment life insurance calls for the payment of premiums over a specified period of time and offers lifetime protection. Many people buy a limited payment life policy to be paid up at age 65, and thus eliminate the payment of premiums out of retirement income. Cash values are accumulated.

Term insurance provides temporary protection for a stated number of years. Should the policyholder die during the term, the full amount of the policy is paid to his beneficiary. If he does not die during the term, the insurance protection ends when the term expires. A cash value is not accumulated. The premium is lower than for other kinds of policies because the risk is for a short period of time. Term insurance is designed to meet temporary needs, rather than for use in a family's permanent protection program.

The endowment policy is used to accumulate a certain amount of money within a certain period of time while at the same time providing life insurance protection. If the policyholder lives, the total amount of the policy is paid to him when the endowment matures or comes due. If he dies before the period has elapsed, the full amount is paid to his beneficiary. An endowment

Taken at Age	Straight Life	Limited Payment Life (Paid Up at Age 65)	Five-Year Term (Renewable and Convertible)	Twenty-Year Endowment
15	$14.10	$14.95	$ 8.85	$46.45
16	14.35	15.30	8.90	46.50
17	14.65	15.60	8.90	46.50
18	14.90	15.95	8.95	46.50
19	15.25	16.30	8.95	46.55
20	15.55	16.65	9.30	46.55
25	17.35	18.85	9.35	46.70
30	19.65	21.85	9.40	47.00
40	26.55	31.70	11.60	48.75
50	37.60	54.65	18.40	53.65

Rates shown are approximate premium payments for life insurance protection for men. Because women live longer, rates for them would be somewhat less. Rates would also be lower per $1,000 of protection if policies were purchased in units of $5,000 or $10,000.

Source: *Money Management for the Young Adult,* Educational Division, Institute of Life Insurance, New York, Revised 1971.

Figure 13-10   Approximate annual premium rates for $1,000 of each of four types of ordinary life insurance.

costs more than other kinds of insurance with the same amount of protection. However, it accumulates cash values more rapidly than do other policies. See Figure 13-10 for a comparison of average premium rates for the four basic types of life insurance.

Combination Policies.   The three kinds of combination policies are family income, family, and retirement income. The family income policy includes straight life and term insurance and is less expensive than if both were bought separately. A family is assured a regular monthly income if the policyholder dies during the stated term (e.g., 5, 10, 15, or 20 years), and the full amount of the policy is paid to the beneficiary. The income is paid from the time the policyholder dies until the end of the particular term. If the insured is alive at the end of the term, the family is still protected for the future by the straight life feature of the policy.

The family policy provides insurance on the lives of every member of the family. The breadwinner is covered by a permanent, straight life policy in the largest amount. The dependents are covered by smaller amounts of term insurance. When the children grow up, they can convert the term to permanent insurance, regardless of their health or occupation at the time.

Under the retirement income policy, financial protection is given the family during the years the insured builds savings in a retirement income policy that will provide him with income for life upon his retirement.

Annuities.   Annuities are not life insurance policies. They merely provide for a periodic payment of money to the owner of the annuity contract beginning at a particular time and continuing for life or for the number of years stated in the contract. Units of an annuity may be purchased over a number of years, or an annuity may be purchased for a lump sum.

Types of Health Insurance.   Under a hospital-expense insurance policy, all or part of the costs of hospital room and board are covered. A specific sum is allowed for each day of hospitalization up to a certain number of days. In addition, benefits are provided to meet other hospital charges, such as medication, X-rays, and the use of the operating room.

A surgical-expense insurance policy provides funds to pay for surgical services in accordance with a schedule of fees based on the severity of the operation.

A general medical-expense policy provides for full or partial payment of doctor's fees for office visits or his calls at the hospital or the home. The maximum number of calls allowed for each sickness or injury is set forth in the policy.

Protection against the major costs of serious or prolonged illness or injury is provided by major medical-expense insurance. Almost every expense is covered, even nursing care both during the critical period and during convalescence. Because ordinary hospital and medical insurance often takes care of initial costs, these policies include a deductible clause. A policyholder pays 20 percent to 25 percent of the charges incurred by his illness over and above the deductible amount. This coinsurance feature gives the insured a direct financial stake in using only necessary services during his illness and recuperation. Benefits may run as high as $15,000 or more.

When a person is unable to work because of sickness or injury, the loss-of-income insurance policy provides cash income to replace part of the lost regular income. The amount of income and the length of time for which payments will be continued depend on the provisions agreed upon when the policy is taken out. Generally, there is a waiting period before benefits begin. Thus, premiums are kept down by the elimination of small claims. Benefits are paid regardless of whether an accident or illness is job connected.

Insurance on Personal Property.   Automobile insurance coverage is the most familiar type of insurance on a person's property that not only protects the property but also provides property damage and personal liability benefits. Insurance companies also offer pleasure craft policies that cover damage to the boat and motor and provide watercraft liability insurance for property damage and bodily injury.

A person purchasing or owning a home usually carries a fire insurance policy to cover replacement costs. The latest trend, however, is to purchase a comprehensive homeowner's policy that covers the house and outbuildings, household goods, and personal property against fire, theft, windstorm and hail, explosion, smoke, vehicle damage, aircraft damage, vandalism, and riot. Additional options would protect against ice, snow, sleet, falling objects, glass breakage, collapse, and bursting pipes. A comprehensive policy also pays for additional living expense or rental value while repairs or rebuilding is in process after a disaster, and provides away-from-home coverage of personal property anywhere in the world against all perils covered in the basic homeowner's policy.

13.4 SECURITIES TRANSACTIONS

Many business men and women invest in stocks, bonds, commodities, or mutual funds; and familiarity with the operation of the securities market will assist them to function more efficiently in it. Equally important is adequate recordkeeping, which is vital in order to comply with Internal Revenue Service regulations about reporting profits and losses on income tax forms. Secretaries and administrative assistants should also understand these financial transactions because they are usually delegated much of the recordkeeping and some business contacts with brokerage firms. This section explains buying and selling, defines special terms, and discusses and illustrates proper recordkeeping. Other financial terms are defined in the "Dictionary of Business Terms," Section 16.10.

Characteristics of Bonds   p. 521
Preferred and Common Stocks   p. 523
Stock Exchanges   p. 524
The Over-the-Counter Market   p. 524
Brokers and Dealers   p. 525
Trading Terms   p. 525
Types of Orders   p. 528
Mutual Funds   p. 529
Stock Market Quotations   p. 530
Sources of Security Information   p. 530
Records to Be Maintained   p. 531
Safeguarding Security Certificates   p. 535

Characteristics of Bonds.   Bonds rank ahead of preferred or common stocks in a corporation's capital structure with prior claim to earnings and assets. Payment is guaranteed of (1) a stated amount at a definite future date, and (2) a series of interest payments at a fixed rate, usually semiannually.

The *face value,* sometimes called *par value,* the amount printed on the bond, is the sum of money the borrower promises to pay the holder. The *coupon rate* is the percentage of the face value that the borrower promises to pay in two interest payments each year. The *date of maturity* is the date when the bond becomes due and at which time the borrower pays the holder the face value of the bond.

Bonds may be purchased through banks and brokerage firms, which trade on regulated exchanges and over-the-counter. The market price of a bond is frequently a different value than its face value. Some bonds trade at a premium, or more than their face value (which is usually $1,000); others trade at a discount, or less than face value. Current yield on a bond is the ratio of its interest to its market value and may be different from the coupon yield.

Bond quotations are listed at a percentage of face value. A bond that trades for "100" may be bought for 100 percent of par, or $1,000. One that trades at "84" is priced at 84 percent of par, or $840. The price of a bond quoted at "108½" is $1,085. To compute the current yield on a 5-percent $1,000 bond purchased at "95," divide the price paid into the yearly interest ($50 ÷ $950). The interest on a *registered bond* is sent by the issuing company directly to the holder on payment dates. The holder of a *coupon bond* detaches the interest coupon and deposits it in his bank for collection.

Types of Bonds.   Eleven types of bonds are usually offered to investors by governments and companies in order to raise capital.

Certificates of indebtedness, issued mainly by national, state, or local governments, are unsecured short-term notes with a maximum maturity of one year.

Collateral trust bonds are secured by collateral security, such as bonds, notes, or stock.

Convertible bonds may be exchanged at the option of the holder for other securities of a corporation.

Debentures are bonds without any specific security other than the general assets and credit of the issuing company.

Discount bills are unsecured short-term obligations (mostly for 91 or 182 days) sold by governments at competitive bidding. No regular interest payments are made, but as these bonds are sold for less than face value, the discount represents interest. They are similar to Series E Savings Bonds, which are also sold at a discount and paid off at full face value at maturity.

Equipment trust certificates are issued by railroads and represent part ownership in specified rolling stock and other equipment. The trustee for the equipment trust leases the rolling stock to the railroad and retains absolute title throughout the term of the contract. Title does not pass to the railroad until the last of the equipment trust certificates have been paid off. Most issues run up to 10 or 15 years and mature serially in amounts calculated to reduce the amount outstanding as the underlying properties depreciate in value.

Guaranteed bonds are backed by a party other than the issuer as to payment of principal or interest, or both.

Income bonds are usually issued in reorganizations to holders of defaulted mortgage bonds. Interest payments are contingent upon earnings. Failure to pay interest, except when earned, does not entitle the bondholder to the right to sue. Interest may be cumulative or noncumulative.

Mortgage bonds are secured by a mortgage on property that may be sold to satisfy the debt if interest or principal is defaulted.

Notes, as the term is applied to securities, are short-term obligations of five years or less.

Tax-exempt bonds are usually issued by the state or a municipality and are exempt, either in part or in entirety, from federal and/or state and local taxation.

Special Features of Bonds.   *Callable bonds* (and some preferred stocks) are redeemable at the option of the issuer. Almost all such issues provide for the payment to the holder of a premium over the par value. Noncallable issues cannot be redeemed prior to maturity.

Coupon bonds are payable to the bearer. The title to the bond passes by delivery without endorsement. One receives the interest by clipping the attached coupons as they mature and presenting them to the bank for payment.

Registered bonds have the owner's name printed on the face and cannot be negotiated except by the endorsement of the owner and the transfer on the books of the company who issued the bonds. If the bond is registered as to principal only, coupons are attached, and interest is collected in the same manner as for coupon bonds. If the bond is registered as to both principal and interest, interest payment is made by check at specified times and mailed to the owner of record by the issuing company.

Serial bonds are payable to the holder in installments. A certain amount of the principal matures each year.

Sinking funds contain funds set aside by the company in the form of a fixed amount or a portion of earnings sufficient to provide for the eventual payment of part or all of an issue of bonds or preferred stock. Payments are usually made to a trust company or a sinking fund trustee, and are as binding on the company as interest payments.

With interest is a term applying to most bonds and notes. It means that accrued interest from the last interest payment date must be paid by the purchaser in addition to the price of the bond or the note on the date of purchase. Income and adjustment bonds, however, are traded *flat,* meaning that no accrued interest must be paid.

Yield is computed by dividing the annual dividend or interest by the price. Computation of the *yield to maturity* on a bond takes into consideration the difference between the purchase price and the value of the bond at maturity. This latter percentage return is readily obtained by use of a yield book.

Preferred and Common Stocks.   Companies having preferred stock give certain preferential treatment, except the voting privilege, over the common shareholder to the preferred shareholder. Preferred stocks receive a fixed dividend before any payment can be made on the common stock and also have prior claim against assets in the event that the company is liquidated. Dividends are usually cumulative. Preferred stocks seem, however, to lack the growth element found in common stocks, and do not appear to be a good hedge against inflation. Yet, they are noted for their price stability, and they rank between bonds and common stocks from the standpoint of safety. Market movements in preferred stock are influenced more by factors governing the bond market than by those affecting common stocks. The yields are usually moderately higher than those on bonds.

Common stocks also represent ownership in a company, and the shareholder is entitled to elect directors, to vote on certain other matters, and to participate in the distribution of earnings after all prior claims (bond interest, preferred-stock dividends, and so on), if any, have been met. Common stock shareowners bear the greatest risk but are in a position to reap the largest profits. Most companies reinvest about 40 percent of their earnings into the business; the remainder is available for distribution to shareowners. A regular dividend rate in good years may be increased or extra dividends declared, and in poor years it may be cut or omitted.

Listed in "Dictionary of Business Terms," Section 16.10, are additional terms that explain the many features of preferred and common stock and define the technical terms used by traders in the securities and commodities markets.

Stock Exchanges. A stock exchange provides a meeting place for buyers and sellers of securities. Brokers and commission houses who are members of the exchange do the actual buying and selling of shares of listed securities for their customers. Exchanges do not trade in securities nor do they fix prices. Prices are determined by a two-way auction system. Federal and state controls regulate the functioning of securities markets and the use of credit therein. The exchanges see that these regulations are followed.

In the United States, there are eighteen exchanges:

American Stock Exchange
Boston Stock Exchange
Chicago Board of Trade
Cincinnati Stock Exchange
Colorado Springs Stock Exchange
Detroit Stock Exchange
Honolulu Stock Exchange
Midwest Stock Exchange
National Stock Exchange
New York Stock Exchange
Pacific Coast Stock Exchange
Philadelphia-Baltimore Stock
  Exchange
Pittsburgh Stock Exchange
Richmond Stock Exchange
Salt Lake Stock Exchange
San Francisco Mining Exchange
Spokane Stock Exchange
Wheeling Stock Exchange

The Over-the-Counter Market. The unlisted, off-board, or over-the-counter market does not provide a meeting place for buyers and sellers in the same manner as the exchanges. A complex network of trading rooms linked by telephone, teletype, and telegraph facilitates the meeting of buyer and seller. A much larger volume is handled on the over-the-counter market than on the listed or exchange market. Prices are arrived at by negotiation. Many times the dealer buys the security himself or sells from his own holdings. Over-the-counter brokers and dealers are subject to federal and state regulations, as well as to the rules of their trade association, the National Association of Securities Dealers, Inc. Investors may not borrow on unlisted securities from a broker, although there is no legal limitation on borrowing from a bank.

Brokers and Dealers.   A *broker* is the middleman who acts as an agent in the execution of orders, receiving a commission for his services. All brokers charge the same commissions but offer different services. (See Figure 13-11 for a recent commission-rate table.)

A *security dealer* is one who acts as the principal in a security transaction, buying and selling for his own account, as distinguished from a broker, who is an intermediary.

A *commission house,* or wire house, acts as a contact with the investing public. It furnishes investment information, accepts and executes orders, reports transactions to customers, and receives and delivers securities.

A *floor broker,* a regular member of an exchange who executes orders for other members on the exchange floor, is a broker's broker.

A *floor partner* is a partner of a commission house who executes orders for his firm on the floor of an exchange of which he is a member.

A *floor trader* is an exchange member who buys and sells listed securities for his own account.

An *odd-lot dealer* buys and sells round lots (most commonly 100 shares) and stands ready to sell stock in odd lots to buyers, and to purchase stock in odd lots from sellers. Odd-lot transactions are geared to the round-lot market price. The odd-lot dealer receives a differential of one-eighth or one-quarter point depending on the price of the security (Figure 13-12).

A *specialist* is an exchange member who remains at one trading post on the exchange floor and accepts orders from other members in the particular securities in which he is registered as a specialist. He sees that orders are properly executed and maintains a close, continuous, and orderly market in the stocks assigned to him. He acts as a broker when executing orders for customer houses, and as a dealer when buying and selling for his own account.

Trading Terms.   A person who invests in stocks and bonds should be familiar with the vocabulary of the securities market. The following terms are commonly used in trading.

Bid and Asked.   The bid price is the amount a prospective buyer will pay for a share. The asked price (also called an *offer*) is the price at which a holder offers to sell.

Stocks Selling at $1.00 and Above

First 1,000 Shares of an Order—100-share units or less:

Money Value	Commission
Under $100	As mutually agreed
$100 to $399	2% plus $ 3.00
$400 to $2,399	1% plus $ 7.00
$2,400 to $4,999	1/2% plus $19.00
$5,000 and above	1/10% plus $39.00

ODD LOT—$2 Less

Portion of Order in Excess of 1,000 Shares—100-share units or less:

Money Involved	Commission
$100 to and including $2,800	1/2% of money involved plus $4.00
Above $2,800 to and including $3,000. .	Compute as $2,800
Above $3,000 to and including $9,000. .	1/2% of money involved plus $3.00
Above $9,000	1/10% of money involved plus $39.00

(Never more than $1.50 per share or $75 per single transaction, nor less than $6)

Surcharge on 1,000 Shares or Less:

In addition to the commission rates, a service charge is levied on transactions of 1,000 shares or less of not less than the lesser of $15 or 50% of such commission.

Bonds
(Except Governmental, Short-Term or Called Bonds)

Selling At	Minimum Commission Per Bond ($1,000)
Less than $10 (1%)	$0.75
$10 (1%) and above but under $100 (10%) . . .	$1.25
$100 (10% and above)	$2.50

(In practice, commissions charged are generally a flat $5 per bond or a minimum of $15 per transaction.)

Figure 13-11 Recent formulas for computing minimum commissions on purchases and sales of securities and bonds.

NEW YORK STOCK EXCHANGE

100-share Unit Stocks

Effective round-lot sale	Odd-lot differential
55 or above	1/4 point
54 7/8 or below	1/8 point
1/8 of a point or less	one half the price of the effective round-lot sale

10-share Unit Stocks

Above 75	3/4 point
75	5/8 point
74 7/8	1/2 point
25 1/8 through 74 3/4	3/8 point
25 or below	1/4 point

AMERICAN STOCK EXCHANGE

	Odd-lot charge
Stocks with a unit trading of 100 shares:	
When the round lot sells below $40 a share	1/8 point
When the round lot sells at $40 and over	1/4 point
Stocks with a unit of trading of 10 shares, regardless of selling price	1/2 point
Stocks with a unit trading of either 25 shares or 50 shares, regardless of selling price	1/4 point
All American depositary receipts, American shares or block shares, regardless of selling price	1/4 point
Stocks selling under 1/2 of a dollar	1/16 point

Figure 13-12 Odd-lot differentials on the New York and American Stock Exchanges.

Eighth Stocks. Stocks in which odd-lot orders (less than 100 shares) are executed at one-eighth point from the next full-lot price.

Even Lot. A round or even lot consists of 100 shares or multiples thereof.

Ex-Dividend. A stock that is quoted ex-dividend reserves the right to the pending or accrued dividend to the seller. The ex-dividend date is the first day that the stock sells without the dividend, usually the fourth full business day before the date the stockholder's name must be on record in order to qualify him for the dividend. The opening price that day shows a decline from the previous day equal to the value of the dividend.

Ex-Rights. Ex-rights is similar to ex-dividend in that the seller retains ownership of the rights.

Margin refers to a credit transaction in which the security buyer pays a portion of the purchase price and borrows the remaining amount from the broker. The margin requirement is the difference between the market value and the maximum loan value. A buyer of stock worth $1,000 must make a minimum cash payment of $700 if the margin requirement is 70 percent; he may borrow only $300. The stock certificate is held by the broker until paid for in full.

Margin Call. Should the price of a stock bought on margin decline, the broker would call for additional funds in order to maintain the margin requirement. If a margin call is not satisfactorily answered, the broker has the right to sell the securities to satisfy the loan.

Odd Lot. A transaction of less than 100 shares is called an odd lot.

Odd-Lot Differential. The prices of odd-lot transactions are determined by the prices of round-lot trades made on the floor of the exchange, modified by a differential. On a purchase, the odd-lot differential is added to the next round-lot sale price or the best offer, if no sale takes place. On a sale, the differential is subtracted from the next round-lot price or the best bid if there is no transaction. Figure 13-12 lists the odd-lot differential in effect on the New York and American stock exchanges.

Point. One point, the unit of measurement for changes in stocks, bonds, or commodity quotations, is equal to $1 a share for stocks or commodities and $10 for a bond of $1,000 denomination.

Quarter Stocks. Stocks in which odd-lot orders are executed at one-quarter point from the next full-lot sales price are the higher-priced listed stocks (see Figure 13-12).

Spread. The difference between the bid and the asked price of a security.

Types of Orders. *At the Opening.* An order left with a broker for execution at the best price obtainable at the opening of the market.

At the Close. An odd-lot order executed on the basis of the final bid and asked prices.

Day Order. An order good only for the day on which it is received, after which it is automatically canceled.

Discretionary Order. An order permitting the broker to use his own judgment in executing it.

G.T.C. An order that is *good till canceled* and may be carried over for several days until the market reaches the price stipulated or the order is canceled. Other time limits may be designated, such as *good this week* or *good this month.*

Limited Order. An order to be executed at a specific price or at a price more favorable to the customer, if possible. In the case of odd lots a limited order to buy at "26" will not be executed until the price for round-lot sales reaches "25 7/8."

Market Order.   An order to be executed at the best price obtainable immediately after its receipt by a broker. If no price is stated, an order is always understood to be *at the market.*

Seller 30.   The seller contracts to deliver securities 30 days after sale. Other delivery periods may be specified.

Stop Order.   An order that does not go into effect until the market price reaches the price specified on the order. It changes from a stop order to a market order at that moment. Execution does not necessarily take place at the stop-order price. Stop orders to buy are usually placed above the current market, whereas stop orders to sell are placed below the current price. A buy stop-order protects the buyer against a sudden advance in price, whereas a sell stop-order limits the loss of a stockholder against a sudden decline in price.

Stop and Limit.   A stop-and-limit order, similar in one aspect to a stop order, limits the price at which it may be executed after going through the stop. The limit price may be the same as the stop price, or a different price may be set.

Mutual Funds.   A mutual fund is an investment company that buys and sells shares of stocks and bonds of many different corporations. Its business is investing, instead of manufacturing or merchandising, and it operates just like any other company, with officers and directors responsible to the shareholders. An investor may buy and sell shares of a mutual fund and thus have his money invested in a variety of companies. In effect, the mutual fund is a kind of middleman who receives the investor's money and buys securities with it. Each mutual fund shareholder owns a tiny part of each security that the fund has purchased. Specialists select, supervise, buy, and sell the securities for mutual fund investors.

The following tasks are performed by the staff of a mutual fund.

The constant surveillance of the market to determine when certain securities are attractively priced.

The analysis of the financial reports of all industries and individual companies within an industry.

The purchase of high-quality securities when their market prices are low.

The sale of securities when they are overpriced or when market prices are about to fall.

The receipt of dividends and interest on the securities and bonds owned by the fund.

The distribution of the proportional share of the fund's income and capital gains to each shareholder.

The sale of new shares of the fund to prospective investors.

The repurchase of shares from owners who wish to sell.

The preparation of periodic reports of the activities of the company for shareholders.

The preparation and filing of reports required by governmental agencies.

Stock Market Quotations. The financial pages of local newspapers, the *Wall Street Journal,* or the *New York Times* usually list daily quotations from the following sources:

New York Stock Exchange
American Stock Exchange
Local or regional exchange
National over-the-counter prices
Regional over-the-counter prices
Commodity market
Investment funds (mutual funds)
Treasury bonds
U.S. and foreign bond markets

All of these tables give at least the bid and asked prices and the net change from the previous day's closing price for each listed item. The stock exchanges include additional information in their lists. On a specific day in 1971, for example, quotes from the New York Stock Exchange stock table appeared as follows.

1971			Sales					Net
High	Low		(in 100s)	Open	High	Low	Close	Chg.
$53\frac{7}{8}$	$47\frac{3}{4}$	Am T&T 2.60	1048	$48\frac{1}{2}$	$48\frac{7}{8}$	$48\frac{1}{8}$	$48\frac{7}{8}$	$+\frac{1}{8}$
$29\frac{1}{4}$	$24\frac{1}{8}$	FluorCP 1.23f	64	27	27	$26\frac{1}{2}$	$26\frac{1}{2}$	$-\frac{1}{4}$
$60\frac{1}{2}$	50	Ill Cen pf3.50	29	$57\frac{3}{4}$	$58\frac{1}{8}$	$57\frac{3}{4}$	$57\frac{3}{4}$	...
$23\frac{1}{4}$	18	McGrwH .60a	146	$20\frac{1}{4}$	21	$20\frac{1}{8}$	21	$+\frac{5}{8}$

The highest price of American Telephone & Telegraph common stock since January 1, 1971, was 53 7/8 per share; the lowest, 47 3/4. AT&T common pays $2.60 per share as an annual dividend. The number of shares sold on that particular day were 104,800. From an opening of $48\frac{1}{2}$, the price fluctuated during trading from a low of 48 1/8 to a high of 48 7/8 and closed at 48 7/8. The stock advanced 1/8 of a point or $.125 from the previous day's close.

The .60a following McGraw-Hill's symbol indicates that the common stock pays a yearly dividend of 60 cents plus an extra dividend, often at the end of the year. Preferred stocks are indicated by the letters *pf* plus the dividend rate as seen in the listing of Illinois Central $3.50 preferred in the preceding table. Most financial pages include information on how to read the stock tables.

Sources of Security Information. Information on all phases of security investment may be secured from two leading services—Moody or Standard & Poor. Each service assembles comprehensive data on individual companies and maintains current figures through loose-leaf periodic cumulations. Also, many brokerage firms publish brochures and newsletters that explain how and where to invest and also list the advantages and the disadvantages of investing in certain securities or commodities. Some brochures offer advice on total investment programs for professionals, single persons, the self-employed, and the retired or soon-to-be retired. A great deal of material is available, but for helpful statistics one should consult the publications of the independent security services.

Moody's Investors Service, 99 Church Street, New York City, issues a semi-weekly cumulative record of dividend payments and corporate meetings, called *Moody's Dividend Record. Moody's Bond Record* is a pocket guide to all types of information on bonds. The American and foreign annual volumes of *Moody's Manual of Investments* contain full information about the following types of issuers of securities: governments and municipalities; banks; insurance companies; real estate enterprises; investment trusts; industrial firms; public utilities; and transportation companies.

Standard & Poor's Corporation, 345 Hudson Street, New York City, supplies complete factual information on major American, Canadian, and foreign corporations and their securities through its *Corporation Records.* Six loose-leaf volumes, revised bimonthly, supply the bulk of the data on balance sheets, earnings, and market prices. Standard & Poor's Trade and Securities Service includes (1) a weekly *Outlook* for securities markets, (2) a monthly earnings and ratings *Stock Guide,* and (3) a monthly loose-leaf *Statistical Section.* Their pocket-size *Bond Guide* lists information for each security on one line. A *Daily Stock Price Index* supplies the price range of a stock for any day beginning with January 1, 1962, up to the current day. It is brought up-to-date four times a year. Their capsule stock sheets list companies traded on the New York Stock Exchange and the American Stock Exchange and over-the-counter, together with the high and low for the year and Standard & Poor's opinion on each company and its future performance.

Records to Be Maintained.   A list of all investments in securities should be compiled. It should be brought up to date weekly, biweekly, or monthly, as desired by the investor, in order to incorporate all changes during the period and to indicate the current market value of each item and the total value of securities investments. The use of the suggested form in Figure 13-13 will allow the investor to see his market position at a glance.

A record of all purchases and sales should be kept and should include the information required by the Internal Revenue Service when one is accounting for short- and long-term capital gains and losses. Without detailed records, the taxpayer will find it difficult to explain his figures in this area to the Internal Revenue Service during an audit. A chart similar to the one in Figure 13-14 should be completed for each company, fund, or governmental agency. Notice how much detailed information is required by Internal Revenue Service regulations.

In order to make an accurate declaration of yearly income, an investor should record interest and dividend income as it is received. Figures 13-15 and 13-16 illustrate charts that are useful for recording income information.

Besides these personal records, which summarize securities transactions,

LIST OF INVESTMENTS IN SECURITIES

as of _____

No. shares or face value	Name	Maturity date (if applicable)	Purchase price	Current market price
Stocks:				
Bonds:				
Investment Funds (Mutual):				
Miscellaneous:				

Total amount originally invested _____

Current value of investments–(Date) _____

Figure 13-13 Chart for listing investments in securities.

RECORD OF SECURITY OR MUTUAL FUND TRANSACTIONS

Name of Security or Fund _____

Exchange on which listed _____

Broker _____ Phone _____

PURCHASES:

No. of Shares	Kind	Date of Purchase	Price per Share	Broker's Commission	Total Purchase Price	Certificate Number	Registered Name(s)	Location of Certificate

SALES:

No. of Shares	Kind	Certificate Number	Date of Sale	Price per Share	Total Sales Price	Commission	Taxes and Other Charges	Capital Gain or Loss (in red)	
								Short Term	Long Term

Figure 13-14 Chart for recording purchases and sales of securities and mutual fund shares.

INTEREST INCOME

January 1, 19__ – December 31, 19__

for _____(Owner(s))

Tax Exempt Bonds

Name	Date	Amount	Total
Nontaxable Interest Income for 19__			

Taxable Interest

Name	Date	Amount	Total
Taxable Interest Income for 19__			

Figure 13-15 Chart for recording interest income.

```
┌─────────────────────────────────────────────────────────────────┐
│                       DIVIDEND INCOME                             │
│                                                                   │
│            January 1, 19 ___ - December 31, 19 ___                │
│                                                                   │
│  for _____(Owner(s))  │
│                                                                   │
```

Security	Quarter				Year's Total
	1st	2nd	3rd	4th	
Total for Quarter					
Total Dividend Income for 19 ___					

Figure 13-16 Chart for recording dividend income.

the Internal Revenue Service requires that the facts be supported by brokers' transaction slips of purchases and sales, brokers' monthly statements, and yearly dividend or interest statements from the issuing companies. These supporting documents should be carefully filed by appropriate subject headings and retained at least three years *after* a security is sold. The year of a security sale is the one in which the outcome of the investment is explained on the investor's income tax form. Income tax declarations may be audited three years after their filing date.

Safeguarding Security Certificates. Stock certificates should be kept in a safe place, preferably in the safe deposit vault of a bank. All nonregistered certificates, those not registered as to the owner's name, should always be kept in a safe deposit box. Often registered certificates are left with the broker so that delivery may be made easily when the security is sold. Some businessmen keep their certificates in the office safe or in a locked file cabinet. There is some risk in this practice, however, because the certificates may become mixed with company documents, and proof of ownership might become a problem later on. Other investors keep their certificates at home in a "safe place." The dangers here, as in an office building, are of fire or theft. Nonregistered certificates may be irretrievably lost, and the reissue of registered certificates takes considerable time. (See Section 13.8 on replacing lost documents.) While waiting for a reissue, the investor is unable to take advantage of stock market movements. Other certificates may be held as security for a loan by a bank. Regardless of where certificates are kept, it is important that their whereabouts be noted on a chart such as the one in Figure 13-14. A simple code may be developed for use in the "Location" column, for example:

SD	Safe deposit box
B	Broker's office
H	Home
O	Office (indicate the location and the file number or subject)
M–( )	Miscellaneous (state the place)

Certificate numbers should be carefully checked before anyone forwards the document to the broker to complete a sale. If certificates are kept at the broker's office, check the certificate number on the transaction slip to see that the first one acquired is the first one sold. This is the general practice in taking advantage of a long-term capital gain or loss. If there is a discrepancy in either the certificate number or the date of acquisition, call the broker for clarification.

13.5   ESTATE PLANNING—THE WILL

The single most important document in an estate plan is a person's will. It guarantees his wishes, conserves his estate, and protects his beneficiaries. If it is properly drawn and up-to-date, a will is a binding document. A person whose financial matters are complicated, encumbered, or extensive should select an attorney in whom he has confidence to draw up the will. The ensuing document will contain the correct legal terminology and will be properly witnessed and notarized.

This section contains estate planning information as listed in this index.

Holographic Wills	p. 537
Division of an Estate in the Absence of a Will	p. 537
Information Needed by Your Attorney and Your Executor	p. 538
Periodic Review of the Will	p. 539
The Executor of a Will	p. 539
Estate, Inheritance, and Gift Taxes	p. 540

Holographic Wills.   A person may write entirely in longhand his own will. To avoid any problems it should be written on a blank sheet of paper, dated, and signed by the testator himself. His intentions must be absolutely clear in order to avoid misinterpretation later. This need alone indicates that the services of an attorney should be considered. If the holographic will is ruled invalid for any reason, no matter how minor, the court will step in and distribute the estate as if there were no will. An example of a temporary will that might be used in a special situation for a short period of time is shown in Figure 13-17.

Division of an Estate in the Absence of a Will.   If a person does not leave a will, his property will be distributed to certain persons related to him in

---

Last Will and Testament of

I, _____ of _____,

City of _____, State of _____,
do hereby make, publish, and declare this to be my last will and testament and I do hereby revoke all former wills and codicils thereto by me at any time made.

First: I desire that my just debts, including the expenses of my last illness and funeral, be paid as soon as may be practical after my death.

Second: All of the residue of my estate, whether real, personal, or mixed, wheresoever situate, and whether now owned or hereafter acquired, I give, devise   and   bequeath   unto   my   beloved   wife   (husband),

_____, for her (his) own use and benefit forever.

Note: If there are children, they should be specifically mentioned, or the will may be set aside.

Third: I appoint as executrix (executor) of my will my wife (husband); I request that she (he) be permitted to serve without sureties on her (his) bond and that, without application to or order of courts, she (he) have full power and authority to sell, transfer, grant, convey, exchange, lease, mortgage, pledge, or otherwise encumber or dispose of, any or all of the real and personal property of my estate

In   Witness   Whereof,   I   have   hereunto   subscribed   my   name   this

_____ day of _____, 19_____.

_____(Signature)

Figure 13-17   Example of the wording of a temporary holographic will.

accordance with state law. The right to intestate succession is not an inherent right, but exists only because the state legislatures have so provided. The legislatures of the individual states have the right to change, modify, or destroy the right to inherit property.

Although intestate distribution varies from state to state, current state laws do exhibit general patterns as follows.

1. Spouses. The surviving spouse, whether husband or wife, will share in the estate. The extent of the share generally depends upon the number of children and other specified heirs. In the absence of surviving blood relations, the surviving spouse usually takes the entire estate.

2. Lineals.   Lineals or lineal descendants are blood descendants of the decedent. The major portion of an estate not distributed to the surviving spouse is generally distributed to lineals, although sometimes parents also have a claim to part of it.

3. Parents. If there are still assets in the estate, the remainder is commonly distributed to the decedent's parents.

4. Collateral heirs. These are persons who are not descendants of the decedent but who are related to him through a common ancestor. Generally, they include his brothers and sisters, and they are next in line after his parents, although in some states they have equal claim with the parents.

Information Needed by Your Attorney and Your Executor.   To simplify the administration of the estate and to avoid delay in its distribution, file a copy of the following information in a safe place with your will. Be sure the information is correct and up-to-date.

Date on which compiled or updated
Your full name
Legal address and temporary addresses
Date of birth
Place of birth
If a naturalized citizen, date and place of naturalization
Date you became a resident of your state
Former residences
Name of present spouse
Date of marriage
Children—names and birth dates
Previous marriage, if any:
  Date
  Name of spouse
  Date marriage terminated
  Reason
  Children—names and birth dates
Social Security number
Name and address of any company having funeral arrangement contract
Mortuary preference
Other remarks or instructions regarding funeral
Persons to be notified at death—names and addresses

Attorney—name, address, and phone number
Physician—name, address, and phone number
Life insurance agent
Accountant
Bank accounts—name and address of bank, account number
Safe deposit boxes—name and address of bank and name under which registered
Brokers' accounts—names and addresses
Location of personal property (securities, automobiles, jewelry, furniture, mortgages, contracts, and so on)
Employer
Description of any employment contracts, compensation due, or other benefits
Names of business associates
Liabilities (describe any debts, including loan or contract payments)
Property in storage—name and address of storage company
Gifts made prior to death
  To whom
  Amount
Tax return—where filed
Interest in trust—name and address of trustee
Armed services information
  Location of discharge and other related documents
  Veterans' organization memberships
Miscellaneous information that might be helpful

Periodic Review of the Will. A will should be reviewed every year and brought up-to-date. Do not make changes by scratching out, adding to, or writing over something. Changes and amendments should be made by an attorney and properly witnessed in the same manner as the original will. Here are some items that should definitely be reviewed.

Death of a beneficiary named in the will
Change of residence to another state
Birth of a child after the making of the will
Extreme rise or drop in the value of the estate
Payment of debts that were listed as collectable
Major changes in tax laws
Sale of stock or other property bequeathed to someone in the will
Change of status of a beneficiary (such as reaching majority), making a change in a trust necessary
Change in purchasing power of the dollar, which may necessitate change in support allowance under a Trust

The Executor of a Will. Banks through their trust departments can act as the executor of a will, or an individual may be named by the testator as the executor. Co-executors may be named, such as a bank and an individual. Naming an individual poses certain problems: he is subject to illnesses, travel, the press of personal business; an individual must post a bond, unless it is specifically waived by the terms of the will; if the individual is also a beneficiary, it may be difficult to convince others that he is impartial in handling the estate; an individual may lack management skills and the facilities to perform all the required duties of an executor.

Duties of an Executor.   Some of the duties an executor must perform in handling the probate of a will are to

Employ an attorney to represent the estate.

Locate and analyze the will with his help.

Apply for appointment as executor.

Arrange living allowances for the decedent's immediate family.

Collect the life insurance payable to the estate.

Assemble and inventory all the assets of the estate.

Have each asset properly appraised.

Provide protection for all property in the estate and maintain adequate insurance on all insurable property.

Keep real property in good repair, maintain the rental of income property, and collect rents.

Pay all real and personal property taxes when due.

Collect dividends and any other income from security or bond investments and attend to all investment matters.

Operate, liquidate, or sell the interest in any business owned by the estate.

File notice to creditors and approve or reject any claims filed against the estate; defend actions on rejected claims; obtain approval from the court to pay claims and pay those so approved.

Sell property in the estate, as necessary, to pay taxes and claims, and pay those so approved.

Prepare Federal Estate Tax and State Inheritance Tax returns; file and pay such taxes at the proper time. Prepare and file final income tax returns and negotiate any audits of prior income tax returns. Obtain clearance of all tax items.

Keep the family informed of all estate matters and consult with beneficiaries on personal matters pertinent to the estate.

Account for all monies received and disbursed and submit a detailed report thereof to the court when the estate is ready to close.

Make final distribution of the estate as directed by the court.

Executor's Fees.   The usual statutory fees for acting as an executor whether as an individual, a bank, or a court-appointed administrator are

On an estate of $100,000: $2,630.

On an estate of $350,000: $6,630.

On an estate of $500,000: $8,880.

The court may also make such further allowances as are just and reasonable for extraordinary services. All of these charges are tax-deductible to the estate.

Estate, Inheritance, and Gift Taxes.   The Federal Estate Tax and the State Inheritance Tax must be paid or provided for before an estate can be distributed. The Federal Estate Tax must be paid within fifteen months after the testator's death. States usually allow more time for payment of the Inheritance Tax. California, for instance, asks for payment within two years. Discounts are often allowed for prepayment of the Inheritance Tax before the due date. Penalties and interest are added to all delinquencies. By consulting Figure 13-18 you may secure an approximate figure for the Federal Estate Tax on an estate. Figure 13-19 gives recent California Inheritance Tax rates and exemptions.

Property that is given away during a person's lifetime is subject to both federal and state gift taxes. However, if the gift is made in *contemplation of death* (to keep the property out of an estate), the transfer is not subject to

FEDERAL ESTATE TAX RATES

(1) Net Estate	(2) Total Tax	(3) Net Estate in Excess of (1)	(4) Rate of Tax on (3)
$ 60,000	$ None	$ 5,000	3%
65,000	150	5,000	7%
70,000	500	10,000	11%
80,000	1,600	10,000	14%
90,000	3,000	10,000	18%
100,000	4,800	10,000	22%
110,000	7,000	10,000	25%
120,000	9,500	40,000	28%
160,000	20,700	150,000	30%
310,000	65,700	250,000	32%
560,000	145,700	250,000	35%
810,000	233,200	250,000	37%
1,060,000	325,700	250,000	39%
1,310,000	423,200	250,000	42%
1,560,000	528,200	500,000	45%
2,060,000	753,200	500,000	49%
2,560,000	998,200	500,000	53%
3,060,000	1,263,200	500,000	56%
3,560,000	1,543,200	500,000	59%
4,060,000	1,838,200	1,000,000	63%
5,060,000	2,468,200	1,000,000	67%
6,060,000	3,138,200	1,000,000	70%
7,060,000	3,838,200	1,000,000	73%
8,060,000	4,568,200	2,000,000	76%
10,060,000	6,088,200	Remainder of estate	77%

Figure 13-18   Federal estate tax table.

California Inheritance Tax Table of Rates

APPLICATION OF RATES TO VALUE OF INHERITANCE OR BEQUESTS [1]

Classification or indication of Relationship	Exemption (To Each Recipient)	On Excess After Deduction of Exemption from $25,000	$25,000 to $50,000	$50,000 to $100,000	$100,000 to $200,000	$200,000 to $300,000	$300,000 to $400,000	Over $400,000
Class A Minor child	$12,000	3%	4%	6%	8%	10%	12%	14%
Husband, wife, lineal ancestor, lineal issue, adopted or mutually acknowledged child (except a minor), lineal issue of such child, adopted child of any lineal issue or child mentioned in Class A	5,000*	*Generally, no community property is subject to inheritance tax on a transfer at death between spouses.						
Class B Brother, sister or descendant of either, wife or widow of a son, husband of a daughter ...	2,000	6%	10%	12%	14%	16%	18%	20%
Class C All others not exempt from taxation**	300	10%	14%	16%	18%	20%	22%	24%

** No tax on gifts for charitable, benevolent, educational or public purposes, either to a domestic corporation or for use within the State, or to societies, institutions and corporations which are exempt by law from taxation; nor on gifts to such institutions in other states whose laws contain reciprocal provisions allowing like exemptions in favor of similar California institutions. No tax on intangibles of non-residents.

Where the inheritance tax is less than 80% credit upon the Federal Estate Tax, or where, because of exemption, no inheritance tax is imposed and a Federal Estate Tax is due, the tax is increased so that the amount due the state is the maximum amount of credit allowed upon Federal Estate Tax.

[1] Where property has been subject to a like tax within five years, a credit is provided if the decedent was a Class A transferee and the present transferee is a Class A transferee.

Figure 13-19 California inheritance tax table.

Based upon your net gift after deducting the annual exclusion of $3,000 and the lifetime exemption of $30,000.

If your net gift is	Your Gift Tax is	plus	on excess to
Up to $ 5,000	2.25%		
5,000	$ 112.50	5.25%	$ 10,000
10,000	375	8.25%	20,000
20,000	1,200	10.50%	30,000
30,000	2,250	13.50%	40,000
40,000	3,600	16.50%	50,000
50,000	5,250	18.75%	60,000
60,000	7,125	21.00%	100,000
100,000	15,525	22.50%	250,000
250,000	49,275	24.00%	500,000
500,000	109,275	26.25%	750,000
750,000	174,900	27.75%	1,000,000
1,000,000	244,275	29.25%	1,250,000

Gifts in excess of $1,250,000 are taxed at rates graduated from 31½% to 57¾%.

Figure 13-20   Federal gift tax table.

regular gift-tax treatment, but instead will be taxed as part of the estate. The federal gift-tax table is shown in Figure 13-20. For a typical state gift-tax table, refer to Figure 13-19 because California's inheritance and gift taxes are the same.

13.6. TAXES

Local, state and federal taxes are payable by all U.S. businesses and citizens and also by aliens who receive income from U.S. sources. The Internal Revenue Service at the federal level, as well as state and local revenue services, stand ready to help individuals and businesses to complete tax forms so that they comply with tax laws. Personnel at local tax offices will advise taxpayers and assist them to complete the necessary tax forms. Published information and instructions are available, free or at a small fee, from the local IRS office or the Superintendent of Documents in Washington, D.C.

A study of the information in this section will clarify many tax issues and will assist you in complying with regulations.

Arrangements for Paying Taxes   p. 544
Tax Publications   p. 544
Tax Calendar   p. 549
Keeping Adequate Tax Records   p. 549
Tax-Deductible Business Expenses   p. 552
Tax Information for Individuals   p. 552

Arrangements for Paying Taxes. The three governments agree that the businessman must take the responsibility to pay taxes owed. It is his duty to locate the most recent tax laws that concern him and his business enterprise and to comply with them. When starting a business, he should immediately contact the tax and permit division of his city government, the tax collector of his county government, and the franchise tax board of his state government, in order to familiarize himself with their requirements and thus avoid penalties. If he is an employer, he will need an employer's identification number from the Internal Revenue Service and will be required to file numerous forms and/or make deposits on specific dates. Compliance is mandatory and ignorance unexcused.

Most cities require one to have a permit to operate a business within their city limits; many have established sales taxes that are collected for them by the retailer; and some have assessed income taxes on individuals and businesses. County governments usually levy property taxes on personal property, real estate, merchandise inventory, office and trade machinery, and other items, such as signs and permanent fixtures. State governments levy income taxes and special taxes on saleable items, such as gasoline. Then there are such things as Social Security taxes, excise taxes, federal and state unemployment taxes, and workmen's compensation premiums that must be collected.

Tax Publications. Because tax laws change from year to year, current regulations, rates, and due dates should be secured from the local, state, and federal revenue services. The local and state tax laws in each of the fifty states are all slightly different. The businessman, therefore, should investigate these for himself in all the states in which he does business and secure explanatory material. The federal tax requirements are the same for everyone and are discussed in some detail in this section.

The Internal Revenue Service publishes pamphlets that answer practically any tax question that might be raised. They may be secured from any one of the 58 IRS field offices or from the nearest Superintendent of Documents office. These offices are listed in the telephone book under "United States Government." A selected group of informative IRS publications is listed in Figure 13-21; a complete list of those available from the IRS may be found in Publication 552.

A *Mr. Businessman's Kit* may be secured free of charge from any IRS office. It contains instructions and samples of forms that indicate when and where to file returns and pay taxes, and it gives answers to commonly asked questions. Two publications in it are of particular value—Circular E (*Employer's Tax Guide*) and Publication 552 (*Recordkeeping Requirements and a Guide to Tax Publications*). Circular E contains definitions of *employer* and *employee;* instructions for securing an employer identification number; explanation of Social Security regulations, taxable wages and tips, withholding regulations, the reporting and payment of quarterly returns, adjustments, and other important regulations. Most importantly, it contains both the percentage and the wage-bracket table method of income tax withholding so that regardless of the payroll period, the paymaster can quickly ascertain the correct sum to withhold. Social Security employee tax tables up to $360.11 in wages per week are also part of the booklet. Publication 552 lists the records that every taxpayer must keep in order to prepare accurate income tax returns or to answer questions for the IRS in case his return is audited. Ordinarily, the statute of limitations for an income tax return expires three years after the return is due to be filed. However, the following records should be retained indefinitely.

Transactions affecting the basis of an asset
Changes in the method of accounting or the adoption of the LIFO method of
   inventory
The basis of property received by gift
An auxiliary record of depreciation for tax purposes

Tax Guide for Small Business, Publication 334, explains, among other things, how income, excise, Social Security, and withholding taxes apply to sole proprietorships, partnerships, and corporations. It answers questions about starting, operating, and disposing of a business. A checklist of business activities shows the kinds of federal taxes to be paid for each, what forms to use, and the page on which each kind of tax is explained (Figure 13-22).

Your Federal Income Tax, Publication 17, explains such things as, how to prepare a return, what exemptions and deductions are allowed, what income is taxable, how to determine income and deductions from investment property, and how to determine capital gains and losses. Publications 334 and 17 are obtainable from the Superintendent of Documents in Washington or the local IRS office for 75 cents each.

Farmer's Tax Guide explains the income tax rules as they apply to farming and may be secured free from county farm agents or IRS offices.

Number	Title	Number	Title
15	Circular E, Employer's Tax Guide		counting Periods and Methods
225	Farmer's Tax Guide	539	Withholding Taxes from Your Employee's Wages
308	Farmer's Gas Tax Credit		
334*	Tax Guide for Small Business	540	Tax Information on Repairs, Replacements, and Improvements
349	Federal Use Tax on Trucks, Truck-Tractors, and Buses	541	Tax Information on Partnership Income and Losses
378	Federal Gas Tax Credit or Refund for Nonhighway and Transit Users	542	Corporations and the Federal Income Tax
463	Travel, Entertainment, and Gift Expenses	543	Tax Information on the Sale of a Business
508	Tax Information on Educational Expenses	544	Sales and Exchanges of Assets
510	Information on Excise Taxes	545	Income Tax Deduction for Interest Expense
511	Sales and Other Dispositions of Depreciable Property	546	Income Tax Deduction for Taxes
512	Credit Sales by Dealers in Personal Property	547	Tax Information on Disasters, Casualty I osses, and Thefts
515	Withholding of Tax on Non-resident Aliens and Foreign Corporations	548	Tax Information on Deduction for Bad Debts
517	Social Security for Clergymen and Religious Workers	549	Condemnations of Private Property for Public Use
521	Moving Expenses—Tax Information for Employees and Employers	551	Tax Information on Cost or Other Basis of Assets
522	Adjustments to Income for Sick Pay	552	Recordkeeping Requirements and a Guide to Tax Publications
533	Information on Self-Employment Tax	556	Appeal Rights and Claims for Refund
534	Depreciation, Investment Credit, Amortization, Depletion	557	How to Apply for Exemption for an Organization
535	Tax Information on Business Expenses	558	Tax Information for Sponsors of Contests and Sporting Events
536	Losses from Operating a Business	560	Retirement Plans for Self-Employed Individuals
538	Tax Information on Ac-	561	Valuation of Donated Property

*A charge of 75¢ is made for this publication.

Figure 13-21 Selected list of informative Internal Revenue Service free publications for the businessman.

TYPE OF BUSINESS

Corporation
Form 1120—Income tax

Corporation electing not to be
taxed
Form 1120-S—Information
return

Partnership
Form 1065—Information return

Sole Proprietor (or partner)
Form 1040—Income tax
Form 1040-ES—Estimated tax
Form 1040—Self-employment
tax

WHICH EMPLOYS:

1 or more persons
Form 941—Income tax with-
holding
Form 941—FICA taxes

4 or more persons
Form 940—FUTA tax

Household workers
Form 942—FICA taxes

FURNISHES SERVICES AND FACILITIES FOR:

Local and toll telephone service
and teletypewriter exchange

Transportation of persons by air
Form 720—Excise tax on
facilities

IMPORTS:

Adulterated or process butter
Form 923—Stamp tax

Filled cheese
Form 923—Stamp tax

Firearms
Form 11—Occupational tax

Marijuana
Form 960—Occupational tax
Form 678—Stamp tax

Narcotic drugs
Form 810—Occupational tax
Form 786—Stamp tax

ISSUES:

Insurance policies (foreign insurer)
Form 720—Excise tax

MAINTAINS FOR USE:

Slot machines
Form 11-B—Occupational tax

Punchboards
Form 11-C—Occupational tax
Form 730—Wagering tax

MANUFACTURES:

Adulterated or process butter
Form 11—Occupational tax
Form 218—Stamp tax

Automobiles, trucks, buses, or
trailers
Form 720—Manufacturers
excise tax

Beer
Form 2034—Excise tax

Cigars, cigarettes, cigarette papers
or tubes
Forms 2137, 3071—Excise tax

Distilled spirits
Forms 2521, 2522, 2523, 2527—
Excise Tax

Filled cheese
Form 11—Occupational tax
Form 218—Stamp tax

Figure 13-22   Checklist of some federal taxes for which businesses may be liable.

Firearms
Form 11—Occupational tax
Form 720—Manufacturers excise tax

Fishing equipment
Form 720—Manufacturers excise tax

Marijuana
Form 678—Occupational tax

Narcotic drugs
Form 678—Occupational tax
Form 786—Stamp tax

Parts and accessories for trucks or buses
Form 720—Manufacturers excise tax

Petroleum products
Form 720—Manufacturers excise tax

Rectified spirits
Form 11—Occupational tax

Stills or condensers for use in distilling distilled spirits
Form 11—Occupational tax

Sugar
Form 720—Manufacturers excise tax

Tires and tubes
Form 720—Manufacturers excise tax

Wine
Forms 2050, 2052, 2523, 2527—Excise tax

OPERATES A:

Brewery
Form 11—Occupational tax

Truck, truck-tractor, or bus on a highway
Form 2290—Federal use tax

Wagering pool, lottery, or otherwise accepts wagers
Form 11-C—Occupational tax
Form 730—Wagering tax

Wholesale liquor dealership
Form 11—Occupational tax

SELLS AT RETAIL:

Adulterated butter
Form 11—Occupational tax

Diesel and special fuels
Form 720—Retailers excise tax

Distilled spirits, wines, or beer
Form 11—Occupational tax

Filled cheese
Form 11—Occupational tax

Marijuana
Form 961—Occupational tax
Form 785—Stamp tax

Narcotic drugs
Form 678—Occupational tax

TRANSFERS:

Firearms
Form 4 (Firearms)—Stamp tax

Marijuana
Form 678—Occupational tax
Form 786—Stamp tax

Narcotic drugs
Form 678—Occupational tax

Figure 13-22 (continued).

Tax Calendar. The three governments (local, state, and federal) require that taxes be paid and deposits made by specific dates. Penalties are assessed for late returns. It is necessary, therefore, for the person in the office who is responsible for payment to add these dates to his tickler file. Individuals should also make notes on their calendars of due dates and should allow ample time to complete forms.

Figure 13-23 shows the due dates for the federal tax returns that are most commonly filed. For a more complete calendar, consult the current *Tax Guide for Small Business*. It will give the exact dates that forms, payments, and deposits are due for that year.

Keeping Adequate Tax Records. Every taxpayer, individual or corporate, must maintain records and keep supporting documents that substantiate entries in these records. The law does not require any particular kinds of records, but they must be permanent, accurate, and complete, and clearly establish income, deductions, credits, inventories, employee information, sales of items subject to excise taxes, and so on. Memorandums or sketchy records that merely approximate income, deductions, or other pertinent items affecting tax liability are not considered adequate for compliance with the law. Paid bills, canceled checks, sales slips, invoices, receipts, and other documents should be filed in an orderly manner and stored in a safe place. Records supporting items on a tax return should be retained until the expiration of the statute of limitations for that return. Ordinarily, the statute of limitations for an income tax return expires three years after the return is due to be filed. However, there are many cases in which all or some records should be retained indefinitely. (See "Importance of a Retention Schedule" in Section 12.1).

Microfilm records containing reproductions of general books of account, such as cash books, journals, voucher registers, ledgers, and so on, do *not* meet the recordkeeping requirements of the law. You need maintain, however, only the microfilm reproductions of supporting records, such as payroll records, canceled checks, invoices, vouchers, and so on, provided the following conditions are met.

1. Microfilmed copies are retained as long as their contents may become material in the administration of any Internal Revenue Service law.

2. Appropriate facilities are provided for preservation of the films and for the ready inspection and location of the particular records, including a projector for viewing the records in the event inspection is necessary for tax purposes.

3. Transcriptions of the information contained on the microfilm may be made when required.

If the records are maintained within an automatic data processing system, the system must include a method for producing from the punched cards or

Title of Form	Form Number	Due Dates[1]			
Employer's Annual Federal Unemployment Tax Return	940	Jan. 31			
Employer's Quarterly Federal Tax Return	941	4th qtr. Jan. 31	1st qtr. Apr. 30	2d qtr. July 31	3d qtr. Oct. 31
		10 addl. days allowed for filing if timely deposits are made in full payment of taxes for the quarter.			
Employer's Quarterly Tax Return for Household Employees	942	4th qtr. Jan. 31	1st qtr. Apr. 30	2d qtr. July 31	3d qtr. Oct. 31
Federal Tax Deposit Withheld Income and FICA Taxes	501	*Monthly Deposits*—Deposit tax for first and second months of quarter within 15 days after end of month. Deposit remaining tax for quarter (if more than $100) by last day of month following close of quarter.			
		Semi-monthly Deposits—Make deposits within 3 banking days after the 15th and last days of each month. Deposit remaining tax for quarter (if more than $100) by last day of month following close of quarter.			
Quarterly Federal Excise Tax Return	720	4th qtr. Jan. 31	1st qtr. Apr. 30	2d qtr. July 31	3d qtr. Oct. 31
		10 addl. days allowed for filing if timely deposits in full payment of taxes for the quarter.			
Federal Tax Deposit Excise Taxes	504	*Monthly Deposits*—Deposit tax for first and second months of quarter within 15 days after end of month. Deposit remaining tax for			

Figure 13-23 Federal tax calendar for returns most commonly filed.

quarter (if more than $100) by last day of month following close of quarter.

Semi-monthly Deposits. Make deposits within 3 banking days after the 15th and last days of each month. Deposit remaining tax for quarter (if more than $100) by last day of month following close of quarter.

Special Tax Return (Mfg. or sale of gaming devices; narcotics; distilled spirits, beer, or wines; firearms; wagering, etc.)	11, 11B, or 11C	July 1[2]			
U.S. Individual Income Tax Return	1040	April 15			
Declaration of Estimated Income for Individuals	1040-ES	April 15			

		Installments			
Estimated Income Tax Payments	1040-ES	4th Jan. 15 of follow- ing year	1st Apr. 15	2d June 15	3d Sept. 15

Federal Use Tax Return on Highway Motor Vehicles	2290[3]	April 30			

		Installments			
Highway Motor Vehicle Use Tax	2290[3]	3d Mar. 31	4th June 30	1st Aug. 31	2d Dec. 31

[1] Due dates falling on a Saturday, Sunday, or legal holiday are postponed until the next day which is not a Saturday, Sunday, or legal holiday.

[2] Only for those currently registered. Others must register and pay tax before commencing such business.

[3] See Publication 349 for filing and paying highway motor vehicle use tax covering vehicles used during other than the month of July.

Figure 13-23 (continued).

tapes visible and legible records that provide adequate information for the verification of the tax liability.

Tax-Deductible Business Expenses. To claim tax deductions for certain business expenses, the company or the businessman must submit adequate records and substantiation to the Internal Revenue Service. For example, a diary, account book, or similar summary of travel and entertainment expenses is required, plus receipts, itemized paid bills, and similar statements for single items exceeding $25. The only possible exception to a receipt for travel expenses over $25 is a canceled check made out to an air, rail, car rental, or steamship transportation company. However, if a paid receipt is available for transportation costs, the IRS prefers such a receipt. Canceled checks are not acceptable for expense items over $25. If a bill or a voucher isn't available, other evidence may have to be presented. Receipts for lodgings are required regardless of amount unless their cost is covered by a per diem allowance of $25 or less.

For travel, entertainment, and gift expenses, a chart similar to the one in Figure 13-24 should be completed as these expenses occur. This procedure plus the filing of supporting documents will ensure compliance with the regulations that are spelled out by the IRS in Publication 463 (Figure 13-25).

Most business expense items are handled by the accountant or bookkeeper, who sets up accounts for all the normal costs of operation. The IRS is concerned that only ordinary and necessary expenses directly connected with or related to the trade, business, or profession be deducted. Not all business expenditures are deductible even though they may be ordinary and necessary. For further information, the following IRS pamphlets, which discuss, list, and supply examples of deductible and nondeductible business expenses, should be consulted.

Travel, Entertainment, and Gift Expenses	#463
Depreciation, Investment Credit, Amortization, Depletion	#534
Tax Information on Business Expenses	#535
Losses from Operating a Business	#536
Tax Information on Deduction for Bad Debts	#548

Tax Information for Individuals. The Internal Revenue Service publishes many pamphlets that explain how to fill out Form 1040 and its supplementary schedules. These are available at the local IRS office or through the Superintendent of Documents in Washington. See Figure 13-26 for a list of those available free of charge or for a small fee.

For complete information and examples, *Your Federal Income Tax,* provided by the Internal Revenue Service, should be consulted for the pertinent year. You may secure it by writing the Superintendent of Documents and enclosing the fee of 75 cents. Another good outline, *Your Income Tax,* by

RECORD OF TRAVEL, ENTERTAINMENT, OR GIFT EXPENSES

January 1, 19_____ —December 31, 19_____

Dates (Event, Gift, Departure and Return)	Place	Business Purpose or Benefit Derived	Names and Business Relationship	COSTS				
				Trans-portation	Gas & Oil	Lodging	Meals	Miscellaneous (Phone, Taxi, etc.)

Figure 13-24   Chart for recording travel, entertainment, or gift expense information to comply with IRS regulations.

Factors to be Proved in Substantiating Elements in Column 1—

Elements to be substantiated (1)	For expenditures for travel away from home (2)	For expenditures for entertainment (3)	For expenditures for gifts (4)
Amount	Amount of each separate expenditure for transportation, lodging, and meals. Permissible to aggregate incidental expenses in reasonable categories, such as gasoline and oil, taxis, daily meals for traveler, etc.	Amount of each separate expenditure. Incidental items such as taxis, telephones, etc., may be aggregated on a daily basis.	Cost of gift to taxpayer.
Time	Dates of departure and return for each trip, and number of days attributable to business activities.	Date of entertainment or use of a facility for entertainment. (Duration of business discussion.)	Date of gift.
Place	Destination by name of city or other appropriate designation.	Name and address or similar designation of place of entertainment, or place of use of a facility in connection with entertainment. Type of entertainment if not otherwise apparent. (Place of business discussion).	Not applicable.
Description ... Business purpose.	Not applicable. Business reason for travel or nature of business benefit derived or expected to be derived.	Not applicable. Business reason or nature of business benefit derived or expected to be derived. Nature of business discussion or activity if entertainment is other than "business meals,"	Description of gift. Business reason for making the gift or nature of business benefit derived or expected to be derived.
Business relationship.....	Not applicable.	Occupations or other information—such as names or other designations—about persons entertained which establishes their business relationship to taxpayer. (Identification of persons entertained who participated in business discussion.)	Occupation or other information— such as name or other designation—about recipient which establishes business relationship to taxpayer.

Figure 13-25 Elements of travel, entertainment, and gift expenses which must be substantiated to Internal Revenue.

554

Free of Charge

#54	Tax Guide for U.S. Citizens Abroad
#501	Your Exemptions and Exemptions for Dependents
#502	Deduction for Medical and Dental Expenses
#503	Child Care and Disabled Dependent Care
#504	Income Tax Deduction for Alimony Payments
#506	Computing Your Tax Under the Income Averaging Method
#507	Tax Information on Scholarships and Fellowships
#513	Tax Information for Visitors to the United States
#514	Foreign Tax Credit for U.S. Citizens and Resident Aliens
#518	Foreign Scholars and Educational and Cultural Exchange Visitors
#519	United States Tax Guide for Aliens
#520	Tax Information for American Scholars Abroad
#523	Tax Information on Selling Your Home
#524	Retirement Income and Retirement Income Credit
#525	Taxable Income and Nontaxable Income
#526	Income Tax Deductions for Contributions
#527	Rental Income and Royalty Income
#529	Other "Page 2" Miscellaneous Deductions
#530	Tax Information on Deductions for Homeowners
#531	Reporting Your Tips for Federal Tax Purposes
#532	Tax Information for Students and Parents
#550	Tax Information on Investment Income and Expenses
#555	Community Property and the Federal Income Tax
#559	Federal Tax Guide for Survivors, Executors, and Administrators

Fee Charged

#17	Your Federal Income Tax
#337	Law and Regulations Relating to Employee Pension, Annuity, Profit-Sharing, Stock Bonus and Bond Purchase Plans, Including Plans for Self-Employed Individuals
#377	Pension Trust Procedures and Guides for Qualification
#448	A Guide to Federal Estate and Gift Taxation Description of Principal Federal Tax Returns, Related Forms, and Publications

Figure 13-26 Internal Revenue publications of interest to individual taxpayers.

J. K. Lasser, published by Simon & Schuster, may be purchased at most bookstores for about $2.

An individual is required to maintain adequate records to substantiate income and deductions. A diary record that gives the details of each transaction is acceptable, if supported by documents. It is especially important to keep separate records on medical expenses, charitable contributions, deductible taxes, and household worker(s) expenses. The secretary who is assigned the task of maintaining these records for her employer should collect the pertinent IRS publications and then construct charts on which to collect the information in chronological order from January 1 to December 31. Files should be set up in which to collect the supporting documents. A systematic approach to the collection of income tax information will eliminate much frustration and work at the end of the year.

13.7. SOCIAL SECURITY

During working years employees, their employers, and self-employed persons pay Social Security contributions into special trust funds. When earnings stop or are reduced because the worker retires, dies, or becomes disabled, monthly cash benefits are paid from these trust funds to replace part of the earnings the family has lost. Also, part of the contributions goes into a separate hospital insurance trust fund so that workers and their dependents, upon reaching age 65, will have help in paying hospital bills. Voluntary medical insurance is available in addition for those 65 or over to help pay doctors' bills and other medical expenses. This latter program is financed out of premiums shared equally by the older people who sign up and the Federal Government (see "Medicare—Hospital and Medical Insurance" in this section).

A list of the main topics covered in this section follows.

How to Qualify for Benefits	p. 557
How to Figure Monthly Benefits	p. 559
How to Apply for Benefits	p. 560
Lump-Sum Payment at Death	p. 562
How to Question or Appeal the Decision on a Claim	p. 562
A Disabled Person	p. 563
Social Security for the Self-Employed	p. 564
Social Security for Citizens Employed by a Foreign Agency in the U.S.A.	p. 565
Reporting Cash Tips	p. 566
How to Check Social Security Earnings Record	p. 566
Social Security for Household Employees	p. 567
Medicare—Hospital and Medical Insurance	p. 567
Benefits of Workers over Age 65	p. 570
Reasons for Discontinuation of Payments	p. 570

How to Qualify for Benefits.   *Credits—Quarters of Coverage.*   To receive monthly cash payments for himself, his family, or his survivors, a worker must first have credit for a certain amount of work under Social Security. Social Security credits are called *quarters of coverage.* A worker receives credit for up to four quarters in a year, one each for the calendar quarters shown here.

Calendar Quarters

January	April
February	May
March	June
July	October
August	November
September	December

Credits are counted in the following manner.

1. A person who works for someone else gets one quarter's coverage for each calendar quarter in which he is paid total wages of $50 or more. In figuring the $50, count cash wages, the cash value of wages in kind (such as meals or a room), and tips of $20 or more in a month while working for one employer. Wages in kind do not count, however, if they are paid for work in private households or on farms.

2. A person who earns the maximum wages creditable for Social Security during the year receives credit for all four quarters of that year even if no wages are received in some of the quarters.

3. A domestic employee in a private household receives credit for only the calendar quarters in which cash payment from one employer amounts to $50 or more.

4. A farm worker, including one who does domestic work in a farmhouse, receives credit for cash pay if (a) at least $150 in cash pay is received from that employer during a year; or (b) the worker is paid in cash on a time basis (by hour, day, week) for twenty or more days during a year, regardless of the amount of pay.
Credit is given for one calendar quarter for each $100 in cash pay in a year under these rules for farm work, up to a maximum of four quarters in any one year.

5. A self-employed person receives credit for four calendar quarters in each taxable year in which he has earned a net profit of $400 or more from self-employment covered by the law. Net profit less than $400 per year does not count. A self-employed farmer, however, receives credit for a year if his gross farm income is $600 or more even if his actual net earnings are less than $400.
Minimum Number of Credits Needed.   To be fully insured, one needs a

minimum number of credits—at least one and one-half and no more than ten years of work. A fully insured status means only that certain kinds of cash benefits may be payable—it does not determine the amount.

1. For retirement. The number of quarters of credit needed to qualify for retirement benefits is shown in Figure 13-27 by date of birth. Also shown in the table is the number of credits needed for hospital insurance under Medicare by people who reach 65. No earnings credits are needed for the medical insurance part of Medicare.

2. For survivors. Benefits may also be available for survivors of a worker under Social Security. If the worker dies before reaching 65 (males) or 62

(1)	(2)	(3) Quarters of Coverage Needed for Retirement Benefits		(4) Quarters of Coverage Needed for Hospital Insurance		(5) Number of Years to Be Counted in Figuring Average Earnings	
Year Born	*Year 65*	*Men*	*Women*	*Men*	*Women*	*Men*	*Women*
1895 or earlier	1960	9	6	0	0	5	5
1896	1961	10	7	0	0	5	5
1897	1962	11	8	0	0	6	5
1898	1963	12	9	0	0	7	5
1899	1964	13	10	0	0	8	5
1900	1965	14	11	0	0	9	6
1901	1966	15	12	0	0	10	7
1902	1967	16	13	0	0	11	8
1903	1968	17	14	3	3	12	9
1904	1969	18	15	6	6	13	10
1905	1970	19	16	9	9	14	11
1906	1971	20	17	12	12	15	12
1907	1972	21	18	15	15	16	13
1908	1973	22	19	18	18	17	14
1909	1974	23	20	21	20	18	15
1910	1975	24	21	24	21	19	16
1911	1976	25	22	25	22	20	17
1912	1977	26	23	26	23	21	18
1913	1978	27	24	27	24	22	19
1917	1982	31	28	31	28	26	23
1921	1986	35	32	35	32	30	27
1925	1990	39	36	39	36	34	31
1929 or later	1994 or later	40	40	40	40	38	35

Figure 13-27   Requirements for retirement and hospital benefits under Social Security.

(females), monthly benefits can go to certain members of the family if the worker has one quarter of coverage for each year after 1950 and up to the year of death if he was born in 1929 or before; or after his twenty-first birthday and up to the year of death if he was born in 1930 or later. Regardless of a worker's birth date, monthly payments can be made to surviving dependent children if the person worked one and one-half years (six quarters) in the three years before death. A widow may also be eligible if she is caring for children entitled to benefits based on the worker's earnings.

3. For disability. Disability benefits depend upon the worker's age when he became disabled. If the person is under 24, he will need credit for one and one-half years of work (six quarters) out of the three-year period ending when the disability begins. If the worker is 24 to 30 years of age, credit is needed for half the period from the time of his 21st birthday until he became disabled. A person 31 or older needs credit for five years of work out of the ten years ending with disability—in other words, twenty quarters of coverage out of the previous forty quarters. Beginning in 1972 for men and 1975 for women, the disabled worker will also need to be fully insured and eligible for retirement benefits as if he had reached retirement age at the time he became disabled.

How to Figure Monthly Benefits.   The amount of benefit depends on average earnings, not on how many quarters of coverage a worker has. Under the Social Security law, benefits are based on average earnings beginning with 1937, or beginning with 1951, whichever will give the higher benefit. Because earnings levels have been higher since 1950, most people will get higher benefits based on average yearly earnings since 1951. For those using wages earned after 1950 to find yearly average, the following computation provides a fairly accurate idea of future benefits.

First, find the number of years that must be counted.

1. For retirement benefits, find the year of birth on Figure 13-27 and in Column 5 ascertain the number of years that must be counted in figuring average earnings.

2. For disability or survivor's benefits, the following steps will establish the number of years to count: (a) a worker born before 1930 should start with 1956; and (b) a worker born after 1929 should start with the year he reached the age of 27; (c) count the starting year and each year up to but *not* including the year of disablement for disability benefits or the year of death for survivor's benefits. At least two years of earnings must be used in either case.

Second, list earnings for all years beginning with 1951. Include earnings in the year of death or the year disability began; but in retirement cases, do not include earnings in the 65th year for men or the 62nd year for women. The maximum that may be counted for any year is listed here.

1951	$3,600	1957	$4,200	1963	$4,800
1952	3,600	1958	4,200	1964	4,800
1953	3,600	1959	4,800	1965	4,800
1954	3,600	1960	4,800	1966	6,600
1955	4,200	1961	4,800	1967	6,600
1956	4,200	1962	4,800	1968	7,800
				1972 and subsequent years	9,000

Third, drop the years of your lowest earnings. Cross off the list the years of lowest earnings until the number remaining is the same as the answer to Step 1. It may be necessary to keep on the list years in which you had no earnings.

Fourth, find the benefit amount. Add up the earnings for the years left on the list and divide by the number of years you must count as determined in Step 1. The result is the average yearly earnings covered by Social Security over this period.

Most workers will not be eligible for the maximum benefits based on the $7,800 average annual wage until after the year 2000. However, Congress has periodically voted a cost-of-living increase to workers covered by the retirement, survivor's, and disability insurance. One may anticipate, therefore, slightly higher benefits than those listed in Figure 13-28.

How to Apply for Benefits. Before one can receive payments from Social Security, an application must be filed with the nearest Social Security office. It is to your advantage to apply before reaching retirement age, even if you do not plan to retire. If you have high earnings that would increase the amount of your benefit in the year you are 65 or later, your benefit amount will be refigured.

When a person who has worked under the Social Security law dies, a member of his family should get in touch with the Social Security office.

A person who is unable to come to the Social Security office should write or telephone and arrange for a representative to visit his home.

Delays in filing an application can cause loss of some benefits, because back payments for monthly cash benefits can be made for no more than 12 months. An application for a lump-sum death payment must be made within two years of the worker's death.

Proofs Needed. The following documents must be produced, whether you are applying for your own Social Security benefits or for benefits based on the earnings of another person.

1. The Social Security card or a record of the number.

2. Proof of age—a birth certificate or a baptismal certificate made at or shortly after birth for the insured and his wife, a widow, a widower, or eligible children.

Average yearly earnings after 1950 subject to Social Security tax	Less than $900	$1800	$3000	$4200	$5400	$6600	$7800	$9000
Retired worker—65 or older } Disabled worker—under 65 }	70.40	111.90	145.60	177.70	208.80	240.30	275.80	295.40
Wife 65 or older	35.20	56.00	72.80	88.90	104.40	120.20	137.90	147.70
Retired worker at 62	56.30	89.50	116.50	142.10	167.10	192.30	220.70	236.40
Wife at 62, no child	26.40	42.00	54.70	66.70	78.30	90.10	103.50	110.80
Widow at 62 or older	70.40	92.40	120.10	146.60	172.30	198.20	227.60	243.80
Widow at 60, no child	61.00	80.10	104.20	127.20	149.40	171.80	197.30	211.30
Disabled widow at 50, no child	42.80	56.10	72.90	89.00	104.50	120.20	138.00	147.80
Wife under 65 and one child	35.20	56.10	77.20	131.30	181.10	194.90	202.20	221.60
Widow under 62 and one child	105.60	167.90	218.50	266.60	313.30	360.40	413.80	443.20
Widow under 62 and two children	105.60	167.90	222.60	308.90	389.80	435.30	477.80	517.00
One child of retired or disabled worker	35.20	56.00	72.80	88.90	104.40	120.20	137.90	147.70
One surviving child	70.40	83.90	109.20	133.30	156.60	180.20	206.90	221.60
Maximum family payment	105.60	167.90	222.60	308.90	389.80	435.30	477.80	517.00

Figure 13-28 Examples of monthly cash payments under Social Security.

3. If applying for wife's, widow's, or widower's benefits, a marriage certificate.

4. The insured worker's Form W-2, "Wage and Tax Statement," from the previous year. If he was self-employed, a copy of the last federal income tax return.

5. Proof of support by a parent or a husband applying for benefits.

Apply immediately for benefits even if all the above proofs are not available. The Social Security office will advise you about other proofs that may be used.

Lump-Sum Payment at Death. The lump-sum payment at a worker's death is ordinarily three times the amount of his monthly retirement benefit at the age of 65, or $255, whichever is less.

How to Question or Appeal the Decision on a Claim. If a worker covered by Social Security feels that the decision on his claim or on any other of his rights under the Social Security law is not correct, he may take the following steps within specified time limits to have his claim reconsidered.

Reconsideration. He may make a request for reconsideration within six months of the date of the mailing of the notice of the initial determination. A thorough examination of all the evidence submitted when the original decision was made plus any additional evidence is made by persons other than those who made the original determination to ensure a new and independent decision. If the worker still disagrees with the reconsidered decision, he may take the next step.

Hearing Before a Hearing Examiner. Within six months of the date of the mailing of the notice of reconsidered determination, the worker may request a personal appearance before a hearing examiner at the nearest Social Security district office. His appearance in person may be waived, if he so desires. A copy of the examiner's written decision is sent to the worker. If this decision is not acceptable, he may request review by the Appeals Council.

Appeals Council Review. The worker may make a request within sixty days of the date of the mailing of the hearing examiner's decision or the dismissal of the hearing request. The Appeals Council may or may not decide to review the case. If the case is to be reviewed, the worker has the right to appear (in Washington, D.C.) and present new evidence and/or to file a written statement. The council sends a copy of its written decision to the worker. If the decision is not correct or if the Appeals Council has declined to review the hearing examiner's decision, the worker may bring suit in a federal district court.

Court Action. The worker may file a complaint in a district court of the United States within sixty days of the date of the mailing of the notice of the Appeals Council's decision or its denial of review.

When the last day of the period for requesting any of the actions falls on a nonworkday (Saturday, Sunday, or a national holiday), the period is extended to the next full workday. Failure to request the appropriate review within the time specified may result in loss of the right to that review and ineligibility to take advantage of the next step in the review process. However, for good cause, such time limits may be extended.

A worker may be represented by a qualified person of his own choice in dealing with the Social Security Administration at any stage of his claim. All Social Security offices have qualified personnel who are willing to discuss a claim and answer questions. All inquiries should start at the local office.

A Disabled Person.   A person is considered disabled only if he has a severe physical or mental condition that prevents him from working and if this condition is expected to last (or has lasted) for at least 12 months or is expected to result in death. A person with a severe medical condition could be eligible even if he manages to do a little work.

Disability protection is provided in three different situations.

1. Disabled workers under the age of 65 and their families.

2. Persons disabled in childhood (before the age of 18) who continue to be disabled. These benefits are payable as early as the age of 18 when a parent receives Social Security retirement or disability benefits.

3. Disabled widows, disabled dependent widowers, and (under certain conditions) disabled surviving divorced wives of workers who were insured at death. These benefits are payable to those as young as fifty.

There are special provisions for the blind. A person whose vision is no better than 20/200 even with glasses (or who has a limited visual field of 20 degrees or less) is considered "blind" under the Social Security law. If a person who meets this test of blindness has worked long enough and recently enough under Social Security, he is eligible for a disability "freeze" even if he is actually working. Under the "freeze," the years in which he had had low earnings (or no earnings) because of disability will not reduce the amount of his future benefits, which are figured from his average earnings. A person 55 to 65 years old who meets this test of blindness and who has worked long enough and recently enough under Social Security can get cash disability benefits if he is unable to perform work requiring skills or abilities comparable to the work he did regularly before he reached 55 or became blind, whichever is later. Benefits are not paid, however, for any month in which he actually performs substantial gainful work. A blind worker under 55 can become entitled to cash benefits only if he is unable to engage in *any* substantial gainful work.

Vocational rehabilitation is available to disabled persons. Everyone who applies for Social Security disability benefits is referred for possible services to his state rehabilitation agency. These services help many people to return to productive employment. Social Security often helps to pay the cost of such services.

Social Security for the Self-Employed. A person who engages in a trade, a business, or a profession, either individually or as a partner, is self-employed. Almost all self-employment is covered by Social Security.

Ministers, Christian Science practitioners, and members of religious orders are automatically covered unless exempted by the Internal Revenue Service.

A self-employed person receives Social Security credit if his net earnings are at least $400 and up to $9,000 in a year, unless he also receives wages from covered employment. If wages are also received, the worker will receive credit only for a sufficient amount of his net earnings from self-employment to bring the combined total up to $9,000.

Gross income from trade or business, less allowable business deductions and depreciation, is considered net income. If the worker is self-employed in more than one activity, the profits or losses from each of the activities must be taken into account when he is figuring total net earnings. Therefore, a net loss in one business will affect the amount of credit received from net earnings in another.

The following kinds of income do *not* count for Social Security credit.

1. Dividends from shares of stock and interest on bonds or other interest-bearing instruments issued by corporations, *unless* received in the course of business as a dealer in stocks and securities.

2. Interest from loans, *unless* the person is engaged in the business of lending money.

3. Rentals from real estate, *unless* the person acts as a real estate dealer (real estate dealers should exclude income from properties held for investment rather than as stock-in-trade) or when he regularly furnishes services primarily for the convenience of the occupant. For information on farm rental income, secure *Farmers Are Asking About Farm Rental Income* at the nearest Social Security Office.

At the end of the year, earnings of $400 or more should be reported on Form 1040 ("U.S. Individual Income Tax Return"), Schedule C ("Profit (or Loss) from Business or Profession"), and Schedule C-3 ("Computation of Social Security Self-Employment Tax"). The income tax return and schedules, along with the self-employment contribution, should be sent to the Internal Revenue Service on or before April 15 of the following year. Also, on or before April 15 of any year for which a self-employed person expects to owe income tax and self-employment contributions (see Figure 13-29 for rates) of $40 or more, a declaration of estimated tax on Form 1040-ES must be filed along with the estimated tax or the first installment of the tax.

A man and wife who operate a business as a *true* partnership or a joint venture should each report their respective shares of the business profits as net earnings from self-employment on separate schedules even though they file a joint tax return. The amount of net earnings each should report depends

Period	Retirement, Survivors, and Disability Insurance	Hospital Insurance	Total
EMPLOYER-EMPLOYEE, Each			
1969-70	4.2%	0.60%	4.8%
1971-72	4.6	.60	5.2
1973-75	5.0	.65	5.65
1976-79	5.0	.70	5.7
1980-86	5.0	.80	5.8
1987 and after	5.0	.90	5.9
SELF-EMPLOYED			
1969-70	6.3	.60	6.9
1971-72	6.9	.60	7.5
1973-75	7.0	.65	7.65
1976-79	7.0	.70	7.7
1980-86	7.0	.80	7.8
1987 and after	7.0	.90	7.9

Note: Maximum taxable earnings base is $9,000.

Figure 13-29 Social Security contribution rate schedule for the employer, the employee, and self-employed persons.

on the terms of the partnership agreement regarding the division of the profits of the business. Each one will receive Social Security credit if each has net earnings of $400 or more.

If a man and wife are not actual business partners, net earnings go only to the one who manages and controls the business. Usually this is the husband, and the net earnings for Social Security purposes should be reported for him alone, even though a joint income tax return is filed. In a community-property state, the earnings are considered the husband's unless the wife exercises practically all management and control of the business.

A parent and his child may work together to conduct a business as partners or joint venturers. In either case, both are self-employed, and each should report his share of the profits of the business as his net earnings.

Social Security for Citizens Employed by a Foreign Agency in the U.S.A. A United States citizen who works for a foreign government, an international organization, or an instrumentality wholly owned by a foreign government within the fifty states and U.S. territories should report his earnings from these employers as though he were self-employed. See "Social Security for the Self-Employed" in this section.

Reporting Cash Tips. Earnings in the form of tips are covered by Social Security. Cash tips that add up to $20 or more a month in the course of work for *one* employer must be reported. If the tips are split or shared with other workers, only the amount finally received counts. If the employer requires customers to pay a service charge and this charge is divided among the employees, the part the employee receives is considered a regular wage and *not* a tip.

The employee must give the employer a written report of tips within ten days after the end of the month if they add up to $20 or more in a month. If the person works for more than one employer during the month, the $20 limit applies separately to the tips received while working for each employer. The Internal Revenue Service provides Form 4070 ("Employee's Report of Tips") to use in making tip reports. Document 5635, in which to keep a record of tips and reports, can be obtained from the IRS. These records of daily and monthly tips should become a part of the worker's personal tax papers. *Non-Cash Tips or Gifts.* Tips received in any form other than cash, such as passes, tickets, or merchandise, should not be included with cash tips. Their value must be reported by the employee, however, on his income tax return. *Payment of Social Security Contribution on Tips.* The employer collects Social Security tax contributions on tips. He may deduct the money either from regular wages he owes the employee or from funds given him by the employee for the purpose of paying contributions. The employer does not match the employee's contribution on tips as he does on regular wages. The employee pays the same tax rate on tips as he pays on his regular wages. (Figure 13-29.)

An employer reports tips and regular wages to the Internal Revenue Service every three months on Form 941(IRS). These returns are later sent to the Social Security Administration, where wages and tips are credited to the employee's record. Tips reported to the employer on Form W-2 ("Wage and Tax Statement") are also reported. Any uncollected Social Security tax contributions due on tips are reported to the IRS by the employer and must be paid by the employee with his income tax return for that year.

How to Check Social Security Earnings Record. A person may check his earnings record by sending a post card to the Social Security Administration, P.O. Box 57, Baltimore, Maryland 21203, or by securing from the local Social Security office a post card form to use in requesting a copy of his record.

If the amounts on the statement received from the SSA do not agree with the worker's records, he should get in touch with his local Social Security office immediately. If this is not feasible, he should write the local office, giving his Social Security number, the periods of work in question, the pay in each period, and the employer's name and address. If the earnings in question were from self-employment, the date of the filing of the tax return and the address of the IRS office to which the return was sent should be given.

Social Security for Household Employees. All household employees, both men and women are covered by Social Security if an employer pays them cash wages of $50 or more in a calendar quarter for household work performed in or about the employer's private home. Household workers include maids, cooks, butlers, cleaning women, gardeners, handymen, and so on. Babysitters, adult or teen-age, are also included if they come to a private home to care for children. People who do similar work in rooming houses, boarding houses, hotels, motels, and so on, are covered even if they are paid less than $50 in a calendar quarter. Workers who perform similar duties on farms operated for profit are also covered, but under different conditions. The local Social Security office can provide information about farm workers.

Contributions are shared equally by the worker and the employer. The same contribution rate applies to these workers as to all other workers (Figure 13-29). The employer may deduct the correct percentage from the worker's cash wages or may pay the worker's contribution together with his contribution. Before the end of the month after the calendar quarter (Figure 13-23), the employer must send these contributions, using either Form 942 or Form 941, with a report of wages paid, to the Internal Revenue Service. The employer must also give each household employee a yearly statement of the total wages paid during the year and the total amount of Social Security contributions deducted (or paid for him) from those wages.

Household work performed as an employee by a child under 21 for his parent, by a husband for his wife, or by a wife for her husband is not covered by the law. Household work performed by a parent in the home of his son or daughter may be covered in some cases but only if specified conditions are met. For details, inquire at the local Social Security office.

Medicare—Hospital and Medical Insurance. *Hospital Insurance.* Everyone who is 65 or older and is entitled to monthly cash Social Security or railroad retirement benefits gets hospital insurance automatically. Even if a person is still working for substantial earnings and does not plan to retire, he still receives hospital insurance protection. Figure 13-27, Column 4, shows the number of quarters of credit needed for hospital insurance at age 65.

To receive hospital protection starting the month in which he reaches 65, a worker must apply two or three months before his 65th birth date. The following services are covered.

1. Up to 90 days in a participating hospital during each *spell of illness.*

For the first 60 days, hospital insurance pays all but the first $50. For the next 30 days, it pays all but $13 a day. (Payment for treatment in a psychiatric hospital is limited to 190 days during a lifetime.)

2. A "lifetime reserve" of 60 additional hospital days that is not renewable after used. Hospital insurance pays all but $26 a day for these additional days.

3. Up to 100 days of care in a participating extended-care facility (a skilled nursing home or a special part of a hospital) that meets the requirements of the law. Hospital insurance pays for all covered services for the first 20 days of care and all but $6.50 daily for the next 80 days. Extended care services are for persons who have been in the hospital for 3 days or longer and enter the facility within 14 days after leaving the hospital. The patient must require skilled nursing in connection with the illness for which he was treated in the hospital.

4. Up to 100 home health visits (within a twelve-month period) by nurses, physical therapists, or certain health workers (not doctors) from a participating home health agency. Services must be in connection with an illness for which treatment of at least 3 days was given in a hospital or extended-care facility, and be part of a plan set up by the doctor within.14 days after the patient has left the hospital or extended-care facility.

(a) Spell of illness. A spell of illness begins on the first day that covered services are received as a patient in a hospital and ends 60 consecutive days after discharge from the hospital or skilled nursing home.

(b) Covered services. These services in a hospital or extended-care facility include the cost of room and meals (including special diets) in semiprivate accommodations (two to four beds); regular nursing services; the use of operating rooms; and the cost of drugs, supplies, appliances, and equipment that are furnished for use in the facility and that are ordinarily furnished to inpatients of the hospital or extended-care facility.

(c) Services not covered. Hospital insurance gives basic protection against the high cost of illness after one reaches the age of 65 but will not pay all health care bills. No payment is made for doctor bills; custodial care; private duty nurses; the cost of the first three pints of blood needed in the hospital during a spell of illness; items furnished for convenience, such as a telephone or television in the room; or services outside the United States or its possessions.

Medical Insurance.   Practically anyone who is 65 or older may sign up for voluntary medical insurance under Medicare, whether he has worked under Social Security or not and whether or not he has retired. Aliens may sign up only if they were lawfully admitted to the United States and have lived here continuously for the last five years. The premium rate is $5.30 a month, and may be increased each year by the government if the current rate is not enough to cover the program's expenses.

1. Sign-up periods. A person may sign up for medical insurance only

during specified periods. The first period begins three months before reaching age 65 and ends three months after the month in which age 65 is reached. The next opportunity to sign up is the first three months of each year. Protection does not begin until the July following the month of enrollment. If a person has not signed up within three years of his first opportunity, he loses the privilege of enrolling for medical insurance.

2. Services provided. Medical insurance helps pay for the following services.

(a) Physicians' services in office, hospital, home, or elsewhere in the United States. (There is a special limitation (approximately $250) on psychiatric care outside of a hospital.)

(b) Up to 100 home health visits each year by nurses, physical therapists, and other health workers from a qualified home health agency. Eligibility does not depend on one's having been hospitalized, but the visits must be arranged by a doctor. These are in addition to the visits available under the hospital insurance plan.

(c) Other medical and health services prescribed by the doctor, such as diagnostic services; X-ray or other radiation treatments; portable X-ray services in the home; surgical dressings and splints, casts, and braces; artificial limbs and eyes; and the rental or purchase of durable medical equipment, such as wheelchairs or hospital beds for use in the home.

(d) Drugs administered by the doctor.

(e) Full reasonable charges for laboratory, and X-ray and other radiology services performed by a physician for a bed patient in a hospital.

(f) Certain services furnished by a hospital or extended-care facility for which hospital insurance cannot pay. Examples are X-ray and laboratory services furnished after hospital insurance benefits in a spell of illness are exhausted.

(g) Outpatient physical therapy services furnished by an approved agency.

(h) All hospital outpatient services, including diagnosis and treatment.

(i) Certain services by podiatrists other than routine foot care or the treatment of flat feet or partial dislocations.

3. Amount paid by medical insurance. Medical insurance pays 80 percent of reasonable charges for all covered services for the year above a $50 deductible.

4. Services not covered. Some services and supplies are not covered, such as routine physical checkups, prescription drugs and patent medicines, eyeglasses or examinations performed for the purpose of fitting eyeglasses, hearing aids, immunizations, dentures and routine dental care, orthopedic shoes, service provided outside the United States, personal comfort items, and the first three pints of blood received other than as a hospital inpatient in each calendar year.

5. Dropping out and reenrollment. A written notice is required to drop medical insurance. Protection and obligation to pay the premium stops at the end of the calendar quarter following the quarter in which the notice is

received. Reenrollment may be made during the first three months of any year within three years after one drops out.

Benefits of Workers over 65. *General Rule.* The conditions under which benefits are paid to people who work after age 65 are as follows.

1. You may earn $1,680 or less in a year and receive all the benefits.

2. If you are under age 72, earnings over $1,680 and up to $2,880 call for a deduction of $1 in benefits for each $2 earned over $1,680. In addition, $1 in benefits will be withheld for each $1 of earnings over $2,880.

Exception to the general rule: Regardless of total earnings in a year, benefits are payable for any month in which you neither earn wages of more than $140 nor perform substantial services in self-employment.

3. If you are 72 or older, benefits are payable for all months regardless of the amount of earnings.

Earnings to Be Counted. Earnings from work of any kind must be counted, whether or not the work is covered by Social Security. Tips amounting to less than $20 a month with any one employer, however, are not counted. Total wages (not just take-home pay) and all net earnings from self-employment must be added together. Income from savings, investments, pensions, insurance, or royalties received after age 65 because of copyrights or patents obtained before age 65, should *not* be counted as earnings.

Reasons for Discontinuation of Payments. Once monthly Social Security payments are started, they continue until stopped for one of the following reasons.

1. Marriage. Benefits for a child, an aged dependent parent, a disabled dependent widower, a divorced wife, a disabled widow, or a widow receiving mother's benefits generally stop when the beneficiary marries a person who is not also getting Social Security dependent's or survivor's benefits.

The exception is for the widow who remarries after reaching age 60. If she could have qualified for benefits on her deceased husband's record, she may still get benefits on that record. She would qualify for one half of her deceased husband's retirement benefit or (at age 62) for the amount of the wife's benefit on her later husband's record, whichever is larger. A similar provision applies to widowers who remarry after age 62.

2. Divorce. Payments to a wife or a dependent husband generally end if a divorce is granted. However, if a wife of 62 or older and her husband are divorced, benefits to the wife may continue if the marriage lasted at least twenty continuous years before the divorce. If a wife under age 65 and her husband are divorced after twenty continuous years of marriage, she may receive benefits at age 62 or later, providing certain conditions are met.

3. No child "in her care." Payment to a wife under age 62 or to a widow or surviving divorced wife under age 60 will generally stop when she no longer has in her care a child under 18 or disabled. A widow or surviving

divorced wife who is age 50 or over and is severely disabled should get in touch with the Social Security office for information about any benefits that may be payable.

4. Child reaches age 18. When a child reaches age 18, his payments stop unless he is disabled or is a full-time, unmarried student. If a student, he is eligible for benefits until he reaches age 22.

5. Adoption. An adopted child's payments end unless he is adopted by his stepparent, grandparent, aunt, uncle, brother, or sister after the death of the person on whose record he is receiving benefits.

6. Death. When any person receiving monthly benefits dies, his or her payments end.

7. Disability benefits. When the benefits payable to a person stop because he is no longer disabled, the benefits payable to his dependents also stop.

If payments end because of any of the above reasons, the last check due is the one for the month *before* the event.

13.8 PROTECTION AND REPLACEMENT OF IMPORTANT DOCUMENTS

To alleviate any future problems, it is wise to know at all times where important documents are located and that they are properly secured. As explained in Section 3.2, the security of classified government documents must conform to government regulations. Important company papers, such as those of incorporation or partnership agreements, must be retained for the life of the company. The proper filing and retention of these types of documents is fully explained in Section 12.1, "Records Management."

Protection of Important Personal Documents. Personal documents require the same careful attention as that given to important papers belonging to a company. Accurate and detailed records should be kept in several places— dates, names, numbers, and so on, of all valuable papers, such as birth, marriage, stock certificates; insurance policies; deeds; credit and charge-account cards; banking records; tax and estate records; all papers having to do with security transactions; employment and Social Security information. A list of the facts pertinent to the personal papers should be kept at home, another copy at the office, and a third copy in a safe deposit box along with irreplaceable documents. This list should be updated every year. Trying to recall or collect information after papers are lost, stolen, or destroyed is difficult and time-consuming. The documents themselves should be kept in the safest place available to the individual—home, office, or bank. The Social Security card, the driver's license, and credit cards are usually carried on one's person. If they are not, they should be filed carefully or locked away until needed. For some documents, you should consider having duplicate copies made and then should store each one in a different place. Hidden items often cause frustration as one hunts for them. Therefore, resist the temptation to bury documents and their copies but merely place them in logical places or file them systematically by cross-referencing.

Replacement of Documents. If documents are lost, stolen, burned, or damaged in any other way, the following suggestions on how to replace them will help you secure copies without too much difficulty.

Birth, Marriage, and Divorce Certificates. Write the bureau of vital statistics, or similar office, in the city where you were born, married, or divorced. Be sure to supply detailed information to assist them in locating the correct record—your name; your present and previous addresses; your parents' names; your maiden name, if necessary; the date of the event; the hospital or church; the doctor, minister, or attorney; and so on. In a large city, there are so many identical names that it is often difficult to isolate the correct person. Most cities charge a fee, which must be paid in advance, for a photostat or copy of the requested certificate.

A person lacking a birth certificate can secure proof of age from the Census Bureau. A letter should be sent to Bureau of the Census, Personal Census Service Branch, Pittsburg, Kansas 66762, asking for an "Age Search Application Form." The form contains instructions for its completion and must be returned with the fee of $4. If a fast reply is needed, the fee is $5.

Checks. If a check you sent someone does not arrive, ask the bank to stop payment. A telephone request must be followed by a letter or a completed bank form for stopping payment. Banks usually levy a small charge for this service. Next, notify the payee not to cash or deposit the check if it does turn up later, but to return it to you. Give him the number and the date of the lost check for identification. Then issue him a new one.

Commercial Checkbook. If you lose blank checks or your entire checkbook, notify the bank immediately. They will need to know the missing check numbers. A caution card will be attached to your records in the bank, and thereafter the bank assumes responsibility in case someone attempts to present one of your checks for payment. Most banks recommend closing the account and opening a new one.

Credit and Charge-Account Cards. Notify immediately by telephone or telegraph the nearest business office of the company issuing the particular credit card. Give your complete name and address; the account or card number; the location and the date when it was lost, stolen, or damaged. If you reported the loss to the police, include this fact. Follow up the verbal contact with a letter giving the same information. You are usually not held responsible for charges made by others to your account after you have properly notified the issuer of the card. By federal law, an individual's maximum liability for the fraudulent use of any kind of credit card is limited to $50 per card.

Keep a separate record of all credit and charge-account cards in your possession so that you will have the number and be able to report the loss immediately. A card case with transparent sections will remind you visually of a missing card.

Deeds to Real Property. If a deed to property is lost or destroyed, a copy may be secured for a small fee from the county recorder where the property is located. Sometimes a deed is not necessary when one is transferring property that has been sold. Sales of real estate that go through escrow do not require a copy of the deed because title to the property is searched by a title company and a new deed issued to the new owner.

Driver's License and Car Registration or Pink Slip. Go to the nearest office of the Department of Motor Vehicles and apply for a duplicate of your driver's license. If you have proper identification, you will receive a duplicate permit immediately. If not, you will be mailed one in a few days. There is a small fee for this service.

If the pink slip for your automobile is lost, take the original registration slip to the Department of Motor Vehicles. They will issue a duplicate pink slip. If the registration slip is lost, take the pink slip in for a new white registration slip. It is best to take care of these losses immediately for your own protection. Also, if you are cited for a traffic violation, there is usually an additional fine for driving without a license.

Government Savings Bonds. Write the Bureau of Public Debt, Division of Loan and Currency, 536 South Clark Street, Chicago, Illinois 60605, for Form PD 1048. List the serial numbers of the bonds, dates issued, and persons to whom issued. Duplicate bonds are forthcoming in about six months and carry the same issue dates as the old ones. In cases of hardship, when prompt replacement is important, a letter should be sent with the completed form explaining the circumstances. Every effort will be made to replace the bonds as quickly as possible.

Income Tax Returns. You may secure a copy of an old tax return by writing the Internal Revenue Service office where the original return was filed. Send adequate identifying information, such as the year of the return, the Social Security number(s), the name(s), and the address. A copy of the return should be forthcoming in about two months for a small fee.

Insurance Policies. Notify your agent or the headquarters of the insurance company by telephone or in writing of the loss of the policy. Include as much pertinent data as possible—the kind, the names in which issued, the number, the dates, and so on. Insurance coverage continues without interruption while a duplicate policy is being processed. The important point here is that the policy or record of it be among the personal papers of a deceased person so that his estate may make claim for any proceeds that may be due.

Mortgage and Other Loan Papers. Notify the company, the bank, or the other institution that loaned the money by telephone or in writing. A photocopy of the agreement will be sent you. If your payment book has been lost, the bank or collecting agent will replace it.

Passport. If you lose your passport abroad, notify the nearest United States embassy or consulate. A duplicate will be issued within a week. Passports lost in this country should be reported to the local passport agency, if there is one, or the local police station. It is important to be able to supply your passport number. For those cities without an office (even though the loss has been reported to the police), write the Passport Agency, Department of State, Washington, DC 20520, giving the number, the date of issue, the name(s) in which issued, and other pertinent facts.

Savings Passbook or Receipt Book. The savings receipt book that has been used since 1967 records only the total of the deposit or the withdrawal. The customer must keep his own record of the current balance in the pages provided at the back of the book. If the savings passbook in which the bank continues to maintain a running balance for the customer or the receipt book is lost, a restriction is placed on the account for thirty days. A new book using the same account number is issued after that time. A new account number may be secured if desired. Usually, the customer is allowed to withdraw some of the funds on deposit before the new book is issued.

Social Security Card. Take the duplicate card given you when you first obtained your Social Security card to the post office or the nearest Social Security office. If you are unable to find the duplicate, secure your Social Security number from your list of important documents, a paycheck receipt, or a copy of your last year's income tax form. At the Social Security office you will be given a replacement application to complete. A new card will be processed within ten days. To find the address of the local Social Security office, look in the phone book under "United States Government, Department of Health, Education and Welfare."

Stock Certificates. Notify the transfer agent immediately. If you do not have a record of the agent, write the company or call a local broker or stock exchange if there is one in your area. The company will alert the transfer agent for the stock or tell you to. The agent, in turn, will put a *stop* against your stock.

Most companies require that you purchase an indemnity bond from a surety company before a replacement certificate is processed. The issuing company is then protected against the sale of the missing certificate by someone else. An indemnity bond premium costs approximately $40 per $1,000 of a stock's current market value. The premium is not returnable.

If you lose the record of the purchase or sale of stock, which information is needed for income tax accounting, contact your broker (he need not be the one through which you purchased or sold the stock). He will contact the exchanges for prices and will also supply the brokerage fees paid on each transaction.

Traveler's Checks. The numbers of traveler's checks should be kept separately from the checks themselves. If any checks are lost, go to the issuing company's branch office or its local representative, such as a bank or travel agent. You will be asked to sign an affidavit listing the numbers of the missing checks and the date and place of their loss. Replacement checks are issued immediately. If you do not have the numbers, you may be given a partial refund only; and the balance will be paid as soon as the agent receives confirmation of your purchase from the issuing office or bank. When traveling abroad, take precautions to safeguard traveler's checks, even though representatives of issuing companies are extremely helpful in cases of emergency.

14

International Trade

The world has become a one-market, low-tariff area, and most countries have entered an era of tremendously expanded international trade. With stepped-up competition in all markets, at home and abroad, U.S. firms will need to compete aggressively in protecting and strengthening both their domestic and their overseas markets. Those who limit their horizons to the U.S. market will find themselves in trouble from foreign competitors. Consequently the government has called upon American businessmen to step up export activity and to increase income from overseas trade. The information in this chapter will provide valuable reference material for the exporter and the businessman interested in becoming an exporter.

CONTENTS

14.1 Doing Business Abroad   p. 576
14.2 Foreign Countries, Their Capitals, and Descriptive National Terms   p. 604
14.3 Foreign Money and Its Value   p. 607
14.4 Customs Regulations   p. 612
14.5 U.S. Foreign Service Posts   p. 621

14.1 DOING BUSINESS ABROAD

Any businessman interested in entering the export market or in increasing the worldwide market for his product should work closely with the Bureau of International Commerce of the Department of Commerce. The prime objective of the Bureau is to increase U.S. exports through these means.

Providing services and information that make it easier for American businessmen to trade abroad.

Operating trade centers, organizing and sponsoring trade missions, and running trade fair exhibits and other marketing devices to promote U.S. goods in markets abroad.

Working with other government agencies and international organizations to create a climate in which international trade and investment can flourish.

Presenting the views of traders and investors in governmental councils.
Working out policies and procedures that make it simpler and more profitable to do
  business abroad.

Following is an index to topics dealt with in this section. You may secure
further information by visiting or writing the Bureau of International Commerce, Fourteenth Street between Constitution Avenue and E Street NW,
Washington, DC 20230, or the nearest Department of Commerce field office.
(See Figure 14-1 for the addresses of field offices.)

Department of Commerce Services	p. 577
Publications of Interest	p. 580
Bibliographies of Interest to the Exporter	p. 584
Stateside (Private) Assistance	p. 585
Assistance Abroad	p. 587
Foreign Market Reports	p. 592
Other Export Considerations	p. 595
Shipping to the Market	p. 599
Foreign-Trade Zones	p. 600
Collecting from the Market	p. 600
Other Market Information	p. 602
Export Reference Guides	p. 603

Department of Commerce Services. *Registration with the Bureau of International Commerce.* Businessmen who register with the Commercial
Intelligence Division of the Bureau of International Commerce are placed on
the Department's mailing list ("American International Traders Index") to
receive information about export trade opportunities applicable to U.S.
firms. A company will also be notified of future program activities covering
its products. Through this service an exporter may keep up-to-date on specific
assistance offered by the Department of Commerce.
Export Counseling Service. All inquiries received by the Department of
Commerce in Washington concerning questions or problems that involve
exporting are directed to the Export Counseling Section of the Export
Business Relations Division for initial discussions to ensure that all relevant
governmental resources are brought to bear in each case. In addition to special
guidance for firms new to export and continual aid to established exporters,
the Division works closely with other divisions of the Commerce Department,
the Departments of Agriculture and Interior, the Agency for International
Development, the Small Business Administration, and the Export-Import
Bank. It will arrange appointments for the exporter throughout these agencies.
   The Division has operational responsibility for the Piggyback Program.
This program is used for the purpose of getting U.S. producers, new to
export, to export through the facilities of other, more experienced U.S.
producers or Combination Export Managers (CEM's), Export Distributors
(ED's), and Intermediary Exporters (IE's) with overseas distribution outlets.
The service offered consists of receiving and recording inquiries from U.S.
producers who as "riders" want to have other U.S. producers distribute their

Albuquerque, NM 87101
U.S. Courthouse
Area Code 505 843-2386

Anchorage, AK 99501
412 Hill Building
632 Sixth Avenue
Area Code 907 272-6531

Atlanta, GA 30303
Home Savings Bldg.
75 Forsyth Street, N.W.
Area Code 404 526-6000

Baltimore, MD 21202
305 U.S. Customhouse
Gay and Lombard Streets
Area Code 301 962-3560

Birmingham, AL 35205
908 S. 20th Street
Area Code 205 325-3327

Boston, MA 02203
John F. Kennedy Federal
  Building
Area Code 617 223-2312

Buffalo, NY 14203
504 Federal Bldg.
117 Ellicott Street
Area Code 716 842-3208

Charleston, SC 29403
Federal Bldg., Suite 631
334 Meeting Street
Area Code 803 577-4171

Charleston, WV 25301
3000 New Federal Office
  Building
500 Quarrier Street
Area Code 304 343-6181

Cheyenne, WY 82001
6022 O'Mahoney Federal
  Center
2120 Capitol Avenue
Area Code 307 778-2220

Chicago, IL 60604
219 S. Dearborn St.
Area Code 312 353-4400

Cincinnati, OH 45202
8028 Federal Office
  Building
550 Main Street
Area Code 513 684-2944

Cleveland, OH 44114
666 Euclid Avenue
Area Code 216 522-4750

Dallas, TX 75202
1114 Commerce Street
Area Code 214 749-3287

Denver, CO 80202
Room 161, New
  Customhouse
19th and Stout Streets
Area Code 303 837-3246

Des Moines, IA 50309
609 Federal Bldg.
210 Walnut Street
Area Code 515 284-4222

Detroit, MI 48226
445 Federal Bldg.
Area Code 313 226-6088

Greensboro, NC 27402
258 Federal Bldg.
P.O. Box 1950
Area Code 919 275-9111

Hartford, CT 06103
Federal Office Bldg.
450 Main Street
Area Code 203 244-3530

Honolulu, HI 96813
286 Alexander Young Bldg.
1015 Bishop Street
Area Code 808 546-5977

Houston, TX 77002
1017 Old Federal Bldg.
201 Fannin Street
Area Code 713 226-4231

Jacksonville, FL 32202
P.O. Box 35087
400 West Bay Street
Area Code 904 791-2796

Kansas City, MO 64106
601 East 12th Street
Room 1840
Area Code 816 374-3141

Los Angeles, CA 90024
11402 Federal Building
11000 Wilshire Blvd.
Area Code 213 824-7691

Memphis, TN 38103
147 Jefferson Ave.
Area Code 901 534-3214

Miami, FL 33130
25 West Flagler St.
Area Code 305 350-5267

Milwaukee, WI 53203
Straus Building
238 W. Wisconsin Ave.
Area Code 414 234-3473

Minneapolis, MN 55401
306 Federal Building
110 S. Fourth Street
Area Code 612 725-2133

New Orleans, LA 70130
909 Federal Office Bldg.
610 South Street
Area Code 504 527-6546

New York, NY 10007
Federal Office Bldg.
Foley Square
Area Code 212 264-0634

Figure 14-1 Locations of field offices of the United States Department of Commerce.

Philadelphia, PA 19107
Jefferson Bldg.
1015 Chestnut Street
Area Code 215 597-2850

Reno, NV 89502
2028 Federal Building
300 Booth Street
Area Code 702 784-5203

San Francisco, CA 94102
Federal Bldg., Box 36013
450 Golden Gate Avenue
Area Code 415 556-5864

Phoenix, AZ 85025
5413 New Federal Bldg.
230 N. First Avenue
Area Code 602 261-3285

Richmond, VA 23240
2105 Federal Bldg.
400 N. 8th Street
Area Code 703 782-2246

San Juan, PR 00902
Rm. 100, Post Office Bldg.
Area Code 809 723-4640

Pittsburgh, PA 15222
431 Federal Bldg.
1000 Liberty Avenue
Area Code 412 644-2850

St. Louis, MO 63103
2511 Federal Bldg.
1520 Market Street
Area Code 314 622-4243

Savannah, GA 31402
125-29 Bull Street
Area Code 912 232-4321

Portland, OR 97204
217 Old U.S. Courthouse
520 S.W. Morrison St.
Area Code 503 226-3361

Salt Lake City, UT 8411
1201 Federal Building
125 South State Street
Area Code 801 524-5116

Seattle, WA 98104
8021 Federal Office Bldg.
909 First Avenue
Area Code 206 442-5815

Figure 14-1   (continued).

lines overseas, or as "carriers" want to distribute in foreign markets the lines of other producers. It also matches riders with appropriate carriers (obviously of lines that are compatible but noncompetitive), and connects the 42 U.S. Department of Commerce field offices with such riders and carriers to provide assistance as needed to ensure productive working relationships between them.

This division is also a central source of information on nongovernment-sponsored foreign fairs and exhibitions, maintaining files of pertinent foreign service despatches, official fair catalogs, pamphlets, and other materials concerning international trade shows that may offer U.S. firms a means of displaying their products and thereby increasing their export sales. It operates an export information office in Washington, located in the lobby of the Commerce Department building on the Fourteenth Street side, between Constitution Avenue and E Street. The telephone numbers are Area Code 202 967-2732, 2733, 3181, or 3182.

Export Market Identification.   The Export Market Identification Division identifies specific export opportunities, by product and country, that have immediate and long-term sales potential. These product/market opportunities are determined by the pulling together and analyzing of market research data from a multitude of sources. The results are disseminated to the U.S. business community in the form of regularly issued publications. They are designed to motivate the new exporter or nonexporter to undertake positive action to capitalize on export potentials identified in the studies.

Concurrently, the EMI develops, on a highly selective basis, several long-term global marketing plans. Each of these plans covers a product or a product category and projects maximum export sales growth on a worldwide basis over a two- to five-year period. The implementation of each global plan is the dual responsibility of industry and government, and industry is encouraged to participate in Commerce Department trade promotional activities in those markets that offer the best sales potential and optimum profit return.

Joint Export Associations.   The Joint Export Associations (JEA) program offers cooperation and financial assistance from the U.S. government to groups of manufacturers joining together to sell abroad. Under the JEAs, the government shares specified costs of overseas market development activities with cooperating groups on a contract basis. The JEAs provide the means for planned, long-term development of selected export markets by joint industry/government action. Industry groups seeking support are required to prepare detailed proposals for promotional activities for which they desire the government to share the costs. They have operational responsibility; the government, through the Bureau of International Commerce, provides planning and other assistance related to trade expansion programs and maintains the degree of supervision necessary to assure fulfillment of the contracts.

The following promotional activities are illustrative of those eligible for government assistance.

Advertising and publicity
Participation in trade exhibitions
Market research
Supplying samples and technical data
Preparing and submitting bids
Overseas promotional visits
Training of sales and service personnel
Product-use familiarization programs
Operation abroad of sales offices, showrooms, warehouses, and service centers

Four general types of business organizations are most adaptable to this program: (1) trade associations or subsidiaries or components thereof; (2) groups of firms operating under the leadership of export management companies; (3) export trade associations organized under the Webb-Pomerene Export Trade Act of 1918; (4) groups of firms specially organized to participate in this program; (5) piggyback arrangements, whereby one manufacturer represents a group of companies with related products.

Publications of Interest.   *Department of Commerce.*   The following publications of the Department of Commerce are helpful to any company engaged in worldwide trade. Most of them may be secured from the field offices or from the Department of Commerce, Publication Sales and Distribution Branch, Office of Administrative Services, Washington, DC 20230.

1. "Exporting—A How to Get Started Handbook" covers most of the services and programs of the Department of Commerce and also contains suggestions for the use of private facilities.

2. "Selling Around the World" covers much the same information as the

"Handbook"; but because it is limited to an explanation of the services of the Department of Commerce, it goes into some of these in greater detail. It is not as comprehensive as the "Handbook," however, in covering all the steps and elements that are necessary for the whole export marketing package.

3. "Low Cost Marketing Aids for Higher Export Profits" is a pamphlet that describes the purposes of trade lists, world-trade directory reports, trade contact surveys, and the agency index. It includes trade list classifications by commodities, and points out that certain countries are covered by general trade lists, known as *business firms lists,* rather than by specific commodity classifications.

4. Twice a year the Bureau of International Commerce puts out a "Checklist" of international publications. In addition to listing all the Commerce Department's general "International Trade" publications, it also gives a detailed listing by country of the economic and commercial reports available for a particular country. This listing is most helpful in identifying those country, and in some cases those product/country, markets of specific interest. Also listed in the "Checklist" are recent reports of the Bureau of the Census concerning imports and exports, and reports on the overseas market for specific products by the industry divisions of the Department's Business and Defense Services Administration. A list of applicable labor law and practice monographs issued by the Department of Labor is included. A company or businessman involved in exporting should ask to be placed on the mailing list.

5. An out-of-print paperback published some years ago by the Department of Commerce, *Export and Import Practice,* is a comprehensive foreign trade guide that contains an excellent glossary of trade terms. It should be obtainable at large public libraries or at university libraries.

6. *International Commerce,* a weekly magazine published by the Department, offers practical, authoritative, and concise international marketing information, news, and reports. It carries feature articles and timetables on significant developments in the U.S. Export Expansion Program. Twice each year an issue is devoted to the world trade outlook. Each week 500 or more export trade opportunities are presented in a semiclassified advertisement style and listed by SIC code numbers. SIC code numbers refer to specific commodities as classified in the Standard Industrial Classification (SIC) Manual, which is available for $2.50 a copy from the Superintendent of Documents, U.S. Government Printing Office, Washington, DC 20402. *International Commerce* keeps an exporter, or potential exporter, constantly informed on what the Department is doing to help the U.S. business community in its international trade activities. Subscription to the magazine costs $20 a year ($6.25 additional for foreign mailing). A single copy costs 40 cents. Domestic subscribers desiring airmail service must submit an additional $28 for postage. Make the remittance payable to the Superintendent of Documents and mail it either to a U.S. Department of Commerce field office or to the Superintendent of Documents.

7. Information about a particular foreign firm mentioned in *International Commerce* is obtainable in the form of a "World Trade Directory" (WTD) report. These reports indicate the type of organization, the sales territory, the size of the business, its sales volume, its trade and financial reputation, and other factors. WTD reports may be ordered for $2 each from the Bureau of International Commerce, BIC 924, U.S. Department of Commerce, Room 6059B, Washington, DC 20230 (Phone: 202-967-4203).

8. The best sources of country information of value to exporters are the Overseas Business Reports (OBR) of the Bureau of International Commerce. Several types of information are available. The "Basic Data" series are the broadest of the group and should be studied first by the prospective exporter. Such basic data on a country as geography, population, government, economic structure, markets, national income, industries, commercial crops, mineral resources, manufacturing, power, transportation, communications, labor force, finance, banking system, foreign trade, import regulations and restrictions, and development plans of the government are included in each report.

The "Foreign Trade Regulations" series of OBR include topics such as the country's trade policy, tariff system, customs provisions, shipping documents, marking and labeling requirements, nontariff import trade controls, export controls, and representation in the United States. These reports also include any import or export controls set up by the United States in regard to the particular country.

The third informational series of the Overseas Business Reports are designed for the firm wishing to open a local plant or office in a foreign country. The "Establishing a Business" series supply current information on the investment climate; the trade factors affecting investment; the extent of foreign investment; the regulations governing investment; patents; trade-marks and copyrights; employment; taxation; the availability of capital; and investment information services. Other OBR series, "Market Profiles for *(Region),*" "Selling in *(Country),*" and "Market Factors in *(Country),*" are helpful in finding and analyzing the market.

A subscription to the Overseas Business Reports (formerly World Trade Information Service) may be entered for $16 a year ($5 additional for foreign mailing) or single copies may be secured for 15 cents each. Order them from any Department of Commerce field office or from the Superintendent of Documents, U.S. Government Printing Office, Washington, DC 20402.

Miscellaneous Sources.   Other publications of help to exporters are available from the following agencies.

1. The Small Business Administration. Of special importance to owner-managers of smaller firms who seek sales in foreign markets is the booklet *Export Marketing for Smaller Firms.* This manual, issued by the SBA, outlines for the management of smaller firms the sequence of steps necessary to determine whether and how to utilize foreign markets as a source of immediate and future profits. It describes the problems facing smaller firms engaged in, or seeking to enter, foreign trade and the many types of assistance available to help them cope with these problems. A step-by-step guide to the appraisal of the sales potential of foreign markets is included. The requirements of local marketing practices and procedures are explained. A copy of the manual may be secured from the Superintendent of Documents for 50 cents.

2. The International Monetary Fund. Another good source of financial information for a country that is a member of the International Monetary Fund is IMF's annual report series entitled *Exchange Restrictions.* The yearly report is an excellent summary of monetary regulations as they pertain to trade and capital transfers. A current copy should be available at a large public library or a university library, or may be obtained from the Fund in Washington, D.C.

3. The Department of State. United States personnel stationed at foreign service posts will perform a variety of services for the businessman engaged in international trade. For instance, the primary responsibility of the Commercial Officer is to promote trade, travel, and private investment interests of the United States. He will help develop trade contacts and export opportunities; arrange appointments for U.S. businessmen and assist in contacts with local government officials; support special overseas activities of the Department of Commerce, such as trade centers, trade missions, and trade fairs; and report on business trends, market potentials, and laws and customs that affect U.S. commercial interests. He also works toward eliminating any discriminatory treatment of U.S. business interests. The Labor Attaché is responsible for following the political and economic activities of the national labor organizations. He is ready to supply information regarding labor and social attitudes and trends, wages, nonwage costs, Social Security regulations, government labor policies and regulations, and labor attitudes toward U.S. business investments. The Department of State Publication 7877, *Key Officers of Foreign Service Posts Guide for Businessmen,* lists the addresses and the telephone numbers of foreign service posts. The names of key officers at these posts are included in the publication, which is brought up to date four times a year. It may be secured from the Superintendent of Documents by subscription for $1 a year or by single copy for 35 cents.

4. Pan American World Airways. Advice for businessmen on how to do business in foreign countries is presented in Richard G. Laurie's *Passports and Profits: Pan American Airways' Guide to Doing Business in 105 Countries.* The book contains current and detailed descriptions of business practices and standards of ethics pertinent to a particular country. Practical suggestions on conduct and amenities are included for the business visitor. You may secure a copy of *Passports and Profits* by writing Pan American, Mail Service Unit, P.O. Box 2212, Boston, MA 02107.

The Kennedy Round and You is a Pan Am publication devoted to an explanation of future tariffs as established by the Kennedy Round. Information in the booklet should help the exporter to make the most of coming world trade developments. For instance, the schedule of important tariff cuts made by the European Economic Community, by the United Kingdom, and by Japan is a useful guide to tariff reductions for a wide range of products (but not all 4,000) classified by the Brussels Tariff Nomenclature (BTN) system. Because a four-digit BTN number may encompass a number of related products, a country may have more than one duty rate per BTN number. Thus, for detailed foreign tariff reduction information, send a complete product description or the identifying BTN or U.S. Schedule B Export Commodity numbers to Kennedy Round Service, Bureau of International Commerce—880, Department of Commerce, Washington, DC 20230. You may obtain a copy of *The Kennedy Round and You* by writing the Manager-Marketing Services, Pan American World Airways, Pan Am Building, New York, NY 10017.

Pan Am also publishes a monthly magazine, *Worldwide Marketing Horizons,* in seven languages with worldwide circulation. Each issue contains foreign trade topics of interest and a comprehensive list of worldwide marketing opportunities. Buyers and sellers around the world are offered free listings each month. For information about listing products or locating names and addresses of firms importing or exporting particular products in other countries, write Pan Am's Manager-Marketing Services. To be placed on the *Horizons* mailing list write The Editor, *Worldwide Marketing Horizons* at the New York address.

Bibliographies of Interest to the Exporter. A list of private publications representative of available important material can be found in the Department of Commerce publication, "Exporting—A How to Get Started Handbook."

The Chamber of Commerce of the United States of America, 1615 H Street, NW, Washington, DC 20006, publishes a foreign commerce handbook that includes a comprehensive bibliography of reference works, books, pamphlets, and periodicals.

The Business Administration Library, Graduate School of Business Administration, University of California, Los Angeles, CA 90024, has compiled several bibliographies of interest to export firms. One monograph, "Sources of Information on Doing Business with Japan," lists reference guides, yearbooks, directories, books, journals and periodicals, specific journal articles, and publishers' addresses. Another monograph lists foreign management journals of Austria and Switzerland; Belgium and the Netherlands; France; Germany; Italy; Spain; Latin America; Scandinavia; India and Pakistan; Great Britain, the Commonwealth (excluding Canada), and Ireland; Japan, Korea, Taiwan; Africa, Malaysia, the Middle East, and the Philippines.

Selective bibliographies are published by the Bureau of International

Commerce Clearinghouse on 300 general subjects of wide industrial interest, such as lubricants, transistors, plastics, welding, and cements. There is a $1-each distribution charge. As a special service, Clearinghouse bibliographers will, upon request, make individual searches on a given topic for approximately $11 an hour. Searches of the technical document collections of the National Aeronautics and Space Administration, the Library of Congress, the Atomic Energy Commission, and the Department of Defense can be arranged at the same rate. For the bibliographies or the "current-awareness search," write the Clearinghouse, U.S. Department of Commerce, Springfield, VA 22151. Make checks payable to the National Bureau of Standards.

An interested businessman may secure a twice-monthly listing of technical translations available from the Clearinghouse and other sources for approximately $12 a year, $4 additional for foreign mailing. The subscription is handled by the Superintendent of Documents, U.S. Government Printing Office, Washington, DC 20402.

Stateside (Private) Assistance. Regional Export Expansion councils are established in the same areas served by the Department of Commerce field offices. The council members are local business leaders appointed by the Secretary of Commerce to work with the Department in promoting world trade. As a group and as individuals, they give advice and guidance to fellow businessmen interested in foreign markets but not yet exporting. These councils, in cooperation with the Department's field offices, work closely with chambers of commerce, trade associations, banks, schools, and the Small Business Administration in arranging courses, seminars, and clinics dealing with exporting procedures. They also provide private consultations between experienced and prospective exporters. Each local field office, as well as the Washington-based Office of Field Services, has a list of members.

Many banks in the United States maintain large international departments that make available to their customers a wide range of services and information. The following New York banks have well-established international departments:

Bankers Trust Company
Chase Manhattan Bank
Chemical Bank
First National City Bank
Manufacturers Hanover Trust Company
Morgan Guaranty Trust Company

If your local bank does not have an international department, it will be able to arrange for one of its correspondent banks either in your city or in New York to help you.

Several foreign banks have stateside branches in the larger cities and are willing to assist the U.S. businessman. A check of the banks listed in the yellow pages of the local telephone directory will indicate where they may be located.

Many airlines and steamship companies offer more extensive services and information to businessmen and representatives of firms than those normally available to ordinary passengers. Special services are available if there is a possibility of joint publicity arrangements and/or substantial freight contracts. Both Pan American Airways and Trans World Airlines maintain departments in international trade to assist the exporter. An examination of Pan Am's World-Wide Marketing Service indicates that ample free marketing information is available. WWMS advises the U.S. businessman, provides foreign marketing facts, finds buyers, explains foreign trade practices, and maintains a staff of trained marketing specialists. One need not first agree to ship via Pan Am to reap the benefits of their World-Wide Marketing Service. To obtain help, direct a letter on company letterhead to the Manager-Marketing Services, Pan American World Airways, Pan Am Building, New York, NY 10017, or telephone your nearest Pan Am district sales office. When writing, indicate whether you're interested in importing or exporting. Include a description of the products you wish to buy or sell and the kind of outlets you're looking for—wholesalers, retailers, processors, sales agents, and so on. Indicate your preference in the market areas also. A brief description of any previous experience in international marketing should be included. Based on the information supplied in the inquiry, a Pan Am marketing specialist will familiarize himself with your marketing goals. Likely markets for your product or promising sources of supply will be suggested. The specialist will also pinpoint the areas that offer the most promise in relation to your marketing objectives. When the most potentially profitable markets have been determined, Pan Am will arrange to transmit your descriptive material (catalogs, specification sheets, brochures, and price lists) to its local marketing service offices in the foreign areas that interest you. Pan Am has over 900 offices around the world and wide business contacts in 122 major markets overseas. The local foreign office will personally search out and contact firms whose manufacturing or sales interests are related to your own. Any solid interest received as a result of these contacts will then be reported to you for further development through correspondence or personal contact. During the seeking-out period, Pan Am can advise you on the establishment of banking and credit connections and the selection of export or import methods, or they can assist you in making any other arrangements needed to close a sale.

Pan Am's monthly trade news, *Worldwide Marketing Horizons,* will be sent to an interested businessman without charge. Published in seven languages— English, Spanish, French, German, Italian, Korean, and Japanese—and read by over 195,000 businessmen around the world, each issue spotlights overseas economic development, new markets, and new suppliers. A firm's products or needs will be advertised without charge in the classified listing of marketing opportunities, a regular feature of *Horizons*. (See "Publications of Interest, Miscellaneous Sources" in this chapter.)

Trans World Airlines provides similar services for the international business firm. A letter addressed to the Manager, MarketAir Planning, 605 Third Avenue, New York, NY 10016, should include the same information suggested for the letter to Pan Am. TWA's marketing services are explained in their "MarketAir Newsletter," which will be sent to interested persons upon request.

Steamship companies, through their freight sales departments, assist the importer/exporter with his marketing problems. For instance, when trading in the South Pacific area including Japan, contact the Matson Navigation Co., 215 Market Street, San Francisco, CA 90746, for information. Worldwide coverage is offered by twelve American steamship lines through their Committee of American Steamship Lines (CASL). These companies have 300 ships visiting 450 major ports regularly. Figure 14-2 lists the principal countries where you will find CASL offices and agents around the world. For the names and addresses of representatives in any city or port in any of the countries listed, write, wire, or phone one of the steamship companies shown opposite the country. The trade expansion program of CASL offers the exporter/importer complimentary overseas marketing information, in such areas as finding new customers overseas, increasing exports, developing new markets, locating new sources of supply, packaging, licensing, and advertising abroad. A "Trade Assistance Request" to CASL or any one of the lines listed in Figure 14-3 will bring a prompt reply.

United States port authorities are also anxious to help the exporter/importer who uses their facilities. For instance, the Massachusetts Port Authority has prepared a directory of sea and air services between Boston and major world points. The booklet contains the names of customs brokers and forwarders in Boston, a glossary of shipping terms, air trade routes, steamship trade routes, cargo ship lines and their agents serving the world from the Port of Boston, and important government addresses and telephone numbers in the Boston area. You may secure one of these booklets by writing the Massachusetts Port Authority, 470 Atlantic Avenue, Boston, MA 02110, or by telephoning 617-482-2030. Contact the port authorities of the ports listed in Figure 14-4 for information or assistance when using their facilities.

Assistance Abroad.   When abroad the U.S. businessman may contact Foreign Service officers at the U.S. embassies or consulates for assistance. Commercial officers are assigned to embassies in countries that are major trading partners of the United States. In other countries, officers assigned to the economic section perform similar functions. Reports prepared by these officers furnish the Department of Commerce with a good part of its country information. Assistance is given to visiting U.S. businessmen and representatives of U.S. firms in a variety of ways. Direct correspondence from the United States is

Algeria (Lykes)
Angola (Delta, Farrell)
Argentina (Delta,
  Moore-McCormack)
Aruba (Farrell, Prudential-Grace,
  Lykes, Moore-McCormack)
Ascension (Farrell,
  Moore-McCormack)
Australia (Farrell, Pacific
  Far East)
Austria (Lykes, U.S. Lines)
Azores (Delta, Farrell, Lykes)

Bahamas (Moore-McCormack)
Barbados (Delta,
  Moore-McCormack)
Basutoland (Farrell, Moore-
  McCormack)
Bechuanaland (Farrell,
  Moore-McCormack)
Belgium (Farrell, Lykes, Moore-
  McCormack, U.S. Lines)
Bermuda (Delta, Farrell, Lykes)
Bolivia (Delta,
  Prudential-Grace,
  Gulf & South American,
  Moore-McCormack)
Brazil (Delta, Moore-
  McCormack)
British Guiana (Delta)
Burma (American Mail,
  Pacific Far East,
  American President)
Burundi (Farrell, Moore-
  McCormack)

Cambodia (American Mail,
  American President,
  Pacific Far East,
  U.S. Lines, States Line)
Cameroon (Delta, Farrell)
Canal Zone (Farrell,
  Prudential-Grace,
  Gulf & South American,
  Lykes, Moore-McCormack)

Canary Islands, Delta,
  Farrell, Lykes)
Cape Verde Islands (Delta,
  Farrell)
Ceylon (American Mail,
  American President)
Chile (Prudential-Grace,
  Gulf & South American)
Colombia (Prudential-Grace,
  Gulf & South American, Lykes
  Moore-McCormack)
Congo-Leopoldville
  (Delta, Farrell,
  Moore-McCormack)
Congo-Brazzaville (Farrell)
Costa Rica (Prudential-Grace)
Curacao (Delta, Farrell,
  Prudential-Grace, Lykes,
  Moore-McCormack)
Czechoslovakia (Lykes,
  Moore-McCormack,
  U.S. Lines)

Dahomey (Delta, Farrell)
Denmark (Lykes, Moore-
  McCormack, U.S. Lines)
Dominican Republic
  (Prudential-Grace, Lykes)

Ecuador (Prudential-Grace,
  Gulf & South American)
Egypt (Lykes)
El Salvador (Prudential-Grace)

Fiji (Farrell, Pacific
  Far East)
Finland (Lykes, Moore-
  McCormack, U.S. Lines)
France (American President,
  Farrell, Lykes, U.S. Lines)

Gabon (Delta, Farrell)
Gambia (Delta, Farrell)
Germany (Farrell, Lykes, Moore-
  McCormack, U.S. Lines)

Figure 14-2 Committee of American Steamship Lines (CASL) offices and agents in principal countries around the world.

Ghana (Delta, Farrell)
Great Britain (Farrell, Lykes,
U.S. Lines)
Greece (Lykes, Prudential-Grace)
Guam (American President,
Pacific Far East)
Guatemala (Prudential-Grace)
Guinea (Delta, Farrell)

Haiti (Prudential-Grace, Lykes)
Honduras (Prudential-Grace)
Hong Kong (American Mail,
American President,
Lykes, Pacific Far East,
States Line, U.S. Lines)
Hungary (Moore-McCormack,
U.S. Lines)

Iceland (Moore-McCormack)
India (American Mail,
American President)
Indonesia (American Mail,
American President, Lykes)
Ireland (Lykes, U.S. Lines)
Israel (Lykes)
Italy (American President,
Lykes, Prudential-Grace)
Ivory Coast (Delta, Farrell)

Jamaica (Prudential-Grace,
Lykes, Moore-McCormack)
Japan (American Mail,
American President,
Lykes, Pacific Far East,
States Line, U.S. Lines)

Kenya (Farrell, Lykes,
Moore-McCormack)
Korea (American Mail,
American President,
Lykes, Pacific Far East,
States Line, U.S. Lines)
Kwajalein (Pacific Far East)

Laos (American President,
States Line, U.S. Lines)

Lebanon (Lykes)
Liberia (Delta, Farrell)
Libya (Lykes)
Luxembourg (Moore-
McCormack, U.S. Lines)

Malagasy Republic
(Madagascar) (Farrell,
Lykes, Moore-McCormack)
Malawi Republic (Farrell,
Moore-McCormack)
Malaysia (American Mail,
American President, Lykes)
Malta (Lykes)
Martinique (Prudential-Grace)
Mauretania (Delta, Farrell)
Mauritius (Farrell, Lykes,
Moore-McCormack)
Midway (States Line)
Mexico (Delta, Farrell,
Prudential-Grace, Lykes,
Moore-McCormack)
Morocco (Lykes)
Mozambique (Farrell, Lykes,
Moore-McCormack)

Netherlands (Farrell, Lykes,
Moore-McCormack, U.S. Lines)
New Britain (Farrell)
New Caledonia (Farrell,
Pacific Far East)
New Guinea (Farrell)
New Zealand (Farrell,
Pacific Far East)
Nicaragua (Prudential-Grace)
Nigeria (Delta, Farrell)
Norway (Lykes, Moore-
McCormack, U.S. Lines)

Okinawa (American Mail,
American President,
Lykes, Pacific Far East,
States Line, U.S. Lines)

Pakistan (American Mail,
American President)

Figure 14-2   (continued).

Panama (Farrell, Prudential-Grace,
  Gulf & South American,
  Lykes, Moore-McCormack)
Paraguay (Delta, Moore-
  McCormack)
Pemba Island (Farrell,
  Moore-McCormack)
Peru (Delta, Prudential-Grace,
  Gulf & South American,
  Moore-McCormack)
Philippine Islands
  (American Mail,
  American President,
  Lykes, Pacific Far East,
  States Line, U.S. Lines)
Poland (Lykes, Moore-
  McCormack, U.S. Lines)
Portugal (Farrell, Lykes,
  U.S. Lines)
Portuguese Guinea (Delta,
  Farrell)
Portuguese West Africa
  (Delta, Farrell)
Puerto Rico (Delta, Lykes)

Reunion Island (Farrell,
  Lykes, Moore-McCormack)
Rhodesia (Farrell, Moore-
  McCormack, Lykes)
Rwanda (Farrell, Moore-
  McCormack)

Samoa (Pacific Far East)
Sarawak (American President,
  States Line)
Senegal (Delta, Farrell)
Sierra Leone (Delta, Farrell)
Singapore (American Mail,
  American President,
  Lykes, U.S. Lines)
Somalia (Farrell, Lykes,
  Moore-McCormack)
South Africa (Farrell,
  Lykes, Moore-McCormack)

South West Africa (Farrell,
  Lykes, Moore-McCormack)
Spain (American President,
  Farrell, Lykes, Prudential-
  Grace, U.S. Lines)
Spanish Guinea (Delta,
  Farrell)
St. Helena (Farrell, Moore-
  McCormack)
Surinam (Delta)
Swaziland (Farrell, Moore-
  McCormack)
Sweden (Lykes, Moore-
  McCormack, U.S. Lines)
Switzerland (Farrell, Lykes,
  Moore-McCormack, U.S. Lines)

Tahiti (Farrell, Pacific
  Far East)
Taiwan (Formosa) (American
  Mail, American President,
  Lykes, Pacific Far East,
  States Line, U.S. Lines)
Tanzania (Farrell, Lykes,
  Moore-McCormack)
Tasmania (Farrell, Pacific
  Far East)
Thailand (American Mail,
  American President,
  Lykes, Pacific Far East,
  States Line, U.S. Lines)
Togo (Delta, Farrell)
Trinidad (Farrell, Lykes,
  Moore-McCormack)
Tunisia (Lykes)
Turkey (Lykes, Prudential-
  Grace)

U.A.R. (Lykes)
Uganda (Farrell, Lykes,
  Moore-McCormack)
Uruguay (Delta,
  Moore-McCormack)

Figure 14-2   (continued).

590

Venezuela (Delta, Prudential-Grace, Lykes, Moore-McCormack) Viet Nam (American Mail, American President, Lykes, Pacific Far East, States Line, U.S. Lines)	Wake Island (Pacific Far East) Yugoslavia (Lykes) Zambia (Farrell, Moore-McCormack)

Figure 14-2   (continued).

discouraged because the information requested is usually already available at the Department of Commerce.

In some foreign cities, local chambers of commerce actively assist the visiting businessman. In others, there are associations of resident U.S. businessmen or joint U.S.-foreign groups that welcome visitors and accord them facilities. For example, there are almost fifty U.S. chambers of commerce abroad (AmChams). These voluntary associations of businessmen and host-country nationals operate in concert with host-country business firms, affiliates, individuals, and governments. Through a wide spectrum of activities, AmChams work (a) to develop mutually prosperous and amicable economic, social, and commercial relations between United States business and industrial interests and those of host countries, (b) to foster and communicate abroad the beneficial concepts of U.S. private enterprise, and (c) to promote local economic and social contributions for the benefit of host countries. AmChams represent their members before the governments, the business communities, and the general publics of host countries.

Besides offering translation services, AmChams frequently provide letters of introduction for U.S. and host-country members planning to visit the United States. They also assist, generally at early stages and on an informal basis, in mitigating or remedying trade disputes between (a) members, (b) members and nonmembers, or (c) U.S. and foreign firms. When the desired solution is not achieved, difficulties are frequently referred to the American Arbitration Association and its affiliates, to the International Chamber of Commerce, or to foreign boards of arbitration. Visiting U.S. businessmen may use AmCham headquarters as bases of operations during visits. AmChams assist in arranging meetings, luncheons, receptions, and business appointments for members of visiting trade missions. Chapters may be found in the following countries.

Far East and Pacific

Melbourne, Australia	Manila, Philippine Islands
Sydney, Australia	Taipei, Taiwan
Tokyo, Japan	Bangkok, Thailand
Seoul, Korea	Saigon, Vietnam
Koza, Okinawa	

Latin America	*Europe*
Buenos Aires, Argentina	Dusseldorf, Germany
Pôrto Alegre, Brazil	Frankfurt/Main, Germany
Recife, Brazil	Hamburg, Germany
Rio de Janeiro, Brazil	Munich, Germany
São Paulo, Brazil	Dublin, Ireland
Santiago, Chile	Florence, Italy
Santo Domingo, Dominican Republic	Milan, Italy
Guatemala City, Guatemala	Rome, Italy
Guadalajara, Mexico	The Hague, The Netherlands
Mexico City, Mexico	Barcelona, Spain
Lima, Peru	Bilbao, Spain
Montevideo, Uruguay	Madrid, Spain
Caracas, Venezuela	Oviedo, Spain
	Seville, Spain
Europe	Valencia, Spain
Brussels, Belgium	Zaragoza, Spain
London, England	Zurich, Switzerland
Paris, France	
Berlin, Germany	*Africa*
Bremen, Germany	Casablanca, Morocco

Foreign Market Reports. Up-to-date information of activity in foreign markets is of paramount importance to the exporter/importer. Several agencies make studies of countries and their industries and gather other economic facts that influence the flow of goods and services. These studies are published in reports and statistical charts that are made available to the U.S. businessman.

Foreign Market Report Service. This service provides the businessman with copies of unclassified Foreign Service reports covering useful marketing information on the status of certain industries in a country plus recent economic developments in that country. A listing of these reports is compiled each month and sent to the Department of Commerce field offices, which perform secondary distribution to interested firms. The Inquiry and Reference Service Section of the Commercial Intelligence Division (CID), which does the compiling, maintains copies of all reports and files them by Standard Industrial Classification number by country. This Section will place an interested firm on its mailing list to receive the monthly compilations.

Share of Market Statistical Studies. These statistics show the U.S. share of the world market for 1,127 commodities (products) and provide a comparison of the value of U.S. trade with that of competing countries. The figures given are the U.S. share of imports into ninety different countries. Also given is the export figure of each of the countries for a particular commodity.

The purpose of these studies is to identify product groups in which the U.S. share of particular foreign markets appears unduly low in relation to the possibilities and to indicate the opportunities for significant increases. These studies also enable the businessman to:

1. Pinpoint the source and strength of foreign competition in world markets.

AMERICAN MAIL LINE, LTD.

1010 Washington Building
Seattle, WA 98101
206 624-4400

AMERICAN PRESIDENT LINES, LTD.

Freight Sales
601 California Street
San Francisco, CA 94108
415 981-6000

DELTA STEAMSHIP LINES, INC.

Vice President—Sales
Post Office Box 50250
New Orleans, LA 70150
504 522-3492

FARRELL LINES, INC.

Manager—Trade Department
1 Whitehall Street
New York, NY 10004
'212 944-7460

GULF & SO. AMERICAN STEAMSHIP CO., INC.

Vice President—Traffic
Post Office Box 50938
New Orleans, LA 70150
504 523-6611

LYKES BROS. STEAMSHIP CO., INC.

Vice President—Traffic
Post Office Box 53068
New Orleans, LA 70150
504 522-6661

MOORE-McCORMACK LINES, INC.

2 Broadway
New York, NY 10004
212 363-6600

PACIFIC FAR EAST LINE, INC.

141 Battery Street
San Francisco, CA 94111
415 392-7600

PRUDENTIAL-GRACE LINES, INC.

Vice President—Traffic
3 Hanover Square
New York, NY 10004
212 344-6000

STATES STEAMSHIP COMPANY

Vice President—Traffic
320 California Street
San Francisco, CA 94104
415 982-6221

UNITED STATES LINES COMPANY

Manager, Trade Development
1 Broadway
New York, NY 10004
212 344-5800

Figure 14-3 Names and addresses of CASL members.

OCEAN AND RIVER PORTS	GREAT LAKES PORTS
Port of New York, New York	Duluth-Superior, Minn., Wis.
New Orleans, Louisiana	Toledo, Ohio
Houston, Texas	Chicago, Illinois
Philadelphia, Pennsylvania	Detroit, Michigan
Norfolk Harbor, Virginia	Indiana Harbor, Indiana
Baltimore, Maryland	Cleveland, Ohio
Beaumont, Texas	Buffalo, New York
Baton Rouge, Louisiana	Calcite, Michigan
Port Arthur, Texas	Ashtabula, Ohio
Los Angeles, California	Gary, Indiana
Boston, Massachusetts	
Corpus Christi, Texas	
Mobile, Alabama	
Texas City, Texas	
Portland, Maine	
Lake Charles, Louisiana	
Richmond, California	
Portland, Oregon	
Tampa, Florida	
Huntington, West Virginia	
Newport News, Virginia	
Seattle, Washington	
Long Beach, California	

Figure 14-4   Major United States ports in order of total tonnage.

2. Determine where specific products sell best, thus ranking the markets so that the most important get prime attention.

3. Identify markets where U.S. exporters are already doing well, thus recognizing the competition and necessitating the determination as to whether more intense market development is worthwhile.

4. Determine whether a company's share is increasing or decreasing relative to comparative U.S. performance. For example, if the U.S. share is increasing but a company's showing is contrary to the trend, it will be useful to the management to know this fact so that corrective action may be taken.

These trade statistics are reported in terms of the Standard International Trade Classification (SITC) system of the United Nations and are currently available at the four- and five-digit levels.

In addition to all the above benefits, these studies provide two of the three elements necessary to determine what a country's current market for a given product is. The total existing market is simply imports plus domestic production less exports. Thus, any U.S. businessman interested in finding out what is the statistical market for his product in a particular country would need only to ascertain the production figures within that country in order to determine the total consumption of his product. In many cases the applicable industry division of the Business and Defense Services Administration will be able to furnish such production figures; if not, the country desk of the Office of International Regional Economics should be consulted; failing to get information in this way would then necessitate making a direct inquiry overseas.

World Trade Annual. A publication of the International Trade Statistics Centre of the United Nations, the *World Trade Annual,* contains detailed trade statistics. The purpose of the Centre is to collect, verify, and standardize trade statistics from as many countries as possible. Data are collected from approximately fifty countries, mostly on a quarterly basis and in terms of the 1,312 items of the United Nations Standard International Trade Classification (SITC). These figures go to a five-digit classification, and are stored on tape in standard units of value (the U.S. dollar) and of quantity (metric units). The Centre arranges for certain publications in printed form and supplies at cost selections and rearrangements of the figures in the form of machine tabulations, punched cards, or magnetic tape.

United Nations statistical publications are available throughout the United States at all United Nations depository libraries, which include the principal public and university libraries. A set for 19 industrial countries is available for reference purposes at the Bureau of International Commerce's International Trade Analysis Division.

Other Export Considerations. *C.I.F. Price Determination.* Foreign businessmen prefer to have prices quoted as c.i.f. rather than f.o.b. The U.S. businessman can figure the total costs more accurately because he knows how far it is to the port of embarkation and the means and routing to use to get the goods there and to the port of debarkation. Many factors beside cost (net amount required by exporter), insurance (marine), and freight (inland plus overseas) have to be considered in the determining of the final market price. The following cost elements should also be determined.

Export packing
Special marking and labeling
Shipping registration, documentation, and other fees
Financing and credit insurance costs, where applicable
Wharfage and pier handling charges
Warehousing, if necessary
Customs clearance, consular, or purchasing fees
Distributor/dealer markups
Duties and taxes

General information on duties (tariffs) and taxes may be found in the Overseas Business Reports series "Foreign Trade Regulations of *(Country)*." For specific information on the exporter's product, the Trade Regulations Section of the respective Office of International Regional Economics geographic division should be consulted.

Nontariff barriers may need to be considered also when one is determining market price. Barriers of a broad scope such as electrical, plumbing, and safety standards; pharmaceutical or pharmacopoeia standards; container sizes; customs surcharges; internal taxes; licensing; and exchange control systems (some countries require import licensing in order to entitle the importer to an exchange permit that allows payment for the goods in dollars) are discussed in the OBR country series.

Electric Current Characteristics. Because most overseas markets operate on different electric current than that in the United States, design and engineering changes in the product may be necessary. A booklet entitled *Electric Current Abroad* may be secured from the Superintendent of Documents or consulted at any of the Department of Commerce field offices.

Selection of an Overseas Outlet. Trade lists are available that contain the names and addresses of firms handling a specific commodity in a particular foreign country. By consulting these lists, U.S. companies may locate agents, distributors, and in some instances potential customers for the particular overseas market. These automated trade lists include also a numerical business code, the type of organization, the year it was established, its size, its number of employees, whether it has U.S. representation, the languages of correspondence, and the date of the source information. Lists are available for $1 per country for each commodity from the Bureau of International Commerce (Commercial Intelligence Division) or from any Department of Commerce field office. After selecting the names of a few firms whose brief description makes them appealing, the businessman may request a "World Trade Directory Report" (WTDR) on each specific company.

Upon special application through the Department of Commerce, an exporter may ask a Foreign Service officer at an overseas post to make an on-the-spot trade contact survey to find two or three, and sometimes more, qualified local firms who are specifically interested in the exporter's product. Each survey costs $50 and averages sixty days to complete. Applications for trade contact surveys, however, will be accepted only after all other efforts to locate a foreign distributor have failed.

Export Distributors. A number of private export agents in this country and abroad are willing to function as exclusive distributors on a worldwide basis or in a certain locale. Many of these firms have a network of foreign representatives, salesmen, and/or distributors. As independent representatives, they generally handle a number of related but noncompetitive lines for several exporters. Most of them work on a commission basis, but many request a retaining fee to develop markets for new products. A directory of the available export agents is available for review in the BIC's Commercial Intelligence Division or at the Department of Commerce field offices.

The functions of an exporter manager closely parallel those of the export agent. The combination export manager prefers to act as the export department for the exporter, doing business in the exporter's name and on the exporter's letterhead. Similarly to the export agent, the combination export manager usually handles a number of related but noncompetitive lines and sells through a network of foreign representatives, salesmen, and/or distributors. These firms generally operate on a minimum retainer plus a commission basis. A directory of these firms is available at the Department of Commerce field offices.

Legislation Favorable to Exporters. The Webb-Pomerene Act affords a limited exemption from antitrust laws for direct exports by allowing exporters to agree on prices, sales, terms, territorial divisions, and other activities in export trade otherwise forbidden by U.S. antitrust laws. The Western Hemisphere Trade Corporation and the China Trade Act are the only recognized forms of tax incentives to aid exporters. To qualify as a Western Hemisphere Trade Center, the firm must be a domestic corporation, all of whose business is done in any country of North, Central, or South America, or in the West Indies, deriving 95 percent of its gross income for a three-year period from sources outside the United States, and 90 percent or more from the active conduct of trade or business. The special rate reduction granted to these corporations amounts to a considerable reduction, accomplished through a special formula deduction against taxable income, which deduction currently amounts to 28 percent.

A U.S. firm that incorporates under the China Trade Act to do business in Hong Kong or Taiwan may be fully exempted from U.S. corporate income tax on dividends distributed to qualified stockholders. Moreover, if the stockholders of a CTA corporation are resident in Hong Kong or Taiwan, they, too, are exempted from U.S. personal income tax on the dividends distributed to them. The articles of incorporation are required to state that a major portion of the corporation's business will be in developing markets for goods produced in the United States. Three or more persons, a majority of whom are U.S. citizens, may apply for CTA incorporation. The company's president, its treasurer, and a majority of the board of directors must be U.S. citizens residing in either Hong Kong or Taiwan. Application forms and additional information may be obtained from the Acting Registrar of the China Trade Act in the Commerce Department. Additional information about these three advantages for exporters may be secured from the BIC's Foreign Business Practices Division.

Trade Fair Participation. Two types of international trade fairs are used by the United States. Commercial exhibitions are held in the more developed areas, which have been selected entirely for their sales potential. Specific market research has been made to pinpoint product classification and the models thereof that are the most saleable. The BIC conducts an extensive promotional campaign to attract buyers and prospective agents for the exhibited products. It designs, constructs, and installs the exhibits; and U.S. businessmen are encouraged to participate. Participation agreements are handled by the Commercial Exhibits Division of the Office of International Trade Promotion, and a telephone call to the Project Officer will elicit the going fee for space charges and other information. Only products of at least 50 percent American origin may be displayed.

United States national exhibitions are put on by the BIC in conjunction with the State Department and the U.S. Information Agency, and are primarily designed to portray the American way of life under the free-enterprise system. Most of these fairs are now concentrated behind the Iron Curtain. The cost of participating in this type of fair is generally nominal. Display space for U.S. products is free, and except where there are commercial overtones for the product on display, there is no charge to an exhibitor for transporting his products from the U.S. dockside to the fair site—and back, in the event that the goods are not sold at the fair. A real effort is made, however, to make sales at the fair, although this is the secondary purpose of the presentation.

Trade Centers.   Permanent trade centers have been established by the Bureau of International Commerce in London, Frankfurt, Paris, Milan, Tokyo, Sydney, Bangkok, and Stockholm. The trade centers are permanent merchandise marts where groups of related U.S. products are placed on exhibition for two to three weeks and then replaced by another exhibit of different U.S. products. A permanent U.S. staff operates each trade center, handles all the necessary advance promotion and publicity, and helps to find agents, distributors, and dealers for the products exhibited. More information about trade fairs and centers can be secured from the Commercial Exhibits Division of OITP or the nearest field office.

Trade Missions.   There are three categories of missions, all with the common objective of assisting the American businessman to initiate or expand trade with overseas markets.

1. Government-organized and -sponsored trade missions are composed of businessmen specialists, selected by the Department of Commerce, and sent abroad at government expense. In this type of mission, business proposals for the products or industries represented may be submitted by a businessman anywhere in the United States in advance of the mission's departure. Such a business proposal, after having been screened for validity by the Commercial Intelligence Division, is discussed in conferences overseas by one businessman talking to another—one from the United States and the other a national of the host country. Mission members agree not to undertake business on behalf of their own interests while in the country.

2. An "industry-organized government-approved trade mission" may represent a state, a city, a chamber of commerce, a trade association, a group

of industries, or a single industry. The selection of the membership is the responsibility of the organizers. The members pay all expenses of the mission and may do business on their own behalf. Department of Commerce approval and sponsorship is granted provided the mission adheres to the criteria set up by the Department.

3. Other privately organized and financed business groups traveling abroad are invited to avail themselves of the services offered. (See the BIC pamphlet "Criteria and Services for Facilitated Group Business Travel.")

Mobile Trade Fairs.   The BIC, through its Office of International Trade Promotion, offers technical and limited financial support to private operators of mobile trade fairs. These fairs are designed to show and sell products of U.S. business and agriculture at foreign ports and other commercial centers throughout the world.

Sample Display Service Program.   An exhibit of a U.S. business firm's merchandise samples and product literature may be set up at designated U.S. Foreign Service posts. At present, sample display facilities are available in Beirut, Nairobi, and Bangkok. The display at each post consists of a small showroom-office (except in Bangkok, which uses the Trade Center) facility that is managed by a U.S. Commercial Attaché and staffed by Foreign Service local employees.

Shipping to the Market.   The procedures for effecting and protecting foreign shipments are more complicated than for domestic shipments. Complete information for handling this particular marketing element can be secured through the Bureau of International Commerce. The Overseas Business Report series "Foreign Trade Regulations of (*Country*)" contain information regarding the marking and labeling of packages and containers.

Use of Freight Forwarders.   Many firms are equipped to perform a variety of services for the exporter, including the handling of the paperwork involved in shipping to and collecting from the market. A freight forwarder can package the items; is familiar with the necessary marking and labeling; can arrange for marine insurance; can prepare any necessary shipping, consular, and other documents; can arrange customs clearances; can handle the inland transportation of the products both here and abroad; can book the necessary freight space; and can oversee the placement of the goods aboard ship. He can also help prepare and will forward banking collection papers. A list of customhouse brokers and foreign freight forwarders can be obtained from the Custom Brokers and Forwarders Association of America, Inc., 8 Bridge Street, New York, NY 10004.

Necessary Documentation.   Export sales may require the following documents:

1. A bill of lading.
2. A commercial invoice.

3. A Consular Invoice describing the merchandise being exported and used to clear the goods through the customs office of the importing country.

4. A certificate of, or the actual policy covering, marine insurance and war risk.

5. Certificates of origin, packing lists, health certificates for certain types of food products, and certificates of quality.

6. The shipper's export declaration.

7. Marine insurance and freight.

Foreign-Trade Zones.   A foreign-trade zone is a controlled area into which may be brought domestic and foreign merchandise without such goods being subject to the U.S. customs laws governing entry or payment of duties. In such a zone a broad range of business activities may be conducted, including manufacturing, assembling, processing, packaging, exhibiting, storing, and other activities. These goods, or the products derived therefrom, may be exported, imported, or transshipped from the zone. Foreign merchandise sent from a zone into U.S. customs territory for consumption is subject to the laws and regulations affecting imports.

The business advantages inherent in a foreign-trade zone operation include opportunities for:

1. Duty-free and quota-free manufacturing for export using foreign materials or components in the production of goods.

2. The employment of U.S. labor, technology, and management at a duty-free U.S. site.

3. A reduction in volume of the outlay of working capital for the payment of customs duties on foreign goods or components destined for U.S. markets. (These are paid only when and if goods enter U.S. customs territory and apply only to the quantity of imported goods that actually enter.)

4. The establishment of production facilities in the United States as an alternative to establishing similar facilities abroad.

5. Immediate export status for U.S. exports placed in a zone solely for export. Such a classification permits prompt customs drawback and refund or exemption from liability for Internal Revenue taxes.

6. The possibility of a saving in ultimate customs duties, particularly on that merchandise shipped abroad from a trade zone.

The ten foreign-trade zones are located in New York City; New Orleans; San Francisco; Seattle; Toledo; Honolulu; Mayagüez, Puerto Rico; and Bay County, Michigan. General inquiries pertaining to their use by business firms should be referred to the Executive Secretary of the Foreign-Trade Zones Board, headquartered at the Bureau of International Commerce.

Collecting from the Market.   Knowledgeable domestic banking facilities, the Export-Import Bank, and the Foreign Credit Insurance Association aid the U.S. businessman in collecting from the foreign market.

Foreign Credit Insurance. Several types of credit insurance are available for export sales under programs administered by the Foreign Credit Insurance Association (FCIA). Insurance can be obtained covering comprehensive risks (credit and political), or political risk alone for short-term (up to six months) transactions and medium-term (six months to five years) transactions. In the case of short-term insurance, the exporter retains from 5 percent to 15 percent of the political risk (the percentage varying according to the country and to the terms of the credit extended) and 10 percent of the credit risk. In the case of medium-term insurance, the customer generally makes a down payment of 20 percent and the exporter carries at least 10 percent of the remainder. Member insurance companies are listed in a booklet issued by the Foreign Credit Insurance Association, 250 Broadway, New York, NY 10007. Policies are available from any insurance broker or agent.

Export-Import Bank. The Export-Import Bank will guarantee medium-term (six months to five years) export transactions to commercial banks or other financial institutions. In the event the exporter cannot get financing through the commercial bank or credit insurance through the Foreign Credit Insurance Association, he may apply directly to the Export-Import Bank for either a guarantee or a direct credit. The exporter is required generally to obtain a 20 percent cash down-payment from his customer and to carry not less than 10 percent of the balance to be financed. Further details on this program, as well as on the FCIA, can be obtained from the International Finance Division of the Office of Commercial and Financial Policy or from any commercial bank with a foreign department.

United States and International Lending Agencies. Two U.S. agencies and several international institutions provide loans that help U.S. exporters and investors. United States exporters and investors seeking financing should become familiar with the differences in purposes and facilities of these lending agencies, as they vary considerably. Generally, however, the company should turn first to the two U.S. government agencies (the EX-IM Bank and the Agency for International Development), as they are more closely concerned with U.S. business operations, and procurement under these programs must—with some exceptions—be in the United States.

Use of Commercial Banks' International Departments. Most of the large banks have active international departments, which are becoming more and more familiar with the details involved in getting paid for exports. If the exporter's local bank does not have an international department, or does not handle import or export papers, it is in all probability a correspondent of a large metropolitan bank that does and can provide assistance in helping to arrange financing for sound export business transactions.

Small Business Administration Loans. In the interest of making an effective contribution to the National Export Expansion Program and of assisting small concerns and individuals in the United States, as defined in the Small Business Act, to enter into and to expand export trade and international commerce, the SBA considers applications for loans, including working capital, to defray the costs of:

1. Professional foreign marketing advice and service.
2. Foreign business travel.
3. Shopping foreign markets.
4. Ocean freight and the insurance of sample merchandise shipped abroad.
5. Participation in U.S. trade center shows and exhibits at international trade fairs.
6. Foreign advertising and the preparation of promotional material.
7. Other related purposes not otherwise described.

The prime collateral required to secure such a loan is a lien on real and/or personal property, inventory, assignments of accounts receivables, and/or monies due under a contractual obligation, all of which are subject to foreclosure, enforcement, and collection in the United States or its possessions.

Other Market Information.   *Export Control.*   No special license is needed to engage in export trade. The U.S. government does, however, control the export of U.S. goods to all foreign countries. With the exception of certain specialized commodities and implements of war, export licensing is handled by the Office of Export Control in the Bureau of International Commerce.

The vast majority of goods can move to free world countries under what is called a *general license.* No formal license application is required, and the shipper's export declaration is all that is required.

The necessity for a *validated license* depends on *what* you are shipping *where*. Validated licenses are necessary for certain types of strategic goods regardless of destination and for all except a select list of *peaceful* items intended for the European Soviet Bloc. To all intents and purposes there is a total embargo on U.S. trade either directly or indirectly with North Korea, North Vietnam, and Cuba. However, there are signs of relaxation on trade with Communist China and Southern Rhodesia. The Office of Export Control or a Department of Commerce field office can give the exporter the necessary information on the status of his particular shipment. In addition, the *Comprehensive Exports Schedule,* an annual publication kept up-to-date with supplementary bulletins, is a compilation of U.S. export-control regulations and policies. It includes complete instructions, interpretations, and explanatory material.

Foreign Business Practices.   An exporter might have problems with foreign business customs and practices stemming either from discriminatory action by trade associations or cartels or from any other form of private, restrictive trade barrier. Any such cases should be reported to the Foreign Business Practices Division of BIC, which will give the proper information and seek corrective action.

Patents and Trademarks.   Information on foreign patent, trademark, and copyright laws and practices, and international treaties concerned therewith, is available from the Foreign Business Practices Division of BIC.

Imitation and Copying Complaints.   Product imitation, trademark piracy, and design copying can be a scourge to the exporter. Instances of this nature should be reported to the Foreign Business Practices Division of BIC.

Licensing and Exchange Control.   Certain countries require import licensing in order to entitle the importer to an exchange permit to allow payment for the goods in dollars.

Trade Dispute Resolutions.   Business practice complaints are handled by the Foreign Business Practices Division in BIC's Office of Commercial and Financial Policy and involve the areas of discriminatory practices, patents and trademarks, and imitation and copying. Disputes with foreign government agencies as well as cases involving the apparent violation of U.S. business-men's rights and privileges under terms of treaties and international agree-ments are handled by the Office of International Regional Economics (OIRE) at BIC. Business transaction disputes other than those over collection between U.S. and foreign firms or individuals are handled by BIC's Commercial Intelligence Division of the Office of International Trade Promotion.

Choice of Language.   Seven-eighths of the world's population do not under-stand English. If you are able to correspond with the foreign businessman in his own language, greater understanding will result. In cases where the foreign businessman requests an answer in his own language, do all you can to oblige. The Department of Commerce field offices can help with transla-tions or can direct you to a linguist competent in the business vocabulary and practices of the foreign nation in which you are interested.

Answering a Foreign Advertisement.   When answering a foreign advertise-ment or selling abroad through correspondence, give the whole story the first time. The unit of sale—whether by foot or by ton—and what kind of ton; the details of the various price lines available if you have such distinctions as *utility, standard,* or *deluxe;* the c.i.f. price including discounts for quantity and for prompt payment; and the delivery schedule and the payment terms. Copies of catalogs and other literature should be sent also.

Use of the Metric System.   Most countries use, or are changing to, the metric system for measurements. When corresponding with foreign importers, quote in metric measurements to facilitate understanding. (See Chapter 18, "Weights and Measures," for an explanation of the metric system.)

Export Reference Guides.   An indispensable reference guide for firms actively engaged in importing and exporting is the *Custom House Guide, Foreign Traders' Encyclopedia.* Published yearly, it contains up-to-date information on United States customs ports, customs tariffs, customs regula-tions, the Revenue Act, and trade agreements. The addresses of United States ports, foreign consuls, steamship companies, surety companies, warehouses, customhouse brokers, and freight forwarders are listed also. The *Custom House Guide* is published by Budd Publications, Inc., 26 Beaver Street, New York, NY 10004, and costs approximately $35 a year.

The *Exporters' Encyclopedia,* published by Dun & Bradstreet, is another guide for exporters worthy of their attention. Besides a comprehensive 850 pages of facts and figures on every facet of foreign trade, the subscriber is offered free consultation on export problems by letter, telegram, or telephone as often as needed. Dun's *World Marketing Newsletter,* a twice-monthly publication, is included in the $75-a-year subscription price. The basic encyclopedia is updated during the year with twice-monthly revisions. Exporters desiring additional information about this guide and its supplemental services should write Dun's Exporters' Encyclopedia, International Business Information Service, P.O. Box 3088, Grand Central Station, New York, NY 10017.

14.2 FOREIGN COUNTRIES, THEIR CAPITALS, AND DESCRIPTIVE NATIONAL TERMS

		Nationality	
Country	Capital	Noun	Adjective
Afghanistan	Kabul	Afghan(s)	Afghan
Albania	Tirana	Albanian(s)	Albanian
Algeria	Algiers	Algerian(s)	Algerian
Andorra	Andorra la Vella	Andorran(s)	Andorran
Argentina	Buenos Aires	Argentine(s)	Argentine
Australia	Canberra	Australian(s)	Australian
Austria	Vienna (Wien)	Austrian(s)	Austrian
Barbados	Bridgetown	Barbadian(s)	Barbadian
Belgium	Brussels	Belgian(s)	Belgian
Bhutan	Thimphu	Bhutanese	Bhutanese
Bolivia	Sucre; La Paz, seat of government	Bolivian(s)	Bolivian
Botswana	Gaberone	Botswana	Botswana
Brazil	Brasília	Brazilian(s)	Brazilian
Bulgaria	Sofia	Bulgarian(s)	Bulgarian
Burma	Rangoon	Burman(s)	Burmese
Burundi	Bujumbura	Burundian(s)	Burundian
Cambodia	Phnom Penh	Cambodian(s)	Cambodian
Cameroon	Yaoundé	Cameroonian(s)	Cameroonian
Canada	Ottawa	Canadian(s)	Canadian
Central African Republic	Bangui	Central African(s)	Central African
Ceylon	Colombo	Ceylonese	Ceylonese
Chad	Fort-Lamy	Chadian(s)	Chadian
Chile	Santiago	Chilean(s)	Chilean
China, People's Republic of	Peking	Chinese	Chinese
China, Republic of	Taipei, Taiwan	Chinese	Chinese
Colombia	Bogotá	Colombian(s)	Colombian

Country	Capital	Nationality	
		Noun	Adjective
Congo, Democratic Republic of	Kinshasa	Congolese	Congolese or Congo
Congo, People's Republic of	Brazzaville	Congolese	Congolese or Congo
Costa Rica	San José	Costa Rican(s)	Costa Rican
Cuba	Havana	Cuban(s)	Cuban
Cyprus	Nicosia	Cypriot(s)	Cypriot
Czechoslovakia	Prague	Czechoslovak(s)	Czechoslovak
Dahomey	Porto Novo	Dahomean(s)	Dahomean
Denmark	Copenhagen	Dane(s)	Danish
Dominican Republic	Santo Domingo	Dominican(s)	Dominican
Ecuador	Quito	Ecuadorean(s)	Ecuadorean
El Salvador	San Salvador	Salvadoran(s)	Salvadoran
Equatorial Guinea	Santa Isabel	Guinean(s)	Guinean
Estonia	Tallinn	Estonian(s)	Estonian
Ethiopia	Addis Ababa	Ethiopian(s)	Ethiopian
Fiji	Suva	Fiji(s)	Fiji
Finland	Helsinki	Finn(s)	Finnish
France	Paris	Frenchman(men)	French
Gabon Republic	Libreville	Gabonese	Gabonese
Gambia, The	Bathurst	Gambian(s)	Gambian
German Democratic Republic	East Berlin	German(s)	German
Germany, Federal Republic of	Bonn	German(s)	German
Ghana	Accra	Ghanaian(s)	Ghanaian
Greece	Athens	Greek(s)	Greek
Guatemala	Guatemala City	Guatemalan(s)	Guatemalan
Guinea	Conakry	Guinean(s)	Guinean
Guyana	Georgetown	Guyanese	Guyanese
Haiti	Port-au-Prince	Haitian(s)	Haitian
Honduras	Tegucigalpa	Honduran(s)	Honduran
Hungary	Budapest	Hungarian(s)	Hungarian
Iceland	Reykjavik	Icelander(s)	Icelandic
India	New Delhi	Indian(s)	Indian
Indonesia	Djakarta	Indonesian(s)	Indonesian
Iran	Tehran	Iranian(s)	Iranian
Iraq	Baghdad	Iraqi(s)	Iraqi
Ireland	Dublin	Irishman(men), Irish (collective plural)	Irish
Israel	Jerusalem	Israeli(s)	Israeli
Italy	Rome	Italian(s)	Italian
Ivory Coast	Abidjan	Ivoirian(s)	Ivoirian
Jamaica	Kingston	Jamaican(s)	Jamaican
Japan	Tokyo	Japanese	Japanese
Jordan	Amman	Jordanian(s)	Jordanian
Kenya	Nairobi	Kenyan(s)	Kenyan
Korea, North	Pyongyang	Korean(s)	Korean
Korea, Republic of	Seoul	Korean(s)	Korean
Kuwait	Kuwait City	Kuwaiti(s)	Kuwaiti
Laos	Vientiane	Lao	Lao or Laotian
Latvia	Riga	Latvian(s)	Latvian

Country	Capital	Nationality	
		Noun	*Adjective*
Lebanon	Beirut	Lebanese	Lebanese
Lesotho	Maseru	Basuto(s)	Basuto
Liberia	Monrovia	Liberian(s)	Liberian
Libya	Benghazi and Tripoli	Libyan(s)	Libyan
Liechtenstein	Vaduz	Liechtensteiner(s)	Liechtenstein
Lithuania	Vilnyus	Lithuanian(s)	Lithuanian
Luxembourg	Luxembourg	Luxembourger(s)	Luxembourg
Malagasy Republic	Tananarive	Malagasy	Malagasy
Malawi	Zomba	Malawian(s)	Malawian
Malaysia	Kuala Lumpur	Malaysian(s)	Malaysian
Maldives, Republic of	Male	Maldivian(s)	Maldivian
Mali	Bamako	Malian(s)	Malian
Malta	Valletta	Maltese	Maltese
Mauritania	Nouakchott	Mauritanian(s)	Mauritanian
Mauritius	Port Louis	Mauritian(s)	Mauritian
Mexico	Mexico City	Mexican(s)	Mexican
Monaco	Monaco	Monacan(s), Monegasque(s)	Monacan or Monegasque
Mongolia	Ulan Bator	Mongol(s)	Mongol
Morocco	Rabat	Moroccan(s)	Moroccan
Muscat and Oman	Muscat	Muscati(s), Omani(s)	Muscati, Omani
Nepal	Katmandu	Nepalese	Nepalese
Netherlands	Amsterdam; The Hague, seat of government	Netherlander(s)	Netherlands
New Zealand	Wellington	New Zealander(s)	New Zealand
Nicaragua	Managua	Nicaraguan(s)	Nicaraguan
Niger	Niamey	Nigerois	Niger
Nigeria	Lagos	Nigerian(s)	Nigerian
Norway	Oslo	Norwegian(s)	Norwegian
Pakistan	Islamabad	Pakistani(s)	Pakistani
Panama	Panama City	Panamanian(s)	Panamanian
Paraguay	Asunción	Paraguayan(s)	Paraguayan
Peru	Lima	Peruvian(s)	Peruvian
Philippines	Quezon City; Manila, seat of government	Filipino(s)	Philippine
Poland	Warsaw	Pole(s)	Polish
Portugal	Lisbon	Portuguese	Portuguese
Rhodesia	Salisbury	Rhodesian(s)	Rhodesian
Romania	Bucharest	Romanian(s)	Romanian
Rwanda	Kigali	Rwandan(s)	Rwandan
San Marino	San Marino	Sanmarinese	Sanmarinese
Saudi Arabia	Riyadh; Jidda, diplomatic center	Saudi	Saudi Arabian or Saudi
Senegal	Dakar	Senegalese	Senegalese
Sierra Leone	Freetown	Sierra Leonean(s)	Sierra Leonean
Singapore	Singapore	Singaporan(s)	Singaporan
Somalia	Mogadishu	Somali(s)	Somali
South Africa, Republic of	Pretoria; Capetown, legislative capital	South African(s)	South African

Country	Capital	Nationality	
		Noun	Adjective
Southern Yemen	Aden	Yemeni(s)	Yemeni
Spain	Madrid	Spaniard(s)	Spanish
Sudan	Khartoum	Sudanese	Sudanese
Swaziland	Mbabane	Swazi(s)	Swazi
Sweden	Stockholm	Swede(s)	Swedish
Switzerland	Bern	Swiss	Swiss
Syria	Damascus	Syrian(s)	Syrian
Tanzania	Dar es Salaam	Tanzanian(s)	Tanzanian
Thailand	Bangkok	Thai	Thai
Togo	Lomé	Togolese	Togolese
Tonga	Nukualofa	Tongan(s)	Tongan
Trinidad and Tobago	Port of Spain	Trinidadian(s), Tobagan(s)	Trinidadian, Tobagan
Tunisia	Tunis	Tunisian(s)	Tunisian
Turkey	Ankara	Turk(s)	Turkish
Uganda	Kampala	Ugandan(s)	Ugandan
Union of Soviet Socialist Republics	Moscow	Soviet(s)	Soviet
United Arab Republic	Cairo	Egyptian(s)	United Arab Republic
United Kingdom	London	Briton(s), British (collective plural) Irishman(men) Scot(s) Welshman(men)	British Irish Scottish Welsh
United States of America	Washington, D.C.	American(s)	American
Upper Volta	Ouagadougou	Upper Voltan(s)	Upper Voltan
Uruguay	Montevideo	Uruguayan(s)	Uruguayan
Venezuela	Caracas	Venezuelan(s)	Venezuelan
Vietnam, Democratic Republic of	Hanoi	Vietnamese	Vietnamese
Vietnam, Republic of	Saigon	Vietnamese	Vietnamese
Western Samoa	Apia	Western Samoan(s)	Western Samoan
Yemen	San'a	Yemeni(s)	Yemeni
Yugoslavia	Belgrade	Yugoslav(s)	Yugoslav
Zambia	Lusaka	Zambian(s)	Zambian

14.3 FOREIGN MONEY AND ITS VALUE[1]

Country or Area	Basic Monetary Units			Name and Number of Principal Fractional Units in Basic Unit
	Name	Symbol	Approx. U.S. Value	
Afghanistan	Afghani	Afg	$.02	100 Puls
Albania	Lek		.20	100 Quintars
Algeria	Dinar	AD	.20	100 Centimes
Andorra	French Franc	Fr	.017	100 Centimes
	Spanish Peseta	Pta	.017	100 Centimos

[1] Rates of exchange are subject to daily fluctuations.

| Country or Area | Basic Monetary Units | | | Name and Number of Principal Fractional Units in Basic Unit |
	Name	Symbol	Approx. U.S. Value	
Argentina	Peso	M$N	.126	100 Centavos
Australia	Dollar	A$	1.20	100 Cents
Austria	Schilling	S	.043	100 Groschen
Bahamas	Dollar	$	1.03	100 Cents
Barbados	East Caribbean Dollar	EC$	.54	100 Cents
Belgium	Franc	BF	.022	100 Centimes
Bhutan	Indian Rupee	R	.132	100 Naya Paisa
Bolivia	Peso Boliviano	B$	.085	100 Centavos
Botswana	S. African Rand	R	1.40	100 Cents
Brazil	Cruzeiro	Cr$	.18	100 Centavos
British Honduras	Lempira	L	.50	100 Cents
Bulgaria	Lev	LV	.86	100 Stotinki
Burma	Kyat	K	.19	100 Pyas
Burundi	Franc	RBF	.011	100 Centimes
Cambodia	Riel		.029	100 Sen
Cameroon	CFA Franc[2]	CFAF	.004	100 Centimes
Canada	Dollar	Can$	1.00	100 Cents
Canary Islands	Peseta	Pta	.017	100 Centimos
Central African Republic	CFA Franc	CFAF	.004	100 Centimes
Ceylon	Rupee	Cey R	.21	100 Cents
Chad	CFA Franc	CFAF	.004	100 Centimes
Chile	Escudo	Esc	0.37	100 Centesimos
China, Republic of (Taiwan)	New Taiwan Dollar	NT$	.025	100 Cents
China, People's Republic of	Yuan	$	.40	100 Fen
Colombia	Peso	Col$	.048	100 Centavos
Congo, People's Republic of	CFA Franc	CFAF	.004	100 Centimes
Congo, Democratic Republic of	Zaire		2.00	100 Makuto
Costa Rica	Colón	CR¢	.15	100 Centimos
Cuba	Peso	Cub$	1.00	100 Centavos
Cyprus	Pound	C£	2.60	1,000 Mils
Czechoslovakia	Koruna	Kcš	.14	100 Hellers
Dahomey	CFA Franc	CFAF	.004	100 Centimes
Denmark	Krone	DKr	.14	100 Øre
Dominican Republic	Peso	RD$	1.00	100 Centavos
Ecuador	Sucre	ES/	.04	100 Centavos
El Salvador	Colón	ES¢	.40	100 Centavos
Equatorial Guinea	Peseta	Pta	.014	100 Centimos
Estonia	Ruble	Rbl	1.20	100 Kopecks
Ethiopia	Dollar	Eth$	.40	100 Cents
Fiji	Dollar	F$	.90	100 Cents
Finland	Markka	Fmk	.24	100 Pennis

[2] Currency of the African Financial Community.

| Country or Area | Basic Monetary Units | | | Name and Number of Principal Fractional Units in Basic Unit |
	Name	Symbol	Approx. U.S. Value	
France	Franc	Fr	.19	100 Centimes
Gabon Republic	CFA Franc	CFAF	.004	100 Centimes
Gambia, The	Dalasi		.52	20 Shillings
German Democratic Republic	DDR Mark	M	.45	100 Pfennig
Germany, Federal Republic of	Deutsche Mark	DM	.31	100 Pfennig
Ghana	New Cedi	¢	.55	100 Pesawa
Greece	Drachma	Dr	.034	100 Lepta
Guatemala	Quetzal(es)	Q	1.00	100 Centavos
Guinea	Franc	GFr	.004	100 Centimes
Guyana	Guyana Dollar	G$ or G	.50	100 Cents
Haiti	Gourde	G	.20	100 Centimes
Honduras	Lempira	L	.50	100 Centavos
Hong Kong	Dollar	HK$	.18	100 Cents
Hungary	Forint	Ft	.086	100 Fillers
Iceland	Króna	IKr	.014	100 Øre (Aurar)
India	Rupee	R	.13	100 Naya Paise
Indonesia	Rupiah	Rp	.02	100 Sen
Iran	Rial	Rl	.013	100 Dinars
Iraq	Dinar	ID	3.00	1,000 Fils
Ireland	Pound	Ire£	2.60	100 Pence
Israel	Pound	I£	.24	100 Agorot (Prutah)
Italy	Lira (Lire)	Lit	.002	100 Centesimi
Ivory Coast	CFA Franc	CFAF	.004	100 Centimes
Jamaica	Dollar	J$	1.30	100 Cents
Japan	Yen	Y	.003	100 Sen
Jordan	Dinar	JD	2.80	1,000 Fils
Kenya	Shilling	Ks	.14	100 Cents
Korea, People's Republic of	Won	W	.39	100 Jun
Korea, Republic of	Won	W	.004	100 Chon
Kuwait	Dinar	KD	3.00	1,000 Fils
Laos	Kip	K	.004	100 At
Latvia	Ruble	Rbl	1.20	100 Kopecks
Lebanon	Pound	L£	.32	100 Piasters
Lesotho	S. African Rand	R	1.40	100 Cents
Liberia	Dollar	Lib$	1.00	100 Cents
Libya	Pound	L£	3.00	100 Piasters
Liechtenstein	Swiss Franc	Sw Fr	.23	100 Centimes
Lithuania	Ruble	Rbl	1.20	100 Kopecks
Luxembourg	Franc	Lux Fr	.02	100 Centimes
Macao	Pataca		.17	100 Avos
Madeira	Escudo	Esc	.035	100 Centavos
Malagasy Republic	Malagasy Franc	FMG	.004	100 Centimes
Malawi	Kwasha	K	1.30	100 Tambala
Malaysia	Dollar	M$	.33	100 Cents

| Country or Area | Basic Monetary Units | | | Name and Number of Principal Fractional Units in Basic Unit |
	Name	Symbol	Approx. U.S. Value	
Maldives, Republic of	Rupee	MR	.168	100 Lari
Mali	Franc	MFr	.004	100 Centimes
Malta	Pound	£	2.60	100 Pence
Marshall Islands	US Dollar	$	1.00	100 Cents
Martinique	Franc	Fr	.16	100 Centimes
Mauritania	CFA Franc	CFAF	.004	100 Centimes
Mauritius	Rupee	R	.18	100 Cents
Mexico	Peso	Mex$	.08	100 Centavos
Monaco	French Franc	Fr	.20	100 Centimes
Montserrat	Dollar	$	.59	100 Cents
Morocco	Dirham	DH	.20	100 Moroccan Francs
Muscat and Oman	Rial Saidi		2.40	1,000 Baiza
Nepal	Rupee	NR	.10	100 Pice
Netherlands	Guilder	G	.31	100 Cents
New Caledonia	Franc	CFP Fr	.0115	100 Centimes
New Guinea	Dollar	A$	1.12	100 Cents
New Zealand	Dollar	NZ$	1.18	100 Cents
Nicaragua	Cordoba	C$	.84	100 Centavos
Niger	CFA Franc	CFAF	.004	100 Centimes
Nigeria	Pound	N£	3.00	20 Shillings
Norway	Krone	NKr	.15	100 Öre
Oceania (French)	Franc	CFP Fr	.0115	100 Centimes
Pakistan	Rupee	PR	.21	100 Paisa
Panama	Balboa	B/	1.00	100 Centesimos
Paraguay	Guarani	PG	.008	100 Centimos
Peru	Sol(es)	PS/	.023	100 Centavos
Philippines	Peso	P	.16	100 Centavos
Poland	Zloty	Zl	.25	100 Grosze
Portugal	Escudo	Esc	.037	100 Centavos
Puerto Rico	US Dollar	$	1.00	100 Cents
Qatar	Gulf Rupee	GR	.21	100 Paise
Reunion Island	Franc	CFA Fr	.004	100 Centimes
Rhodesia	Dollar	R$	2.77	100 Cents
Romania	Leu (Lei)	L	.17	100 Bani
Rwanda	Franc	RBF	.01	100 Centimes
Ryukyu Islands	US Dollar	$	1.00	100 Cents
Samoa	Dollar	S$	.70	100 Cents
San Marino	Italian Lira	Lit	.002	100 Centesimi
Saudi Arabia	Riyal	SRl	.22	20 Gurshes
Senegal	CFA Franc	CFAF	.004	100 Centimes
Sierra Leone	Leone	Le	1.30	100 Cents
Singapore	Dollar	S$	.35	100 Cents
Somalia	Somali Shilling	SSh	.14	100 Centesimi
South Africa, Republic of	Rand	R	1.40	100 Cents
Southern Yemen	Dinar	SYD	2.39	1,000 Fils
Spain	Peseta	Pta	.015	100 Centimos
Sudan	Pound	Sd£	2.87	100 Piasters

| | Basic Monetary Units | | | Name and Number of Principal |
Country or Area	Name	Symbol	Approx. U.S. Value	Fractional Units in Basic Unit
Swaziland	Rand	R	1.40	100 Cents
Sweden	Krona	SKr	.21	100 Öre
Switzerland	Franc	Sw Fr	.26	100 Centimes
Syria	Pound	S£	.45	100 Piasters
Tanzania	Shilling	Sh	.14	100 Cents
Thailand	Baht	B	.048	100 Satang
Togo	CFA Franc	CFAF	.004	100 Centimes
Trinidad and Tobago	TT Dollar	TT$	.59	100 Cents
Tunisia	Dinar	D	2.06	1,000 Mils
Turkey	Lira	TL	.066	100 Piasters
Uganda	Shilling	USh	.14	100 Cents
Union of Soviet Socialist Republics	Ruble	Rbl	1.20	100 Kopecks
United Arab Republic	Pound	E£	2.87	100 Piasters
United Kingdom[3]	Pound	£	2.60	100 Pence
United States	Dollar	$	1.00	100 Cents
Upper Volta	CFA Franc	CFAF	.004	100 Centimes
Uruguay	Peso	Ur$	.002	100 Centesimos
Venezuela	Bolivar	B	.23	100 Centimos
Vietnam, Democratic Republic of	Dong		.18	100 Sau
Vietnam, Republic of	Piastre	VN$	.029	100 Cents
Virgin Islands (US)	US Dollar	$	1.00	100 Cents
Western Samoa	Tala	WS$	1.40	100 Cents
Yemen	Yemeni Rial		.935	40 Bogshas
Yugoslavia	Dinar	Din	.06	100 Paras
Zambia	Kwacha	ZK	1.40	100 Ngwee

[3] The United Kingdom Monetary System, effective February 15, 1971. A pound (£) note and penny system consisting of:

CURRENCY	APPROX. U.S. VALUE
Paper	
£ note = 100p	$2.60
Coins	
50p	1.30
10p	.26
5p	.13
2p	.052
1p	.026
½p	.013

14.4 CUSTOMS REGULATIONS

The U.S. government has established the Customs Service to enforce the customs regulations passed by Congress. Any person intending to travel outside the boundaries of the United States or any company intending to import materials should be familiar with these rather precise regulations. This chapter outlines a few of them, such as exemptions for travelers, declaration procedures, and prohibited or restricted items for importation. You may obtain additional information from your local customs officer or by writing to the Bureau of Customs, Treasury Department, Washington, DC 20226.

Customs Exemptions. Exemptions may be applied only to articles you bring with you at the time of your return to the United States if you are a returning resident who has not abandoned permanent residence in the United States and taken up permanent residence abroad.

One-Hundred-Dollar Exemption. This exemption applies if you are returning from a stay abroad of at least 48 hours (an exact computation). Exception: If you return from Mexico, there is no minimum time requirement, unless you have used this $100 exemption, or part of it, within the preceding thirty-day period.

Articles totaling $100 (based on the fair *retail* value of each item in the country where it was acquired) may be entered free of duty, subject to limitations on liquors and cigars, if:

1. They accompany you at the time of your return.
2. They were acquired as an incident of your trip.
3. They are for your personal or household use.
4. They are properly declared to customs.

Cigars and Cigarettes. There is no limitation on the number of cigarettes that may be imported for personal use. However, not more than 100 cigars may be included. This exemption is available to each person regardless of age.

Liquor. One quart of alcoholic beverages may be included in this exemption if you are 21 years of age or older, subject to state and federal restrictions.

Ten-Dollar Exemption. If you are not entitled to the $100 exemption because of the 30-day or 48-hour minimum limitations, you may bring in free of duty and tax articles acquired abroad for your personal or household use if the total fair retail value does not exceed $10. This is an individual exemption and may not be grouped with articles brought in by other members of your family on one customs declaration. Any of the following may be included: 50 cigarettes, 10 cigars, one-half pound of manufactured tobacco, 4 ounces of alcoholic beverages, or 4 ounces of alcoholic perfume. CAUTION: If any article is subject to duty or tax, or if the total value of all articles exceeds $10, no article may be exempted from duty or tax.

Importation in Excess of Exemption. Articles in excess of your customs exemption may be imported unless they are prohibited from entering the

United States (see "Prohibited and Restricted Articles" in this section). Items not entitled to free entry will be subject to customs duty. An abbreviated list of the usual rates of duty on popular tourist items appears in Figure 14-5.

Traveling Back and Forth Across Borders.   After you have crossed the U.S. boundary at one point and swing back into the U.S. to travel to another point in the foreign country, you run the risk of losing your customs exemption unless you meet certain requirements. If you make a *swing back,* be sure to ask the nearest customs officer about these requirements.

Virgin Islands of United States, American Samoa, Guam.   If returning directly or indirectly from the Virgin Islands, American Samoa, or Guam, you may receive a customs exemption of $200, based on the fair retail value of the articles in the country where they were acquired, *provided* not more than $100 of this exemption is applied to merchandise obtained elsewhere than in these islands. The Virgin Islands are excepted from the 48-hour minimum-time requirement. Residents 21 years of age or older may enter one wine gallon of alcoholic beverages free of duty and tax, *provided* not more than one quart of this amount is acquired elsewhere than in these islands.

Customs Declaration.   You must declare to U.S. Customs, either orally or in writing, ALL articles acquired abroad and in your possession at the time of return. Include:

1. Items another person requested you to bring home.

2. Any article you intend to sell or use in your business.

3. Alterations or repairs made to articles taken abroad.

4. Gifts presented to you while abroad, such as wedding or birthday presents.

The wearing or use of an article acquired abroad does not exempt it from duty, and it must be declared at the price you paid for it. The customs officer will make an appropriate reduction in its value for wear and use.

Written Declaration.   All articles acquired abroad must be declared to customs in writing when:

1. Their total fair retail value (including alterations and repairs) exceeds $100.

2. More than one quart of alcoholic beverages or more than 100 cigars are included.

3. Some of the items are not intended for your personal or household use, such as commercial samples, items for sale or use in your business, or articles you are bringing home for another person.

4. A customs duty or Internal Revenue tax is collectible on any article in your possession.

Family Declaration.   The head of a family may make a joint declaration for all members residing in the same household and returning with him to the

DESCRIPTION	RATE*	DESCRIPTION	RATE*
Alcoholic beverages (See discussion)		Clocks:	
Antiques:		valued over $5 but not over $10 each	$1.50 ea. + 32½%
over 100 years old	Free	valued over $10 each	$2.25 ea. + 32½%
Automobiles, passenger	6½%		
Bags, hand, leather	20%	Cork, manufactures of	36%
Bamboo, manufactures of	25%		
Beads:		Dolls and parts	35%
imitation precious and semi-precious stones	14 to 26%	Drawings (graphics):	
ivory	20%	originals	Free
Binoculars, prism	30%	copies	8%
Books:		Earthenware tableware, available in 77-piece sets:	
foreign author	3%	valued not over $3.30/set	10¢ doz. + 28%
foreign language	Free	valued over $3.30 but not over $7/set	10¢ doz. + 37%
Cameras:		valued over $7/set	10¢ doz. + 21%
motion picture, over $50	12%		
still, over $10	15%		
cases, leather	20%	Figurines, china	45%
lenses	25%	Flax, manufactures of	13.5%
Candy:		Flowers, artificial, plastic	28%
sweetened chocolate	10%	Fruit, prepared	35% or under
other	14%		
Chess Sets	20%	Fur:	
China:		wearing apparel	17 to 37½%
bone	35%	other manufactures of	17%
nonbone, other than tableware	45%	Furniture:	
nonbone, available in 77-piece sets:		wood, chairs	17%
		wood, other than chairs	10.6%
valued not over $10/set	10¢ doz. + 48%	Glass tableware valued not over $1 ea.	40 - 50%
valued over $10 but not over $24/set	10¢ doz. + 55%	Gloves:	
		not lace or net, plain, vegetable fibers, woven	25%
valued over $24/set	10¢ doz. + 36%	wool, over $4/doz.	37.5¢ lb. +25%
Cigarette lighters:		fur	20%
pocket, valued over 42¢ ea.	45%	horsehide or cowhide	15%
table	24%	Golf balls	12.5%

Figure 14-5 Advisory guide of tariff rates for popular tourist items.

Handkerchiefs:		Slippers, leather	10%
cotton, plain	30%	Sterling flatware and tableware:	
other vegetable fiber, plain	18%	knives and forks	8¢ ea.
			+ 17.5%
Iron, travel type, electric	11.5%	spoons and tableware	25%
Ivory, manufactures of	12%	Stones, cut but not set:	
		diamonds not over 1/2 carat	8%
Jade, cut but not set	5%	diamonds over 1/2 carat	10%
Jewelry, precious metal or		other	3 to 10%
stone:		Sweaters, wool, over $5/lb.	37.5¢ lb.
silver chief value, valued			+ 20%
not over $18/doz.	55%	Tape recorders	11.5 to 15%
other	24%	Toilet preparations:	
		not containing alcohol	15%
Mah jong sets	20%	containing alcohol	16¢ lb. + 15%
Mother of pearl, manufactures	17.5%	Toys	35%
Motorcycles	10%	Truffles	Free
Mushrooms, dried	4¢ lb.		
	+ 20%	Vegetables prepared	17.5%
Musical instruments:			
music boxes, wood	16%	Watches, on $100 watch duty	
woodwind	15%	varies from	$8 to $15
		Wearing apparel:	
Paintings (works of art):		embroidered or	
original	Free	ornamented	42.5%
copies	8%	not embroidered, not orna-	
Paper, manufactures of	17.5%	mented:	
Pearls:		cotton, knit	25%
loose or temporarily strung:		cotton, not knit	10 to 25%
genuine	3%	linen, not knit	15%
cultured	5%	manmade fiber, knit	25¢ lb.
imitation	40%		+ 32.5%
permanently strung	24 to 55%	manmade fiber, not	
Perfume	16¢ lb.	knit	25¢ lb.
	+ 15%		+ 32.5%
Postage stamps	Free	silk knit	20%
Printed matter, foreign author	4%	silk, not knit	32.5%
		wool, knit	37.5¢ lb.
Radios	12.5%		+ 20 to 32%
Rattan:		wool, not knit	25 to 37.5¢
furniture	18%		lb. + 21%
other manufactures of	25%		
Records, phonograph	10%	Wood:	
Rubber, manufactures of	12.5%	carvings	16 2/3%
		manufactures of	16 2/3%
Shaver, electric	13.75%		
Shell, manufactures of	17.5%		
Shoes, leather	5 to 20%		

Figure 14-5 (continued).

United States as a group. A family of four, for instance, may bring in articles free of duty valued up to $400 fair retail value on one declaration, even if the articles acquired by one member of the family exceed his $100 exemption. Infants and children returning to the United States are entitled to the same exemption as adults (except for alcoholic beverages). Children born abroad, who have never resided in the United States, are not eligible for the exemption.

How to Avoid Customs Penalties. Don't rely on advice given by persons outside the Customs Service. It is well known that some merchants abroad offer travelers invoices or bills of sale showing false and understated values. This practice only delays your customs examination and may prove costly. Current commercial prices on foreign items are available at all times and on-the-spot comparisons of these values are made.

Listing, Packing, and Opening Your Baggage. Make a list of the articles acquired before you reach the port of entry. Retain sales slips and purchase orders covering these items and have them available for ready examination by the customs officer. Pack your baggage in a manner that will make inspection easy. Pack separately articles acquired abroad. If asked to open your luggage or the trunk of your car, comply without hesitation.

Other Customs Exemptions. *Foreign-Made Articles Taken Abroad.* Articles of foreign origin, such as cameras, watches, jewelry, and plumage, are dutiable upon each importation into the United States unless you can *prove* to the customs officer that you possessed the items in this country before your departure. Bills of sale or receipts for purchase, repair, or cleaning will be reasonable proof of prior possession. Register valuable articles of foreign origin before your departure by taking them to any customs office in the United States for identification. This may also be done when you leave the country at the port of embarkation.

Gifts. Gifts accompanying you are considered to be for your personal use and may be included within your exemption. Included are those given you by others while you were abroad and those you intend to give to others after your return. Gifts intended for business or promotional purposes may not be included.

While you are abroad you may send gifts totaling $10 fair retail value to friends or relatives in the United States without payment of duty and tax, provided the addressee does not receive in a single day gift parcels exceeding the $10 limitation. Write GIFT ENCLOSED in large letters and the fair retail value of the contents on the outside of the package. Alcoholic beverages and tobacco products are not included in this privilege, nor are perfumes valued at more than $1.

Personal Belongings Sent Home. Personal effects of United States origin are entitled to entry free of duty. They may be sent home by mail before you return and receive free entry if a statement is placed on the outside wrapper or enclosed in the package explaining that the articles were taken out of the United States as personal effects and are being returned without having been altered or repaired while abroad.

Automobiles, Boats, Airplanes.   Automobiles, boats, planes, or other vehicles taken abroad for noncommercial use may be returned duty free if you can prove to the customs officer that they were taken out of the United States. This proof may be the state registration card for an automobile, the Department of Commerce certificate for an aircraft, a yacht license or motorboat identification certificate for a pleasure boat, or a customs certificate of registration obtained before departure. Dutiable repairs or accessories acquired abroad for these vehicles must be declared on your return.

A leaflet, *Imported Automobiles,* may be obtained from a customs office near you or from the Bureau of Customs, Treasury Department, Washington, DC 20226, if you are considering the purchase of a foreign-made car during your travel abroad.

Antiques.   Antiques are free of duty if they were made at least 100 years ago. Antique furniture, unless brought in as personal and household effects, must be inspected for free entry by the antique examiners located at most of the major ports of entry.

Household Effects.   Household effects, professional books, or tools of trade or occupation that you prove were taken out of the United States are duty free at the time you return, if properly declared and entered.

Books, furniture, carpets, paintings, tableware, linens, and similar household furnishings acquired abroad may be imported free of duty if:

1. They are not imported for another person.

2. They are not imported for sale.

3. They have been used abroad by you for not less than one year, or were available for use in a household in which you were a resident member for one year. This privilege does not include articles placed in storage outside the home.

The year of use need not be continuous, nor does it need to be the year immediately preceding the date of importation. Vehicles, consumable supplies, and office furniture cannot be passed free of duty as household effects.

A customs declaration must be made by the owner to avoid the posting of an entry bond to secure release of the goods without a deposit of duties. This declaration may be made only at the time of, or after, your arrival in the United States. To keep broker charges to a minimum, arrive home before your shipment so that you can mail your customs declaration to the carrier to speed clearance of your goods through customs. Otherwise, the broker must furnish a bond to produce the declaration of the owner. There are times when the carrier is unable to obtain the services of a broker willing to furnish the bond. When this happens, the goods must either be held at the port of arrival, where storage and handling fees accrue, or be shipped in bond to an interior port where customs clearance must be arranged.

Prohibited and Restricted Articles. Articles considered injurious or detrimental to the general welfare of the United States are prohibited entry by law. Among these are narcotics, drugs containing narcotics in any amount (including prescriptions and preparations such as cough and headache remedies), obscene articles and publications, lottery tickets, wild birds, and the feathers and eggs of wild birds.

Special Requirements for Specific Items. Other items must meet the special requirements described here before they can be released by a customs officer.

1. Trademarked articles. Any foreign article bearing a trademark recorded in the Treasury Department, e.g., perfumes, cameras, watches, musical instruments, and so on, cannot be brought into the United States without the consent of the trademark owner. If the trademark is removed or obliterated, there is no restriction. A list of trademarked articles may be obtained from the nearest U.S. consular officer or from the Commissioner of Customs, Washington, DC 20226.

2. Fruits, vegetables, plants, and plant products. The Department of Agriculture is responsible for preventing the entry of injurious pests and plant diseases into the United States. Fruits, vegetables, plants, cuttings, seeds, and unprocessed plant products are the hosts for these pests and diseases. Consequently, these items either are prohibited from entering the country or require an import permit. Permits should be obtained in advance of importation. Applications for import permits or information should be addressed to the Import and Permit Section, Plant Quarantine Division, 209 River Street, Hoboken, NJ 07030.

3. Livestock, meats, and poultry. The customs officer also enforces for the Department of Agriculture the rules and regulations that prevent the importation of animal diseases into the United States—including rinderpest and foot-and-mouth disease, a threat to our livestock industry. Because animal diseases exist in most countries of the world, for all practical purposes the following animals, animal products, and poultry are prohibited from entering the United States.

(a) Fresh, chilled, frozen, or dried meat.

(b) Cured and cooked meats, such as bacon, hams, sausages, bologna, salami, and similar products.

(c) Organs, glands, extracts, secretions, untanned hides and skins, wool, hair, and so on.

(d) Cattle, sheep, goats, swine, deer, horses, mules and burros, and dogs for use around livestock.

(e) Chickens, ducks, geese, swans, pheasants, grouse, partridges, quail, guinea fowl, and pea fowl, including eggs for hatching purposes.

If you are considering either bringing or sending any of the above items to the United States, write for detailed requirements to the Animal Inspection and Quarantine Division, Agricultural Research Service, Department of Agriculture, Washington, DC 20250.

Pets. The leaflet "So You Want to Import a Pet" explains the general import requirements for cats, dogs, monkeys, and psittacine birds. A copy may be secured from the customs field office near you or the Commissioner of Customs, Washington, DC 20226. For more specific information, write to the Division of Foreign Quarantine, U.S. Public Health Service, Silver Springs, MD 20910. Questions on wild birds and migratory game birds should be addressed to the Fish and Wildlife Service, Department of Interior, Washington, DC 20240.

Biological Materials. Biological materials of public health importance (disease organisms and vectors for research and educational purposes) require import permits. Write to the Division of Foreign Quarantine Program, U.S. Public Health Service, Center for Disease Control, Atlanta, Georgia 30333.

Merchandise Prohibited by Foreign Assets Control Regulations. The importation (as well as the purchase abroad) of all merchandise originating in Communist China, North Korea, North Vietnam, or Cuba and all goods containing Cuban components is prohibited without a Treasury license. These licenses are strictly controlled and, for all practical purposes, may be considered unavailable to tourists.

The importation or purchase of other specified commodities of a type or kind that was traditionally imported from mainland China is prohibited without a Treasury license. However, many such specified commodities may be purchased and imported if a "Comprehensive Certificate of Origin," issued by the Hong Kong government and appropriate for Foreign Assets Control purposes, is obtained at the time of purchase. If the required certificate of origin cannot be produced at the time of importation, the goods are liable to seizure. Before making purchases in Far Eastern countries, check with the local U.S. consulate.

Copies of the Foreign Assets Control Regulations, listing the commodities affected and explaining the certification procedures, and copies of the Cuban Assets Control Regulations may be obtained from the Federal Reserve Bank of New York or from the Office of Foreign Assets Control, Treasury Department, Washington, DC 20220.

Gold Coins and Medals. The Treasury Department gold regulations prohibit the importation of gold bullion or gold coins except under license. Gold medals, other than special award medals, are prohibited entry. Gold-coin jewelry is restricted and may be imported only if it meets certain requirements. Gold-coin jewelry and gold coins taken out of the United States cannot be returned without special authorization. For information, write the Director, Office of Domestic Gold and Silver Operations, Treasury Department, Washington, DC 20220.

Firearms and Ammunition. Firearms and ammunition are subject to restrictions and licenses. Travelers entering and leaving the United States are permitted for personal use three firearms (nonautomatic rifles, carbines, revolvers, and pistols) and 1,000 rounds of ammunition as part of their

	Internal Revenue Tax	Customs Duty
Beer	$ 9 bbl. (31 gal.)	$0.12½ per gal.
Brandy	$10.50[1]	$1.25[1] to $5.00[1]
Gin	$10.50[1]	1.00[1]
Liqueurs	$10.50[1]	1.00[1]
Rum	$10.50[1]	1.75[1]
Whisky[2]		
Scotch	$10.50[1]	1.02[1]
Irish	$10.50[1]	1.02[1]
Other	$10.50[1]	1.25[1]
Wine		
Sparkling	$2.40 to $3.40	1.50
Still	$ .17 to $2.25	.37½ to $1

[1] Proof gallon.
[2] If under 100 proof, duty and tax are based on wine gallon.

Figure 14-6   Rates of duty and tax on alcoholic beverages.

accompanied or unaccompanied baggage. These firearms must be declared with customs at the time of departure from the U.S. A special license from the Office of Munitions Control, State Department, Washington, DC 20520, is required for additional firearms and ammunition. Pistols, revolvers, and other firearms capable of being concealed on the person, and all types of ammunition are prohibited by law from being shipped in the mails.

Importation of Alcoholic Beverages.   Liquor may not be imported into a state of the United States in violation of its laws. Information on state restrictions and state taxes should be obtained from the state government.

United States postal laws prohibit the shipment of alcoholic beverages by mail.

Alcoholic beverages forwarded to persons in the United States are not entitled to free entry under the $10 gift exemption, and any carried in by travelers in excess of the one-quart limitation are subject to duty and Internal Revenue tax. The usual rates of duty and tax are shown in Figure 14-6.

14.5   UNITED STATES FOREIGN SERVICE POSTS

To assist U.S. business interests abroad, the Department of State provides key officers at all foreign service posts around the world who act as liaison between the particular country and the businessman. The following description of the variety of services offered by the officers at these posts will aid the businessman in selecting the correct person to contact for assistance. When seeking information, he should write directly to the officer responsible for the area of endeavor in which he is interested.

Key Officers at Foreign Service Posts

Chief of Mission, with the title of "Ambassador" or "Minister," and *Deputy Chief of Mission.* Both officers are responsible for the entire U.S. mission within a country, including all consular posts as well as the embassy.

Political officers participate in negotiations to further U.S. political objectives. They analyze and report on political developments of internal or international significance.

Economic officers take part in negotiations relating to our economic policy objectives and analyze and report on economic matters. At the smaller posts they also perform the functions of the commercial officer.

The *commercial officer*'s primary responsibility is to promote trade, travel, and the private investment interests of the United States. He helps to develop trade contacts and export opportunities; arrange appointments for U.S. businessmen and assist in contacts with local government officials; support special overseas activities of the Department of Commerce, such as trade centers, trade missions, and trade fairs; and report on business trends, market potentials, and laws and customs that affect U.S. commercial interests. He also works toward eliminating any discriminatory treatment of U.S. business interests.

The *labor attaché,* or labor officer, is responsible for following the political and economic activities of the national labor organizations. He is ready to supply information regarding labor and social attitudes and trends, wages, nonwage costs, Social Security regulations, government labor policies and regulations, and labor attitudes toward American business investments.

Consular officers extend to U.S. citizens and their property abroad the protection of the U.S. government; maintain lists of local attorneys; and act as a liaison with customs, tax, and policy officials. Consular officers have the authority to notarize documents and authenticate the signatures and seals of foreign officials. In troubled areas, the U.S. businessman is advised to register with the consular officer.

The *administrative officer* is responsible for the management of the post, including such matters as personnel, budget, operations, and so on. This officer is in charge of purchasing for the post and would be the individual to contact regarding sales to the post, its commissary, or its personnel.

ACM	Assistant chief of mission	L	Legation
ADM	Administrative section	LAB	Labor officer
AGR	Agricultural section	M	Mission
AID	Agency for International	MIN	Minister
	Development	NATO	North Atlantic Treaty
AMB	Ambassador		Organization
BO	Branch office of embassy	OAS	Organization of American
C	Consulate		States
CAO	Cultural affairs officer	OIC	Officer in charge
CG	Consul general, consulate general	PAO	Public affairs officer
COM	Commercial section		(USIA)
CON	Consul, consular section	PO	Principal officer
COUN	Counselor	POL	Political section
CRD	Mission coordinator	USEC	US Mission to European
DCM	Deputy chief of mission		Communities
DEP	Deputy	USIA	US Information Agency
DPO	Deputy principal officer	USRO	US Mission to North Atlantic
E	Embassy		Treaty Organization and
ECO	Economic section		European Regional
FAO	Food and Agriculture Organization		Organizations
IAEA	International Atomic Energy Agency	USUN	US Mission to United
ICAO	International Civil Aviation		Nations
	Organization	VC	Vice consul

Figure 14-7 Foreign service abbreviations.

The *agricultural attaché,* the officer of the U.S. Department of Agriculture attached to the post, reports on agricultural production, trade policy, and market developments in his area and promotes U.S. agricultural exports.

The *AID Mission Director* is responsible for the Agency for International Development programs, including dollar and local currency loans to governments and private enterprises, grants, investment guaranties, technical assistance, and fellowships.

The *public affairs officer,* an officer of the U.S. Information Agency, is responsible for U.S. informational and cultural programs in the host country. Although not specifically charged with assisting U.S. business abroad, this officer is ready to advise American companies on general public relations programs.

Foreign service abbreviations are listed in Figure 14-7.

Directory of Foreign Service Posts.   A list of the addresses and the telephone numbers of foreign service posts may be found in the Department of State Publication 7877, *Key Officers of Foreign Service Posts Guide for Businessmen.* This publication includes the names of key officers at these posts and is brought up-to-date four times a year. A single copy may be secured from the Superintendent of Documents for 35 cents, or a yearly subscription may be entered for $1.

15

Postal Regulations

Postal regulations change frequently. Consequently, the latest bulletins of the U.S. Postal Service should be kept in the office. These may be obtained from any post office free of charge. Also indispensable to every regular user of the mails is the *Postal Manual.* The *Manual,* which may be ordered from the Superintendent of Documents, gives the details of postal regulations governing domestic and foreign mail of all types. For a small fee, it is kept up-to-date with inserts issued by the Postal Service and automatically sent to subscribers.

Many companies issue their own regulations for the handling of outgoing letters and parcels. These regulations are designed to speed the mail, ensure its arrival in good condition, and save money. (See Figure 15-1.)

This chapter provides information from Post Office sources for all companies engaged in domestic or foreign trade.

CONTENTS

15.1 Domestic Mail   p. 623
15.2 International Mail   p. 641
15.3 Nonmail Postal Services   p. 653

15.1 DOMESTIC MAIL

Airmail	p. 631	Precanceled Stamps	p. 635
Bulk Mail	p. 637	Priority Mail	p. 631
Certified Mail	p. 634	Recall of Mail	p. 639
COD Mail	p. 633	Registered, Insured, and COD claims	p. 634
First Class	p. 626	Registered Mail	p. 631
Forwarding of Mail	p. 638	Return of Mail to Sender	p. 638
Fourth Class (Parcel Post)	p. 628	Return Receipts	p. 635
Insured Mail	p. 633	Second Class	p. 626
Meter Stamps	p. 636	Special Delivery	p. 631
Military Mail Within the United States	p. 639	Stamps, Envelopes, and Postal Cards	p. 635
		Third Class	p. 627
Nonmailable Matter	p. 640	Tracing Mail	p. 639
Permit Imprints	p. 636	Undeliverable Mail	p. 640

First Class Mail

Sealed matter partly or wholly in *writing*:

Typed or handwritten originals and carbons.

Bills, statements, invoices.

Orders.

Printed forms that are filled in.

Printed price lists with handwritten corrections.

Punched tabulating cards.

Exceptions:

Manuscripts for books, articles, music (4th Class).

Reproductions of handwritten or typed matter when mailed in minimum quantity of 20 pieces in unsealed envelopes (3d Class).

Reproductions of bills, invoices, statements (3d Class).

Any printing—except by typewriter—when not in nature of correspondence (3d Class). Advertising included.

Foreign Mail

Use air mail for all letters and important packages. Surface mail often takes as long as six weeks to two months to reach its destination. Aerogrammes available from the Post Office are adequate for most business messages.

If company stationery must be used because of length of message, always use air mail envelopes and tissue sheets. Within the ½ ounce basic limit, three full size 8½ x 11 tissue sheets may be enclosed in the air mail envelope. Place a paper clip where stamp should be to alert mailroom to the need for foreign postage.

Use inexpensive AO rate for

(a) commercial papers (invoices, waybills, music manuscripts, legal papers)

(b) printed matter (newspapers, books, pamphlets, music, printing proofs, catalogs, advertising brochures)

(c) merchandising samples

Do not seal foreign-bound packages but tie them securely with string.

Bulk Mail

Flap envelopes by opening the flaps slightly and folding them one inside the other. This arrangement speeds them through the stamping machine and insures that none goes unsealed.

Use a single size envelope for multiple pieces to eliminate the need for sorting and meter adjustments for different sizes.

Oversize Envelopes

When a large manila envelope contains first class matter, mark it *First Class Mail* just below the postage area to insure that it goes the fastest way possible.

Third Class Mail

Use 3d Class for catalogs, price lists, pads of forms and other salesman supplies, brochures, advertising, and booklets with less than 24 pages. To save postage, use 4th Class if the 3d Class matter weighs more than 16 oz.

Seal 3d Class envelopes if *Third Class* is written on front or back. Leave unsealed if not identified. A

Figure 15-1 Practical hints on preparing company mail.

clasp, tuck-in flap, or glue spot envelope qualifies as unsealed.

Use a return address with the endorsement *Return Requested* only when it is imperative to secure the return of the contents. The charge for each returned piece is 10¢ or more.

Postcards

Use postcards for short messages. As 1st Class mail, they receive the same handling as letters for less postage. Repetitive messages should be printed on them to save time. The cost of using expensive letterheads and envelopes is avoided also.

Air Mail

Air mail receives first priority in leaving the airport on the first available plane and being processed first on arrival at its destination. Never use air mail on Fridays nor during winter months in areas that always have bad weather. Flights may be delayed or diverted to alternate airports.

Except in emergencies, do *not* use air mail for letters within the continental United States. All 1st Class mail traveling more than 200 miles goes by air; that traveling less goes by surface mail even if it carries air mail postage.

Special Delivery

Use special delivery only when extra speed is vital. Never use it:

(a) on Fridays unless Saturday delivery is imperative.

(b) to a P.O. Box address.

(c) unless the addressee will be at the address to receive it.

Special delivery does not travel faster than 1st Class or air mail. It is dispatched from the addressee's post office during working hours only, and in 90 percent of cases reaches him only a few hours ahead of regular mail.

Special Handling

Use special handling to speed the delivery of 4th Class mail. About two days are saved, and costs are less than Air Parcel.

Mixed Classes of Mail

Mark *First Class Mail Enclosed* on all packages in 3d and 4th Class which contain written material. Postage is then computed at the lowest rate and one 1st Class stamp is affixed in addition to cover the 1st Class matter.

Return Receipt

Ask for a return receipt only when proof of delivery is vital. It cannot be obtained unless the letter or package is sent by registered, insured, or certified mail. The cost of the return receipt must be added to the regular postage and fee for these services

A better alternative is to request a *Certificate of Mailing* from the post office when the letter or package is accepted by them. This service is available to all classes of mail for 5¢.

Figure 15-1 (continued).

	Rate
First Class. Letters, bills and statements of account, and other written matter wholly or partially in writing or typewriting and including carbon copies, sealed against inspection, and weighing 12 ounces or less, except postal and post cards	8¢ an ounce
Over 12 ounces	Priority mail rates apply
Single and double postal cards sold by the post office	6¢ each half
Single and double private post cards (reply half of double post cards does not have to bear postage when originally mailed)	6¢ each half
Business-reply mail:	
Cards	8¢ each
Other than cards:	
Weight not over 2 ounces	8¢ per ounce or fraction of an ounce plus 2¢ per piece
Weight over 2 ounces	8¢ per ounce or fraction of an ounce plus 5¢ per piece
Over 12 ounces	Priority mail rates plus 5¢ per piece

Restrictions on Size, Shape and Weight of First-Class Mail. Each piece may not exceed 100 inches in length and girth combined (Figure 15-2). Envelopes, cards, and self-mailers are nonmailable if they are less than 3 inches in width (height) or $4\frac{1}{4}$ inches in length, have shapes other than rectangular, or have a thickness of less than 0.006 of an inch. It is recommended that pieces be sealed or secured on all four edges in order that they may be handled by machines.

Second Class. Newspapers, magazines, and other periodicals. Single-copy mailings by general public	6¢ for first 2 ounces, 1¢ each addl. ounce or fraction thereof or fourth-class rate, whichever is lower
Quantity mailings containing notice of second-class entry	Consult postmaster

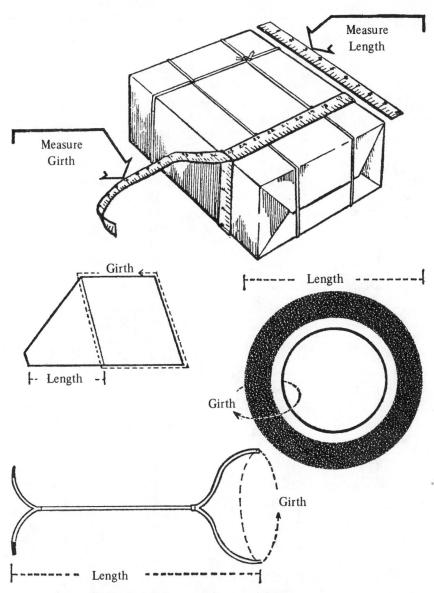

Figure 15-2   How to compute the size of a package.

Third Class.   Circulars, books, catalogs, and other printed matter, merchandise, seeds, cuttings, bulbs, roots, scions, and plants, weighing less than 16 ounces.

Single rate: 8¢ first 2 ounces, 2¢ addl. for 3d, 6th, 9th, 12th, and 15th ounce or fraction, 3¢ addl. for 4th, 5th, 7th, 8th, 10th, 11th, 13th, 14th, 16th ounce or fraction.

Bulk rate . . . . See "Bulk Mail" in this section

Keys, identification cards, identification tags, or similar identification devices, without cover and containing or securely attached to the name and complete post office address of a person, organization, or concern, with instructions to return to such address and a statement guaranteeing payment of postage due on delivery . . . . 14¢ first 2 ounces, 8¢ each addl. 2 ounces or fraction

Fourth Class (Parcel Post). Merchandise, books, printed matter, and so on, weighing over 16 ounces.

Fourth-Class (Parcel Post) Zone Rates

Weight— 1 pound and not exceeding (pounds)	Local	1 and 2	3	4	5	6	7	8
2....	$0.60	$0.65	$0.70	$0.75	$0.80	$0.90	$1.00	$1.05
3....	.60	.75	.80	.85	.95	1.10	1.20	1.35
4....	.65	.80	.85	.95	1.10	1.30	1.40	1.60
5....	.70	.85	.90	1.05	1.20	1.45	1.65	1.90
6....	.70	.95	1.00	1.15	1.35	1.60	1.85	2 10
7....	.75	1.05	1.10	1.25	1.50	1.75	2.10	2.35
8....	.75	1.10	1.15	1.35	1.60	1.90	2.30	2.60
9....	.80	1.15	1.20	1.45	1.75	2.05	2.45	2.85
10....	.80	1.20	1.30	1.55	1.90	2.20	2.65	3.10
11....	.80	1.25	1.35	1.60	2.00	2.30	2.85	3.35
12....	.85	1.30	1.45	1.70	2.10	2.45	3.05	3.55
13....	.85	1.35	1.55	1.80	2.20	2.60	3.25	3.80
14....	.90	1.40	1.60	1.90	2.35	2.75	3.45	4.00
15....	.90	1.45	1 65	2.00	2.45	2.85	3.60	4.20
16....	.95	1.55	1.75	2.05	2.55	2.95	3.80	4.40
17....	1.00	1.60	1.80	2.15	2.65	3.10	3.95	4.60
18....	1.00	1.65	1.90	2.20	2.75	3.20	4.15	4.80
19....	1.05	1.70	2.00	2.30	2.85	3.35	4.30	5.00
20....	1.05	1.75	2.05	2.40	2.95	3.50	4.50	5.20
21....	1.10	1.85	2.10	2.45	3.05	3.65	4.65	5.40
22....	1.15	1.90	2.15	2.55	3.15	3.75	4.85	5.60
23....	1.15	1.95	2.20	2.60	3.25	3.90	5.00	5.80
24....	1.20	2.00	2.25	2.65	3.35	4.05	5.15	6.00
25....	1.20	2.05	2.30	2.75	3.45	4.15	5.35	6.20
26....	1.20	2.10	2.35	2.85	3.55	4.30	5.50	6.40
27....	1.25	2.15	2.40	2.90	3.70	4.45	5.65	6.60
28....	1.25	2.20	2.45	2.95	3.80	4.60	5.80	6.80
29....	1.30	2.25	2.50	3.05	3.90	4.70	5.95	7.00
30....	1.30	2.30	2.55	3.10	4.00	4.85	6.10	7.20
31....	1.35	2.35	2.65	3.20	4.10	5.00	6.25	7.40
32....	1.40	2.40	2.70	3.30	4.20	5.15	6.45	7.60
33....	1.40	2.45	2.75	3.35	4.30	5.25	6.60	7.80
34....	1.45	2.50	2.80	3.40	4.40	5.40	6.75	8.00
35....	1.45	2.55	2.85	3.45	4.50	5.55	6.90	8.20

Weight— 1 pound and not exceeding (pounds)	Local	1 and 2	3	4	5	6	7	8
36....	$1.45	$2.60	$2.90	$3.55	$4.60	$5.65	$ 7.10	$8.40
37....	1.50	2.65	3.00	3.65	4.70	5.75	7.25	8.60
38....	1.50	2.70	3.05	3.70	4.80	5.90	7.45	8.80
39....	1.55	2.75	3.10	3.80	4.90	6.05	7.60	9.00
40....	1.55	2.80	3.15	3.85	5.00	6.15	7.75	9.20
CONSULT POSTMASTER FOR WEIGHT AND SIZE LIMITS								
41....	1.60	2.85	3.20	3.95	5.15	6.25	7.95	9.40
42....	1.65	2.90	3.25	4.00	5.25	6.40	8.10	9.60
43....	1.65	2.95	3.30	4.10	5.35	6.55	8.25	9.80
44....	1.70	3.00	3.35	4.15	5.45	6.65	8.40	10.00
45....	1.70	3.05	3.40	4.20	5.55	6.80	8.55	10.20
46....	1.70	3.10	3.50	4.30	5.65	6.90	8.70	10.40
47....	1.75	3.10	3.55	4.40	5.75	7.00	8.90	10.60
48....	1.75	3.15	3.60	4.45	5.85	7.15	9.05	10.80
49....	1.80	3.20	3.65	4.50	5.95	7.30	9.20	11.00
50....	1.80	3.25	3.70	4.60	6.05	7.40	9.35	11.15
51....	1.85	3.30	3.80	4.70	6.15	7.50	9.50	11.35
52....	1.90	3.35	3.85	4.75	6.25	7.65	9.65	11.55
53....	1.90	3.40	3.90	4.80	6.35	7.80	9.80	11.75
54....	1.95	3.40	3.95	4.90	6.45	7.90	9.95	11.90
55....	1.95	3.45	4.00	4.95	6.55	8.00	10.10	12.10
56....	1.95	3.50	4.10	5.05	6.60	8.10	10.25	12.25
57....	2.00	3.55	4.15	5.15	6.70	8.25	10.40	12.45
58....	2.00	3.60	4.20	5.20	6.80	8.40	10.55	12.60
59....	2.05	3.65	4.25	5.25	6.90	8.50	10.70	12.80
60....	2.05	3.65	4.30	5.35	7.00	8.60	10.85	12.95
61....	2.10	3.70	4.35	5.45	7.05	8.70	11.00	13.10
62....	2.15	3.70	4.40	5.50	7.15	8.85	11.15	13.30
63....	2.15	3.75	4.45	5.55	7.25	9.00	11.30	13.45
64....	2.20	3.80	4.50	5.60	7.35	9.10	11.45	13.65
65....	2.20	3.85	4.60	5.70	7.45	9.20	11.60	13.80
66....	2.20	3.90	4.65	5.80	7.50	9.30	11.75	13.95
67....	2.25	3.90	4.70	5.85	7.60	9.40	11.85	14.15
68....	2.25	3.95	4.75	5.90	7.70	9.55	12.00	14.30
69....	2.30	4.00	4.80	5.95	7.75	9.65	12.15	14.50
70....	2.30	4.05	4.85	6.05	7.85	9.75	12.25	14.65

Figure 15-3 Fourth-class (parcel post) zone rates.

	16 ounces or more but not exceeding	Maximum length and girth
Parcels mailed between first-class post offices in the 48 contiguous states of the United States	40 pounds	84 inches
Parcels mailed at or to: Any second, third, or fourth class post office. Any rural or star route. Any Army, Air Force, or Fleet post office. Any post office in Alaska or Hawaii. Any post office in the Commonwealth of Puerto Rico. Any post office in a territory or possession of the U.S., including the Canal Zone and Trust Territory of the Pacific Islands. Any post office when contents are baby poultry, nursery stock, agricultural commodities; books, Braille writers, and other appliances for the blind. (The term *agricultural commodities* includes any product grown or produced incident to an agricultural activity on a farm or in a garden, orchard, nursery, or forest, but does not include articles manufactured or processed from these commodities.)	70 pounds	100 inches

Figure 15-4   Parcel post weight and size limits.

On parcels measuring more than 84 inches but not more than 100 inches in length and girth combined the minimum charge shall be the zone charge that would apply to a 10-pound parcel. (See Figure 15-3 for rates and Figure 15-4 for weight and size limits.)

Combination Mailings. Letters may be placed in second-, third-, or fourth-class mail provided first-class postage is paid for them. The words, *FIRST CLASS MAIL ENCLOSED,* should be written on the outside of the parcel. Or the sealed letter may be securely fastened to the outside (Figure 15-5).

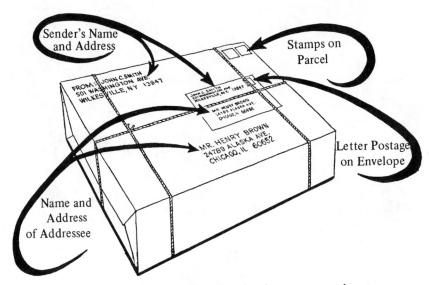

Figure 15-5   How to affix a first-class letter on a parcel.

Special Handling.   Assures first-class handling to the point of destination for third- and fourth-class mail. Fees are in addition to postage.

Not more than 2 pounds	25¢
More than 2 pounds but not more than 10 pounds	35¢
More than 10 pounds	50¢

Special Fourth-Class Rates.   Medical information for distribution to doctors, hospitals, medical schools, and medical students when it is contained in books, 16mm or narrower-width films, and catalogs (rate applies for films and catalogs except when mailed to or from commercial theaters); printed music, printed objective test materials, sound recordings, playscripts and manuscripts for books, periodicals, and music; printed educational reference charts permanently processed for preservation; loose-leaf pages, and binders therefor .   14¢ first pound, 7¢ each addl. pound or fraction

The *library rate* may be used for specific items loaned or exchanged between schools, colleges, or universities and public libraries, museums and herbaria, and non-profit religious, educational, scientific, philanthropic, agricultural, labor, veterans, or fraternal organizations; or when cooperatively processed by libraries; or loaned or exchanged between libraries, organizations, or associations, and their members, readers, or borrowers. The specific items covered by this rate include books; printed music; bound academic theses; periodicals; sound recordings; museum materials; 16mm or narrower-width films, filmstrips, transparencies, slides, microfilms; scientific or mathematical kits, instruments, or other devices; catalogs of the materials . .   6¢ first pound or fraction, 2¢ each addl. pound or fraction

Airmail.

Air postal or post cards	9¢ each
Letters and packages 8 ounces or less	11¢ an ounce

Business reply:

Air cards	11¢ each

Airmail other than cards:

Weight not over 2 ounces	11¢ an ounce, plus 2¢ per piece
Weight over 2 ounces	11¢ an ounce, plus 5¢ per piece
Weight over 8 ounces	Priority mail rates plus 5¢ per piece

Priority Mail.   Priority mail includes first-class pieces weighing more than 12 ounces and airmail pieces weighing more than 8 ounces. Such mail is carried as one class on a most expeditious basis. See schedule of rates in Figure 15-6.

Special Delivery.   All classes of mail may use special delivery upon payment of a fee in addition to regular postage. The fees are the same for both domestic and international mail.

First-class, airmail, and air parcel post	2 pounds or less 60¢ Up to 10 lbs. 75¢ Over 10 lbs. 90¢
All other classes	2 lbs. or less 80¢ Up to 10 lbs. 90¢ Over 10 lbs. $1.05

Registered Mail.   All mailable matter prepaid with postage at the first-class or airmail rate may be registered. The sender is required by law to declare the full value of the item presented for registration, as outlined here.

Item being mailed	*Valued to be declared*
Negotiable instruments—instruments payable to bearer, and matured interest coupons.	Market value.
Nonnegotiable instruments—all registered bonds, warehouse receipts, checks, drafts, deeds, wills, abstracts, and similar documents. Certificates of stock, including those endorsed in blank, are considered nonnegotiable.	No value, or replacement cost if postal insurance coverage is desired.
Money.	Full value.
Jewelry, gems, precious metals.	Market value or cost.
Merchandise.	Market value or cost.
Nonvaluables—matter not having intrinsic value, such as letters, files, and records, and so on.	No value or replacement cost if postal insurance coverage is desired.

Weight over 8 ounces and not exceeding: (Lbs.)	Local Zones 1, 2, and 3	Zone 4	Zone 5	Zone 6	Zone 7	Zone 8
1....	1.00	1.00	1.00	1.00	1.00	1.00
1-½..	1.20	1.22	1.25	1.30	1.40	1.50
2....	1.40	1.43	1.51	1.60	1.68	1.77
2-½..	1.60	1.65	1.76	1.90	2.02	2.16
3....	1.80	1.86	2.01	2.20	2.36	2.54
3-½..	2.00	2.08	2.26	2.49	2.69	2.93
4....	2.20	2.30	2.52	2.79	3.03	3.31
4-½..	2.40	2.51	2.77	3.09	3.37	3.70
5....	2.60	2.73	3.02	3.39	3.71	4.08
6....	3.08	3.23	3.58	4.03	4.43	4.88
7....	3.56	3.73	4.14	4.67	5.15	5.68
8....	4.04	4.23	4.70	5.31	5.87	6.48
9....	4.52	4.73	5.26	5.95	6.59	7.28
10....	5.00	5.23	5.82	6.59	7.31	8.08
11....	5.48	5.73	6.38	7.23	8.03	8.88
12....	5.96	6.23	6.94	7.87	8.75	9.68
13....	6.44	6.73	7.50	8.51	9.47	10.48
14....	6.92	7.23	8.06	9.15	10.19	11.28
15....	7.40	7.73	8.62	9.79	10.91	12.08
16....	7.88	8.23	9.18	10.43	11.63	12.88
17....	8.36	8.73	9.74	11.07	12.35	13.68
18....	8.84	9.23	10.30	11.71	13.07	14.48
19....	9.32	9.73	10.86	12.35	13.79	15.28
20....	9.80	10.23	11.42	12.99	14.51	16.08
21....	10.28	10.73	11.98	13.63	15.23	16.88
22....	10.76	11.23	12.54	14.27	15.95	17.68
23....	11.24	11.73	13.10	14.91	16.67	18.48
24....	11.72	12.23	13.66	15.55	17.39	19.28
25....	12.20	12.73	14.22	16.19	18.11	20.08
26....	12.68	13.23	14.78	16.83	18.83	20.88
27....	13.16	13.73	15.34	17.47	19.55	21.68
28....	13.64	14.23	15.90	18.11	20.27	22.48
29....	14.12	14.73	16.46	18.75	20.99	23.28
30....	14.60	15.23	17.02	19.39	21.71	24.08
31....	15.08	15.73	17.58	20.03	22.43	24.88
32....	15.56	16.23	18.14	20.67	23.15	25.68
33....	16.04	16.73	18.70	21.31	23.87	26.48
34....	16.52	17.23	19.26	21.95	24.59	27.28
35....	17.00	17.73	19.82	22.59	25.31	28.08
36....	17.48	18.23	20.38	23.23	26.03	28.88
37....	17.96	18.73	20.94	23.87	26.75	29.68
38....	18.44	19.23	21.50	24.51	27.47	30.48
39....	18.92	19.73	22.06	25.15	28.19	31.28
40....	19.40	20.23	22.62	25.79	28.91	32.08
41....	19.88	20.73	23.18	26.43	29.63	32.88
42....	20.36	21.23	23.74	27.07	30.35	33.68
43....	20.84	21.73	24.30	27.71	31.07	34.48
44....	21.32	22.23	24.86	28.35	31.79	35.28
45....	21.80	22.73	25.42	28.99	32.51	36.08
46....	22.28	23.23	25.98	29.63	33.23	36.88
47....	22.76	23.73	26.54	30.27	33.95	37.68
48....	23.24	24.23	27.10	30.91	34.67	38.48
49....	23.72	24.73	27.66	31.55	35.39	39.28
50....	24.20	25.23	28.22	32.19	36.11	40.08
51....	24.68	25.73	28.78	32.83	36.83	40.88
52....	25.16	26.23	29.34	33.47	37.55	41.68
53....	25.64	26.73	29.90	34.11	38.27	42.48
54....	26.12	27.23	30.46	34.75	38.99	43.28
55....	26.60	27.73	31.02	35.39	39.71	44.08
56....	27.08	28.23	31.58	36.03	40.43	44.88
57....	27.56	28.73	32.14	36.67	41.15	45.68
58....	28.04	29.23	32.70	37.31	41.87	46.48
59....	28.52	29.73	33.26	37.95	42.59	47.28
60....	29.00	30.23	33.82	38.59	43.31	48.08
61....	29.48	30.73	34.38	39.23	44.03	48.88
62....	29.96	31.23	34.94	39.87	44.75	49.68
63....	30.44	31.73	35.50	40.51	45.47	50.48
64....	30.92	32.23	36.06	41.15	46.19	51.28
65....	31.40	32.73	36.62	41.79	46.91	52.08
66....	31.88	33.23	37.18	42.43	47.63	52.88
67....	32.36	33.73	37.74	43.07	48.35	53.68
68....	32.84	34.23	38.30	43.71	49.07	54.48
69....	33.32	34.73	38.86	44.35	49.79	55.28
70....	33.80	35.23	39.42	44.99	50.51	56.08

Figure 15-6 Rates for priority mail (first-class mail weighing over 12 ounces and airmail weighing over 8 ounces).

Registry fees (in addition to postage).

Declared Actual Value (No Limit)	Articles either Not Covered or Covered by Commercial or Other Insurance	Postal Liability
$0.00 to $100	$0.95	Without commercial
$100.01 to $200	1.25	or other insurance —declared value.
$200.01 to $400	1.55	With commercial or
$400.01 to $600	1.85	other insurance—
$600.01 to $800	2.15	declared value or
$800.01 to $1,000	2.45	prorated.

Maximum postal insurance for shipments NOT commercially insured $10,000
Maximum postal insurance for shipments commercially insured . $1,000
Restricted delivery to a named person only . . . . . Addl. fee 50¢

Insured Mail.   Only third- and fourth-class mail or airmail that contains third- and fourth-class matter may be insured. The fees in addition to postage are:

Liability	Fee
$0.01 to $15	$0.20
$15.01 to $50	0.30
$50.01 to $100	0.40
$100.01 to $150	0.50
$150.01 to $200	0.60

Liability for insured mail is limited to $200. Restricted delivery is available for an additional 50¢ fee for mail insured for $15.01 or more. Return receipts are available for an additional fee for mail insured for $15.01 or more.

The sender may obtain payment for loss of, rifling of, or damage to domestic mail by having it insured. The mail must bear the complete names and addresses of the sender and the addressee. Not acceptable for insurance are parcels containing matter offered for sale and addressed to prospective purchasers who have not ordered or authorized their sending, nonmailable matter, articles that are so fragile as to prevent their safe carriage in the mail regardless of packaging, and articles not adequately prepared to withstand normal handling in the mail.

COD Mail.   First-, third-, and fourth-class matter may be sent as COD mail. The U.S. Postal Service will collect the price and the cost of the postage from the addressee when the article is delivered. The amount collected is returned to the mailer by a postal money order. The fees for COD service include insurance against loss of, rifling of, or damage to the article and failure to receive the amount collected from the addressee. The fees in addition to postage are:

Amount to Be Collected	COD Fee
$0.01 to $10	$0.70
$10.01 to $25	0.80
$25.01 to $50	0.90
$50.01 to $100	1.00
$100.01 to $200 (Maximum)	1.10

Registered, Insured, and COD Claims. Claims by either the mailer or the addressee for damage to insured matter or for the nondelivery of an insured parcel should be made on Form 3812, "Request for Payment of Domestic Postal Insurance." The completed form may be filed at any post office, branch, or station and need not be filed at the office of mailing or of address. The following periods, plus transportation time, must be observed before a claim is filed.

Registered Mail	10 days
Insured Mail	15 days
COD Mail	30 days

Evidence that the mail was registered, insured, or sent COD must be submitted—the receipt issued at time of mailing, an exact copy thereof made by any photographic process, a notarized copy of the original, or the wrapper or envelope of the article bearing the names and addresses of the sender and the addressee and the endorsement that the mail was sent registered, insured, or COD. The claimant must make a definite statement showing the actual value of lost or irreparably damaged articles or the cost of repairing partially damaged articles. Allowance must be made for any depreciation due to age or wear or for repairs needed at time of shipment. Statements of the value of lost or completely damaged articles should be supported by receipted bills or prices, if practicable. In the case of articles that can be repaired, a receipted bill for repairs already made, or an estimate of the cost of repairs obtained from a reliable repairman, must accompany the claim. When a lost registered, insured, or COD article is recovered, the payee may accept the article and reimburse the United States for the full amount paid if the article is undamaged, or such amount as may be determined equitable by the U.S. Postal Service if the article is damaged or has depreciated in value or if the contents are not intact.

Certified Mail. Certified mail service provides for a receipt to the sender and a record of delivery at the office of address. No record is kept at the office at which mailed. It is handled in the ordinary mail and no insurance coverage is provided. Any mailable matter of no intrinsic value on which postage at the first-class rate has been paid will be accepted as certified mail. This does not exclude articles of a nonnegotiable character and other matter that would involve a cost of duplication if lost or destroyed. The mail may be sent by air, and special delivery service is available. The fee is currently

30¢, in addition to the regular postage. Restricted delivery may be secured for a fee of 50¢.

Return Receipts.   A postal card verifying receipt of certified, insured, and registered mail may be secured for the following additional fees.
Requested at time of mailing:

Showing to whom and date delivered . . . . 15¢
Showing to whom, date, and address where delivered . . . . 35¢

Requested after mailing:

Showing to whom and date delivered . . . . 25¢

Stamps, Envelopes, and Postal Cards.   Ordinary postage is available singly or in sheets in the following denominations: 1¢, 2¢, 3¢, 4¢, 5¢, 6¢, 8¢, 10¢, 12¢, 13¢, 15¢, 16¢, 20¢, 25¢, 30¢, 40¢, and 50¢; $1 and $5. Airmail postage is sold singly or in sheets in denominations of 9¢, 11¢, 15¢, 17¢, 20¢, 21¢, and 25¢. Two books of stamps are available.

24 8¢ stamps $1.92
8 11¢ airmail stamps and 6 2¢ stamps 1.00

Three sizes of coils are available in the following denominations.

100 stamps . . . .   6¢, 8¢, 25¢, and 11¢ airmail
500 stamps . . . .   1¢, 5¢, 6¢, 8¢, and 11¢ airmail
3,000 stamps . . . .   1¢, 5¢, 6¢, 8¢, and 11¢ airmail

Both regular and window envelopes with postage affixed may be purchased in either the small size, 6¾ inches in length, or the large size, 10 inches in length as follows.

8¢ regular or window envelope, small or large . . . . 10¢ each
11¢ airmail regular or window envelope, small or large . . . . . 13¢ each

Single postal cards sell for 6¢; airmail single, 9¢; and double-reply (6¢ each half), 12¢.

Precanceled Stamps.   Precanceling means the cancellation of postage stamps, stamped envelopes, or postal cards in advance of mailing. Adhesive postage stamps may be precanceled only by the post office. The use of precanceled postage reduces the time and costs of mail handling. Precanceled mail, sorted and tied in packages by the mailer, requires less processing time in the post office and is therefore dispatched more quickly.

Precanceled stamps may be used to pay postage on post cards, but on no other first-class mail, unless specifically authorized by the postmaster on Form 3620; and on second-, third-, and fourth-class mail. Any number of pieces may be mailed at one time, regardless of whether they are identical, except for third-class bulk mailings. Matter bearing precanceled stamps may be mailed only at the post office that sold the stamps.

Meter Stamps.   Postage may be paid by printed meter stamps with a postage meter on any class of mail. Metered mail is entitled to all privileges and subject to all conditions applying to the various classes of mail. Postage meters facilitate the purchase, control, and affixing of postage. Metered mail does not require facing, canceling, and postmarking in the post office and can therefore be dispatched more quickly.

Postage meters print single, several, or all denominations of postage. They contain in one sealed unit the printing die or dies and two recording counters. One adds and keeps a total of all postage printed by the meter. The other subtracts and shows the balance of postage remaining in the meter, after the use of which it will lock. From time to time, mailers take the meter to the post office to have the counter set for additional postage, which is added to the balance remaining. Payment must be made for each additional setting.

Meters may be leased from the following authorized manufacturers:

The Singer Co., Friden Div.	National Cash Register Co.
2350 Washington Ave.	Dayton, OH 45409
San Leandro, CA 94577	Pitney-Bowes, Inc.
For the following meters:	Pacific and Walnut Sts.
Commercial Controls Corp.	Stamford, CT 06904
Friden, Inc.	Postalia Corp.
International Postal Supply Co.	32–31 57th Street
The Singer Co., Friden Div.	Woodwide, Flushing, NY 11377

A license to use a postage meter may be obtained at the post office where the metered mail will be deposited. No fee is charged. The application must specify the make and model of the meter.

Permit Imprints.   A permit to use permit imprints and pay postage in cash at the time of mailing may be obtained by the submitting of Form 3601, "Application to Mail Without Affixing Postage Stamp," with a fee of $15, to the post office where mailings will be made. The applicant must also pay an annual bulk mailing fee if he mails third-class matter at bulk rates.

Permit imprints may be made by printing press, handstamp, lithography, mimeograph, multigraph, addressograph, or similar devices. They may not be typewritten or hand-drawn. The imprint must be prepared both as to style and content in one of the forms shown in Figure 15-7. No other forms of imprints may be used. The imprint must be legible and must be of a color that contrasts sufficiently with the paper to make the imprint readable. The entire imprint must be placed in the upper right corner of the address side of each piece, parallel with the length of the piece.

The minimum quantities required to be mailed at one time are as follows.

First-class mail . . . . 300 pieces of identical weight.
Second- and third-class mail . . . . . . 300 pieces of identical matter, except 50 pounds or 200 pieces of identical third-class bulk mail.
Fourth-class mail . . . . 250 pieces of identical matter.
International mail . . . . 300 pieces of identical matter. (See "International Mail," Section 15.2.)

Bulk Mail. The bulk rate is applied to mailings of identical pieces separately addressed to different addressees in quantities of not less than 50 pounds or 200 pieces. All the pieces in a bulk mailing must be identical as to size, weight, and number of enclosures, but the printed textual matter need not be identical. Postage is computed at pound rates on the entire bulk mailed at one time, except that in no case shall less than the minimum charge per piece be paid. The annual bulk mailing fee of $30 must be paid at or before the first mailing each calendar year. Each piece may weigh up to but not including 16 ounces, and there is no maximum limit of size. Postage must be prepaid by meter

First-Class Mail

Second-, Third-, and Fourth-Class Mail
(Date and First-Class Mail omitted)

Bulk Third-Class Mail

Authorized Nonprofit Organization Mailings Only

Figure 15-7 Authorized permit imprints.

stamps, precanceled stamps or precanceled stamped envelopes, or by permit imprints. The identifying words *Bulk Rate* or the abbreviation *Blk. Rt.* must be printed or rubber-stamped by the mailer either in or immediately adjacent to permit imprints, meter stamps, or precanceled stamps. Qualified nonprofit organizations should print the words *Nonprofit Organization* or the abbreviation *Nonprofit Org.* in the same place. Bulk rates were as follows as of December 1971.

	Nonprofit Organizations	All Other Mailers
Books and catalogs having 24 or more bound pages with at least 22 printed; seeds, cuttings, bulbs, roots, scions, and plants.	8¢ per pound or fraction	17¢ per pound or fraction
All matter not listed above nor included in first or second class.	11¢ per pound or fraction	23¢ per pound or fraction
Minimum rate per piece.	1.7¢	4¢

If the total postage computed at the pound rate does not amount to the minimum rate per piece or more, postage must be computed at the minimum charge per piece.

Return of Mail to Sender.   Undelivered first-class mail will be returned to the sender without additional postage. The rules governing the return of second-class matter are complicated and may be obtained from your local post office. Third- and fourth-class matter will be returned to the sender and return postage collected on delivery. The notation *Return Postage Guaranteed* may be put on these two classes by the sender.

Forwarding of Mail.   First-class mail will be forwarded from one post office to another without additional charge. Second-, third-, and fourth-class will be forwarded but the person to whom it is addressed will be charged additional postage, except when it is forwarded within the same postal district. Airmail will be forwarded without additional charge. Special delivery mail will be forwarded but will not be delivered "special" to the second address, unless additional postage has been guaranteed by the sender for this purpose when it is mailed.

To have mail delivered to a new address, file Form 3575, "Change of Address Order," which is available at any post office or from any carrier. A written and signed order or a telegram is acceptable and must be sent by the patron, his agent, or the person in whose care mail will be addressed. The old and new addresses must always be furnished, including the ZIP Code numbers, if known. Mail received at the old address will be handled as follows.

1. All first-class mail, all official mail, and all third- and fourth-class parcels of obvious value will be forwarded.

2. Second-class, other fourth-class, and other third-class mail of obvious value will be forwarded only when specifically requested by the order.

3. Third-class matter of no obvious value and mail addressed to "Occupant" or "Postal Patron" will NOT be forwarded.

4. Mail bearing specific instructions of the sender *DO NOT FORWARD* will not be forwarded.

The order to forward mail constitutes the pledge of the addressee to pay forwarding postage. The order to forward also covers registered, certified, insured, and COD mail unless the sender has given other instructions or unless the addressee has moved outside the United States.

Recall of Mail.   Mail deposited in a post office or box may be recalled by the sender, by the parent or guardian of a minor child, or by the guardian of a person of unsound mind. An application form, "Sender's Application for Recall of Mail," which is obtainable at any post office, should be submitted. The mailer pays all the expenses of recalling mail, including the cost of any necessary telegrams, and the regular rate of return postage (except for first-class mail, which is returned without additional postage). If the mail has been delivered before receipt of the recall application, the mailer is notified. The addressee is not informed that recall has been requested.

Tracing Mail.   Letters and packages that have become lost in the mails may be traced by the sender or the addressee by the filing of a request form with the post office. The form must be filed within a year from the date of mailing and must include all pertinent information to facilitate the tracing of the item.

Military Mail Within the United States.   Mail to military personnel is subject to the usual postal fees for the type of matter mailed. It is important that the address be complete and accurate. For all branches of the service, show grade, full name, including first and middle name or initial, service number, organization, military installation, and the ZIP Code. Examples:

Pvt. Wilbur B. Doe, RA 34000001
Co. B. 1st Bn., 12th Infantry
Fort Lewis, WA 98433

M/SGT Manuel A. Garcia, 1243165 USMC
Headquarters Battalion
Headquarters U.S. Marine Corps
Henderson Hall
Arlington, VA 22214

Mail addressed to dependents for delivery through the sponsor's military *unit* should be addressed in care of the sponsor. Example:

Master Robert Thompson
c/o Lt. Col. Douglas G. Thompson RA
Company A 6th Bn., 10th Inf.
Fort Benning, GA 30905

Mail addressed to dependents for delivery at the sponsor's military *quarters* need not be addressed in care of the sponsor. Example:

Master Robert Thompson
2519 C Street
Wright-Patterson AFB, OH 45433

Undeliverable Mail. First-class mail, except postal and post cards, is returned to the sender if it bears a return address. Only postal and post cards that bear the sender's address and a request for return are returned, and postage at the card rate is collected on delivery to the sender. Copies of second-class publications bearing the old local address shall be delivered to the new local address without charge for a period of three months, even though the copies bear the request of the sender for return. Second-class publications will not be forwarded to an address outside the local area unless the addressee has pledged to pay forwarding postage. Third- and fourth-class undeliverable mail having obvious value or bearing the words *Return Requested* will be returned to the sender, and a charge of 8¢ or postage at the single-piece third- or fourth-class rate, whichever is higher, will be collected on delivery.

Airmail weighing 8 ounces or less will be returned by the same transportation as first-class mail at no additional charge. Airmail weighing more than 8 ounces will be returned by surface transportation at the appropriate rate according to class of mail. If the mail bears instructions of the sender to return by airmail, it will be returned at the airmail rate to be collected on delivery to the sender.

When registered, certified, insured, and COD mail is undeliverable as addressed and cannot be forwarded, a notice is sent to the mailer on Form 3858, "Notice of Undeliverable or Abandoned Mail," showing the reason. By completing the form and returning it immediately in an envelope bearing first-class postage, the mailer may tell the postmaster what to do with the mail. Mail will be returned to the mailer if there is no response.

Nonmailable Matter. A defective address, insufficient postage, or an overweight or oversize item may cause a letter or package to be unmailable. Also, the Post Office Department is restrained from handling the following nonmailable matter.

Any articles, compositions, or materials that may kill or injure another, or injure the mail or other property. This includes but is not limited to (a) all kinds of poison or matter containing poison; (b) all poisonous animals, except scorpions (see P.M. 125.35), all poisonous insects, all poisonous reptiles, and all kinds of snakes; (c) all disease germs or scabs; and (d) all explosives, flammable material, infernal machines and mechanical, chemical, or other devices or compositions that may ignite or explode.

Radioactive materials other than those described in P.M. 125.24. Any package of radioactive matter that bears an Interstate Commerce Commission red or blue label as *CLASS D POISON* or that is marked to indicate that it contains radioactive matter in excess of the quantities listed in 125.24.

Spirituous, vinous, malted, fermented, or other intoxicating liquors of any kind containing more than 3.2 percent of alcohol by weight. Shipment of liquors containing not more than 3.2 percent of alcohol may not be mailed into a territory or district of the United States the laws of which prohibit the manufacture or sale therein of alcoholic beverages of that content. Beer, lager beer, ale, porter, wine, or other liquors, regardless of alcoholic content, may not be mailed to Indian wards anywhere or into any Indian reservation.

Any mail containing any filthy, vile, or indecent thing.

Anything intended to prevent conception or produce abortion.

Any matter tending to incite arson, murder, or assassination.

Any letter, package, postal card, or circular concerning any lottery, gift enterprise, or similar scheme offering prizes dependent in whole or in part on lot or chance.

Anything mailed in pursuance of any scheme for obtaining money or property of any kind through the mail by means of false or fraudulent pretenses, representations, or promises.

Any matter addressed to a person using any fictitious, false, or assumed name, title, or address in conducting, promoting, or carrying on or assisting therein, through the mail, any business scheme or device in violation of the law.

Any matter otherwise mailable that has on its outside wrapper or envelope, or any postal card or post card carrying on it:
1. Any libelous, scurrilous, defamatory, or threatening language, whether written or printed, or any language that by its manner or style of display is obviously intended to reflect injuriously on the character or conduct of another.
2. Any language asking for payment of a bill that by its manner or style of display is defamatory and reflects injuriously on the character of the addressee.

Any letter, publication, or thing containing any matter advocating or urging treason, insurrection, or forcible resistance to any law of the United States.

Any letter or other matter containing any threat to take the life of, or to inflict bodily harm upon, the President of the United States.

Publications that violate copyrights granted by the United States.

Matter addressed to foreign countries, posted in violation of law or treaty stipulations.

Matter of any kind giving or offering to give information concerning procurement of a divorce in a foreign country and designed to solicit business in connection with such procurement.

15.2 INTERNATIONAL MAIL

Airmail and Surface Rates	p. 645	Preparing and Addressing	p. 642
COD Mail	p. 653	Parcel Post (Packing)	p. 645
Customs Forms	p. 643	Prepayment of Replies from	
Parcel Post	p. 645	Other Countries	p. 644
Dimensions	p. 642	Prohibited Articles	p. 644
Parcel Post	p. 645	Sealing	p. 642
Endorsements	p. 642	Parcel Post	p. 645
Parcel Post	p. 645	Special Services Available	p. 644
Postal Union Mail	p. 642	Parcel Post	p. 645
		Undeliverable Articles	p. 644

International mail is divided into two categories: postal union mail and parcel post. Postal union mail is divided into two groups, LC mail and AO mail. LC mail (letters and cards) consists of letters, letter packages, areogrammes, and post cards. AO mail (other articles) includes printed matter, matter for the blind, and small packets.

Postal Union Mail. The International Service Division, Bureau of Transportation and International Services, U.S. Postal Service, Washington, DC 20260, is responsible for all phases of international postal service except money-order business and investigations handled by the Postal Inspection Service. Inquiries regarding special situations should be directed to that Division.

Preparing and Addressing. Articles must be securely sealed or wrapped because international mail is handled more often and subjected to greater pressure and friction than domestic mail. Use strong envelopes and wrapping papers and stout twine for tying packages. Reserve at least the entire right half of the front side for the addressee's address, the stamps, and the service labels and notations. Make out the address legibly and completely, using *roman* letters and *arabic* figures placed lengthwise on *one* side of the article only. Give the house number and the street or box number when mail is for towns or cities. Show the names of the post office and the country of destination in *capital* letters. An address in a foreign language is permissible *provided* the names of the post office, the province, and the country are in English; or, if the English form is not known, are in *roman* characters. Addressing international mail to "Boxholder" or "Householder" is not permissible. The sender's name and complete address should be shown in the upper left corner of the address side.

Dimensions. The maximum size permissible for union mail is 36 inches in combined length, breadth, and thickness. The greatest length permissible is 24 inches. Unless one surface is at least $5\frac{1}{2}$ by $3\frac{1}{2}$ inches, the article must be provided with a strong rectangular address tag whose dimensions are not less than 4 by $2\frac{3}{4}$ inches. For articles in the form of a roll, the maximum length is 36 inches, and the maximum size is 42 inches in length plus twice the diameter. If the roll is less than 4 inches in length or $6\frac{3}{4}$ inches in length plus twice the diameter, a strong rectangular address tag must be attached whose dimensions are not less than 4 by $2\frac{3}{4}$ inches.

Sealing. Registered letters and registered letter packages must be sealed, and ordinary letters and letter packages may be sealed. All other postal union articles are required to be left unsealed, even if registered.

Endorsements. The envelopes or wrappers of postal union articles, except letters and cards, must be endorsed to show the classification under which they are mailed, for instance, *Small Packet*. Endorse envelopes or wrappers *Printed Matter* when mailing prints at regular printed matter rates, and *Printed Matter—Books* or *Printed Matter—Sheet Music* when mailing at the special rates prescribed for these categories. The words *Letter (lettre)* should be added on the address side of letters or letter packages that, because of their size or manner of preparation, may be mistaken for matter of another classification. In addition, airmail articles should be plainly endorsed *Par Avion* or have a *Par Avion* label affixed. Articles intended for special delivery should have a red international *Expres* label affixed or be marked boldly in red *Expres (Special Delivery)*.

Customs Forms.   Small packets, letters, and letter packages containing dutiable merchandise must have the green customs label, Form 2976, affixed, or the top part of the label affixed to the cover and a paper form of customs declaration, Form 2976-A, enclosed. The forms are furnished free at post offices.

Merchandise subject to duty or restricted entry differs from country to country. In the United States, all foreign mail believed to contain merchandise, including articles of U.S. origin, and printed matter are subject to U.S. customs examination. See Section 14.4. Articles believed liable to duty are submitted immediately to customs officers for inspection. Airmail articles receive preferential treatment and are submitted separately from surface mail. Upon return from customs, dispatch will be by air if it will expedite delivery. In the absence of an endorsement permitting the customs officer to open a sealed letter or letter package, the post office will obtain the addressee's signed authority before opening. Two notices are sent at 15-day intervals; and if no response is received, the article is marked *Unclaimed* and returned to its origin. Sealed parcel post is opened without the permission of the addressee.

An addressee is *not* permitted to examine the contents of dutiable articles until duty is paid. You may claim a refund for damage within 60 days from the date of entry by forwarding the article with the application through post office channels. If the addressee wishes to abandon the article to the government, he should so state in his application. To file a claim for indemnity with the U.S. Postal Service, an addressee must present the contents, the container, and the complete wrapping to the post office for inspection.

Refund of duties paid will be considered by the Customs Service if the abandoned merchandise represents 5 percent or more of the total value of all merchandise of the same kind entered in the invoice in which the item appears, and is delivered within 60 days to the customs office where entry was made. Refund of duties paid less one percent will also be considered if merchandise is found not to conform to sample or specification or was shipped without the consent of the consignee. Such merchandise must be returned to customs custody for exportation within 90 days, unless the Secretary of Treasury authorizes in writing a longer time. The postal charges incident to returning the merchandise to the sender must be paid by the addressee.

An addressee may object to the assessed value, rate, or amount of duty charged in one of three ways.

1. He may take delivery, pay the duty and postal fees, and make formal protest in writing within 60 days directly to the customs port of entry.

2. He may refuse the package pending review of entry by the customs

service. To do this, he must state his objections in writing to the postmaster and submit any evidence he may have substantiating his claim (invoice, declaration of value, and so on). The package is marked *Addressee protests duty* and returned to customs to be held awaiting receipt of the addressee's written protest.

3. An addressee may refuse the package if he does not wish to pay the duty or does not wish to protest the assessment. The package is disposed of immediately as undeliverable and is returned to the sender.

Section 14.4, "Customs Regulations," discusses other facets of this subject. Additional information concerning rates of duty on articles imported into the United States or concerning other customs procedures may be obtained from Customs Service offices located in various cities through the country, or from the Commissioner of Customs, Treasury Department, Washington, DC 20226.
Prohibited Articles. Articles of a dangerous or objectionable nature are generally prohibited in international mail. Also prohibited are matches, most live or dead creatures, poisons including narcotics, firearms capable of being concealed on the person, combustible liquids having a flash point of 150°F. or lower but above 80°F., and radioactive materials. Each country prohibits or restricts the importation of various articles in addition to those generally prohibited. Information on these special *country* prohibitions or restrictions appears in the *Directory of International Mail* or may be secured at a local post office. Failure to investigate these limitations before you mail may result in the seizure of packages in the country of address.
Prepayment of Replies from Other Countries. A mailer who wishes to prepay a reply by letter from another country may do so by sending his correspondent one or more international reply coupons, which may be purchased in U.S. post offices. One coupon, costing 22 cents in the United States, is exchangeable in member countries of the Universal Postal Union for a stamp or stamps of the country sufficient to prepay a surface letter of the first unit of weight (usually one ounce or 20 grams) to the United States. If prepayment by airmail is desired, the appropriate number of coupons for the anticipated weight should be obtained from the local post office.

International reply-paid postal cards are no longer accepted. United States *business* reply cards or envelopes are also not accepted in the international mails.
Undeliverable Articles. Postal union mail is generally returned to the sender if delivery cannot be made. However, post cards that do not bear the return address of the sender are not returned. Neither are undeliverable, unregistered printed-matter articles (other than books) returned unless they bear the sender's request for return.
Special Services Available. Letters and letter packets may be *registered* to practically all countries for a fee of 95 cents. The maximum indemnity, payable only in the case of complete loss (of both the contents and the wrapper), is $100 in the case of Canada and $13.07 in the case of other countries.

A *return receipt* may be requested only at the time of mailing for a fee of 20 cents.

Special delivery is available to most countries. For post cards, letter mail, and airmail *other articles,* the fees are 60¢ up to 2 pounds, 75¢ over 2 and less than 10 pounds, and 90¢ over 10 pounds. For surface *other articles,* the fees are 80¢, 90¢, and $1.05 respectively.

Airmail and Surface Rates.   Daily *airmail* service is available to practically all countries. See Figure 15-8 for international air rates and surface parcel rates and Figure 15-9 for postal union surface rates.

Parcel Post.   Packages in international mail must adhere to most of the general regulations for postal union mail. There is a definite weight limit to other countries as noted on the parcel post table of international rates (Figure 15-8). Special regulations for parcel post are explained in the following sections.

Dimension Limits.   Greatest length, $3\frac{1}{2}$ feet; greatest length and girth combined, 6 feet. To some countries parcels may measure 4 feet in length if not more than 16 inches in girth. Consult the post office.

Packing.   Containers should be used that are strong enough to protect the contents from the weight of other mail, pressure and friction, climatic changes, and the repeated handlings to which parcels are subjected. When using fiberboard or double-faced corrugated boxes, use only those made of good-quality material. Containers of 275-pound test, with contents solidly packed, are preferred. Cushioning material should be used. When sending liquids or easily liquefiable substances, place sufficient absorbent material between the inner and outer containers to absorb all the liquid contents in case of breakage.

Sealing.   Registered or insured parcels must be sealed. The sealing of ordinary parcels is optional to some countries and compulsory to others. Consult the post office.

Customs Forms.   A parcel post sticker, Form 2922, and two customs declaration forms, 2966 and 2972, are required for parcel post packages (surface or air) mailed to another country. The following countries do not require a Form 2972.

Bolivia	Indonesia	Portugal
Chile	Martinique	
Iceland	Nepal	
India	Panama	

Special Parcel Post Services.   *Registration* is available to only a few countries. *Insurance* is available to many countries, and *air service* is possible to most countries.

Special handling, which entitles parcels to priority handling between the mailing point and the United States point of dispatch, may be had for the

Country (1)	Merchandise admitted in letter packages (2)	Special delivery service available (3)	Air Rates				Parcel post insurance available (6)	Max. weight for parcel post (surface and air) (7)
			AO Mail (4)		Parcel Post (5)			
			First 2 oz.	Each additional 2 oz. or fraction	First 4 oz.	Each additional 4 oz. or fraction		
								Lbs.
Afghanistan	Yes	Yes	$0.60	$0.30	$2.20	$0.83	No	22
Albania	No	Yes	.50	.20	2.33	.54	No	22
Algeria	Yes	Yes	.50	.20	1.89	.55	No	44
Andorra (Rep. of)	Yes	No	.50	.20	1.95	.48	$330	44
Angola (Port. West Africa)	Yes	Yes	.60	.30	2.05	.70	16.33	22
Antigua (Leeward Is.)	Yes	No	.40	.10	1.24	.25	100	22
Argentina	Yes[1]	Yes	.50	.20	1.72	.74	165	44
Aruba (Neth. Antilles)	Yes	No	.40	.10	1.45	.31	165	44
Ascension	Yes	No	.50	.20	(4)		No	22
Australia	Yes	Yes	.60	.30	1.83	.84	170	22
Austria	Yes	Yes	.50	.20	1.88	.51	330	44
Azores	Yes	Yes	.50	.20	1.36	.39	165	22
Bahamas	Yes	Yes	.40	.10	1.53	.18	100	22
Bahrain	Yes	No	.60	.30	1.69	.72	100	22
Barbados	Yes	No	.40	.10	1.33	.35	100	22
Barbuda (Leeward Is.)	Yes	No	.40	.10	1.24	.25	100	22
Belgium	Yes	Yes	.50	.20	1.68	.46	165	44
Bermuda	Yes	No	.40	.10	1.23	.24	No	33
Bhutan	No	Yes	.60	.30	(4)		No	(5)
Bolivia	No	No	.50	.20	1.73	.47	No	44
Bonaire (Neth. Ant.)	Yes	No	.40	.10	1.45	.31	165	44
Botswana	Yes	Yes	.60	.30	1.86	.88	No	22
Brazil	No	Yes	.50	.20	2.06	.54	No	44
British Honduras	Yes	Yes[1]	.40	.10	1.32	.33	No	22
British Virgin Is. (Leeward Is.).	Yes	No	.40	.10	1.24	.25	100	22
Brunei	Yes	No	.60	.30	2.10	1.02	No	22
Bulgaria	Yes	Yes	.50	.20	1.50	.52	No	22
Burma	Yes	No	.60	.30	2.31	1.00	No	22
Burundi	Yes	Yes	.60	.30	1.93	.74	No	22
Cambodia (Khmer Republic)	Yes	Yes	.60	.30	(4)		No	22
Cameroon	Yes	Yes	.60	.30	1.95	.64	No	22
Canada (3)	Yes	Yes[1]	(6)		(6)		200	25
Cape Verde Islands	Yes	Yes	.60	.30	1.90	.56	16.33	22
Central African Republic	Yes	No	.60	.30	1.93	.74	No	44
Ceylon	Yes	Yes	.60	.30	2.33	.89	165	22
Chad	Yes	No	.60	.30	1.93	.74	No	44
Chile	Yes	Yes	.50	.20	2.04	.61	No	22
China:								
Republic of China (Taiwan, Penghu, Quemoy and Matsu Islands).	No	Yes	.60	.30	1.72	.73	165	44
Continental China (7)	No	No	.60	.30	(4)		No	(5)
Colombia	No	Yes[1]	.50	.20	2.00	.34	165	44
Comoro Islands	Yes	No	.60	.30	2.19	1.00	No	44
Congo (People's Rep.) (Brazzaville).	Yes	No	.60	.30	1.93	.74	No	44

See footnotes at end of table.

Figure 15-8 Table of international postal rates and parcel post weight limits.

Country	Merchandise admitted in letter packages	Special delivery service available	Air Rates				Parcel post insurance available	Max. weight for parcel post (surface and air)
			AO Mail (4)		Parcel Post (5)			
			First 2 oz.	Each additional 2 oz. or fraction	First 4 oz.	Each additional 4 oz. or fraction		
(1)	(2)	(3)					(6)	(7)
								Lbs.
Congo, Democratic Republic (Kinshasa).	Yes	Yes	$0.60	$0.30	$1.93	$0.74	No	44
Corsica	Yes	Yes	.50	.20	2.08	.46	330	44
Costa Rica	Yes	Yes	.40	.10	1.44	.29	No	44
Cuba	No	No	1 .40	.10	(4)	--------	No	(5)
Curacao (Neth. Ant.)	Yes	No	.40	.10	1.45	.31	165	44
Cyprus	Yes	Yes 1	.60	.30	2.01	.59	No	22
Czechoslovakia	Yes	Yes	.50	.20	1.52	.53	200	44
Dahomey	Yes	Yes	.60	.30	1.65	.59	No	44
Denmark	Yes	Yes	.50	.20	1.49	.50	330	44
Dominica (Windward Is.)	Yes	No	.40	.10	1.67	.33	100	22
Dominican Republic	No	Yes	.40	.10	1.56	.25	No	44
Ecuador	Yes 1	Yes 1	.50	.20	1.94	.33	50	44
El Salvador	Yes	No	.40	.10	1.54	.30	No	44
Equatorial Guinea	No	Yes	.60	.30	1.97	.85	No	44
Estonia 2	No	Yes	.60	.30	1.99	.66	165	44
Ethiopia (incl. Eritrea)	Yes	Yes	.60	.30	1.98	.76	165	44
Falkland Islands	Yes	No	.50	.20	2.09	.59	No	22
Faroe Islands	Yes	No	.50	.20	1.49	.49	330	44
Fiji	Yes	No	.60	.30	1.95	.62	100	22
Finland	Yes	Yes	.50	.20	1.52	.54	330	44
France, including Monaco	Yes	Yes	.50	.20	2.08	.46	330	44
French Guiana	Yes	Yes	.50	.20	1.53	.39	No	44
French Polynesia	Yes	Yes	.60	.30	1.88	.53	330	44
French Territory of the Afars and Issas.	Yes	Yes	.60	.30	2.02	.72	330	44
Gabon	Yes	No	.60	.30	1.93	.74	No	44
Gambia	Yes	Yes	.60	.30	1.67	.53	No	22
Germany, including Saar	Yes	Yes	.50	.20	1.47	.48	1 330	44
Ghana	Yes	Yes	.60	.30	2.04	.64	80	22
Gibraltar	Yes	Yes	.50	.20	1.51	.52	50	22
Gilbert and Ellice Islands	Yes	No	.60	.30	1.86	.69	No	22
Great Britain and Northern Ireland.	Yes	Yes	.50	.20	1.45	.46	1,000	22
Greece, incl. Crete and Dodecanese Islands.	Yes	Yes	.50	.20	1.83	.58	165	22
Greenland	Yes	No	.50	.20	1.64	.65	330	44
Grenada and The Grenadines	Yes	No	.40	.10	1.67	.33	100	22
Guadeloupe	Yes	Yes	.40	.10	1.40	.25	No	22
Guatemala	No	Yes	.40	.10	1.75	.32	100	44
Guinea, Rep. of	Yes	No	.60	.30	1.72	.67	No	44
Guyana	Yes	Yes	.50	.20	1.69	.34	165	22
Haiti	Yes	No	.40	.10	1.57	.24	No	44
Honduras (Rep.)	Yes	Yes	.40	.10	1.49	.32	No	1 44
Hong Kong	Yes	No	.60	.30	1.85	.87	330	22
Hungary	Yes	Yes	.50	.20	1.51	.53	100	44
Iceland	Yes	Yes	.50	.20	1.86	.39	330	44
India	Yes	Yes 1	.60	.30	1.87	.88	165	1 44
Indonesia	Yes	Yes	.60	.30	2.43	1.06	No	22
Iran	Yes	Yes 1	.60	.30	1.87	.67	165	44

See footnotes at end of table.

Figure 15-8 (continued).

Country	Merchandise admitted in letter packages	Special delivery service available	Air Rates				Parcel post insurance available	Max. weight for parcel post (surface and air)
			AO Mail (4)		Parcel Post (5)			
			First 2 oz.	Each additional 2 oz. or fraction	First 4 oz.	Each additional 4 oz. or fraction		
(1)	(2)	(3)					(6)	(7)
								Lbs.
Iraq	Yes	No	$0.60	$0.30	$2.08	$0.66	No	44
Ireland (Eire)	Yes	Yes	.50	.20	1.44	.46	1,000	22
Israel	Yes	Yes	.60	.30	2.05	.63	No	22
Italy, incl. San Marino	No	Yes	.50	.20	1.84	.54	100	44
Ivory Coast	Yes	Yes	.60	.30	1.72	.66	No	44
Jamaica	Yes	No	.40	.10	1.65	.22	No	22
Japan	Yes	Yes	.60	.30	1.53	.55	330	22
Jordan, including Central Arab Palestine.	Yes	Yes	.60	.30	1.90	.62	No	22
Kenya	Yes	Yes	.60	.30	2.05	.76	No	22
Korea:								
Republic of	Yes [1]	Yes [1]	.60	.30	1.57	.59	100	22
North Korea [1]	No	No	.60	.30	(4)	-------	No	(5)
Kuwait	Yes	Yes	.60	.30	1.67	.69	165	22
Laos	Yes	Yes	.60	.30	2.34	.95	No	22
Latvia [2]	No	Yes	.60	.30	1.99	.66	165	44
Lebanon	Yes	No	.60	.30	1.90	.62	No	[1] 44
Leeward Islands	Yes	No	.40	.10	1.24	.25	100	22
Lesotho	Yes	Yes	.60	.30	1.86	.88	No	22
Liberia	Yes	Yes	.60	.30	1.56	.58	80	22
Libya	Yes [1]	Yes	.60	.30	1.88	.59	No	44
Liechtenstein	Yes	Yes	.50	.20	1.67	.47	330	44
Lithuania [2]	No	Yes	.60	.30	1.99	.66	165	44
Luxembourg	Yes	Yes	.50	.20	1.73	.45	165	44
Macao	Yes	Yes	.60	.30	2.24	.87	No	22
Madagascar (Malagasy Rep.)	Yes	No	.60	.30	2.16	.85	No	44
Madeira Islands	Yes	Yes	.50	.20	1.47	.50	165	22
Malawi	Yes	No	.60	.30	1.86	.87	No	22
Malaysia	Yes	No	.60	.30	2.26	.99	100	22
Maldives, Rep. of	No	No	.60	.30	2.51	.90	No	22
Mali	Yes	Yes	.60	.30	2.42	.57	No	44
Malta	Yes	Yes	.50	.20	1.82	.54	No	22
Martinique	Yes	Yes	.40	.10	1.40	.25	No	44
Mauritania	Yes	Yes	.60	.30	1.65	.54	No	44
Mauritius	Yes	No	.60	.30	2.10	.90	No	22
Mexico	Yes	Yes	.40	.10	1.23	.24	No	44
Montserrat (Leeward Islands)	Yes	No	.40	.10	1.24	.25	100	22
Morocco	Yes	Yes	.50	.20	1.84	.54	No	44
Muscat	Yes	No	.60	.30	1.69	.72	100	22
Nauru, Rep. of	Yes	Yes	.60	.30	1.83	.84	170	22
Nepal	Yes [1]	No	.60	.30	1.86	.88	No	22
Netherlands	Yes	Yes	.50	.20	1.65	.46	330	44
Netherlands Antilles	Yes	No	.40	.10	1.45	.31	165	44
Nevis (Leeward Is.)	Yes	No	.40	.10	1.24	.25	100	22
New Caledonia	Yes	Yes	.60	.30	1.96	.65	330	44
New Guinea Territory	Yes	No	.60	.30	1.90	.92	80	22
New Hebrides	Yes	No	.60	.30	1.85	.65	No	44
New Zealand	Yes	No	.60	.30	2.08	.74	165	22
Nicaragua	Yes	No	.40	.10	1.45	.29	165	44
Niger	Yes	Yes	.60	.30	2.41	.55	No	44

See footnotes at end of table.

Figure 15-8 (continued).

648

Country	Merchandise admitted in letter packages	Special delivery service available	AO Mail (4)		Parcel Post (5)		Parcel post insurance available	Max. weight for parcel post (surface and air)
			First 2 oz.	Each additional 2 oz. or fraction	First 4 oz.	Each additional 4 oz. or fraction		
(1)	(2)	(3)					(6)	(7)
								Lbs.
Nigeria	Yes	Yes	$0.60	$0.30	$2.20	$0.65	No	22
Norway, incl. Spitzbergen	Yes	Yes	.50	.20	1.49	.50	330	44
Outer Mongolia	No	No	.60	.30	(4)	....	No	(5)
Pakistan	Yes	Yes [1]	.60	.30	2.42	.85	165	22
Palestine (Western Arab)	Yes	No	.60	.30	2.05	.63	No	11
Panama (Rep.)	Yes [1]	Yes	.40	.10	1.74	.31	No	[1] 70
Papua	Yes	No	.60	.30	1.90	.92	80	22
Paraguay	Yes	Yes	.50	.20	1.73	.47	No	44
Peru	Yes	No	.50	.20	2.01	.41	No	44
Philippines	Yes	Yes	.60	.30	2.12	.81	165	[1] 44
Pitcairn Islands	Yes	No	.60	.30	2.02	.72	No	22
Poland	Yes	Yes	.50	.20	1.82	.52	No	44
Portugal	Yes	Yes	.50	.20	1.43	.44	165	22
Portuguese E. Africa (Mozambique).	Yes	Yes	.60	.30	2.40	.89	100	22
Portuguese Guinea (Port. W. Africa).	Yes	Yes	.60	.30	2.05	.70	16.33	22
Portuguese Timor	Yes	Yes	.60	.30	2.54	1.20	No	22
Portuguese West Africa	Yes	Yes	.60	.30	2.05	.70	16.33	22
Qatar	Yes	No	.60	.30	1.69	.72	100	22
Reunion	Yes	Yes	.60	.30	2.02	.88	No	44
Rhodesia	Yes	No	.60	.30	1.86	.87	No	22
Rumania	No [1]	Yes	.50	.20	1.69	.54	No	22
Rwanda	Yes	Yes	.60	.30	1.93	.74	No	22
Ryukyu Islands	No	No	.60	.60	1.57	.59	165	22
Saba (Neth. Antilles)	Yes	No	.40	.10	1.45	.31	165	44
St. Christopher(WindwardIs.)	Yes	No	.40	.10	1.67	.33	100	22
St. Eustatius (Neth. Antilles)	Yes	No	.40	.10	1.45	.31	165	44
St. Helena	Yes	No	.60	.30	2.10	.85	No	22
St. Lucia (Windward Is.)	Yes	No	.40	.10	1.67	.33	100	22
St. Pierre and Miquelon	Yes	Yes	.40	.10	1.20	.24	No	44
St. Vincent (Windward Is.)	Yes	No	.40	.10	1.67	.33	100	22
Santa Cruz Islands	Yes	No	.60	.30	2.17	.97	No	22
Saudi Arabia	No	No	.60	.30	2.17	.69	No	22
Senegal	Yes	Yes	.60	.30	1.63	.52	No	44
Seychelles	Yes	No	.60	.30	1.77	.78	No	22
Sierra Leone	Yes	Yes	.60	.30	2.16	.56	No	22
Singapore	Yes	No	.60	.30	2.26	.99	100	22
Solomon Islands	Yes	No	.60	.30	2.18	.97	No	22
Somalia	Yes	No	.60	.30	[1] 2.26	.79	No	22
South Africa (Rep.)	Yes	Yes	.60	.30	1.86	.88	No	22
Spain, incl. Canary and Balearic Islands and Spanish offices in N. Africa.	Yes	Yes	.50	.20	1.95	.48	165	[1] 44
Spanish Sahara	No	Yes	.60	.30	1.96	.56	No	[1] 44
Sudan	Yes	No	.60	.30	2.19	.70	No	22
Surinam	Yes	No	.50	.20	1.56	.38	100	44
Swaziland	Yes	Yes	.60	.30	1.86	.86	No	22
Sweden	Yes	Yes	.50	.20	1.49	.50	330	44
Switzerland	Yes	Yes	.50	.20	1.67	.47	330	44

See footnotes at end of table.

Figure 15-8 (continued).

Country	Merchandise admitted in letter packages	Special delivery service available	Air Rates				Parcel post insurance available	Max. weight for parcel post (surface and air)
			AO Mail (4)		Parcel Post (5)			
			First 2 oz.	Each additional 2 oz. or fraction	First 4 oz.	Each additional 4 oz. or fraction		
(1)	(2)	(3)					(6)	(7)
								Lbs.
Syria	Yes	No	$0.60	$0.30	$1.73	$0.64	165	[1] 44
Tanzania	Yes	Yes	.60	.30	2.09	.80	No	22
Thailand	Yes	Yes	.60	.30	2.29	.81	100	22
Togo	Yes	Yes [1]	.60	.30	1.80	.66	No	44
Tongo (Friendly) Islands	Yes	No	.60	.30	1.63	.65	No	22
Trinidad and Tobago	Yes	No	.40	.10	1.66	.31	120	22
Tristan da Cunha	Yes	No	.60	.30	1.98	.84	No	22
Trucial States	Yes	No	.60	.30	1.69	.72	100	22
Tunisia	Yes	Yes	.50	.20	1.83	.52	No	44
Turkey	Yes	Yes	.50	.20	1.58	.59	165	44
Turks Islands	Yes	No	.40	.10	1.57	.22	No	22
Uganda	Yes	Yes	.60	.30	2.05	.76	No	22
Union of Soviet Socialist Republics.[2]	No	Yes	.60	.30	1.99	.66	165	44
United Arab Republic (Egypt).	Yes	Yes	.50	.20	1.62	.64	165	44
Upper Volta	Yes	Yes	.60	.30	1.90	.61	No	44
Uruguay	Yes	No	.50	.20	2.05	.62	No	44
Vatican City State	Yes	Yes	.50	.20	1.69	.51	No	44
Venezuela	No	Yes	.50	.20	1.89	.29	No	44
Vietnam:								
Republic of	Yes	Yes	.60	.30	2.30	.90	No	22
North Vietnam	No	No	.60	.30	(4)	--------	No	(5)
Western Samoa	Yes	No	.60	.30	1.89	.55	165	22
Windward Islands	Yes	No	.40	.10	1.67	.33	100	22
Yeman (Aden)	Yes	No	.60	.30	1.96	.76	No	22
Yeman (Sanaa)	Yes [1]	No	.60	.30	(4)	--------	No	(5)
Yugoslavia	Yes	Yes	.50	.20	1.52	.54	165	44
Zambia	Yes	No	.60	.30	1.86	.87	No	22

[1] Restrictions apply. Consult post office.

[2] To facilitate distribution and delivery, include "Union of Soviet Socialist Republics" or "U.S.S.R." as part of the address.

[3] Small packets weight limit 1 pound.

[4] No air parcel post service.

[5] No surface parcel post service.

[6] No airmail AO or air parcel post to Canada. Prepare and prepay all airmail packages as letter mail.

[7] The Continental China postal authorities will not deliver articles unless addressed to show name of the country as "People's Republic of China;" also acceptable spelling of capital is "Peking."

Figure 15-8 (continued).

Classifications	*Countries*	*Surface Rates*

Letter mail
  Weight limit 4 lbs.,
  except Canada 60 lbs.
	Canada and Mexico	8¢ per ounce up to 12 ozs.
		Eighth zone priority rate over 12 ozs.

	All other countries	15¢ for first ounce 26¢ for 1 oz. but not over 2 ozs. 34¢ over 2 ozs. but not over 4 ozs. 76¢ over 4 ozs. but not over 8 ozs. $1.44 over 8 ozs. but not over 1 lb. $2.40 over 1 lb. but not over 2 lbs. $3.84 over 2 lbs. but not over 4 lbs.
Post cards—single only	Canada and Mexico All other countries	6¢ 10¢

Printed matter:
  a. Regular—not stated
     in b, c, or d
	Canada and Mexico	8¢ first 2 ozs.
		2¢ each addl. ounce or fraction

	All other countries	8¢ first 2 ozs. 12¢ over 2 ozs. but not over 4 ozs. 19¢ over 4 ozs. but not over 8 ozs. 33¢ over 8 ozs. but not over 1 lb. 57¢ over 1 lb. but not over 2 lbs. 96¢ over 2 lbs. but not over 4 lbs. 48¢ each addl. 2 lbs. or fraction

Figure 15-9   Postal union mail surface rates.

Classification	Countries	Surface Rates
b. Books and sheet music	Canada, Mexico, Central and South America	14¢ not exceeding 8 ozs. 17¢ over 8 ozs. but not over 1 lb. 21¢ over 1 but not over 2 lbs. 36¢ over 2 but not over 4 lbs. 18¢ each addl. 2 lbs. or fraction
	All other countries	14¢ not over 8 ozs. 17¢ over 8 ozs. but not over 1 lb. 28¢ over 1 but not over 2 lbs. 48¢ over 2 but not over 4 lbs. 24¢ each addl. 2 lbs. or fraction
c. Matter for the blind Weight limit 15 lbs.	All countries admitting	Free
d. Controlled circulation publications and publishers' 2d class.	Consult post office for rates and conditions	
Small packets of merchandise and samples Weight limit 2 lbs. except Canada 1 lb.	Canada and Mexico	8¢ first 2 ozs. 2¢ each addl. ounce or fraction
	All other countries	15¢ up to 4 ozs. 29¢ over 4 but not over 8 ozs. 48¢ over 8 ozs. but not over 1 lb. 86¢ over 1 but not over 2 lbs.

Figure 15-9   (continued).

following fees: 25¢ for parcels to 2 pounds, 35¢ over 2 pounds to 10 pounds, and 50¢ over 10 pounds.

COD Mail.   It is not possible to send parcels to other countries via COD mail.

15.3   NONMAIL POSTAL SERVICES

Box Rental	p. 656
Documentary Internal Revenue Stamps	p. 655
Migratory-Bird Hunting Stamps	p. 655
Money Orders	p. 653
Postal Savings	p. 656
U.S. Savings Bonds and Stamps	p. 655

Money Orders.   Domestic money orders may be purchased at all post offices and branches. International money orders may be purchased at almost all first-class and some second-, third-, and fourth-class post offices. The maximum amount for a single money order is $100. The fees are as follows:

Amount of Money Order	Domestic Fee	International Fee
$0.01 to $10	$0.25	$0.45
$10.01 to $50	0.35	0.65
$50.01 to $100	0.40	0.75

Payment must be made in U.S. money. Postmasters may accept, at their own risk, from a person whose endorsement is acceptable, a Federal Government check in payment for a money order. The postal clerk enters the amount, the date, and his initials in the spaces provided in the form. The purchaser must fill in his name and address and the full name of the person or organization to whom the money order is to be paid. Other identification data may be added by the purchaser to ensure proper credit by the payee. He should complete the form promptly to protect his rights in the event the order is lost. The U.S. Postal Service assumes no responsibility for money orders lost before the completion of the form by the purchaser.

International money orders will be issued to addressees in those countries that have agreed with the United States to conduct such business. In most cases the amount is written in United States dollars and converted into foreign currency in the country where payable. If the purchaser requests it, however, the order may be written in foreign currency. The payee's address should include the name of the canton, department, or district in which his city, town, or village is located. Also, if the payee is a woman, her marital status (single, married, or widowed) should appear after her name.

The domestic money-order form is used for the following countries, and the transaction is handled in the same manner as U.S. domestic orders.

Antigua	Dominica
Bahamas	Grenada
Barbados	Jamaica
Bermuda	Montserrat
British Honduras	Saint Kitts-Nevis-Anguilla
British Virgin Islands	Saint Lucia
Canada	Saint Vincent
Canal Zone	Trinidad and Tobago

An international money-order form is completed for all other foreign countries. The purchaser is given a receipt and the order is sent abroad by the International Money Order Branch, U.S. Postal Service, General Accounting Office Building, Washington, DC 20260. Direct exchange is conducted between the U.S. office and the foreign exchange office of the places named in the following list.

Argentina	Ireland
Australia, Commonwealth of:	Italy
New South Wales	Japan
Queensland	Lebanon
South Australia	Luxembourg
Tasmania	Mexico
Victoria	Morocco
Western Australia	Netherlands
Austria	Netherlands Antilles
Belgium	New Zealand
Chile	Norway
China (Taiwan)	Peru
Colombia	Philippines
Costa Rica	Poland
Czechoslovakia	Ryukyu Islands (Okinawa)
Denmark	South Africa, Republic of
El Salvador	Surinam
Finland	Sweden
Germany	Switzerland
Great Britain and	Syria
Northern Ireland	Thailand
Greece	Tunisia
Guatemala	United Arab Republic
Guyana	Uruguay
Hungary	Vatican City
Iceland	Yugoslavia

In all other countries, service is available on an indirect exchange basis through an intermediary country, which reserves the right to deduct a fee for its service.

The life of a money order is limited. International money orders are valid for one year from the last day of the month of original issue. Domestic money orders are invalid after 20 years from the last day of the month of original issue.

To be cashed at any post office or bank, the card money order must be endorsed in the presence of a postal clerk or bank teller, who will ask for identification, such as a driver's permit, a military identification card, or other credentials showing the signature of the bearer and having serial numbers or other indicia that can be traced to the holder. The old-style paper money order is cashed by the Money Order Division, U.S. Postal Service, Washington, DC 20260, and must be accompanied by a completed Form 6401, "Inquiry as to Payment of Money Order." A post office will accept a stamped signature provided an agreement is filed in advance regarding the responsibility for the correctness of such payments. A stamped signature is acceptable as an endorsement on a money order drawn in favor of a firm, a corporation, an association, a society, or an individual, provided the money order is presented to a bank for payment.

Money orders completed by a purchaser to show more than one firm or person as payee may be paid to any one of them. The payee or the purchaser of a money order may transfer it to any other person or firm by endorsement. Money orders will not be paid when there are two endorsements, neither of which is a transfer. The local post office will issue a duplicate if the first endorser wishes to give the money order to another for the payment of an obligation. A photostat of a paid money order will be furnished to the purchaser, the payee, or the endorsee by the Money Order Division upon payment of a charge of 30 cents. The photostat will be mailed directly to the applicant, who completes Form 6065, "Request for Photo Copy of Money Order," at his local post office.

U.S. Savings Bonds and Stamps.   The Post Office Department acts as the agent of the Treasury Department for the sales of Series E savings bonds and stamps at post offices in communities where no banks sell them or where there are no other issuing agents.

Documentary Internal Revenue Stamps.   Documentary Internal Revenue stamps are sold at all first- and second-class post offices, and at third- and fourth-class offices located in county seats. These stamps are used for the payment of taxes on the following documents: (a) issuance of capital stock and certificates of indebtedness of a corporation; (b) sales or transfers of capital stock and certificates of indebtedness of a corporation; (c) real estate conveyances, deeds, and so on; (d) steamship passage tickets; and (e) policies by foreign insurers. The stamps may be purchased in the following denominations: 1¢, 2¢, 3¢, 4¢, 5¢, 8¢, 10¢, 20¢, 25¢, 40¢, 50¢, 55¢, and 80¢; $1.00, $1.10, $1.65, $2.00, $2.20, $2.75, $3.00, $3.30, $4.00, $5.00, $10.00, $20.00, $30.00, $50.00, $60.00, $100.00, $500.00, and $1,000.00. The $30, $50, $60, $100, $500, $1,000 stamps are each furnished in books of 40 stamps, and the other denominations are furnished in sheets of 100.

Migratory-Bird Hunting Stamps.   Migratory-bird hunting stamps cost $3 each and are sold at all first- and second-class post offices, and at certain designated third- and fourth-class offices where there is a demand for them.

Postal Savings.   The Postal Savings System was discontinued by Public Law 89-377 on April 27, 1966. All funds not withdrawn by July 1, 1967 have been turned over to the Treasury Department, and claim for payment must be made to that office.

Box Rental.   Boxes and drawers are provided at most post offices for the convenience of individuals and companies. The service provides privacy and permits the pickup of mail during the hours the lobby is kept open. To rent a box the patron submits Form 1093, "Application for Post Office Box." A box is assigned immediately to a known qualified applicant upon payment of rent. An unknown applicant must present his driver's license, Social Security card, military identification card, or some other identification document. After the postmaster verifies that the applicant resides or conducts business at the addresses shown and is served by the telephone number shown, the application is approved.

Box rents vary according to the classification of the post office and are payable quarterly in advance. The quarterly box rental schedule in Figure 15-10 may be used as a guide.

Post office groups	Rate per quarter						
	Call boxes		Lockboxes and drawers				
	Size No.		Size No.				
	1	2	1	2	3	4	5
	Cubic-inch capacity		Cubic-inch capacity				
	To 225	225 to 500	To 225	225 to	500 to	900 to	3,000 and over
Offices with city carrier service:							
Group A	$2.25	$3.00	$4.50	$6.00	$8.00	$10.00	$12.00
Group B	1.50	2.25	3.00	4.50	6.00	7.50	9.00
Group C	1.10	1.50	2.25	3.00	4.50	6.00	7.50
Group D	.80	1.10	1.70	2.25	3.00	4.50	6.00
Group E	.65	.80	1.20	1.50	2.25	3.00	4.50
Offices without city carrier service:							
Group F	.50	.65	.90	1.10	1.50	2.25	3.00
Group G	.35	.50	.70	.90	1.10	1.50	2.25
Group H	.20	.30	.50	.65	.90	1.10	1.50
Group I	.15	.20	.35	.50	.65	.90	1.10

Figure 15-10   Schedule of quarterly box rentals in main post offices.

16

Dictionary of Business Terms

Definitions of selected terms in ten important fields. **Boldface** terms in the definitions can be located in the alphabetical listing.

CONTENTS

16.1	Accounting	p. 657
16.2	Banking	p. 662
16.3	Data Processing	p. 668
16.4	Economics	p. 678
16.5	Government	p. 682
16.6	Insurance	p. 684
16.7	Law	p. 688
16.8	Marketing	p. 694
16.9	Personnel	p. 699
16.10	Stock Market	p. 705

16.1 ACCOUNTING

account A ledger record of a specific transaction or series of related transactions entered as money or some other appropriate unit.

accountancy Theoretical and practical accounting; its purpose, conventional standards, and general applications.

accountant An accounting specialist. A public accountant serves the public. A Certified Public Accountant meets the statutory requirements of a state or other political subdivision of the United States and is registered or licensed to practice public accounting and use the initials *CPA* after his name. A private accountant is employed by a single organization.

accounting The recording and reporting of transactions; including design of systems, bookkeeping, and auditing.

accrue To increase in worth; to accumulate.

adjusting entry An accounting transaction recorded to correct an error or to enter supplementary information, such as accruals, write-offs, depreciation, and bad debts.

allowance for bad debts A valuation account set up to reduce the recorded amount of notes and accounts receivable to that considered collectable. Also called *allowance for credit losses* or *reserve for bad debts*.

allowance for depreciation The credit derived from net depreciation provisions; the account in which these items appear. See **depreciation**.

asset Any physical object (tangible) or right (intangible) having value, expressed in terms of its cost, depreciated cost, or as it benefits present or future worth.

auditing An exploratory review by a public accountant of the internal controls and accounting records of a business or economic unit, before he gives an opinion of the propriety of its financial statements.

auditor Either a regular employee or an outside professional, who audits accounting records kept by others.

bad debt An uncollectable receivable.

balance sheet A business financial position statement disclosing assets, liabilities, and the equity of owners.

bank reconciliation A statement of the items of difference between an account balance reported by a bank and the account being kept by the bank's customer. Such items include outstanding checks and deposits in transit.

bank service charge A bank charge to a customer for collection, protest fees, exchange, checks drawn, or other services, exclusive of interest and discount.

bank statement A deposit and withdrawal statement (usually monthly) sent by a bank to the holder of a checking account.

bond A written certificate of indebtedness. Bonds may be in the form of coupon or bearer instruments, or registered in the name of the owner as to principal only (registered coupon bonds) or as to both principal and interest (registered bonds).

bookkeeping Analyzing, classifying, and recording transactions in accordance with an accounting plan.

budget A periodic financial plan to estimate and control expenditures.

canceled check A check paid by the bank and returned to the writer. It supports the bank's charge against the account and is the depositor's receipt of payment.

capital Invested amount plus retained income (or earned surplus); net worth; net assets; stockholders' equity.

capital stock Shares representing ownership in a corporation.

cash discount An amount allowed for the prompt cash payment of a purchase.

closing entry At the end of an accounting period, a final entry eliminating the year's revenue and expense accounts, their net total being carried to **earned surplus** or other proprietorship accounts.

comparative statement   A statement of assets and liabilities, operations, or other data, giving figures in comparative form for more than one date or period or organization.

control account   An account containing the totals of a series of transactions, the details of which are kept in a subsidiary ledger. Its balance equals the sum of the balances of the detailed accounts.

controller (comptroller)   An accountant in charge, who has been given that title by the management or board of directors.

cost accountant   One skilled in cost accounting.

cost accounting   The branch of accounting dealing with the classification, recording, allocation, summarization, and reporting of current and prospective costs.

cost of goods sold   The total cost of goods sold, ascertained from invoices and other expense records.

credit   A bookkeeping entry recording the reduction in an asset or an expense, or an addition to a liability or item of net worth or revenue; an entry on the right side of an account. Compare with **debit**. The balance of a liability, net worth, revenue, or credit account.

current asset   May be any one or all of the following: cash and items that are the equivalent of cash; inventories of merchandise, raw materials, goods in process, finished goods, operating supplies, and ordinary maintenance material and parts; trade accounts, notes, and acceptances receivable; receivables from officers, employees, affiliates, and others, if collectable within a year; installment or deferred accounts and notes receivable, if payment is to be received within the year; marketable securities; and prepaid expenses.

current liability   An obligation or short-term debt that will become due in the near future.

debit   A bookkeeping entry recording the creation of or the addition to an asset or an expense, or the reduction of a liability, credit account, or item of net worth or revenue; an entry on the left side of an account. Compare with **credit**. The balance of an asset, expense, or debit valuation account.

deposit   Currency, checks, or coupons presented to a bank by or for a customer for credit to his account.

depositor   One who makes a deposit or for whom a deposit is made.

depreciation   Lost usefulness; expired utility; the diminution of service from a fixed asset that cannot be restored by repairs or by the replacement of parts, caused by wear and tear from use, disuse, poor maintenance, obsolescence, or inadequacy.

discount on purchases   An amount allowed for the prompt settlement of a debt arising out of a purchase.

dishonor   To refuse to accept a check or other commercial paper in payment.

draft   A written order drawn by one party (drawer) ordering a second party (drawee) to pay a specified amount of money to a third party (payee).

earned surplus Accumulated net income, less distributions to stockholders. Also known as **retained earnings**.

equity Any right or claim to assets. An equity holder may be a creditor or a proprietor.

financial statement A balance sheet, an income statement, a statement of application of funds, or any supporting statement of financial data derived from accounting records.

fixed asset Any tangible item of the plant held for the services it provides in the production of other goods and services.

flow chart A graphic presentation of operational sequences in the handling of materials or documents.

freight in Freight charges paid on incoming shipments; treated as an item of the cost of the goods received.

goodwill An intangible asset, such as the value of the company name, its reputation, or its location. Shown only when one company purchases another.

gross profit Sales, less the cost of the goods sold and inventory losses, and before the deduction of selling, administrative, and general expenses, and income taxes.

income Money, or its equivalent, earned or accrued during an accounting period that increases the total of previously existing net assets.

income statement A summary of the revenues and expenses for an accounting period.

journal A book of original entry in which a condensed record of each transaction is entered in chronological order.

journal voucher A filled-in form that supports a noncash transaction. A file of journal vouchers may take the place of a general journal, or vouchers may be summarized periodically in the general journal.

ledger A book of final entry to which the sums entered in the journals are transferred under account names.

liability An amount owed by one person (a debtor) to another (a creditor), payable in money or in goods and/or services.

liquid asset Cash in banks and on hand or a readily marketable investment. The term is somewhat more restrictive than **cash asset** and much more restrictive than **quick asset**.

long-term liability An obligation that will become due after a year or more has elapsed. Examples: mortgages; mortgage bonds and debentures; secured-note issues; and funded debt generally.

margin on sales See **gross profit**.

outstanding checks Uncollected or unpaid checks that have been sent to the payees but have not cleared the drawee's bank.

perpetual inventory Inventory kept in continuous agreement with stock on hand by means of a detailed record that could serve as a subsidiary ledger if dollar amounts as well as physical quantities are maintained.

petty cash   A relatively small sum of money on hand or on deposit, which may be used for minor disbursements.

petty cash voucher   A document that serves as authority to disburse petty cash and as evidence of payment.

physical inventory   The actual counting, weighing, or measuring of tangible items.

posting   The bookkeeping process of transferring dollar amounts and other information from a document or book of original entry to a ledger.

profit and loss statement   See **income statement**.

quick asset   A current asset convertible into cash within a relatively short period of time. Examples: a call loan, a marketable security, a customer's account, or a commodity immediately saleable at quoted prices on the open market.

register   A record of the consecutive entry of similar transactions, with space for notations of essential information that may be needed for future reference.

reserve for bad debts   See **allowance for bad debts**.

reserve for depreciation   See **allowance for depreciation**.

retained earnings   See **earned surplus**. A more meaningful term for use on the balance sheet.

revenue   Income from the sale of products, merchandise, and services; and earnings from interest, dividends, rents, and wages.

sales returns and allowances   Goods sent back to the seller, the amount being deducted from his gross sales.

sight draft   A draft payable by the drawee upon demand or presentation; distinguished from **time draft** or *acceptance*.

sole proprietorship   A business enterprise whose net worth belongs entirely to one individual.

subsidiary ledger   A supporting ledger consisting of a group of accounts the total of which is in agreement with a control account. Examples: customers' ledger, creditors' ledger, factory ledger, expense ledger, and departmental ledger.

surplus   Stockholders' equity in a corporation in excess of the par or stated value of capital stock. Always used with a qualifying adjective in the balance sheet.

tickler   A file or record of maturing obligations or other items of interest maintained in such a manner as to call attention to each item at the proper time. Examples: in a bank, the note tickler; in an insurance office, the policy-expiration or premiums-due tickler.

time draft   A draft payable within a specified time after acceptance by the drawee, usually thirty days.

treasury stock   Fully paid capital stock reacquired by the issuing company through gift, purchase, or some other means, and available for resale or cancelation.

trial balance A list of the balances, or of total debits and total credits, of the accounts in a ledger. Its purpose is to show the equality of posted debits and credits and to provide a basic summary for financial statements.

working capital Capital in current use in the operation of a business in excess of current assets over current liabilities.

16.2 BANKING

See Section 13.1 for information on banking.

ABA number The number assigned by the American Bankers Association to a bank. The top figures designate the city and state and the number of the individual bank; the bottom figures signify the Federal Reserve district and other routing symbols, e.g., $\frac{16\text{-}5}{1220}$. Only the bank number (16-5) is written on a deposit slip.

acceleration clause A contractual clause that provides that if interest or an installment is not paid when due, the entire debt becomes payable at once.

amortization The making of periodic payments to eliminate a debt. Each payment includes interest on the outstanding debt and a repayment of part of the principal.

bank discount The interest charge made by a bank on a loan or for converting commercial paper into cash before maturity.

bank draft An order by one bank on another authorizing the latter to pay a stated sum of money to the order of the person named in the draft.

bank statement The monthly statement supplied by the bank to checking-account customers.

callable loan A bank loan that may be repaid at any time by the borrower but that must be repaid upon the lender's demand.

canceled check A check paid by the bank and returned to its depositor. It is listed on the bank statement as a withdrawal from the account, and serves as the depositor's receipt from the payee.

cashier's check A check drawn by a bank on its own funds. A customer may purchase one of these checks for a fee in order to meet the demands of a supplier for such a check. Used especially in international trade.

certificate of deposit A depositor may place a certain sum of money with the bank to be redeemed on demand or on a specified date. He will be issued a certificate as a receipt, and may not draw against the money until the certificate is returned to the bank.

certified check The depositor's own check, which has been guaranteed as to the amount by the bank on which it is drawn. A fee is charged; and to stop payment on it, the maker must post a bond. Because funds have been set aside to cover the check, an unused one should be endorsed by the maker with the statement "Not used for purpose intended" and deposited in his account.

clearing house   A voluntary association of banks, usually citywide, to facilitate the settlement of interbank debits and credits. Besides checks, money orders, bond coupons, and other paper are cleared.

comaker   A person who signs a note or check of another and thereby also assumes responsibility for payment.

commercial bank   A general banking business primarily engaged in financing businesses on short-term or seasonal loans. It may also have savings and trust departments depending on the state law.

commercial credit   Loans made by commercial banks to business concerns for relatively short periods of time.

commercial draft   A written order by one party directing another party to pay a sum of money to a third party.

commercial letter of credit   The importer arranges for a sufficient amount of credit to meet his obligations on a certain purchase of goods. His bank notifies a bank in the seller's city by a letter of credit that credit has been established. The seller may then draw a draft and receive his money before he ships the goods.

correspondent bank   A bank in another location with which the local bank has established a working relationship to facilitate the handling of customers' needs. Often the local bank has established a line of credit or opened an account with the correspondent bank.

days of grace   Extra days within which to meet an obligation without penalty. Usually no grace is allowed on notes and bills.

deceased account   No transactions may be made in an account of a deceased person after the bank has been notified of the death. A bank is not liable in case checks clear the account before notification.

demand deposit   A deposit in a checking account that may be withdrawn at any time without previous notice. The majority of deposits are demand deposits, and no interest is paid on them.

deposits   The following items may be deposited in either savings or checking accounts: cash, checks, interest coupons, money orders, traveler's checks, drafts, and promissory notes.

drawee   The person named in the draft who pays its amount to the drawer.

drawer   The person who draws a draft asking for payment.

endorsements   See Section 13.1 for a description of acceptable endorsements.

escrow   The delivery of funds or other security to a third person, such as a bank, to be held until the happening of some event or the performance of some act, under the terms of an escrow agreement.

estate taxes   An excise tax on the right to transfer property from the dead to the living.

exchange rate   The monetary rate at which one country can exchange its money for the money of another country.

excise taxes Federal, state, and local taxes imposed on acts rather than on property.

Federal Deposit Insurance Corporation (FDIC) A federal agency that insures bank deposits.

Federal Home Loan Bank System Savings and loan associations are members of this System.

Federal Reserve System The banking system established by Congress to provide an elastic currency and to unify banking. The United States is divided into twelve districts with a Federal Reserve bank in each district. These banks deal only with member banks.

Federal Savings and Loan Insurance Corporation A federal agency that insures deposits in savings and loan associations.

fee simple The absolute ownership of real property that the owner has the right to dispose of as he wishes.

foreign bill A commercial draft drawn in one state or country on a person or business in another state or country.

forged or raised check A check on which the drawer's name, the endorser's name, or the amount has been written by another in order to defraud. A bank is liable to a depositor for payment of a forged or raised check, if the bank is notified within one year after the return to the depositor of a forged or raised paid check.

frozen account An account in which no transactions may take place because of a court order or the demise of the account holder.

gift tax A federal or state excise tax on the transfer of money or property from one person to another without a return in money or other value.

gold certificates Certificates issued by the government and held by the Treasury or Federal Reserve banks; none are used by the public.

gold standard A monetary unit expressed as a weight of gold. U.S. currency cannot be redeemed for gold, because the United States went off the gold standard in 1933.

grantee and grantor The parties to a deed are (1) the grantor, who gives his interest in the property to the grantee, and (2) the grantee, who in return gives a consideration to the grantor.

inheritance tax Excise tax levied by states on the right of the living to receive property from the dead.

interest Payment for the use of another's money.

inter vivos trust A trust created by the grantor during his lifetime, also known as a living trust. The grantor or another person may be the beneficiary, and the trust may be either irrevocable or revocable.

investment bank A firm that buys large blocks of securities and sells them to the public in small amounts, thus supplying immediate capital to businesses.

investment trust A financial organization that sells shares of the trust to the public and invests the funds thus obtained in high-grade securities.

irrevocable trust An irrevocable trust occurs when the grantor gives away assets without any right to or control over the income and without the right of repossession of the assets. There is no right to alter, amend, or revoke the trust. Because their revocable trust is in the nature of a gift, gift taxes apply. The income earned by the trust fund is taxable to the trust.

joint account A checking or savings account in the names of two or more people. See **joint tenants** and **tenants in common**.

joint tenants Depositors who open a bank account as joint tenants may each deposit or withdraw from the account. If one of the depositors dies, the other is entitled to the balance of the account (the right of survivorship). Persons may also own other types of assets as joint tenants. (See also **tenants in common**.)

kiting The illegal practice of writing checks against a bank account in which there are insufficient funds to cover them but fully expecting to deposit funds to cover the amount drawn before the checks are presented to the bank for payment.

letter of credit A letter from one bank to another, or from a company to its bank or business associates, stating that a specified amount of credit has been established by the named person or company.

liquidity The maintaining of cash reserves against unforeseeable needs and as capital for future investment.

living trust An agreement whereby the trustor, while he is alive, engages a trustee to take care of his property on behalf of beneficiaries, who may include himself, or any other person, group, or organization.

loan The temporary use of another's money at interest, with repayment usually secured by a promissory note or a mortgage on real property.

medium of exchange Anything used as the basis for the exchange of goods or services. Money is the most frequently used medium of exchange.

member bank A national or state bank or a trust company that is a member of the Federal Reserve System.

money orders The purchase of a checklike form for a certain sum at a bank, post office, or telegraph office. Money orders are used for payments under a maximum set by the issuing institution. A fee is charged according to the amount of the order.

night depository A lock-box of a type that permits a depositor to come to the bank after it is closed and drop his deposit in it. The bank then assumes the responsibility for safekeeping until its opening the next day.

notary public A person commissioned by the state to administer oaths, certify to the genuineness of documents, witness signatures, and take acknowledgments.

note A written promise to pay a specified sum of money on demand or at a named future date. It may be made payable to a person's order or to the bearer and thus becomes negotiable by endorsement. The payee may deposit the note with the collection teller at his bank, who will place the collected amount in his account upon receipt.

per stirpes The distribution of the principal of a trust fund in accordance with ancestral lines. Grandchildren would receive the prorated share that their parents had a claim to.

pour-over trust A person who has established a living trust may make provision in his will for the assets remaining at his death to "pour over" into the living trust.

private bank A commercial bank, privately owned, that lends money to finance international projects in addition to the usual commercial banking activities.

promissory note See **note**

protest A formal notification that the maker has not made payment when due on a note, a draft, or other paper. A notary public or a responsible person in the presence of two witnesses may draw up the protest certificate that lists the facts in the case. A copy is served on all parties whose names appear on the instrument as drawer and endorsers. An endorser may write "Protest waived" above his signature if he is willing to assume liability should the drawer default.

reconciliation See Section 13.1 for instructions for the reconciliation of a bank statement.

rediscount rate The rate charged by the Federal Reserve banks for discounting commercial paper presented by member banks. The Federal Reserve banks set their own rediscount rates, subject to review by the Federal Reserve Board. The Board often uses the rediscount rate to control credit by raising the rate to limit borrowing and lowering it to encourage borrowing.

revocable trust A trust containing the revocable clause may be terminated at any time or at a certain specified time. No gift tax applies at the time of creation because control is retained over the assets of the trust. The income tax laws regarding revocable trusts are very strict.

revolving letter of credit A letter of credit issued by a bank to a traveler in return for cash or established credit at the bank in the amount stated in the letter. When the traveler presents the letter of credit to any of the listed foreign banks, he is entitled to draw checks or drafts against the credit. The amount of each withdrawal is entered on the letter until the full amount has been used. Any unused portion should be returned by the traveler to his account at the bank that issued the letter.

savings and loan association A savings institution established primarily for the deposit and investment of savings and the loaning of money to builders and buyers of homes.

sight draft Payment on this type of draft is immediate—at sight or on demand. These payment terms are stated in the draft when drawn.

stale check   An old check, usually one with a date more than six months old. Many banks refuse to honor a stale check.

stop payment   See Section 13.1 for the stopping of payment of checks.

straight loan   A short-term loan (three to five years) on real estate for a definite number of years at a specific interest rate. It is payable in full at maturity, but interest is paid periodically during the life of the loan.

tenants in common   Depositors who open a **joint account** as tenants in common may all make deposits, but the signatures of all tenants are required for withdrawals. At the death of one of them, the survivors are entitled to their share only, and the decedent's heirs are entitled to his interest. (See also **joint tenants**.)

testamentary trust   A trust fund set up in a will that takes effect upon the death of the testator. The major reason for its creation is to protect the beneficiary from his or her own inexperience. A simple testamentary trust clause might be stated as follows.

All the rest, residue, and remainder of my estate, I give, devise and bequeath to my Trustee, hereinafter named, IN TRUST, nevertheless for the following purposes and uses: To collect and receive the income and to pay or apply the net income therefrom not less frequently than monthly, to my beloved wife, Mary Smith, during her life. Upon her death my Trustee shall pay and distribute the principal remaining, if any, of said trust, equally share and share alike to my children, and to my children's children *per stirpes* for those of my children who are deceased.

time deposits   Savings and thrift accounts are time deposits and are not subject to withdrawals by checks. The record of deposits is kept in a passbook, or certificates of deposit are issued for the amount on deposit. These accounts earn interest.

time draft   A draft ordering payment at a certain time after receipt, acceptance, or date. The drawee writes "accepted," the date, the place payable, and his signature on the face of the draft. He usually has 24 hours to examine the goods and the papers attached to the draft and to decide whether or not to accept the draft and the merchandise.

title insurance   An assurance by a title insurance company that property is clear at the time of transfer. Such a company will make good to the beneficiary any loss, up to a fixed amount, sustained through defects in the title.

traveler's checks   Checks that must be purchased from firms such as the American Express Company, the Bank of America, the First National City Bank of New York, and Thos. Cook & Son. They are available in denominations of $10, $20, $50, and $100 for a fee. When purchased they must be signed in the presence of the company representative, and when cashed they must be signed again in the presence of the person who is accepting them in lieu of cash.

traveler's letter of credit   See **revolving letter of credit**.

trust   The holding of property by a trustee (a bank, trust company, or persons) who manages it for the benefit of the named beneficiaries. See **living trust, irrevocable trust, revocable trust,** and **testamentary trust**.

voucher check   A check with a detachable stub on which are listed the items for which payment is being made. A voucher is a receipt for or a proof of a business expenditure, and the stub of the check is considered to be a voucher.

warrant   In banking, a written order to pay money.

16.3   DATA PROCESSING

A discussion of data processing and its uses in the office will be found in Section 5.1.

access time   The time it takes a computer to locate information in storage and transfer it to the **arithmetic unit**.

address   An identification—name, label, or number—for the location of information in storage.

ADP (automated data-processing)   A system of electronic machines so interconnected and interacting that there is minimum need for human intervention.

ALGOL (algorithmic language)   A system by which numerical procedures may be precisely presented to a computer in a standard form.

algorithm   A set of finite steps or processes for the solution of a problem.

analog computer   A computer that measures physical relationships in processing data, in contrast to a **digital computer**, which represents relationships numerically.

analyzer   A routine used to analyze a program written for the same or a different computer.

arithmetic function   The computational steps involved in data processing.

arithmetic unit   The portion of the hardware of a computer in which arithmetical and logical operations are performed.

artificial language   A language specifically designed for ease of communication in a particular area of endeavor.

assembler   A computer program that translates symbolic programming language into machine language.

asynchronous computer   A computer in which each operation starts as a result of a signal indicating that the previous operation has been completed or that the parts of the computer required for the next operation are available. Also, a computer that is able to go directly to stored data at any point in storage.

audio-response unit   A device that provides verbal replies to questions directed to the computer through a dial telephone input unit.

autocoder   A **symbolic coding** system for writing instructions that must be translated into **machine language** before they can be executed by a computer.

automation   A self-regulating process in which work is done with a minimum of human effort; also, the investigation, design, development, and application of methods of rendering processes automatic.

BCD (binary-coded decimal system)   A system of representing decimal digits so that each appears as a combination of four binary digits (**bits**). For example: the number *thirty-two* is represented as *0011 0010;* whereas in a pure binary system, *32* is represented as *100000.*

binary coding system   A system having only two possibilities—on or off, yes or no, go or no go, open or closed.

binary number   A number of two characters or digits (usually *1* and *0*).

bionics   Knowledge gained from analysis of living systems applied to the creation of computer circuits.

bit (binary digit)   A single digit in a binary number.

block   Set of things, such as words, characters, or digits, handled as a unit.

block diagram   A schematic chart setting forth the detailed sequence of internal operations for the computer to perform. Used as a tool in programming.

block transfer   The movement of a group of consecutive words from one place to another.

branch   Program movement to a step that is not the next sequential one.

breakpoint   A point in a computer **program** that permits a visual check of progress or some other analysis.

buffer storage   An intermediate storage unit used to hold information being transmitted between two units of a computer.

card column   One of the vertical areas on a **punch card** in which a digit, letter, or symbol may be recorded. A standard IBM card has 80 columns; the Univac has 80 or 90; and the IBM System 3 has 96 columns.

card-punch machine   A machine that records data by punching holes in cards.

card read-punch unit   A device that reads information punched in cards into the processing unit of the computer. It also punches data that have been processed by the computer into the same card or a new set of cards.

card-to-tape converter   A device that converts information directly from punched cards to punch or **magnetic tape**.

card verifier   A machine used to check the accuracy of holes punched into a card. It is similar in appearance to a **card-punch machine**.

cell   A storage unit in a computer.

cell address   The number or symbol designating the location of a cell in which information is stored.

chad   The small pieces of paper that are removed when holes are punched in cards or tape.

character density   The number of characters that can be stored per inch.

character reader A device that converts type fonts or scripts directly into **machine language**.

check bit A bit used by the computer in checking its own accuracy in transmitting data.

check indicator A device that indicates that an error has been made.

classifying The process of coding similar types of data.

COBOL (*common business oriented language***)** A language used to present a business program to a computer.

coded program A program expressed in the code or language of a specific machine.

collator A device used to collate or merge sets of cards in sequence.

common machine language Information presented in a manner common to a related group of machines.

compiler A special computer program that translates programs written in symbolic form to machine-language form. It can generate more than one machine instruction for each symbolic statement as well as perform the functions of a processor program.

configuration Machines interconnected and programmed to operate as a system.

console The part of the computer that provides information to the operator about the performance of the system and that is used to put information into the system manually, to alter content when necessary, and to start and stop the machine.

constant An item of information, such as a total, stored in the computer in a fixed location and used repeatedly during the running of the program.

control board or panel A removable grid or plate on which wires for controlling the computer must be assembled manually.

control sequence The order of instructions to a machine.

correction seal A small rectangle of tape placed over an incorrect punch to correct a minor error on cards used only once or twice.

CPU (central processing unit) An electronic machine capable of receiving and storing instructions, receiving and storing data to be processed, transferring and editing data already stored, making arithmetic computations, making decisions of logic, and directing the action of the input and output units.

crosstalk Unwanted signals in a channel that originate from other channels in the same system.

cryogenics The field of technology dealing with the properties of elements at very low temperatures.

cybernetics The technology involved in the comparative study of information-handling machines.

cycle The frequency with which any given set of data is processed.

data conversion The changing of information from one form of representation to another.

data processing (or data handling) The processing of source material containing basic information by classifying, sorting, calculating, summarizing, and recording.

d-character   The last character in computer instructions. Its function is to ask questions—Has the last card been processed? Is the page filled on which output is being printed? or, What is the definition of the operation being performed?

debug   The location and correction of errors in a computer program.

deceleration time (or stop time)   The elapsed time between completion of the reading or the writing of a tape and the cessation of its motion.

decision symbol   A symbol denoting the need to verify the existence or non-existence of a given condition and for determining future action.

decoder   A device that interprets a set of signals and initiates appropriate computer operation.

detail printing   A printout on the final computer report of all information on each card that entered the computer.

diagnostic routine (also called malfunction routine)   A procedure for locating computer **malfunction**.

digital computer   A computer that uses numbers in processing data. Compare with **analog computer**.

down time   The time during which a computer is out of service because of mechanical or electronic failure.

EBDIC (extended binary coded decimal interchange code)   A code that converts two sets of four binary digits into hexadecimal code, unique to IBM/360 computers.

EDP   Electronic data-processing.

EDST   Elastic diaphragm switch technology.

11 position (or "X" position)   The position immediately below the 12 position of a standard punch card.

EOF   *End of file* or the point of completion of a quantity of data.

equal sequence   An arrangement whereby the value of a particular **field** on one card may be equal to the value of the same field on a succeeding card.

erasable storage   Data stored on magnetic tapes, drums, and cores, and subject to alteration during the course of a computation.

error-detection routine   A routine used to detect whether an error has occurred in the internal or external transfer of information.

excess-three code   A coding system derived from the **binary-coded decimal** system, in which each decimal digit is represented by its binary equivalent plus 3. A fixed number of four **bits** is used to express each digit.

execution time   The time required to do a job.

fast-access storage   The section of storage from which data may be obtained most rapidly.

field   One set of positions on a punch card, tape, or disc that is always used to record similar data.

fixed-count coding   Coding in which a fixed number of **bits** (usually two) are moved. Computers using this coding system are primarily designed for numeric processing.

fixed-data area   An area of the computer set aside for information common to all processing requirements.

fixed word-length   A term describing data treated in units of a fixed number of characters or **bits** (as contrasted with variable word-lengths).

flow chart   A graph of the physical movement of data.

FORTRAN   A programming language for problems expressed in algebraic notation.

gigo   A term used to explain what happens when incorrect information is fed to the computer. It means "garbage in, garbage out."

grandfather tape   Old information (from preceding processing cycles) retained as backup in case of future need.

graph plotter   An output device capable of displaying the results of a computation in graph form.

grouping   The process of bringing together related bits of information.

hardware   The physical equipment making up a data-processing system.

heuristic   Pertaining to trial and error as applied to the solution of problems.

hexadecimal   A base of 16 that requires 16 symbols to represent 16 number values. Hexadecimal code is used on IBM/360 computers.

high-order position   The position at the extreme left of a **field**.

high sequence   An arrangement whereby the value of a particular **field** in one card may be less than the value of the same field in another card following it.

hollerith code   A system used by IBM for representing data by rectangular holes punched in an 80-column card.

housekeeping routine   The initial instructions executed only once in a program.

IDP (integrated data processing)   A sequence of data-processing steps integrated into a complete system.

immediate access   A storage device that handles input or output data in a short period of time.

incremental computer   A computer in which changes in the variables are recorded rather than the variables themselves.

information processing system   The seven-step procedure of classifying, sorting, calculating, summarizing, recording, communicating, and storing information.

information retrieval   The recovery of specified information or data from a collection of records.

input   The original placement of data in the computer.

input media   The forms on which data to be processed are recorded.

instruction format   The order in which instructions are written for the computer.

instruction time   The time required by the computer to perform on instruction.

internal storage (or internal memory) A data storage device that is an integral part of the computer.

interpreter A machine that prints on a punch card the data already punched in the card.

iterative process Calculation by means of a repeating cycle of operations.

key punch A perforating device used to put information on cards or tape.

key sort A method of processing data that uses cards with holes punched around the four edges. Notches are made in the holes and used as codes for sorting data.

loading routine A stored routine for bringing other information into storage from cards or tapes.

logic function The machine process of comparing numbers and testing the data being processed to ascertain that certain conditions have been met.

loop The repetition of a group of instructions in a routine until certain conditions are reached.

low-order position The position at the extreme right of a word.

low sequence An arrangement whereby the value of a particular **field** in one card may be greater than the value of the same field in a succeeding card.

LPM "Lines per minute."

machine language A language designed for use by a machine without translation.

macro instruction An instruction in symbolic language that is the same as a specified sequence of machine-language instructions.

magnetic disc or tape A storage (input and output) medium on whose magnetized surface data are recorded.

malfunction A failure in the hardware of a computer.

mark-sensed card A special card, having 27 vertical positions, on which information is recorded by the use of a graphite pencil. Special equipment converts the pencil marks into punched holes.

master card A punched card containing standard information that applies to a group of cards, such as program number and customer's name, address and code number.

matching process A process whereby two decks of punched cards arranged in sequential order are compared. Unmatched cards are removed, and the two matched decks are either kept separate or collated in order.

memory That part of the computer that stores programs, intermediate results, and various constant data.

merging process A process whereby two decks of punched cards arranged in sequential order are brought together in one sequenced set.

microsecond One millionth of a second.

millisecond One thousandth of a second.

minuend The quantity from which another quantity is subtracted.

MIT A "master instruction tape" on which all programs for a system of runs are recorded.

mnemonic operation code A code that abbreviates the names of operations; e.g., *CLR* for "clear storage" and *SQR* for "square root."

Monte Carlo method Repeated trial-and-error calculations used to discover the best solution to a problem.

move-and-edit function A process that edits data as they are moved from storage to the printing area of the computer.

multiple-address instruction An instruction consisting of an operation code and two or more addresses.

multiprogramming A technique used for the simultaneous handling of a number of programs.

nanosecond One billionth of a second

9 edge The bottom edge of a standard punch card.

no-address instruction An instruction for an operation the computer can perform without referring to its storage unit.

nonerasable storage Stored information that cannot be erased during computation.

numeric code Numerical abbreviations used to prepare **input** information.

off-line equipment The peripheral or auxiliary devices not in direct communication with the **central processing unit** of a computer.

on-line processing The passage of information to the central unit as activity occurs through the input and output devices under the direct control of the central processing unit.

operand An instruction that designates the location or **address** of the data to be processed.

operating ratio Hours of correct machine operation in relation to the hours of scheduled operation.

optical-mark page reader A machine that senses marks made by pencil or pen on a specially designed form.

optical scanner A device that photoelectrically speed-reads data from a page directly into the computer.

optical scanning The reading of data into a computer through the use of magnetic ink or optical marks.

optimize To arrange the instructions or the data in storage for a minimum of time-consuming jumps or transfers when the program is run.

output The data processed from internal storage to printed sheets, cards, tapes, or some other output media.

overpunch The addition of holes to a card column that already contains one or more holes.

parallel storage The equally available storage of data, including all **bits**, characters, or words.

parameter A quantity to which different values may be assigned, which usually remains the same throughout a particular program.

parity (or odd-even) check A process that determines whether the number of ones (or zeros) in an array of binary digits is odd or even.

perforation rate   The rate at which characters, rows, or words are punched in a paper tape.

peripheral equipment   Auxiliary machines under the control of the central computer.

permanent storage   The storage of intermediate or final results usually in the form of punched cards or magnetic tape outside the computer.

pinboard   A control panel using jacks or pins instead of wires to control the operation of a computer.

PL/1   A programming language having increased capability and combining the best aspects of COBOL and FORTRAN. It is a single language that can be effectively used by both commercial and scientific programmers.

plus zone   The coded **bit** positions that represent the algebraic plus sign.

polyvalent number   A number made up of several digits, each digit representing one of several characteristics being described.

postedit   To edit the results of a previous computation.

post-mortem routine   A routine for analyzing the cause of a failure.

predicate   To affirm or deny, using mathematical logic.

probability   The likelihood of the occurrence of an event.

problem-oriented language   A language designed for the convenience of a problem statement rather than for easy machine instruction.

processor program   A program formulated by the computer manufacturer that may be used to translate a source program into a **machine language** program.

program   A set of instructions for solving a problem that directs the computer in its operations.

program chart   The form on which the program for a computer is written.

program language   The code used by programmers to write computer programs.

programmer   A person who plans the steps and the order of the operations for the solution of the problem and who **debugs** the program, if necessary.

programming   The process of planning and writing the program.

program register   A device in which the instruction of a program is stored.

propagated error   An error in one operation that spreads through and influences later operations.

punch card   A stiff card upon which data may be stored as punched holes.

punch tape   Paper tape on which data may be stored as punched holes.

random-access storage (or RAM for "random-access memory")   A storage device in which each record with a specific **address** may be reached directly.

raw data   Facts that have not been processed and that may or may not be in **machine language**.

read-in   To transmit external information to internal storage in the computer.

reading rate   The number of characters, words, **fields, blocks,** or cards transmitted by a sensing device per unit of time.

read-out   To transmit internally stored information out of the computer.

real-time   The processing of individual transactions at the time they occur rather than collecting them for future processing.

recursive   Repetitive.

repertory instruction   The set of instructions that a computer is capable of following.

rerun routine (or rollback routine)   A set of instructions designed to be used after a computer **malfunction** to reconstitute a routine from the last rerun point.

rounding error (or round-off error)   The error that results from rounding off a quantity by deleting some significant digits, e.g., 0.3853 can be rounded to 0.385 with a rounding error of .0003.

RPG (report program generator)   A fixed-form language for simplified programming that is then translated into machine language.

scanner   An instruction that automatically samples or interrogates various processes or files and initiates action as required.

scratch date   A calendar date assigned to any group of data, after which day the stored information may be destroyed.

secondary storage   Magnetic drums and tapes that are not part of the computer but are connected to and controlled by it.

sequential operation   A series of steps or instructions in a program that the computer will perform one after the other without interruption.

serial operation   Information flow through a computer in sequence using only one digit, word, line, or channel at a time.

serial programming   A computer operation that permits only one arithmetical or logical function at a time.

serial transmission   Data movement in sequence, one character at a time.

servomechanism   A device used to monitor and control an operation as it proceeds.

seven-bit alphameric code   A coding system that is an outgrowth of the binary-coded decimal system. Four **bits** are used to express the digits and two more bits to express alphabetic and special characters. The seventh bit is a **parity check**.

signal attenuation   Reduction in the strength of electrical signals.

signal-to-noise ratio   The relationship of information signals to random signals not conveying information.

skip instructions   Directions to a computer to proceed to another instruction in the storage portion.

sophisticated vocabulary   Advanced or elaborate instructions requiring complex mathematical processes.

sorter (or sequencer)   A machine that sorts information into a particular order or into similar groups.

source machine   The computer on which the **source program** is translated into the object program.

source program   A program coded in other than **machine language**, which must be translated into machine language before use.

SPS (symbolic programming system)   A programming language using **mnemonic** substitutes for easier programming of operation codes and storage addresses.

statement   An instruction to the computer to perform some sequence of operations.

storage allocation   The reservation of blocks of storage for specific blocks of information.

storage cycle   The sequence of occurrences when information is transferred to or from the storage unit of a computer.

store   To place data in a location in storage so that it may be retrieved for later use.

stored-program computer   A **digital computer** that, under the control of internally stored instructions, can synthesize, alter, and store instructions as though they were data and can subsequently carry out these new instructions.

subprogram   A part of a larger program that can be independently processed or compiled.

subroutine   Instructions for carrying out a well-defined mathematical or logical operation that may be included in other programs requiring the particular operation.

subroutine library   A set of **subroutine** instructions kept on file for later use.

subscript   A notation used to specify a particular member of a series of items (not necessarily arranged in a meaningful pattern) when the name for the group of items does not identify each item.

symbolic coding   Writing programs in any language other than absolute machine language.

tape-to-card converter   A device that transfers information punched into paper tape or recorded on magnetic tape to punched cards.

tape-to-tape reproducer   A device that transfers information on paper or magnetic tape to other sections of tape.

terminating symbol   A symbol on the tape that indicates the end of a block of information.

test routine   Instructions designed to show whether a computer is functioning properly.

time-sharing   An arrangement whereby more than one user share the same computer.

transducer   A device that converts a signal from one form to another.

transfer   To terminate one sequence of instructions and begin another sequence.

transfer check   A test process to verify that information is transferred correctly.

transfer operation An instruction that moves information from one storage location to another.

trouble location problem A test problem for locating faulty equipment.

12 edge The term used to designate the top edge of a punch card.

12 position (or "Y" position) The punching position nearest the top or **12 edge** of the standard punch card.

unconditional branch An instruction that switches or branches the computer to another instruction, regardless of conditions.

Univac A computer system manufactured by the Univac Division of the Sperry-Rand Corporation.

up-time The time during which equipment is available for productive work.

utility A standard program, usually provided by the manufacturer, that performs the functions commonly required by all computer installations, such as card-to-tape and tape-to-printer programs.

variable A symbol whose numeric value changes from one run of a program to the next or changes within each run of a program.

variable word-length Some computers accept machine words in variable word-lengths; others can accept only a fixed number of characters in each machine word. With variable word-length, the end of each word must be indicated.

verifier A device on which a record can be compared as to identity, character by character, with a retranscription or copy.

word A single character or a group of characters representing a complete unit of information.

word mark A **bit** used to signal the beginning or the end of a **word**.

write To transfer information, usually from main storage to an **output** device.

"X" position See **11 position**.

"Y" position See **12 position**.

zero position The topmost printed digit position on a standard card. A punch in this position represents the digit *zero*. When used with another punched number, the zero punch represents a letter of the alphabet or a symbol.

zero suppression The elimination before printing of nonsignificant zeros to the left of significant digits.

zone bits The **bits** used in combination with digit bits in a **cell** to represent the letters of the alphabet as well as some special signs and symbols.

16.4 ECONOMICS

absolute advantage The ability to supply a product or service at a cost lower than that of a competitor.

actuary A statistician who determines the annual retirement of plants and equipment.

affluent society A community in which most persons enjoy an abundance of material things.

arbitrage   The act of simultaneously purchasing foreign exchange, securities, commodities, or other goods in one market and selling them in another market at a higher price.

balanced budget   The equalization of revenues and expenditures.

bankruptcy   A legal declaration of the insolvency of individuals, partnerships, or corporations, discharging the debtor from his debts and assuring creditors of an orderly process of liquidation.

basic research   Scientific investigation undertaken for the advancement of knowledge, not gain.

book value   The net value of a corporation according to its accounting records.

budget deficit   An excess of expenditures over revenues.

capital budget   A company budget that involves the planning and controlling of capital expenditures.

capital goods   Goods needed in the production of other goods; e.g., factory buildings, machinery, trucks, and so on.

circular flow   The continual movement of money and goods in the economy.

circulating capital   Goods that can be used only at one time or over a relatively short period of time.

closed corporation   A corporation in which all or almost all of the stock is owned by a small number of people.

collateral   Property pledged to secure a loan.

commercial paper   The unsecured promissory notes of companies with a high credit rating.

commodity exchange   An association of traders who buy and sell contracts for the delivery of commodities.

convenience goods   Inexpensive items that the consumer purchases frequently near his home or place of business.

credit card   A card of identification that allows the purchase of goods and services and payment for them at a later date.

creeping inflation   Slow upward movement in the general price level.

depletion allowance   A tax allowance extended to the owners of exhaustible natural resources.

direct cost   A cost that can be identified with a specific unit of output.

discount rate (or rediscount rate)   The interest a Federal Reserve bank charges a commercial bank for a loan.

econometrics   The application of statistical and mathematical techniques in testing and demonstrating economic theories.

economic analysis or economic theory   A study of the cause-and-effect relationships of economic phenomena.

economic policy   A course of action based on economic analysis and influenced by political, military, and social policies.

economics   A systematic study of matters relating to the efforts of people to satisfy their wants by the use of goods and services. Such matters as the production, distribution, and consumption of goods and services are studied.

entrepreneur A business operator who introduces a new product, a new productive process, or an improved organization and raises the necessary capital, assembles the factors of production, and sets up the management of a business.

equity capital The total investment in a business of all its owners.

escalator clause A contractual provision that requires the payment of automatic increases or decreases in the event of price changes.

escrow A deed, bond, or other written document adopted by two parties and deposited with a third party for safekeeping, to be held until the grantee fulfills specific conditions.

excess-profits tax A tax on corporate profits above a specified normal level.

fair-trade law A state resale price-maintenance law that permits manufacturers to set minimum retail prices for their products.

fiscal year The accounting year, which may start at any time in the calendar year.

fringe benefit Nonwage benefits or payments to workers in addition to their wages, e.g., pensions, travel pay, vacation pay, health insurance, and so on.

frozen asset An asset that is not readily convertible into cash or would be sold at a loss.

funded debt The long-term indebtedness of a corporation or a government, usually in the form of interest-bearing bonds.

garnishment A court order requiring an employer to pay part or all of an employee's wages to a court officer for the benefit of a creditor.

goodwill The money value of the reputation of a company.

horizontal combination The bringing under control of one company several firms engaged in the sale of the same product or similar products.

indirect cost Any cost not consistently identified with a specific product unit.

installment credit Credit in which repayment, including interest charges, is made by regular periodic payments.

limited liability Restriction of an owner's loss in his business to the amount of his invested capital.

long-term forecast A forecast that extends at least five years ahead.

macroeconomics A study of the problems of the economy as a whole or a general equilibrium analysis of total employment, total production, business cycles, inflation, and the effects of changes in the rate of economic growth.

Malthusian theory "The world's population increases faster than does the means of subsistence."

marginal cost The additional cost of making one additional unit of output.

microeconomics The study of the problems of individuals, firms, and industries; in other words, a partial equilibrium analysis concerned with only part of the total economy.

minimum wage The lowest wage rate allowed by law.

mixed economy A system composed of both unplanned economy and **planned economy** by a centralized authority, either public or private.

monetary system The kinds of money used in a nation.

mutual company A corporation without capital stock in which profits are divided among the members in proportion to the business that each has done with the company.

net worth The excess of assets over liabilities, representing the equity, or values, of the owners' interest in the assets.

operations research An analytic approach by a team or group to the study of the operation of a system or an integrated set of actions. It uses the talents of different specialists, utilizes mathematical analysis, seeks underlying principles, and forms conclusions that indicate the probable results of various courses of action. It is most useful in solving complex problems involving many factors that can be measured and described in quantitative terms.

overhead A cost that a firm incurs for general and administrative expenses.

parent company A corporation that owns the majority of the stock of another company, called its *subsidiary*.

planned economy An economy in which some central authority or power sets the goals for production and allocates the available productive resources to uses that are intended to result in the attainment of those goals.

price control Government regulation of prices of goods and services designed to stabilize the cost of living.

price-earnings ratio The current market price of a company's stock expressed as a multiple of the company's per-share earnings.

profiteering Unreasonably large profit-taking on the sale of goods and services.

profit sharing A bonus for workers above their regular wage, based on a certain percentage of the profits of their employer.

profit squeeze Reduced profits due to rising costs and stable prices.

proprietorship An organization in which one individual owns the business.

quantify To express in terms of number, force, or weight, or some other indication of measurement.

quantitative analysis The use of descriptive statistics—the collection, organization, and presentation of empirical data in the form of tables and charts—and analytical statistics—the formulation of general relationships or conclusions from the data.

simulation games The acting out of real-life business situations by management trainees to provide experience in the operations of a business.

soft goods (or nondurable goods) Consumer items that last a short time, usually under three years.

stabilizer An economic policy designed to control rapid upward and downward movements in the economy over the long run.

statistics The collection, classification, and use of numerical facts.

symbolic reasoning A system in which mathematical symbols and their manipulation are used to state and solve logic problems. Just as arithmetic can be put into verbal terms, so verbal logic may be represented by mathematical symbols.

tax-free carryforward A provision permitting businesses and individuals to use the losses of one year to offset the income of succeeding years.

technological unemployment The displacement of labor by machinery and improved methods of production.

time study The determination of the time required by an experienced person, working at a normal pace, to do a specified task.

trademark Any word, name, symbol, or device used by a manufacturer or merchant to identify his goods and services.

trusts The control by a group of trustees of corporations whose stock certificates have been exchanged for certificates of the trust.

unemployment rate The number of jobless persons expressed as a percentage of the total labor force.

variable cost The cost of production other than fixed costs, such as labor and materials.

vertical combination The corporate combination of several companies engaged in different steps in manufacturing or marketing a product.

16.5 GOVERNMENT

anarchism A political doctrine advocating the overthrow of organized authority.

authoritarian A term used to describe a dictatorlike government.

autonomy Self-government.

balance of payments The difference between a country's payments for imports and its receipts for exports.

balance of power The strength of one group of nations equal to the strength of an opposing group.

bilateral agreement An agreement between two parties.

bipartisan foreign policy A foreign policy in which two nations agree.

boondoggling Wasteful use of public funds.

bossism Control by political bosses.

bourgeoisie Marx so denoted the middle class—proprietors, manufacturers, merchants, and so on.

brainwashing Systematic indoctrination that tends to change or undermine a person's political beliefs.

buffer state A state or country situated between two other states that lessens the danger of direct conflicts between them.

bureaucracy Government by bureaus or departments; the excessive use of bureaus.

by-election   An election to fill an unexpired term.

capitalism   An economic system in which businesses for the most part are owned and operated for private profit.

caucus   A meeting of political party members to select candidates and plan campaigns.

censure   A resolution by a legislative body disapproving the actions of a public official.

checks and balances   The division of power among the legislative, executive, and judiciary branches of government.

civil rights   The individual rights guaranteed by the Constitution.

cloture rule   A parliamentary procedure to stop debate in order to secure a vote.

common law   Law based on custom, precedent, and tradition.

Congressional Record   An official publication of proceedings in Congress.

contraband   Goods that are banned for export or import.

coup d'état   Sudden overthrow of a government by force.

de facto   Actually existing.

de jure   By legal right.

détente   The easing of strained relations between states.

due process of law   Legal method for determining guilt in a criminal or civil offense.

eminent domain   The state's right to buy private property for public use.

extradition   Surrender of a wanted person by one state to another state where the person is suspected of committing a crime.

filibuster   A delaying tactic in Congress to prevent the passage of a bill.

franchise   The right to vote.

gerrymandering   Uneven apportionment of election districts used expressly to benefit a political candidate.

grass roots   The common people or electorate.

gross national product (GNP)   The total market value of a nation's goods and services.

imperialism   The policy of a nation seeking to extend its power, territories, or dominion.

incumbent   An officeholder running for reelection.

isolationism   Opposition to national involvement in international affairs.

legislation   An enacted law or the act of making laws.

logrolling   Vote trading among legislators to obtain passage of bills in which they have an interest.

mandamus   A court order to a public official to perform his duty.

mugwump   One who votes his conviction, regardless of party.

municipality   An incorporated town, borough, or city.

national debt   The amount owed by a nation.

nationalization   The transfer of private property to the state.

naturalization   The procedure by which an alien becomes a citizen.

nihilism   A revolt against all authority.

nonaggression pact   An agreement between two nations to refrain from the use of force against each other.

nonpartisan   Not supporting any of the regularly established political parties.

partisanship   The support of a political party.

pigeonhole   To file away.

pivotal state   A state with a large electoral vote that might swing the outcome of the election from one party to another.

plebiscite   The vote of the people on an issue.

plurality   The votes one candidate receives in excess of those received by his opponent.

precinct   A voting district.

pressure group   A group influencing legislators toward its own interests.

primary election   A vote in which party members choose their candidates.

proletariat   Wage earners with little or no property.

quorum   The fewest members of a body that must be present to transact business legally.

rapprochement   The reestablishment of good relations between states.

reapportion   To change the boundaries of districts within the state so that they are more equal as to residents.

referendum   Referral of legislation to the voters.

states' rights   The rights of individual states, as opposed to the rights of the Federal Government.

subpoena   An order to appear as a witness.

16.6   INSURANCE

See Section 13.3 for a discussion of business and personal insurance.

accident and health insurance   Personal insurance that pays benefits for illness, accidental injury, or accidental death.

accidental-death benefit   Also known as *double indemnity*. A clause in a life insurance policy that offers an additional amount in case of accidental death.

actuary   A professionally trained person who works out the technical aspects of insurance and its mathematics, such as the calculation of premiums and the determination of risks, reserves, and other values.

adjuster   One who acts for an insurance company in settling claims arising out of insurance contracts, by determining the amount payable for a loss.

agent   A salesman for an insurance company or a single proprietorship that sells and services insurance from one or more companies to its clients.

annuity   A contract that provides a given amount of income payable for a specified number of years at regular intervals, based on the previous deposit of a certain sum of money.

assignee   The person to whom the interest in a policy is transferred.

assigner   The person who transfers the interest in the policy.

automatic premium loan   A provision in the policy that authorizes the payment of premiums from the loan value of the policy if payment is not made by the end of the grace period.

beneficiary   The person named in a policy or a trust account to receive the benefits on the death of the insured or the depositor.

binder   Notification from an agent to an applicant that his insurance is in force even though the policy is still to be issued.

blanket policy   The coverage of an entire group under one policy.

borrower's protective insurance   Insurance in the amount of an indebtedness of a debtor, payable to a creditor as the beneficiary.

broker   A sales and service representative who sells insurance for several companies and handles many insurance needs for clients. May also be known as an **agent**.

business life or health insurance   Policies issued on the life and health of executives to minimize the company's loss of the services of key personnel. The company is named as beneficiary.

cancelation   The termination of an insurance policy before its expiration.

cash option   When certain kinds of policies mature, the policyholder may elect to take an amount in cash in lieu of some other settlement.

cash surrender value   The cash amount a policyholder would receive upon the voluntary termination of a policy before maturity or death.

casualty insurance   Protection against loss from injuries to a third party for which the insured is responsible, such as automobile and public liability insurance; injury or illness to the insured himself, such as accident, health, hospital, and medical expense insurance; damage or loss to certain types of property owned by the insured, such as burglary, theft, and robbery insurance, and plate glass insurance.

claimant   The policyholder who presents a claim for a loss covered by an insurance contract.

coinsurance   An arrangement whereby property is insured for a certain percentage of its cash value in case of loss. If the owner does not insure up to this value, he becomes his own insurer by assuming part of the risk. Also, in the case of extremely expensive properties, two or more insurance companies might share the risk on the same terms and conditions.

common carrier's insurance   A policy to cover the liability of transportation companies for loss of, or damage to, cargo or property being transported by them.

credit insurance   A policy to insure wholesalers, manufacturers, and jobbers against excess or abnormal loss from credit accounts.

credit life insurance   A policy issued through a lender to cover the payment of a loan, installment contract, or some other obligation in the event of death.

declination   The refusal of a life insurance company to insure a person for reasons of health or occupational hazard.

deferred group annuity   The purchase of paid-up deferred annuities for each member of the group, who will receive the total amount purchased for him at his retirement.

dividend   A share of the profit paid to a policyholder in a participating insurance company.

dividend accumulations   The adding of dividends to the cash value of a policy.

dividend additions   The use of dividends to purchase additional insurance that is added to the face value of the policy.

effective date   The date on which an insurance contract goes into effect. Later known as the *policy anniversary date*.

endorsement   An amendment that changes the original coverage in some way either by adding or subtracting some feature.

endowment policy   A policy with an investment or savings feature whereby the holder pays in a certain sum that will be repaid to him after a certain number of years as a lump sum or in periodic payments. In case of death prior to expiration of the period, his heirs would benefit.

equity   The portion or value of a policy in excess of liens or other charges against it.

exclusions   Conditions in an insurance contract excluding coverage under certain conditions or in certain situations.

expiration date   The date on which a policy matures and no longer covers the conditions for which it was taken out.

extended coverage   The addition of an endorsement or rider that extends coverage to include risks not already covered in the basic policy.

fidelity bond   A policy or bond that an employer may purchase to insure himself against loss through the dishonesty of an employee in a position of trust.

floater policy   The insurance of property that is changeable in quantity, value, and/or location.

general average   A general charge made against parties who hold an interest in a cargo or ship that has been sacrificed for the common safety.

grace period   A specified number of days after the premium due date when the insured may still pay without a penalty or loss of coverage.

group insurance   Insurance covering a group of persons under one policy, e.g., group life, hospital and major medical, and so on.

HR-10 (Keogh Retirement Plans)   A plan, approved by federal legislation, whereby self-employed persons can set up retirement programs and receive certain tax advantages. Available through insurance companies, banks, and mutual funds.

indemnify   To make good a loss.

insurable interest   In order for a contract to be enforceable, a person or business must have an insurable interest by being financially injured by the occurrence of the event insured against.

insurance examiner   An employee of the state insurance department who audits and examines the affairs of an insurance company.

Keogh Retirement Plans   See **HR-10.**

lapsed policy   A policy that has been canceled because of nonpayment of the premium.

legal reserve   The portion of its assets set aside by an insurance company to meet the liabilities on its policies.

liability insurance   See **casualty insurance.**

loss-of-income policy   An insurance policy that provides cash income if the insured is unable to work because of sickness or injury.

major medical insurance   Insurance coverage of specific medical costs in addition to hospital costs.

maturity date   The date on which a policy matures or proceeds may be paid out.

mutual life insurance company   An insurance company owned and operated by the policyholders, and one that issues participating insurance.

ocean marine insurance   Insurance that protects the owners of ships and cargoes against losses at sea or in transit.

paid-up policy   One on which premiums have been paid in full.

participating insurance   A contract that entitles the policyholder to receive dividends when the actual costs are lower than the premiums paid.

pension and profit-sharing plans   An incentive plan set up by employers to reward employees through the creation of a retirement plan or other kinds of profit sharing.

policy   A printed document that states the terms of an insurance contract and guarantees certain kinds of protection.

policy loan   A loan by the insurance company to the policyholder on the security of the cash value of a policy.

preauthorized premium payment plan   The arrangement by the policyholder with his bank for the automatic payment of premiums from his checking account.

premium   The regular periodic payment that a policyholder agrees to make for insurance coverage.

premium loan   A loan on the cash value of the policy for the purpose of paying premiums.

property insurance   Insurance that protects property against risks, such as fire, flood, theft, and collision.

rider   See **endorsement.**

straight life insurance   A life insurance policy on which premiums are payable for life.

underwriting   The study by underwriters of each application for insurance and the determination of whether the insurance company should assume the risk. Their main principle is to scatter or diversify risks so that no single loss can endanger the company's financial stability.

waiver of premiums   A provision in the policy that keeps the insurance in force without payment of premiums if such a condition as disability occurs.

workmen's compensation   The payment of funds to workmen injured on the job from liability insurance purchased by their employers as required by the Workmen's Compensation Law.

16.7   LAW

abrogate   To abolish or annul (a law or custom) by an authoritative act; repeal; do away with.

abscond   To go away suddenly and secretly; go off and hide.

abstract   A short statement giving the main information of a larger treatise.

abstract of title   A written summary of important facts concerning title to land.

acceptance   Agreement by a person to be bound by the terms of an offer.

accessory (before, during, after the fact)   One who aids a known felon.

accommodation endorser   A person who signs negotiable paper for another to allow the other to receive credit.

accroach   To exercise power without due authority.

acknowledgment   Affirmation before a public officer that one has executed an instrument by his free act and deed.

acquiescence   Giving consent by failing to make an objection.

adjudicate   To determine by judgment after weighing the evidence and hearing the argument.

administrator   A person appointed by the court to administer the **estate** and distribute the property of a decedent who fails to leave a will.

affidavit   A statement sworn to before a notary public.

agent   One party acts for or in the place of another, called the *principal*, in doing business with third parties.

antitrust laws   Statutes that outlaw or control business practices that restrain trade and impede free competition.

appellant   A person who takes an appeal from one court to another.

apportionment   Division or distribution of proportionate parts.

artisan's lien   A legal right of a skilled worker to retain possession of something he has made or worked on until paid.

assignment   The transfer of a right.

attachment   Legal proceeding by which a creditor acquires a **lien** against a debtor's property as security for payment of any **judgment** he may recover.

attorney at law   A person licensed to practice law.

attorney in fact   A person designated in writing as an **agent**.

bailment   The delivery of personal property by the owner to another in **trust** for a specific purpose.

bankruptcy   The state of a person who is unable to pay his debts; a legal procedure whereby a bankrupt person is permitted to have available assets distributed to creditors, thereby releasing him from further obligation.

bilateral contract   A **contract** in which there is an exchange of mutual promises.

bill of exchange   An unconditional written order from one person to another, signed by the offeror, requiring the offeree to pay on demand, or at a fixed or determinable future time, a sum of money to order or to the bearer.

bill of sale   A written agreement transferring title to personal property.

binder   A written notation that is in effect only until the execution of the formal agreement.

bogus   Counterfeit, sham. A check drawn by a person on a bank in which he has no funds is called a *bogus check*.

brief   A discussion of the facts and points of law that are to be pleaded in court when a case comes to trial.

capacity   Competence to enter into binding contractual relationships. A minor or a mentally ill person lacks legal capacity.

chattel   Any article of personal property.

chattels real   Interest in land or a building for a limited time, such as a lease.

chose in action   A person's right to recover money or property from another by judicial proceedings. Such a right arises out of **contracts**, claims for debt, or rights against property. Stock certificates and notes are examples of choses in action.

circumstantial evidence   Evidence that tends to prove a fact by proving related facts and thus establishing a reasonable basis for the occurrence of the fact in question.

civil   Pertaining to the private rights of individuals and the legal proceedings connected with these rights.

claimant   One who voluntarily makes a claim for justice.

codicil   An addition to an executed last will and testament.

collateral   Security placed by a borrower with a creditor to assure performance or reimbursement of the obligation.

collusion   A secret alliance between two or more persons to defraud another or to secure something forbidden by law.

common law   Law based on **precedents** stemming from previous court decisions.

compensatory damage   Payment for loss in direct proportion to the amount of value lost.

complaint   The allegations made by one who institutes a suit at law.

condemnation   Taking of private property for public use.

conditional sale   A transaction whereby the seller retains title and the goods are delivered to the buyer until some condition is performed. Upon payment of the purchase price or some other act, the buyer is given title. If the buyer defaults, the possession of the goods reverts to the seller.

condition precedent   Condition that must be fulfilled before one becomes entitled to some right.

confusion of goods   The intermingling of the goods of two or more persons by any of the owners so that the property of an individual owner cannot be separated.

consideration   An item of value given in exchange for a promise.

contract   A legal agreement between two or more persons made voluntarily in good faith and with **consideration**.

conveyance   A written instrument by which title or interest in land is transferred from one person to another.

copyright   An author's right, upon registration with the Federal Government, to publish, use, and sell his writings exclusively for a period of twenty-eight years, with the privilege of renewal for an additional twenty-eight years.

court of appeals   A court that reviews the proceedings and findings of a lower court.

court of equity   A court legally qualified to hear and act in equity cases—those based on the natural law of fairness and justice.

court of law   A court governed by the rules and principles of common law—hears cases based on written law and prior court decisions.

covenant   An agreement in writing under seal.

damages   The monetary compensation that A must pay to B under a court ruling that A, by violating a legal duty owed to B, is responsible for B's loss or suffering.

deed   A written agreement by which an owner transfers his interest in land to a new owner.

de facto **corporation**   A corporation that fails to comply with one or more requirements of the incorporation law but is still recognized as a corporation in fact if not in law.

defalcation   Both **embezzlement** and misappropriation are included, but it is a broader term than either.

defamation of character   An attack upon the good name of a person; **slander**.

defective title   Title obtained by **fraud**, force, or fear, or other unlawful means, or the negotiation of such title in breach of faith.

defendant   A person who has been sued in a court of law.

de jure   By right and just title.

de jure **corporation**   A corporation that complies fully with the incorporation laws.

demurrage   Compensation for the delay of a vessel or railroad car beyond the time allowed for loading, unloading, or transit.

demurrer   A pleading that raises a question of law. It might be a motion to dismiss for failure to state a cause of action.

deposition   Testimony taken outside the court that is written and witnessed and that will be used if the case goes to court.

discharge A court order to cancel, dismiss, or set aside the obligation of a **contract**.

dissolution The stage at which a company or partnership ceases to exist as a legal entity.

documentary evidence Written documents of all kinds, as contrasted to oral **evidence**.

draft A written request by a person to a second person for the payment of a specific sum of money to a third party on demand or at a future time.

duress Compelling by threat or imprisonment a person to enter into a **contract** or perform some act.

earnest money Money given by one **contracting** party to another to bind the bargain.

easement The right to use the land of another.

ejectment Action to recover the possession of real property.

embezzlement Fraudulent appropriation by a person of the property entrusted to him.

eminent domain The right of the Federal Government or a state, county, city, school, or other public body to take private property for public use upon payment of just compensation.

enjoin To command or forbid by **injunction**.

escheat The return of property to the state, when no one makes a claim thereto.

estate An interest in property.

estate in fee simple An inherited **estate** in which the owner may use the entire property with unconditional power of disposition during his life and passing to his heirs upon his death intestate.

estoppel The legal principle that says a person is legally barred, because of his prior conduct, from asserting certain facts or doing certain acts.

evidence Any factual data that is presented to a trial court as a means of ascertaining the truth, such as through witnesses, objects, documents, or records.

executory contract An agreement that has not yet been executed because something still needs to be done.

exemplary damages The awarding of **damages** beyond actual loss to punish and make an example of the offender.

feasance The doing or performing of a condition or duty.

fiduciary relationship A relationship involving a high degree of trust and confidence. One who holds goods in **trust** for another or one who holds a position of trust and confidence has a fiduciary duty.

fixture Personal property that is annexed to realty and thus becomes part of it.

franchise A privilege or right granted by a government, a manufacturer, or a corporation.

fraud In contract law, the making of false and misleading statements to induce another to enter into a **contract**.

garnishee To attach a person's property or wages and hold them until the results of a law suit are known.

guarantor One that signs a guaranty that is a promise to answer for the debt, default, or miscarriage of another.

hearsay evidence Evidence given by a witness who testifies about information learned from another person and not from his own knowledge.

holder in due course The holder of a bill, note, check, or other **negotiable instrument** who is legally entitled to receive payment.

hypothecate To pledge without delivery of title or possession.

inchoate Recently begun but incomplete. **Contracts** are inchoate until they are signed.

indictment A written accusation by a grand jury charging a person with the performance of an act that by law is a public offense.

injunction A court order **enjoining** a person from doing a particular act that will be detrimental to another.

interpolation The act of inserting new words in a document.

irrevocable Unalterable.

judgment A decision by a court.

jointly and severally Pertaining to several defendants who may all be sued simultaneously or each separately as the plaintiff desires.

kite To issue or negotiate worthless paper and then redeem it with the proceeds of similar paper.

libel Anything written, printed, or published that is intended to expose another to public hatred or ridicule.

lien A legal right to retain the goods of another until certain conditions are satisfied.

limited liability Under corporate law, a stockholder is liable for the debts of the corporation only to the limit of the amount he paid or agreed to pay for his shares of stock.

liquidate To clear up the affairs of a **bankruptcy**; to close out a business.

litigate To contest a suit in court.

malfeasance The performance of an unlawful act.

malice aforethought A predetermination to commit a wrongful act toward some person.

mandamus A writ issued by a court directing the performance of specific acts.

misfeasance Improper performance of a lawful act.

mitigation of damages A reduction in **damages** because of extenuating circumstances.

negligence Failure to exercise proper care.

negotiable instrument An instrument such as a promissory note, bill of exchange, check, or security that may be transferred freely from one person to another by endorsement and delivery or, in some cases, by delivery alone.

nominal damages A small sum given for the violation of a right where no actual loss has resulted.

nonfeasance Omission or failure of an **agent** to perform some distinct duty or obligation that he has agreed to do.

nonsuit Failure to establish a case in court.

offer The communication of a proposal by the offeror (the person making the offer) to the offeree (the person receiving the offer).

overt Open; public.

patent A grant by the Federal Government to the inventor of a new device, not previously patented, of exclusive right to reproduce, use, and sell the device for 17 years.

pecuniary damages Monetary **damages**.

plat A map or drawing showing the dimensions and locations of sections of land.

pleadings The exchange of legal documents by the parties to a lawsuit— plaintiff's complaint and **defendant**'s answer.

pledge The offer of personal property as security for the payment of a debt or the performance of an obligation.

power of attorney A document authorizing another to act as one's attorney.

precedent A previous decision that may be relied on in the deciding of similar or analogous future cases.

prerogative An exclusive or special right or privilege.

proxy Authority to act for another in some matter.

punitive damages More than ordinary **damages**.

quasi-legal A matter that has some legal implications but is not genuinely legal.

quo warranto A proceeding in court used for trying title to a corporate or other type of **franchise**, or to a public or corporate office.

ratification The approval of an act that previously had not been binding.

recrimination A countercharge against the accuser.

replevin An action used to recover the possession of goods unlawfully taken or held.

rescission The cancelation of a **contract** and the restoration of each party to his original position.

restraint of trade Business practices that tend to interfere with free competition.

revocation The recall of some power or thing granted.

set-off In a suit for **damages** when both parties owe something to the other, the amount recovered is reduced by the respective debt.

slander The speaking of defamatory words tending to prejudice.

solvent Able to pay all that is owed.

sound and disposing mind   The normal condition of the mind. A phrase usually found in a will to indicate the testator's competency.

statute of frauds   A statute that calls for **contracts** and certain agreements to be in writing, in order to be enforced in court.

statute of limitations   A statute that imposes a time limit on when an action may be instituted in certain cases.

subpoena   A process that compels a witness to appear and give testimony.

subrogation   The substitution of one person for another, who then succeeds to the other's debt or claim.

surety   A promise to answer for the debt of another.

tort   A **civil** wrong other than a breach of contract.

transcript   An official copy of the original proceedings in a court trial.

trust   A relationship between persons by which one holds property for the use and benefit of the other.

turpitude   Anything done contrary to right, honesty, or modesty.

ultra vires   An act or **contract** that a corporation has no legal power to do or make.

undue influence   Influence that destroys free will and substitutes the will of another.

unilateral contract   A **contract** in which only one party makes an offer or promise of performance.

usury   An excess interest charge for the use of money; interest charged above the rate allowed by law.

venue   The place in which a case is to be tried.

verdict   The decision of the jury or of a judge acting without a jury.

waiver   The voluntary relinquishment of a known right.

writ of attachment   A writ issued for the seizure of property pending court action.

16.8   MARKETING

ad valorem   A term applied to duty on imports or exports based on their value.

advertising agency   A professional organization that prepares and places copy in media for an advertiser.

advertising copy   The text of an advertisement written as an attempt to influence prospective buyers.

advertising media   Newspapers, magazines, radio, television, direct mail, throwaways, and billboards that present advertising copy to potential buyers.

bill of lading (or B/L)   A receipt and contract from a **common carrier** for the transportation of goods.

brand name   Words or letters that identify a seller's product.

break-even point The volume at which a seller covers all his costs but makes no profit.

buying habits Recognizable patterns that indicate how people buy.

buying motives Reasons for buying goods and services.

buying power The total purchasing power of consumers in a particular product area.

buyer's commission A percentage payment given to an agent for negotiating the purchase of merchandise.

carload (c.l.) rate Freight charges for a full carload of freight; lower than the less-than-carload rate.

cartel An agreement among foreign businesses to regulate competition and fix prices.

cash discount A discount allowed a buyer for paying his bill within a specified period of time.

caveat emptor "Let the buyer beware"; implies purchase at the buyer's own risk.

cease-and-desist order Usually refers to a restraining order issued by the Federal Trade Commission to cease questionable marketing practices.

central merchandising Chain-store buying by a central office, which then distributes the merchandise to its individual stores.

certificate of origin A certificate attached to a draft covering the shipment of goods, testifying to the origin of the material or labor used in producing the merchandise.

c.o.d. (cash on delivery) Upon the delivery of goods, the buyer must make immediate payment to the bearer.

commissary A company store.

commodity exchange A market for buyers and sellers of certain commodities.

common carriers Transportation companies that offer services for hire to the general public.

consignee The receiver of a shipment of goods.

consignor The one who ships goods to a **consignee**.

consul general The top official appointed to a foreign country to facilitate the affairs and trade of the country sending him and to look out for the commercial interests of its citizens.

consumer cooperative An organized collective association that buys goods for resale within the group.

consumer goods Products used by the consumer without further processing, e.g., tools.

consumer research The analysis and classification of **buying habits, buying motives,** and other important data for the purpose of determining the consumer's willingness and ability to buy a product.

copy testing A survey made to test the selling power of advertisements.

corporate chain A group of branch stores that are controlled by the parent organization.

cost price   The actual price paid for a commodity or product.

customhouse   The building where customs and duties are paid and where vessels are cleared.

customs inspector   A person who inspects vessels and reports violations of neutrality laws to the customs collector of the port.

damageable   Capable of being broken or disfigured and thus being reduced in value.

declaration   A full report of goods so that duty or taxes may be determined.

demurrage   A freight charge levied against a receiver of goods when he fails to unload a freight car within a specified time.

departmentalizing   Organizing units in the company according to product lines.

depth interview   A probe into a respondent's attitudes or opinions.

discount house   A retail store where merchandise is sold below the usual price.

distribution cost-analysis   A study of the costs or the profitability of various distribution methods.

e.o.m. (end of month)   A term used in the processing of invoices.

exclusive agent   One who has the exclusive selling privileges for a product or products in a designated territory.

Federal Trade Commission (FTC)   The federal agency that deals with unfair marketing practices.

f.o.b. (free on board)   A term that indicates that the merchandise has been delivered to the carrier without extra charge to the buyer.

franchise agreement   A contract between a manufacturer and a **jobber** or a **retailer** that sets forth the responsibilities of the **exclusive agent**.

freight forwarders   **Middlemen** who consolidate **less-than-carload** shipments into full carloads, thereby taking advantage of special **mixed-car rates** and offering better service to the shippers.

futures contract   A **commodity exchange** transaction that involves delivery at some specified future date.

futures trading   The buying and selling of **futures contracts**.

grade labeling   A letter or number placed on the product label to indicate the quality of the contents.

group buying   Cooperative buying by independent stores.

hand-to-mouth buying   The practice of buying only enough merchandise to serve immediate needs.

information aggregation   A method of maintaining two types of detailed information in the **system** data files. Micro data maintenance is concerned with individual items whereas macro is concerned with the mass of data and what it shows as trends, share of the market, six-month reports, and so on.

information recency   The time between the occurrence of an event and the inclusion of data describing that event in the **system**.

jobber (or wholesaler)   A **middleman** who buys goods in bulk from a manufacturer or importer for resale to **retailers**.

less-than-carload (l.c.l.) rate   The freight charge for shipping less than a carload of merchandise; usually higher than the **carload rate**.

loss leaders   Items sold below cost to attract trade and increase traffic in a store.

markdown   A reduction in the selling price of an item.

market analysis   An investigation of the market to determine the quantity of the product that might be sold in it.

market information system   A continuous arrangement for collecting market facts about operational areas, such as advertising, distribution, **market research**, product development, and sales.

marketing concept   The coordination of the entire marketing process with production, finance, accounting, statistical control, and personnel.

marketing fundamentals   Five interrelated marketing functions: product design, manufacturing, advertising and sales, physical distribution, and billing and collection.

marketing mix   Involves the integration of product planning, pricing, distribution, and promotion.

market potential   The expected sales for a particular product in a given area during a particular period of time.

market research   The identification of the firm's customers, its trading area, the consumers' desires and attitudes, the sales potential for the industry and the firm, the effectiveness of a sales promotion program, and the most profitable channels of distribution.

markup   The difference between the cost price of an item and its selling price.

media   Includes newspapers, magazines, trade journals, radio, television, billboards, handouts, throwaways, or any other means by which a manufacturer or retailer may advertise his product to the buying public.

merchandise control   The analysis of sales, inventory, and prices in order to establish a profitable relationship between inventory and sales.

metropolitan area   A central city and its suburbs.

middlemen   The persons or organizations who buy in bulk from producers and sell to **retailers** or consumers.

mixed-car rate   The freight charge that a shipper pays for shipping a full car of several commodities to the same destination, somewhat less expensive than the combined **less-than-carload rate**.

motivation research   The study of people's behavior in order to understand their preferences, buying habits, and so on.

open system   One that receives and sends out messages, such as a business organization that interacts with customers, competitors, labor organizations, suppliers, and government agencies.

piggyback service   The practice of hauling loaded truck trailers on special railroad flatcars in order to reduce freight handling and increase speed of delivery.

premiums Coupons, trading stamps, box tops, or gifts of merchandise or cash given with the purchase of goods.

price discrimination An unfair trade practice in which varying prices are given to different buyers and are not based on differences in manufacturing, selling, or delivery costs.

price fixing The agreement among competitors, a monopoly, or a government agency on a set price for a product.

private brand A name that is owned and sponsored by a **jobber** or a **retailer.**

product line The group of similar products that a manufacturer has for sale.

product research The study of a product to determine if it will meet the demands of the consumer market.

promotions Special endeavors to sell the product, such as special TV exposure, free samples, refund coupons, and demonstrations, which supplement the regular advertising campaign.

raw materials The unprocessed products of farms, forests, or mines used in the manufacture of products.

receipt of goods (or r.o.g.) A term that means that the **cash discount** period begins on the day the goods are received by the buyer, not on the date the goods are shipped.

resident buyer A buying organization located in a central wholesale market to serve clients who are too far away or too small to have buyers in the market at all times.

retailer A merchant **middleman** between the manufacturer and the customer or between the **jobber** and the customer.

retail trade A general term that includes all the activities of businesses primarily engaged in selling merchandise for personal, household, or farm consumption.

sales analysis The study of the sales records of a company.

sales forecast The prediction of the amount of sales during a particular period and/or from a given area.

sales potential The share of the total market that a company hopes to corner.

sales quota A goal set to encourage a salesman or a sales force to equal or exceed a predetermined level of activity.

sales territory A defined geographic area that is assigned to a salesman, branch office, or manufacturer's agent.

shopping center A concentration of small retail establishments outside the central business district.

short sales A contract made by a seller promising future delivery of goods he does not yet have.

specialty store An establishment that sells only one class of goods.

speculation The sale and/or purchase of inventory or **futures contracts** for the purpose of making profits from price changes.

standardization   The establishment of grades for different classes of products.

stock control   The maintenance of a profitable relationship between inventories and sales by the budgeting of inventories and purchases.

stock turnover   The ratio of sales to average inventory.

survey method   The use of questionnaires to gather market data.

system   An on-going process or a set of objects with a given set of relationships between the objects and their attributes.

systems analysis   A decision-making process of systematically investigating objectives; comparing the costs, the effectiveness, and the risks associated with alternative policies or the strategies for achieving them; and formulating additional alternatives, if necessary.

terms of sale   The conditions of sale, excluding price, that accompany a price quotation.

trademark   A name, design, or symbol used by a merchant or manufacturer to identify his goods and distinguish them from those made or sold by others.

variable-price policy   A pricing policy whereby the purchase price is determined at the time of sale.

variety stores   Retail stores that carry a large variety of low-cost merchandise.

vertical integration   The single ownership of production and marketing facilities.

warehouse receipt   A document issued to the owner of goods stored in a warehouse. Usually, the receipt may be used as collateral for a loan.

zone pricing   A pricing method whereby all buyers located within a given geographic area pay the same price for goods.

16.9 PERSONNEL

ability   The capacity to perform; includes such things as attitudes, personality, configuration skill, education, and knowledge, and skills gained from experience.

accident proneness   The tendency to have more than the average number of accidents.

arbitration   The settlement by a third party of a **grievance** between an employee and his employer or between the union and the company.

attitude survey   A questionnaire survey that attempts to find out how an employee feels about his job, his **supervisor**, company policies, or the company as a whole.

authority   The right to proceed on one's own cognizance, or the power to command others in order to further departmental or company purpose.

bargaining   A meeting between a group representing the workers and a group representing management to talk things over and to make compromises in an effort to settle problems or to secure acceptance of proposed changes.

blue-collar workers   Factory workers or manual laborers.

brainstorming   The process of expressing ideas as they occur without evaluating their appropriateness as possible solutions to a problem.

bumping   The seniority principle that allows a person released in one department because of low seniority among the workers there to displace a worker in another department with less seniority than he has.

by-passing   The process of ignoring intermediate worker or supervisory levels and going to a higher or lower level for a decision or information.

centralization   An organizational policy that states that almost every decision must go through many levels for approval.

change   The phenomenon of constant introduction of new technology, processes, ideas, and so on, which cause a shift from the present condition.

clerical workers   Those employees who work mainly with routine tasks involving forms, ledgers, and periodic reports, reproduced by hand, on the typewriter, or on some other office machine; a **white-collar worker**.

communication downward   Information passing from the top level or from some lower rung of management through all subsequent levels to the lowest **subordinate**.

communication upward   Messages from lower levels being passed up through all supervisory levels to top-level management.

conference   A meeting of persons with similar interests who come together to discuss mutual problems and who tend to contribute to the discussion. Conferees usually come from a number of companies or from different departments within a company.

decentralization   A policy whereby interrelated jobs are grouped in order to complete the total operation. The workers are given autonomy to make decisions as they coordinate the effort and cooperate in reaching the goal.

delegation of authority   The delegation by a superior to a **subordinate** of the right or freedom within specified limits to solve a problem or to proceed on an assignment.

discipline   Corrective action taken to maintain standards of performance. Progressive discipline calls for increasingly severe penalties—an oral warning followed by a written one, then disciplinary layoff, and finally discharge.

distortions downward   Messages are liable to changes or distortions as they move downward if subtle shades of meaning are involved.

downtime   The pay a worker receives when he is unable to earn his regular incentive pay because of a breakdown in machinery or of his placement on special assignment.

fatigue   The product of chemical and physical changes in the nerves and muscles of the body that make it difficult to continue work.

featherbedding   The requirement by the union of unneeded workmen or the slowdown of workers to stretch the job out.

feedback   Messages that management receives from workers about their performance, understandings, insecurities, confidence in the company, and so on. Also refers to the ability of certain systems to check on their own performance and to correct it, if necessary.

first-line supervisor   The foreman or **supervisor** whose **subordinates** are production workers, office people, engineers, and so on, who are doing the actual work of the organization.

flow charts   Charts or drawings that plot the progress of a product through the plant from raw material to finished product. They may also be used to show the progress of a piece of paper or a report.

fringe benefits   All of the employee benefits—insurance, holidays, paid vacations, overtime pay, pensions, and so on—provided by the employer in addition to direct-wage payments.

grapevine   A flexible informal system of communications among employees of a company for the passage of information by word of mouth.

grievance   A complaint by an employee who disagrees with his **supervisor**'s decision in any matter concerning him personally. He may file a **grievance** claiming that management is acting in violation of either the contract or of past practice (the equivalent of the contract).

group cohesion   Unity; a group of workers may have a greater or lesser degree of unity or cohesion in adhering to group standards.

group norm   The standards of attitudes or common points of view adopted by a group of people working closely together that are shared by each member of the group. These attitudes may have no basis in fact but are accepted by the group as facts.

group standards   The standards of behavior set up by the group to which each member is pressured to conform.

human relations   The human aspect of management that attempts to understand people and help them to work together to accomplish company objectives.

incentive pay   Payment in addition to a basic wage for production exceeding a stated quota. Used in mass-production industries where the work is standardized, the units of output are measurable, and the quantity of output is proportional to employee effort and attention.

industrial relations   The area concerned with the relations between a worker and his boss. Another term for *personnel management*.

interview   Primarily thought of as the initial meeting between a prospective employee and a member of the personnel department. A meeting between a worker and his superior for a variety of reasons, the purpose being to draw the worker out, to discover what he really wants to say, and to give him a chance to express himself fully.

job classification   Jobs with roughly similar requirements of experience, training, and skill, or with similar types of tasks, are grouped as a job classification or labor grade. Each job within the classification receives the same rate of pay.

job description   A list of the duties and responsibilities of a job.

job evaluation A method of determining the relationship between wage rates that enables management to determine how much one job should pay relative to others.

job specification A statement written from the job description of specific qualifications needed by the individual who will fill the job. Such things are included as knowledge, experience, judgment, initiative, manual dexterity, accuracy, physical activity, strength, and years of schooling.

management development A continuing program of training designed to help all managers perform more adequately on their present job and to prepare for more responsible positions.

merit increases Increases in salary above the minimum rate set by the job evaluation as recognition of outstanding performance.

merit rating A periodic review of a worker by his **supervisor** on a merit-rating form on which are summarized the employee's strong and weak points. A merit-rating interview is usually held by the supervisor with the employee to communicate the results of the merit rating.

micromotion charts Slow-motion film of a worker performing a task is analyzed on micromotion charts, in order to discover the number and complexity of motions.

mobility The ability of a person to move upward in a company or to move from one job to another.

motion study The determination of the most efficient method of production; industrial engineering. The motion study of individual workers involves an analysis of how the job is performed today, whether steps may be eliminated or combined, and how the job might be performed more quickly and easily.

motivation An attempt to encourage **subordinates** to perform more effectively and efficiently in a situation in which they can satisfy their own **needs** while working toward the goals of the company.

needs Every worker desires or needs certain things for his own fulfillment; he may need money, advancement, security, a sense of accomplishment, a sense of creativity, productiveness, a certain amount of autonomy, knowledge, and certain social needs.

negative transfer The negative effect on present learning because of previous learning.

nondirective interview An **interview** in which the interviewer encourages the interviewee to express his own thoughts with considerable freedom—contrasted to directive interviewing in which the interviewer asks questions and keeps the discussion within certain limits.

open-door policy A policy whereby every employee may walk into the office of any manager at any level to voice his complaints.

open-end question A question that allows and encourages a respondent to answer in his own words.

operations chart   A diagram of the manner in which an operator performs his task and that indicates what he does with each hand. An attempt to understand the motion involved in the performance of a task in order to simplify, substitute, or rearrange the motions.

organization man   A person deeply involved in the company and its goals, who intends to stay with it and work his way up.

Parkinson's Law   The tendency to expand work to fill the time available.

paternalism   A situation in which management emphasizes how much it has given its employees, thus implying that employees might lose these benefits if they fail to show proper appreciation.

pension   An allowance for past services.

perception   The perceiving of a situation according to one's prejudices, stereotypes, and past experiences or beliefs.

power test   A test designed to measure ability that is not limited in time.

process chart   An analysis of the steps taken during the progress of a product or a piece of paper by the use of special symbols to highlight the various steps.

professional   A person who has specialized and lengthy training in a recognized field and who adheres to a code of ethics advocated by his own profession or by professionals in general. Some established professional groups are engineers, doctors, lawyers, economists, accountants, and educators, who identify themselves with a national organization that promotes high standards of performance and behavior and lengthy training as a prerequisite to membership.

profit sharing   A bonus paid to workers based on a percentage of the company's profits beyond some fixed minimum.

rate busting   The outcome when a worker ignores the level of output established by the work group and produces at a level substantially above the agreed-on ceiling.

rate range   Instead of a single wage or salary rate for the job, the company establishes a wage range that is divided into a series of steps. Rate ranges normally overlap with the highest step in one **job classification**, paying more than the lowest step in the next job classification.

recruitment   The active search for employees to fill jobs and positions at all levels.

role playing   The technique of acting out parts as one would in a real business situation.

sensitivity training   A group situation in which the discussion centers on what is happening within the group itself. Each person is helped when he becomes aware of how he actually does behave so that he can decide how he should behave.

span of control   The number of workers and/or departments for which a **supervisor** is responsible.

specialization The breaking down of a single job into several separate jobs and the restricting of an employee to a single task.

staff The *staff* employee provides advice and information to the supervisor; the *line* makes decisions.

status A certain standing within a company that is measured by title, pay, the type of work performed, symbols, size of office, secretarial assistance, and other factors.

subordinate A person who is responsible to a higher level of supervision. Every company employee is subordinate to someone; the president is subordinate to the board of directors and the board of directors is answerable to the stockholders.

supervisor The person who directs the activities of a group of workers.

symbolic meanings Meanings attached to a word that are different from person to person; no clear-cut definition is accepted by everyone.

tests A means of measuring the qualifications of job applicants as well as candidates for transfer or promotion.

time study A means of determining the standard output of a worker within a given period. These standards aid the **supervisor** to allocate work fairly, to judge a man's performance, and to estimate costs. They also serve as the basis for piece-work and incentive plans. Time studies are often made in conjunction with **motion studies**.

unemployment insurance State insurance plans that pay the worker who has been laid off and is actively looking for another job a weekly benefit for a specified number of weeks. Most of these plans are designed in such a way that companies with an unstable employment record pay more into the fund than companies with a stable record.

union shop A company in which all employees belong to the union that has won bargaining rights. The union security agreement states that an employee who fails to join within a brief probationary period must forfeit his job.

union steward An employee who represents the union within the plant, consults with supervision about proposed changes, handles **grievances**, and conducts other union business on company time. He usually does not work on the production line although he is paid by the company.

vestibule training Off-the-job training.

wage and salary administration A systematic procedure for establishing a sound compensation structure that makes use of wage and salary surveys, job evaluations, merit ratings, and incentives.

white-collar worker An office worker below the ranks of management.

workmen's compensation A public system that provides social insurance against the costs of medical care and the loss of income arising out of industrial accidents. The employer pays the insurance premium, which is based on the average number of accidents in the plant and the type of accident prevention fostered by the company.

16.10 STOCK MARKET

In Section 13.4, "Securities Transactions," many terms, in addition to those listed below, are defined in the explanation of the functions of the securities field.

arrears The term used to refer to unpaid dividends on **cumulative** preferred stock or unpaid interest on cumulative income bonds.

averaging down The practice of purchasing additional shares of a security at more favorable prices than the original commitment. The purpose is to lower the average cost of the combined purchases.

bear A person who believes that security or commodity prices will decline and liquidates a **long** position or goes *short*.

blue-chip stock A stock that has a high degree of popularity or preference and commands a high price relative to its earnings because of its stature or reputation.

blue-sky laws State laws that protect the public against securities frauds.

board room A customers' room in a broker's office where quotations are electronically posted on a board while the exchanges are open.

book value The stated value of the assets of a corporation after the deduction of all liabilities and any arrears on the preferred stock. It is usually expressed in terms of dollars per common share, after the deduction of the preferred stock, if any, at its involuntary liquidating value. It does not necessarily represent the amount that would be realized in liquidation.

borrowing demand This situation occurs when a person *short* of the market looks for stocks to borrow in order to make a needed delivery.

bull A person who believes that prices will rise and buys on that assumption.

businessman's investment An intrinsically sound security that is affected by business conditions and therefore should be watched closely.

call money Loans that are good only from day to day and are subject to demand payment at any time.

capital stock All classes of stock issued by a company. Where only one class of stock is outstanding, it is often called capital, rather than common, stock.

carrying charge The fee charged by brokers for carrying customers' securities on margin.

cats and dogs An expression used for highly speculative securities.

Class A and Class B stock A labeling device used to indicate that one stock may have voting power and the other none or that one may participate in dividends to a greater extent than the other.

convertible preferred A preferred stock that may be exchanged, at the option of the holder, before a certain time for a specified number of common shares.

cumulative A preferred stock feature that guarantees the shareholder the receipt of full dividends regardless of how long they have not been paid. Not all preferred stocks bear this feature; some are noncumulative.

distress selling   Forced sale brought about when an owner's equity in stocks purchased on margin has been impaired or eliminated by declining prices.

Dow-Jones Averages   An average price of 65 stocks—30 industrials, 20 railroads, and 15 utilities. They are indications as to whether the market has advanced or declined since the previous day.

futures   Contracts in which the seller agrees to deliver commodities, foreign exchange, or securities at a specified future date.

growth stock   The stock of a company whose sales and profits have been rising faster than those for corporations generally.

guaranteed stocks   Stocks in which the dividends are guaranteed by a company other than the one issuing them. Railroad issues of leased lines usually contain this feature.

hedging   The process of protecting a **long** transaction by means of a *short* transaction to prevent loss through price fluctuation. It is commonly practiced in grains and foreign exchange. In the commodity markets, it takes the form of selling a futures contract in an amount equal to cash purchases.

in and out   A transaction turned over quickly—within a day, a week, or even a month.

insider   A person close to a corporation who has intimate knowledge of financial developments before they become public knowledge.

intrinsic value   The value of a security based on its underlying worth. Its market value may be either higher or lower than its intrinsic value.

loan crowd   Brokers who desire to borrow or to lend stocks in connection with **short sales**.

long   The position of a person who has bought and is holding stocks or bonds, as distinguished from one who has sold **short**.

major trend   The long-term trend of prices, even though interrupted by temporary **rallies** or reactions.

melon   A stock dividend or extraordinarily large special cash dividend. Declaration of such a dividend is called *cutting a melon*.

overbought   When a weak technical market results from active speculative buying and advanced prices, speculative holders of stock who are concerned that they have overbought, tend to sell and accept the profits.

oversold   The reverse of **overbought**, particularly when a holder with short interests is anxious to cover.

overstay   A speculator is said to have overstayed his market when he has failed to accept a paper profit at its highest point.

par value   The face value assigned to a security when issued. It has nothing to do with the market value of the security. Some companies issue no par stock.

penny stocks   Those that sell for less than $1 and are quoted in cents.

portfolio   The total security holdings of an individual or an institution.

price-earnings ratio   A measure of investment values that is regarded as more reliable than straight earnings per share. Found by dividing the earnings per share into the current market price of the stock. Earnings per share are included in the company's quarterly and annual reports to stockholders.

profit taking   The realizing of profit by either the selling of a **long** holding or the covering of a **short** position.

proxy   A statement that, when signed by the registered owner, gives another person the right to vote his stock at the annual meeting.

puts and calls   Options purchased by a speculator that give him the right to decide whether to exercise them. A *put* is a right to sell 100 shares of a certain stock within a given time at a price fixed in the contract. A *call* is the right to buy 100 shares of a certain stock at a set price within a given period of time.

pyramiding   The purchase of additional securities through the use of unrealized profits as additional margin.

rally   A temporary price advance after a decline.

reaction   A temporary price decline following an advance.

rights   The privilege extended to a shareholder of subscribing to additional stock of the same or another class or to bonds, usually at a price below the market and in an amount proportional to the number of shares already held. Rights must be exercised within a time limit and may be sold if the holder does not wish to purchase additional shares.

risks   The chances taken when capital is invested. *Business risk* refers to the stability and earning power of the issuing company. *Market risk* is determined by the general market conditions that affect the saleability and market price of a security. Fluctuating interest rates create a *money rate risk*. For instance, in a period of rising interest rates, bond prices decline, and vice versa. A rise in prices of goods and services, *price level risk,* means a loss of real income to holders of bonds and preferred stock with a fixed return.

scale buying   The placing of buy orders at regular price intervals above prevailing quotations.

secondary distribution   The sale of a block of stock off the floor of an exchange by a securities firm or a group of such firms at a fixed price geared to the current market price. Firms must have the approval of their exchange to participate in a secondary distribution of a listed stock.

secular trend   The long-term trend judged to be normal.

selling against the box   Another term for a sale of stock without delivery of the certificate. As a short operation, it may be covered through the repurchase of the stock sold or delivery of certificates already owned.

short   In a declining market, a person may sell a security or commodity he does not own and buy it at a lower price later on. In the case of securities, the person borrows the securities sold to make delivery.

short covering   The purchase of securities or commodities to complete a short transaction.

special offering   A large block of stock sold in a particular market at a special time for a fixed price. Announcement is made on the exchange ticker tape of the offering at a fixed price based on the last transaction in the regular auction market. Member firms may buy the stock for customers directly from the seller's broker during trading hours. Only the seller pays a commission.

squeeze The event that occurs when a short seller is forced to cover his contract in a rising market for fear that the advance will continue.

Standard & Poor's Index An hourly stock market index based on the prices of five-hundred stocks, similar to the Dow-Jones Averages, that shows the movement of the market.

stock dividend Shares of the issuing company declared in lieu of a cash dividend.

stock purchase warrant An agreement whereby the stockholders may purchase a certain number of shares of the corporation based on the number of warrants held for a fixed price, with or without a time limit.

stock split The division of the outstanding shares of a company that results in an increase in the number of shares, usually by some round-number multiple, such as two for one or three for one. The chief purpose of a stock split is to reduce the market value of each share to make possible a wider ownership.

street certificate A stock certificate that has been endorsed in blank by the registered owner and guaranteed by a responsible broker. It may then be bought and sold without being transferred on the books of the company. Such certificates are used as collateral in margin accounts.

swings Movements up or down in security or commodity prices, business activity, money rates, and so forth. In stock, there are primary or major swings and secondary or minor swings.

technical position A condition of the market affected by immediate supply of and demand for stocks without regard to external factors.

trading market A market in which the range of price movements is relatively narrow for a considerable period of time. It has profit possibilities only for those who trade actively to take advantage of smaller price movements.

voting trust certificates A negotiable receipt for stock certificates deposited with a trustee. Stockholders retain all rights in the stock except voting power, which is delegated to the trustee. Many states limit the term of the voting trust agreement to five years.

List of Standard Abbreviations

For rules governing the use of abbreviations, see "Abbreviations," Section 10.1.

Common abbreviations of government agencies are listed at the end of the Chapter on pp. 750–752.

NOTE: There is considerable variation in the use of capitals and periods with abbreviations. In the list that follows, generally accepted practice is observed.

A

a   are (metric); ampere (see *amp.*)

@   at; to (in market reports)

A, A., A.U.   angstrom unit (of light)

A.   Army; acre(s); absolute (temperature); answer (in court writings); area

A-1   first-class

A.A.   Associate in Arts

aa   author's alterations (printing)

AAA   American Automobile Association

AAAS   American Association for the Advancement of Science

AAR   against all risks (insurance)

A.A.S.   Fellow of the American Academy (*Academiae Americanae Socius*)

AAU   Amateur Athletic Union

ab.   about; absent

A.B.   Bachelor of Arts (see *B.A.*)

ABA   American Bankers Association; American Bar Association

abbr., abbrev.   abbreviation; abbreviated

ABC   American Broadcasting Company

abr.   abridged

abs.   absolute; abstract; absent

Abs., A.   absolute (temperature)

abst.   abstract

abt., ab.   about
a.c.   alternating current
a/c, acct.   account
A/C   account current
A.C.   Air Corps
A/cs Pay.   accounts payable
A/cs Rec.   accounts receivable
accum.   accumulative
ack.   acknowledgment
act.   active; actual
Actg.   Acting (officer or official)
a/d   after date
ad   advertisement (pl. *ads*)
a.d.   before the day
A.D.   in the year of our Lord (L. *anno Domini*) (e.g., *A.D. 1972* or *1972 A.D.*)
add., ads.   address
A-D-C., ADC   Aide-de-Camp
addl.   additional
ad fin.   to the end (L. *ad finem*)
ad inf.   to infinity (L. *ad infinitum*)
ad init.   at the beginning (L. *ad initium*)
ad int., a.i.   in the meantime or meanwhile (L. *ad interim*)
adj.   adjective; adjustment (bonds)
Adj.   Adjutant
Adj. Gen., A.G.   Adjutant General
ad lib.   at one's pleasure; freely (L. *ad libitum*)
ad loc.   to or at the place (L. *ad locum*)
Adm.   Admiral, -ty
adm.   administration, -tive
Admr.   Administrator
Admx.   Administratrix
adv.   adverb
ad val.   according to value (L. *ad valorem*)
adv. chgs.   advance charges
advtg.   advertising
A.E.   Agricultural Engineer
AEC   Atomic Energy Commission
a.f., AF   audio frequency
Af., Afr.   African; Africa
aff., affd., aff'd   affirmative; affirmed
afft.   affidavit
A/1C   Airman 1st Class; A/2C; A/3C
AFL-CIO   American Federation of Labor and Congress of Industrial
   Organizations

AFRes.   Air Force Reserve
AFTR   American Federal Tax Reports
A.G., Adj. Gen.   Adjutant General
a.g.b.   a good brand
agcy.   agency
agr., ag., agri.   agriculture; agricultural
agr.   agreement
agt.   agent; against
a-h   ampere-hour
AIAA   American Institute of Aeronautics and Astronautics
AIB   American Institute of Banking
AIEE   American Institute of Electrical Engineers
AK, Alas.   Alaska
AL, Ala.   Alabama
ALA   American Library Association
alt.   altitude; alternate; alteration
Alta.   Alberta, Canada
a.m., A.M.   before noon (L. *ante meridian*)
Am.   America; American
AM   amplitude modulation (radio)
AMA   American Medical Association
Amb.   Ambassador
amp., a   ampere(s)
amp-hr.   ampere-hour
amt.   amount
AMVETS   American Veterans of World War II
a.n.   arrival notice (shipping)
anal.   analysis; analytic; analogy
anon.   anonymous
ANPA   American Newspaper Publishers Association
ans.   answer; answered
A. to O.C.   attach(ed) to other correspondence
AP   Associated Press
A/P   authority to pay or purchase; additional premium (insurance)
Apd.   assessment paid
API   American Petroleum Institute
APO   Army Post Office
app.   appendix; applied; apparatus
appd.   approved
appl.   application
approx.   approximately
appt.   appointment; appointed
Apr.   April
apt.   apartment

aq.   water; aqueous
ar., arr.   arrive
A/R   all risks; against all risks (marine insurance)
AR, Ark.   Arkansas
A.R.   Army Regulations
ARA   American Railway Association
ARC   American National Red Cross
arch.   architect; architecture
Arch.E.   Architectural Engineer
arr.   arranged
art.   article
a.s.   at sight
A.S.   Academy of Science; Apprentice Seaman
ASA   American Standards Association
A.S.A.   American Statistical Association
ASCAP   American Society of Composers, Authors, and Publishers
ASCE   American Society of Civil Engineers
asgd.   assigned
asgmt.   assignment
ASME   American Society of Mechanical Engineers
A.S.N.   Army Service Number
assn., ass'n   association
assoc.   associate
asst.   assistant
AST, AT   Atlantic Standard Time
ASTA   American Society of Travel Agents, Inc.
ASTM   American Society for Testing Materials
astr.   astronomy; astronomical
A/T   American terms (grain trade)
Atl.   Atlantic
atm.   atmosphere(s); atmospheric
at. no.   atomic number
att.   attached
attn., atten.   attention
atty.   attorney (pl. *attys.*)
Atty. Gen.   Attorney General
at. vol.   atomic volume
at. wt.   atomic weight
au.   author
Aug.   August
Aus., Austl.   Australian; Australia
AUS   Army of the United States
auth.   author; authorized
aux.   auxiliary

A.V.   Authorized Version
A/V   according to value (L. *ad valorem*)
avdp.   avoirdupois
Ave., Av.   Avenue
avg., av.   average
avn.   aviation
A/W   actual weight; all water (transportation)
A.W.G.   American wire guage
a.w.l.   absent with leave
a.w.o.l., AWOL   absent without leave
AZ, Ariz.   Arizona

B

b.   born
b7d, b10d, etc.   buyer 7 days to take up (stocks and bonds)
B.A.   Bachelor of Arts
bal.   balance
bar.   barometer; barometric
b.b.   bail bond; bill book; break bulk
BBC   British Broadcasting Corporation
bbl.   barrel(s)
bbls/day, b/d   barrels per day
B.C.   before Christ (e.g., 100 B.C.); British Columbia, Canada
B/C   bill of collection
bch.   bunch (pl. *bchs.*)
bd.   board; bond; bound
B/D   bank draft; bar draft (grain trade)
bd. ft., b. ft.   board foot or feet
Bd. of Rev.   Board of Review
bdl.   bundle
bdy.   boundary
B/E   bill of exchange; bill of entry
bet.   between
Bev.   billion electron volts
bf.   boldface
b.f.   board foot or feet
B/F   brought forward (bookkeeping)
b. hp., bhp.   brake horsepower
B/H   bill of health
bibliog.   bibliography, -er, -ical
biog.   biography, -er, -ical
biol.   biology, -ical, -ist
bk.   bank; book

bkg.   banking
bkkp.   bookkeeping
bkpt.   bankrupt
bkt, bsk.   basket(s)
B/L   bill of lading (pl. *Bs/L*)
bl.   bale(s); black
B/L Att.   bill of lading attached
Bldg.   Building
bldr.   builder
blk.   block (pl. *blks.*); black; bulk
B.L.S.   Bachelor of Library Science
Blvd.   Boulevard
b.m.   board measure
B/M   bill of material(s)
b.o.   buyer's option; back order
b/o   brought over
B.O.   branch office
Bor.   borough
bot.   bottle(s); bottom; bought
BOT   Board of Trade
bp., Bp., BP   blueprint
b.p., bp   boiling point; boiler pressure
B/P, b. pay., B. Pay.   bills payable
b.p.b.   bank post bill
b.p.d., bpd, b/d, bbls/day   barrels per day
B.Pd.   Bachelor of Pedagogy
Br.   British; Branch; Brother
B/R   bills receivable; builders' risks
b. rec.   bills receivable
Brig. Gen.   Brigadier General
Brit.   British; Britain
Bro.   Brother
Bros.   Brothers
brt. fwd., b.f.   brought forward
B.S.   Bachelor of Science
B/S   bill of sale
bsk, bkt.   basket
B/St.   bill of sight
bt.   bought; boat
BTA   Board of Tax Appeals
BTU   British Thermal Unit(s)
bu.   bushel(s)
bul.   bulletin
Bur., Bu   Bureau

bus.   business; bushels
Bus. Mgr.   Business Manager
b.v., B/v   book value
B.W.G.   Birmingham wire gauge
bx.   box (pl. *bxs.*)

C

c   carat (metric); cycle (electrical); candle
C.   Celsius; Centigrade; Congress
©, Copr.   copyright
¢, c., ct.   cent(s)
c/   case(s)
ca.   circa; about; centiare
C.A.   Chartered Accountant
C/A   capital account; credit account; current account; commercial agent
CA, Calif.   California
C a/c   current account
c.a.f.   cost, assurance, and freight
cal.   small calorie; calendar; caliber
Can.   Canadian; Canada
canc.   canceled; cancellation
cap.   capital; capacity
caps   capital letters
Capt.   Captain
cart.   cartage
cat.   catalog
C/B   cash book
c.b.d., C.B.D.   cash before delivery
CBS   Columbia Broadcasting System
cc, cc.   carbon copy; cubic centimeter
cd.   cord
cd. ft.   cord foot
c/d   carried down
C/D   certificate of deposit; consular declaration; commercial dock
c. & d.   collection and delivery
cem.   cement
cen.   center; central; century
Cen. Am., C.A.   Central America
cert., ct., ctf.   certificate, -tion; certified
cf.   compare, certificate
c/f   carried forward (bookkeeping)
c. & f.   cost and freight

C.F.C.   Consolidated Freight Classification
c.f.i.   cost, freight, and insurance
cfm (cfs)   cubic feet per minute (second)
c.f.o.   cost for orders
cg, cgm   centigram(s)
c.g.   center of gravity
C.G.   Consul General; Commanding General; Coast Guard
cge. pd.   carriage paid
ch.   chain; chapter; channel (television); chemical; chart
c.-h.   candle-hour
Ch.   Chinese; China; Chaplain; Church
CH., c.h.   customhouse; courthouse
C.H.   Clearing House
chap., chapt., ch., C. (with number)   chapter (pl. *chaps.* or *chs.*)
Ch. Clk.   Chief Clerk
Ch.E., Chem.E.   Chemical Engineer
chem., ch.   chemical, chemistry
chf.   chief
chg.   charge; change (pl. *chgs.*)
C.I.   consular invoice
c.i.f.   cost, insurance, and freight
CIR   Commissioner of Internal Revenue
cir.   circle; circular; circumference
cit.   citation; citizen
civ.   civil; civilian
ck.   check; cask
ckt.   circuit
cl   centiliter (metric)
cl.   class; classification; clause
c.l.   carload
c/l   craft loss
cld.   colored; cleared; called (bonds)
clk.   clerk
clr.   clear; clearance; color
clt.   collateral trust (bonds)
cm   centimeter (metric)
cm^2 square centimeter
cm^3, cc   cubic centimeter
c.m., cir. mils   circular mils (wire measure)
cml.   commercial
cm. pf.   cumulative preferred (stocks)
C/N   credit note; consignment note; circular note
cn.   consolidated (bonds)
CO   Commanding Officer

C/O   cash order; certificate of origin; case oil
CO, Colo.   Colorado
Co.   Company (pl. *Cos.*); County
c/o, %   carried over (bookkeeping); in care of
c.o.d.   certificates of deposit; cash on delivery (also *C.O.D.*)
coef.   coefficient (mathematics)
C. of C.   Chamber of Commerce
col.   column
Col.   Colonel; College
coll.   collection; collateral
colloq.   colloquial
coll. tr., clt.   collateral trust (bonds)
com., comm.   commerce; commission, -er; committee; communication
Comdr.   Commander
Comdt.   Commandant (Navy and Marine)
coml., cml.   commercial
Commo.   Commodore
Com'r, Comm.   Commissioner
con.   continued
conc.   concentrate
cond.   conductivity (electrical); condition
Cong., C.   Congress; Congressional
cons.   consolidated; consign, -ed, -ment
const.   constant; construction
Const.   Constitution
cont.   contract; contents; continent
contd., cont., con.   continued
Contl.   Continental
CONUS   Continental United States
conv.   convertible
coop, co-op   cooperative
Copr., ©   copyright
cor.   corner; correct, -ed
Corp.   Corporation
corr.   corrected; corresponding, -ence
Cor. Sec.   Corresponding Secretary
c.o.s.   cash on shipment
cp.   compare; coupon
c-p   candle power
C.P.A., CPA   Certified Public Accountant
CPFF   cost-plus-fixed-fee
CPI   Consumer Price Index
Cpl.   Corporal
c.p.m., cpm (cps)   cycles per minute (second)

cpn., cp.   coupon
cp. off (on)   coupon off (on) (bonds)
C.P.S.   Certified Professional Secretary
cr.   credit; creditor
C.R.   class rate; current rate; company's risk; carrier's risk
CRP   C-reactive protein
crt.   crate (pl. *crts.*)
cs   centistere (metric)
cs., c/s   cases
csc   cosecant
csch   hyperbolic cosecant
CST, C.S.T.   Central Standard Time
Ct.   court
CT, Conn.   Connecticut
CT, C.T.   Central Time
ctf., ct.   certificate (pl. *ctfs.*)
ctg.   cartage
ctn.   carton
ctr.   center; counter
cu.   cubic
cu. cm   cubic centimeter(s)
cu. ft.   cubic foot or feet
cu. in.   cubic inch(es)
cu. mi.   cubic mile(s)
cum., cm.   cumulative
cum d., cum div.   with dividend
cum. pfd., cu. pf.   cumulative preferred (stock)
cur.   current; currency
cust.   customer
cu. yd.   cubic yard(s)
cv., cvt.   convertible (securities)
cv. db.   convertible debentures (securities)
cv. pf.   convertible preferred (securities)
C.W.   commercial weight
c.w.o.   cash with order
CWO   Chief Warrant Officer
cwt.   hundredweight
CZ, C.Z.   Canal Zone

D

d   dyne
d.   date; died; density; distance; daughter

D.   Democrat; diameter
D.A.   District Attorney
d/a   days after acceptance
D/A   deposit account; documents against acceptance; discharge afloat
DAR   Daughters of the American Revolution
db   decibel (unit of sound)
dbu   decibel unit
d.b.a.   doing business as (company name)
d.b.h.   diameter at breast height
db. rts.   debenture rights (securities)
d.c.   direct current
DC, D.C.   District of Columbia
D/C   deviation clause
D.C.L.   Doctor of Civil Law
D.Cn.L.   Doctor of Canon Law
dd.   delivered
D.D.   Doctor of Divinity (honorary)
D/D   demand draft; delivered at docks; delivered at destination; dock dues
D/d   days after date
d.d. in d.   from day to day
D.D.S.   Doctor of Dental Surgery
D.D.Sc.   Doctor of Dental Science
DDT   Dichlorodiphenyltrichloroethane
D.E., D.Eng.   Doctor of Engineering
DE, Del.   Delaware
deb.   debenture
dec.   decrease; deceased; decimal; declination
Dec.   December
def.   deferred (securities); definition; defense
deg., °   degree(s)
del.   deliver, -y
Dem., D.   Democrat
dep.   deposit; deputy; depot; departure
dep. ctfs.   deposit certificates
dept.   department (pl. *depts.*)
det.   detached; detachment; detective
dev.   deviation
DEW   distant early warning (*DEW line*)
d.f.   dead freight
D.F.A.   Division Freight Agent
dft., Dft.   draft; defendant
dg.   decigram(s)
dia., diam.   diameter
diag.   diagram; diagonal

dict.   dictionary
dir.   director
dis.   discount; discharge
disch.   discharge
dist.   district; distance; distribution
div.   dividend; division (pl. *divs.*)
D.J.S.   Doctor of Juridical Science
dk.   dock; deck
dkg   dekagram (metric)
dkl   dekaliter (metric)
dkm   dekameter (metric)
dks   dekastere (metric)
dkt.   docket
dl   deciliter (metric)
DL   day letter
D/L   demand loan
dld.   delivered
D.Lit., D.Litt.   Doctor of Literature or Letters
d.l.o.   dispatch loading only
D.L.O.   Dead Letter Office
dls/shr   dollars per share
dm, decim.   decimeter(s)
D.M.D.   Doctor of Dental Medicine
D. Mus., D.M.   Doctor of Music
D/N   debit note
do.   ditto *(the same)*
D/O   delivery order
D.O.   Doctor of Osteopathy
doc.   document (pl. *docs.*)
dol., dl., $ dollar (pl. *dols.* or *dls.*)
dom.   dominion; domestic
doz.   dozen
d.p.   direct port
DP   dew point
D/P   documents against payment
D.P.H.   Doctor of Public Health
D.P.Hy.   Doctor of Public Hygiene
dr.   debit; debtor; dram
Dr.   Doctor (pl. *Drs.*); Drive
dr. ap.   apothecaries' dram(s)
dr. av.   dram(s) avoirdupois
D.R.E.   Doctor of Religious Education
D/s   days after sight

ds   decistere (metric)
D.Sc., D.S.   Doctor of Science
D.S.C.   Distinguished Service Cross
D.S.M.   Distinguished Service Medal
D.S.O.   Distinguished Service Order (British)
d.s.p.   died without issue (L. *decessit sine prole*)
DST, D.S.T.   Daylight Saving Time; Doctor of Sacred Theology
dstn.   destination
dtd.   dated
D.V.M.   Doctor of Veterinary Medicine
D/W   dock warrant
d.w.   dead weight
d.w.c.   deadweight capacity
d.w.t.   deadweight tons
dwg.   drawing
dwt.   pennyweight(s)
d.w.t.f.   daily and weekly till forbidden (advertising)
D/y   delivery
dz.   dozen

E

e   erg
E.   east
ea.   each
E.A.O.N.   except as otherwise noted
ed.   editor; education; edition (pl. *eds.*)
Ed. Note   Editorial Note
EDT, E.D.T.   Eastern Daylight Time
educ.   education, -al
e.e.   errors excepted
E.E.   Electrical Engineer
eff.   effective
e.g.   for example (L. *exempli gratia*)
EHF   extremely high frequency
el.   elevation
elec.   electric, -al, -ian, -ity
E. Long.   east longitude
E.M.   Engineer of Mines (see *M.E.*)
e.m.f.   electromotive force
e.m.p.   end of month payment
enc., encl.   enclosure(s)

encyc.   encyclopedia
end.   endorse, -d, -ment
ENE   east-northeast
eng.   engine; engineer; engraved
Eng.   England; English
engg.   engineering
engr.   engineer; engraver, -ing
Ens.   Ensign
entd.   entered
env.   envelope(s)
e.o.d.   every other day (advertising)
E. & O.E.   errors and omissions excepted
e.o.   ex officio
e.o.h.p.   except as otherwise herein provided
e.o.m.   end of month
eq.   equal; equivalent; equation
equip., eqpt.   equipment
ESE   east-southeast
esp.   especially
Esq.   Esquire
est.   establish, -ed, -ment; estimate; estate
EST, E.S.T.   Eastern Standard Time
e.s.u.   electrostatic unit
et al.   and others (L. *et alii*)
etc.   and so forth (L. *et cetera*)
et seq.   and the following (L. *et sequens*)
et ux.   and wife (L. *et uxor*)
et vir   and husband (L.)
Eur.   Europe; European
Euratom   European Atomic Energy Community
ex   out of or from (e.g., *ex warehouse, ex officio*)
ex   without or not including (e.g., *ex interest, ex dividend*)
ex.   example; extra
ex cp. or x/cp   without the coupon
ex d. or ex div.   without the dividend
exam.   examination; examined
exch.   exchange
exec.   executive
ex. fcy.   extra fancy
ex int.   without the interest
exp.   express; expense; export
expt.   experiment, -al
ex r.   ex rights or without rights
exr.   executor

exrx. executrix

ext. exterior; extended; extension; extract; external; extinct

F

F. Fahrenheit; franc(s); French

f. farad; force

f., ff. and following page(s)

f.a.a. free of all average (insurance)

F.A.A.A.S. Fellow of the American Association for the Advancement of Science

fac. facsimile

F.A.C.S. Fellow of the American College of Surgeons

F.A.G.S. Fellow of the American Geographical Society

F.A.I.A. Fellow of the American Institute of Architects

f.a.q. fair average quality; free at quay

f.a.s. free alongside ship

fath., fm., f. fathom

f.b. freight bill

fbm feet board measure

fcp. foolscap

f.c. & s. free of capture and seizure (insurance)

fcy, pks. fancy packs

f.d. free discharge; free delivery; free dispatch

f. & d. freight and demurrage

fd. fund; funding

fdg. funding (bonds)

fdy. foundry

Feb. February

Fed. Federal; Federated; Federation

fem., f. feminine; female

ff. and the following [pages]; folios

f.f.a. free from alongside; free foreign agency

Fid. Fidelity; Fiduciary

fifo first in, first out (merchandise)

fig. figure (pl. *figs.*)

fin. financial; finance; finish

Fin. Sec. Financial Secretary

f.i.o. free in and out

f.i.t. free of income tax; free in truck

FL, Fla. Florida

fl. fluid; floor

fl. dr. fluid dram

fl. oz. fluid ounce

flt. flight; fleet
fm. fathom; from; form
FM frequency modulation
fn., ftnt. footnote
fn. p., fnp fusion point
f°, fol., f. folio (pl. *ff.*)
f.o. for orders; firm offer; full out terms (grain trade)
f.o.b. free on board
f.o.d. free of damage
f.o.f. free on field (airmail)
fol. follow, -ing; folio
f.o.q. free on quay
f.o.r. free on rail
for. forward; foreign; forestry
f.o.t. free on truck
f.p., fp freezing point
F.P. floating policy; fully paid
f.p.a. free of particular average (insurance)
f. pd. fully paid
f.p.m. feet per minute
FPO fleet post office
f.p.s. feet per second; frames per second
FR full-rate (telegram and cables)
F/R freight release
FRB Federal Reserve Bank
Fri. Friday (F. in tabulations)
f.r.o.f. fire risk on freight
FRS Federal Reserve System
frt. freight
Ft. Fort
ft. foot or feet
f.t. full terms
ft-c foot-candle
ft-L foot-lambert
ft-lb. foot-pound(s)
ft/sec. feet per second
ft-tn foot-ton
fur. furlong
furn. furnished; furniture
fut. futures (exchange)
f.v. on the back of the page (L. *folio verso*)
fwd. forward
FX foreign exchange
F.Y.I. for your information

G

g   gram (metric)

g.   gold; gauge; gulf; gravity

g.a.   general average

GA, Ga.   Georgia

gal.   gallon(s)

GAW   guaranteed annual wage

GCA   ground control approach

g-cal   gram-calorie

GCD, g.c.d.   greatest common divisor

GCI   ground control intercept

G.C.T., GCT   Greenwich Civil Time

gds.   goods

g.f.a.   good fair average

G.F.A.   General Freight Agent

gen.   general; generator; genus or kind

Gen.   General (pl. *Gens.*)

geog.   geography, -ic, -ical, -er

geol.   geology, -ic, -ical, -ist

g. gr.   great gross (144 dozen)

GHQ   General Headquarters (military)

GI   government issue; general issue

gi.   gill(s)

gm.   gram(s) (*g* is preferred)

GMAT, G.M.A.T.   Greenwich Mean Astronomical Time

GMT, G.M.T.   Greenwich Mean Time

G.N.   Graduate Nurse

GNP   gross national product

G.O.P., GOP   Republican Party (Grand Old Party)

Gov.   Governor

govt.   government

G.P.A.   General Passenger Agent

g.p.m.   gallons per minute

GPO   Government Printing Office

g.p.s.   gallons per second

gr.   grain; gross

gr. wt.   gross weight

grad.   graduate, -ed, -tion

g.s.   ground speed (aviation)

Gt. Br.   Great Britain

GTC   good till canceled (brokerage order)

GTM   good this month (brokerage order)

GTW   good this week (becomes void on Saturday)

guar.   guarantee; guaranteed

H

h   henry (electricity); hours, as *8h* or *12h*
ha   hectare (metric)
h.c.f.   highest common factor
hd.   head
hdbk.   handbook
hdkf.   handkerchief(s)
hdqrs.   headquarters
hdw., hdwr.   hardware
H. Doc. (with number)   House of Representatives document
HE   high explosive
HEW   Department of Health, Education, and Welfare
hf.   half
h-f., HF   high frequency
H.F.M.   hold for money
hg   hectogram
hhd.   hogshead(s)
HI, Ha.   Hawaii; Hawaiian Islands
hist.   history, -ical, -ian
hl   hectoliter (metric)
hm   hectometer (metric)
Hon.   Honorable
hosp.   hospital
hp.   horsepower
h.p.   high pressure
h-p. cyl.   high-pressure cycle
hp-hr.   horsepower-hour
hq.   headquarters
hr.   hour
H.R.   House of Representatives; House bill (with number)
H.R.H.   His, or Her, Royal Highness
H.S.S.   Fellow of the Historical Society
ht.   height; heat
hund., C   hundred
H.W.   high water
H.W.M.   high water mark
Hwy., Hy.   Highway
hyp.   hypothesis

I

I.   Island(s); Isle(s)
IA, Ia.   Iowa
ib., ibid.   in the same place (footnote) (L. *ibidem*)

I.B.   invoice book; in bond
I.B.I.   invoice book, inwards
i.b.p., ibp   initial boiling point
I.C. & C.   invoice cost and charges
id.   the same (L. *idem*)
ID   Idaho (*also* Ida.); identification
i.e.   that is (L. *id est*)
IES   Illuminating Engineering Society
ign.   unknown; ignition
i. hp.   indicated horsepower
IL, Ill.   Illinois
ill., illus.   illustration; illustrated
ILO   International Labor Organization
imp.   improvement; implement; imperial; import, -ing, -ed, -er
imp. gal.   imperial gallon(s)
in., "   inch(es)
IN, Ind.   Indiana
Inc.   Incorporated
inc.   increase; income, -ing
incl.   inclusive; including
incog.   incognito; unknown; unofficially; in secret
ind.   industrial; industry; independent
Ind.E.   Industrial Engineer
inf.   inferior; below (L. *infra*)
init.   initial
in-lb.   inch-pound
in loc.   in the proper place (L. *in loco*)
INP   International News Photos
ins.   insurance; inspector
INS   International News Service
inst.   instant; instrument; installment
Inst.   Institute, -tion
int.   interest; interior
intl., intnatl.   international
inv.   invoice; investment; inventor, -tion
invt.   inventory
I O U   I owe you
i.p.   intermediate pressure; i-p (adj.)
i.p.s., ips   inches per second
I.Q.   Intelligence Quotient
IRC   Internal Revenue Code
iss.   issue
ital.   italics
i.v.   invoice value; increased value

J

j   joule (electricity)
J.   Judge; Justice
J.A.   Judge Advocate
J/A   joint account
J.A.G.   Judge Advocate General
Jan.   January
jato   jet-assisted takeoff
jc., jct., junc.   junction
J.C.D.   Doctor of Canon or Civil Law
J.C.L.   Licentiate in Canon Law
J.D.   Doctor of Laws
jg.   junior grade
JJ.   Justices
jnt. stk.   joint stock
jour.   journal
J.P.   Justice of the Peace
Jr.   Junior; journal
J.S.D.   Doctor of Juristic Science (law)
jt.   joint
J.U.D.   Doctor of both Canon and Civil Laws
junc., jct.   junction

K

K   karat (gold measure); kilo
K.   Kelvin (absolute scale of temperature)
kc   kilocycle
kcal   kilocalorie
kcps, kc/s   kilocycles per second
K.D.   knocked down (freight)
kg   kilogram (metric)
kg.   keg(s)
kl   kiloliter
km   kilometer
km^2 square kilometer
km^3 cubic kilometer
kn.   knot
KS, Kans.   Kansas
kt.   karat; kiloton
kv   kilovolt
kv-a   kilovolt-ampere
kw   kilowatt

kw-hr.   kilowatt-hour
KY, Ky.   Kentucky

L

l   liter (metric)
l.   line (pl. *ll.*); left; length; lumen (light measure)
L   listed (securities); fifty; lire
L.   Latin; law(s); ledger
£   pound sterling (British)
la., lge.   large
LA, La.   Louisiana
l.a.   law agent
L/A   letter of authority; landing account; Lloyd's agent
lab.   laboratory; labor
lang.   language
lat., ϕ latitude
lb.   pound(s)
lb. ap.   pound, apothecary's
lb. av.   pound, avoirdupois
lb-ft.   pound-foot
lb/ft²   pounds per square foot
lb-in.   pound-inch
lb/in²   pounds per square inch (see *p.s.i.*)
lbr.   lumber
lb. t.   pound, troy
lc.   lowercase
l.c.   in the place cited (see *loc. cit.*)
LC   deferred cable
L/C   letter of credit (pl. *Ls/C*)
l.c.l.   less than carload lot(s) (pl. *l.c.l.s.*)
l.c.m.   least common multiple
l.c.t.   long calcined ton
ldg.   loading
ldg. & dely.   landing and delivery
lds.   loads
L.D.S.   Licentiate in Dental Surgery
l.d.t.   long dry ton
lea.   league
L. Ed.   Lawyer's Edition (Supreme Court reports)
leg.   legal
legis.   legislature, -tion
lf.   lightface
LF   low frequency

l.f.   ledger folio
lge., la.   large
lg.tn., l.t. ˙ long ton(s)
l.h.   left hand
L.H.D.   Doctor of the Humanities or Doctor of Humane Letters
l-hr   lumen-hour
li.   link
L.I.   Long Island
lib.   library
Lieut., Lt.   Lieutenant (pl. *Lts.*)
lifo   last in, first out (merchandise)
lin.   linear
lin. ft.   linear foot
L.I.P.   life insurance policy
liq.   liquid; liquor
lit.   literature; literally; liter
lkg. & bkg.   leakage and breakage
LL   leased line (securities)
LL.B.   Bachelor of Laws
LL.D.   Doctor of Laws
L.M.S.C.   let me see correspondence
ln.   lien; loan
loc.   location; local
loc. cit.   in the place cited (L. *loco citato*)
log   logarithm
long.   longitude
loran   long-range navigation
lox   liquid oxygen
l.p., lp   low pressure; long-playing (records)
LPG   liquefied petroleum gas
lpw, l/w   lumens per watt
l.s.   left side
L.S.   place of the seal
l.s.t., LST   local standard time
lt.   light; left
l.t.   local time; long ton
LT   letter message (cables)
Lt., Lieut.   Lieutenant (pl. *Lts.*)
Lt. Col.   Lieutenant Colonel
Lt. Comdr.   Lieutenant Commander
ltd., Ltd.   limited; Limited (British)
Lt. Gen.   Lieutenant General
Lt. Gov.   Lieutenant Governor
Lt. (jg)   Lieutenant (junior grade) (Navy)

Lt.-V   light vessel
ltr.   letter
lv.   leave
l.w.l.   load waterline
l.w.m.   low watermark

M

m   minutes, meter (metric)
m.   noon; married; masculine; month; male
M   thousand (1,000); 2M (2,000), and so on
M.   Master (degree); Monday; Monsieur (pl. *MM.* or *Messrs.*)
ma   milliampere
m/a   my account
MA, Mass.   Massachusetts
M.A.   Master of Arts
mach.   machine; machinery
mag.   magazine; magnitude
maj.   majority
Maj.   Major
Maj. Gen.   Major General
Man.   Manhattan; Manitoba, Canada
man.   manager; manual
mar.   market; maritime; married
Mar.   Marine; March
mat.   maturity (bonds); matinee
math.   mathematics, -cian, -cal
max.   maximum
max. cap.   maximum capacity
mb   millibar
M b.m.   thousand (feet) board measure
mc   megacycle
m.c.   marked capacity
M.C.   Master of Ceremonies; Member of Congress; Military Cross
M/C   marginal credit
Mcf   million cubic feet (gas lines)
M c.f.   thousand cubic feet
mch., mach.   machine
m.c.p.s.   megacycles per second; millicycles per second
m/d   months after date
MD, Md.   Maryland
M.D.   Doctor of Medicine
M/D   memorandum of deposit
mdse.   merchandise

ME, Me.   Maine
M.E.   Mechanical Engineer; Military Engineer; Mining Engineer; Managing
  Editor
meas.   measure, -ment
mech.   mechanic, -s, -al
med.   medium; medicine; medical
memo   memorandum(s)
m.e.p., mep   mean effective pressure
meq   milliequivalent
mer.   mercantile; meridian
Messrs., MM.   Misters (Messieurs)
met.   metropolitan; meteorological; metal
metal., met.   metallurgy
Met.E.   Metallurgical Engineer
Mev.   million electron volts
Mex.   Mexican; Mexico
mf   millifarad (electricity)
mfd.   manufactured
mfg.   manufacturing
mfr.   manufacture, -r (pl. *mfrs.*)
mfst.   manifest
mg   milligram (metric)
m.g.d.   million gallons per day
mgr.   manager
Mgr., Monsig., Msgr.   Monseigneur; Monsignor
mh   millihenry
M.H.   Medal of Honor
mhcp   mean horizontal candlepower
mi.   mile(s), mill
MI, Mich.   Michigan
mid., mdnt.   midnight
Mid'n   Midshipman
mil.   military; mileage; million
min.   minute(s); minimum; minority; minister
min. B/L   minimum bill of lading
M.I.P.   marine insurance policy
misc.   miscellaneous
M.I.T.   Massachusetts Institute of Technology
mkt.   market
ml   milliliter (metric)
mL   millilambert
Mlle.   Mademoiselle (Miss)
mm   millimeter(s)
mm^2 square millimeter

mm³   cubic millimeter
Mme.   Madame (pl. *Mmes.*)
m.m.f.   magnetomotive force
mmfd   micromicrofarad
MN, Minn.   Minnesota
M.N.A.S.   Member of the National Academy of Sciences
mng.   managing
mo.   month(s) (pl. *mos.*)
MO, Mo.   Missouri
m.o.   money order; mail order
mod.   modified; moderate
mol. wt.   molecular weight
m.o.m.   middle of month
Mon.   Monday (M. in tabulations)
mot.   motor
MP   Military Police
M.P.   Member of Parliament (Britain); Mounted Police (Canada)
m.p.   melting point
M.P.C.   Member of Parliament, Canada
m.p.g., mpg   miles per gallon
m.p.h., mph   miles per hour
mr   milliroentgen
Mr.   Mister (pl. *Messrs.*)
Mrs.   Mistress or Madam (pl. *Mmes.*)
ms.,   megasecond, manuscript
MS., MSS.   manuscript; manuscripts
M/s, m/s   months after sight; meters per second
Ms.   Miss or Mrs.
MS, Miss.   Mississippi
M.S.   Master of Science
m.s.cp., mscp   mean spherical candlepower
msg.   message
Msgr., msgr.   Monsignor; messenger
M. Sgt., M/Sgt.   Master Sergeant
m.s.l.   mean sea level
MST, M.S.T.   Mountain Standard Time
Mt.   Mount; Mountain (pl. *Mts.*)
mt.   empty; megaton
MT, Mont.   Montana
MT, M.T.   mountain time
mt. ct. cp.   mortgage certificate coupon (securities)
mtg.   mortgage; meeting
mun.   municipal
mus.   museum; music; musical

m.v. market value
MV motor vessel

N

n. net; news; normal; north; noon; note; noun; number
N. north; Navy
na, NA not available
N.A., n/a no account (banking)
N.A., N.Am. North America
N.A.M., NAM National Association of Manufacturers
NANA North American Newspaper Alliance, Inc.
NAS National Academy of Sciences
nat., natl. national
naut. nautical
nav. naval; navigation
n.b., N.B. note well; take notice (L. *nota bene*)
NB, Neb. Nebraska; northbound
NBC National Broadcasting Company
NC, N.C. North Carolina
n-c, NC non callable (bonds)
N/C new charter; new crop
NCO noncommissioned officer
n.c.u.p. no commission until paid
N.C.V. no commercial value
n.d. no date; next day's delivery
ND, N. Dak. North Dakota
n.e. not exceeding
NE northeast
N.E., N. Eng. New England
NEA Newspapers Enterprise Association
NEA National Education Association; National Editorial Association
n.e.c. not elsewhere classified
NEC National Electrical Code
NED New English Dictionary (the Oxford English Dictionary)
neg. negative, -ly
n.e.s. not elsewhere specified
neut., n. neuter
n/f no funds (banking)
n.-f.e. nitrogen-free extract
n.g. no good
N.G., NG National Guard
NH, N.H. New Hampshire
n. hp., N. HP nominal horsepower

NJ, N.J.   New Jersey
n.l.   natural log or logarithm; new line
NL   night letter (telegram)
N. Lat., n. lat.   north latitude
NLT   night letter cable
NM   night message
NM, N. Mex.   New Mexico
n/m   no mark
n. mi.   nautical mile(s)
NNE   north-northeast
NNW   north-northwest
No., no., Nos., nos.   number, numbers
No., N.   North; northern
n/o   in the name of (finance)
N/O   no orders (banking)
N.O.E.   not otherwise enumerated
N.O.H.P.   not otherwise herein provided
nom.   nominal; nominative
nom. std.   nominal standard
non pros.   he does not prosecute
non seq.   it does not follow (L. *non sequitur*)
n.o.p.   not otherwise provided for
n.o.s., N.O.S.   not otherwise specified
nos.   numbers
Nov.   November
np   nonparticipating (stocks)
n.p. or d.   no place or date
N.P.   Notary Public; no protest (banking)
n/p   net proceeds
N.P.L.   nonpersonal liability
n.p.t.   normal pressure and temperature
nr.   near
n.r.   no risk; net register
n.r.a.d.   no risk after discharge
n/s, n.s.   not specified; not sufficient; new series; new style
N.S.F.   not sufficient funds (banking)
n.t.   net ton; new terms (grain trade)
nth   indefinite (e.g., *nth degree*)
n.t.p.   no title page
nt. wt.   net weight
n.u.   name unknown
nv   nonvoting (stocks)
NV, Nev.   Nevada
NW   northwest

NY, N.Y.   New York
NYC   New York City

O

o.   order; old
O   pint, apothecaries'
oa., OA   overall
o/a   on account of
OASI   old-age and survivors insurance
ob.   died (L. *obiit*)
obit.   obituary (pl. *obits.*)
O.B/L, ob/l   order bill of lading
obs.   obsolete; observatory
ob.s.p.   died without issue (L. *obiit sine prole*)
oc.   ocean; overcharge
o/c   over-the-counter; overcharge
Oct.   October
o/d   on demand; overdraft
o.d.   olive drab
o.e.   omissions excepted
OE   Old English
OED   Oxford English Dictionary
off.   office; officer
OH, O.   Ohio
OK, Okla.   Oklahoma
OK, OK'd, OK'ing, OK's   correct
Ont.   Ontario, Canada
O/o   order of
op., opp.   opinion; opposite
o.p.   out of print
O.P., OP   open, or floating, policy
op. cit.   in the work cited (L. *opere citato*)
opd.   opened (stocks)
opr.   operate, -ing, -ion(s)
opt.   optional; optician
OR, Ore., Oreg.   Oregon
o.r.   owner's risk (shipping)
o. & r.   ocean and rail (transp.)
O.R.C., ORC   Officers' Reserve Corps
ord.   ordinance; order; ordinary
org.   organization; organic
orig.   original, -ly
o/s, OS   out of stock

O/S   on sample; on sale or return
o.s. & d.   over, short, and damaged (transportation)
o.t.   overtime
o/t   old terms (grain trade); on truck
o.w., OW   one way (fare)
oz.   ounce(s)
oz. ap.   ounce, apothecaries'
oz. av.   ounce, avoirdupois
oz-ft.   ounce-foot
oz-in.   ounce-inch
oz. t.   ounce, troy

P

p.   page (pl. *pp.*); parallel; pence; per; pico (one trillionth); population; pressure
¶, ℙ   paragraph
PA,   Pennsylvania (also *Pa.*, *Penn.*, *Penna.*)
pa.   paper
p.a.   private account; particular average; by the year (L. *per annum*)
P.A.   purchasing agent; press agent; public-address system
P/A   power of attorney
P/Av.   particular average
Pac.   Pacific
P.a.C.   put and call (stock market)
p. ae.   equal parts (L. *partes aequales*)
pam.   pamphlet
paren.   parenthesis (pl. *parens.*)
part.   participating (securities); particular
pat.   patent, -ed
Pat. Off.   Patent Office
pat. pend.   patent pending
payt.   payment
PBX   telephone switchboard (private branch exchange)
pc.   piece (pl. *pcs.*)
P/C   price current; petty cash
p.c.   post card
pcl.   parcel
pct.   percent
pd.   paid; passed
per an., p.a.   by the year (L. *per annum*)
perp.   perpetual (bonds)
Per Pro., P.P.   on behalf of; by proxy (L. *per procurationem*)
pert.   pertaining

pet., petr.   petroleum

petn.   petition

pfd.   preferred (securities)

pF   picofarad (electricity)

Pfc.   private, first class

ph., PH   phase (1PH = single-phase)

Phar.D.   Doctor of Pharmacy

pharm.   pharmacist; pharmacy

Ph.B., B.Ph.   Bachelor of Philosophy

Ph.C.   Pharmaceutical Chemist

Ph.D.   Doctor of Philosophy

Ph.G.   Graduate in Pharmacy

P.I.   Philippine Islands

p. & i.   protection and indemnity

pk.   peck(s); pack, -ing; park (pl. *pks.*)

pkg.   package (pl. *pkgs.*)

Pkwy.   Parkway

p.l.   partial loss

pl.   place; plural; plate (pl. *pls.*)

P.L.   Public Law

P. & L., P/L   profit and loss

p.m.   afternoon

P.M.   Provost Marshal, afternoon

PM.   Postmaster

pm., prem.   premium

p.n., P/N   promissory note

P.O.   Post Office

PO   Petty Officer

P.O.D.   pay on delivery; payable on death

pol.   politics; political

p.o.o.   post office order

pop.   population

P.O.R., p.o.r.   pay on return

pos.   positive

pot.   potential

pow.   power

POW   prisoner of war

pp.   pages

p.p., P.P.   parcel post

ppd.   prepaid

PPI   plan position indicator

p.p.i.   parcel post insured; policy proof of interest

p.p.m.   parts per million

pr.   pair; price; printed

PR, P.R.   Puerto Rico; payroll
pref., pf.   preferred; preference; preface
prem.   premium
prep.   preposition; preparation
Pres.   President
prin.   principal
prob.   problem
prod.   product; produce, -d
Prof.   Professor (pl. *Profs.*)
pron.   pronunciation; pronounced; pronoun
prop.   property; proposition
Prot.   Protestant
pro tem.   temporarily
prov.   province; provision, -al
prox.   of the next month; proximo
pr. pf.   prior preferred (stocks)
prs.   pairs
P.S., P.P.S.   postscript; post-postscript
P/S   public sale
p.s.f., psf   pounds per square foot
psgr., pass.   passenger
p.s.i., psi   pounds per square inch
P.S.T., PST   Pacific Standard Time
pt.   part; pint; point; port (pl. *pts.*)
p.t.   private terms
P.T., PT   Pacific Time
P.T.A., PTA   Parent-Teacher Association (pl. *P.T.A.s, PTAs*)
ptg.   printing
p.t.o.   please turn over
pt. pf.   participating preferred (stocks)
pub.   public, -ation; published, -ing, -er
pur.   purchase, -r; purchasing
Pvt.   Private
p.w.   packed weight (transp.)
pwr., pow.   power
pwt.   pennyweight
P.X., p.x.   please exchange
PX   post exchange (pl. *PXs*)

Q

q   quintal (metric)
q., Q.   quart; query; question; quire

Q.E.D., q.e.d.   which was to be proved or demonstrated (L. *quod erat demon-strandum*)

Q.E.F., q.e.f.   which was to be done (L. *quod erat faciendum*)

Q.E.I., q.e.i.   which was to be ascertained (L. *quod erat inveniendum*)

qly.   quality

Q.M.   Quartermaster

qr.   quarter, -ly; quire

qt.   quart (pl. *qts.*)

qtr.   quarter, -ly

qty.   quantity

quad.   quadrant; quadrangle

ques.   question(s)

q.v.   which see (pl. *qq.v*) (L. *quod vide*)

qy.   query

R

r.   road; right

R.   Republic, -an; river; radius; Reaumur (thermometric scale)

®   Registered in U.S. Patent Office

R.A.   Rear Admiral; Royal Academy; regular army

R/A   refer to acceptor

racon   radar beacon

radar   radio detection and ranging

R. & D.   research and development

R.C.   Red Cross; Roman Catholic

R/C   reconsigned

rcd., recd.   received

rd.   road; rod; round

r.d.   running days

R.D.   rural delivery

rdp.   redemption

re   in regard to

R.E.   real estate

Rear Adm.   Rear Admiral

rec.   receipt; record; recipe

recd., rcd.   received

Rec. Sec.   Recording Secretary

ref.   reference; referred; referee; refunding

refr.   refrigerate, -ed, -ing, -or

reg.   regular; regulation; register, -ed

reg. sess.   regular session (of legislature)

R.E.O.   real estate owned (banking)

rep.   report; repeat; repair

Rep.   Republican; Republic; Representative (pl. *Reps.*)
req.   requisition; required
res.   reserve; residence; resort; resolution
ret.   retired; return
retd.   returned
rev.   review; revenue; revolution; revise, -ed, -ion
Rev.   Reverend (pl. *Revs.*)
rev. A/C   revenue account
revd., rev'd   reversed
revg., rev'g   reversing
rf., rfg.   refunding (bonds); refining (oil)
RF   radio frequency
R.F.D.   rural free delivery (see *R.D.*)
rg., reg.   registered
r.h.   right hand; relative humidity
rhp, RHP   rated horsepower
RI, R.I.   Rhode Island
R.I.   reinsurance
r. & l.   rail and lake (transportation)
r.l. & r.   rail, lake, and rail (transportation)
rm.   ream; room (pl. *rms.*)
r.m.s.   root mean square
R.N.   Registered Nurse
r. & o.   rail and ocean (transportation)
R.O.G.   receipt of goods
Rom., rom.   Roman; Romance; roman (type)
ROP   run of paper
ROTC   Reserve Officers' Training Corps
rotn. no.   rotation number
RP   reply paid (cables)
R.P.   return premium
R/p   return of post for orders
R.P.D.   Doctor of Political Science
r.p.m., rpm, r/m   revolutions per minute
R.P.O., RPO   Railway Post Office
r.p.s., rps, r/s   revolutions per second
RR   railroad (pl. *RRs*)
r.s.   right side
R.S.V.P.   please reply (F. *répondez s'il vous plait*)
rt.   right (pl. *rts.*); round trip
Rte., Rt.   Route
Rt. Rev.   Right Reverend
rva   reactive volt-ampere (see *var.*)
R/W   right of way

r. & w.   rail and water (transportation)

Ry.   railway (pl. *Rys.*)

S

s   stere (metric); seconds (e.g., *10″* or *10s*)

s.   silver; stock; shilling; son

S.   south; Senate bill (with number)

/S/   signed (before a typed signature)

s7d   seller 7 days to deliver (securities)

s/a   subject to approval; safe arrival

S.A.   South America; South Africa; Salvation Army; an incorporated company in France; a stock company in Spain.

SAE   Society of Automotive Engineers

SAGE   semiautomatic ground environment

S.A.I.   an incorporated company in Italy

S. Am.   South America, -n

s.a.n.r.   subject to approval, no risk (no risk until insurance is confirmed)

San.D.   Doctor of Sanitation

s. ap., sc., ℈   scruple, apothecaries'

s. and s.c.   sized and supercalendered

SAR   Sons of the American Revolution

Sat.   Saturday (Sa. in tabulations)

sav.   saving(s)

SB   southbound

s.b.   salesbook

S.B.   Senate Bill (State); short bill

S/B   statement of billing (transp.)

s.c.   small capital letters; same case (legal); sized and calendered; single circuit (electrical)

sc., sci.   science

sc., scil.   namely, to wit (see also *ss*)

SC, S.C.   South Carolina

S.C.   salvage charges

s. & c.   shipper and carrier

Sc.D.   Doctor of Science

sch.   schedule; school

S. Con. Res.   Senate concurrent resolution (with number)

s.cp., scp   spherical candlepower

s.d.   without date (L. *sine die*)

SD, S. Dak.   South Dakota

S. Doc.   Senate document (with number)

S.D.B.L.   sight draft, bill of lading attached

SE   southeast

sec   secant

sec., sect.   second; section (pl. *secs., sects.*)

sec., secy.   secretary

sec.-ft.   second-foot

sech   hyperbolic secant

sel.   selected, -tion

Sen.   Senate; Senator (pl. *Sens.*)

sep.   separate

Sept.   September (*Sep.* in tabulations)

seq.   the following; in sequence (pl. *seqq.*)

ser.   series; serial; service

serv.   service

sess.   session

S. & F.A.   shipping and forwarding

s.f.   sinking fund

Slc.   Seaman, first class

Sfc.   Sergeant, first class

sg., sig.   signature

S.G.   Surgeon General

sgd.   signed (see /S/)

Sgt.   Sergeant

sh.   share (pl. *shs.*)

SHF   superhigh frequency

shoran   short range (radio)

s. hp., shp   shaft horsepower

shpt.   shipment

shtg.   shortage

sh. tn.   short ton

sic   thus (Latin; no period)

sig.   signature

sin   sine (mathematics)

sing.   singular

sinh   hyperbolic sine

s.i.t.   stopping in transit (transportation)

S.J.D.   Doctor of Juridical Science (law) (see *J.S.D.*)

sk.   sack (pl. *sx*)

s.l.   salvage loss

S. Lat.   south latitude

sld.   sold; sealed; sailed

sltx, SLTX   sales tax

sm.   small

Sn., SN   Seaman

S/N   shipping note

s.o., S.O.   seller's option; shipping order; ship's option

So., S.   southern; south

soc.   society

sofar   sound fixing and ranging

sol.   solution; soluble; solicitor(s)

Sol. Op.   Solicitor's Opinion

S.O.L.   Shipowner's liability

sonar   sound, navigation and ranging

SOP   standard operating procedure

S O S   Help! (distress signal)

S.O.S.   Service of Supply (military)

sp.   species; special; spelling

s.p.   without issue (L. *sine prole;* law); single-phase

SP   shore patrol

S.P.   supra protest

SPAR   Coast Guard Women's Reserve

s.p.d.   steamer pays dues

spec.   specification(s); specimen(s)

spg.   spring (pl. *spgs.*)

sp. gr.   specific gravity

sp. ht.   specific heat

Sp. Op.   special opinion

s.p.s.   without surviving issue (L. *sine prole superstite;* law)

spt.   seaport

sp. term   special term (of court)

sq.   square (e.g., *sq. ft., sq. in.,* and so on)

sq.   the following (L. *sequens*) (pl. *sqq.*)

Sq.   Square (street)

Sr.   Senior; Señor; Sister

S. Rept.   Senate report (with number)

S. Res.   Senate resolution (with number)

SRO   standing room only

ss   namely (L. *scilicet;* law)

ss.   sections

SS.   steamship (pl. *SSs.*)

S. to S.   station to station

SSE   south-southeast

S.Sgt., S/Sgt.   Staff Sergeant

SSW   south-southwest

S.S.U.   standard Saybolt universal

St., Ste.,   Saint, Sainte (pl. SS.)

St.   Street; State; Store; Strait (pl. *Sts.*)

sta.   station; stamped (securities)

stat.   statistics; statutes

std.   standard

S.T.D.   Doctor of Sacred Theology
std. c.f.   standard cubic foot (feet)
stet   let it stand (L.)
stg.   storage; sterling
stk.   stock
Stk. Ex.   Stock Exchange
Stk. Mkt.   stock market
S.T.Lr.   Lector in Sacred Theology
st. mi.   statute mile(s)
stp.   stamped
S.T.P.   Professor of Sacred Theology
str.   steamer; store (pl. *strs.*)
S.U.   set up (freight)
sub.   substitute; suburb; subscriber, -ption
subj.   subject
subs.   subsidiary; subscription
Sun.   Sunday (*Su.* in tabulations)
sup.   superior; supply; above (L. *supra*)
supp.   supplement (pl. *supps.*)
supt.   superintendent
surg.   surgeon; surgery; surgical
s.v.   sailing vessel; under the word (L. *sub verbo*)
svc.   service
s.v.p.   if you please (F. *s'il vous plait*)
SW   southwest
S.W.   shipper's weights
S.W.G., SWG   standard wire gauge
sx   sacks
syl.   syllable(s)
syn.   synonymous
synd.   syndicate
sys., syst.   system

T

t   metric ton (*tn.* or *T.*, ordinary ton)
t.   temperature; town; troy; time
T., Tp.   township (pl. *Tps.*)
T.A.   Traffic Agent
tab.   table(s); tabulation(s)
T.A.G.   The Adjutant General
t.a.w.   twice a week (advertising)
t.b., T.B.   trial balance
TB   tuberculosis

tbsp., tbs., T.   tablespoon(s)
TC   Tax Court of the United States
T/C   until countermanded
T.D.   trust deed; Treasury Decisions
T/D   time deposit
TDN   total digestible nutrients
T.E.   Topographical Engineer; trade expenses
tech.   technical
tel.   telephone; telegraph; telegram
temp.   temperature; temporary
Ter.   Territory; territorial; terrace
tf., t.f.   till forbidden (advertising)
tg.   telegraph
tgm.   telegram
thou.   thousand
3-D   three-dimensional
Thurs., Thu.   Thursday (*Th.* in tabulations)
tkr.   tanker
T/L   time loan
t.l.o.   total loss only (marine insurance)
t.m.   true mean; trade-mark
tn., T.   ton (metric ton is *t*); town; train
TN, Tenn.   Tennessee
tn. mi.   ton mile (air freight)
T/O   transfer order
tonn.   tonnage
t.p.   title page
tr.   trust; trustee; transit; transfer; transpose
T.R.   tons registered (shipping)
trans.   translated, -tion, -tor
transp.   transportation
Treas., Tr.   Treasurer; Treasury
t.s., ts   tensile strength
T. Sgt., T/Sgt.   Technical Sergeant
tsp., t.   teaspoon(s)
TT   teletype, -writer
T.T.s.   telegraphic transfers (of money)
Tues., Tue.   Tuesday (*Tu.* in tabulations)
TV   television; terminal velocity
Twad.   Twaddell (hydrometer)
Twp.   township (see *T.*)
TWX   teletypewriter exchange
tx.   tax(es); text, -book
TX, Tex.   Texas

U

U., Univ.   University
U/A   underwriting account (marine insurance)
uc.; u.c.   uppercase
u.d., ut dict.   as directed (L. *ut dictum*)
UGT   urgent (cable)
UHF   ultra-high-frequency (television)
u.i.   as below (L. *ut infra*)
U.K.   United Kingdom
ult.   last month (L. *ultimo*); ultimate
un.   unifying; unified (bonds)
Un.   Union; United
UN, U.N.   United Nations
univ.   university; universal
unl.   unlimited; unlisted (securities)
up.   underproof (alcohols)
UP   United Press
u.s.   as above (L. *ut supra*)
U.S.   United States
U.S.A.   United States of America
USA   U.S. Army
USAF   U.S. Airforce
USAREUR   U.S. Army, Europe
U.S.C.   United States Code
USCG   U.S. Coast Guard
U.S.D.J.   United States District Judge
USMC   U.S. Marine Corps
USN   U.S. Navy
USNR   U.S. Naval Reserve
U.S.P.   United States Pharmacopeia
U.S.S.   United States Senate; U.S. ship
ut.   utilities
u.t., UT   universal time
UT, Ut.   Utah
U/w   underwriter

V

v.   volt; versus (also *vs.*); verb; volume
V.   valve; velocity
va, v-a   volt-ampere (electricity)
VA, Va.   Virginia
vac.   vacuum

val.   value; valuation
var   reactive volt-ampere
var.   variety; various; variant; variation
V.C.   valuation clause; Vice Consul
vel.   velocity
Ven.   Venerable
v.f., VF   video frequency (television)
VHF   very high frequency (television)
v.i.   see below (L. *vide infra*)
VI, V.I.   Virgin Islands
Vice Adm.   Vice Admiral
Vice Pres., V.P.   Vice President
vid.   see (L. *vide*)
VIP   very important person (pl. *VIPs*)
vis.   visibility (aviation)
viz.   namely (L. *videlicet*)
V.M.D.   Doctor of Veterinary Medicine
vol.   volume (pl. *vols.*)
v.o.p.   value as in original policy
vou.   voucher
voy.   voyage
v.p., vt. pl.   voting pool (stocks)
vs.   verse; versus
v.s.   see above (L. *vide supra*); volumetric solution
V.S.   Veterinary Surgeon
VT, Vt.   Vermont
vt.   voting (stock)
vv.   verses
v.v.   vice versa

W

w.   watt (electricity); week
W.   west
WA, Wash.   Washington (State) (Spell out Washington, D.C.)
w.a.   with average (insurance)
WAC   Women's Army Corps (pl. *WACs*)
w.a.e.   when actually employed
WAF   Women in the Air Force
war.   warrant (securities); warranted
WAVES   Women Accepted for Volunteer Emergency Service (Navy)
wb.   wheelbase
WB   waybill; westbound
w.d., wd   when distributed (securities)

w/d   warranted
W.D.   Western District
Wed.   Wednesday (*W.* in tabulations)
wf   wrong font (printing)
w.g.   wire gauge; weight guaranteed
wh, w-hr., whr.   watt-hour (electricity)
whf.   wharf
whge.   wharfage
whs.   warehouse
whsle.   wholesale
w.i.   when issued (securities)
WI, Wis.   Wisconsin
wk.   week (pl. *wks.*); work
w.l.   wave length (electricity)
W. Long.   west longitude
W/M   weight and/or measurement
WNW   west-northwest
WO   Warrant Officer
w.o.c.   without compensation
w.p.   without predjudice; weather permitting
wpc, w/c   watts per candle
w.p.p.   waterproof paper packing
w.r., wr   with rights (securities)
w. & r.   water and rail (transportation)
W.R., whr. rec.   warehouse receipt
WSW   west-southwest
wt.   weight; warrant (pl. *wts.*)
WV, W. Va.   West Virginia
w.w., ww   with warrants (securities)
W/W   warehouse warrant
WY, Wyo.   Wyoming

X

x   box(es); by (*4 × 6*); cross (*X-roads*); extra (*x-lge.*)
xc, xcp, x-c, x-cp   ex or without coupon
Xch., X   exchange
xd, xdiv., x-d, x-div.   ex or without dividend
x in., x-i, x-in., x-int.   ex or without interest
x pr., x-pr.   ex or without privileges
xr, x rts., x-rts.   ex or without rights
Xtal, xtl.   crystal
xw   ex or without warrants
XQ   cross-question

Y

yb.   yearbook
yd.   yard (pl. *yds.*)
yd², sq. yd.   square yard(s)
yd³, cu. yd.   cubic yard(s)
YMCA   Young Men's Christian Association
yr., y.   year (pl. *yrs.*); your; younger
YWCA   Young Women's Christian Association

Z

z., Z.   zone; zero; zenith distance
zool   zoology, -ical

A list of common government abbreviations follows:

ACDA	Arms Control and Disarmament
AEC	Atomic Energy Commission
AID	Agency for International Development
ARPA	Advanced Research Projects Agency (Defense)
ARS	Agricultural Research Service
BDSA	Business and Defense Services Administration
BEC	Bureau of Employees' Compensation
BIS	Bank for International Settlements
BLS	Bureau of Labor Statistics
CAB	Civil Aeronautics Board
CAP	Civil Air Patrol
CARE	Cooperative for American Remittances to Everywhere, Inc.
CCC	Commodity Credit Corporation
CCR	Commission on Civil Rights
CEA	Council of Economic Advisers
CENTO	Central Treaty Organization
CEP	Concentrated Employment Programs
CIA	Central Intelligence Agency
CMS	Consumer and Marketing Service
CONUS	Continental United States
CSC	Civil Service Commission
DASA	Defense Atomic Support Agency
EEC	European Economic Community
ESSA	Environmental Science Services Administration
FAA	Federal Aviation Agency
FAO	Food and Agriculture Organization (UN)
FAS	Foreign Agricultural Service

FBI	Federal Bureau of Investigation
FCA	Farm Credit Administration
FCC	Federal Communications Commission
FDA	Food and Drug Administration
FDIC	Federal Deposit Insurance Corporation
FHA	Federal Housing Administration
	Farmers Home Administration
FHLBB	Federal Home Loan Bank Board
FIA	Federal Insurance Administration
FMC	Federal Maritime Commission
FMCS	Federal Mediation and Conciliation Service
FNMA	Federal National Mortgage Association
FPC	Federal Power Commission
FRS	Federal Reserve System
FTC	Federal Trade Commission
GAO	General Accounting Office
GATT	General Agreement on Tariffs and Trade
GPO	Government Printing Office
GSA	General Services Administration
HEW	Department of Health, Education and Welfare
HHFA	Housing and Home Finance Agency
HUD	Department of Housing and Urban Development
IADB	Inter-American Defense Board
IAEA	International Atomic Energy Agency
ICC	Interstate Commerce Commission
	Indian Claims Commission
ICEM	Intergovernmental Committee for European Migration
IDA	International Development Association
IFC	International Finance Corporation
ILO	International Labor Organization
IRO	International Refugee Organization
IRS	Internal Revenue Service
ITO	International Trade Organization
JOBS	Job Opportunity in the Business Sector
MA	Maritime Administration
MAC	Military Airlift Command
MDTA	Manpower Development and Training Act
NAB	National Alliance of Businessmen
NARS	National Archives and Records Service
NASA	National Aeronautics and Space Administration
NATO	North Atlantic Treaty Organization
NBS	National Bureau of Standards
NIH	National Institutes of Health
NLRB	National Labor Relations Board

NMB	National Mediation Board
NOVS	National Office of Vital Statistics
NSA	National Shipping Authority
NSC	National Security Council
NSF	National Science Foundation
NYC	Neighborhood Youth Corps
OAS	Organization of American States
OECD	Organization for Economic Cooperation and Development
OEO	Office of Economic Opportunity
OEP	Office of Emergency Preparedness
OJT	On-the-Job Training Program
PBS	Public Buildings Service
PHA	Public Housing Administration
PHS	Public Health Service
RB	Renegotiation Board
REA	Rural Electrification Administration
RRB	Railroad Retirement Board
SBA	Small Business Administration
SEATO	Southeast Asia Treaty Organization
SEC	Securities and Exchange Commission
SSA	Social Security Administration
SSS	Selective Service System
SUNFED	Special United Nations Fund for Economic Development
TVA	Tennessee Valley Authority
UMTS	Universal Military Training Service (or System)
UN	United Nations
UNESCO	United Nations Educational, Scientific, and Cultural Organization
UNICEF	United Nations Children's Fund
USES	United States Employment Service
USIA	United States Information Agency
USTES	United States Training and Employment Service
VA	Veterans Administration
VISTA	Volunteers in Service to America
WHO	World Health Organization
WIN	Work Incentive Program

18

Weights and Measures

Standard weights and measures are used in measuring lengths, quantities, and volumes and in determining avoirdupois, troy, and apothecary weights. The National Bureau of Standards is responsible for setting and encouraging acceptance of these standards in the United States. The weights and measures that follow correspond to those established by the Bureau.

CONTENTS

Weights	p. 754
Avoirdupois	p. 754
Troy	p. 754
Apothecaries'	p. 754
Precious Stones	p. 754
Measures	p. 755
The Metric System	p. 755
Circular or Angular Measure	p. 755
Metric Measures—Length, Area, Volume, Cubic, and Mass	p. 756
Linear Measure—United States	p. 758
Linear Measure—Metric System	p. 758
Square Measure—United States	p. 759
Square Measure—Metric System	p. 759
Capacity—United States: Liquid and Dry Measures	p. 760
Capacity—Metric System	p. 761
Common Units	p. 761
Paper Measure	p. 761
Time Measure	p. 761
Temperature—Centigrade and Fahrenheit	p. 762
British Standard Measurement	p. 762
Common Measures and Their Metric Equivalents	p. 763
Miscellaneous Units of Measurement	p. 764
Conversion Tables—Lengths, Areas, Volumes or Capacities, Volumes or Cubic Measure, and Masses	p. 766

WEIGHTS
(The grain is the same in all systems.)

Avoirdupois Weight

27 11/32 grains = 1 dram (dr.)
16 drams = 437.5 grains = 1 ounce (oz.)
16 ounces = 7,000 grains = 1 pound (lb.)
25 pounds = 1 quarter
4 quarters or 100 pounds (U.S.) = 1 hundredweight (cwt.)
2,000 pounds = 1 short ton (T.)
2,240 pounds = 1 long ton
2,204.62 pounds = 1 metric ton
1 std. lime bbl., small = 180 lb. net
1 std. lime bbl., large = 280 lb. net

In Great Britain:

14 pounds = 1 stone
2 stone = 28 pounds = 1 quarter
4 quarters = 112 pounds = 1 hundredweight
2,240 pounds = 20 hundredweight = 1 long ton

Troy Weight

24 grains (gr.) = 1 pennyweight (pwt. or dwt.)
20 pennyweights = 480 grains = 1 ounce (oz.t.)
12 ounces = 5,760 grains = 1 pound troy (lb.t.)
1 assay ton = 29,167 milligrams, or as many
milligrams as there are troy
ounces in a ton of 2,000 lb.
avoirdupois.
3,168 grains = 1 carat
(Pure gold is 24 carats fine.   Gold marked 14 carats is 14/24 pure
gold by weight and 10/24 alloy by weight.)

Apothecaries' Weight

20 grains = 1 scruple (sc., ℈)
3 scruples = 60 grains = 1 dram (dr., ℨ)
8 drams = 1 ounce (oz., ℥)
12 ounces = 5,760 grains = 1 pound (lb.)

Weight for Precious Stones
1 carat = 200 milligrams

MEASURES

The Metric System. In the United States, Great Britain and Russia, the metric system is used mainly for scientific work whereas in most other countries it is the national system used for all measurements. The metric system is a decimal system of counting that may be learned in a few hours of study. All figures are based on a scale of tens. Metric system units are all subdivisions or multiples of the following units:

meter (m) — length
gram (g) — weight
liter (l) — capacity
are (a) — area
stere (s) — volume

To these roots, the following prefixes are attached:

pico- — 1/1,000,000,000,000
nano- — 1/1,000,000,000
micro- (μ) — 1/1,000,000
milli- (m) — 1/1,000
centi- (c) — 1/100
deci- (d) — 1/10
deka- (dk) — 10
hecto- (h) — 100
kilo- (k) — 1,000
myria- (my) — 10,000
mega- (mg) — 1,000,000
giga- — 1,000,000,000
tera- — 1,000,000,000,000

Metric abbreviations are the same for both singular and plural and are written in lower-case letters without periods. Square and cubic may be indicated by the exponents ^{2} and ^{3}. Because it is possible that in the near future the metric system will be adopted as the United States national measurement system, Figures 18–1 through 18–4, which list the U.S. system, also include the metric equivalent.

Circular or Angular Measure.

60 seconds (″)	= 1 minute (′)
60 minutes	= 1 degree (°)
30 degrees	= 1 sign (1/12 of a circle)
60 degrees	= 1 sextant (1/6 of a circle)
90 degrees	= 1 quadrant or right angle (1/4 of a circle)
360 degrees	= 1 circle (cir.)

Length

Unit	Symbol	Value in meters
Micron	μ	0.000001
Millimeter	mm	0.001
Centimeter	cm	0.01
Decimeter	dm	0.1
Meter	m	1.0
Dekameter	dkm	10.0
Hectometer	hm	100.0
Kilometer	km	1,000.0
Myriameter	Mm	10,000.0
Megameter	—	1,000,000.0

Area

Unit	Symbol	Value in sq. meters
Sq millimeter	mm^2	0.000001
Sq centimeter	cm^2	0.0001
Sq decimeter	dm^2	0.01
Sq meter (centiare)	m^2	1.0
Sq dekameter (are)	a	100.0
Hectare	ha	10,000.0
Sq kilometer	km^2	1,000,000.0

Volume

Unit	Symbol	Value in liters
Milliliter	ml	0.001
Liter	l	1.0
Kiloliter	kl	1,000.0
Also		
Centiliter	cl	0.01
Deciliter	dl	0.1
Dekaliter	dkl	10.0
Hectoliter	hl	100.0

Cubic measure

Unit	Symbol	Value in cubic meters
Cubic kilometer	km^3	10^9
Cubic hectometer	hm^3	10^6
Cubic dekameter	dkm^3	10^3
Cubic meter	m^3	1
Cubic decimeter	dm^3	10^{-3}
Cubic centimeter	cm^3	10^{-6}
Cubic millimeter	mm^3	10^{-9}
Cubic micron	μ^3	10^{-18}

Mass

Unit	Symbol	Value in grams	Unit	Symbol	Value in grams
Microgram	µg	0.000001	Dekagram	dkg	10.0
Milligram	mg	0.001	Hectogram	hg	100.0
Centigram	cg	0.01	Kilogram	kg	1,000.0
Decigram	dg	0.1	Myriagram	Mg	10,000.0
Gram	g	1.0	Quintal	q	100,000.0
			Ton	t	1,000,000.0

Figure 18-1 Metric measures—length, area, volume, cubic, and mass.

757

United States

Name	Abbreviation	Common Equivalent	Metric Equivalent
1 inch	in. or "	1,000 mils	2.54 centimeters
1 foot	ft. or '	12 inches	30.48 centimeters, 0.3048 meters
1 yard	yd.	3 feet (36 in.)	0.9144 meters
1 rod or 1 pole	rd., p.	5 1/2 yards (16 1/2 ft.)	5.0292 meters
1 furlong	fur.	40 rods or 1/8 mile (220 yds.)	201.168 meters
1 mile	mi.	8 furlongs or 320 rods (1760 yds., 5,280 ft.)	1609.3 meters 1.6093 kilometers
1 league		3 miles	4.828 kilometers

Metric System

Name	Abbreviation	Metric Equivalent	Common Equivalent
1 millimeter	mm	1/1000 m	0.03937 inches
1 centimeter	cm	1/100 m	0.3937 inches
1 decimeter	dm	1/10 m	3.937 inches
1 METER	m		39.37 inches 3.2808 feet 1.0936 yards
1 dekameter*	dkm	10 m	393.7 inches 32.8083 feet
1 hectometer	hm	100 m	328 ft. and 1 in. 109.36 yards
1 kilometer	km	1,000 m	3280.833 feet 0.62137 miles
1 myriameter	mym	10,000 m or 10 km	6.2127 miles

*also spelled decameter

Conversion of meters to feet or feet to meters:
Multiply meters by 3.28 in order to convert them to feet.
Divide feet by 3.28 in order to convert them to meters.

Figure 18-2   Linear measure.

United States			
Name	Abbreviation	Common Equivalent	Metric Equivalent
1 square inch	sq. in.		6.4516 cm²
1 square foot	sq. ft.	144 sq. in.	929.034 cm² or 0.0929 m²
1 square yard	sq. yd.	9 sq. ft. 1,296 sq. in.	0.8361 m²
1 square rod	sq. rd.	30 1/4 sq. yd. 272 1/4 sq. ft.	25.2930 m²
1 acre	A.	160 sq. rd. 43,560 sq. ft.	40.4687 ares or 0.4047 hectares
1 square mile or 1 section	sq. mi. sec.	640 acres	258.9998 hectares or 2.5900 km²
1 township	T. or Tp.	36 sq. mi.	9324.0 hectares

Metric System			
Name	Abbreviation	Metric Equivalent	Common Equivalent
1 square centimeter	cm²	1/10000 square meter	0.1550 sq. in.
1 centare (also centiare or centar)	ca	1 square meter	1550 sq. in.
1 are	a	100 square meters	119.6 sq. yd.
1 hectare (also hectar)	ha	10,000 square meters	2.4710 acres
1 square kilometer	km²	1,000,000 square meters	247.104 acres or 0.3861 sq. mi.
1 myriare	mya	10 square kilometers	3.861 sq. mi.

Figure 18-3 Square measure.

United States

Liquid Measure			
Name	Abbreviation	Common Equivalent	Metric Equivalent
1 gill	gi.	32 fluid grams; 4 fluid ounces or 7.219 cu. ins.	0.1183 liter
1 pint	pt.	4 gills or 28.875 cu. ins.	0.4732 liter
1 quart	qt.	2 pints or 57.75 cu. ins.	0.9463 liter
1 gallon	gal.	4 quarts or 231 cu. ins.	3.7853 liters
1 barrel	bbl.	31 1/2 gals. (32 gals. in some states; 42 gals. for oil)	119.238 liters
1 hogshead	hhd.	2 barrels or 63 gals.	238.476 liters
Dry Measure			
1 pint	pt.	1/2 quart or 33.60 cu. ins.	0.5506 liter
1 quart	qt.	2 pints or 67.30 cu. ins.	1.1012 liters
1 peck	pk.	8 quarts or 537.605 cu. ins.	8.8096 liters
1 bushel	bu.	4 pecks or 2150.42 cu. ins.	35.2383 liters
1 barrel	bbl.	105 dry quarts or 7056 cu. ins.	115.6260 liters

Figure 18-4 Capacity

Metric System				
Name	Abbre-viation	Metric Equivalent	Dry Measure	Liquid Measure
1 milliliter	ml	1/1000 liter	0.0610 cu. in.	0.2705 fluid dram
1 centiliter	cl	10 milliliters	0.61025 cu. in.	0.3381 fluid ounce
1 deciliter	dl	10 centiliters	6.1025 cu. in.	0.8454 gill
1 LITER	1	10 deciliters	0.9081 qt.	1.0567 quarts
1 dekaliter	dkl	10 liters	1.1351 pecks	2.64178 gals.
1 hectoliter	hl	10 dekaliters	2.8378 bushels	26.4178 gals.
1 kiloliter	kl	1 stere	1.308 cu. yds.	264.178 gals.
1 myrialiter	myl	10 kiloliters	13.80 cu. yds.	2641.78 gals.

Figure 18-4 (continued).

Common Units.

$$12 \text{ units} = 1 \text{ dozen (doz.)}$$
$$12 \text{ dozen} = 1 \text{ gross (gr.)}$$
$$144 \text{ units} = 1 \text{ gross}$$
$$12 \text{ gross} = 1 \text{ great gross (great gr.)}$$
$$20 \text{ units} = 1 \text{ score}$$

Paper Measure.

$$24 \text{ sheets} = 1 \text{ quire (qr.)}$$
$$20 \text{ quires} = 1 \text{ ream (480 sheets) (rm.)}$$
$$500 \text{ sheets} = 1 \text{ commercial ream}$$
$$2 \text{ reams} = 1 \text{ bundle (bdl.)}$$
$$5 \text{ bundles} = 1 \text{ bale (bl.)}$$

Time Measure.

$$60 \text{ seconds (sec.)} = 1 \text{ minute (min.)}$$
$$60 \text{ minutes} = 1 \text{ hour (hr.)}$$
$$24 \text{ hours} = 1 \text{ day (da.)}$$
$$7 \text{ days} = 1 \text{ week (wk.)}$$
$$14 \text{ days} = 1 \text{ fortnight}$$
$$4 \ 1/3 \text{ weeks} = \text{an average month}$$

30 days = April, June, September, November
31 days = January, March, May, July, August,
          October, December
28 days = February (except for leap year
          every four years [1972], when it
          has 29 days)
365 days = 1 common year (yr.)
52 weeks = 1 year
12 months = 1 year
366 days = 1 leap year
10 years = 1 decade
100 years = 1 century
1,000 years = 1 millennium

Temperature.

CENTIGRADE	FAHRENHEIT
0°	32° (Freezing point)
5°	41°
10°	50°
20°	68°
30°	86°
37°	98° (Normal body temperature)
40°	104°
50°	122°
60°	140°
70°	158°
80°	176°
90°	194°
100°	212° (Boiling point)

To compute Fahrenheit:

Multiply Centigrade by 1.8 and add 32.

To compute Centigrade:

Subtract 32 from Fahrenheit and divide by 1.8.

British Standard Measurement.

DISTANCE

1 kilometer = 0.621 mile	1 chain = 66 feet
1 furlong = 660 feet	1 hand = 4 inches
1 land League = 3 miles	1 mile = 1.609 kilometers

WEIGHT
1 stone = 14 lbs.
1 cwt. = 112 lbs.
1 kilogram = 2.2 lbs.

VOLUME
1 fluid ounce (Br.) = 0.961 fluid ounce (U.S.)
1 quart (Br.) = 1.201 liquid qts. (U.S.)
1 gallon (Br.) = 1.20094 gals. (U.S.)
1 bushel (Br.) = 1.032 bushels (U.S.)
1 quarter (Br.) = 8.256 bushels (U.S.)

Common Measures and Their Metric Equivalents.

COMMON MEASURE	EQUIVALENT
inch	2.54 centimeters
foot	0.3048 meter
yard	0.9144 meter
rod	5.029 meters
mile	1.6093 kilometers
square inch	6.452 square centimeters
square foot	0.0929 square meter
square yard	0.836 square meter
square rod	25.29 square meters
acre	0.4047 hectare
square mile	259 hectare
cubic inch	16.39 cubic centimeters
cubic foot	0.0283 cubic meter
cubic yard	0.7646 cubic meter
cord	3.625 steres
liquid quart (U.S.)	0.9463 liter
dry quart (U.S.)	1.101 liters
quart, imperial	1.136 liters
gallon (U.S.)	3.785 liters
gallon, imperial	4.546 liters
peck (U.S.)	8.810 liters
peck, imperial	9.092 liters
bushel (U.S.)	35.24 liters
bushel, imperial	36.37 liters
ounce, avoirdupois	28.35 grams
pound, avoirdupois	0.4536 kilogram
ton, long	1.0160 metric tons
ton, short	0.9072 metric ton

grain .   .   .   .   0.0648 gram
ounce, troy   .   .   .   . 31.103 grams
pound, troy   .   .   .   .   0.3732 kilogram

Miscellaneous Units of Measurement.

agate.   A size of type between pearl and nonpareil, approximately 5 1/2 points.

Angstrom.   One ten-billionth of a meter; used to calculate the length of light waves.

bale.   A large compact bundle of goods; used as a unit of measure for certain commodities at fixed amounts, for example, a bale of cotton weighs 500 pounds.

bushel.   A unit of dry capacity used in the United States equal to 2,219.36 cubic inches.

board foot.   A unit of quantity for lumber equal to the volume of a board 12″ × 12″ × 1″.

British Thermal Unit (BTU).   A measure of heat equal to 252 calories or 0.00029 kilowatt-hours.

cable length.   A maritime unit of length based on the length of a ship's cable and variously reckoned as equal to 100 fathoms, 1/10 of a nautical mile or 6,080 feet, or 120 fathoms.

calorie.   A unit of heat equal to the quantity of heat required to raise one gram of water from 14.5°C to 15.5°C.

carat.   An international unit of weight for precious stones equal to 200 milligrams; also used to indicate the purity of precious metals, such as 24 carats for pure gold.

chain.   Often referred to as Gunter's Chain, it is a chain of 66 feet consisting of 100 links of 7.92 inches each; the unit of length used by surveyors.

decibel.   A unit for measuring the loudness of sounds; it is equal to the smallest degree of sound detectable by the human ear. The human auditory range is about 130 decibels on a scale beginning at 1 for the faintest audible sound.

ell.   A unit for measuring cloth, such as the English ell of 45 inches, the Dutch or Flemish of about 27 inches, or the Scottish unit of about 37 inches.

fathom.   A unit of length equal to 6 feet based on the distance between the fingertips of a man's outstretched arms; used mainly for measuring the depth of water.

foot-pound.   A unit of work equal to the raising of one pound of weight through a distance of one foot against the force of gravity.

freight ton.   Cargo measuring less than 40 cubic feet per long ton or weighing less than 56 pounds per cubic foot.

great gross.   A unit of quantity equal to 12 gross or 1,728.

gross.   A unit of quantity equal to 12 dozen or 144.

hand. A unit of measure equal to 4 inches, used mainly for stating the height of horses.

hogshead. A large cask or barrel containing from 63 to 140 gallons.

horsepower. A unit of power equal in the United States to 746 watts and nearly equivalent to the English gravitational unit of the same name that equals 550 foot-pounds of work per second.

knot. One nautical mile per hour; used to express the speed of seagoing ships and of airplanes, to indicate the strength of water currents and the degree of intensity of air currents.

league. An English unit of about 3 miles.

link. One of the standardized links of a surveyor's chain, 7.92 inches long; serves as a measure of length.

magnum. A large wine bottle holding about 2/5 of a gallon.

micron. A unit of length equal to 1/1000 of a millimeter or about 0.000039 inch.

mil. A unit of length equal to 1/1000 inch or 0.0254 millimeter; used for measuring the diameter of wire.

nautical mile. Any of several units of distance used for sea and air navigation based on the length of a minute of arc of a great circle of the earth and differing because the earth is not a perfect sphere. The official international unit is 1,852 meters or 6,076.12 feet.

pica. A size of type equivalent to 12 points and a unit equal to 1/6 inch. Used in measuring composing materials, line and cut widths, and type-page dimensions.

point. A unit used to measure the size of type in printing that is equivalent to about 1/72 of an inch.

quintal. Any of various units of weight used primarily in Latin American and the Mediterranean countries; in the metric system a unit of measure equal to 220.46 pounds.

quire. A collection of 24 or 25 sheets of paper of the same size and quality, either not folded or having a single fold.

ream. Twenty quires or 480 sheets of paper, unless newsprint or book paper, which comprises 500 sheets.

span. The distance from the end of the thumb to the end of the little finger of the spread hand, or 9 inches.

stone. An official British unit equal to 14 pounds.

township. A piece of land that is bounded on the east and west by meridians 6 miles apart as its south border, has a north-south length of 6 miles, and forms one of the chief divisions of a U.S. public-land survey; 36 sections of 640 acres or 1 square mile each.

watt. A unit of electrical power equal to one volt multiplied by one ampere.

Conversion Tables. The following five tables (Figure 18–5) provide for easy conversion from one unit of measure to another.

Conversion of Lengths

	Inches to milli-meters	Milli-meters to inches	Feet to meters	Meters to feet	Yards to meters	Meters to yards	Miles to kilo-meters	Kilo-meters to miles
1	25.4	0.03937	0.3048	3.281	0.9144	1.094	1.609	0.6214
2	50.8	0.07874	0.6096	6.562	1.829	2.187	3.219	1.243
3	76.2	0.1181	0.9144	9.842	2.743	3.281	4.828	1.864
4	101.6	0.1575	1.219	13.12	3.658	4.374	6.437	2.485
5	127.0	0.1968	1.524	16.40	4.572	5.468	8.047	3.107
6	152.4	0.2362	1.829	19.68	5.486	6.562	9.656	3.728
7	177.8	0.2756	2.134	22.97	6.401	7.655	11.27	4.350
8	203.2	0.3150	2.438	26.25	7.315	8.749	12.87	4.971
9	228.6	0.3543	2.743	29.53	8.230	9.842	14.48	5.592

Example: 1 in. = 25.4 mm

Figure 18-5 Conversion tables.

Conversion of Areas

	Sq. in. to sq. cm	Sq. cm to sq. in.	Sq. ft. to sq. m.	Sq. m. to sq. ft.	Sq. yd. to sq. m.	Sq. m. to sq. yd.	Acres to hec- tares	Hec- tares to acres	Sq. mi to sq. km	Sq. km to sq. mi.
1	6.452	0.155	0.0929	10.76	0.8361	1.196	0.4047	2.471	2.59	0.3861
2	12.90	0.310	0.1858	21.53	1.672	2.392	0.8094	4.942	5.18	0.7722
3	19.35	0.465	0.2787	32.29	2.508	3.588	1.214	7.413	7.77	1.158
4	25.81	0.620	0.3716	43.06	3.345	4.784	1.619	9.884	10.36	1.544
5	32.26	0.775	0.4645	53.82	4.181	5.980	2.023	12.355	12.95	1.931
6	38.71	0.930	0.5574	64.58	5.017	7.176	2.428	14.826	15.54	2.317
7	45.16	1.085	0.6503	75.35	5.853	8.372	2.833	17.297	18.13	2.703
8	51.61	1.240	0.7432	86.11	6.689	9.568	3.237	19.768	20.72	3.089
9	58.06	1.395	0.8361	96.87	7.525	10.764	3.642	22.239	23.31	3.475

Example: 1 sq. in = 6.452 sq. cm

Figure 18-5 (continued).

Conversion of Volumes or Capacities

	Fluid ounces to cu. cm.	Cu. cm. to fluid ounces	Liquid pints to liters	Liters to liquid pints	Liquid quarts to liters	Liters to liquid quarts	Gallons to liters	Liters to gallons	Bushels to hecto-liters	Hecto-liters to bushels
1	29.57	0.03381	0.4732	2.113	0.9463	1.057	3.785	0.2642	0.3524	2.838
2	59.15	0.06763	0.9463	4.227	1.893	2.113	7.571	0.5284	0.7048	5.676
3	88.72	0.1014	1.420	6.340	2.839	3.170	11.36	0.7925	1.057	8.513
4	118.3	0.1353	1.893	8.454	3.785	4.227	15.14	1.057	1.410	11.35
5	147.9	0.1691	2.366	10.57	4.732	5.284	18.93	1.321	1.762	14.19
6	177.4	0.2092	2.839	12.68	5.678	6.340	22.71	1.585	2.114	17.03
7	207.0	0.2367	3.312	14.79	6.624	7.397	26.50	1.849	2.467	19.86
8	236.6	0.2705	3.785	16.91	7.571	8.454	30.28	2.113	2.819	22.70
9	266.2	2.3043	4.259	19.02	8.517	9.510	34.07	2.378	3.171	25.54

Example: 1 fluid oz. = 29.57 cu. cm.

Figure 18-5 (continued).

Conversion of Volumes or Cubic Measure

	Cu. in. to cu. cm.	Cu. cm. to cu. in.	Cu. ft. to cu. m.	Cu. m. to cu. ft.	Cu. yd. to cu. m.	Cu. m. to cu. yd.	Gallons to cu. ft.	Cu. ft. to gallons
1	16.39	0.06102	0.02832	35.31	0.7646	1.308	0.1337	7.481
2	32.77	0.1220	0.05663	70.63	1.529	2.616	0.2674	14.96
3	49.16	0.1831	0.08495	105.9	2.294	3.924	0.4010	22.44
4	65.55	0.2441	0.1133	141.3	3.058	5.232	0.5347	29.92
5	81.94	0.3051	0.1416	176.6	3.823	6.540	0.6684	37.40
6	98.32	0.3661	0.1699	211.9	4.587	7.848	0.8021	44.88
7	114.7	0.4272	0.1982	247.2	5.352	9.156	0.9358	52.36
8	131.1	0.4882	0.2265	282.5	6.116	10.46	1.069	59.84
9	147.5	0.5492	0.2549	317.8	6.881	11.77	1.203	67.32

Example: 1 cu. in. = 16.39 cu. cm.

Figure 18-5 (continued).

Conversion of Masses

	Grains to grams	Grams to grains	Ounces (avoir.) to grams	Grams to ounces (avoir.)	Pounds (avoir.) to kilograms	Kilograms to pounds (avoir.)	Short tons (2000 lb.) to metric tons	Metric tons (1000 kg) to short tons	Long tons (2240 lb.) to metric tons	Metric tons to long tons
1	0.0648	15.43	28.35	0.03527	0.4536	2.205	0.907	1.102	1.016	0.984
2	0.1296	30.86	56.70	0.07055	0.9072	4.409	1.814	2.205	2.032	1.968
3	0.1944	46.30	85.05	0.1058	1.361	6.614	2.722	3.307	3.048	2.953
4	0.2592	61.73	113.40	0.1411	1.814	8.818	3.629	4.409	4.064	3.937
5	0.3240	77.16	141.75	0.1764	2.268	11.02	4.536	5.512	5.080	4.921
6	0.3888	92.59	170.10	0.2116	2.722	13.23	5.443	6.614	6.096	5.905
7	0.4536	108.03	198.45	0.2469	3.175	15.43	6.350	7.716	7.112	6.889
8	0.5184	123.46	226.80	0.2822	3.629	17.64	7.257	8.818	8.128	7.874
9	0.5832	138.89	255.15	0.3175	4.082	19.84	8.165	9.921	9.144	8.858

Example: 1 grain = 0.0648 gr

Figure 18-5 (continued).

Signs and Symbols

+	plus		≐	approaches
−	minus		→	approaches limit of
±	plus or minus		∝	varies as
∓	minus or plus		‖	parallel
×	multiplied by; by (3″ × 4″)		⊥	perpendicular
·	multiplied by		∠	angle
÷	divided by		∟	right angle
=	equal to		△	triangle
≠	or ≠ ; not equal to		□	square
≈	or ≒ ; nearly equal to		▭	rectangle
≡	identical with		▱	parallelogram
≢	not identical with		○	circle; Ⓢ circles
⇔	equivalent		⌒	arc of circle
~	difference		⟂	equilateral
≅	congruent to		≜	equiangular
>	greater than		√	radical; root; square root
≯	not greater than		∛	cube root
<	less than		∜	fourth root
≮	not less than		Σ	summation sign
≧	or ≥; greater than or equal to		!	or ∟; factorial product
≦	or ≤; less than or equal to		∞	infinity
‖	absolute value		∫	integral; ∫ extended integral
∪	logical sum or union		f	function
∩	logical product or intersection		∂	or δ; differential; variation
⊂	is contained in		π	pi
⊃	excluded from		∴	therefore
∈	is a member of; dielectric constant; mean error		∵	because
			‾	vinculum (above letter)
:	is to; ratio		( )	parentheses
::	as; proportion		[ ]	brackets

{ }	braces	♀	Venus
°	degree	⊖	or ⊕ ; Earth
′	minute; prime	♂	Mars
″	second; double prime	♃	Jupiter
‴	triple prime	h	Saturn
ℋ	horsepower	♅	Uranus
Δ	increment	♇	or ♆ ; Neptune
ω	angular frequency, solid angle	♇	Pluto
Ω	ohm	♈	Aries
μΩ	microhm	♉	Taurus
MΩ	megohm	♊	Gemini
Φ	magnetic flux; farad	♋	Cancer
Ψ	dielectric flux; electrostatic flux	♌	Leo
ρ	resistivity	♍	Virgo
γ	conductivity	♎	Libra
Λ	equivalent conductivity	♏	Scorpio
ℛ	reluctance	♐	Sagittarius
⇌	electrical current	♑	Capricornus
⟨_⟩	benzene ring	♒	Aquarius
→	yields; direction of flow	♓	Pisces
⇌	reversible reaction	☌	conjunction
↓	precipitate	☍	opposition
↑	gas	△	trine
‰	salinity	□	quadrature
⊙	or ☺ ; Sun	✳	sextile
●	or ◍ ; New moon	☊	dragon's head, ascending node
☽	First quarter	☋	dragon's tail, descending node
○	or ⊗ ; Full moon	①	Ceres
☾	Last quarter	②	Pallas
☿	Mercury	③	Juno

④	Vesta	Ꜫ	scruple
◑	rain	o	pint
*	snow	ƒ℥	fluid ounce
⊠	snow on ground	ƒ ʒ	fluid dram
←	floating ice crystals	ɱ	minim
▲	hail	&	or ℰ ; and; ampersand
△	sleet	℔	per
v	frostwork	#	number (before number);
‿	hoarfrost		pounds (after number)
≡	fog	/	virgule; solidus; separatrix; shilling; per
∞	haze; dust haze	%	percent
ᛐ	thunder	®	registered in U.S. Patent Office
⦗	sheet lightning	©	copyright
☉	solar corona	c/o	care of
⊕	solar halo	a/c	account of
⦦	thunderstorm	@	at
`	direction	¢	cent
O	or ⊙ , or ⊚ ; annual	*	asterisk
∞	or ② ; biennial	†	dagger
♃	perennial	‡	double dagger
♂	or ♂ male	§	section
♀	female	☞	index
□	male, in charts	´	acute
○	female, in charts	`	grave
℞	take (L. recipe); response (church)	~	tilde
A̅A̅	or A̅, or āā; of each	^	circumflex
	(doctor's prescription)	—	macron
℔	pound	ᴜ	breve
ʒ	ounce	¨	dieresis
ʒ	dram	ꜜ	cedilla

$\wedge$	caret	$^\circ\,'\,''$	degrees, minutes, seconds of an arc
$\vee$	caron	&c	and so forth; etc.
$\sqrt{}$	check	¶	paragraph
$\sqrt[v]{}$	double check	₵	center line
$\square''$	square inches;	⬡	hexagon
$\square'$	square feet	$\langle\,\rangle$	an order set
$\#/\square''$	pounds per square inch	Π	product sign

Greek Alphabet

Name	Capital	Lower Case
Alpha	A	α
Beta	B	β
Gamma	Γ	γ
Delta	Δ	δ
Epsilon	E	ϵ
Zeta	Z	ζ
Eta	H	η
Theta	Θ	θ
Iota	I	ι
Kappa	K	κ
Lambda	Λ	λ
Mu	M	μ
Nu	N	ν
Xi	Ξ	ξ
Omicron	O	o
Pi	Π	π
Rho	P	ρ
Sigma	Σ	σ, ς
Tau	T	τ
Upsilon	Υ	υ
Phi	Φ	φ, ϕ
Chi	X	χ
Psi	Ψ	ψ
Omega	Ω	ω

Six-Year Holiday Timetable

(Includes provisions of the Uniform Holiday Bill, effective January 1, 1971)

	1972	1973	1974	1975	1976	1977
New Year's Day	S Jan 1	M Jan 1	T Jan 1	W Jan 1	Th Jan 1	S Jan 1
Lincoln's Birthday	S Feb 12	M Feb 12	T Feb 12	W Feb 12	Th Feb 12	S Feb 12
St. Valentine's Day	M Feb 14	W Feb 14	Th Feb 14	F Feb 14	S Feb 14	M Feb 14
Washington's Birthday	M Feb 21	M Feb 19	M Feb 18	M Feb 17	M Feb 23	M Feb 21
Ash Wednesday	W Feb 16	W Mar 7	W Feb 27	W Feb 12	W Mar 3	W Feb 23
Good Friday	F Mar 31	F Apr 20	F Apr 12	F Mar 28	F Apr 16	F Apr 8
Jewish Passover	Th Mar 30- / Th Apr 6	T Apr 17- / T Apr 24	Su Apr 7- / Su Apr 14	Th Mar 27- / Th Apr 3	Th Apr 15- / Th Apr 22	Su Apr 3- / Su Apr 10
Easter Sunday	Su Apr 2	Su Apr 22	Su Apr 14	Su Mar 30	Su Apr 18	Su Apr 10
Mother's Day	Su May 14	Su May 13	Su May 12	Su May 11	Su May 9	Su May 8
Memorial Day	M May 29	M May 28	M May 27	M May 26	M May 31	M May 30
Father's Day	Su June 18	Su June 17	Su June 16	Su June 15	Su June 20	Su June 19
Independence Day	T July 4	M July 4	Th July 4	F July 4	Su July 4	M July 4
Labor Day	M Sept 4	M Sept 3	M Sept 2	M Sept 1	M Sept 6	M Sept 5

Jewish New Year	S	Sept 9	Th	Sept 27	T	Sept 17	S	Sept 6	S	Sept 25	T	Sept 13
Jewish Yom Kippur	M	Sept 18	S	Oct 6	Th	Sept 26	M	Sept 15	M	Oct 4	Th	Sept 22
World Series	1st wk Oct		1st wk Oct		1st wk Oct		1st wk Oct		1st wk Oct		1st wk Oct	
Columbus Day	M	Oct 9	M	Oct 8	M	Oct 14	M	Oct 13	M	Oct 11	M	Oct 10
Veterans Day	M	Oct 23	M	Oct 22	M	Oct 28	M	Oct 27	M	Oct 25	M	Oct 31
Election Day	T	Nov 7	T	Nov 6	T	Nov 5	T	Nov 4	T	Nov 2	T	Nov 1
Thanksgiving	Th	Nov 23	Th	Nov 22	Th	Nov 28	Th	Nov 27	Th	Nov 25	Th	Nov 24
Jewish Hanukah	F	Dec 1-	Th	Dec 20-	M	Dec 9-	S	Nov 29-	F	Dec 17-	M	Dec 5-
	F	Dec 8	Th	Dec 27	M	Dec 16	S	Dec 6	F	Dec 24	M	Dec 12
Christmas	M	Dec 25	T	Dec 25	W	Dec 25	Th	Dec 25	S	Dec 25	Su	Dec 25

Legal holidays:

New Year's Day
Lincoln's Birthday
Washington's Birthday
Memorial Day
Independence Day
Labor Day
Columbus Day
Veterans Day
Thanksgiving
Christmas

Three-day Weekends:

Washington's Birthday
Memorial Day
Labor Day
Columbus Day
Veterans Day
And any other legal holiday which falls on
    Friday, Saturday, Sunday, or Monday.

D

State Holidays

Note: When the holiday falls on Sunday, the Monday following is usually observed.

ALABAMA

Jan. 1, 19
Feb. 22
Mardi Gras*
April 13, 26
June 3
July 4
Labor Day
Oct. 12
Nov. 11
Thanksgiving
Dec. 25

ALASKA

Jan. 1
Feb. 12, 22
March 30
May 30
July 4
Labor Day
General election
Oct. 18
Nov. 11
Thanksgiving
Dec. 25

ARIZONA

Jan. 1
Feb. 12, 14, 22
May 30
July 4
Labor Day
Oct. 12
Election day
Nov. 11
Thanksgiving
Dec. 25

ARKANSAS

Jan. 1, 19
Feb. 22
May 30
July 4

Labor Day
Election days
Nov. 11
Thanksgiving
Dec. 25

CALIFORNIA

Jan. 1
Feb. 12, 22
Good Friday (noon to 3 p.m.)
May 30
July 4
Labor Day
Sept. 9
Oct. 12
General election
Nov. 11
Thanksgiving
Dec. 25

COLORADO

Jan. 1
Feb. 12, 22
May 30
July 4
Aug. 1
Labor Day
Oct. 12
General election
Nov. 11
Thanksgiving
Dec. 25

CONNECTICUT

Jan. 1
Feb. 12, 22
Good Friday
May 30
July 4
Labor Day
Oct. 12
Nov. 11

Thanksgiving
Dec. 25

DELAWARE

Jan. 1
Feb. 12, 22
Good Friday
May 30
July 4
Labor Day
Oct. 12
Election day
Nov. 11
Thanksgiving
Dec. 25

DISTRICT OF COLUMBIA

Jan. 1
Inauguration Day
Feb. 22
May 30
July 4
Labor Day
Nov. 11
Thanksgiving
Dec. 25

FLORIDA

Jan. 1, 19, Arbor Day
Feb. 22
April 26
Good Friday
May 30
June 3
July 4
Labor Day
Oct. 12
Nov. 11
General election
Thanksgiving
Dec. 25

*Held on Shrove Tuesday, the day before Ash Wednesday.

GEORGIA

Jan. 1, 19
Feb. 22
April 26
June 3
July 4
Labor Day
Oct. 12
Nov. 11
Thanksgiving
Dec. 25

HAWAII

Jan. 1, 30
Feb. 12, 22
Good Friday
May 30
June 11
July 4
Labor Day
Regatta Day
Primary and
   general elections
Nov. 11
Thanksgiving
Dec. 25

IDAHO

Jan. 1
May 30
July 4
Labor Day
Nov. 11
Thanksgiving
Dec. 25

ILLINOIS

Jan. 1
Feb. 12, 22
Good Friday
May 30
July 4
Labor Day

Oct. 12
Nov. 11
Thanksgiving
Dec. 25

INDIANA

Jan. 1
Feb. 12, 22
Good Friday
May 30
July 4
Labor Day
Oct. 12
Election day
Nov. 11
Thanksgiving
Dec. 25

IOWA

Jan. 1
Feb. 12, 22
May 30
July 4
Labor Day
Nov. 11
Thanksgiving
Dec. 25

KANSAS

Jan. 1
Feb. 12, 22
May 30
July 4
Labor Day
Oct. 12
Nov. 11
Thanksgiving
Dec. 25

KENTUCKY

Jan. 1, 19, 30
Feb. 12, 22
May 30

June 3
July 4
Labor Day
Oct. 12
Nov. 11
Thanksgiving
Dec. 25

LOUISIANA

Jan. 1, 8, 19
Feb. 22
Mardi Gras in
   New Orleans, etc.*
Good Friday
May 30
June 3
July 4
Aug. 30
Labor Day
Oct. 12
Nov. 1, 11
Thanksgiving
Dec. 25
Sat. P.M.

MAINE

Jan. 1
Feb. 22
April 19
May 30
July 4
Labor Day
Nov. 11
Thanksgiving
Dec. 25

MARYLAND

Jan. 1
Feb. 12, 22
Mar. 25
Good Friday
May 30
July 4
Labor Day
Sept. 12

*Held on Shrove Tuesday, the day before Ash Wednesday;

Oct. 12
Election day
Nov. 11
Thanksgiving
Dec. 25
Sat. P.M. (local)

MASSACHUSETTS

Jan. 1
Feb. 22
March 17 (local)
April 19
May 30
June 17 (local)
July 4
Labor Day
Oct. 12
Nov. 11
Thanksgiving
Dec. 25

MICHIGAN

Jan. 1
Feb. 12, 22
May 30
July 4
Labor Day
Oct. 12
Election days
Nov. 11
Thanksgiving
Dec. 25

MINNESOTA

Jan. 1
Feb. 12, 22
Good Friday
May 30
July 4
Labor Day
Oct. 12
Nov. 11
Thanksgiving
Dec. 25

MISSISSIPPI

Jan. 1, 19
Feb. 22
April 26
June 3
July 4
Labor Day
Nov. 11
Thanksgiving
Dec. 25

MISSOURI

Jan. 1
Feb. 12, 22
April 13
May 30
July 4
Labor Day
Oct. 12
Election days
Nov. 11
Thanksgiving
Dec. 25

MONTANA

Jan. 1
Feb. 12, 22
May 30
July 4
Labor Day
Oct. 12
General election
Nov. 11
Thanksgiving
Dec. 25

NEBRASKA

Jan. 1
Feb. 12, 22
April 22
May 30
July 4
Labor Day

Oct. 12
Nov. 11
Thanksgiving
Dec. 25

NEVADA

Jan. 1
Feb. 12, 22
May 30
July 4
Labor Day
Primary election
Oct. 12, 31
General election
Nov. 11
Thanksgiving
Dec. 25

NEW HAMPSHIRE

Jan. 1
Feb. 22
Fast Day
May 30
July 4
Labor Day
Oct. 12
General election
Nov. 11
Thanksgiving
Dec. 25

NEW JERSEY

Jan. 1
Feb. 12, 22
Good Friday
May 30
July 4
Labor Day
Oct. 12
General election
Nov. 11
Thanksgiving
Dec. 25
Sats.—Bank holidays

NEW MEXICO

Jan. 1
Feb. 22
May 30
July 4
Labor Day
Oct. 12
Nov. 11
Thanksgiving
Dec. 25

NEW YORK

Jan. 1
Feb. 12, 22
May 30
July 4
Labor Day
Oct. 12
General election
Nov. 11
Thanksgiving
Dec. 25

NORTH CAROLINA

Jan. 1, 19
Feb. 22
Easter Monday
April 12
May 10, 20, 30
July 4
Labor Day
Election day
Nov. 11
Thanksgiving
Dec. 25

NORTH DAKOTA

Jan. 1
Feb. 12, 22
Good Friday
May 30
July 4
Labor Day
Oct. 12
General election

Nov. 11
Thanksgiving
Dec. 25

OHIO

Jan. 1
Feb. 12, 22
May 30
July 4
Labor Day
Oct. 12
General election (P.M.)
Nov. 11
Thanksgiving
Dec. 25
Sat. P.M.

OKLAHOMA

Jan. 1
Feb. 22
April 13, 22
May 30
July 4
Labor Day
Oct. 12
Election day
Nov. 11
Thanksgiving
Dec. 25

OREGON

Jan. 1
Feb. 12, 22
Primary Day
May 30
July 4
Labor Day
Oct. 12
General election
Nov. 11
Thanksgiving
Dec. 25

PENNSYLVANIA

Jan. 1

Feb. 12, 22
Good Friday
May 30
June 14
July 4
Labor Day
Oct. 12
General election
Nov. 11
Thanksgiving
Dec. 25
Sat. P.M.

PUERTO RICO

Jan. 1, 6, 11
Feb. 22
Mar. 22
Good Friday
April 16
May 30
July 4, 17, 25, 27
Labor Day
Oct. 12
Election day
Nov. 11, 19
Thanksgiving
Dec. 25

RHODE ISLAND

Jan. 1
Feb. 22
May 4, 30
July 4
Labor Day
Oct. 12
General election
Nov. 11
Thanksgiving
Dec. 25

SOUTH CAROLINA

Jan. 1, 19
Feb. 22
June 3
July 4

Labor Day
General election
Nov. 11
Thanksgiving
Dec. 25

SOUTH DAKOTA

Jan. 1
Feb. 12, 22
May 30
July 4
Labor Day
General election
Nov. 11
Thanksgiving
Dec. 25

TENNESSEE

Jan. 1, 19
Feb. 12, 22
March 15
Good Friday
May 30
June 3
July 4, 13
Labor Day
Nov. 11
General election
Thanksgiving
Dec. 25

TEXAS

Jan. 1, 19
Feb. 12, 22
March 2
April 21
May 30
June 3
July 4
Labor Day
Oct. 12
Nov. 11
Thanksgiving
Dec. 25

UTAH

Jan. 1
Feb. 12, 22
Arbor Day
May 30
July 4, 24
Labor Day
Oct. 12
Nov. 11
Thanksgiving
Dec. 25

VERMONT

Jan. 1
Feb. 12, 22
May 30
July 4
August 16
Labor Day
Oct. 12
Nov. 11
Thanksgiving
Dec. 25

VIRGINIA

Jan. 1, 19
Feb. 22
April 13
May 30
June 3
July 4
Labor Day
Oct. 12
General election
Nov. 11
Thanksgiving
Dec. 25

WASHINGTON

Jan. 1
Feb. 12, 22
May 30
July 4
Labor Day

Oct. 12
General election
Nov. 11
Thanksgiving
Dec. 25

WEST VIRGINIA

Jan. 1
Feb. 12, 22
May 30
June 20
July 4
Labor Day
Oct. 12
General and
    special election
Nov. 11
Thanksgiving
Dec. 25
Sat. P.M.

WISCONSIN

Jan. 1
Feb. 12, 22
May 30
July 4
Labor Day
Oct. 12
Election days
Nov. 11
Thanksgiving
Dec. 25

WYOMING

Jan. 1
Feb. 12, 22
Arbor Day
May 30
July 4
Labor Day
General election
Nov. 11
Thanksgiving
Dec. 25

Twenty-four-Hour Military Time

The following chart compares the standard 12-hour time with the equivalent 24-hour military time. Only the first hour shown illustrates how the odd minutes of an hour compare. The same system applies to all hours.

12-hour Time	24-hour Time	12-hour Time	24-hour Time
1:00 a.m.	0100	11:00 a.m.	1100
1:07 a.m.	0107	12:00 noon	1200
1:15 a.m.	0115	1:00 p.m.	1300
1:30 a.m.	0130	2:00 p.m.	1400
1:52 a.m.	0152	3:00 p.m.	1500
2:00 a.m.	0200	4:00 p.m.	1600
3:00 a.m.	0300	5:00 p.m.	1700
4:00 a.m.	0400	6:00 p.m.	1800
5:00 a.m.	0500	7:00 p.m.	1900
6:00 a.m.	0600	8:00 p.m.	2000
7:00 a.m.	0700	9:00 p.m.	2100
8:00 a.m.	0800	10:00 p.m.	2200
9:00 a.m.	0900	11:00 p.m.	2300
10:00 a.m.	1000	12:00 midnight	2400

When speaking of military time, say:

0 one hundred, for 0100
0 one 0 seven, for 0107
0 one fifteen, for 0115
0 one thirty, for 0130
0 one fifty-two, for 0152
0 two hundred, for 0200
ten hundred, for 1000
ten 0 seven, for 1007
twenty-one fifteen, for 2115, etc.

Number of Days Between Dates

From Any Day of	To the Same Day of the Next											
	Jan.	Feb.	Mar.	Apr.	May	June	July	Aug.	Sept.	Oct.	Nov.	Dec.
January	365	31	59	90	120	151	181	212	243	273	304	334
February	334	365	28	59	89	120	150	181	212	242	273	303
March	306	337	365	31	61	92	122	153	184	214	245	275
April	275	306	334	365	30	61	91	122	153	183	214	244
May	245	276	304	335	365	31	61	92	123	153	184	214
June	214	245	273	304	334	365	30	61	92	122	153	183
July	184	215	243	274	304	335	365	31	62	92	123	153
August	153	184	212	243	273	304	334	365	31	61	92	122
September	122	153	181	212	242	273	303	334	365	30	61	91
October	92	123	151	182	212	243	273	304	335	365	31	61
November	61	92	120	151	181	212	242	273	304	334	365	30
December	31	62	90	121	151	182	212	243	274	304	335	365

When February has 29 days, add one day to the figure in the chart.

Simple Interest Tables *G*

Time	1/4%	1/2%	3/4%	1%	4%	5%	6%	7%
1 Day	.0007	.0014	.0021	.0028	.0111	.0139	.0167	.0195
2	.0014	.0028	.0042	.0056	.0222	.0278	.0333	.0389
3	.0021	.0042	.0063	.0083	.0333	.0417	.0500	.0583
4	.0028	.0056	.0084	.0111	.0444	.0556	.0667	.0778
5	.0035	.0070	.0105	.0139	.0556	.0694	.0833	.0972
6	.0042	.0083	.0125	.0167	.0667	.0833	.1000	.1167
7	.0043	.0097	.0146	.0195	.0778	.0972	.1167	.1362
8	.0056	.0111	.0167	.0223	.0889	.1111	.1333	.1556
9	.0063	.0125	.0188	.0250	.1000	.1250	.1500	.1750
10	.0070	.0139	.0209	.0278	.1111	.1389	.1667	.1945
1 Month	.0208	.0417	.0625	.0833	.3333	.4167	.5000	.5833
2	.0417	.0833	.1250	.1667	.6667	.8333	1.0000	1.1667
3	.0625	.1250	.1875	.2500	1.0000	1.2500	1.5000	1.7500
4	.0833	.1667	.2500	.3333	1.3333	1.6667	2.0000	2.3333
5	.1042	.2083	.3125	.4167	1.6667	2.0833	2.5000	2.9167
6	.1250	.2500	.3750	.5000	2.0000	2.5000	3.0000	3.5000

Example: To find interest at 5 3/4% for 7 months and 20 days

	5%	3/4%
Add intererest for 6 months	2.5000	.3750
1 month	.4160	.0625
10 days	.1389	.0209
10 days	.1389	.0209
	3.1938	.4793
	.4793	
	3.6731	

Interest on $100 at 5 3/4% for 7 months and 20 days = $3.67

H

Decimal Equivalents of Fractions

	1	2	3	4	5	6	7	8	9	10	11	12	13	14	15	16
2nds	.5															
3rds	.3333	.6667														
4ths	.25	.5	.75													
5ths	.2	.4	.6	.8												
6ths	.1667	.3333	.5	.6667	.8333											
7ths	.1429	.2857	.4296	.5714	.7143	.8571										
8ths	.125	.25	.375	.5	.625	.75	.875									
9ths	.1111	.2222	.3333	.4444	.5556	.6667	.7778	.8889								
10ths	.1	.2	.3	.4	.5	.6	.7	.8	.9							
11ths	.0909	.1818	.2727	.3636	.4545	.5455	.6364	.7273	.8182	.9091						
12ths	.0833	.1667	.25	.3333	.4167	.5	.5833	.6667	.75	.8333	.9167					
13ths	.0769	.1538	.2308	.3977	.3846	.4615	.5385	.6154	.6923	.7692	.8462	.9231				
14ths	.0714	.1429	.2143	.2857	.3571	.4286	.5	.5714	.6429	.7143	.7857	.8571	.9286			
15ths	.0667	.1333	.2	.2667	.3333	.4	.4667	.5333	.6	.6667	.7333	.8	.8667	.9333		
16ths	.0625	.125	.1875	.25	.3125	.375	.4375	.5	.5626	.625	.6875	.75	.8125	.875	.9375	1.

Common Volume Formulas

l

Figure	Formula	Meaning of Letters
Rectangle	$A = ab$	a = base, b = height
Square	$A = a^2$	a = one side
Triangle	$A = \dfrac{ab}{2}$	a = base, b = height
Parallelogram	$A = ab$	a = base, b = height
Regular pentagon	$A = 1.720a^2$	a = one side
Regular hexagon	$A = 2.598a^2$	a = one side
Regular octagon	$A = 4.828a^2$	a = one side
Circle	$A = \pi r^2$	$\pi = 3.1416$, r = radius

J

Common Area Formulas

Figure	Formula	Meaning of Letters
Cube	$V = a^3$	a = one side
Pyramid	$V = \dfrac{ah}{3}$	a = area of base, h = height
Cylinder	$V = \pi r^2 h$	π = 3.1416, h = height, r = radius of the base
Cone	$V = \dfrac{\pi r^2 h}{3}$	π = 3.1416, r = radius of the base, h = height
Sphere	$V = \dfrac{4\pi r^3}{3}$	π = 3.1416, r = radius

Index

Abbreviations, 94–95, 110, 205, 221, 355, 362–65, 372, 381, 709–52
  capitalization of, 363
  company names, 365
  dates, numbers, time, 205
  diagonal, use with, 364
  division of, 381
  footnotes, 221
  general rules, 362–65
  government, 750–52
  individual's name, 365
  inside address of letters, 94–95
  list of, 709–50
  misuses, 365
  numbers with, 372
  periods with, 355, 363–64
  plurals of, 364
  spacing of, 363
  states with ZIP code, 110
  titles, 364–65
Absenteeism, 41
Accounting terms, 657–62
Acknowledgments, 165, 174–77
Address lines, military, 120–23
Addresses, 93–96, 106–10, 134–43
  envelope, 106–10
  forms of, 134–43
  general practices, 134–35
  important titles in, 137–43
  inside address, 93–96
  military, 135–36
  return address, 108 (figure)
  special titles in, 135–37
  titles in, 134–43
  ZIP Code use, 109–10
Addressing machines, 441
Adjectives, 320–21
Administrative assistant, 25–40, 144–59, 164–74, 194–210, 238–65, 409–83, 657–708
  data processing, 194–210
  dictation techniques, 155–59
  dictionary of business terms, 657–708
  duplicating and copying, 431–41
  improving correspondence procedures, 164–74
  letter writing, 144–55
  records management, 409–31
  reports, 238–65
  supervision, 25–40

telephone and wire services, 442–66
  travel arrangements, 466–83
Adverbs, 321–22
Agenda, 57–58
Airmail, 631, 645, 646 (table)
Alphabetizing, 410–15
Annuities, 520
Apostrophe, 340–41
Appointments and visitors, 4–11, 177
  business associates, 9
  calendar and schedules, 5–7
  drop-in visitors, 8–9
  ending the visit, 9–10
  greeting visitors, 8–11
  hosting visitors, 10–11
  interruptions, 9
  letters setting up, 177
  luncheons, 5
  making appointments, 4–5
  records of, 5–8
  refreshments, 9
Area formulas, 788
Automation, impact of, 2–3

Banking procedures, 484–94
  cashing checks, 490
  check writing, 485–86
  checking accounts, 485–90
  corrections or changes, 486
  deposits, 490–91
  endorsements, 486–87
  reconciling bank statement, 488–89
  savings accounts, 491–94
  stopping payment, 487–88
Banking services, 494–95
Banking terms, 662–68
Bibliographies, 226–28, 261
Blueline, 438–39
Bonds, 521–23
Brackets, 341
Brokers and dealers, 525
Business expenses, tax deductible, 552–54
Business terms, 657–708

Calendars, 6 (figure)
Capitalization, 94, 365–72
  calendar periods, 366
  company name, 94, 365
  compound proper names, 366
  departments in company, 366

Capitalization (*cont.*)
  derivatives of proper names, 366–67
  emphasis, 367
  geographic names, 367
  governmental units, 367
  headings and titles, 367–68
  historical periods, 368
  hyphenated words, 368
  legal references, 369
  letter parts, 369
  literary usage, 369
  numerical and alphabetical references, 369
  prefixed names, 369–70
  proper names, 370
  publications, 370
  quotations, 358, 370
  religious names, 370
  shortened names, 370–71
  the, 371
  titles of persons, 371
  trade names, 372
Capitals after colon, 342
Carbon paper, 391–92, 436
Centrex telephone service, 442–43
Chambers of commerce abroad, 591–92
Charts, *see* Graphs and charts
Checking accounts, 485–91
  deposits, 490–91
  endorsing checks, 486–87
  making changes on checks, 486
  reconciling bank statement, 488–89
  signing checks, 486
  stopping payment, 487–88
  writing checks, 485–86
Civic titles, 134–43
Classified government information, 116–33, 460–63
Colon, 95, 241–42
Comma, 343–47, 373
Communication, 32–33
  empathy, 32–33
  feedback, 32–33
  in supervision, 32–33
  two-way, 32–33
Company car, use of, 478
Company documents, security of, 129
Company mail, 624–25 (*figure*)
Company name, 365
Comparison, adjectives and adverbs, 320–22
Complimentary close, 98–99
Compound words with hyphen, 349–53
Computers, *see* Data processing
Conciseness, 249
Conferences and meetings, 19, 20–25 51–78, *see also* Conventions
  agenda, 57–58

arrangements, 52–60
chairing a meeting, 22–23
conference calls, 19
dictionary of conference terms, 21 (*figure*)
duties during meeting, 59
formal, 55–60
giving a talk, 23–24
informal, 52–54
introductions, 24–25
minutes and notes, 59, 60 (*figure*)
parliamentary procedure, 60–65
participant's responsibility, 20–22
post–meeting functions, 56–60
preliminary plans, 55–58
types of, 51–52
Confidential information, 41–42
Consumer Credit Protection Act, 496–97
Conventions, 78–85, *see also* Conferences and meetings
  audio-visual equipment, 83
  chairman's duties, 78–79
  exhibits, 85
  food service, 84
  hospitality, 82
  hotel liaison, 80–81
  location, 79–80
  meeting rooms, 81
  office arrangements, 81
  planning, 79
  platform, 83
  post-convention duties, 85
  printing and duplicating, 81
  publicity, 85
  registration, 81–82
  staff assistance, 84
Copytron, 437–38
Correspondence, 164–74, *see also* Letters
  acknowledgments, 165
  copies, 165
  follow-ups, 165–66
  form letters, 166–68
  handwritten, 167–69
  improving procedures, 164–74
  printed enclosures, 169
  reply copy, 169
  return address and telephone number, 169
  return envelope, 169
  routing slips, 169
  sheet size, 169
  speed letters, 171
  telephone in place of, 171–72
  training manual and bulletins, 172–74
Courtesy, 8–10, 12–16, 42
  in the office, 42
  on the telephone, 12–16

with visitors, 8–10
Credit information, 496–511
adverse information, life of, 510
advertising limitations and penalties, 498
charges, additional, 504, 506
closed-end accounts, 498
Consumer Credit Protection Act, 496–97
correcting errors in file, 509
cost of, 500–501
credit ratings, 507–509
Fair Credit Reporting Act, 509–11
open-end accounts, 497–98, 499 (*figure*)
recipients of credit reports, 510–11
Regulation Z, 497
repayment schedule, 502 (*table*)
sources of credit, 500–504
automobile dealers, 504
banks and savings and loan, 501–502
consumer finance and small loan companies, 502–503
credit unions, 503
insurance companies, 504
pawnbrokers, 503
retail stores, 503–504, 505 (*figure*)
Truth-in-Lending Act, 497
use of credit, 506–507
Criticism, 42–43
Customs regulations, 612–20

Dash, 347–48
Data processing, 2–3, 194–210, 668–78
applications, 195–97
computer configuration, 207–208
electronic, 205–206
impact of automation, 2–3
input-output, 197
integrated systems, 201–202
language of, 202–205
manual processing, 198
mechanical processing, 198–99
need for, 195
operating systems, 209–210
programming, 208–209
punched card processing, 199–201
steps in, 197
terms, 668–78
time sharing, 209–10
Daylight saving time, 448
Days between dates, 784
Decimal equivalents of fractions, 786
Declassifying military correspondence, 119–20, 130–33 (*table*)
Diagonal line, 364
Dictation, 155–64
machine, 157–59

model dictation, 158–59
person-to-person, 156–57
taking dictation, 159–62
techniques, 155–59
transcribing, 162–64
Dictionaries, 284, 286–87 (*figure*)
Dictionary of business terms, 657–708
Diplomatic letters, 106, 107 (*figure*)
Diplomatic titles, 134–35, 137–43
Ditto, 436
Documents, replacement of, 572–75
Domestic mail, 623–41
Dun & Bradstreet, 507–508
Duplicating and copying, 431–41
addressing machines, 441
comparative costs of processes, 432–35 (*table*)
copying processes, 437–41
blueline, 438–39
copyflo xerox, 438
copytron, 437–38
multilith, 439–40
ozalid, 439
photographic, 440
readyprint, 437
thermofax, 437
xerography, 438
duplicating processes, 436–37
automatic typewriters, 436
carbon paper, 436
spirit process, 436
stencil duplicating, 436–37
equipment, auxiliary, 441
Justowriter, 441
reproduction department, 431
Vari-typer, 441

Economics terms, 678–82
Editing, 271–78
content and structure, 272–73
copy for printer, 275–78
cropping and scaling pictures, 277 (*figure*)
editor's functions, 271–72
making corrections, 275
manuscript edited, 274 (*figure*)
reference tools, 273, 275
type styles, 276 (*figure*)
effect, affect, 294
ei, ie, 288–89
Elite type, 87, 392
Ellipsis, 348
Empathy, 32–33
Employee relations, 26–38, 41–50, 172–74
bulletins, 174
business etiquette, 41–50
cooperation, 42

Employee relations (*cont.*)
 courtesy, 42
 criticism, 42–43
 discipline, 37
 employer-secretary, 44
 exit interviews, 37–38
 grievances, 35–37
 husband-wife, 45
 interviewing, 26–28
 merit ratings, 34–35
 morale, 33–34
 motivation, 34
 parties, company, 47
 personal habits, 47–48
 training, 28–31, 172–74
Enclosures, 104, 110, 169
 inserting in envelope, 110
 listing of, 104
 printed, 169
English usage, 284–339
 dictionary, use of, 287
 ei and *ie,* 288–89
 grammar review, 308–22
 grammatical terms, 303–308
 plurals, 289–93
 spelling guide, 285–93
 suffixes and prefixes, 285–89
 words
  confusing, 293–303
  correct use, 323–39
Envelopes, 106–10, 112, 169
 addressing, 106–10
 chain-feeding, 112
 notations on, 107–108
 position of address, 110
 prepaid return envelope, 169
 return address, 106
 room, suite, or apartment number, 110
 state abbreviation with ZIP code, 109–10
 window, 108
Equations and formulas, typing of, 400–408
Estate planning—the will, 536–43
 division of estate without will, 537–38
 estate, inheritance, gift taxes, 540–43
 executor, 539–40
 holographic wills, 537
 information for attorney and executor, 538–39
 periodic review of will, 539
Etiquette, 41–50
 absenteeism, 41
 borrowing, 41
 cafeteria, 41
 complaints, personal, 42
 confidential matters, 41–42
 cooperation, 42

 counseling female subordinates, 42
 courtesy, 42
 criticism, 42–43
 death, 43
 dining out, 43
 elevator, 44
 employer-secretary, 44
 gifts, 44
 grooming, 44–45
 husband–wife working together, 45
 introductions, 45–47
 names, use of, 47
 neatness, 47
 office parties, 47
 personal habits, 47–48
 personal phone calls, 48
 personal visitors, 48
 precedence, 48
 private dining room, 48–49
 punctuality, 49
 rising in deference, 49
 romance in office, 49
 tipping, 50
 traveling with secretary, 50
Exclamation point, 348
Expense records, 471–75

Fair Credit Reporting Act, 509–11
Feedback, 32–33
Filing, 409–31, 516
 alphabetical, 410–15
 centralized files, 426
 charge-outs, 425
 chronological, 417
 coding, 420
 departmental files, 425
 equipment, 419
 geographical area, 415
 indexing, 420–21
 indexing rules, 421–25
 microfilming, 428–31
 by name, 410
 numerical, 415–17
 phonetic, 417, 419
 planning the system, 419–20
 retention schedule, 426–27
 sorting, 421
 storing, 421
 subject, 410
 tickler file, 418 (*figure*), 516
 transfer of files, 428
Financial information, 484–536
 banking, 484–95
 credit, 496–511
 insurance, 511–21
 office cash, 495–96
 securities, 521–36
Footnotes, 219–26, 231

abbreviations, 221 (*figure*)
content, 222
copy for printer, 276 (*figure*)
Latin terms, 221
law cases, 225–26
public documents, 222–26
style, 219–22, 223 (*figure*)
in tables, 231
Foreign countries and capitals, 604–607
Foreign currency, 483, 607–11
value and nomenclature, 607–11
where to buy, 483
Foreign travel, 480–83
Foreign words, plural of, 292–93
Form letters and paragraphs, 166–68
Forms of address, 134–43
alphabetical list of important titles, 137–43
general practices, 134–35, 137
military titles, 135–37
special titles, 135
Fractions, decimal equivalents, 786
further, farther, 298

Galley proof, 279–83
Geographic names, 367
Gerunds, possessive with, 320
Gift tax table, 543 (*table*)
Government abbreviations, 750–52
Government correspondence, 115–28
Government publications, 215–17, 544–46, 580–83
Government terms, 682–84
Grammar review, 308–22
adjectives, 320–21
adverbs, 321–22
gerunds, 320
infinitives, 319
participles, 319–20
possessive, 315–17
prepositions, 322
pronouns, 313–15
sentence structure, 309–11
subject-verb agreement, 312–13
verbs, 317–19
Grammatical terms, 303–308
Graphs and charts, 231–37
bar and column charts, 234 (*table*), 236–37
line charts, 237
materials needed, 232
pie charts, 233 (*figure*), 235–36
techniques for making, 232–35
Greek alphabet, 775

Headings, titles, 251, 367–68, 382, 394–98
Head-to-head, 431
Health insurance, 520

Hectograph, 436
Holiday 6-year timetable, 776–77
Holidays, state, 778–82
Hyphen, 349–53, 375–76

ie, ei, 288–89
Importing, 613–20
alcoholic beverages, 620
antiques, 617
automobiles, 617
customs declaration, 613, 616
household effects, 617
prohibited and restricted articles, 618–20
tariff rates, 614–15 (*table*)
Index in a report, 261
Indexing minutes, 71
Indexing rules, 421–25
Infinitives, 319
Information sources, 210–219
atlases, dictionaries, encyclopedias, 218–19
company files, 211–12
directories, 217
economic and financial, 217–18
footnotes and bibliographies, 219
government publications, 215–17
international references, 219
library, 212–15
personal inquiry, 211
private records, 212
Insurance, 511–21, 684–88
annuities, 520
business, 511–14
health, 520
personal, 518–21
personal property, 520–21
protection of policies, 514
records, 514–17
terms, 684–88
Interest tables, 785
International mail, 641–53
International time, 455–56
International trade, 576–622
customs regulations, 612–20
doing business abroad, 576–604
American shipping lines, 593 (*table*)
assistance abroad, 587, 591–92
bibliographies for exporters, 584–85
CASL agents abroad, 588–91 (*table*)
C.I.F. price determination, 595–96
collecting from the market, 600–602
Department of Commerce services, 577–80
electric current abroad, 596
export distributors, 596–97
export reference guides, 603–604
foreign market reports, 592, 594–95

International trade (*cont.*)
   foreign-trade zones, 600
   legislation favorable to exporters, 597
   major U.S. ports, 594 (*table*)
   other market information, 602–603
   publications of interest, 580–84
   selecting overseas outlets, 596
   shipping to the market, 599–600
   stateside assistance, 585–87
   trade centers, 598
   trade fairs, 597–98
   trade missions, 598–99
  foreign capitals and descriptive terms, 604–607
  foreign money and its value, 607–11
  U.S. foreign service posts, 621–22
Interviewing, 26–28, 37–38, *see also* Employee relations
Introductions, 24–25, 45–47
  acknowledging, 47
  group, 46
  individuals, 45–46
  self, 46
  speaker, 24–25
Internal communications, 112–15
International telegraph service, 454–60
Italics, 380
Itinerary, 467, 470 (*figure*)

Judicial titles, 139, 141
Justowriter, 441

Law terms, 688–94
Letters, 86–107, 115–29, 134–43, 167–69, 171, 174–93
  attention line, 101–102
  block style, 87, 89 (*figure*)
  body of letter, 96–98
  carbon copy notation, 104–105
  complimentary close, 98–99
  correspondence procedures, 164–74
  date line, 93
  enclosures, 104
  executive stationery, 108 (*figure*)
  firm name in close, 99
  folding, 110–11
  form letters, 166–67, 168 (*figure*)
  format or style, 87–91
  forms of address, 134–43
  full block, 90 (*figure*), 91
  handwritten, 167, 169
  hanging-indented style, 90 (*figure*), 91
  indented style, 90 (*figure*), 91
  identification initials, 101
  inside address, 93–95
  mailing notation, 104

  military letters, 115–29
  model letters, 174–93
  personal or confidential, 101
  personal or diplomatic, 105–106, 107 (*figure*)
  placement of message, 87, 88 (*figure*)
  postage, *see* Postal regulations
  postscripts, 105
  principal parts, 93–105
  proofreading, 110
  punctuation patterns, 91–93
  quoted and enumerated matter, 97–98
  salutation, 95–96
  second and subsequent pages, 105
  semiblock style, 87, 90 (*figure*)
  signature lines, 100–101
  simplified style, 90, 92, (*figure*), 98
  spacing body of letter, 96–98
  speed letters, 171
  subject or reference line, 102–104
  tabulated material in, 98
  transcribing, 162–64
  ZIP code, 95
Letter models, 174–93
  acknowledgments, 174–77
  appointment, 177
  appreciation, 178
  complaint, 178–79
  condolence, 179–80
  confirmation, 180–81
  congratulatory, 181–83
  follow-up, 183–84
  introduction, 184–85
  invitation, 185–87
  recommendation, 187–88
  reference, 188
  refusal, 188–89
  request, 189–90
  sympathy, 190
  ticket order, 191
  transmittal, 191–92
  travel arrangements, 192–93
Letter parts, capitalization of, 369
Letter writing, 146–59, 164–93
  beginning, the, 146–49
  conciseness, 147 (*figure*)
  dictation techniques, 155–59
  editing another's letter, 153
  effective letters, 144–45
  ending, the, 148–49
  improving correspondence procedures, 164–74
  language, 150–53
  model letters, 174–93
  planning the letter, 146
  positive and negative, 154 (*figure*)
  signed by secretary, 153–55
  writing for employer's signature, 153

Library information, 213–15
　books in print, 214
　cumulative book index, 214
　general catalog, 213–14
　general guides, 214–15
　indexes, 214
　vertical file index, 214
Limited, 129
Listening, effective, 33 (*figure*)
Long distance telephone calls, 18–20
Lost documents, 572–75

Machine dictation, 157–59
Mail, *see* Postal regulations
Mailing classified material, 127–28
Marketing terms, 694–99
Marking classified military correspond-
　ence, 117–20
Manuscript, 238–83
Measures, 755–64
　British standard, 762–63
　capacity
　　metric, 761 (*table*)
　　U.S. liquid and dry, 760–61 (*tables*)
　circular or angular, 755
　common measures and metric equiva-
　　lents, 763–64
　common units, 761
　conversion tables, 766–70 (*tables*)
　linear, U.S. and metric, 758 (*table*)
　metric length, area, volume, cubic,
　　mass, 756–57 (*tables*)
　metric system, 755
　miscellaneous units, 764–65
　paper, 761
　square, U.S. and metric, 759 (*table*)
　temperature, 762
　time, 761–62
Medicare, 567–70
Meetings, *see* Conferences and meetings
Memorandums, 112–15, 261–65
　classified, 115
　copies, list of, 114
　distribution list, 114
　file copies, 115
　format, 262
　heading of, 112–13
　language, 265
　organization of data, 262–65
　second page, 115
　spacing, 112–13
　subjects treated, 261–62
　uses of, 261
Metric system, 755–61
Microfilm or microform, 428–31, 440
　legality of microfilm documents, 430–
　　31
　microcard and microfiche, 429–30

Military correspondence, 116–29, 130–
　33 (*table*)
　carbon copies, 124–25
　classifying, 117–20, 121 (*table*)
　company control numbers, 116–17
　copies, 125
　declassifying, 119–20
　destruction of, 128–29
　enclosures, 124
　format, 120–27
　mailing of, 127–28
　procedures for handling, 130–33 (*ta-
　　ble*)
　reference line, 123
　salutation, 123
　second-page heading, 126 (*figure*)
　security, 116
　transmittal receipt, 125, 127
Military time, 783
Military titles, 135–37
Minutes and notes, 59, 60 (*figure*), 66–
　67 (*figure*), 68–78
　content, 69–70
　corporation, 71–78
　corrections to, 70–71
　directors' meeting, 77–78
　formal meeting, 66–67 (*figure*)
　indexing, 71
　language, 70
　mechanics, 59, 60 (*figure*), 69
　minute book, 76
　stockholders' meetings, 72–75 (*figure*),
　　76
Money orders, 451–52, 653–55
　postal, 653–55
　telegraph, 451–52
Morale, 33–37
Multilith, 439–40
Mutual funds, 529

Natural language, 250
New York Times Index, 214
Nouns, 289–93, 304, 307, 315–17, 350–
　51, 366–71, 382–83
　common, 291, 304, 371
　compound, 290–91, 350–51, 366, 383
　foreign, 292–93
　plural, 289–93
　possessive, 315–17
　predicate noun, 307
　proper, 291–92, 307, 366–71, 382
　words as, 292
Numbering pages in manuscript, 278
Numbers, 351, 372–79
　abbreviations with, 372
　alignment of, 372
　cents, 372
　commas with, 373

Numbers (*cont.*)
  dates, 374
  decimals, 374
  dollars, 374–75
  fractions, 375
  general usage, 372
  hyphenated, 375–76
  hyphenation of, 351
  in legal documents, 374
  measurements, 376
  ordinal, 376
  percentages, 377
  plural usage, 377
  reading numbers, 373 (*figure*)
  roman numerals, 378
  round numbers, 378–79
  sentence beginning, 379
  words and figures, 376

Office routine, 38–40, 495–96
  housekeeping, 40
  machine maintenance, 39–40
  methods and procedures, 38–39
  petty cash, 495–96
  supervision, 25–40
  supplies, 40
Office services, 409–83
  duplicating and copying, 431–41
  records management, 409–31
  telephone and wires, 442–66
  travel arrangements, 466–83
Opportunities in the office, 1–4
Out-of-town telephone calls, 18–20
  appointment and sequence, 18–19
  charges, 20
  collect, 19
  conference, 19
  mobile and marine, 19
  overseas, 19–20
  person-to-person, 18
  station-to-station, 19
  WATS, 19
Outlining, 242–46
Over-the-counter market, 524–25
Ozalid, 439

Page proof, 283
Paragraphing in reports, 248–49
Parentheses, 353–54
Parliamentary procedures, 60–65
  basic principles, 60–61
  conduct of business, 62–65
  motions and resolutions, 62–65
  order of business, 61–62
Participles, dangling, 319–20
Passport, 482
Per diem, 472–73
Period, 355–56

Personal effectiveness, 1–50
  appointments and visitors, 4–11
  attending meetings, 20–22
  business etiquette, 41–50
  cooperation, 3, 42
  opportunities in the office, 1–4
  supervising, 25–40
  talking to groups, 20–25
  training, 3–4
  using the telephone, 11–20
Personal letters, 106
Personal property insurance, 520–21
Personnel terms, 699–704
Petty cash fund, 495–96
Photo-offset, 440
Photographs, cropping, 277 (*figure*), 278
Photostats, 440
Pica Type, 87, 392
Plurals, 289–93, 364, 377
Political titles, 134–43
Possessive nouns, 316–17
Possessive pronouns, 316
Postal regulations, 112, 623–56
  ascertaining correct postage, 112
  computing size of package, 627 (*figure*)
  domestic mail, 626–41
    airmail, 631, 632 (*table*)
    bulk mail, 637–38
    certified, 634–35
    claims, 634
    COD mail, 633–34
    forwarding, 638–39
    first class, 626, 632 (*table*)
    fourth class parcel post, 628–31
    insured, 633
    meter stamps, 636
    military, 639–40
    nonmailable matter, 640–41
    permit imprints, 636–37
    precanceled stamps, 635–36
    priority mail, 631, 632 (*table*)
    recall of, 639
    registered, 631–33
    return of, 638
    return receipts, 635
    second class, 626
    special delivery, 631
    stamps, stamped envelopes, postal cards, 635
    third class, 627–28
    tracing, 639
    undeliverable, 640
  international mail, 641–53
    parcel post, 645–53
    postal union mail, 642–45
    rates and weight limits, 646–50 (*table*)

surface rates, 651–52 (*table*)
nonmail services, 653–56
  box rental, 656
  documentary internal revenue stamps,
    655
  migratory-bird hunting stamps, 655
  money orders, 653–55
  postal savings, 656
  U.S. savings bonds and stamps, 655
  preparing company mail, 624–25 (*table*)
Prefixes, hyphen with, 351–53
Prepositions, end of sentence, 322
Press releases, 266–71
  mechanical form, 267–69
  photographs, 271, 277 (*figure*), 278
  subjects, 267
  writing, 269–71
Pronouns, 313–16
Pronunciation key, 294
Proofreading, 110, 278–83, 394
  galley proofs, 279, 283
  hints on, 394
  letters, 110
  page proofs, 283
  proofreader's marks, 279, 280–81 (*figure*)
  typeset page, 282 (*figure*)
Proprietary information, 129
Protection of documents, 571–72
Publicity and editorial work, 266–83
Punctuation, 340–61
  apostrophe, 340–41
  brackets, 341
  colon, 341–42
  comma, 343–47
  exclamation point, 348
  hyphen, 349–53
  parentheses, 353–54
  question mark, 356
  quotation marks, 357–60
  semicolon, 360–61

Question mark, 356
Quotation marks, 357–60
Quotations and quoted matter, 97–98,
    252, 270, 278, 357–60
  capitalization of, 358
  in edited manuscripts, 278
  in letters, 97–98
  in press releases, 270
  punctuation of, 357–60
  in reports, 252

Readyprint, 437
Reconciliation of bank statement, 488–89
Records management, 409–31
  alphabetical filing systems, 410–15

centralized versus decentralized, 425–26
commercial filing systems, 419
control of records, 425
equipment needs, 419
filing process, 420–21
important or vital records, 428
indexing rules, 421–25
microform, 428–31
nonalphabetical filing systems, 415–19
planning the file system, 419–20
retention schedule, 426–27
storage of records, 410
transfer and disposal of records, 428
Religious titles, 134–43
Replacement of documents, 572–75
Reports, 238–65
  appendix, 261
  assembling, 256–61
  bibliography, 261
  binding, 251
  connecting ideas, 247–48
  cover, 258
  criteria of, 240 (*figure*)
  data, locating, 239–41
  exhibits, 252, 255–56, 261
  footnotes, 252
  headings, degrees of, 251–52
  index, 261
  introduction, 257–58 (*figure*), 262
  language, 246–47
  letter of transmittal, 254 (*figure*), 260
  margins, 251
  memorandums as, 261–65
  organization of data, 241–42
  outlining, 242–46
  page numbers, 252
  paragraphing, 248–49
  planning, 238–39
  preface, 261
  primary data, 239–40
  quotations, 252
  secondary data, 240
  sentences in, 249
  spacing, 252
  summary, 261
  table of contents, 255 (*figure*), 256 (*figure*), 261
  title page, 253 (*figure*), 258
  typing of, 250–61
  word use, 250
  writing of, 239 (*figure*), 246–50
Retail installment contract, 505 (*figure*)
Roman numerals, 378
Routing slips, 169, 170 (*figure*)

Salutation, 95–96, 123, 137–43
  correspondence, 95–96

Salutation (*cont.*)
   important persons, 137–43
   military, 123
Savings accounts, 491–94
   insurance of, 492–94
   interest paid, 491–92
Second-page heading, 125
Secret material, 128–29
Secretary, 30–31, 41–50, 55–60, 66–68,
      78–85, 144–55, 159–62, 164–93,
      466–83, 507–09, 514–17, 535–36,
      552–54
   backup secretary, 30–31
   business etiquette, 41–50
   conference duties, 59
   conventions, 78–85
   correspondence procedures, 164–74
   dictation, 159–62
   expense records, 471–75, 552–54
   insurance records, 514–17
   letter-writing, 144–55
   minutes, 66–68
   model letters, 174–93
   planning conferences, 55–58
   polishing another's letters, 153
   post-meeting duties, 59–60
   preparing material for dictator's sig-
      nature, 163–64
   protection of insurance policies, 514
   safeguarding security certificates, 535–
      36
   securities records, 531–35
   supplying credit information, 507–509
   tax records, 549, 552, 553 (*table*)
   ticket orders, 191
   transcribing notes and tapes, 162–64
   travel arrangements, 192–93, 466–83
   writing for employer's signature, 153
   writing for own signature, 153–55
Securities transactions, 521–36, 705–708
   bonds, 521–23
   brokers and dealers, 525
   commission table, 526 (*table*)
   mutual funds, 529
   odd-lot differentials, 527 (*table*)
   orders, types of, 528–29
   over-the-counter market, 524–25
   preferred and common stocks, 523–24
   quotations, 530
   records, 531–35
   safeguarding certificates, 535–36
   sources of information, 530–31
   stock exchanges, 524
   stock market terms, 705–708
   trading terms, 525, 527–28
Security of company documents, 129
Security of military correspondence, 116
Semicolon, 360–61

Sensitive information, 129
Sentences, 248–49, 309–11, 379
   completeness, 310–11
   conciseness, 249
   fragment, 309
   numbers in, 379
   parallel construction, 310
   report writing, 249
   run-on, 309
   structure of, 309–10
   topic, 248
shall, will, 336–37
should, would, 337
Signatures, 100, 486–87
   on checks, 486–87
   signing for another, 100
   women's, 100
Signs and symbols, 771–74
Simplified letter style, 90, 92 (*figure*), 98
Slant, 364
Small Business Administration, 216
Social security, 556–71
   appealing decisions, 562–63
   applying for benefits, 560, 562
   cash tips, reporting of, 566
   checking earnings record, 566–67
   contribution rate schedule, 565 (*table*)
   death payment, 562
   disabled person, 563
   discontinuation of payments, 570–71
   employment by foreign agency in USA,
      565–66
   figuring monthly benefits, 559–60
   household employees, 567
   medicare, 567–70
   monthly cash payments, 561 (*table*)
   qualifying for benefits, 557–59
   quarters of coverage, 557
   self-employed, 564–65
   workers over 65, 570
Sources of information, *see* Information
      sources
Speechmaking, 23–24
Speed letters, 171
Split infinitives, 319
State abbreviations with ZIP code, 110
State holidays, 778–79
Statistical typing, 228–31, 394–408
   centering headings, 394–96
   formulas and equations, 400–408
   horizontal placement, 397–400
      centering method, 397
      columnar entries, 398–400
      columnar headings, 398
      use of leaders, 400
   reference table, 229 (*figure*), 396–97
   spot table, 229 (*figure*), 396
   tabulations, 228–31

underscoring and spacing headings, 395–96
vertical placement, 396–97
Stencils, 436–37
Stenographer, *see* Secretary
Stilted language, 250
Stock market terms, 705–708
Stockholders' minutes, 72–75 (*figure*), 76
Stocks and bonds, 523–24
Subject-verb agreement, 312–13, 318 ·
Subscripts and superscripts, 405–406
Superintendent of Documents, 216
Supervision, 3–4, 25–40, 42–43, 172–74
communications, 32–33
counseling female subordinates, 42
criticism, 42–43
discipline, 37
employment interview, 27–28
exit interview, 37–38
grievances, 35, 37
interviewing, 26–28
merit ratings, 34–35, 36 (*table*)
morale, 33–34
motivation, 34
office, 25–38
office routine, 38–40
training, 3–4, 28–31, 172–74
Suspension hyphen, 353

Table of contents, 255 (*figure*), 256 (*figure*)
Tables, graphs, and charts, 228–37, 394–400
columns, 231
design of, 228–31
footnotes, 231
placement in reports, 252, 255–56
stub, 231
title, 231
typing of, 394–400
Tabulations, 97–98, 228–31
in letters, 97–98
in tables, 228–31
Talking to groups, 20–25
chairing a meeting, 22–23
giving a talk, 23–24
introducing a speaker, 24–25
participating as a delegate, 20–22
Tariff rates, 614–15 (*table*)
Taxes, 471–72, 480, 543–56
arrangements for paying, 544
business expenses, deductible, 552, 554 (*table*)
calendar, 549, 550–51 (*table*)
estate, inheritance and gift, 540–43
federal business taxes, 547–48 (*table*)
information for individuals, 552, 555

(*table*), 556
keeping records, 549, 552, 553 (*table*)
living abroad, 480
publications on, 544–46
travel and entertainment, 471–72
Telegraph services, 447–66
choosing the service, 447–51
costs, 450–51
copies of wires, 461 (*figure*)
counting words, 448–51
day letter, 447–48
direct wire, 452
errand service, 452
format of government wires, 462 (*figure*), 463 (*figure*)
government information via wire, 460–63
incoming wires, 460
international service, 454–60
classes of service, 454–55
costs, 454, 456
counting words, 456–60
delivery instructions, 458–60
time considerations, 455–56
in-transit service, 452
mailgram, 452
money orders, 451–52
night letter, 448
second-page heading, 464 (*figure*)
telegram, 447
time zone map, 449 (*figure*)
typing telegrams, 452–54
WUX, TWX, TELEX, 463–66
Telephone services, 442–46
centrex, 442–43
equipment, 443–46
call commander, 444
card dialer, 445
code call, 445
data-phone, 446
dataspeed, 446
electronic secretary, 444
electrowriter, 445–46
executive quick call, 444
Magicall electronic dialer, 445
P-A-B-X, 445
PBX, 444
speakerphone, 444
touch-tone, 446
Wide Area Telephone Service (WATS), 443
Telephone usage, 11–20, 171–72
appointment and sequence calls, 18–19
clear speech, 11–12
collect calls, 19
conference calls, 19
courtesy, 12–18
directories and lists, 12–13

Telephone usage (*cont.*)
  incoming calls, 13–17
  in place of correspondence, 171–72
  long distance charges, 20
  mobile and marine service, 19
  outgoing calls, 17–18
  out-of-town calls, 18–20
  overseas calls, 19–20
  person-to-person calls, 18
  phrasing telephone numbers, 12 (*figure*)
  priority calls, 16–17
  screening calls, 15–17
  spelling names, 11–12
  station-to-station calls, 19
  taking messages, 16
  transferring calls, 15
  WATS, 19
TELEX, 464–66
Thermofax, 437
Ticket orders, 191
Tickler file, 418 (*figure*), 516
Time, military, 783
Time, worldwide, 455–56
Time zones, U.S., 448–49
Titles, 134–43, 357, 364–65, 367–71, 379–80
  abbreviation of, 364–65
  capitalization of, 367–71
  forms of address, 134–43
  inside address, 94–95
  punctuation of, 357
  salutations, 95–96
  underlining, 379–80
Trade names, 372
Training, 3–4, 28–31, 172–74
  backup secretary, 30–31
  correspondence manual, 172–74
  induction, 28
  need for, 3–4
  on-the-job, 28–30
Transcribing notes and tapes, 162–64
Travel arrangements, 192–93, 466–83
  authorization form, 468–69 (*table*)
  classified trip, 475, 476 (*table*)
  collecting trip information, 466–67
  company policy, 472–75
  expense reports, 471–75
  foreign travel, 480–83
  itinerary, 467, 470 (*figure*)
  model letter, 192–93
  per diem, 472–73
  professional meetings, 475, 477 (*table*)
  travel agents, 466
  trip preparations, 467, 470–71
  use of company or personal car, 478–80
Traveler's checks, 482–83

Truth-in-Lending Act, 497
Tumblehead, 431
TWX, 464
Type styles, 276 (*figure*)
Typewriters, automatic, 436
Typewriting, 250–62, 267–69, 275–78, 452–54
  copy for printer, 275–78
  memorandums, 262
  numbering manuscript pages, 278
  press releases, 267–69
  reports, 250–61
  telegrams, 452–54
Typing pointers, 384–408
  carbon paper hints, 388–89, 391–92
  changing ribbons, 390
  chain-feeding, 387–88
  correcting bound manuscripts, 386
  correcting originals and carbon copies, 385–86
  even right margins, 390
  formulas and equations, 400–408
  improving typing efficiency, 384–94
  individual labels, 388
  last-line corrections, 390
  locating typing line, 386–87
  posture and chair height, 385
  proofreading, 394
  ruled lines, 387
  selecting the ribbon, 392
  special characters, 400–401
  special keys and levers, 390–91
  two-column copy, 393 (*figure*), 394
  typing on printed forms, 392–94
  typing statistical material, 394–400
  uniform bottom margins, 387
  using a copyholder, 385
  word substitutions, 389–90
  writing between lines, 385

Underlining, 379–80
United Nations titles, 143
U.S. Department of Commerce field offices, 578–79 (*table*)
U.S. Foreign Service, 621–22
  abbreviations, 622 (*table*)
  directory, 622
  posts, 621–22
U.S. Government abbreviations, 750–52

Vari-Typer, 441
Verbal noun, *see* Gerund
Verbs, 317–19
Visitors, 8–11
Volume formulas, 787

Wall Street Journal Index, 214
WATS telephone service, 443

Weights and measures, 365, 753–70
  abbreviations of, 365
  apothecaries', 754
  avoirdupois, 754
  conversion tables, 766–70
  measures, 755–64
  miscellaneous units of measurement, 764–65
  precious stones, 754
  troy, 754
who, whom, 339
will, shall, 336–37
Wills, holographic, 537
Window envelopes, 108
Wire services, 447–66
Women's signatures and titles, 96, 100, 424–25
Word division, 380–83
  abbreviations, 381
  affixes, 381
  contractions, 381
  dates, 381
  double consonants, 381
  figures, 383
  foreign words, 382
  general usage, 381–81

  headings, 382
  hyphenated words, 382
  last words, 382
  mispronunciation, 382
  proper names, 382
  solid compounds, 383
  successive lines, 383
  vowels, 383
Words, 248, 250, 293–303, 323–339
  confusing, 293–303
  connecting, 248
  correct usage, 323–339
  in reports, 250
would, should, 337
Writing, 144–53, 246–50, 261–65, 269–71, 308–22
  grammar review, 308–22
  letters, 144–53
  memorandums, 261–65
  press releases, 269–71
  reports, 246–50
WUX, 463

Xerography, 438

ZIP code, 95, 106–10

Quick Reference
to Frequently Consulted Subjects

(Contents on pages xi–xiv—Full Index on page 789)

Abbreviation style	362	Data processing methods	194
Abbreviations listed	709	Data processing terms	668
Accounting terms	657	Days between dates	784
Acknowledgments	174	Decimal-fraction equivalents	786
Agenda	57	Dictation techniques	155
Airmail	631	Duplicating and copying	431
Alphabetizing	410	Editing	271
Apostrophe	340	Ellipsis	348
Appointments and visitors	4	Employee relations	26
Area formulas	788	Envelope addresses	106
Banking procedures	484	Equations, typing	401
Banking terms	662	Estate planning	536
Bibliographies	226	Estate taxes	540
Brackets	341	Etiquette	41
Business terms defined	657	Exclamation point	348
Cables	454	Expense vouchers	552
Calendar of appointments	5	Export information	576
Capitals	365	Filing	409
Chain-feeding envelopes	387	Financial information	484
Chairing a meeting	22	Footnotes	219
Check endorsements	486	Foreign countries and capitals	604
Checking accounts	485	Foreign money	607
Classified documents	115	Foreign words, plurals	292
Colon	341	Form letters	166
Comma	343	Forms of address	134
Communication	32	Formulas and equations,	
Complaint letters	178	typing	401
Computers	205	Government agencies,	
Condolence letters	179	abbreviations	750
Conference arrangements	52	Government correspondence	115
Congratulatory letters	181	Government trade assistance	577
Convention procedures	78	Grammar review	308
Conversion tables	766	Grammatical terms defined	303
Copying machines	437	Graphic presentation	231
Correcting typed material	385	Greek alphabet	775
Correspondence procedures	164	Headings, styles	251
Credit information sources	507	Holidays	776
Credit procedures	496	Hyphen	349
Customs regulations	612	Indexing	421
Dash	347	Information sources	210